Foreword

THE ACS SYMPOSIUM SERIES was founded in 1974 to provide a medium for publishing symposia quickly in book form. The format of the Series parallels that of the continuing ADVANCES IN CHEMISTRY SERIES except that, in order to save time, the papers are not typeset, but are reproduced as they are submitted by the authors in camera-ready form. Papers are reviewed under the supervision of the editors with the assistance of the Advisory Board and are selected to maintain the integrity of the symposia. Both reviews and reports of research are acceptable, because symposia may embrace both types of presentation. However, verbatim reproductions of previously published papers are not accepted.

Contents

THE AQUATIC COMPONENT

THE TERRESTRIAL COMPONENT

INDEXES

Preface

ENVIRONMENTAL SCIENCE (along with other forms of raised consciousness) came to national prominence during the 1960s and, with assistance from the worldwide media, rapidly grew in name recognition. Many colleges and universities established environmental chemistry, environmental engineering, and other environmental science programs. In 1963, the U.S. Congress passed the first Clean Air Act. In 1970, the United States expanded local and statewide efforts to combat air and water pollution to the national level by establishing the Environmental Protection Agency (EPA). The first version of the Clean Water Act passed the U.S. Congress in 1972. The EPA promulgated national standards for air and water quality. Significant progress was made in the reduction of emissions of harmful substances into the air and water, both in the United States and in other developed countries worldwide. Some particularly insidious environmental contaminants, such as DDT, were banned completely by some countries.

Following national environmental initiatives in the United States and other industrialized countries, an awareness arose that air and water pollution problems transcended not only state geographical and political boundaries but also national boundaries. The problem of acid precipitation in the Scandinavian countries is caused partly by emissions from other countries, and oil spills pollute waters or beaches without regard to the offending vessel's country of registry. However, the potential global proportions of human pollution were largely unrecognized until the discovery that supersonic aircraft flights might disrupt the chemical balance of the stratosphere. Although the focus of this problem has changed from the SSTs to the chlorofluorocarbons (CFCs), significant stratospheric ozone depletion is now a reality and is expected to worsen into the next century. In contrast to the CFC problem (whose emissions can be eliminated) problems of global warming are immensely more difficult to deal with. Many view global warming as the foremost environmental issue for the next century. Carbon dioxide, once viewed as a benign emission, is now recognized as a global air pollutant. Add in global deforestation and desertification, problems of feeding the increasing world population, and so on, and it is clear that humanity must come to grips with its future.

Our goal in this volume, as editors and chemists, has been to bring together researchers who could address the major worldwide environmental problems, which contain some element of chemistry. Although chemists like to view chemistry as the central discipline and chemistry plays an essential role in most of this book's chapters, many of the authors are not chemists. Biology, geophysics, and other disciplines are prominent. *Biogeochemistry* is becoming a catchword for the 1990s. People are now aware that (as Mark Twain said) "everything is connected to everything else". Environmental problems can never again be considered separately from one another. While enough of the natural world remains for study, scientists must develop an understanding of its internal interconnected workings. The chapter authors describe important elements of these inner workings.

Although we have attempted to include chapters relevant to all major issues of environmental concern, gaps in coverage occur. These will be obvious to those whose area is not included and to those with a broad perspective of environmental issues. We hope that these omissions will not detract too much from the presented material.

The targeted readership for this book is the scientifically literate nonspecialist. We encouraged the authors to present their material in a scientifically accurate and critically evaluated fashion understandable to those outside their discipline. This is always a very difficult task, and different authors took different approaches. Issues of disciplinarity are addressed by Brian Mar in his introduction.

The editorial effort demanded by this book did not seem formidable at the onset, but we definitely underestimated the amount of work involved. We would not have been able to finish without the dedicated efforts of several people, including Peg Pankratz, Monica Striker, and Karen McNeil, who worked far beyond the call of duty in preparing not only our contributions but also submissions for a number of other authors. We are grateful to Christopher O'Brien for editorial assistance and to the Portland State University Chemistry Department for support.

We are indebted to Mostafa Tolba, Executive Director of the United Nations Environmental Programme, for his overview. Dr. Tolba's perspective on environmental issues is clearly a global one. We take this opportunity to thank Clayton Callis, past ACS president, for his support of the symposium upon which this book is based, and the Electric Power Research Institute and the ACS Division of Environmental Chemistry for financial assistance with speakers' travel to that symposium.

Finally, we want to acknowledge individually the reviewers who took the time to comment on the chapters contained herein. Their comments, although not always favorable, were invariably useful and often quite detailed and have in many cases greatly improved the content and clarity of the chapters. These people, in random order, include the following: Paul Lioy, William Wilson, David Boone, Ramesh Reddy, John Hardy, Herman Gucinski, D. E. Ryan, Emmanuel Mendez Palma, Gerald Akland, Garcia Moreno, Reid Bryson, Curt Covey, Clayton Reitan, Charles Kolb, David Horn, Thomas Culliney, Aslam Khalil, Thomas Hard, Wayne Willford, J. R. Vallentyne, Glenn Shaw, John Firor, Mal-

vern Gilmartin, David Perry, R. J. Paterson, J. M. Bewers, R. Pockling-
ton, Judith Weis, John Disinger, Marat Khabibullov, John Winchester,
Dan Lashof, R. A. Houghton, Jeffrey Weitz, William Becker, Peter
Felker, John Ludwig, Paul Singh, Gregory Patton, Paul Ringold, and P. J.
Dillon.

DAVID A. DUNNETTE
Environmental Sciences and Resources Program
Portland State University
Portland, OR 97207

ROBERT J. O'BRIEN
Chemistry Department and Environmental Sciences Doctoral Program
Portland State University
Portland, OR 97207

September 30, 1991

The Global Environment

An Overview

Mostafa K. Tolba

Executive Director, United Nations Environment Program, Nairobi, Kenya

Interconnections

Global environmental chemistry today involves a rapidly expanding need both for new research, and for the development of an interdisciplinary approach to the multiplicity of interconnected environmental problems which now confront us. Every area of our planet's life support system -- air, land, water and natural ecosystems -- is showing signs of damage from the combined effects of too many humans and too little care. Growing quantities of wastes poison land, air and water. Water supplies become ever scarcer; soil degradation continues apace; the state of coastal zones deteriorates ever more rapidly; deforestation continues to take its toll, both in terms of land degradation and in terms of its contribution to climatic change. Now, global warming has been added to ozone depletion and environmental degradation as a major threat to the health and survival of future generations.

As we contemplate both the effects of human actions, and their solutions, we are forced increasingly to recognize the inextricably interconnected nature of life on Earth. The behavior of individual chemical constituents depends on many other constituents and environmental variables. Individual species depend for their survival on the existence and health of a network of other species within their own ecosystems; ecosystems depend in turn on the health of other ecosystems. Interactions in the oceans are affected by, and affect, processes on land and in the atmosphere. Increasingly, science is recognizing that it cannot understand the individual parts which make up life on this planet without considering the whole. It is becoming apparent that solutions to the environmental degradation now witnessed world-wide must involve a cooperative and holistic global effort. Environmental problems and their solutions pose huge challenges to the scientific community. Traditionally, scientific knowledge has been accumulated through painstaking and precise study of specific areas of science. Today, however, understanding of global environmental problems demands an interdisciplinary approach.

Need for Scientific Understanding

At present, we do not understand how the interactive physical, chemical and biological processes regulate the total Earth system. Nor do we know how this system will respond to anthropogenic influences. To develop this understanding, science must develop a knowledge base that embraces many disciplines and accommodates many cultures. Such a knowledge base is urgently needed. Global change brought about by human activities is likely to approach critical dimensions within 50 years, as the combined impacts of climate change, ozone depletion, population pressure and general environmental degradation compound each individual problem. Already, policymakers are demanding a firmer base for the national and international decisions that must be made. What is needed is the development of an initiative which considers all relevant dimensions of the driving forces of global change, including the social sciences and engineering. Ultimately, it will be a combination of scientific knowledge, public understanding and political will, which begin the actions that can preserve our planet for future generations. And this is where bodies such as the American Chemical Society assume such importance.

Legislation and public actions cannot succeed without scientific understanding. Yet the United Nations alone cannot provide this scientific understanding. UNEP's role is that of a catalyst, to spur others to act, working through and with other organizations. It is to bodies such as the American Chemical Society that UNEP looks, to provide the essential research without which neither legislation nor restorative actions can succeed. Texts such as this, which span a range of disciplines and look in detail at a variety of environmental problems and research activities will play an increasingly important role as the various scientific disciplines begin the attempts to gain an adequate understanding of knowledge in other fields.

At the same time the chemical industry has to make more readily available its research findings on the environmental health effects of the substances it produces, and information on the contaminants which may remain in its products. Only with meaningful cooperation between universities, institutes and the industrial communities will we be able to resolve these outstanding issues. Antagonisms and suspicions must be replaced by a greater willingness to work together to help overcome the major global environmental problems that affect us all.

Public Policy Implications

As the demand for a greater interdisciplinary approach expands, information and communication of information will become more important. Scientists in many disciplines, policymakers, industry and members of the public all need clear information on research findings and predictions. The demands for a closer liaison between scientists and policymakers presents particular challenges. Policymakers receive their information after it has been filtered through the media, or through their own staff. This process gives ample scope for error and distortion. Yet the very nature of scientific writing, which aims at complete clarity for the reader through the correct use of technical terms, renders it incomprehensible to many politicians, few of whom have any scientific training.

This particular challenge has yet to be adequately taken up by the scientific community, even though it is one which urgently requires resolution. There is a pressing need for action on a variety of environmental fronts, but this action will not be forthcoming until the public and politicians alike understand the reasons for the urgency. This understanding will only come through renewed efforts on the part of the scientific community.

The new demands for scientists to assist in the political sphere compound the challenge to scientists. Politics and science have in the past been near absolute opposites. Today, scientific knowledge is providing the impetus for political decisions aimed at rectifying the environmental damage which human activities have caused. Yet the knowledge gap between science and politics continues to cause concern. The scientific ethic demands the clear definition of remaining uncertainties. Politics demands certainty and is uncomfortable with uncertainty. Just as there is a need for scientific information to be communicated more broadly, so there is a need for science to communicate its certainties and its doubts more clearly to policymakers -- and for policymakers to understand and act upon what science is saying.

State of the Global Environment

The first step in planetary management is to find out exactly what is going wrong and why, and whether it is getting worse. The second is to make this information available to those who can do something about it. We now know a great deal about what is going wrong with our global environment, and why. We know that much of the observed environmental damage is worsening. And increasingly, we realize that these global problems and their solutions are inextricably interconnected.

The state of our global environment should be of deep concern. More than three hundred million tonnes of hazardous wastes produced each year affect the health of human and natural communities. Half of Europe's forests are affected to some degree by acid rain and other air pollution effects, as are large expanses of forests in North America. Destruction of tropical rainforests continues to degrade land and destroy natural resources.

A quarter of the world's population lacks safe drinking water. Each day, 35,000 people die because of lack of clean water. Each year, diarrhea resulting from unsafe water kills 4.6 million children under the age of five. Existing water supplies are dwindling, or becoming contaminated. Salinization of water supplies is already a problem in several parts of Africa, the arid belt from West Asia to India, and in Australia. Each year, salinization, alkalinization and erosion render almost ten million hectares of agricultural land unproductive.

Heavy metal and synthetic organic pollution cause severe problems in many major rivers around the world. Heavy metals and persistent organic compounds make soil and groundwater unusable. The effects of these pollutants can be long-lasting. Groundwater nitrate levels exceed World Health Organization guidelines for drinking water in parts of Western Europe and the United States. Contamination by organic pesticides, PCBs and other synthetic organics is widespread and locally serious in high and low income countries alike.

Marine pollution is worsening. Coral reefs are being destroyed by excessive quantities of silt washed down from deforested and eroding highlands, and by the increasing quantities of nutrients arising from sewage and agricultural run-off. Human activity already puts as great a quantity of nutrients into coastal waters as comes from natural sources. Within two or three decades, these quantities are expected to exceed natural background levels by several times, with serious consequences such as eutrophication and red tides.

Air pollution threatens the health of over one billion people, particularly in cities of the developing world. On top of the health problems such pollution causes, we now face the longer-term and even more serious threats of stratospheric ozone depletion and global warming. Ozone depletion is now an established fact. Even if the ban on ozone-depleting chemicals were implemented fully tomorrow, the long residence times of these chemicals in the atmosphere mean the world would be committed to continuing ozone depletion for at least a century.

Global warming now threatens to further unsettle our global environmental security. The scientific consensus is that global warming is inevitable and will be irreversible. Without urgent and drastic action, future generations will face increasingly savage impacts throughout the next century and beyond.

Conclusions

Environmental problems in the past have mainly impacted at the local or regional levels. Even disasters of the scale of Chernobyl were not felt globally. Now, however, human activity has managed to create truly global impacts on our environment and any solution demands a global, interdisciplinary approach.

A variety of research initiatives are already under way, forced by the nature of the problems themselves to involve many scientific disciplines. The effects on planetary systems of the environmental damage we have caused need to be understood, to allow the world to plan to minimize and repair the damage. And they can only be understood through a pooling of knowledge from a wide variety of sources.

We are being forced, in fact, to develop patterns of behavior that mirror the interconnectedness of our planet's natural systems. To understand the problems we have caused, and devise solutions, we must cooperate, as individuals, as scientists, as nations. The difficulties are great - as are the challenges our overburdened environment is now presenting to us. Yet it is only through taking up these challenges, and confronting them in a spirit of partnership, that we will succeed in preserving this planet of ours for future generations in a form that at least resembles the world we know today.

RECEIVED September 30, 1991

Chapter 1

Global Environmental Chemistry
The Connections

Brian W. Mar

Environmental Engineering and Science Program, Department of Civil Engineering, University of Washington, Seattle, WA 98195

Scientists working to improve the understanding of human impacts on global environmental systems are today challenged to synthesize fragmented studies into a global perspective (1,2). The challenge arises because these scientists must work with partial information. Scientists by nature are reductionist and tend to isolate a few variables for study and ignore the rest (3). The goal of this paper is to provide a guide for synthesis of the information presented in the papers that follow. It is critical that researchers explicitly define the boundaries of the domains they study, their selected temporal and spatial resolution, their specific variables, and the units they employ. A discussion of the papers in this volume is used to demonstrate how these characteristics are critical to synthesizing fragmented studies of the global environment.

There is a growing concern that human activities have increased to the level that they are 1) causing global warming, 2) allowing damaging levels of ultraviolet radiation to reach the earth's surface, 3) polluting the oceans, and 4) reducing our ability to produce enough food for the growing human population. In response, scientists are accelerating their efforts to understand global environmental sciences (4). The papers in this volume focus on environmental chemistry and related disciplines. Each effort can be viewed as a piece of a jigsaw puzzle that, when completed, may form a comprehensive view of Global Environmental Chemistry. While the ability to understand global environmental chemistry may be necessary to understand the behavior of the global natural environment, it is not sufficient. Scientists are attempting to piece together jigsaw puzzles of the chemistry, the geophysics, the biology, and other science disciplines describing global behavior. Does a puzzle piece resulting from a specific

0097–6156/92/0483–0005$06.00/0

study fit into the global chemistry puzzle (read model)? How can a piece of the global chemistry puzzle be tailored to fit into a global geophysics puzzle? The first step in integration (putting the puzzle pieces together), is to understand the boundaries, resolution, and focus of each research effort. These characteristics are the ones that define the size and shape of a puzzle piece described by a study or subset of knowledge.

Interdisciplinary Issues

Paradigms. Each scientific discipline bounds their domain of study and selects their level of spatial and temporal resolution. Kuhn (5) introduced the concept of paradigms of science that form the basic concepts, assumptions, and goals of a discipline. He observed that the progress of science is marked by shifts in paradigms. In addition to paradigm shifts by scientific disciplines, splintering of disciplines into subgroups with alternative paradigms is also a common event. There now appears to be a paradigm shift in global environmental studies where disciplinary efforts are giving way to interdisciplinary efforts. These interdisciplinary efforts will probably result in new disciplines as they mature. How will the discipline of chemistry respond to these changing paradigms?

Any interdisciplinary team studying global environmental changes must adopt a common nomenclature, a paradigm, and a set of spatial and temporal units if their contributions are to be successfully synthesized. Each discipline may use a different paradigm and may establish unique nomenclature to establish their identity. Ergo, adoption of a common set of nomenclature and a common paradigm are difficult tasks for any interdisciplinary team. The basic problem is that training in any discipline provides an individual with a paradigm that establishes what is important and unimportant to that discipline and a nomenclature that discipline members can use for communication of their ideas.

When individuals from several disciplines try to address a common problem, how do they communicate with each other and what process do they select for their paradigm? If each individual believes that their paradigm is the only one to use and that every one must use that nomenclature and process, major confrontations can arise. If there is a dominate personality that forces everyone on the team to learn the leaders' paradigm, language, and process, then a learning period of several years may be required before the team can be effective. An alternative is to create a compromise language acceptable to the team, but this can create a communication barrier between the team and the traditional disciplines.

These paradigm and people problems are not limited to disciplinary groups (6). Groups in industry and government are interdisciplinary in composition, since individuals are faced with the option of cooperating or leaving. This threat does not exist for tenured faculty in the university setting, which exacerbates interdisciplinary approaches to environmental problems. Organizational groups in industry and government provide functional services such as research and development in particular subjects such as materials, waste handling, unit operations, or service functions. Service functions may encompass such diverse areas as instrumentation, data analysis, clinical services, monitoring, and resource management. They develop their own paradigm, language, and culture. The integration of interorganizational teams presents the same type of problems encountered in the management of interdisciplinary teams in the university setting (7).

Temporal and Spatial Resolution.   Once the issue of nomenclature is resolved, the team must select a baseline temporal and spatial resolution. Scientists studying plate deformations and the behavior of internal earth processes use time scales of millions and billions of years.   Scientists studying the dynamics at the surface of the earth are concerned with solar driven processes and use time scales ranging from days to centuries. These researchers may assume that internal earth processes are static for purposes of their studies.   If the temporal baseline selected is days, then those researchers interested in phenomena that require years or centuries will withdraw from the team.

Spatial resolution for global studies can be based on a division of the earth into atmospheric, aquatic, and terrestrial components as shown in Figure 1, and this is the organizational structure used in this book. Another decomposition strategy used in global environmental studies is to examine the cycling of the various forms of a chemical element. Carbon, nitrogen, phosphorus, and sulfur cycling have been most widely investigated. Such studies employ mass balances and material flows to describe the fluxes, sinks and sources of interacting forms of the element.

In the past, disciplinary researchers have bounded their study area in space and time and assumed that their interfaces with the other disciplines are given and independent of each other. Disciplinary researchers strive to decompose and increase the resolution of their selected research topic. There are few researchers that try to integrate findings from different disciplines and explore the interface issues that often are ignored by the pure disciplines, since their parent disciplines view such efforts as inconsistent with disciplinary goals. The need to integrate disciplinary studies to create a synthesis of global environmental behavior arose with the threat that human activities could alter the global environment.   For example, scientists investigating the atmosphere and the oceans study circulation and temperatures. Only in the last few decades have they joined forces to study the interfaces and dynamics of the fluxes between the atmosphere and the oceans.   Terrestrial scientists studying productivity, nutrient cycling, and biome extent at local and regional scales, tend to assume that atmospheric and oceanic systems are givens or that the processes that they study do not impact the global environment.   Even the study of water has been decomposed into many disciplinary efforts such as hydrology, oceanography, geochemistry, limnology, or civil and environmental engineering. There is not a single discipline that synthesizes the knowledge-base associated with water.   The fragmentation of science and the creation of many specialty disciplines to cope with the complex and massive knowledge base generated

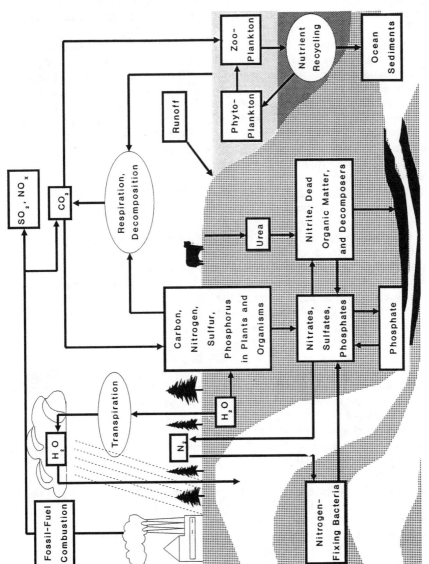

Figure 1. Global Environment Cycles and Spatial Partitions.

by scientists is a major barrier to synthesizing knowledge required to understand the global environment.

Defining the Problem and Integrating the Findings. Even when interdisciplinary or interorganizational groups develop effective communication, they may spend too little time defining their problem and may develop the right answer to the wrong problem, or that they devote too much time to problem definition and never solve the problem. Other interdisciplinary groups enjoy each other so much that they create a new discipline and spend all their efforts defending their new found field rather than contributing their knowledge to address the larger global issues.

The scientific process of hypothesis formulation, testing, and validation by separate scientific disciplines is difficult to implement in large, complex, global environmental studies. Scientists, especially those attempting large scale interdisciplinary efforts associated with global studies, have serious problems defining their problems and orchestrating their efforts. Large scale interdisciplinary research efforts also have the problem that they cannot be duplicated and verified because of costs.

Such problems are common to many interdisciplinary research efforts. When I began my studies, I found that problems I had observed were reported earlier by Holling and Chambers (8) and have existed for a long time. I have been studying the behavior of interdisciplinary and interorganizational groups for several decades and observe slow progress in understanding how to manage interdisciplinary efforts (6,7); hopefully global environmental scientists will do better.

Any effort to integrate the findings of partial global environmental system studies into a comprehensive holistic view requires:

- a common set of time and spatial scales to be used in the analysis,
- the ability to aggregate or disaggregate existing knowledge to these time scales,
- the ability to monitor or transform data at this scale of resolution,
- the ability to formulate and validate models at this resolution, and
- the ability to aggregate and disaggregate knowledge to the elected level of resolution.

System Concepts

A system is a convenient concept that is used to describe how the individual parts of anything (a system) are perceived to interact. System concepts are used by many disciplines and may form a common framework to support global environmental studies. A system definition must start with the identification of the boundaries of the system of interest. Next, the inputs and outputs to that system must be identified. The inputs and outputs of subsystems are the conventional linkages to other subsystems and facilitate the integration of any part of the system into the whole. As discussed previously, it is important that a common and consistent set of units be selected to describe these inputs and outputs. Once the inputs and outputs are selected, the next task is to discover or describe the processes that transform the inputs into outputs.

Some investigators use the term *box* for system. Box models are abstractions of the real world, where parts of the real world such as an ocean, a continent, a nation, or a city are isolated in an imaginary box for analysis. Other researchers use the term *compartment* rather than the box or system. *Biome* is a term ecologists use to describe and isolate ecosystems of interest such as forest, desert, or grassland. Each of these bounding concepts has the common property of isolating a part of the global environment for study. Another abstraction commonly used to bound a system is to select a chemical compound or element of interest. Studies of global environmental chemistry may select organic or inorganic compounds or elements of interest and ignore others when they define a system.

System Properties and Components. It is important to explicitly identify what is assumed to remain constant, what is to be neglected, and what has been abstracted. For example, if those interested in the atmosphere ignore the contributions from the oceans, or those studying the lakes, rivers, and oceans ignore atmospheric input, then mass, energy, and element balances will be incorrect. In the long run, it is the ignored inputs and outputs that limit the value of global system studies. Scientists should employ system concepts to improve the understanding of the scope, limitations, assumptions, and significance of various global environmental system studies. Since any scientific study is an abstraction of the real world and only addresses the researcher's view of the global environmental system, linkages must be created to permit these partial views to be integrated into a whole. There are two basic types of study performed on bounded components of the global environment, 1) a static view providing an inventory or a mass balance of inputs, outputs, and storage in the system at a point in time or integrated over a time period, and 2) a dynamic view describing the rates of change of inputs, outputs, transformations, and storage as a function of time.

Decomposability. The most important concept provided by system science is that an entire system can be decomposed into its parts, and that the integration of the parts should describe the whole. The danger of a bottom-up strategy in global studies (studying particular parts of the system and then synthesizing knowledge of these parts) is that if all the parts of the system are not identified, the synthesized view will be incomplete. The top-down approach to system analysis avoids these problems of omission with a parity check for all the parts that must make up the whole. In top-down analysis there is always a part called *the rest of the system*, to which unknown or forgotten parts are assigned. In most system studies, the rest of the system (the parts not addressed by the study) is described by assumptions that are made to reduce the study to a manageable size. Explicit descriptions of all assumptions used to bound the study are critical, since these assumptions form the linkages that allow that study to be synthesized into a total system description.

Global Environmental Systems

Five major cycles that drive global biogeochemistry and the atmospheric interactions are illustrated in Figure 2 (4). In the past, studies of terrestrial systems have been carried out, but more efforts are now underway to study ocean systems. The basic processes described in this illustration are 1) the hydrologic cycle, 2) the solar driven biological cycles converting inorganic forms of chemicals into plant biomass, 3) the conversion of plant matter into animal biomass, 4) the subsequent decomposition of plant and animal matter back to inorganic chemicals, and 5) reaction processes that convert fossil and living biomass into carbon dioxide and water. The hydrologic cycle is usually a separate system view of global processes. It describes the magnitude and dynamics of the earth's water as it evaporates from the oceans and terrestrial surface waters, as it condenses in cloud formation and is transported by earth's weather systems, precipitates in the form of snow or rain, and drains from higher elevations, eroding and transporting rocks and sediment towards the ocean floor. The hydrologic cycle is a buffer for solar energy input to the earth's surface and is the transport mechanism to redistribute moisture to the land. While cycling of carbon, nitrogen, sulfur, and phosphorus is fairly well understood in the laboratory, on farms, and in waste water treatment plants, estimating the global magnitude and dynamics of the pools for these elements in their various chemical species is not a simple task. Past terrestrial studies have focused on biomes, continents, biosphere reserves, but not on a global scale. Most of these studies take the hydrologic cycle, the topology, and the climate as givens that are not impacted by the ecosystem being studied.

The oceans contain more than 90% of the Earth's nonsedimentary carbon and nutrients (4) yet the role and magnitude of the ocean in cycling carbon and nutrients is less understood than is the contribution of terrestrial biological activity. In fact, the knowledge base available to understand the circulation of waters in the oceans is still incomplete. Lacking an understanding of transport processes, it is no wonder than biological productivity in the oceans is not well understood. Yet if global cycles are to be examined, there is a need to define biological activity on the surface of the earth, combining terrestrial and ocean contributions. Only when this system view is taken, can the pools and fluxes most important to biogeochemical cycles be identified.

Land/atmospheric interfacial processes which impact climate and biological activity on earth are illustrated in Figure 3. Emissions of carbon dioxide, methane, nitrogen dioxide, and chlorofluorocarbons (CFCs) have been linked to the transmission of solar radiation to the surface of the earth as well as to the transmission of terrestrial radiation to space. Should solar radiation be an internal process or an external driver of the hydrologic cycle, weather, and air surface temperatures? Compounds of sulfur and nitrogen are associated with acidic precipitation and damage to vegetation, aquatic life, and physical structures.

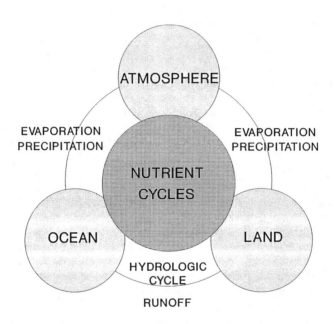

Figure 2. Five Basic Biogeochemical Cycles.

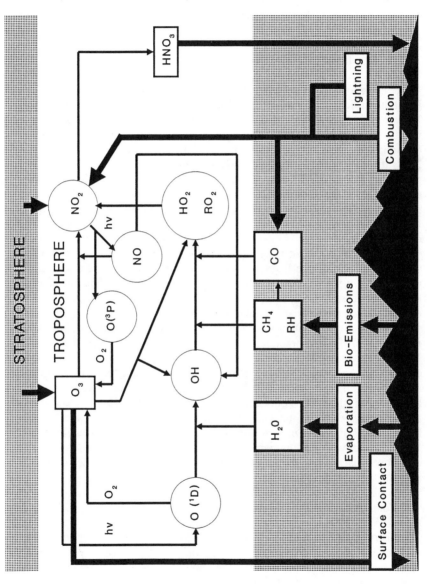

Figure 3. Land /Atmosphere Interfacial Processes.

A representation of the stratospheric system that shields terrestrial life from excessive solar ultraviolet radiation is presented in Figure 4. Our primary concern is the decrease of stratospheric ozone, most striking in the Antarctic, which has been linked to increases in CFCs from the troposphere, and the possible increased transport of these compounds between the stratosphere and the troposphere by increased temperature driven circulation.

The Human Interface

There is a strong interaction between natural global environmental processes and human activities, and many global environmental studies need to view human activities as part of the system being studied and not as external inputs. The economic, social, geopolitical behavior of global systems is dynamic and has strong feedback with the natural environment. The integration of the "hard science" chemical, physical, and biological studies of global environments with the "soft science" studies of human economic, social, and political behavior is a new challenge. I have stressed the need to include a technological sector in global environmental models (2,9), since the interactions between human activities and the natural environment are dynamic.

Political decisions do not always rely on scientific knowledge and, even when scientific proof of cause and effect is established, corrective actions may be slow and inadequate. If we wait until there is sufficient scientific basis to understand the impacts of human activities on the biogeochemical cycles or climate change, the environment may be so degraded that it cannot support the level of human activity that now exists. A trade-off must be made by global environmental researchers between 1) the use of a coarser spatial and temporal resolution to allow the linking of human behavior and chemical cycling and 2) the reduction of boundaries to gain more temporal and/or spatial resolution of the physical circulation systems or the biogeochemical cycles. Politically, the question for scientists should be "can human activities alter the global processes such as weather and natural biogeochemical cycles in a nonreversible direction that will cause major economic damage and human suffering?" If the answer is yes, then the question must follow: "what alternative policies can be implemented to mitigate or minimize these global impacts?"

The Components and the Connections

Chemistry may be a unifying force for studies of global environmental phenomena, since chemists have a common paradigm and may be able to facilitate the aggregation or disaggregation of data to the temporal and spatial resolutions needed for global studies more rapidly than other disciplines. The American Chemical Society might provide a forum for

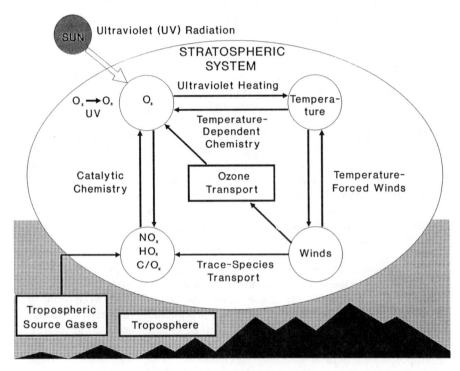

Figure 4. Processes that Control Ozone in the Stratosphere.

chemists involved with global environmental studies to establish a universal set of boundaries and units used in the study of global environmental processes. Standard methods could be established for the conversion of information from partial system studies to global system concepts. Such concepts could provide a unifying framework for synthesis. The search for connections may be facilitated by appropriate definitions of space, time, and chemical boundaries as the common dimensions.

The global system studies described by NASA (4) were presented to illustrate the variation in inputs and outputs, temporal and spatial scales, processes, and boundary interfaces associated with different aspects of global environmental studies. The reader should attempt to define these same characteristics for each paper in this volume. I will try to suggest important connections that may be of interest in these papers. How do each of these papers contribute to the understanding of global environmental chemistry? What piece of the overall puzzle is provided by each of these papers? Can the finding of each paper be tailored to form a piece in a different puzzle?

The Table of Contents for this collection will facilitate this discussion. Notice that the papers are grouped into the categories of Atmospheric, Aquatic and Terrestrial Components, Global Carbon Cycle and Climate Change, and Global Environmental Science Education. The reader may want to consider the various chemical species studied in each paper. Next, the reader may wish to group the papers by whether they address the source or the receptor, the transport or transformation processes for the chemical species. Finally, the reader needs to establish the time scales and the spatial resolution used.

The Atmospheric Component. Using the above strategy to search for connections in the set of papers in the Atmospheric Component group, the chemicals of interest are those associated with ozone production or depletion, and those associated with acid precipitation. Molina and Molina address stratospheric ozone destruction while O'Brien and George address inputs that may influence tropospheric ozone production or the troposphere's natural cleansing mechanisms. The other papers in the Atmospheric Component group address air pollution impacts on humans and the environment. The chemicals of concern are fossil fuel combustion products. The spatial resolution examined ranges from the urban scale study of Mexico City by Garfias and Gonzalez to the global assessment of urban air quality by Akland et al. A "connection" issue is how to aggregate urban level studies to the global level. The transport of air pollutants from one location to another on a regional scale is reported by Moser et al. Elder examines those components that are related to acidic precipitation. The reader may wish to identify those chemical species common to these papers and to consider the more detailed resolution studies synthesized to address global issues. Neither CO_2 nor carbon are addressed in these papers, yet they are an implicit in the chemistry of the chemicals in this set of papers.

The Aquatic Component. These papers demonstrate the need for consistent spatial and temporal characteristics to connect research results. At the local or urban scale, Pavoni *et al.* examine water quality in the Venice lagoon related to eutrophication and other pollution problems. Williams reports on Great lakes Water Quality and Dunnette examines global river water quality issues with the Willamette River as a case study. El-Sayed and Stephens examine productivity in the Southern Ocean. While all of these efforts include productivity, none present convenient linkages to the others. For example, do nutrients released in urban areas flush to rivers and then to the oceans in significant amounts to alter fluxes, pools, or dynamics of nutrients? Are nutrients the major concern in eutrophication problems or may light or toxicity be limiting? Unless these studies clearly define the bounds and assumption used, it is difficult to synthesize or extrapolate their findings. Levy's paper on marine debris raises the question "where does all the plastic come from?" Should researchers examining urban, river and lake water quality include plastics and study their transport to the oceans? Carbon dioxide and carbon are implicit in this set of papers, but can these papers contribute to the global carbon balance or to ozone depletion studies? The answer is that if the time and spatial dimensions and units are defined and the boundaries and chemicals are clearly identified such connections are possible.

The Terrestrial Component. These papers illustrate the application of temporal, spatial, and domain connectivity. Chemicals associated with people, food eaten by people, insects, and other organisms that compete with people for food, and other biomass must be identified. Since most of these chemical groups are terrestrial, spatial boundaries such as urban, biome, regional, and global are used. From a system perspective, these boundaries exclude water and air and require that they be placed in the "rest of the system" category. This type of boundary introduces the assumption that food, competitors for food, or any chemical that is discharged to or harvested from the air or water is ignored or assumed to be external to the system studied.

Examination of each set of papers may reveal that more questions than answers are provided. For example, none of the papers in the Terrestrial Component section examine a complete global cycling of food. A problem of food production is poor storage and transportation--how much food decomposes or is destroyed before it can be consumed by people? How would improvement of storage and transportation impact fossil fuel usage? How does this, in turn, impact air pollution or water pollution. Will air and water pollution impact crop production? One obvious connection is methane--several of the papers in this group address biomethanogenesis as a link between food production and air quality related problems--methane is an increasingly important component of both the troposphere and the stratosphere.

A more difficult question to explore is how much food an individual requires to be happy. A simpler question is how much food does a human need to function at different levels of efficiency. These questions must be approached by examining the direct inputs to a human, and then expanded to examine the indirect inputs associated with the direct inputs. For example, the paper by Pimentel addresses the issue of food production and the effectiveness of pesticides, chemical fertilizers, and other chemicals in producing food for humans. Extrapolating these data into the long term future requires additional studies that address issues other than food and people. Food production requires energy to irrigate, cultivate, harvest, transport, and store food products; and land area for it's production. Hall addresses the energy needed to produce food, while Chynoweth's studies of biomethanogenesis provide insights to the question. The loss of forests caused by land clearing for food production has positive as well as negative global impacts. Kauffman *et al.* analyze the biogeochemistry of deforestation and the resulting loss of soil productivity and increase of runoff pollution to streams, lakes, and the oceans. Fergusson examines dust in the environment and stimulates concern for decreased food production associated with increased particulate matter in the atmosphere. Kline describes the impact of acid deposition on forest decline and Whitford examines the decoupling of elemental cycles that results in desertification.

Global Carbon Cycle and Climate Change. Two major human activities, in addition to food production, have increased in magnitude to become threats to the global environment. The combustion of fossil fuels to provide energy to transport people, to power the industrial complex, and to provide heat, light, and other forms of energy to support human activities all create many forms of pollution, including runoff from extraction activities, water and air pollution from refining or processing activities, and water, land, and air pollution from energy producing activities. The reactions and reaction rates of fossil fuel related pollutants must be identified if sources, sinks, and fates of these pollutants are to be understood and controlled. There are many pieces to a puzzle describing global carbon cycles. People, food, and forests are only a few of the carbon pools that have been identified. Chynoweth examines biomethanogenesis as an important biochemical reaction for global environmental studies since there is increasing concern regarding the role of methane in the global atmosphere and interest in methane as an alternative energy source. The role of methanogenesis at a global scale requires estimation of all the pools and fluxes for methane.

Post *et al.* and Moran examine the global warming issue--the sources, reactions, and fate of greenhouse gases linked to global warming. Simpson and Botkin describe efforts to estimate North American and global forest biomass. Estimating rates of input and output of carbon in forests requires not only understanding of natural processes, but impacts of human actions such as land clearing for food production and pollutants released by human activity. El-Sayed's paper examines the response of phytoplankton to UV radiation, providing a linkage between food production and ozone depletion issues. A reduced ozone shield which permits increasing levels of UV radiation to reach the surface of the earth may alter photosynthetic activity of phytoplankton. Since phytoplankton form the base of the food web, changes in phytoplankton biomass and productivity will impact the amount of food that can be consumed by humans. Any of these issues cannot be separated from the energy/food/people issues, since the chemicals contributing to ozone depletion and global warming are products of food/energy/people activities.

The Educational Component. The papers in this book addressing educational agendas should be read to learn how to synthesize information, and to learn how researchers can provide connecting information in their publications. The educational agenda should stress learning how to find and use existing knowledge, how to adequately define the boundaries, inputs, and outputs used in a study, how to clearly state research hypotheses and results, how to identify the role of the various disciplines in global environmental science, and how scientists can provide the unifying force for global environmental studies at any educational level. Kupchella discusses the education of environmental specialists and generalists in American universities, while Winchester describes a unique undergraduate college program in global change. Finally, Stearns discusses the integration of one aspect of global environmental science (environmental chemistry) into secondary school curricula.

While understanding chemical reactions is a necessary first step, integrating knowledge of reactions with knowledge of sources, sinks, and transport of chemicals is also necessary. In addition to this "hard science" understanding, there is also the need to incorporate social science understanding of human use or abuse of our environmental resources.

Conclusions

Chemistry can be a unifying force for studies of the global environment, but chemists must learn to identify the boundaries, assumptions, and focus of their studies. Examination of past interdisciplinary efforts such as NASA's global environmental studies, and the papers in this collection, reveals that in order to conduct global environmental chemistry studies, the fluxes and pools of chemicals must be estimated. Since most studies abstract the real problem into systems that can be addressed, the study results may be more sensitive to changes in assumptions than to the variables, spatial domain, or time period selected for study. Investigations of food production without examination of the impact of water or air pollution created by food production will overestimate food production. By focusing on the damages that may result from global warming, and ignoring the potential benefits, the wrong management actions may be prescribed. Even comprehensive interdisciplinary studies of the global environment must include simplifying assumptions, and select spatial and temporal scales that will highlight certain phenomena while ignoring others. Facilitating the connections between researchers and research efforts is one of the most important activities in global environmental studies, and chemists and other environmental scientists must step forward and provide this linkage. The key to integration of subsystem studies is to be able to reconcile and support the heterogeneous sets of temporal and spatial scales of analysis used in the various global environmental system studies that are underway. This integration capability is essential to those that have to assemble, teach, and use this knowledge to allocate research funding. Thus there is an opportunity for chemists and other scientists to provide the integrative role for global environmental studies.

Literature Cited

1. Botkin, D.B., Caswell, M.F., Estes, J.E., and Orio, A.A., Eds. Changing the Global Environment - Perspectives on Human Involvement; Academic Press, Inc, Boston, 1989.
2. Mar, B.W., "Technology and the Environment, Workshop on Science Policy for Developing Countries", Cocoyoc, Mexico 1991.
3. Weaver, W., American Scientist, 1948, 36, No. 1.
4. NASA, Earth System Science - A Closer View, Earth System Sciences Committee, NASA, Washington, D.C., 1988.
5. Kuhn, T, The Structure of Scientific Revolutions, 2nd edition, Chicago, University of Chicago Press, 1970.
6. Mar, B.W., Regional Environmental Systems - Assessment of RANN Projects, University of Washington, NSF project NSF/ENV/76-04273. Seattle, WA, 1978.
7. Mar, B.W., Newell, W.T., Saxberg, B.O., Eds.; Managing High Technology -An Interdisciplinary Perspective, North-Holland, Amsterdam, 1985.
8. Holling, C.W. and Chambers, A.D., BioScience, 1973, 23, pp 13-20.
9. Mar, B W., In Changing the Global Environment - Perspectives on Human Involvement; Botkin, D.B., Caswell, M.F., Estes,J.E., and Orio,A.A., Eds; Academic Press, Inc, Boston, 1989, pp 403-418.

RECEIVED September 25, 1991

The Atmospheric Component
An Overview

Robert J. O'Brien

Environmental Sciences Program, Chemistry Department, Portland State University, Portland, OR 97207

Earth's atmosphere was perhaps the first medium to give rise to the fear of global pollution. Air knows no political boundaries and one country's emissions may be another country's lot to deal with. This was first recognized with acid precipitation in Europe and later in North America. However, the first intimation of an air pollution problem of truly *global* proportions arose with the proposal to fly commercial supersonic aircraft (SSTs) in the lower stratosphere. Initial concern over water vapor in aircraft exhaust (the stratosphere is very dry) intensified with the possibility that aircraft-emitted nitrogen oxides could play an increased catalytic role in destroying stratospheric ozone (1,2). Concern for stratospheric ozone simmered for awhile after the US decided against entering the SST race. It resurfaced with a vengeance with the realization (3) that chlorofluorocarbons (CFCs) could provide a much more ominous threat to the earth's stratosphere than nitrogen oxides. However, even this heightened threat had faded in the public mind until the discovery (4) of the Antarctic *ozone hole*. This alarming symptom of human technology has finally provoked a global response by the world's nations, as related by Molina and Molina in their review here of stratospheric ozone chemistry and its implications.

The global proportions of this problem were brought home to me when I testified on behalf of a bill before the Oregon Legislature to ban non-essential uses of CFCs in 1976. I was asked by a senate member and future governor whether we could preserve the stratosphere over Oregon if we banned CFC use in our state. It is a credit to my home state that its legislature was the first governmental body to limit CFC usage--in spite of the fact that our small step forward wouldn't do much for Oregon's *piece* of the stratosphere.

Air pollution, responsible for about 4000 excess deaths in London's *pea-soup* smog of 1952 (5), and identified in a now more common oxidizing form by A.J. Haagen-Smit about the same time in Los Angeles (6), was at one time considered a *local* problem to be solved by dispersing emissions with taller smokestacks. The folly of this approach was brought home to Scandinavians as the average pH of rain in southern Norway and

0097–6156/92/0483–0021$06.00/0

Sweden dropped from a background value of 5.5-6.0 in 1956 to about 4.5 in 1975 (7), up to a 10-fold increase in acidity. Much of this *acid rain* results from emissions in upwind countries. The United States and Canada have debated a problem of almost identical proportions for many years, but the U.S. has recently taken steps to reduce sulfur dioxide emissions significantly (8). The multitudinous ramifications of North American acid deposition are discussed in this section by Elder.

The U.S. Clean Air Act Amendments of 1970 instructed the U.S. Environmental Protection Agency to establish national standards for a number of *criteria* air pollutants, ozone among them. The original ozone standard of 80 ppb has since been increased to 120 ppb, but even this standard is exceeded more than 50% of the time in Los Angeles, and other major U.S. population centers have ozone levels which are not expected to come into compliance with the standard in the foreseeable future. Ozone air pollution is a problem in most major population centers of the world, and here Garfias and Gonzalez discuss Mexico City's experience with ozone and other pollutants. A measure of the extent to which emission controls may go are the proposals in Los Angeles for widespread use of *alternate* automotive fuels, such as methanol, and for the regulation of ozone precursors as seemingly insignificant as charcoal lighter fluid for backyard barbecues.

It is ironic that molecular ozone is being formed in unhealthy amounts in numerous regions of the planet's lower atmosphere, and at the same time is being destroyed in significant amounts in the global stratosphere. Both processes are the result of atmospheric chemical reactions which have been the subject of intense study in recent decades. At the present time, sufficient knowledge of the chemical driving forces exists that regulatory actions can be undertaken. But knowledge is still insufficient to allow an unequivocal knowledge of the future outcome of such actions.

In contrast to stratospheric ozone depletion, recently documented over large regions of the stratosphere (9), atmospheric oxidants and acids are not yet evenly distributed over the globe. The atmosphere's cleansing mechanisms still allow many regions of the world to achieve air which has the semblance of its pre-industrial purity. The free-radical chemical processes which bring us both the intermediate reaction products of human emissions (smog) and the end product (*clean* air) are discussed here by O'Brien and George. Unfortunately, the old adage *what goes up must come down* still applies, and the accumulation of a variety of toxic air pollutants, deposited far from their emission sources, is of concern to global ecosystems, as discussed by Moser, Barker and Tingey.

Although pollution of the global troposphere has not yet reached alarming levels, urban and regional air pollution is clearly a problem of global proportions. The status of global urban air quality is addressed by Akland, de Koning, Mage, and Ozoline. Their analysis of data collected by the United Nations Environmental Programme (UNEP) and the World Health Organization (WHO) through the Global Environment Monitoring Systems (GEMS) Network is presented here. Sadly, they find that less than 20% of the world's urban dwellers enjoy healthy levels of sulfur dioxide and suspended particulate matter, as defined by WHO guidelines. Other pollutants analyzed are nitrogen dioxide, carbon monoxide and lead. Unfortunately, data for ozone are not yet available in a form appropriate for a global analysis.

Atmospheric particulate matter (dust or aerosol) is a good example of the global commonality of air composition, and Fergusson gives a comprehensive analysis of worldwide data for the elemental composition of *dust*. The similar composition found worldwide is attributed to a combination of common sources, efficient atmospheric mixing, and the prevalence of soil and crustal material as a leveling factor.

What does the future hold for global air quality? It is relatively certain that even with a complete cessation of CFC production by the year 2000, stratospheric ozone depletion will continue well into the next century (10). The extent of maximum depletion is still difficult to predict with confidence, but is likely to be small over the tropics and no more than 5% at high latitudes (11). With tropospheric air pollutants, it seems likely that pollutant concentrations in the so-called developed countries may decrease, in spite of contined increase in emission sources associated with population or industrial growth. These countries have the financial resources (and the political will) to invest in emission controls. The extent of future decrease is hard to foresee though, and the decrease may apply mostly to emissions in urban regions with known air quality problems. Total emissions from developed countries are less a matter of current concern, and could increase as emission sources are dispersed away from population centers with existing air quality problems. The situation is even less sanguine in the developing countries, in spite of increasing global efforts to reduce levels of air pollutants, because of these countries' desire to *catch-up* with the industrialized countries, and the role laxer emission standards may play in giving such countries a competitive edge. Stratospheric ozone is now a problem of widely acknowledged global import. It seems likely that global tropospheric pollution, although not here yet, is a concern for the future.

Literature Cited

1.   Crutzen, P.J. *Q.J.R. Meteorol. Soc.* **1070**, 96, 320-325.
2.   Johnston, H.S. *Science* **1971**, 173, 517-522.
3.   Molina, M.J.; Rowland, F.S. *Nature* **1974**, 249, 810-812.
4.   Farman, J.C.; Gardiner, B.G.; Shanklin, J.D. *Nature* **1985**, 315, 207-210.
5.   Logan, W.P.D. *Lancet* **1953**, 264, 336-338.
6.   Haagen-Smit, A.J. *Ind. Eng. Chem.* **1952**, 44, 1342.
7.   Overrein, L.N.; Seip, J.M.; Tollan, A. *Acid Precipitation - Effects on Forest and Fish*; RECLAMO, Oslo, Norway, 1980.
8.   United States Clean Air Ammendments, 1990.
9.   *Report of the International Ozone Trends Panel 1988*, Global Ozone Research and Monitoring Project Report No. 18, World Meteorological Organization, Geneva, Switzerland, 1988.
10. Prather, M.J.; Watson, R.T. *Nature* **1990**, 344, 729-735.
11. World Meteorological Association, *Scientific assessment of stratospheric ozone: 1989, Report 20*, Global Ozone Research and Monitoring Project, Geneva, 1990.

RECEIVED September 30, 1991

Chapter 2

Stratospheric Ozone

Mario J. Molina and Luisa T. Molina

Department of Earth and Planetary Sciences, 54–1312, Massachusetts Institute of Technology, Cambridge, MA 02139

The ozone layer is a very important component of the atmosphere which shields the earth's surface from damaging ultraviolet radiation from the sun. Ozone is continuously being generated by the action of solar radiation on atmospheric oxygen, and it is destroyed by catalytic processes involving trace amounts of free radical species such as nitrogen oxides. More than a decade ago the release of chlorofluorocarbons (CFCs) of industrial origin was predicted to lead to stratospheric ozone depletion. Photodecomposition of the CFCs in the stratosphere produces significant amounts of chlorine free radicals, which are very efficient catalysts for the destruction of ozone. Recent observations have established clearly that the rapid decline in ozone over Antarctica in the spring months is indeed caused by man-made chlorine species.

Ozone (O_3) is continuously being generated in the atmosphere by the action of solar ultraviolet radiation of wavelengths shorter than about 220 nm on molecular oxygen (O_2) to form atomic oxygen (O), followed by the recombination of O-atoms with O_2:

$$O_2 + h\nu \rightarrow O + O \tag{1}$$

$$O + O_2 \rightarrow O_3. \tag{2}$$

Ozone is a relatively unstable species which is easily destroyed by various chemical processes. Its peak concentration is several parts of ozone per million parts of air, and it is found primarily in the stratosphere, the region between about 10 and 50 km above the Earth's surface.

Ozone absorbs ultraviolet radiation very efficiently in the wavelength range between 200 and 300 nm, where molecular oxygen and nitrogen are

0097–6156/92/0483–0024$06.00/0

practically transparent. Hence, one of the important functions of the stratospheric ozone layer is to shield the surface of the Earth from solar ultraviolet radiation, which is harmful to living organisms. This ultraviolet radiation is known to cause human skin cancer as well as pose a threat to certain crops, forests, and ecological systems. In the process of absorbing this radiation the ozone molecule is destroyed:

$$O_3 + hv \rightarrow O_2 + O \tag{3}$$

This process does not lead to net ozone depletion because it is rapidly followed by reaction 2, which regenerates the ozone. Reactions 2 and 3 have, however, another important function, namely the absorption of solar energy; as a result, the temperature increases with altitude, and this *inverted* temperature profile gives rise to the stratosphere (see Figure 1). In the lower layer, the troposphere, the temperature decreases with altitude and vertical mixing occurs on a relatively short time scale. In contrast, the stratosphere is very stable towards vertical mixing because of its inverted temperature profile.

The oxygen atoms, formed in the stratosphere predominantly by reaction 3, occasionally react with ozone instead of adding to molecular oxygen:

$$O + O_3 \rightarrow O_2 + O_2 \tag{4}$$

Reactions 1 to 4 are known collectively as the *Chapman mechanism,* (first outlined by Sidney Chapman (1) in 1930. They basically explain how ozone can exist in the stratosphere in a dynamic balance; it is continuously being produced by the action of solar ultraviolet radiation on oxygen molecules and destroyed by several natural chemical processes in the atmosphere.

Catalytic ozone destruction cycles

The concentration of ozone in the stratosphere is lower than predicted from reactions 1 - 4. This is due to the presence of trace amounts of some reactive species known as free radicals. These species have an odd number of electrons and they can speed up reaction 4 by means of catalytic chain reactions. Nitrogen oxides, NO and NO_2, which are naturally present in the stratosphere at levels of a few parts per billion (ppb), are the most important catalysts in this respect. The reactions, first suggested by Paul Crutzen (2) and by Harold Johnston (3) in the early 1970's, are as follows:

$$NO + O_3 \rightarrow NO_2 + O_2 \tag{5}$$

$$NO_2 + O \rightarrow NO + O_2 \tag{6}$$

Net reaction: $$O + O_3 \rightarrow O_2 + O_2. \tag{4}$$

Reactions 5 and 6 constitute a catalytic cycle because the radical NO that attacks O_3 is regenerated by the reaction of NO_2 with an O-atom. The net effect is the removal of one O_3 molecule and one O-atom. Thus, although the concentration of NO and NO_2 (or NOx) in the stratosphere is small, each NO molecule can destroy thousands of ozone molecules before being scavenged by a reaction such as the following:

$$OH + NO_2 \rightarrow HNO_3 \qquad (7)$$

Other important catalysts are the free radicals OH and HO_2, produced in the stratosphere by the decomposition of water vapor.

Chlorine atoms are also very efficient ozone destruction catalysts, as noted originally by Stolarski and Cicerone (4):

$$Cl + O_3 \rightarrow ClO + O_2 \qquad (8)$$

$$ClO + O \rightarrow Cl + O_2 \qquad (9)$$

Net reaction: $O + O_3 \rightarrow O_2 + O_2. \qquad (4)$

The stratosphere contains, however, only small amounts--a few tenths of a ppb--of chlorine free radicals of natural origin. They are produced by the decomposition of methyl chloride, CH_3Cl. The nitrogen oxides (NO and NO_2) are more abundant and are produced in the stratosphere by the decomposition of nitrous oxide, N_2O. Both CH_3Cl and N_2O are of biological origin: these compounds, released at the Earth's surface, are sufficiently stable to reach the stratosphere in significant amounts.

The Role of Chlorofluorocarbons

In 1974, Molina and Rowland (5) suggested that chlorofluorocarbons (CFCs) could provide an important source of chlorine free radicals to the stratosphere and hence would pose a threat to the ozone layer. The CFCs are man-made chemicals used as refrigerants, solvents, propellants for spray cans, blowing agents for plastic foam, etc. The two most important ones are CFC-11 ($CFCl_3$) and CFC-12 (CF_2Cl_2). These compounds are chemically inert and insoluble in water; thus, they are not removed in the lower atmosphere, in contrast to most other gases released to the environment at the Earth's surface. Instead, the CFCs rise into the stratosphere, where they are eventually destroyed by short-wavelength solar ultraviolet radiation of the type that is shielded by the ozone layer. Because diffusion into the stratosphere is very slow, the residence time for the CFCs in the environment is of the order of a century.

The photodecomposition of the CFCs leads to the release of chlorine atoms in the ozone layer. These atoms can then participate in reactions 8 and 9, as well as in other chemical and photochemical reactions. A schematic representation of the more important reactions is shown in Figure 2. The ClOx catalytic chain mechanism (Reactions 8 and 9) may be interrupted, for example, by reaction of the Cl atom with methane (CH_4) to produce the relatively stable hydrogen chloride molecule (HCl); or by reaction of chlorine monoxide (ClO) with NO_2 or HO_2 to produce $ClONO_2$ (chlorine nitrate) or HOCl (hypochlorous acid):

$$Cl + CH_4 \rightarrow HCl + CH_3 \tag{10}$$

$$ClO + NO_2 \rightarrow ClONO_2 \tag{11}$$

$$ClO + HO_2 \rightarrow HOCl + O_2. \tag{12}$$

The chlorine-containing product species (HCl, $ClONO_2$, HOCl) are "inert reservoirs" because they are not directly involved in ozone depletion; however, they eventually break down by absorbing solar radiation or by reaction with other free radicals, returning chlorine to its catalytically active form. Ozone is formed fastest in the upper stratosphere at tropical latitudes (by reactions 1 and 2), and in those regions a few percent of the chlorine is in its active "free radical" form; the rest is in the "inert reservoir" form (see Figure 3).

In order to estimate the extent of ozone depletion caused by a given release of CFCs, computer models of the atmosphere are employed. These models incorporate information on atmospheric motions and on the rates of over a hundred chemical and photochemical reactions. The results of measurements of the various trace species in the atmosphere are then used to test the models. Because of the complexity of atmospheric transport, the calculations were carried out initially with one-dimensional models, averaging the motions and the concentrations of chemical species over latitude and longitude, leaving only their dependency on altitude and time. More recently, two-dimensional models have been developed, in which the averaging is over longitude only.

The fundamental aspects of the problem are well established: the measured concentrations of the CFCs indicate that they accumulate in the lower atmosphere and that they reach the stratosphere. As expected, chlorine atoms and ClO radicals are found in the stratosphere together with other species such as O, OH, HO_2, NO, NO_2, HCl, $ClONO_2$, HOCl, etc. The observed concentrations are in reasonable agreement with the model predictions if the limitations of the models, as well as atmospheric variability, are taken into account.

Observed Stratospheric Ozone Trends

It is only recently that a decrease in stratospheric ozone levels attributable to the CFCs has been observed. In spite of the relatively large natural

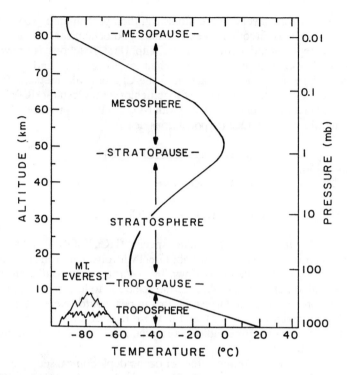

Figure 1. Average temperature profile of air above the earth's surface.

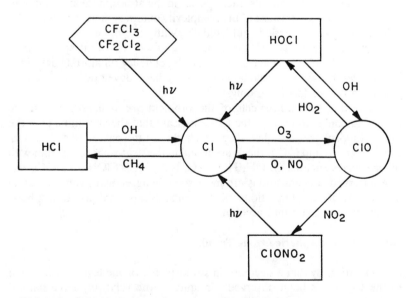

Figure 2. Schematic representation of the more important reactions and compounds in the stratospheric chemistry of chlorine at low and mid-latitudes.

fluctuations in ozone levels, it has been possible to show, by careful examination of the records over the last two decades, that statistically significant changes have occurred in the winter months at high latitudes (6). Furthermore, as first pointed out by Farman and co-workers (7), the ozone levels over Antarctica have dropped dramatically in the spring months starting in the early 1980's (see Figure 4). This Antarctic *ozone hole* was not predicted by earlier models; its cause was not clear until recent years, when laboratory experiments, field measurements over Antarctica and model calculations provided very strong indications that the ozone loss can indeed be traced to man-made CFCs.

Polar Ozone Chemistry

The high-latitude (polar) stratosphere has several unique characteristics. High-energy solar UV radiation is scarce over the poles, thus ozone is not generated there. However, the total ozone column abundance is large in this region because ozone is transported towards the poles from lower latitudes and higher altitudes. Furthermore, temperatures over the poles are very low. The catalytic cycles responsible for ozone destruction are active mainly at higher temperatures and in the presence of abundant solar UV radiation; thus ozone is predicted to be very stable over the poles based on conventional gas phase chemistry, and a chemical explanation of Antarctic ozone depletion requires a different mechanism.

The stratosphere is very dry; clouds do not form at lower latitudes because the temperature is not low enough. However, the stratosphere over Antarctica is distinctive: the temperature can drop to below -90° Celsius during the winter and spring months, leading to the condensation of water vapor and nitric acid vapor, that is, to the formation of ice clouds (polar stratospheric clouds or PSCs).

Several authors (8,9) suggested that PSCs could play a major role in the depletion of ozone over Antarctica by promoting the release of active chlorine from its reservoir species, mainly by the following reaction:

$$HCl + ClONO_2 \rightarrow Cl_2 + HNO_3. \qquad (13)$$

Laboratory experiments by our group showed that reaction 13 occurs very slowly in the gas phase (10). However, in the presence of ice surfaces the reaction proceeds very efficiently: the product Cl_2 is immediately released to the gas phase, whereas HNO_3 remains frozen in the ice (11). Other groups also found that this heterogeneous (i.e., multiphase) process occurs efficiently (12,13), and that a similar reaction also occurs with N_2O_5 as a reactant:

$$HCl + N_2O_5 \rightarrow ClNO_2 + HNO_3 \qquad (14)$$

Both Cl_2 and $ClNO_2$ absorb visible and near ultraviolet radiation, so that they can readily photolyze even with the faint amount of sunlight

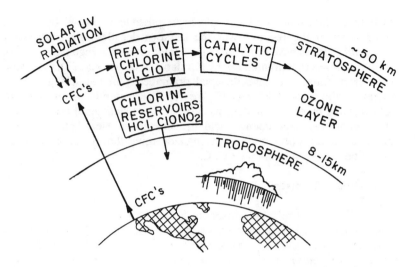

Figure 3. Simplified diagram of the atmospheric behavior of chlorofluorocarbons.

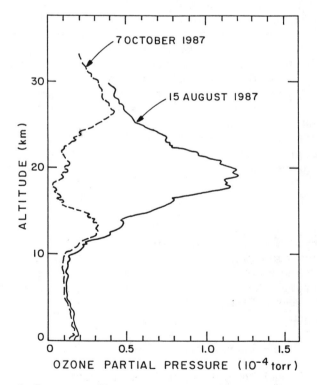

Figure 4. Ozone profiles measured in 1987 over Halley Bay, Antarctica, by Farman (20).

available in the early spring over Antarctica. This process releases free chlorine atoms which react rapidly with ozone, producing oxygen molecules and chlorine monoxide (reaction 8).

The mechanism for reaction 13 is not well established yet, but it is likely to proceed through ionic intermediates (11): the Cl atom in chlorine nitrate is slightly electropositive, so that it readily combines with negative chloride ions to produce Cl_2; the HCl on ice is expected to be at least partially ionized. We have found that HCl has a very high mobility on the ice surface, so that even small amounts of HCl will enable reaction 13 to occur. It is also possible for this reaction to proceed in two steps: the initial step is the reaction of chlorine nitrate with ice; it is followed by the reaction of the product HOCl with HCl on the ice substrate:

$$ClONO_2 + H_2O \rightarrow HOCl + HNO_3 \qquad (15)$$

$$HOCl + HCl \rightarrow H_2O + Cl_2 \qquad (16)$$

Laboratory experiments have shown that reaction 15 occurs on ice in the absence of HCl (11-13); furthermore, the product HOCl appears on a time scale of minutes, in contrast to Cl_2 in reaction 13, which is produced on at most a millisecond time scale (11). Thus, in this mechanism HOCl serves as an intermediate: if there is enough HCl on the ice, HOCl will react with HCl while still on the ice surface; otherwise the HOCl will desorb, eventually finding an HCl molecule in the ice, perhaps after several adsorption-desorption cycles.

The presence of PSCs also leads to the removal of nitrogen oxides (NO and NO_2) from the gas phase. As long as there are significant amounts of NO_2 it will react with chlorine monoxide (ClO) to produce chlorine nitrate (reaction 11). This species subsequently reacts with HCl on PSC surfaces to produce nitric acid (reaction 13), which remains in the condensed phase. Also, nitric acid directly condenses with water to form nitric acid trihydrate particles, hence it is not available to regenerate NO_2 by photochemical processes, as it does when it is in the gas phase.

The catalytic cycle described earlier (reactions 8 and 9) cannot explain the rapid depletion of ozone over the South Pole, because reaction 9 requires free oxygen atoms, which are too scarce in the polar stratosphere to react at any appreciable rate with ClO. Several catalytic cycles that do not require oxygen atoms have been suggested as being at work over Antarctica.

In 1986 we proposed a cycle that involves the self reaction of chlorine monoxide radicals, without requiring free oxygen atoms to regenerate the chlorine atoms (14):

$$ClO + ClO \rightarrow Cl_2O_2 \tag{17}$$

$$2 (Cl + O_3 \rightarrow ClO + O_2) \tag{8}$$

$$Cl_2O_2 + hv \rightarrow Cl + ClOO \tag{18}$$

$$ClOO \rightarrow Cl + O_2 \tag{19}$$

Net reaction: $2O_3 + hv \rightarrow 3O_2$ $\hspace{2cm}$ (20)

Much has been learned in recent years about the "ClO dimer", Cl_2O_2, produced in reaction 17. It is actually dichlorine peroxide, ClOOCl; its geometry is now well established from submillimeter wave spectroscopy (15). Photolysis of ClOOCl around 310 nm -- the atmospherically important wavelengths -- yields chlorine atoms and ClOO radicals (16), as given in reaction 18, rather than two ClO radicals, even though ClO-OCl is the weakest bond (it has a strength of about 17 Kcal/mol (17)). Thermal decomposition of ClOOCl (the reverse of reaction 17) occurs very fast at room temperature, but more slowly at polar stratospheric temperatures. Hence, photolysis is the predominant destruction path for ClOOCl in the polar stratosphere and two Cl atoms are produced for each ultraviolet photon absorbed.

McElroy *et al.* (18) suggested a cycle in which chlorine and bromine are coupled in the destruction of ozone:

$$ClO + BrO \rightarrow Cl + Br + O_2 \tag{21}$$

$$Br + O_3 \rightarrow BrO + O_2 \tag{22}$$

$$Cl + O_3 \rightarrow ClO + O_2 \tag{23}$$

Net reaction: $2O_3 + hv \rightarrow 3O_2$ $\hspace{2cm}$ (20)

There are natural sources of brominated hydrocarbons as well as man-made sources, such as the "halons", which are used in fire extinguishers. Reaction 21 is very fast and generates Cl and Br atoms directly; the cycle does not require a photolytic step. Although this cycle occurs with high efficiency, it is less important than the chlorine peroxide cycle because of the much smaller concentrations of bromine compounds in the stratosphere--parts per trillion vs. parts per billion for the chlorine compounds.

These catalytic cycles proceed efficiently as long as the NO_2 levels are low; otherwise NO_2 reacts with ClO (reaction 11), interfering with reactions 17 and 21. Thus, PSCs are important not only because they release chlorine from inert reservoirs, but also because they scavenge nitrogen oxides from the gas phase, thereby setting the stage for rapid ozone destruction.

Atmospheric Measurements in the Polar Stratosphere

Several key expeditions have been launched in the last few years to measure trace species in the stratosphere over Antarctica as well as over the Arctic. The results provide very convincing evidence for the occurrence of the chemical reactions discussed above and demonstrate the critical role played by man-made chlorine in the formation of the Antarctic "ozone hole". (See, for instance, *J. Geophys. Res. 94*, Nos. D9 and D14, **1989**, for a collection of articles on the Antarctic expedition of 1987, and *Geophys. Res. Lett. 17*, No. 4, **1990**, for the Arctic expedition of 1989). When ozone is being depleted in the spring months over Antarctica, a very large fraction of the chlorine is present as the free radical ClO (see Figure 5); NOx levels are very low; there are cloud particles and they contain nitrate; etc. Over the Arctic a large fraction of the chlorine is also activated, but ozone depletion is less severe because the temperatures are not as low as over Antarctica: the active chlorine remains in contact with ozone only briefly before the Arctic air masses mix with warmer air from lower latitudes. This air also contains NO_2, which passivates the chlorine.

A detailed analysis of the atmospheric measurements over Antarctica by Anderson *et al.* (19) indicates that the cycle comprising reactions 17 - 19 (the chlorine peroxide cycle) accounts for about 75% of the observed ozone depletion, and reactions 21 - 23 account for the rest. While a clear overall picture of polar ozone depletion is emerging, much remains to be learned. For example, the physical chemistry of the acid ices that constitute polar stratospheric clouds needs to be better understood before reliable predictions can be made of future ozone depletion, particularly at northern latitudes, where the chemical changes are more subtle and occur over a larger geographical area.

The Montreal Protocol

Under the auspices of the United Nations Environment Programme, many countries--including the industrialized nations of the world--signed an agreement in 1985 in Vienna to regulate the production of CFCs. This initial agreement was followed by the *Montreal Protocol* in 1987, which called only for a reduction of 50% in the manufacture of CFCs by the end of the century. In view of the strength of the scientific evidence linking stratospheric ozone depletion with the release of CFCs, the initial provisions were strengthened in 1990 through the *London Amendments* to the protocol: the CFCs will be essentially phased out by the end of the century. Other compounds, such as the halons, carbon tetrachloride (CCl_4) and methyl chloroform (CH_3CCl_3), which were not included in the initial negotiations, will also be regulated. Because of the long residence times of the CFCs in the atmosphere, even if the protocol were fully enforced, ozone depletion would continue well into the next century.

In terms of the uses of CFCs, roughly a third of the amount now produced will be replaced with hydrochlorofluorocarbons (HCFCs) or hydrofluorocarbons (HFCs), which are compounds with chemical and physical properties similar to those of the CFCs, except that their molecules contains hydrogen atoms. They are destroyed predominantly in the troposphere by reaction with the hydroxyl radical (OH), forming water and an organic free radical which rapidly photo-oxidizes to yield water-soluble products. Hence, only a small fraction of their release reaches the stratosphere. Another third of the CFC usage will be replaced by "not in kind" compounds; for example, FC-113, which is used to clean electronic boards, can be replaced in many instances by soap-and-water-based or terpene-based solvents. Finally, the last third of the usage will be dealt with by conservation: current practices lead to an unnecessarily large release of CFCs to the environment for certain uses such as cleaning solvents or as refrigerants for automobile air conditioning .

The CFC-ozone depletion issue has demonstrated that mankind has the potential to seriously modify the atmosphere on a global scale. We need to learn much more about the environment to prevent its inadvertent deterioration by human activities.

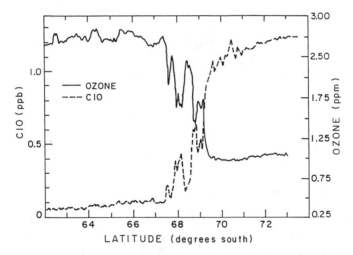

Figure 5. Measurements of chlorine monoxide by Anderson *et al.* (19) and of ozone by Proffitt *et al.* (21) carried out in 1987 during the Airborne Antarctic Ozone Experiment.

Literature Cited

1.   Chapman, S. *Mem. R. Meteorol. Soc.*, **1930**, *3*, pp. 103-105.
2.   Crutzen, P. J. *Q. J. R. Meteorol. Soc.*, **1970**, *96*, pp. 320-325.
3.   Johnston, H. *Science*, **1971**, *173*, pp. 517-522.
4.   Stolarski, R. S.; Cicerone, R. J. *Can. J. Chem.*, **1974**, *52*, pp. 1610-15.
5.   Molina, M. J.; Rowland, F. S. *Nature*, **1974**, *249*, pp. 810-812.

6.   *Report of the International Ozone Trends Panel 1988*, Global Ozone Research and Monitoring Project Report No. 18, World Meteorological Organization, Geneva, Switzerland, **1988**.
7.   Farman, J.C.; Gardiner, B.G.; Shanklin, J.D. *Nature*, **1985**, *315*, pp. 207-210.
8.   Solomon, S.; Garcia, R.R.; Rowland, F.S.; Wuebbles, D. J. *Nature*, **1986**, *321*, pp. 755-758.
9.   Toon, O.B.; Hamill, P.; Turco, R.P., Pinto, J. *Geophys. Res. Lett.*, **1986**, *13*, pp. 1284-1287.
10. Molina, L.T.; Molina, M.J.; Stachnik, R.A.; Tom, R.D. *J. Phys. Chem.*, **1985**, *89*, 3779-3781.
11. Molina, M.J., Tso, T.-L., Molina, L.T.; Wang, F.C.-Y. *Science*, **1987**, *238*, pp. 1253-1257.
12. Leu, M.T. *Geophys. Res. Lett.*, **1988**, *15*, pp. 17-20.
13. Tolbert, M.A.; Rossi, M.J.; Malhotra, R.; Golden, M.D. *Science*, **1987**, *238*, pp. 1258-1260.
14. Molina, L.T.; Molina, M.J. *J. Phys. Chem.*, **1987**, *91*, pp. 433-436.
15. Birk, M.; Friedl, R.R.; Cohen, E.A.; Pickett, H.M. *J. Chem. Phys.*, **1989**, *91*, pp. 6588-6597.
16. Molina, M.J.; Colussi, A.J.; Molina, L.T.; Schindler, R.N.; Tso, T.-L. *Chem. Phys. Lett.*, **1990**, *1973*, pp. 310-315.
17. Cox, R.A.; Hayman, G.D. *Nature*, **1988**, *322*, pp. 796-800.
18. McElroy, M.B.; Salawitch, R.J.; Wofsy, S.C.; Logan, J.A. *Nature*, **1986**, *321*, pp. 759-762.
19. Anderson, J.G.; Toohey, D.W.; Brune, W.H. *Science*, **1991**, *251*, pp. 39-46.
20. Farman, J.C. *New Scientist*, **1987**, *12*, pp. 50-54.
21. Proffitt, M.H.; Steinkamp, M.J.; Powell, J.A.; McLaughlin, R.J.; Mills, O.A.; Schmeltekopf, A.L.; Thompson, T.L.; Tuck, A.F.; Tyler, T.; Winker, R.H.; Chan, K.R. *J. Geophys. Res.*, **1989**, *94*, pp. 16,547-16,555.

RECEIVED October 7, 1991

Chapter 3

Acid Deposition

Acidification of the Environment

Floyd C. Elder[1]

Environment Canada, National Water Research Institute, Burlington, Ontario, Canada L7R 4A6

Acid deposition has been known to exist since early in the industrial age. The principle pollutants responsible for the elevated levels of acidity are the oxidized forms of sulphur and nitrogen that have been emitted as by-products from non-ferrous smelters, fossil-fueled power generating stations, and motor vehicles. The pollutants are transported substantial distances from the source areas by the atmosphere. They are deposited on receptor regions remote from the sources as acidic rain, snow, and fog or as gasses and dry particulates.

Sensitive ecosystems that cannot neutralize the unnatural levels of acidity are adversely affected. Soil nutrient systems may be altered with a resulting direct or indirect damage to forest. Aquatic habitats have been chemically altered and many lakes and streams no longer support the traditional life forms. Fish have been lost from many lakes with a resulting affect on other food-web elements.

Human respiratory functions may be impaired. Elevated levels of metals have been observed in some foods and drinking water in some locations. Masonry works, stone structures and heritage sculptures are subject to accelerated rates of erosion.

Control and reduction of emissions of acidifying pollutants have been legislated in United States, Canada and in some European nations. When these reductions are affected, a reduction of about 60,000 in the number of acidified lakes is expected to be achieved in Canada. However, many highly sensitive lakes will be expected to remain acidified.

---

[1]Current address: 5360 Salem Road, Burlington, Ontario, Canada L7L 3X3

0097–6156/92/0483–0036$08.00/0
© 1992 American Chemical Society

Acid Rain and The Environment

Recognizing The Problem. Over one hundred years ago a British chemist, Robert Angus Smith, used the term "acid rain" in his book "Air and Rain: The Beginnings of Chemical Climatology" (*1*). Although working with what we would now consider primitive technology, he identified several of the issues or questions which even today constitute the basis of public and scientific concern. (a) What is the origin of acidified precipitation? (b) What role does the burning of fossil fuels have? (c) How does the intensity of the precipitation affect the acidity of the receptor? Smith's work ultimately showed great perception in recognizing that the fuel sources that powered the industrial revolution released various unwanted by-products. The smoke and fumes carried substances which caused significant changes in the chemical composition of precipitation, and these changes could indeed be detected "in the town", "in the suburbs",and "in the fields at a distance". He also identified some of the deleterious effects of acid rain such as the bleaching of coloured fabrics, the corrosion of metal surfaces, the deterioration of building materials, and the die-back of vegetation.

Acid rain was not identified as an environmental concern in Canada until the 1950s. While working at Dalhousie University, Dr. Eville Gorham (*2*) studied the chemistry of precipitation and of lakes in Nova Scotia and attributed the "abnormal acidity" that he detected in each of these to airborne pollutants possibly derived from distant sources. Junge and Wertz (*3*) published measurements of the chemistry of precipitation for several locations in the United States in 1958 that indicated elevated levels of dissolved substances including sulphate. The surface water surveys and monitoring that were undertaken by the Canada Department of Mines and Technical Surveys (*4*) provided a valuable baseline for early documentation of the trends and environmental consequences of acidification. In 1966, Dr. Harold Harvey at the University of Toronto detected severe losses of fish populations in the lakes of the La Cloche Mountains of Ontario and ascribed these losses to acidification of the waters by acid rain (*5*). Findings of the National Precipitation Sampling Network of the United States were published by Lodge et al. (*6*) in 1968, also indicating abnormal acidity to be prevalent. The International Joint Commission Reference Studies on the Great Lakes (*7*), and the Ontario Ministries of Environment and Natural Resources, Sudbury Environmental Study (*8*), both produced reports that identified this state of abnormal chemistry of precipitation, particularly in Ontario. These research findings and others from abroad prompted the convening of an International Symposium on Acid Precipitation and the Forest Ecosystem in 1975 as reported by Dochinger and Seliga (*9*). A second symposium convened in the same year in Canada on the "Atmospheric Contribution to the Chemistry of Lake Waters", reported by Matheson and Elder (*10*) indicated an awakening concern for environmental acidification. A report by the National Academy of Sciences, 1975 (*11*) identified these concerns and led to directive by Deputy Minister, Environment Canada (*12*) of the trans-national environmental implications.

Characteristics of Acidic Deposition. In the semi-technical and popular literature, the term "acid rain" has often been used synonymously for acidic deposition. Acidic deposition is associated with many forms of air-borne acidic pollutants. They are transported and deposited via the atmosphere not just in the form of rain but as snow, cloud and fog as well as gases and dust during dry periods. Often, the latter two are referred to as "dry" forms and the first three as "wet" forms of deposition. The proportion of the acidic materials that is deposited by the several mechanisms varies by location. As an example, Schemenauer et al. (13) has estimated that at higher elevations in southern Quebec, sulphate and nitrate deposition due to fog and cloud may be about equivalent to that due to direct precipitation at lower elevations in the region. The deposition of dry materials is dependent on the chemical species and differs with surface characteristic and meteorological conditions. While direct measurements of dry deposition are not generally feasible, estimates have been calculated for eastern Canada as about 15% of the total deposition for sulphate (14). This value is estimated to be as great as 40-50% near strong emission sources.

Rain and snow are types of deposition most commonly measured for quantity and for chemical quality. Measurements derived over more than a decade at many remote locations around the earth have provided evidence that normal or unpolluted precipitation will be slightly acidic, having a "pH" ranging from 5.6 to 5.0 (15) (Figure 1). The slight acidity of normal precipitation (i.e., pH 5.6) is due to atmospheric carbon dioxide and other acidic materials including sulphate of natural origin which are adsorbed during the precipitation processes. Precipitation over eastern North America and over much of Europe has acidity values that are up to ten times greater than normal primarily due to the incorporation of airborne pollutants of man-made origin. As an example, the average pH of precipitation in central Ontario is about 4.2 (14). Measurements of the acidity of cloud water droplets atop Whiteface Mountain in New York have been as acidic as pH 2.6 (16). This cloud moisture is about one thousand times as acidic as normal rain. In some areas, the pH of precipitation may exceed 5.6 (14) as in the Canadian prairie provinces where wind-blown alkaline soil materials actually reduce the natural acidity levels.

Extensive monitoring of the chemistry of precipitation is now available from networks in both North America and Europe. Representative values of the major soluble species that account for most of the measured conductance of the samples at three United States sites are shown in (Table I) (17). It will be noted that the acidity, which is measured directly as pH, is due primarily to the presence of nitrate and sulphate ions that are not balanced by associated cations. While direct pH measurements are a valid measure of precipitation acidity, Reuss (18) has proposed that a balance of the principle ionic species, as in Equation 1 would provide a more appropriate definition of the acidity in relation to possible ecosystem responses.

$$e = 2(SO_4^{--}) + (NO_3^-) + (Cl^-) - 2(Ca^{++}) - 2(mg^{++}) - (Na^+) - (K^+) - (NH_4^+)$$

$$(1)$$

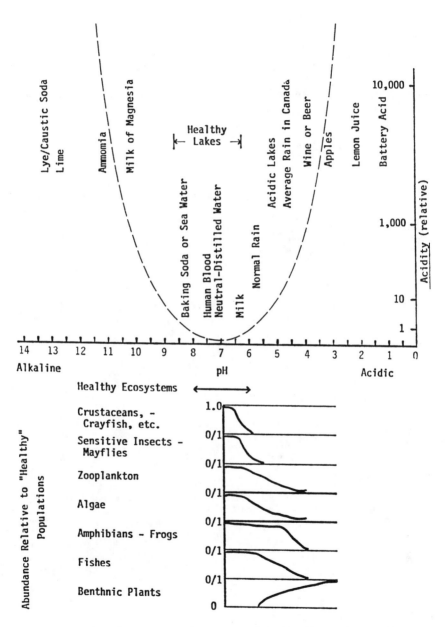

Figure 1. Acidity of Common Substances and the Decline and Loss of Species as Related to Acidity.

Table I. Median Ion Concentrations for Precipitation at Three United States Sites for 1979, (ueq/L), adapted from reference 17.

Ion	GA (42 Samples)[a]	MN (37 Samples)[b]	NY (49 Samples)[c]
SO_4^{--}	38.9	45.8	44.8
NO_3^-	11.6	24.2	25.0
Cl^-	8.2	4.2	4.2
HCO_3 (Calculated)	0.3	10.3	0.1
Anions	59.0	84.5	74.1
NH_4^+	5.5	37.7	8.3
Ca^{++}	5.0	28.9	6.5
Mg^{++}	2.4	6.1	1.9
K^+	0.7	2.0	0.4
Na^+	17.6	13.7	4.9
H^+	17.8	0.5	45.7
Cations	49.0	88.9	67.7
Median pH	4.75	6.31	4.34

[a]The Georgia Station site in west central Georgia.
[b]The Lamberton site in southwestern Minnesota.
[c]The Huntington Wildlife site in northeastern New York.

Where e is the excess acid in mol/L and ionic concentrations are expressed as mol/L. While this more precise definition may apply in some strictly chemical responses such as soil erosion, Brydges and Summers (*19*) have considered the more complete reactions including biological ionic utilizations and have defined an "acidifying potential" of precipitation as:

$$AP = (SO_4^{--}) - (Ca^{++} + Mg^{++}) \tag{2}$$

The nitrogen species (NO_3^- and NH_4^+) are generally utilized as a nutrient by the biological system. The biological assimilation of NO_3 results in production of acid neutralizing capacity while assimiation of NH_4 produces acidity. Where nitrogen is all assimilated and the NO_3/NH_4 ratio is about one, the net acidifying result is nearly neutral (*19*). Cases of excess nitrogen are reported in Europe (*20*) and may become a greater issue in North America as assimilative capacity is reached (*14*). Thus the ionic concentration of sulphate in precipitation is useful as an operational surrogate for the environmental acidification potential.

Sources of Acidic Pollutants. A discussion of the specific ecosystem functions that are affected by acidic deposition must include the fundamental source(s) of the problem. Acidic deposition, whether in "wet" forms such as rain, snow, and cloud or fog droplets, or in "dry" forms of gases and particulates (dust), derives its acidic properties from the airborne pollutants which it carries (*14*). The pollutants are caused primarily by the emissions of sulphur and nitrogen oxides into the atmosphere. The smelting or refining of sulphur-bearing metal ores and the burning of fossil fuels to provide energy to our industrial society are the main emission sources. The sulphur and nitrogen oxides eventually appear as sulphuric and nitric acids in rain, snow, or cloud droplets. Nitrogen oxides also contribute to the formation of ozone in the air near the earth's surface; the ozone may act in conjunction with acidic deposition to harm sensitive plants including forest growth and may be of concern to health. The formation and effects of ozone are beyond the cope of this chapter.

While natural emissions of sulphur and nitrogen exist, over 95% of the sulphur emissions in eastern North America are of man-made origin. Natural sources of nitrogen are less well established but are estimated to be small when compared to the man-made emissions (*21*). The distribution of North American sources of sulphur dioxide and nitrogen oxides are shown in Figure 2. In 1980, which has served as the base period for the assessment of emissions,it was estimated that sulphur dioxide emissions were: Canada - 4.8 million tonnes (metric) and the United States - 24 million tonnes; nitrogen oxides emissions were: Canada - 1.8 million tonnes and the United States - 20 million tonnes. The more recent trends for sulphur dioxide emissions in Canada and the emission control limits are shown in Figure 3 (*14*).

In 1985, about 70% of the sulphur dioxide in the United States was emitted from fossil-fueled generating stations while in Canada, about 50% was

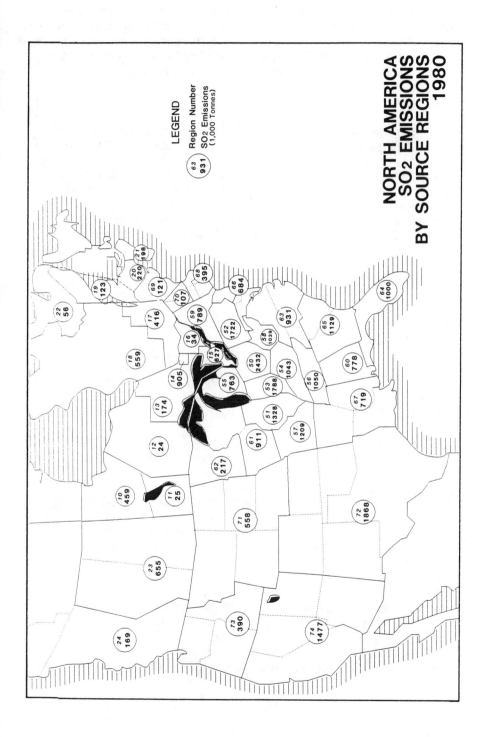

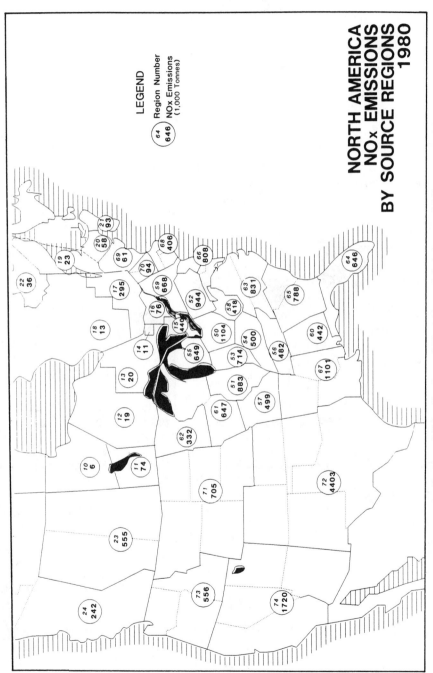

Figure 2. Regional Distribution of Emission of Sulphur and Nitrogen Oxides for North America, 1980, adapted from reference 14.

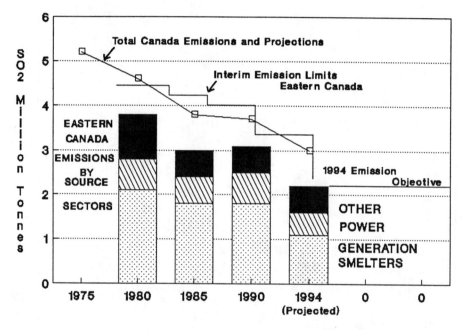

Figure 3. Emission of Sulphur Dioxide in Eastern Canada by Source Sectors; Total Canadian Emissions and Projections to 2000; and Eastern Canada Control Limits, adapted from reference 14.

emitted from ore smelters and about 20% from fossil-fueled generating stations. Figure 3 shows Canadian sulphur dioxide emissions by major sectors of activity. Trends and future projections are shown for emissions in Eastern Canada and for the whole of Canada. Sulphur emissions in both United States and in Canada tend to be concentrated in a relatively few locations (see Figure 2) associated with power generation or ore smelting, Contrastingly, in Canada about 63% of nitrogen oxides come from the transportation sector, about 13% from fossil-fueled generating stations and the balance from other combustion processes (*14*).

As treated in other chapters of this book, air masses often transport acidic pollutants thousands of kilometres from their original source prior to deposition. Because air mass and storm movements tend to follow regular patterns, there is a strong linkage between the sources of pollutants and the areas that receive the acidic deposition. In eastern North America, the air mass movements and storm tracks are, on the average, from southwest towards the northeast. This serves to carry the emitted pollutants from the industrial "heart-land" over the more rural and comparatively pristine area of the   northeast United States and southeastern Canada (*14*). The spatial distribution   of sulphate deposition over the eastern United States and Canada in 1980 is shown in Figure 4 (*17*).

Atmospheric emissions of sulphur dioxide are either measured or estimated at their source and are thus calculated on a provincial or state basis for both Canada and the United States (Figure 2). While much research and debate continues, computer-based simulation models can use this emission information to provide reasonable estimates of how sulphur dioxide and sulphate (the final oxidized form of sulphur dioxide) are transported, transformed, and deposited via atmospheric air masses to selected regions. Such "source-receptor" models are of varying complexity but all are evaluated on their ability to reproduce the measured pattern of sulphate deposition over a network of acid rain monitoring stations across United States and Canada. In a joint effort of the U.S. Environmental Protection Agency and the Canadian Atmospheric Environment Service, eleven linear-chemistry atmospheric models of sulphur deposition were evaluated using data from 1980. It was found that on an annual basis, all but three models were able to simulate the observed deposition patterns within the uncertainty limits of the observations (*22*).

Through the application of atmospheric simulation models, the contribution of emissions from a specific source region to the total deposition at another region can be approximated. By this method,for example,it is estimated that about 50% of the sulphate deposited in Canada is derived from emissions from the United States (*14*). The regional pattern of deposition or annual loading rates for sulphate,as derived from measurements of the precipitation network in 1980, are shown in Figure 4. The industrial mid-western states, the lower Great Lakes region and the St.Lawrence valley receive the highest levels of sulphate deposition. The amount of acidic deposition that is measured to occur in a given region is used to compare with ecosystem damages that are observed in the same region. Ecosystem responses that can be expected from differing levels of emission and subsequent deposition, can thus be developed.

The acidic deposition monitoring network has been operating over North America since about 1979. This program has provided a measurement of the changes or trends that have occurred during that period. Figure 5 (*14*) shows that sulphate deposition in precipitation in Eastern North America, while still at undesirable levels throughout many regions, has declined at an approximately steady rate. When averaged over Eastern North America, the decline in sulphate deposition shows a nearly direct proportion to the decline of the emission of sulphur dioxide. A reduction of sulphur emissions of 16% in Europe between 1980 and 1986 has also been shown to have resulted in 18% decline in sulphur dioxide concentrations and a 15% decline in particulate sulphate deposition (*23*). These correlations provide support to the proposition that if emissions are reduced,a reduction in the levels of acidic pollutants or their precursors in the environment will occur.

Ecological Effects of Acidification

Sensitivity of Ecosystems. When acidic pollutants are deposited over a region, they enter into a variety of complex and interrelated ecosystem processes. Figure 6 illustrates this from a typical" watershed" or "catchment" perspective, showing the pathways of water flow and how these interact with the biophysical processes that are affected by acidic deposition. The contact and interactions of the abnormally acidic water with trees, soils, rocks, grasses,or land and water dwelling organisms all combine and interrelate to determine the ultimate ecosystem responses to the acidic deposition. At each stage of interaction, the chemical characteristics of the water may be altered. The resulting abnormal acidic character of the water may induce a response that may modify the environment as a whole. Tree growth, for instance, may be affected, soil nutrients and trace metals may be altered, soil organisms may be harmed, rock weathering rates may be altered, or living organisms associated with the land and water may be affected. The inability of a particular system to resist deleterious effects due to the acidic deposition is termed its "sensitivity to acidification".

The sensitivity of a region to acidic deposition is related primarily to its capacity to reduce or chemically neutralize acidity. If there is an ability to quickly and effectively return conditions to nearly normal, the effects of the deposition will be minimized and the ecosystem is not considered to be sensitive. However, if there is little or no capacity to reduce the acidity, the ecosystem is highly sensitive and severe damage can occur if the acidic deposition is significant.

Cowell and Lucas (*24*) demonstrated that the capacity of a region to reduce or neutralize acidity is determined primarily by the soil and bedrock characteristics. These scientists developed a sensitivity model that makes use

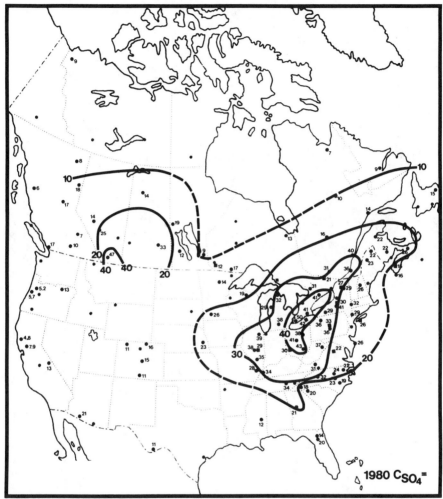

Figure 4. Regional Deposition Rate of Sulphate for North America, 1980, adapted from reference 17.

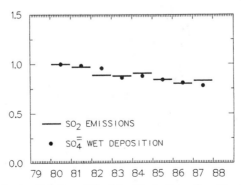

Figure 5. Trends in Sulphur Dioxide Emissions for North America and Associated Trends in Sulphate Deposition, adapted from reference 14.

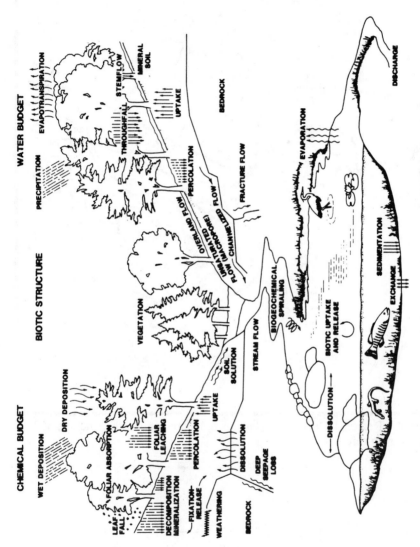

Figure 6. Watershed Flow Chart Showing Key Hydrological and Biochemical Processes that Affect Acidification, adapted from reference 52.

of available information from terrain, soil and ecological land inventories to classify Canadian landscapes into three sensitivity classes --- high, moderate, or low potential to reduce the acidity of acidic deposition. This model has been applied (25) to all of Canada. Figure 7 illustrates the regions of Canada that have a low capacity to reduce acidity and thus are highly sensitive to acidification. These highly sensitive regions conform closely with the Canadian Shield, which is dominated by granitic bedrock and thin, poorly developed soils. Forty-six percent of Canada's landscape or 4,000,000 square kilometres are considered to be sensitive to acidification. This vast area coincides closely with Canada's wealth of lakes and wetlands.

When high levels of acidic deposition occur on regions having a low neutralizing capacity, the water resources of that region retain the elevated levels of acidity, resulting in an abnormal condition which may induce adverse responses in the ecosystem. Figure 4 shows the levels of wet sulphate deposition that were observed over eastern North America in 1980. The coincidence of sensitive terrain and high deposition, as shown in Figure 7, defines that part of Canada of greatest concern with respect to acidic deposition. A level of greater than 10 kg/ha/yr of sulphate was being deposited over areas of sensitive landscape in Ontario, Quebec, the Atlantic Provinces, and to a lesser extent, over southwestern British Columbia. Significant and, in some cases severe ecological responses to acidic deposition are found in these regions (14).

Terrestrial Responses.   Figure 6 depicts the water flow pathways of a watershed and how acidification can interact within the watershed ecosystem. The foliage of the upper canopy as well as ground cover intercepts and collects portions of the acidic substances directly. For dry particulates and gases in particular, the canopy acts as a filter, collecting pollutants from the air. When acidic substances which free fall to the ground and those which alternatively trickle down plant stems and tree trunks finally enter the soil and root zone, both plant nutrient and soil weathering cycles are affected. The presence of elevated acidity in soil water alters the rates of reactions in these cycles. It also induces types of reactions to which the ecosystem is not adapted. The principal reaction caused by the augmented acidity is an increased demand and release of basic (i.e., alkaline) elements such as calcium and magnesium to the soil water solution itself. "Basic" nutrients thus are leached away from plant roots and from soil particles. When the rate of leaching exceeds the availability of basic elements, the water remains acidic and more biologically toxic metals such as aluminum are dissolved, becoming free to move through ground water to streams and lakes. Hence, the soil environment in which the plants must grow can become quite modified, in some cases to the detriment of the existing types of vegetation. Because many Canadian soils have minimal reserves of basic elements (part of what defines terrain as "sensitive"), the acidity cannot always be neutralized.   Thus, the soil or ground waters may remain acidic (26), presenting adverse conditions for many forms of biological life.

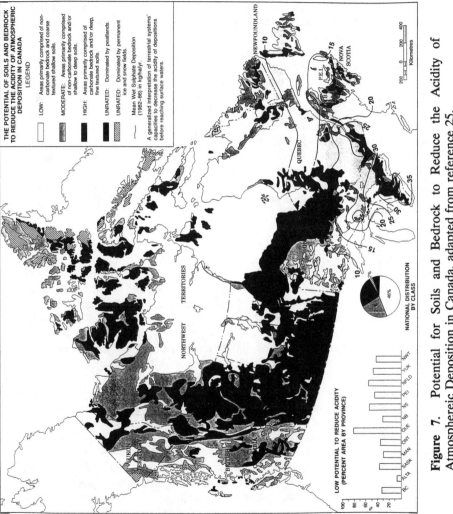

Figure 7. Potential for Soils and Bedrock to Reduce the Acidity of Atmospheric Deposition in Canada, adapted from reference 25.

Biological Responses. Extensive declines and serious die-backs within forests in Europe have raised concerns that acidic pollutants are responsible (27). In the United States, serious die-backs have also occurred, especially on the higher regions of the eastern mountains (28). In Canada, 96% of the land that has been mapped as having high forest capability have been subject to high levels of acidic deposition (29). These are primarily the hardwood and mixedwood forests, comprising approximately 15 million ha that are exposed to significant regional sulfate and nitrate deposition (14). Important die-back and growth rate declines have been documented for Sugar Maple groves that coincide with high levels of acidic deposition and other air pollutants such as ozone. The decline of growth rates of maples appears to begin with the onset of industrialization in Ontario. White Birch decline is evident on the shores of the Bay of Fundy and of Lake Superior (14) where acidic fog frequently occurs.

The potential effects of acidic and related atmospheric pollutants on vegetation are believed to occur through direct plant contacts and indirectly through modification of the plant nutrient supply from the soil. The wax like protective surfaces of leaves and the capacity of guard-cells to function have been shown to be altered in controlled experiments. The implications of these changes to growth functions of trees are not well understood but are believed to decrease the resistance to invasion by diseases. Germination of pollen and thereby the regrowth of species may also be inhibited (14).

Plants may be affected by indirect modifications of the environment. Soil acidification, for example, can cause the leaching of nutrients, and the release of toxic aluminum. These effects may operate together to produce nutrient deficiencies or imbalances to plants. High soil concentrations of aluminum may prevent uptake and utilization of nutrients by plants.Increased availability of aluminum in soils has been implicated as a cause of forest declines in both Europe and the United States, possibly through the toxic effects on small feeder roots (14).

Forests in particular must endure the combined stresses imposed by climatic extremes/changes, invasion of insects and diseases, and forest management practices in addition to the added stress of acidic pollutants. All of these stresses modify forest health and productivity. Under this complex situation, it has not been possible to establish the exact role that acidification has had on forest decline nor to develop critical deposition levels at which damages are believed to become important (14). However, the geographical coincidence of forest decline and elevated levels of acidic pollutants offer strong evidence that a linkages exists.

Surveys of Sugar Maple decline have been conducted in both Quebec and in Ontario. If these declines continue over the long term, the damages will undoubtedly become dramatic and serious. In a survey in Quebec between 1985 and 1987, of over 2 million hectares of stands, 47% exhibited light decline symptoms (11 to 25% defoliation), 3% showed severe decline (25% defoliation), while the remaining 50% revealed only marginal symptoms (10% defoliation). In Ontario, surveys have found that the highest decline occurs across the northern hardwood forest range but significant symptoms of decline are found throughout the range. White Birch forests in some areas may be in an even more serious situation. In the Bay of Fundy region, nearly all birch trees exhibit some damage while, by 1988, about 10% of trees had already died (14). Trees are subject to many other forms of damage such as insect infestations; even when they do not show serious symptoms from acid rain, they may be in a weakened situation and far less able to withstand invasion of insects or disease. The types of damage that we have seen to date are comparatively short term effects for trees. Little is known of the effects on trees of many years of accumulated acidic deposition (14).

Experimental exposure of several agricultural crops to ambient levels of acidic pollutants has not established measurable yield responses although foliar damage has been observed. Complex interactions with other airborne pollutants, particularly ozone, makes it difficult to exactly establish the damages that may be attributed to acidic deposition (14). It has not been possible to establish any critical level of acidic deposition in relation to crop damages.

The effects of acidic deposition on terrestrial wildlife are even more difficult to assess as they would occur indirectly through habitat alteration or through influences on food resources. Damage to or loss of trees, for example, could alter bird habitat. European studies indicate that the altered cycle for calcium nutrients in soils and waters cause dietary deficiencies and may result in fragile egg shells and poor reproductive success (30). In Canada, evidence exists that increased metals in the food (e.g.,mosses and lichens) of ungulates such as moose may accumulate in the liver. The concentration of cadmium in livers of moose has been found to be high enough that humans should avoid or limit their consumption of these organs (14).

Lake and Stream Responses.   The freshwater resources of North America in regions that experience significant acidic deposition are large. In Canada, about 7.6 % of the country is covered by freshwater. A recent satellite study of water bodies (31) was conducted for the region of Canada that is presently subject to acidic pollution (i.e. those regions east of the Ontario-Manitoba border and south of 52 degrees north latitude). In this region, over 775,000 waterbodies were identified that were greater than 0.18 ha in area. This freshwater habitat is dominated by small lakes; 54 % of the total have an area less than one hectare. While these small lakes contribute a relatively small proportion of the total water area, they are a highly important habitat for waterfowl populations and aquatic organisms (32).   Of the total lake resource in eastern Canada, chemical analyses are available for only 8500 lakes or streams, or about one percent of the total. Within these, some chemical information is available for as far back as the 1950's, but the more systematic surveys have only been conducted during the last decade. This limited sampling base, however, has been shown to be a reasonably good representation of the chemistry of the entire water resource (14).

The chemistry of surface waters is determined by the interaction of precipitation with the geological and biological conditions that exist over a given region. Surface waters that have been derived from normal, unpolluted precipitation, that flow through weathered soils and rocks prior to appearing in streams and lakes will contain dissolved basic elements like calcium and magnesium along with a chemical balance of bicarbonate (for more detail, see standard texts on water chemistry, e.g. reference 33). The concentration of these chemicals is determined largely by the geological properties of the watershed. Waters having low concentrations are commonly termed "soft" whereas high concentrations are termed "hard". A large portion of the nonpolluted waters in eastern North America are naturally extremely soft (*21* and *34*) due to the bedrock and soil characteristics of the catchments. The same terrain characteristics that produce soft waters also define areas that are sensitive to acidic deposition. Such waters,unless otherwise polluted, will have a near neutral acidity of about pH6 to somewhat greater than pH 7, and will have only trace amounts of sulphate or nitrate (*14*).

When acidic pollutants containing sulphuric and nitric acids are introduced into soft waters, the acids are first neutralized (buffered) by a loss of the bicarbonate and (to some extent) the release of elements including aluminum. The evidence of such acidification is most easily detected by the loss of bicarbonate and the appearance of sulphate in the water. Nitrate that is deposited is usually assimilated as a nutrient by vegetation and contributes to acidification of surface or ground water only when vegetation and other organisms cannot assimilate all that is deposited. When all of the available bicarbonate supplied by the local weathering has been exhausted, the waters become acidic and will have a pH of 5 or less. The waters will then contain the basic elements like calcium, magnesium, probably some aluminum along with a chemical balance of sulphate. Bicarbonate is absent. The relative amount of bicarbonate and sulphate in water is therefore a measure of the degree of acidification that has taken place (*34*). The increase of aluminum in acidified waters is important because it is toxic to many organisms (*14*).

To measure the spatial extent of acidification in southeastern Canada, waters from over 8500 lakes have been surveyed and analyzed for their chemical contents (*14*). Figure 8 (*34*) summarizes the geographical distribution of waters having various relative amounts of bicarbonate and sulphate for eastern Canada. Areas where the ratio is less than 1.0 have experienced serious acidification. It would be expected that many acidic waters having a pH less than 5 would be found in areas having a ratio less than 0.2. Figure 8 shows that very large portions of Ontario, Quebec and the Atlantic Provinces are in these classes. It may also be observed that the ratio exceeds the value of 1.0 where acidic deposition is small (see Figure 4).

In addition to the long-term acidification of waters, "episodic" or short duration events can have severe consequences for living organisms. In Canada, large amounts of the total annual precipitation are deposited through storm events or as snowfall. The large volumes of pollutants which can be released

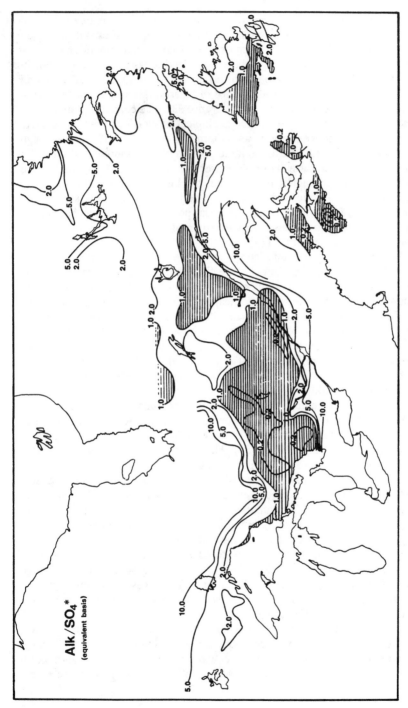

Figure 8. Geographical Distribution of Bicarbonate/Sulphate Ratio in the Surface Waters of Eastern Canada Indicating the Regions of Significant Acidification, adapted from reference 34.

through sudden snow melts in the spring or through storm runoffs have the potential to release large amounts of acidity in a short time.Such events cause "pulses" of increased acidity in the local streams and lakes. These pulses or "acidic shocks" have been shown to kill fish (*35*). Because acidity in this form is not given time to be slowly assimilated into the environment, it is of particular concern even for areas where long-term acidification has not yet reached what would normally be considered serious levels. Contributions of nitrogen are also generally of greater concern during such episodes where assimilation has not been important (*35*).

Responses of Aquatic Organisms. The interactions between aquatic organisms and the chemistry of their water habitats are extremely complex. If a species or a group of species increases or declines in numbers in response to acidification, then the biological structure of the entire water body is likely to be affected. Reactions of organisms to stress such as acidification can be termed a "dose-response" reaction (i.e. a certain dose of acidifying pollutant induces a certain response).

Acidification can also cause changes in any portion of the food web and thereby modify the fundamental food chain or predator-prey relationships. These latter indirect effects make assessments of the biological damages very difficult as one really must first clearly understand the direct effects to draw absolute conclusions. Serious damages often have occurred in the aquatic system before they become obvious through biological responses such as losses of given fish stocks.

Knowledge relating the biological responses to habitat acidification has been obtained from controlled bioassays (laboratory or small-scale controlled experiments), whole ecosystem experiments (entire lakes are artificially acidified), and extensive field surveys and monitoring. By combining these sources of information, quite a precise understanding of effects on aquatic biota has been obtained (*14*). The causes of species declines are complex, involving both direct effects related to acidity of the habitat or increased concentrations of aluminum or other toxic metals, and indirect effects such as losses of lower food-chain organisms.

For organisms, the acidification of lakes may cause stealthy and almost imperceptible effects. At first, only very small changes can be detected, but as the waters become increasingly acidic, more and more species are eliminated. A pH of greater than 6 in a lake is required to ensure that most of the aquatic organisms will thrive. As a pH of less than 5 is reached, only a small number of very hardy plant and animal species survive. Figure 1 illustrates this progressive decline.

Losses of crustaceans, crayfish, mayflies, and some algal and zooplankton species occur as the pH approaches 6, but most fish are largely unaffected. In the range from pH 6 to 5, major population losses are experienced. Major changes of plankton species happen while progressive loss of fish species is likely. Fish decline is often reflected in a failure of the species to reproduce leaving only older individuals; when these fish die,there appears to be a sudden disappearance of the species from a lake. At this stage of pH decline, less desirable species of mosses and plankton may begin to invade the lakes. When the pH decreases to less than 5, the lake is largely devoid of fish, the lake bottom is covered by undecayed material and the near-shore waters are sometimes dominated by mosses. The lake, once alive and rich in species, has gradually become an impoverished environment (36).

Amphibians such as frogs and salamanders depend heavily on temporary ponds for breeding. These ponds are highly vulnerable to the "acid shock" events associated with storms or snowmelt. In several studies, reproduction of amphibians has been shown to be seriously restricted when acidity of their habitat decreases to a pH value of less than 5 (14).

Water birds have not been shown to be directly affected by acidification. However, the prey of waterbirds may be of concern as these lower food-chain organisms may have elevated levels of toxic metals related to acidification of their habitat. Moreover, most water birds rely on some component of the aquatic food-chain for their high protein diet. Invertebrates that normally supply calcium to egg-laying birds or their growing chicks are among the first to disappear as lakes acidify. As these food sources are reduced or eliminated due to acidification, bird habitat is reduced and reproductive rate of the birds is affected. The Common Loon is able to raise fewer chicks, or none at all, on acidic lakes where fish populations are reduced (37 and 38). However, in some isolated cases, food supplies can be increased when competitive species are eliminated (e.g., Common Goldeneye ducks can better exploit insects as food when competition from fish is eliminated). The collective influences of acidification are difficult to quantify on a specific area basis but for species that rely on a healthy aquatic ecosystem to breed, acidification remains a continuing threat in thousands of lakes across eastern North America (14).

Human Health and Man-Made Structures: The Effects

Implications to Humans. Acidic precipitation has not been observed with concentrations that pose a concern to human exposure. The acidic airborne pollutants in the particulate or gaseous forms such as the oxides of sulphur and of nitrogen, and the associated photochemical oxidant ozone, are inhaled. This may lead to the irritation of the respiratory tract, and subsequently to impaired lung function, aggravated asthma and bronchitis.

Humans may also be indirectly affected through exposure to increased levels of toxic metals in drinking water and food. Increased levels of toxic metal are a consequence of direct deposition of pollutants into water sources, increased leaching of metal from soils and lake sediments, and increased corrosion of water pipes.

Evidence for this human health linkage has been suggested from (a) epidemiologic studies of exposed human populations, (b) human volunteer studies, and (c) animal experiments (14). Air pollution levels measured in southwestern Ontario, for instance, have been compared with hospital admissions in the same area, and positive associations were found between respiratory illness and levels of sulphate, ozone, and temperature. The diminished lung function of girls attending a summer camp in southern Ontario, a region that experiences high levels of acidic pollution, was shown to correlate with episodes of elevated pollution (*39*). The lung function of children (aged 7-12) in Tillsonburg, Ontario, and Portage la Prairie, Manitoba, was tested. The recorded response of a diminished lung capacity was shown to be statistically lower by about 2% for the more heavily polluted city. In a subsequent cross-sectional study of 10 towns in Canada, a lung function decrement of about 2% was observed in populations of the towns having higher air pollution levels. The difference appears to be due to acidic sulphate which differed by the greatest amount between the two exposure populations (*40*).

As with other animals, humans can be affected by food-chain linkages. Elevated levels of mercury have been found in fish taken from acidified waters. The mercury may be deposited by direct atmospheric transport or from increased availability due to acidification of the waters (*41*). Drinking water from acidified, untreated sources has been observed with elevated levels of metals primarily derived from corrosion of plumbing systems by the acidified water (*42*). Levels of lead and cadmium, which are highly toxic, may be higher than acceptable if the water from acidified sources stands in plumbing systems for several hours. The elevated metal problem is addressed by adjusting the pH of water in urban water treatment facilities; in some rural or cottage settings where water may be drawn directly from acidified sources, correcting the problem is dependent upon the individual's own efforts such as installing adequate filtering devices or,in cases of contamination from the plumbing, flushing the water supply system to remove built-up contaminants (*14*).

Buildings, Monuments and Materials.   Many materials used in man-made structures are subject to deterioration from normal weathering such as dissolution, mechanical fracture, erosion, and photochemical reactions. However, as shown by Amoroso and Fassina (*43*), the rates of deterioration have increased drastically since the advent of industrial pollution. Losses to Canadian heritage sites such as the federal parliament buildings has been significant and have been described by Weaver (*44*).

It has long been recognized that local environmental characteristics influence the rates of material corrosion. After two years of measurements at 39 sites in Europe and North America, significant relationships have been shown between corrosion rates of building materials and atmospheric pollutants(*45*). While direction of exposure relative to weather and other factors such as frequency and duration of wetting significantly influence corrosion, Kucera (*46*) has shown that sulphur oxides are strongly correlated with deterioration of structural materials.

Modern building materials have been developed to reduce the rates of environmental deterioration. However, stone, brick, and masonry constitute the structure of many of the historic buildings and statues that make up our cultural heritage. The reaction of sulphur-based solutions on the surfaces and in the pore structure of these materials produces increased rates of erosion, chipping, fracture, and discoloration. While general lack of long-term measurements has hindered development of precise relationships, it is now well known that acidic pollutants are the cause of the rapid increase in the decay of historic structures (44).

Environmental Acidification and The Future

Environmental benefits of Emission Controls. Information in Figure 5 illustrate that the emission of sulphur in eastern North America has declined over the past decade. This decline allows for a possible verification of the dose-response relationships on which the environmental concerns for emissions have been based. A decline in sulphate deposition in Nova Scotia has apparently resulted in a decrease in acidity of eleven rivers over the period 1971-73 to 1981-82 (47). In the Sudbury, Ontario area where emissions have declined by over 50% between 1974-76 and 1981-83, a resurvey of 209 lakes shows that most lakes have now become less acidic. Twenty-one lakes that had a pH < 5.5 in 1974-76 showed an average decline in acidity of 0.3 pH units over the period (48). Surveys of 54 lakes in the Algoma region of Ontario have shown a rapid response to a decline in sulphate deposition. Two lakes without fish in 1979 have recovered populations as pH of the water moved above 5.5 (49). Evidence is accumulating to support the hypothesis of benefits that were projected as a consequence of emission controls. This provides increased confidence in the projections.

Legislation enacted by both Canada and the United States (see the US-Canada Air Quality Accord, 1991) will, when implemented, reduce the North American emissions of sulphur dioxide by about 50% based upon the 1980 baseline. These projected emission fields have been appplied in the atmospheric source-receptor models that were described above, to provide a projected deposition field for acidic sulphate that would be expected (14). The predicted sulphate deposition fields have then subsequently been applied in aquatic effects models that provide estimates of regional surface water acidification distributions (50). The regional acidification profiles have then been used in a model of fish species richness (51) that results in an estimate of the expected presence of fish species as compared to that expected in an unacidified case.

The projected benefit of the control strategies is shown for different regions of eastern Canada in Figure 9. The benefits in this case are expressed in terms of damage to fish. Models have been applied to calculate the percentage of lakes in each region that would be expected to retain less than 90% of their fish potential species. The models indicate that emission controls will provide a much greater benefit to waters of the Ontario-Quebec area than to the highly sensitive lakes of the Atlantic Provinces. Even with the United States and Canadian controls in place, some sensitive regions will still be expected to have greater than a 10% loss of species in over 30% of the surface

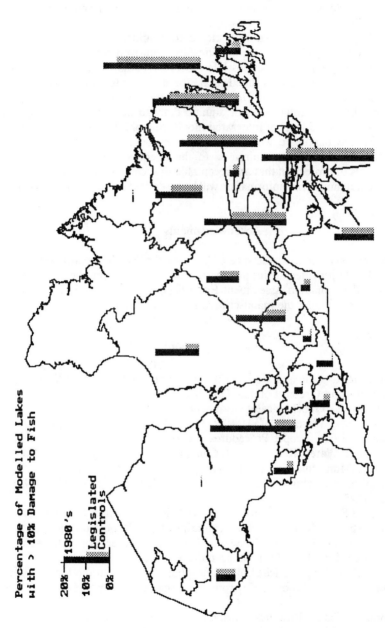

Figure 9. Projected Benefit of Emission Controls Reducing Fish Damage in Eastern Canada, adapted from reference 14.

waters. For the whole of Eastern Canada, the estimated damage level decreases from about 13% (about 100,000 lakes) to about 5% (about 39,000 lakes) for emission reductions of 50% from the 1980 emission levels of both Canada and the United States.

It has been established with increased confidence that reductions of sulphur emissions will result in significantly improved aquatic habitat. No quantitative projections are yet possible for forest, human health, or materials damage but it must be assumed that there will also be a qualitative improvement in these concerns. However, even after the present control targets are achieved, a substantial level of aquatic damage due to acidification will remain. A continued level of integrated monitoring of all concerns is essential to establish the degree to which the actual response follows the predicted. Future judgments will be required as to the adequacy of conrol actions to achieve levels of protection that are acceptable to society. Detailed and reliable environmental monitoring information will be essential for those judgments (14).

Acknowledgments

I wish to acknowledge the assistance of Dr. T.G. Brydges in preparation of this manuscript. He provided advice and made available the comprehensive subject material of the Canadian Assessment Reports (Reference 14). The assistance of Ruth Tung in typing the manuscript is also recognized.

Literature Cited

1. Smith, R.A. "Air and Rain"; The Beginnings of Chemical Climatology; Logmans and Green: London, UK, 1872.
2. Gorham, E. Geochimica et Cosmochimica Acta, **1955**, 7, 231-239.
3. Junge, G.E.; Wertz, R. J. Meteor. **1958**, 15, pp 417-425.
4. Thomas, J.F.J. Scope, Procedures and Interpretation of Survey Studies, Industrial Water Resources of Canada, Water Survey Report No. 1, Canada Mines and Technical Surveys, Ottawa, Ontario, 1986.
5. Beamish, R.J.; Harvey, H.H. J. Fish. Res. Brd. (Canada), **1972**, 29, pp 1131-1143.
6. Lodge, J.P.; Pate, W.; Swanson, G.S.; Hill, K.C.; Lorange, E.; Lazrus, A.L. Chemistry of United States Precipitation, Final Report on the National Precipitation Sampling Network, National Center for Atmospheric Research, Boulder, CO, 1968, pp 66.
7. Acres Consulting Services Ltd., Atmospheric Loading to the Upper Great Lakes, Contract Report to Environment Canada, Burlington, Ontario, 1975.
8. Ontario Water Resources Commission, Preliminary Report on the Influence of Industrial Activity on the Sudbury Area Lakes, Ontario Water Resources Commission, Toronto, Ontario, 1972, pp 78.

9. Dochinger, L.S.; Seliga, T.A.; Eds.; Proceedings First International Symposium on Acid Precipitation and the Forest Ecopsystems, USDA Forest Service, Gen. Tech. Rept. N23, Northeast For. Exp. Stn.; Upper Darby, PA; 1976; pp 1079.

10. Matheson, D.H.; Elder, F.C., Eds.; Atmospheric Contribution to the Chemistry of Lake Waters, J. Great Lakes Res., Suppliment 2, pp 225.

11. National Academy of Science, Air Quality and Stationary Source Emission Control, Comm. on Nat. Resources, National Academy of Sciences, National Research Council, U.S. Gov't Print. Office, Washington, DC, 1975.

12. Whelpdale, D.M. (Chair) Long-Range Transport of Air Pollutants: A Summary Report of the Ad Hoc Committee, Atmospheric Environment Service, Environment Canada, Downsview, Ontario, 1976.

13. Schemenauer, R.S., Schuepp, P., Kermasha, S., and Cereceda, P. In NATO Advanced Research Workshop: Acid Deposition Processes at high Elevation Sites, D. Reidel Publisher, 1988, pp. 359-374.

14. Long-Range Transport of Airborne Pollutants, Research and Monitoring Coordinating Committee, Canada LRTAP Assessment, Atmospheric Environment Service, Environment Canada, Downsview, Ontario, 1990, 7 Volumes.

15. Galloway, J.N.; Likens, G.E.; Hawley, M.E. Science, **1984**, 226, pp 829-831.

16. Castillo, R. An Investigation of the Acidity of Stratus Cloud Water and Its Relationship to Droplet Distribution, pH of Rain and Weather Parameters, Ph.D. Thesis, Dept. Atmos. Sci., State University of New York, Albany, NY, 1979.

17. Stensland, Gary J.; Whelpdale, D.M.; Oehlert, G. Precipitation Chemistry, In ACID DEPOSITION; LONG TERM TRENDS, National Academy of Sciences Press, Washington, DC, 1986, pp 128-199.

18. Reuss, J.O. EPA Ecological Research Report Series, Rept. No. EPA 660/3-75-032,1975, Corvallis, OR, pp 46.

19. Brydges, T.G., and Summers, P.W. Water, Air and Soil Pollution, **1989**, 43, pp 249-263.

20. Grennfelt, P. and Hultberg, H. Water, Air and Soil Pollution, **1986**, 30, pp 945.

21. Irving, P. Ed.; Acidic deposition: State of science and technology, National Acid Precipitation Assessment Program, Washington, DC, 1990.

22. Clark, T.L., Denise, R.L., Seilhop, S.K., Voldner, E.C., Olson, M.P., and Alvo, M. International sulfur desposition model evaluation, Atmospheric Environment Service, Publication No. ARD-87-1, 1987, Downsview, Ontario, Canada.

23 Mylona, Sophia N. Detection of sulphur emission reductions in Europe during the period 1979-1986. EMEP Report MSC-W, 1/89, Norwegian Meteorolgoical Institute, 1989, Blindern, Norway.

24. Cowell. D.W.; Lucas, A.E. Potential of soils and bedrock to reduce acidity of incoming acidic deposition in Ontario, In Assessment of Aquatic and Terrestrial Acid Precipitation Sensitivities for Ontario, Ontario Ministry of

Environment, APIOS Rept. 009/86, 1986, Toronto, Ontario, pp 37 and map.

25. Acid Rain: A National Sensitivity Assessment, Inland Waters Directorate, Environment Canada, Ottawa, Ontario, Fact Sheet and maps, 1988.

26. Berden, M.; Nilsson, S.I.; Rosen, K.; Tyler, G. Soil Acidification: Extent, Causes, and Consequences, National Swedish Environmental Protection Board, Rept. 3292, 1987, pp 164.

27. Krause, G.H.M.; Arndt, U.; Brandt, C.J.; Bucher, J.; Kenk, G.; Matzner, E. Water, Air, and Soil Pollution, 1986, 31, pp 647-668.

28. Johnson, A.H.; Friedland, A.J.; Dushoff, J.G. Recent and Historic Red Spruce Mortality: Evidence of Climatic Influences, Water, Air, and Soil Pollution, 1986, 30, pp 319-330.

29. Lynch-Stewart, P.; Wiken, E.B.; Ironside, G. Acid Deposition on Prime Resource Lands in Eastern Canada, Canada Land Inventory Rept, No. 18, Lands Directorate, Environment Canada, Ottawa, Ontario, 1987.

30. Drent, P.J. and Woldendorp, J.W. Nature, 339, pp 431.

31. Helie, R.G.; Wickware, D.G. Quantitative Assessment of the Water Resources at Risk to Acidification in Eastern Canada, Paper No.6, Sustainable Development Branch, Environment Canada, Ottawa, Ontario, 1990.

32. McNicol, D.K.; Bendell, B.E.; and Ross, R.K. Studies of the effects of acidification on aquatic wildlife in Canada: Waterfowl and Trophic Relationships in Small Lakes in Northern Ontario, Occasional Paper No. 62, Canadian Wildlife Service, Environment Canada, Ottawa, Ontario, 1987, pp 76.

33. Stum, M.; and Morgan, J. Aquatic Chemistry, Wiley-Interscience, New York, NY, 1970.

34. Jeffries, D.S. Impact of acid rain on lake water quality, In Intermedia Pollutant Transport; Allen, D.T., Cohen, Y., and Kaplan, I.R., Eds; Plenum Press, 1989, New York, pp 41-53.

35. Marmorek, D.R.; Thornton, K.W.; Baker, J.P.; Bernard, D.P.; Jones, M.L.; Reuber,B. Acidic Episodes in Surface Waters: The State of Science, Final Rept., US/EPA, Corvallis, OR, 1987.

36. Schindler, D.W.; Mills, K.H.; Malley, D.F.; Findlay, D.L.; Shearer, J.A.; Davies,I.J.; Turner,M.A.; Linsey,G.A.; Cruikshank, D.R. Science, 1985, 228, pp 1395-1401.

37. Alvo, R.; Hussell, D.J.T.; Berrill, M. Canadian J. of Zool., 1988, 66, pp 746-751.

38. Wayland, M.; McNicol, D.K. Status Report on Effects of Acid Precipitation on Common Loon Reproduction in Ontario: The Ontario Loon Survey, Can. Wildlife Serv., Tech. Rept. Ser., No. 92, Ottawa, Ontario, 1990.

39. Bates, D.V.; Sizto, R. The Ontario Air Pollution Study: Identification of the Causative Agents, Health and Environmental Perspectives, 1989, 79, pp 69-72.

40. Stern, B.L.; Jones, L.; Raizenne, M.; Burnett, R., Meranger, J.C., Franklin, C.A. Environmental Research, **1989**, 49, pp 20.
41. Merger, S.A. Water, Air and Soil Pollution, **1986**, 30, pp 411-419.
42. Meranger, J.C.; Kahn, T.R.; Viro, C.; Jackson, R.; Wan Chi Li Internat. J.Environ. Anal. Chem., **1986**, 15, pp 185.
43. Amorosa, G.G.; Fassina, V. Stone Decay and Conservation, Materials Science Monograph 11, Elsevier Science Publishers, 1983, New York, NY pp 453.
44. Weaver, M. Can. Heritage, **1985**, Feb/Mar, pp 24-31.
45. International Co-operative Programme on Effects on Materials Including Historic and Cultural Monuments, Progress Report, 1990, Swedish Corrosion Institute, Stockholm, Sweden, pp 8 and figures.
46. Kucera,V. The Effects of Acidification of the Environment on the Corrosion of the Atmosphere, Water, and Soil, Proc. 9th Scandinavian Corrosion Congress, Copenhagen, Denmark, 1983.
47. Thompson, M.E. Water, Air, and Soil Pollution, **1986**, 31, pp 17-26.
48. Keller, W.; Pitblado, J.R. Water, Air, and Soil Pollution, **1986**, 29, pp 285-296.
49. Kelso, J.M.R.; Jeffries, D.S. J. Fish. and Aquatic Sci., **1988**, 45, pp 1905.
50. Lam, D.C.L.; Swayne, D.A.; Storey, J.; Fraser, A.S. Ecol. Modelling, **1989**, 47, pp 131.
51. Matuszek, J.E.; Biggs, G.L. Canadian J. Fish Aquat. Science, **1988**, 45, pp 1931.
52. Cook, R.B.; Jones, M.L.; Mamorek, D.R.; Elwood, J.W.; Malanchuk, J.L.; Turner, R.S.; Smol, J.P. The Effects of Acidic Deposition on Aquatic Resources in Canada: An analysis of Past, Present, and Future Effects, Oak Ridge National Laboratories, Publication 2894, 1988, Oak Ridge,TE pp 145.

RECEIVED October 1, 1991

Chapter 4

Tropospheric Chemical Reactivity and Its Consequences for Clean and Polluted Air

Robert J. O'Brien and Linda A. George

Chemistry Department and Environmental Sciences Doctoral Program, Portland State University, Portland, OR 97207

The trace free radicals HO and HO_2 (collectively HO_x) play central roles in chemical processes in the lower atmosphere. On the one hand, they are active in controlling buildup of atmospheric trace-gas concentrations that could have marked effects on earth's climate or habitability. On the other hand, they are responsible for the symptoms of anthropogenic gaseous emissions known as acid precipitation or photochemical smog. We review the characteristic chemical processes of the lower atmosphere from the perspective of HO_x free-radical chemistry. The discussion incorporates chemical processes both in the natural atmosphere and in polluted air. Uncertainties in our chemical understanding of tropospheric HO_x processes are enumerated, along with the role that HO_x measurements may play in exploring these uncertainties. Finally, we examine the role of HO and HO_2 in controlling trace-gas concentrations and the reciprocal control that hydrocarbons and oxides of nitrogen exert on these radicals.

The troposphere, in which all earth's creatures live, is a region of the atmosphere where temperature generally decreases with altitude. This decrease, brought about by thermodynamic cooling of an air mass as it rises in earth's gravitational field, persists to the tropopause at an altitude that varies from 18 km at the equator to 8 km at the poles. Although the troposphere contains all non-airborne and non-aquatic life on earth, it barely contains Mt. Everest at 8.848 km. At the tropopause, the temperature profile *pauses* before reversing direction to increase with altitude through earth's next atmospheric layer, the stratosphere or *ozone layer*. Thus the stratosphere functions as a stratified air layer, warmed by ozone's absorption of incoming ultraviolet (uv) light, riding on top of the troposphere. As a result of this temperature inversion, atmospheric mixing up through the stratosphere is inefficient, requiring many decades. In contrast, mixing throughout the troposphere is considerably faster, requiring several days for transport up to the tropopause, several weeks for transport east and west around the globe, several months for mixing throughout a hemisphere, and

0097–6156/92/0483–0064$14.25/0

several years for mixing across the equator. Thus, a substance emitted at the earth's surface may be subjected to many years' assault by tropospheric physical and chemical forces for its removal back to the earth's surface. Chief among these forces is removal in precipitation: *washout*, whereby a gas or particle is absorbed into falling rain or snow; or *rainout*, whereby clouds form around a preexisting particle. In order for washout to be effective in removing an atmospheric gas, it must be significantly soluble in water. Generally less efficient mechanisms for removal of gases or particles to earth's surface include deposition to vegetation, bare earth, or bodies of water. In the case of gases, low vapor pressure, water solubility, or chemical reactivity facilitate deposition.

Upward diffusion of water vapor through the cold temperatures of the tropopause is very inefficient; in fact, the upper limit of cloud formation often occurs at the tropopause. Thus the stratosphere is so dry as to prevent rain formation, and particles and gases have very much longer residence times there than in the troposphere. Stratospheric removal requires diffusion back through the tropopause, which then may be followed by precipitation scavenging.

Tropospheric Oxidation. Many species are emitted into the troposphere in chemical forms that are not very water soluble and that have very limited chemical reactivity. Direct atmospheric removal is therefore inefficient so that other forces come into play. Chief among these is the oxidative capacity of the atmosphere, that transforms unreactive, insoluble molecular forms into new, usually more soluble, molecular entities. Examples of this process include the oxidation of nitric oxide (NO) to nitrogen dioxide (NO_2) and on to nitric acid (HNO_3), sulfur dioxide (SO_2) to sulfuric acid (H_2SO_4), and the oxidation of hydrocarbons to oxygenated substances (aldehydes, ketones, peroxides, CO, and CO_2). All of these products (except CO) are much more soluble than their oxidative precursors, and all but CO and CO_2 can be removed from the atmosphere by rain or deposition within a few weeks. Not all emitted substances are subject to these oxidative processes. It is those oxidation-resistant species that survive the decades necessary for transport to high elevations in the stratosphere where short-wavelength uv light can initiate their decomposition. There is apparently only a single significant *natural* or biogenic trace gas released at the earth's surface that is completely immune to tropospheric removal. This is nitrous oxide (N_2O), a byproduct of bacterial nitrogen fixation in the soil. Nitrous oxide plays a major role in controlling ozone concentrations in the unperturbed stratosphere. Humans, on the other hand, have been releasing since the early 1950's significant quantities of chlorofluorocarbons (CFC's *e.g.* CF_2Cl_2 and $CFCl_3$) that have been shown to have a pronounced and dramatic effect on stratospheric ozone concentrations (Molina, M.J.; Molina, L.T. this volume and references 1,2). In the context of this paper, *natural* refers to processes that are not directly due to the intervention of humankind, although some might argue that humans are *natural* inhabitants of earth.

Naturally-occurring Trace Gases. The naturally emitted gaseous species subject to atmospheric oxidation include:

➤methane CH_4, largely produced in anaerobic aquatic or terrestrial environments and by ruminants (Chynoweth, D.P., this volume and references 3,4);

►hydrogen H_2, largely a product of methane's atmospheric degradation (4,5);

►terpene hydrocarbons, from vegetation (the smell of pine forests or sagebrush consists of these terpenes); the simplest is $CH_2=C(CH_3)CH=CH_2$; many are cyclic alkenes such as α-pinene (6);

►carbon monoxide CO, from natural combustion such as range or forest fires, from processes in the soil, and from tropospheric methane and terpene oxidation (7,8,9,10,11);

►hydrogen sulfide H_2S, from anaerobic aquatic environments and to a lesser extent from volcanic emanations (12,13); and

►dimethyl sulfide $(CH_3)_2S$, from biological processes in ocean surface waters (14,15).

Air Pollution. To the natural background of tropospheric trace gases, people add their share via industry, transportation, agriculture, etc. Many of these air pollutants are the same substances (*e.g.* hydrocarbons and oxides of nitrogen and sulfur) as emitted naturally. On a localized scale, anthropogenic emissions of air pollutants may dwarf natural emissions. The troposphere's oxidative capability has led air pollution scientists to distinguish two classifications of air pollutants: primary (those species directly emitted, such as sulfur dioxide) and secondary (those species, such as sulfuric acid, produced in chemical reaction of the primary pollutants). The primary air pollutants would number in the hundreds or more, but the U.S. Environmental Protection Agency has chosen to consider a small number sufficiently abundant and dangerous to promulgate National Ambient Air Quality Standards (NAAQS) for them.   These pollutants include carbon monoxide and sulfur dioxide. Previously, there was a standard for hydrocarbons because of their role in the generation of the secondary *criteria* air pollutants, ozone and nitrogen dioxide.   Control of ozone in the U.S. is carried out by limiting emissions of the precursor pollutants, hydrocarbons and nitric oxide (16,17,18,19).

Tropospheric Chemistry, the Role of HO_x

The troposphere's natural cleansing mechanism by precipitation is augmented by its oxidative capability to convert water insoluble species to soluble forms. Since all of tropospheric chemical reactivity arises from the influence of sunlight on the atmosphere, it is crucial to understand the mechanism whereby this radiant energy induces chemical processes. Only then can we understand how human activities can change the atmosphere. Very few tropospheric trace gases have significant photochemical reactivity resulting from the direct absorption of the solar wavelengths that penetrate to the troposphere (wavelengths longer than about 290 nm). Chief among these absorbers are NO_2, O_3, and many oxygenated hydrocarbons (*e.g.* aldehydes, ketones, peroxides).   Their tropospheric photochemistry is discussed below.

HO_x refers to the two radicals HO· (or OH) and HO_2·. Radicals are molecules with an unpaired electron, indicated hereafter by a dot ($\cdot$). They generally have high chemical reactivity, ultimately resulting in the combination of two radicals to form new molecules with all electrons paired in bonds, as in reactions R8 and R32 below. Relatively stable tropospheric radicals include $NO\cdot$ and $NO_2\cdot$. Their radical nature allows them to combine directly with HO_x species, for instance in reactions R19 and R23.

Tropospheric HO_x Chemistry. In the unpolluted troposphere, chemical reactivity largely originates from ozone photolysis to form the first excited state of the oxygen atom, $O(^1D)$ (20). Breaking of a molecular bond by light is called photolysis or photodissociation, $h\nu$ is the symbol for a photon (or particle) of light (R1). This process requires wavelengths shorter than about 310 nm, at the short-wavelength end of the tropospheric solar spectrum. Although ozone absorbs and photodissociates throughout the uv and visible spectrum, the ground state oxygen atom so produced simply recombines with O_2 to regenerate O_3. In contrast, $O(^1D)$ formed in

$$O_3 + h\nu \text{-----> } O(^1D) + O_2 \tag{R1}$$

is energetic enough to abstract a hydrogen atom from water,

$$O(^1D) + H_2O \text{-----> } 2\ HO\cdot. \tag{R2}$$

The $HO\cdot$ formation reaction R2 is in competition with electronic deactivation back to the ground state of the oxygen atom

$$O(^1D) + (N_2 \text{ or } O_2) \text{-----> } O + (N_2 \text{ or } O_2), \tag{R3}$$

followed by the recombination of O to reform ozone in R15 with no net change other than atmospheric heating. In warm, humid air about 10% of $O(^1D)$ follows R2 to generate $HO\cdot$.

Most of the troposphere's oxidative capability resides in the hydroxyl radical $HO\cdot$ produced in R2 and by other processes. Due to its high reactivity, hydroxyl is typically present at a mixing ratio of 10^{-12}-10^{-14} in sunlit air, and is believed to be present at much lower and generally insignificant levels at night. [Mixing ratio is the same as mole fraction. Atmospheric scientists use units of ppm, ppb, ppt for 10^{-6}, 10^{-9}, 10^{-12}, these are equivalent on a mole, molecule, volume, or partial pressure basis]. In clean air, $HO\cdot$ is derived primarily from atmospheric water vapor and much of its reactivity consists of the reacquisition of a hydrogen atom to reform H_2O. A major source of hydrogen atoms is organic compounds, such as methane and the higher hydrocarbons.

Methane and the Nonmethane Hydrocarbons. It is traditional to distinguish CH_4 from all other atmospheric hydrocarbons. Methane is by far the most abundant atmospheric hydrocarbon and has very large natural emissions. Its abundance in auto exhaust but low atmospheric reactivity has led air pollution scientists to enact controls on nonmethane hydrocarbons NMHC (also called VOC for volatile organic compounds, which include oxygenated hydrocarbons).

Methane. At a background concentration of 1.7 ppm (3,21), methane is typically much more abundant in either clean or polluted air than all the other hydrocarbons combined. The dominant source of this gas is anaerobic biological activity (methane has been known as swamp gas for centuries), that degrades organic material to this reduced carbon form rather than to CO_2, as happens in aerobic biological activity and in combustion. Wetland ecosystems are major contributors to the global methane budget (22,23). Anaerobic biological processes in rice fields appear to be a major anthropogenic source (3,24,25). Other sources that have been suggested are bacterial digestion of vegetation or cellulose in ruminants (26,27) and in termites (3,28,29,30,31); seepage from petroleum deposits and coal mines; transfer or venting of natural gas (largely methane) (4,32); and biomass burning (33). Methane is the most abundant hydrocarbon in auto exhaust, where it is formed by cracking of fuel hydrocarbons.

Methane is the atmospheric hydrocarbon least reactive with $HO\cdot$, losing a hydrogen after an atmospheric lifetime of about a decade:

$$HO\cdot + CH_4 \text{-----}> H_2O + CH_3\cdot. \tag{R4}$$

The methyl radical reacts further to form either formaldehyde CH_2O or methyl hydroperoxide CH_3OOH, depending upon the nitric oxide $NO\cdot$ concentration:

$$CH_3\cdot + O_2 \text{-----}> CH_3O_2\cdot \tag{R5}$$
$$CH_3O_2\cdot + NO\cdot \text{-----}> NO_2\cdot + CH_3O\cdot \tag{R6}$$
$$CH_3O\cdot + O_2 \text{-----}> HO_2\cdot + CH_2O \tag{R7}$$
$$CH_3O_2\cdot + HO_2\cdot \text{-----}> CH_3OOH + O_2. \tag{R8}$$

Although both of these oxygenated methanes are subject to precipitation removal, they are also photochemically labile, photodissociating in bright sunlight to regenerate $HO\cdot$ or form $HO_2\cdot$ in about 0.5 and 2.5 days for CH_2O and CH_3OOH respectively:

$$CH_2O + h\nu \text{-----}> CO + H_2 \tag{R9}$$
$$CH_2O + h\nu \xrightarrow{O_2} CO + 2 HO_2\cdot \tag{R10}$$
$$CH_3OOH + h\nu \text{-----}> CH_3O\cdot + HO\cdot. \tag{R11}$$

[Reactions with molecular species above the arrow (*e.g.* R10) involve subsequent reactions with these species to produce the indicated products. In most cases the reactants shown to the left of the arrow participate in the slowest or *rate-determining* step]. The $CH_3O\cdot$ radical formed in R11 then follows reaction R7. The $HO_2\cdot$ radical formed in R10 is the other member of the HO_x family and is linked with $HO\cdot$ in a variety of chain reactions. These radicals are produced following $HO\cdot$ attack on hydrocarbons or by photodissociation of oxygenated hydrocarbons such as formaldehyde (R10) and acetaldehyde:

$$CH_3CHO + h\nu \longrightarrow CH_3\cdot + CHO\cdot, \qquad (R12)$$

where the two photo-fragments generate $HO_2\cdot$ via R5-R7. Acetaldehyde is produced in HO-oxidation of ethane, propene and many higher hydrocarbons. Although $HO_2\cdot$ has a number of other sources, oxygen abstraction of a hydrogen atom from an oxygenated organic radical, as in R7, represents a major generation step, especially in polluted air with its greater abundance of organic trace gases.

Methane is an important greenhouse gas (34), whose concentration has been found to be increasing on the order of 1% annually for the last 3 decades (21,35,36,37,38); see Figure 1. Currently, methane represents ~15% of the anthropogenic contribution to radiative warming of the earth's atmosphere (39). The breakdown of causes for this increase between increasing emissions, and suppression of the *natural* tropospheric HO· concentration via R4 and R27, has been the subject of study, as has the global methane budget (3,36,40,41). Model simulations indicate that with a 1% annual increase in CH_4, HO will decrease by 10% over a 50 year model scenario (42). Analysis of methane data suggest that HO may have decreased by 20-25% as a result of increasing methane emissions (36,40).

NMHC. A large number of hydrocarbons are present in petroleum deposits, and their release during refining or use of fuels and solvents, or during the combustion of fuels, results in the presence of more than a hundred different hydrocarbons in polluted air (43,44). These *unnatural* hydrocarbons join the *natural* terpenes such as isoprene and the pinenes in their reactions with tropospheric hydroxyl radical. In saturated hydrocarbons (containing all single carbon-carbon bonds) abstraction of a hydrogen (*e.g.* R4) is the sole tropospheric reaction, but in unsaturated hydrocarbons HO-addition to a carbon-carbon double bond is usually the dominant reaction pathway.

As might be imagined, the detailed mechanisms of all these reactions are exceedingly complex (45,46). For instance, toluene (one of the most abundant constituents of gasoline in the U.S.) leads to more than 25 unique oxidation products (reference 47 and Myton, D.M.; O'Brien, R.J.; submitted to Anal. Chem. 1991). In general, though, the reaction pathways bear much resemblance to the oxidation scheme for methane, but produce a variety of aldehydes, ketones, peroxides, nitrates and other oxygenates as intermediate products in what could be termed low-temperature combustion. These partial oxidation products have higher water solubility than their precursors and may be removed in precipitation; many of them may photodissociate to initiate free radical processes (*e.g.* R10, R11, R12); or they may react further with HO· (*e.g.* R20). Those that survive precipitation scavenging will ultimately oxidize to CO and CO_2.

In addition to reactions with HO·, tropospheric organic compounds may be oxidized by ozone (via ozonation of non-aromatic carbon/carbon double bonds, Atkinson 1990) and in some cases by reaction with nitrate radical, described below. Table I gives representative trace-gas removal rates for these three processes. In spite of these competing reactions, HO· largely serves as

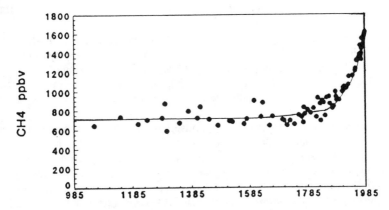

Figure 1. Atmospheric methane increases over the last 300 years. Points are annual averages; the concentrations before 1960 are from ice core analyses; more recent data from atmospheric measurements. From Khalil and Rasmussen (40).

Table I. Trace gas rate constants and lifetimes for reaction with ozone, hydroxyl radical, and nitrate radical. Lifetimes are based upon $[O_3]=40ppb$; $[HO\cdot]=1.0x10^6$ molecules cm^{-3} (daytime); $[NO_3\cdot]=10ppt$ (nighttime).

	Rate constants (cm^{-3} molec s^{-1})			Tropospheric Lifetimes (days)		
	k(HO)	k(O3)	k(NO3)	HO	O3	NO3
methane	8.5E-15	7E-24	4E-19	1362	1.7E6	1.2E5
CO	2.8E-13	4E-25	4E-16	42	3E7	116
CH_2O	9.8E-12	2.1E-24	6.8E-16	1	5.6E6	68
methanol	9.3E-13	very small	2.1E-16	12	--	220
ethane	2.7E-13	1E-20	8E-18	43	1200	5787
propane	1.1E-12	1E-20	very small	11	1200	--
isoprene	1E-10	1.4E-20	8.2E-13	0.12	843	0.06
a-pinene	5E-11	8E-17	6.2E-12	0.23	0.15	0.01
n-butane	2.7E-12	1E-20	5.5E-17	4	1200	843
ethene	2.5E-12	1.9E-18	2E-16	5	6.2	231
propene	2.5E-11	1.1E-17	9.5E-15	0.46	1	5
acetylene	7E-13	7.8E-21	5.1E-17	17	1513	908
benzene	1.2E-12	7E-23	3.2E-17	10	1.7E5	1448
toluene	6.4E-12	1.5E-22	6.9E-17	2	7.9E4	671
$(CH_3)_2S$	9.8E-12	8E-19	9.7E-13	1	15	0.05
ammonia	1.6E-13	very small	6E-16	72	--	77
NO_2	1.1E-11	3.2E-17	1.2E-12	1	0.37	0.04

nature's police officer in maintaining the relatively low and stable tropospheric trace-gas concentrations that have apparently persisted for centuries up until the industrial revolution; see Figure 1 (3,40,48,49,50,51,52,53). For this reason, any potential atmospheric changes which could impact the HO· concentration are matters of concern.

Nitrogen Oxides (NO$_x$ and NO$_y$) and Ozone. The nitrogen oxide family is the other major ingredient of the tropospheric oxidative scheme. This family is classified into two groups, relatively stable free-radical NO$_x$ = NO· + NO$_2$· (nitric oxide and nitrogen dioxide); and NO$_y$ that includes (mostly nonradical species) nitrous, nitric, and pernitric acids, peroxyacetyl nitrate (PAN) and other pernitrates and organic nitrates (NO$_y$ = NO$_x$ + HNO$_2$ + HNO$_3$ + HNO$_4$ + N$_2$O$_5$ + PAN + other organic nitrates and pernitrates).

Nitric oxide involved in R6 is the dominant fixed-nitrogen form produced in combustion and lightning. NO· is the molecular form stable at high temperature and is produced directly from air in the net reaction N$_2$ + O$_2$ ===> 2NO·. Any nitrogen present in a fuel is also largely oxidized to NO·. Fossil fuel combustion and biomass burning have been estimated at about 70% of the total emission sources for NO$_x$ of which ~95% is NO· and ~5% is NO$_2$·. (54,55). The remaining sources of NO$_x$ emissions are microbial activity in soils and lightning discharges, but estimates of the magnitude of the latter source have been significantly increased recently (56).

In addition to reactions such as R6, NO· is oxidized to the NO$_2$· species (thermodynamically more stable at atmospheric temperatures) by the reaction

$$HO_2\cdot \; + \; NO\cdot \; \text{-----}> \; HO\cdot \; + \; NO_2\cdot. \tag{R13}$$

The measurement of R13 about 15 years ago (57) revealed that this reaction was ~10 times faster than it was previously thought to be. This meant that in more polluted regions, with higher levels of nitric oxide, recycling of HO$_2$· in R13 can be a significant source of HO·. (58,59). Thus while hydrocarbon oxidation effectively converts HO· to HO$_2$·, nitric oxide provides a means of regenerating HO· from intermediate radical products of hydrocarbon oxidation. This reaction is important both in regenerating HO· and in oxidizing NO· to NO$_2$·.

In sunlight, NO$_2$· is rapidly photodissociated

$$NO_2\cdot \; + \; h\nu \; \text{-----}> \; NO\cdot \; + \; O, \tag{R14}$$

but is regenerated by

$$O + O_2 \; \text{-----}> \; O_3 \tag{R15}$$
$$NO\cdot \; + \; O_3 \; \text{-----}> \; NO_2\cdot \; + \; O_2. \tag{R16}$$

Reactions R14-R16 are termed the NO·/NO$_2$·/O$_3$ photostationary state PSS, and reach equilibrium levels of NO·, NO$_2$·, and O$_3$ in a few minutes in sunlight. At night, the more abundant of NO· or O_3 titrates out its less abundant partner in R16. Reaction R14 + R15 serve as the only known source of ozone in the troposphere, since uv wavelengths sufficiently energetic to dissociate oxygen (O_2 + $h\nu$ ---> 2O) are completely absorbed above the tropopause.

Ozone production occurs when the PSS is perturbed by reactions such as R13 or R6. These peroxyl radical reactions *save* an *incipient* O_3 molecule from reduction back to O_2 in R16, and result in the gradual photooxidation of NO· to NO_2·, followed by the accumulation of O_3. Figure 2a presents a typical profile for the photooxidation of NO· to NO_2·, with its concomitant formation of ozone, such as occurs in polluted air exposed to sunlight. The horizontal axis represents the exposure time of fresh emissions to sunlight, but could be transformed by an average wind speed to give downwind distance traveled. Globally, it is believed that about 50% of tropospheric ozone results from chemical production and 50% from transport out of the stratosphere (59,60). Locally or regionally produced ozone is a major air pollutant that may reach ten times the natural background concentration.

A steady-state analysis of R13-R16 provides a means of understanding the role of peroxyl radicals such as HO_2 in ozone formation:

$$J_{NO2} [NO_2\cdot] = k_{16}[NO\cdot][O_3] + k_{13}[NO\cdot][HO_2] + k[RO_2][NO\cdot]   \text{(E1)}$$

[Square brackets around a molecular species indicate atmospheric concentration. The rate constants k times the reactant concentration product refers to the rates of the chemical reactions of the indicated number. The photolytic flux term J_{14} refers to the photodissociation rate of NO_2· in Reaction R14, its value is proportional to solar intensity.]. RO_2 stands for an organic peroxyl radical (R is an organic group) that is capable of oxidizing NO to NO_2. Hydrocarbons oxidize to form a very large number of different RO_2 species; the simplest of the family is methylperoxyl radical involved in R5, R6 and R8.

At high concentrations of NO·, its reaction with O_3 dominates NO· oxidation and controls the PSS. Under conditions of low [NO·] or large sources of HO_2· or RO_2· (*i.e.* high hydrocarbon oxidation rates) the last two terms in Equation E1 can be large enough to be determined as an imbalance of the PSS. Such measurements require precise determinations of J_{NO2}, [NO_2·], [NO·], and [O_3], followed by analysis using Equation E1. Under very low [NO·] conditions, HO_2· can reach high enough concentrations to destroy ozone via

$$HO_2\cdot + O_3 \text{-----> } HO\cdot + 2O_2.   \text{(R17)}$$

Existence of the PSS was predicted theoretically by Leighton (61), and experimental studies of this relationship date back almost 20 years. These experiments have been accomplished in smog chambers (62), polluted urban air (63,64,65), rural environments (66), and in the free troposphere (67). The goal of these experiments has been to verify that our understanding of NO_x chemistry is fundamentally correct, and to verify the role of HO_2· and RO_2· in ozone formation. Studies in polluted air seem to confirm the dominance

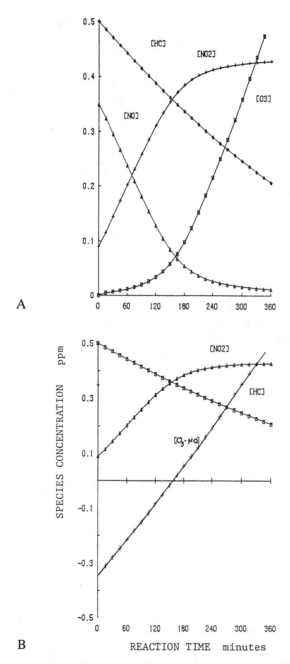

Figure 2. Typical *photochemical smog* cycle in which hydrocarbons HC are consumed, NO· is photooxidized to NO₂·, and O₃ accumulates. A. Typical variables. B. Showing transformed variable [O₃-NO·]. Adapted from Moshiri (75).

of R16 over R13 or other processes for NO· reaction. Analysis of the PSS in rural environment indicates the presence of an additional oxidant, such as HO_2 or RO_2, contributing significantly to the oxidation of NO·. The most comprehensive study of the clean-air PSS, conducted at Mauna Loa on the island of Hawaii, has found a perturbation of the PSS that may be consistent with clean air peroxyl radical concentrations of 80ppt (67), although confirmation by actual HO_2/RO_2 measurements would be useful. Preliminary analysis of the Mauna Loa results indicates sufficiently low [NO·] that net photochemical destruction of ozone is occurring in the free troposphere (67), that is, Reaction R17 is occurring faster than Reaction R13.

The nitrate radical NO_3· is formed by the reaction of NO_2· and O_3

$$NO_2· + O_3 \text{-----}> NO_3· + O_2. \tag{R18}$$

NO_3· reacts rapidly with NO· to regenerate $2NO_2$· and is photodissociated rapidly in daylight, but may have significant chemistry at night if NO· is absent, as will be the case via R16 if ozone is more abundant than nitric oxide. NO_3· reacts with some atmospheric organic compounds, particularly terpenes (see below) and may be a significant agent for their removal (68,69,70). However NO_3· seems to be absent in humid air (70) (where its reaction product with NO_2·, N_2O_5, can be hydrolyzed to nitric acid), and its exact role in tropospheric chemistry remains to be quantified. Reactions of NO_3· more or less mimic those of HO· and often result in the formation of nitric acid HNO_3. PAN and nitrous and pernitric acids are formed in radical combination reactions but serve as reservoirs for both HO_x and NO_x that may be *drawn upon* by re-dissociation or photodissociation, *e.g.*

$$HO_2· + NO_2· \rightleftharpoons HNO_4. \tag{R19}$$

PAN may be formed from a number of hydrocarbons once they have been partially oxidized; the simplest generation is from acetaldehyde in the sequence

$$CH_3CHO + HO· \text{-----}> H_2O + CH_3CO· \tag{R20}$$
$$CH_3CO· + O_2 \text{-----}> CH_3C(O)O_2· \tag{R21}$$

$$CH_3C(O)O_2· + NO_2· \rightleftharpoons CH_3C(O)O_2NO_2 \text{ (PAN)}. \tag{R22}$$

Higher members of the peroxyaclnitrate family are less abundant than PAN but probably significant in total.

PAN is resistant to HO· attack and has low water solubility, which allows it to transport NO_y for periods longer than the atmospheric scavenging time of most other nitrogen oxide species. PAN thus serves as a source of NO_x (by dissociating in the reverse of R22) in the remote troposphere where NO· is a limiting reagent in the generation of ozone. The role of NO· may be seen in comparison of R6 vs. R8 and R13 vs. R33; peroxyl radicals (HO_2·, RO_2·) are shunted to other *oxidants* such as H_2O_2, CH_3OOH or PAN when the NO·

concentration is low, or they may continue to degrade in the process $2RO_2\cdot$ --->
$2RO\cdot + O_2$ (95).

HO· and Acid Precipitation. Hydroxyl radical is also active in the transformations of the key nitrogen and sulfur species that dominate acidified precipitation:

$$HO\cdot + NO_2\cdot \text{-----> } HNO_3 \qquad (R23)$$

$$HO\cdot + SO_2 \xrightarrow{\quad O_2,\ H_2O \quad} H_2SO_4 + HO_2\cdot. \qquad (R24)$$

R23 is the only significant removal process for $NO_2\cdot$ and serves as well as a radical sink reaction for HO_x. Sulfur dioxide (with higher water solubility than $NO_2\cdot$) is also oxidized to sulfuric acid in aerosols and fog droplets (71,72,73,74); its gas-phase oxidation via R24 does not constitute a radical sink, since $HO_2\cdot$ is regenerated.

Oxidant Formation. The role of HO· in controlling the time-scale and severity of tropospheric oxidant pollution may be seen from the parameterization of O'Brien and co-workers (75,76). The simplest possible mechanism for *oxidant (i.e.* ozone, PAN, H_2O_2, etc.) formation consists simply of the reaction of an individual $NMHC_i$ with HO· to convert the $NMHC_i$ to a generic product(s) $PROD_i$, followed by removal of the product by HO· (PROD photolysis may be important, but is ignored here)

$$NMHC_i + HO\cdot \xrightarrow{\quad k_{NMHCi} \quad} PROD_i + \alpha_i\ HO_2\cdot \qquad (R25)$$

$$PROD_i + HO\cdot \xrightarrow{\quad k_{PRODi} \quad} \beta_i\ HO_2\cdot. \qquad (R26)$$

HO-oxidation of an individual $NMHC_i$ produces $HO_2\cdot$ radicals with a yield α_i, and oxidation of the NMHC oxidation product produces $HO_2\cdot$ in stoichiometric amount β_i. The *lumped* coefficients or yields α and β need not be integers, and represent the effectiveness of a particular $NMHC_i$ in producing $RO_2\cdot$ and $HO_2\cdot$ radicals (lumped together as HO_2) that will then oxidize NO· to $NO_2\cdot$ in processes such as R6 and R13, producing one net ozone molecule each. Alternatively, when the NO· concentration is low, peroxyl radicals may form PAN (as in R22) or hydrogen peroxide (as in R33) which are other oxidant species. In this formulation, transport is expressed by an overall dilution rate of the polluted air mass into unpolluted air with a rate constant k_d (units = reciprocal time; dilution lifetime=$1/k_d$). This rate constant includes scavenging processes such as precipitation removal as well as mixing with *clean* air.

When combined with reactions R13 and R14-R16 (the PSS), this highly simplified mechanism describes the elements of ozone and other oxidant formation. By defining net ozone $[O_3\text{-}NO\cdot]$ it is recognized that oxidant formation is a continuous process that must first oxidize nitric oxide to nitrogen dioxide, followed by the accumulation of ozone and other oxidants. Figure 2b illustrates the quantity $[O_3\text{-}NO\cdot]$.

Chemical kinetic analysis of these simplified reactions allows net ozone formation to be directly related to hydrocarbon consumption by $HO\cdot$ on a time-independent basis

$$\frac{d[O_3\text{-}NO\cdot]}{d[NMHC_i]} = \frac{-\alpha_i}{S_i+1} - \frac{\beta_i Q_i}{(S_i+1)(Q_i+1)}\left[1 - \left(\frac{[NMHC_i]}{[NMHC_i]_0}\right)^{\frac{Q_i-1}{S_i+1}}\right] + \frac{S_i}{S_i-1}[O_3\text{-}NO\cdot] \quad (E2)$$

The competition between dilution of $NMHC_i$ (here $[NMHC_i]_0$ represents the initial hydrocarbon concentration) and its reaction with $HO\cdot$ to generate an oxidant molecule enters through the dimensionless parameter $S=k_d/k_{25}[HO\cdot]$ that compares the rate of the HO reaction to the rate of dilution. Also important is the relative reactivity of the oxidation product PROD to the parent hydrocarbon as defined by the dimensionless parameter $Q=k_{26}/k_{25}$. If the oxidation products are more reactive, they will have a greater oxidant yield before suffering dilution themselves. Ignoring $RO_2\cdot/RO_2\cdot$ termination reactions in this simplified treatment causes the quantity $[O_3\text{-}NO\cdot]$ to include other oxidants, such as PAN and hydrogen peroxide, formed by recombination of peroxyl radicals. The oxidant forming potential of an individual NMHC is a function of the stoichiometry parameters α_i and β_i that represent individual or *lumped* hydrocarbon reactivity, the relative reactivity of the $NMHC_i$ oxidation product $PROD_i$ expressed through Q, and the competition between dilution and reaction with $HO\cdot$ expressed through S_i. Thus, oxidant=$[O_3\text{-}NO\cdot]$ is a function of the four parameters α_i, β_i, Q_i, and S_i)]. Low values of α, β, and Q correlate with low ozone yields, as does a large value of S. The quantitative behavior of this equation (obtained by numerical integration of Equation E2) is shown in Figure 3. The course of a photooxidation starts at the right-hand end of each curve, at the starting NMHC concentration. The vertical axis expresses $[O_3\text{-}NO\cdot]$ and is initially negative, corresponding to a beginning [NO] due to fresh emissions (here 200ppb). The horizontal axis (right to left) expresses decreasing NMHC concentration as NMHC is removed by dilution (k_d) and reaction with $HO\cdot$; reaction time is indicated on this axis in units of the NMHC atmospheric concentration lifetime τ given by $1/(k_d+k_{25}[HO\cdot])$. For low values of the dilution parameter S and large values of the product reactivity parameter Q, a near stoichiometric yield of *oxidant* equal to $(\alpha+\beta)[NMHC]_0 = 2\text{x}500\text{ppb} = [800\text{-}(\text{-}200)] = 1000$ ppb is produced when the NMHC is completely consumed; upper curve in Figure 3b. Increasing dilution and reduced product reactivity lower ozone yields. [Equation E2 has an asymptote of zero oxidant $[O_3\text{-}NO\cdot]$, but this may easily be shifted to an appropriate background ozone level]. Thus, ozone yields in photochemical smog are implicitly tied to high $HO\cdot$ concentrations, commonly associated with strong sunlight, and low mixing with clean air, or air stagnation.

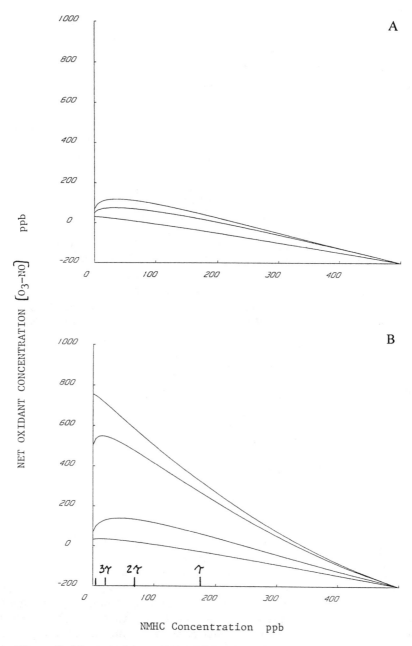

Figure 3. Numerical integration of Equation E2 showing net oxidant [O₃-NO·] yields from an initial [NMHC]ₒ = 500ppb. A. Variation with the product reactivity parameter Q; here $\alpha=\beta=1$ and S=1. B. Variation with the dilution parameter S; here $\alpha=\beta=1$, Q=1. When S is small, a nearly stoichiometric yield of oxidant=1000ppb is achieved; at higher values of S, oxidant and reactants are diluted with less oxidant accumulation.

An illustration of the significance of Equation E2 may be seen in the concept of *hydrocarbon reactivity* that was defined and measured early in the study of photochemical air pollution in Los Angeles. Following Haagen-Smit's (77) pioneering studies, it was recognized that some hydrocarbons were far worse than others in promoting oxidant formation. Scales of hydrocarbon reactivity were based upon maximum ozone concentration, time when $[NO\cdot]=[NO_2\cdot]$ in $NO\cdot$ photooxidation (Figure 2a), or other parameters, all of which were measured in smog chamber experiments with individual hydrocarbons, as discussed below. With the realization of the role of $HO\cdot$ in smog formation, Darnall *et al.* (78) proposed k_{25} for an individual NMHC as a useful measure of hydrocarbon reactivity. The significance of this rate constant is apparent in the parameter S in Equation E2, as is the relative reactivity of $HO\cdot$ with the NMHC oxidation product PROD, as expressed in the parameter Q. However, the peroxyl radical yields as expressed by α and β are equally important in Equation E2.

One strategy in limiting the formation of ozone and other photochemical oxidants has been the use (in the past) of low reactivity fuels in internal combustion engines. More recently, alternate fuels (methanol, for instance) have been proposed for regions that suffer from elevated levels of photochemical air pollution. The effect of switching to such a *low-reactivity* fuel may be seen in Equation E2 for methanol, which has a simple atmospheric reaction mechanism.

$$CH_3OH + HO\cdot \longrightarrow H_2O + CH_3O\cdot \qquad (R27)$$
$$CH_3O\cdot + O_2 \longrightarrow HO_2\cdot + CH_2O \qquad (R28)$$

When these two reactions are coupled with the PSS, the net reaction is simply

$$CH_3OH + 2 O_2 \overset{HO\cdot}{====} \Longrightarrow CH_2O + O_3 + H_2O. \qquad (R29)$$

Thus α is unity for methanol, although formaldehyde (PROD) reacts rapidly $(Q\approx10)$

$$CH_2O + HO\cdot \overset{O_2}{\longrightarrow} H_2O + CO + HO_2. \qquad (R30)$$

Thus β is also unity. CO has a sufficiently slow reaction with HO that it plays a minor role in local photochemistry. Methanol is an attractive automotive fuel from the standpoint of smog reactivity because of its slow reaction with HO and its minimal yield of peroxyl radicals $(\alpha+\beta=2)$ compared with current gasoline constituents. Low reactivity, and the solubility of methanol in precipitation (larger value of k_d), both produce a low value of S in Equation E2. The chief concerns associated with its use in fuel have to do with the reactivity (and toxicity) of its oxidation product CH_2O. Formaldehyde may be an exhaust constituent present in higher concentrations than with current fuels, depending upon the effectiveness of the exhaust catalyst. In addition to its relatively high reactivity with $HO\cdot$, CH_2O also increases HO_x concentrations through photodissociation in R10.

There has been variation of opinion on the importance of hydrocarbon reactivity in the generation of oxidants. In the early days of Los Angeles smog control, the Los Angeles Air Pollution Control District limited fuel and solvent photochemical reactivity (*Rule 66* of the LAAPCD). Subsequently, EPA downplayed the significance of hydrocarbon reactivity in the belief that even low-reactivity hydrocarbons would ultimately generate ozone, albeit farther downwind during the transport process. More recently, with the move toward alternate fuels such as methanol, the argument seems to have come full circle.

Certainly, photochemical air pollution is not merely a local problem. Indeed, spread of anthropogenic *smog plumes* away from urban centers results in regional scale oxidant problems, such as found in the NE United States and many southern States. Ozone production has also been connected with biomass burning in the tropics (79,80,81). Transport of large-scale tropospheric ozone plumes over large distances has been documented from satellite measurements of total atmospheric ozone (82,83,84), originally taken to study stratospheric ozone depletion.

On a local or regional basis, terpenes may contribute significantly to oxidant problems (16,60,85,86,87,88), making control of anthropogenic hydrocarbons problematical. The question of relative controls on hydrocarbon and NO_x emissions from automobiles and industry has been a matter of long-standing controversy and debate in the US, particularly because of the potential role of biogenic hydrocarbons in oxidant production (16,89,90). This controversy is yet unresolved.

Catalytic HO_x Cycles. In the unpolluted troposphere, the two step sequence R1, R2 was early recognized as the dominant source of HO· (20,91,92) and HO· as the dominant reactant for CO removal (93,94).

$$HO· + CO \xrightarrow{\;O_2\;} HO_2· + CO_2. \tag{R31}$$

HO· oxidation of CO is much faster than the reaction with methane, resulting in a mean CO lifetime of about two months, but considerably slower than reaction with the majority of the nonmethane hydrocarbons. Table I gives representative removal rates for a number of atmospheric organic compounds; their atmospheric lifetimes are the reciprocals of these removal rates (see Equation E4, below). The reaction sequence R31, R13, R14, R15 constitutes one of many tropospheric chain reactions that use CO or hydrocarbons as fuel in the production of tropospheric ozone. These four reactions (if not diverted through other pathways) produce the net reaction

$$CO + 2 O_2 \xRightarrow{\;HO·\;} CO_2 + O_3, \tag{R32}$$

in which HO· and $HO_2·$ (and NO· and $NO_2·$) are neither consumed or created. Other catalytic pathways, more competitive with R23 at low nitric oxide concentration, may destroy ozone or leave ozone unaffected in the oxidation of

CO to CO_2 (*e.g.* Finlayson-Pitts and Pitts 1986). The role of HO_x in any of these atmospheric cleansing and oxidant formation pathways is a catalytic one, but the generation of ozone is strongly dependent upon the nitric oxide concentration.

Actual ambient concentrations of $HO\cdot$ and $HO_2\cdot$ will be determined by the balance of radical generation steps (photolysis) and radical termination steps such as R8, R23, and R33

$$2\ HO_2\cdot\ \text{-----}>\ H_2O_2 + O_2. \qquad\qquad\qquad (R33)$$

R8 is the simplest of a large suite of peroxyl radical combination reactions, generalized as $RO_2\cdot + HO_2\cdot$ and $RO_2\cdot + RO_2\cdot$ that generate poorly characterized radical and non-radical reaction products. Such reactions are of greatest significance in air with low nitric oxide concentration where the $RO_2\cdot$ species can reach elevated concentrations (95). The dependence of $[HO_2\cdot]$ upon the tropospheric $NO\cdot$ concentration is discussed below.

Sulfur Chemistry. Reduced sulfur species, such as hydrogen sulfide H_2S, react with $HO\cdot$ via H atom abstraction, similar to hydrocarbons. With H_2S, SO_2 is produced as an oxidation product. Dimethyl sulfide, $(CH_3)_2S$ or DMS, is an important biogenic gas emitted as a metabolic byproduct from marine surface waters. Its oxidation by $HO\cdot$ produces methanesulfonic acid and other products that can condense from the gas phase to form aerosols (96). Such aerosols are important in the formation of clouds in remote regions (97). Global warming may induce greater biological activity in surface waters. If so, DMS production may increase, and the resultant increase in cloud cover may cause negative feedback to global warming by reflecting greater quantities of incoming solar radiation back into space (98). This sequence is one of the more striking interconnections between physical, biological, and chemical processes, but its magnitude depends, in part, upon future HO concentrations in a warmer world.

Halocarbons. Halocarbons are hydrocarbons containing one or more of the halogen atoms F, Cl, Br, I. Methyl chloride CH_3Cl is an important biogenic compound produced in the combustion of vegetation and biomass (79) and released from the oceans. Methylchloroform CH_3CCl_3 is a common industrial solvent also released in large quantities. Both these chlorine compounds lose an H-atom to $HO\cdot$ in relatively slow reactions, and both may introduce significant quantities of catalytically active Cl-atoms into the stratosphere. In contrast, completely halogenated hydrocarbons, *e.g.* CFC's such as CCl_2F_2 and $CFCl_3$, do not react with $HO\cdot$ and present such an ominous threat to the stratosphere that their production has been globally banned by the year 2000 according to the United Nations Montreal Protocol of 1987 and the 1990 Amendments (Molina, M.J.; Molina, L.T. this volume).

Since the recognition of the role of chlorine in catalytic ozone destruction, increasing effort has been devoted to finding replacements. In most cases reported so far, the replacements are partially halogenated molecules that retain one or more hydrogen atoms (HCFC's and HFC's). The presence of H-atoms gives $HO\cdot$ a *handle* (via H-atom abstractions such as R4) for their tropospheric removal. Nevertheless, many such compounds react slowly with HO·, therefore have quite long tropospheric lifetimes, and are not completely innocuous to stratospheric ozone (99).

Summary. Although R1-R33, along with similar reactions for the higher hydrocarbons, represent a portion of *natural* tropospheric chemistry, the high levels of hydrocarbons and oxides of nitrogen and sulfur associated with human activities lead to elevated levels of intermediates such as oxygenated hydrocarbons, nitric and sulfuric acids, that are collectively referred to as *photochemical smog* or *acid rain*. Particularly undesirable products of this photochemistry (in addition to the acids) include ozone (for which a U.S. NAAQS of 120 ppb has been promulgated) and peroxyacetyl nitrate PAN (100), a potent eye-irritant that causes damage to a wide array of native and agricultural plants.

As a result of this photochemistry, federal and state governments in the US have mandated reductions in hydrocarbon and/or nitrogen oxide emissions that are the precursors to ozone generation. In spite of these reductions, or as a consequence of growing numbers of *cleaner* pollution sources (*e.g.* motor vehicles), many areas of the US are designated *non-attainment* areas for ozone, and some areas may not come into compliance in the foreseeable future (*e.g.* the Los Angeles Basin exceeds the standard on two days out of three). All major world population centers in regions of photochemical activity suffer from ozone or oxidant pollution, Mexico City being a notable example (Garfias, J.; Gonzales, R., this volume). Meeting the ozone standard will be difficult in many areas of the US, and ultimately, the rest of the world. Several oxidant control issues discussed above (alternate or low-reactivity fuels, biogenic NMHC's, relative controls on NMHC vs. NO_x emissions) have been around a long time and show no signs of going away. Other approaches, such as limiting automobile use by a variety of societal approaches, are often equally as effective, and may carry such additional benefits as a reduction in traffic congestion, and reduced imports of petroleum, etc.

Tropospheric Trace-gas Lifetimes and Time Scales

Trace-gas Lifetimes. The time scales for tropospheric chemical reactivity depend upon the hydroxyl radical concentration [HO·] and upon the rate of the HO/trace gas reaction, which generally represents the slowest or *rate-determining* chemical step in the removal of an individual, insoluble, molecular species. These rates are determined by the rate constant, *e.g.* k_{25}, for the fundamental reaction with HO, a quantity that in general must be determined experimentally. The average lifetime τ_T of a trace gas T removed solely by its reaction with HO,

$$\text{HO·} + \text{T} \longrightarrow \text{removal of T,} \tag{R34}$$

may be defined by the rate equation

$$d[T]/dt = -k_T [\text{HO·}][T] \equiv [T]/\tau_T. \tag{E3}$$

The lifetime of T is an inverse function of the hydroxyl radical concentration [HO·] and the rate constant k_T for its reaction with a particular trace gas

$$\tau_T = 1/(k_T[\text{HO·}]). \qquad \qquad \text{(E4)}$$

The rate constants k_i defined above are usually functions of temperature, and in some cases depend upon total atmospheric pressure as well. A large suite of pertinent rate constants for HO· reactions have been determined, and are regularly reviewed and reevaluated (46,101). Values of k for individual trace gases span many orders of magnitude; some representative values are given in Table I. In order to obtain an atmospheric trace gas lifetime from Equation E4, an appropriate average tropospheric HO· concentration must be employed. HO· concentrations may be expressed as clear-day maxima (maximum normally near noon, when solar intensity is strongest), daily average (nighttime values normally considered to be negligibly small, equinoxial daily average≈1/4 daily maximum), or some type of annual average that takes into account the seasonal solar cycle. Typical HO· concentrations (daytime values in the range of 10^5-10^7 molecules cm^{-3}) may be obtained from tropospheric photochemical models, observation of actual trace gas removal rates or lifetimes (often employing budget calculations) or by direct *in situ* measurement using a variety of chemical techniques. All three of these approaches have been the subject of extensive effort in atmospheric chemistry, as discussed below.

Relative Trace-gas Oxidation Rates. Following the observations of Haagen-Smit (102) that a combination of NMHC's and NO_x resulted in the photochemical formation of ozone, it was observed that NMHC's reacted faster than could be accounted for by the reaction rates of oxidants known to be present in polluted air (ozone and oxygen atoms). This effect was referred to as the *excess rate of olefin (alkene) consumption*. In 1961 Leighton (61) speculated that this excess rate might be attributed to the presence of HO·. Experimental evidence for the presence and dominant role of HO· in controlling tropospheric trace gas removal was later obtained in relative oxidation rate measurements for a variety of NMHC's (46,103) and for NO_2· (104). In such experiments, two or more trace gases are present together in a simulated atmosphere. During illumination with simulated sunlight, the individual trace gases are observed to photooxidize (react to form products) with relative disappearance rates proportional to the rate constants for their individual reactions with HO·. Rate constants calculated from the measured disappearance rates using an equation equivalent to Equation E3 are found to be in excellent agreement with absolute rate constant measurements made using a variety of chemical techniques, which corroborates the concept that hydroxyl radical is the agent responsible for the individual trace gas removal.

Measurements of Tropospheric HO_x Concentrations

In a sense, the difficulty in measuring [HO·] or [HO_2·] in the troposphere is best demonstrated by the number and complexity of the different measurement schemes that have been devised over the past 25 years, and the controversies that have surrounded some of these measurements. It is also an indication of the importance atmospheric scientists have placed on the measurement of tropospheric HO_x. Since both these radicals are highly reactive, they are easily lost in sampling or collection, and few techniques allow sample concentration or storage, as is common for stable atmospheric trace gases. Most measurements involve *in situ* determination of some chemical or electronic signal proportional to concentration. No one technique has yet emerged as suitable for the rigorous demands of sensitivity, accuracy, rapidity of measurement, flexibility and ease of implementation. Hence, while one technique may be appropriate for one or more of these criteria, another technique has been developed to overcome some other deficiency.

Measurements of tropospheric HO· and HO_2· concentrations have been accomplished by both direct and indirect means. Direct techniques are based on the measurement of the hydroxyl or hydroperoxyl radical using some physical property of the radicals themselves *e.g.* optical absorption. Indirect techniques refer to methods based on the measurement of compounds that are uniquely and/or quantitatively formed from or destroyed by HO· or HO_2·. Examples of these techniques for both [HO·] and [HO_2·] will be given.

Direct Measurement of HO_x in the Troposphere. Techniques to measure tropospheric concentrations of HO· have been reviewed (O'Brien & Hard, submitted to Advances in Chemistry, 1991) so only a summary will be given here. The most extensively researched technique for [HO·] measurement in the troposphere is based on laser-induced fluorescence (LIF) of HO. This approach has been developed in many configurations: directing the laser into the free atmosphere and collecting fluorescence back scatter (LIDAR) (105,106,107); LIF of air sampled at atmospheric pressure (108,109) and LIF of air sampled at reduced pressure so that the background signal is reduced (110,111,112). The principal concern with all of these laser-based techniques is the production of spurious HO· by the laser pulse itself. In most configurations, the exciting laser operates at a wavelength of 282nm where the efficiency of HO· production via R1 and R2 is very high. This source of interference has been studied at great length (113,114,115,116,117,118,119,120, and Hard,T.M.; Mehrabzadeh, A.A.; Chan, C.Y.; O'Brien, R.J. *J. Geophys. Res.* in press, 1991,) and methods for its reduction to acceptable levels have been discussed (120)and implemented (112). A number of LIF [HO·] measurements have been made from NASA aircraft (121), and the long averaging times (typically about an hour) mean the concentration is averaged over a large volume of air. Ground-based LIF measurements have used comparable averaging times from a single location, except for the laboratory studies of Chan *et al.* (112, 127) that achieved adequate sensitivity with averaging times of a few minutes.

Long-path absorption measurements for [HO·] have been primarily developed by researchers in Germany (122,123,124,125). This approach measures the uv absorption by HO· over a pathlength up to several kilometers. The result is an HO· concentration spatially averaged over the region of the light path and temporally averaged on the order of one hour, comparable to the LIF measurements. The main difficulty encountered in this technique is disruption of the laser beam by atmospheric turbulence or scattering by haze. Recently, a possible improvement to the above system, using a folded light path within a shorter absolute point-to-point distance, has been developed and has the potential for greater sensitivity and reduced susceptibility to atmospheric conditions (126). This approach would greatly reduce the effective averaging volume for the HO· concentration as well.

Direct measurement of [HO$_2$·] has been accomplished by cryogenic trapping of air samples in a D$_2$O matrix, followed by a measurement of the electron spin resonance (ESR) signal due to the radicals present in the matrix (127,128). Considerable effort has gone into distinguishing and quantifying the various free radicals contributing to the signal (112, 127). The trapping procedure (~1hr collection time) and laboratory based analysis procedure limits this system to making infrequent measurements but could provide an accurate absolute calibration for other techniques.

Indirect Measurements of Tropospheric HO. There are two principal means of making indirect measurements of [HO·] or [HO$_2$·]· in the troposphere - either by the measurement of the chemical lifetimes of compounds that react uniquely with HO· or HO$_2$· or by chemical conversion of HO· or HO$_2$· to more readily measurable species.

Budget Calculations. Weinstock (93) proposed that HO· oxidation might be the primary sink for CO in the troposphere. Combining his budget analysis with a primary loss due to reaction with HO, an average HO· concentration was derived for the spatial domain of the budget analysis (94,129). Previously, this calculation was performed for the stratosphere (130). The recognition of the primary importance of HO· in the photochemistry of the troposphere has led to the development of trace gas budget analyses as a means of determining spatially averaged tropospheric HO· concentrations (92,131,132). Methylchloroform budgets have been used extensively in determining HO· concentrations (133,134,135,136). Methylchloroform budgets are, in principle, straightforward to develop since the sources (a function of industrial production and sales) are believed to be well quantified.

The combination of known global emission rates for a budget species (HO-chemical tracer) and its averaged global concentrations can lead to a *global* HO· concentration averaged implicitly over the temperature, pressure, and transport regimes appropriate to the tracer. In its simplest manifestation, the measured rate of tropospheric concentration growth (usually close to zero), the estimated emission or source rate, and the tropospheric trace gas concentration combine in the relationship

$$[HO·]_{avg} = \frac{\text{Source rate - Growth rate}}{k_{T,avg} [T]_{avg}} \tag{E5}$$

In using Equation E5 to calculate an average [HO·], an appropriate average for the rate constant k_T must be taken over the representative range of atmospheric temperatures and pressures. For reactions with strong temperature or pressure dependencies, this procedure may be quite elaborate, ultimately requiring the use of a multidimensional atmospheric photochemical model for most accurate calculation. For such a model, the source rate would represent influx from emission or transport to the particular grid point, transport of T away from the grid point would have to be incorporated, the growth rate might be set to zero or explicitly calculated, and k and [T] would be appropriate for the temperature and pressure of the grid point. In this way, the averaging would represent the region of the grid point.

Prinn *et al.* (136) have compiled a record of CH_3CCl_3 measurements taken throughout the world since 1978. This record was used in conjunction with a two-dimensional transport model to calculate longitudinally averaged [HO·]. These results are reproduced in Table II. These values can be compared with a global annual average of 6.5 (+3,-2) x 10^5 cm^{-3} by Volz *et al.* (137) derived from ^{14}CO.

Table II.

HO Concentrations Derived From Methyl Chloroform Distribution; [HO] (in units of 10^6 molecules cm^{-3}).

Latitude	90°-30°N	30°N-0°	0°-30°S	30°-90°S
[HO·]	0.49±0.09	1.04±0.19	0.98±0.18	0.54±0.1

Adapted from Prinn *et al.* (136).

Although Equation E3 is written to calculate an average [HO·], it could be rearranged to calculate an average trace-gas concentration $[T]_{avg}$ from $[HO·]_{avg}$, or to determine total source rates for a trace gas with poorly characterized sources, such as methane (4,138) using averaging procedures appropriate for the species T. Once an accurate method of determining $[HO·]_{avg}$ is determined (via a tropospheric model of suitable dimensionality) much information about trace-gas budgets can be obtained.

Some attempts have been made to use reactive hydrocarbons in conjunction with inert chemical tracers to deduce HO· concentrations in urban plumes (139,140,141). Difficulties in deducing [HO·] from these experiments have been studied by McKeen *et al.* (142), who conclude that such experiments can underpredict HO· concentrations by a factor of 2 when more reactive hydrocarbons are used and parameterization of transport processes is not properly accounted for.

Point Tracer Measurements.   Campbell   and   co-workers

(143,144,145) have capitalized on the uniqueness of hydroxyl radical oxidation of CO to CO_2. By introducing radioactive ^{14}CO to an air stream in a flowing reactor and freezing out the resultant $^{14}CO_2$, after a several second reaction time, the hydroxyl radical concentration can be deduced from a variant of Equation E5. The radioactive $^{14}CO_2$ can be quantified with high sensitivity for sample collection times of about a minute by subsequent decay event counting. This results in a sensitive indirect technique for [HO·], provided that surface-initiated ^{14}CO oxidation and sample contamination by other radio-nuclides can be controlled (145). In contrast to ambient-air, reactive-hydrocarbon-tracer experiments, this technique introduces a tracer into a system in which transport processes can be readily controlled, and produces a point measurement in time and space. However, the current implementation of the system requires careful and time-consuming sample preparation and post-measurement radiocounting that limits its realtime measurement capabilities.

Eisele and Tanner (146) have devised a similar scheme for the measurement of [HO·] via the chemical conversion of HO· to $H_2^{34}SO_4$ by the addition of $^{34}SO_2$ to a flowing reactor followed by chemical ionization of gas-phase sulfuric acid to $H^{34}SO_4^-$. The $H^{34}SO_4^-$ ion is uniquely identified and quantified in the flowing gas sample by a mass spectrometer. This technique is capable of sensitive, realtime measurement of [HO·], and although relatively new, appears to be perhaps the best overall technique devised to date.

Hard et al. (reference 110, 125, and submitted to J. Geophys. Res. 1991) have developed a system for the chemical conversion of HO_2· to HO· via the reaction HO_2· + NO· ---> HO· + NO_2·. The hydroxyl radical is then measured by their low-pressure laser-induced-fluorescence instrument. Their multi-sample-channel LIF FAGE system is thus capable of simultaneous measurements of [HO·] (directly) and [HO_2·] (by conversion to HO·).

Photochemical Modelling of Tropospheric HO_x

Tropospheric Photochemical Models. Photochemical models are essential tools in predicting the nature and magnitude of effects due to the emission of anthropogenic and biogenic compounds into the atmosphere. Their utility ranges from quantifying the sources of atmospheric acids or oxidants (so that effective emission controls may be applied) to predicting the composition of past or future atmospheres. Such models must implicitly yield accurate concentrations of HO· and HO_2·. These models consist simply of an appropriate reaction mechanism, including (in part) most of the reactions discussed in this paper. Using the chemical reaction mechanism, a continuity equation is written for each chemical species that incorporates emissions, chemical and physical transformations, and transport by diffusion or winds.

One goal of tropospheric [HO·] or [HO_2·] measurements is the generation of data for comparison with model calculations--to test or validate the models. Due to its high reactivity, HO· comes into rapid photochemical equilibrium with its surroundings. Thus a test of a photochemical model, which compares measured and calculated HO· concentrations, is mainly a test of the chemical mechanism that the model contains, and is relatively independent of transport or other physical processes. In making the test it is necessary to simultaneously measure other chemical species concentrations and appropriate photolysis rates so that all chemical contributors to HO formation or loss are quantified. For example, all quantities in Equation E6 (below) must be determined (from measurement or theoretical calculation) to compare a measured HO concentration with a model calculation. In spite of numerous measurements of tropospheric HO· concentrations (see review by Altshuller, 147) only a few have been claimed as tests of a tropospheric photochemical model rather than tests for the presumed presence and diurnal behavior of HO, or perhaps tests of the measurement devices themselves. A model test is really a test of the accuracy of our understanding of tropospheric chemistry.

Although more experimentation, including a larger suite of supporting measurements of other atmospheric species and photodissociation rates are necessary, it may be fairly concluded from experiment (105,106,107,108,110,111,123,124,143,144,145,146,148,149) that HO· is indeed present in the troposphere, undergoes a diurnal cycle in concert with solar intensity, and is not greatly at odds with calculated model concentrations. The *error bars* on the comparisons remain rather large; but in cases where agreement between measurement and calculation were not claimed, the measured concentrations have generally been lower than those predicted by the models (125,150). If the measurements and the model calculations were performed properly, this would indicate at least an insufficient knowledge of HO· removal processes, and might implicate heterogeneous loss processes for HO_x species that were not properly accounted for by the model (151). Although our knowledge of heterogeneous tropospheric processes is conceded to be relatively primitive, the possibility of a so-far-unrecognized homogeneous gas-phase source or sink reaction for HO· or HO_2· cannot yet be discounted.

Since monitoring of HO's global distribution is not yet a reality, direct evidence of the impact of changing tropospheric composition on HO· cannot be verified. Nevertheless, photochemical models can be used to simulate the response of [HO·] to local and global changes in atmospheric composition. They can also be used to rationalize measured changes in global tropospheric concentration of long-lived trace gases such as methane and methyl chloroform.

Clean and Polluted Air. In the development of atmospheric chemistry, there has been an historic separation between those studying processes in the natural or unpolluted atmosphere, and those more concerned with air pollution chemistry. As the field has matured, these distinctions have begun to disappear, and with this disappearance has come the realization that few regions of the troposphere are completely unaffected by anthropogenic emissions. An operational definition of clean air could be based upon either the NMHC concentration, or upon the NO_x concentration.

A definition based upon the NMHC concentration might require nonmethane hydrocarbons to contribute insignificantly to atmospheric reactivity. Such a region might still contain very low concentrations of nonmethane hydrocarbons, so long as their sum total reactivity does not significantly contribute to that of methane and carbon monoxide. This is to say, in *clean* air the total rate of HO· reaction with all nonmethane hydrocarbons is much less than the sum of the rates of its reaction with CO and methane. (The reaction with CO usually dominates, see Table III). Such a definition would exclude terpene chemistry as well, even though terpenes are *natural* tropospheric constituents. This definition implicitly requires that nonmethane hydrocarbons do not affect the ambient HO· concentration even though they would continue to be removed by their reaction with HO. *Clean air* conditions that comply with the definition based upon NMHC have been observed (152,153); see Table III.

A definition of *clean air* based upon NO_x concentrations is more difficult to obtain, because of the ubiquitous natural source in lightning (56,154), and because NO· may influence HO· concentration even at the lowest tropospheric NO· levels (a few ppt) that have been observed. An operational definition might require that the rate of the HO_2· self-reaction R33 be much faster than its reaction with NO·, R13. At NO_x concentrations below about 1 ppb, $[HO_2·]$ is relatively independent of [NO·], while [HO·] may increase with [NO·]. Above this level, both $[HO_2·]$ and [HO·] fall with increasing $[NO_x]$. These $[HO_x]$ dependencies on [NO·] are shown in Figure 4 (58) and discussed further in the last section.

At levels of nonmethane hydrocarbons where their reaction rates with HO· are a significant fraction of the reaction rate of HO· with CO and methane, it may happen that the clean-air HO· concentration remains unchanged. This would result if the increase in HO· removal by NMHC's is compensated by increasing HO_x sources such as aldehyde or ketone photolysis and reactions such as R21. These considerations are examined below.

Clean air tropospheric models are designed to test current understanding of background photochemical processes while polluted air models are generally used to predict tropospheric oxidant (ozone, PAN and other oxidizing species) and acid formation. In their simplest form, box-models or zero-dimensional models consider only chemical processes and physical transformations, ignoring transport. Even at this level, the differences in mechanistic details encompass a variety of parameters such as hydrocarbon oxidation mechanism, heterogeneous formation or loss processes and photolysis rates. These factors can affect the simulated hydroxyl radical concentration profile. One, two and three dimensional models of the troposphere also have been developed and can give important information on global [HO·] distribution with respect to altitude, latitude and longitude. Latitudinal considerations generally refer to the effect of solar zenith angle while longitudinal factors are generally based on continental versus marine environments. In either case, emission variations with latitude and longitude may be incorporated.

Clean Air Models. Models developed to simulate clean air chemistry generally have the least amount of chemical parameterization. Several recent zero-dimensional models (95,155,156) and one-dimensional models (157,158) have presented calculated HO· concentrations for clean air. Two dimensional models have also provided predictions for global [HO·] (58,159,160,161). Three dimensional models that provide information

Table III. Comparison of trace gas reaction removal rates with HO, sealevel Oregon Coast, 45°N, 25 August 1987. This day had the lowest NMHC of 9 samples taken 1986-87.

Trace Gas	k(HO)	Concentration	Rate (molec cm^{-3} s^{-1})
methane	8.5(-15)	1705	229
carbon monoxide	2.8(-13)	113	775
ethane	2.8(-13)	0.58	4
propane	1.2(-12)	0.07	2
isoprene	1.0(-10)		
a-pinene	5.3(-11)		
n-butane	2.6(-12)		
ethene	8.5(-12)	0.36	75
propene	2.6(-11)	0.11	70
acetylene	7(-13)	0.04	0.7
benzene	1.2(-12)	0.03	0.9
toluene	6.4(-12)	0.21	33
isopentane		0.03	
other alkanes		0.03	
other alkenes		0.10	
terpenes		0.03	
Total NMHC rate			200
Percent total HO rate			17%

Sample analysis provided by J. Greenberg, National Center for Atmospheric Research.

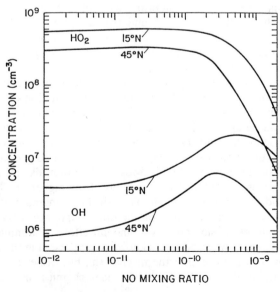

Figure 4.   Model-calculated variation of [HO·] and [HO$_2$·] with nitric oxide concentration for air without NMHC's. From Logan *et al.* (58).

on global [HO·] distributions have been developed (162). In order to make meaningful estimates of [HO·] in clean air, model calculations must utilize estimates of global CO, CH_4, O_3, and NO_x distributions so that representative concentrations of these chemical species may be incorporated. The models must also specify water vapor concentration and solar spectral irradiance. Table IV summarizes the results of model predictions for [HO]. Variations in the estimates derived for similar regions partially stem from differing interpretations of measured distributions of trace gases and water vapor.

In a sense, the lack of *parameterization* of homogeneous processes for clean air photochemical models means that competing models cannot exist--as new homogeneous chemical information becomes available it should be incorporated into any model. Heterogeneous processes are incorporated into zero-dimensional models via first-order removal processes for species soluble in rain or subject to significant deposition at the earth's surface. The chief area of uncertainty lies in the parameterization of heterogeneous processes in clouds themselves. Rates of gaseous species uptake and release by cloud droplets, and concurrent chemical processes occurring within cloud droplets are vastly more complex than clean-air homogeneous processes, and are often still omitted entirely from clean-air models.

Polluted Air Models. Inclusion of NMHC chemistry into a zero-dimensional model introduces an element of uncertainty into the modeling results, both because of inadequate knowledge about the nature of homogeneous processes, and because of the difficulty of even including the voluminous amount of known information. Mechanisms that include NMHC chemistry, originally applied to understanding processes in polluted air, are now routinely applied to understanding the chemistry of the remote troposphere as it has become clear that NMHC can have significant effects on background chemistry (60). In general, inorganic and methane chemistry, as explicitly represented in these mechanisms, is believed to be well understood. For NMHC chemistry, mechanisms have varying degrees and types of parameterizations or simplifications and are of three fundamental types--explicit, lumped (or condensed) and surrogate (163,164,165).

Explicit mechanisms attempt to include all nonmethane hydrocarbons believed present in the system with an explicit representation of their known chemical reactions. Atmospheric simulation experiments with controlled NMHC concentrations can be used to develop explicit mechanisms. Examples of these are Leone and Seinfeld (164), Hough (165) and Atkinson *et al.* (169). Rate constants for homogeneous (gas-phase) reactions and photolytic processes are fairly well established for many NMHC. Most of the lower alkanes and alkenes have been extensively studied, and the reactions of the higher family members, although little studied, should be comparable to the lower members of the family. Terpenes and aromatic hydrocarbons, on the other hand, are still inadequately understood, in spite of considerable experimental effort. Parameterization of NMHC chemistry results when NMHC's known to be present in the atmosphere are not explicitly incorporated into the mechanism, but rather are assigned to augment the concentration of NMHC's of similar chemical nature which the

Table IV. Predicted HO concentrations near the surface of the Northern Hemisphere. Average values obtained from tropospheric models. Taken from Altshuller (147) (see that paper for table references 20 and 24).

		OH Concentrations, $\times 10^6$ mol. cm^{-3}				
Season	Time of Day	15°N	30°N	45°N	60°N	NH avg.[a]
Summer[b]	noon	~6	~5	~3	<2	NR
Summer[c]	diurnal avg.	~1	NR	0.7	NR	NR
Winter[b]	noon	3	2	<1	NR	NR
Winter[c]	diurnal avg.	0.6	NR	0.08	NR	NR
Fall[c]	diurnal avg.	0.9	NR	0.3	NR	NR
Spring[c]	diurnal avg.	0.8	NR	0.2	NR	NR
Annual avg.[b,d]	diurnal avg.	1-1.5	1	0.4-0.5	0.2-0.3	0.4
July 1[e]	diurnal avg.	1-2	~1	0.5-1	~0.5	0.8
Jan. 1[e]	diurnal avg.	0.5-1	~0.5	~0.05	<0.05	0.4
July	daylight avg.	~2	~2.5	~2	1	1.3[f]
Jan.	daylight avg.	1-1.5	~1	0.5	<0.5	0.7[g]
Oct.	daylight avg.	1-1.5	1-1.5	0.5	<0.5	0.9[h]
April	daylight avg.	1.5-2	2	1	<0.5	1[i]

a. Hemispheric average for entire troposphere.

b. Based upon standard model.

c. Based upon standard model with NO_x concentrations assumed to be representative of marine air.

d. Adjusted to an approximate 8-year CH_3CCl_3 tropospheric chemical lifetime in the standard model.

e. Based on standard model for CH_3CCl_3 in which the HO values for the Northern Hemisphere (reference 24) are multiplied by 0.5. Since model-calculated values in reference 20 were multiplied by 1.66 to adjust to ^{14}CO values, the net results are Northern Hemisphere values 83% of adjusted HO values calculated from model.

f. June-September period of day.

g. December-March.

h. October-November.

i. April-May, values for daylight.

mechanism does explicitly include. Parameterization also results when NMHC's of poorly understood chemistry (e.g. aromatic hydrocarbons and many terpenes) are included explicitly with chemical processes that are not well established.

The second model type, surrogate, is further simplified to parameterize groups of not necessarily related hydrocarbons into one species. Examples of such approaches are found in references 75, 76, and 166. These highly simplified mechanisms allow *closed form* solutions of simultaneous differential equations resulting in algebraic equations that provide insight into the relationships between chemical species. Finally, lumped mechanisms combine hydrocarbons based on structural components (e.g. single bonds, 167), general classification (e.g. alkane or aldehyde, 168), or provide specific surrogate species (e.g. propane is a surrogate for itself and for benzene, (169,182)) to represent groups of compounds. These lumped mechanisms are designed to deal with the different reactivities of various hydrocarbons but have classified them with various schemes to reduce the computational requirements.

In contrast to clean-air photochemical mechanisms, where it has been presumed that testing must be conducted in the open atmosphere, polluted-air models are extensively tested in simulation experiments, sometimes termed smog chamber experiments. In these tests a wide range of NMHC concentrations, singly and in combinations, are exposed with oxides of nitrogen to simulated sunlight. A battery of instruments provide intermittent or continuous measurements of a variety of species including $NO\cdot$, $NO_2\cdot$, O_3, CO, individual NMHC, aldehydes, etc. Such chambers (see review by Finlayson-Pitts and Pitts 163) range from small laboratory glass vessels to huge outdoor teflon-film chambers. In order to eliminate cross-contamination from one simulated atmospheric reaction to another, some chambers are *cleaned* by evacuation to low pressures. Illumination sources range from natural sunlight (not absorbed by teflon), to uv fluorescent tubes, to xenon-lamp "search lights". Such chambers generate their *own reactivity* via the production of free radicals (170,171,172,173); NO_x or NO_y; or organic compounds (174); and therefore are not suitable for studying *clean* air, but in many experiments the added concentrations of NMHC and NO_x are sufficiently high as to swamp most *native* photochemistry. Experiments performed in many such vessels over the last several decades provide a data base for *model validation* (45,169,175,176,177,178).

Uncertainties in Photochemical Models. The ability of photochemical models to accurately predict HO_x concentrations is undoubtedly more reliable in clean vs. polluted air, since the number of processes that affect $[HO\cdot]$ and $[HO_2\cdot]$ is much greater in the presence of NMHC. Logan *et al.* (58) have obtained simplified equations for $[HO\cdot]$ and $[HO_2\cdot]$ for conditions where NMHC chemistry can be ignored. The equation for $HO\cdot$ concentration is given in Equation E6. The first term in the numerator refers to the fraction of excited oxygen atoms formed in R1 that react to form HO; *J* refers to the photodissociation of hydrogen peroxide to form 2 $HO\cdot$ molecules; other rate constants refer to numbered reactions above.

$$[HO\cdot] = \cfrac{\cfrac{2J_1[O3]k_2[H_2O]}{k_3[N_2+O_2]} + [HO_2\cdot]\Big(k_{13}[NO\cdot]+k_{17}[O_3]\Big) + 2J[H_2O_2]}{k_{31}[CO] + k_4[CH_4]} \qquad (E6)$$

The $[HO_2\cdot]$ equation is comparable to Equation E6 but is not reproduced since it includes several chemical reactions not included in R1-R33.

These equations identify the dominant source and loss processes for $HO\cdot$ and $HO_2\cdot$ when NMHC reactions are unimportant. Imprecisions inherent in the laboratory measured rate coefficients used in atmospheric mechanisms (for instance, the rate constants in Equation E6) can, themselves, add considerable uncertainty to computed concentrations of atmospheric constituents. A Monte-Carlo technique was used to propagate rate coefficient uncertainties to calculated concentrations (179,180). For hydroxyl radical, uncertainties in published rate constants propagate to modelled $[HO\cdot]$ uncertainties that range from 25% under low-latitude marine conditions to 72% under urban mid-latitude conditions. A large part of this uncertainty is due to the uncertainty ($1\sigma=40\%$) in the photolysis rate of $O(_3)$ to form O^1D, J_1.

When NMHC are significant in concentration, differences in their oxidation mechanisms such as how the NMHC chemistry was parameterized, details of $RO_2\cdot/RO_2\cdot$ recombination (95), and heterogenous chemistry also contribute to differences in computed $[HO\cdot]$. Recently, the sensitivity of $[HO\cdot]$ to non-methane hydrocarbon oxidation was studied in the context of the remote marine boundary-layer (156). It was concluded that differences in radical-radical recombination mechanisms $(RO_2\cdot/RO_2\cdot)$ can cause significant differences in computed $[HO\cdot]$ in regions of low NO_x and NMHC levels. The effect of cloud chemistry in the troposphere has also recently been studied (151, 180). The rapid aqueous-phase breakdown of formaldehyde in the presence of clouds reduces the source of HO_x due to R10. In addition, the dissolution in clouds of a NO_x reservoir (N_2O_5) at night reduces the formation of HO_x and CH_2O due to R6-R10 and R13. Predictions for HO and HO_2 concentrations with cloud chemistry considered compared to predictions without cloud chemistry are 10-40% lower for HO and 10-45% lower for HO_2.

Model Intercomparisons. The uncertainties in polluted-air chemical models regarding $HO\cdot$ radical concentration profiles, although often overlooked in comparisons of pollutant (*e.g.* ozone) profiles, form the essence of the models' accuracy. A comparison of three prominent models (Dodge, 181) found them to yield nearly identical predictions for ozone, peroxyacetylnitrate, and nitric acid under most conditions. Models compared were the Carbon Bond IV Mechanism CB4 (167); and the mechanisms of Lurmann *et al.* CAL (182); and Stockwell RADM (183). Agreement between mechanisms extends to most but not all conditions of $NMHC/NO_x$ ratio and temperature. Although model agreement is encouraging, it was noted that the mechanism developers relied on the same kinetic data evaluation sources when they constructed their mechanisms, and even for processes that have significant uncertainties, there generally is a consensus among modelers on how to treat these processes. Thus Dodge notes "the fact that different mechanisms yield comparable predictions is no assurance that the predictions are correct".

The last several decades have seen the development of numerous polluted-air photochemical models. A comprehensive intercomparison of 20 such models (165) was designed to test the differences in hydrocarbon oxidation schemes with respect to the production of photochemical oxidants. These mechanisms range from highly parameterized (4 organic reactions, 2 organic species) to explicit representations (272 organic reactions, 157 organic species). By standardizing the inorganic chemical mechanism, rate constants, photolytic and heterogenous processes, the effect of different hydrocarbon oxidation schemes was analyzed for a scenario that involved the transport of an clean air parcel over an polluted urban area and into a rural environment. The diurnal variations of [HO·] simulated by the 20 models during the second day of simulation are shown in Figure 5. Although there is general similarity in the results of all mechanisms for [HO·], shifts of the time of peak [HO] result from differences in the organic oxidation processes. Even among the most recently developed models (models 1-9, see Figure 6) which have been most extensively tested with laboratory smog chamber measurements, a variation in the time of peak concentration of [HO·] of about 2 hours is evident. This variation in time of peak concentration is also evident in simulated HO_2 concentration (see Figure 6).

We note several areas of potential concern regarding polluted air chemical models.

Heterogeneous HO_x Sources and Sinks. Heterogeneous radical loss processes have been discussed above, but radical sources have been documented as well. One area of difficulty in validating NMHC oxidation mechanisms has been in fitting the inferred [HO·] temporal profile. It is generally conceded that purely homogeneous chemical processes cannot account for the observed hydroxyl radical concentrations in smog chambers, where experimental data are used to develop tropospheric oxidation mechanisms. The HO· concentrations are straightforward to obtain from equations equivalent to Equation E3 (see the HO-calibration procedure in Chan et al., 112). Accurate HO· temporal profiles are implicitly required to correctly model the individual NMHC decay profiles in these experiments, and are usually obtained by the incorporation of heterogeneous radical generation processes. Although considerable uncertainty in the exact nature of these radical source (or loss) processes remains, one fairly well quantified source (184,185) is the disproportionation reaction

$$2\ NO_2\cdot + H_2O \longrightarrow HNO_2 + HNO_3 \qquad (R35)$$

which is believed to occur on the reaction vessel walls. The nitric acid product is stable, but nitrous acid photodissociates within several minutes

$$HNO_2 + h\nu \longrightarrow HO\cdot + NO\cdot. \qquad (R36)$$

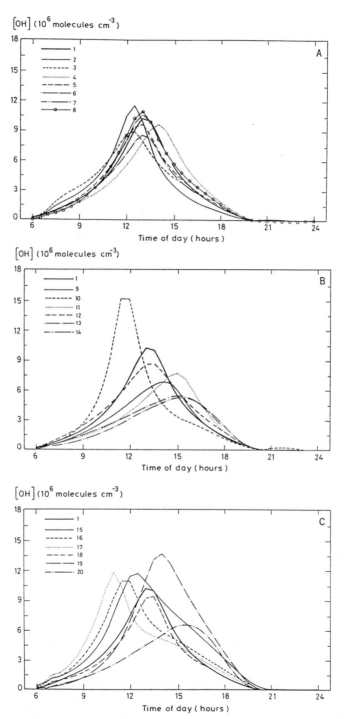

Figure 5. Diurnal HO profiles as predicted by 20 polluted air chemical models. From Hough (165); see that reference for model identities.

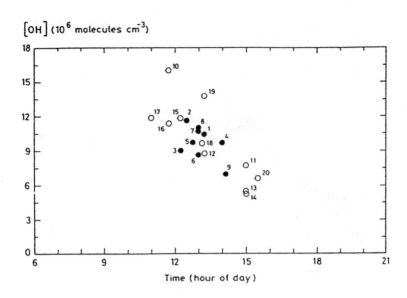

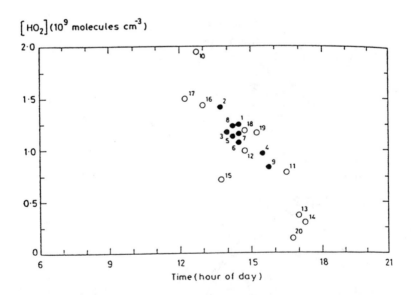

Figure 6. Variation of calculated maximum daily [HO·] and [HO₂·] using 20 different polluted air chemical models. From Hough (165); see that reference for model identities.

R35 can occur in the dark before illumination begins, which will accumulate the radical precursor and help to *start* the photochemistry when illumination commences. It can also occur continuously during the simulated reaction, maintaining a higher steady-state radical concentration than purely homogeneous processes. Another process of uncertain occurrence, cited in older work, is

$$NO\cdot + NO_2\cdot + H_2O ----> 2\ HNO_2. \tag{R37}$$

This reaction, like R35, is thermodynamically favored but of negligible rate unless surface catalyzed. The dark accumulation of HNO_2 can be accounted for in modeling by an *adjustable* starting HNO_2 concentration, while the continuous production is most significant with NMHC of low reactivity. The significance of either of these processes in the open atmosphere, where they may occur on the surface of, or within, aerosol particles is poorly understood.

$RO_2\cdot/RO_2\cdot$ Recombinations. Another area of uncertainty is the peroxyl radical recombination reactions described above, which become especially significant when the $NO\cdot$ concentration is low. This can occur late in the photooxidation of polluted air undergoing transport, as in some rural environments (60,85) and in *clean* air. Although reactions of $HO_2\cdot$ with itself (R33) are reasonably well understood (their rate depends upon total pressure and upon water vapor concentration), reactions of $HO_2\cdot$ with $RO_2\cdot$ species and the $RO_2\cdot$ self reaction are much less well quantified. Since these serve as important radical sink processes under low $NO\cdot$ conditions, their accurate portrayal is important for accurate prediction of HO_x concentrations.

Dicarbonyls. A third area of uncertainty is the treatment of dicarbonyls formed from aromatic or terpene hydrocarbon oxidation. (The simplest is glyoxal, CHOCHO, but a large number have been identified, 47. The yields and subsequent reactions of these compounds represent a major area of uncertainty in urban air photochemistry (186) and since they may be a significant source of HO_x through photolysis, inaccuracies in their portrayal may result in errors in calculated values of $HO\cdot$ and $HO_2\cdot$.

Wall Loss of Oxidation Products. It is known that some classes of hydrocarbons (the higher terpenes, for instance) are prolific aerosol formers when subjected to atmospheric oxidation. Other classes, aromatic hydrocarbons for instance, although they do not form large amounts of suspended aerosol, have been shown to lose (at least under some conditions) large amounts of oxidation products to the reaction vessel walls. The fate of these oxidation products in the open atmosphere remains open to question, as does the extent to which they continue to participate in gas-phase chemistry (187).

Model Uncertainty Estimates. In spite of the complexity of the 3 models compared by Dodge, (CB4, CAL and RADM employ 81, 132, and 154 chemical steps and 34, 51 and 57 chemical species, respectively), it is possible to gain useful information about radical interrelationships by considering approximate relationships. Sillman *et al.* (86) have obtained several such relations. In considering oxidant formation, these authors derive the following relationship for the HO_x balance; the left-hand side refers to radical sources and the right-hand side to radical loss processes.

$$A[O_3]+B_1[RH]+B_2[HO\cdot][RH] =$$

$$2k_{33}[HO_2\cdot]^2+2k_{HO2/RO2}[HO_2\cdot][RO_2\cdot]+k_{23}[[HO\cdot][NO_2\cdot]] \qquad (E7)$$

Here the rate constants k refer to the rates of the numbered reactions above; the value $k_{HO2/RO2}$ is an average for different $RO_2\cdot$ entities. The A term accounts for HO_x production via ozone photolysis R1-R3, the B_1 term accounts approximately for the source from aldehyde photolysis (R12 plus higher aldehydes), and the B_2 term is a composite source from formaldehyde (R10) and dicarbonyls (C_1) less the HO_x sink from PAN formation (R22) (C_2)(*i.e.*, $B_2=C_1-C_2$). Values for B_1, C_1, and C_2 depend upon the hydrocarbon mix, temperature, radiation, and details of the chemical mechanism. Sillman *et al.* (86) determine typical noon values for the CAL (182) mechanism: $A=4\times10^{-6}$ s^{-1}; $B_1=3\times10^{-6}$ s^{-1}; $C_1=2\times10^{-13}$ cm^3 s^{-1}, $C_2=5.5\times10^{-13}$ cm^{3}molecule^{-1} s^{-1}.

From the magnitude of these terms, it is seen that the uncertain dicarbonyl source C_1 is significant, as is the poorly characterized $RO_2\cdot/HO_2\cdot$ reaction. No provision is made for the heterogeneous radical source (182) used in fitting smog chamber data, nor for the possibility of heterogeneous radical loss processes suggested by Perner *et al.* (110, 125). Lurmann *et al.* (182) give a value of 2×10^{-6} s^{-1} for the pseudo-first order rate constant (incorporating 2% H_2O) for the HONO producing process analogous to R35. This value is 1/2 the A term of Sillman *et al.* above. It is unclear whether such a process would have a rate this large in the ambient atmosphere, but polluted-air aerosol-surface/air-volume ratios can be comparable to the surface/volume ratios of large smog chambers.

Regarding processes within aerosols, Zellner *et al.* (188) have determined $HO\cdot$ quantum yields in aqueous photolysis of nitrate, nitrite, and H_2O_2, for which they find respective values of 1.1×10^{-6}, 5.2×10^{-5}, and 9.2×10^{-6} s^{-1}. Although their work was directed chiefly toward experimental measurement of these values, they conclude that from the standpoint of the aerosol phase the estimated aqueous $HO\cdot$ generation rate is comparable to the estimated aerosol $HO\cdot$ deposition rate from the gas phase. Although they do not address the potential gas-phase $HO\cdot$ source strength via evaporation of $HO\cdot$ from aerosol particles, $HO\cdot$ desorbtion may be significant if the liquid phase generation rate is higher that the deposition rate. In their summary, Zellner *et al.* conclude that *in situ* $HO\cdot$ generation is of roughly comparable importance with $HO\cdot$ deposition, and that the nitrate source should be the largest source with the sum of nitrite and peroxide comparable to nitrate. For a nitrate aerosol mass loading of 50 μg/m^3, we can estimate that the liquid phase $HO\cdot$ generation rate would be about 10^6 molecule s^{-1} per cm^3 of air. This may be compared with the A term of Sillman *et al.* by calculating the ozone concentration that would give a gaseous $HO\cdot$ source rate equal to the liquid phase generation rate. Equating $A[O_3]$ to 10^6 molecule cm$^{-3\cdot1}$ results in $[O_3]=1\times10^{12}$, or about 40ppb. Thus, the estimated nitrate liquid phase source should be roughly comparable to 40ppb of gas phase ozone, when compared for equal air volumes. This value would be roughly doubled when nitrite and peroxide were added in, and it is likely that heterogeneous $HO_2\cdot$ sources (*e.g.* dissolved formaldehyde or other aldehydes, condensed organic oxidation products such as dicarbonyls) would also be significant. The above calculations are admittedly rough, but nevertheless it seems unsafe to exclude aerosols as a potential source of gas-phase HO_x.

Dependence of HO· and HO_2· on NMHC and NO_x

A number of studies, *e.g.* (58), have examined the variation of HO_x concentrations with NO_x levels in the absence of NMHC. Several studies have examined past variation in tropospheric [HO·] brought about by the measured increases in tropospheric [CH_4] that have occurred over the last several hundred years (Figure 1). Ignoring NMHC chemistry, Logan *et al.* (58) find that [$HO_2\cdot$] is relatively independent of NO_x concentrations from very low values up to about 0.2 ppb, at which point [$HO_2\cdot$] drops in concentration, due largely to R13 (Figure 4). [HO·], on the other hand, increases in concentration with [NO·] (due largely to the increasing importance of R13) until it too falls in concentration around [NO·]=0.2 ppb (Figure 4). The falloff is largely due to the increasing importance of HO· scavenging by NO_2 to form nitric acid in R23.

Several studies have examined the effects of [NMHC] on [HO_x] concentrations. Kasting and Singh (157) have examined the role of NMHC in marine (very low NO_x) and continental (moderate NO_x) models, incorporating seasonal and diurnal variations in light intensity, water vapor, temperature, etc. Their models predict a significant impact of NMHC's on HO_x for wintertime photochemistry over the continents, but little effect in summer. An increase of HO and HO_2 by factors of 5 and 50, respectively, are induced by the oxidation of NMHC and by the formation of PAN during the wintertime over the continents (157). Donahue and Prinn (156) have explored the role of NMHC in the remote marine boundary layer (very low NO_x) utilizing an explicit mechanism incorporating 750 chemical reactions. Rationalization of observed NMHC concentrations to NMHC fluxes places the remote marine boundary layer, according to their model, in a chemical regime in which [HO] is sensitive to NMHC fluxes. Their analysis predicts that [HO] decreases in response to increasing NMHC flux in the remote marine boundary layer. Interestingly, they find that [HO·] is relatively insensitive to the number of carbon atoms in the distribution of NMHC (*i.e.* light vs. heavy), but sensitive to the total number of hydrocarbon molecules.

We have previously examined the mutual dependence of [HO·] upon [NO_x] and [NMHC] as calculated by a combined clean/polluted air chemical mechanism (76), and extend those calculations here to the more modern CAL mechanism of Lurmann *et al.* (182). To do this we have combined the NO_x/NMHC chemical reactions of the CAL mechanism with the methane chemistry of Logan *et al.* (58). The results of these calculations are shown as *contour maps* or isopleths for [O_3], [HO·], and [$HO_2\cdot$] in Figure 7. Figure 7a, for ozone, is similar to isopleths used to determine reductions in NMHC and/or

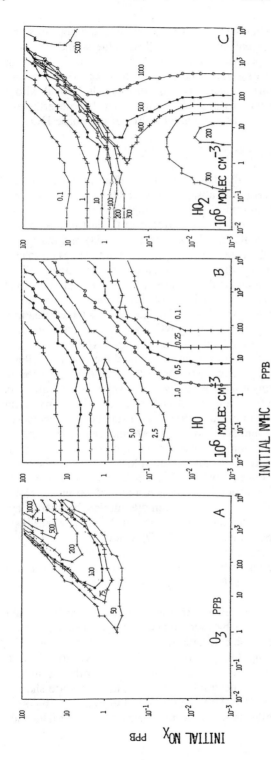

Figure 7. Ozone, hydroxyl, and hydroperoxyl isopleths calculated using a combined clean/polluted air chemical mechanism. A. [O$_3$] contours, ppb. B. [HO•] contours, 10^6 molecules cm^{-3}. C. [HO$_2$•] contours, 10^6 molecules cm^{-3}. Contours are maximum concentrations achieved in one day exposure to sunlight from starting [NMHC] and [NO$_x$] concentrations on axes.

NO_x emissions required for meeting the ozone air quality standard, (*e.g.* reference 16), and is calculated in a similar fashion. However, in this case the calculations are extended into the region of completely *unpolluted* air and are plotted on logarithmic scales covering 5 decades of NMHC concentration and 6 decades of $[NO_x]$. This exploratory model examines only changes in the tropospheric chemical system and thus excludes possible feedbacks to these changes from the stratosphere or biosphere. Tropospheric changes which result in changes in uv radiation intensity or distribution, or changes in temperature or transport will obviously carry strong feed-back features.

One-day Isopleth Calculations. The contours in Figure 7 were obtained by integrating the chemical mechanism numerically for each of the starting conditions described by the horizontal and vertical axis, a total of 304 simulations, with three calculations per decade initial NO_x and NMHC concentration. The initial $[NO_x]$ was 25% NO_2 and 75% NO. In each simulation, a sinusoidal variation of light intensity for 12 hours daylight was followed by 12 hours of darkness. Light intensities appropriate for the equinox at 45° latitude were used. Surface atmospheric pressure was employed, since most reactions occur fastest near the earth's surface. Methane and carbon monoxide concentrations of 1.4 and 0.2 ppm respectively defined *clean* air, and were present in all calculations. Due to its long atmospheric lifetime, atmospheric methane concentrations fluctuate little, but CO may vary by a factor or 2 or more in *clean* air (189). The NMHC distribution chosen for the actual and surrogate species of the CAL mechanism is given in Table V.

TABLE V. NMHC composition for isopleth calculations.

NMHC	percent of total NMHC (molecular basis)
H_2CO (formaldehyde)	4
ALD2 (generic aldehyde)	3
ALKA (generic alkane)	21
C_2H_6 (ethane)	14
C_3H_8 (propane)	14
ALKE (generic alkene)	11
ETHE (ethene)	4
AROM (generic aromatic HC)	28

Each isopleth describes the maximum species concentration achieved during the simulation. In all isopleths, the contours are horizontal at the left-hand edges, indicating that NMHC starting concentrations were reduced sufficiently so that they did not affect the calculated concentration of the species displayed.

Ozone Isopleths. As seen in Figure 7a, the initial ozone concentration of 30 ppb is not augmented by a single-day irradiation of low starting concentrations of NO_x and NMHC, but typical *ozone isopleth* behavior is seen at sufficiently high concentrations, in the upper right-hand corner of the isopleth. This is the region commonly treated in trying to arrive at emission reduction strategies for NMHC and NO_x in meeting air quality standards for ozone. In this concentration regime, ozone maxima occur in the afternoon of the simulations, following the photooxidation of $NO\cdot$ to $NO_2\cdot$, and the subsequent accumulation of ozone as illustrated in Figure 2.

[HO·] Isopleths. Hydroxyl radical contours shown in Figure 7b are horizontal (independent of [NMHC]) in the region [NMHC]<1ppb and $[NO_x]>0.1$ppb. At lower $[NO_x]$, [HO·] is very weakly dependent upon [NMHC]. Maximum [HO·]$=5\times10^6$ molecules cm^{-3} occurs at low [NMHC] between 0.2 and 0.8 ppb total starting NO_x in general agreement with previous calculations that excluded NMHC. The maximum [HO·] feature becomes a ridge that turns and moves diagonally toward higher [NMHC] and $[NO_x]$, falling off in [HO·] by only a factor of two along the ridge-top, but declining more steeply on either side.

[HO₂·] Isopleths. The hydroperoxyl radical contours in Figure 7c show a large area where [HO$_2$·] is very weakly dependent upon either $[NO_x]$ or [NMHC]. In this region (bounded roughly by [NMHC]<50ppb and $[NO_x]<0.5$ppb), [HO$_2$·] varies only by a factor of 2, from $2-4\times10^8$ molecules cm^{-3}. At higher starting $[NO_x]$, [HO$_2$·] declines steeply with increasing $[NO_x]$ (largely due to R9). An increase in [HO$_2$·] with [NMHC] produces a steep diagonal ridge of HO_2 concentration leading to a plateau at high [NMHC]. The diagonal [HO$_2$·] *cliff* corresponds to the ridge on the [HO·] contours.

[HO·] and [HO$_2$·] contours calculated from other NMHC mechanisms give results qualitatively similar to those illustrated here, although there are significant quantitative differences.

The calculations used to generate Figure 7 correspond to an air mass that moves over a pollution source (a city), and then travels downwind for a day without further emissions. Extending the calculations to several days downwind transport results in similar qualitative behavior of the contours, although there are quantitative differences in concentrations achieved on subsequent days. Thus, low concentrations of NMHC and NO_x can generate significant ozone after several days exposure to sunlight, depending upon the dilution rate with *clean* air.

Steady-state Isopleth Calculations. A more interesting simulation results from a change in the boundary conditions of the calculation. Instead of starting with initial [NMHC] and $[NO_x]$, sources for these two controlling variables are introduced into the mechanism, which is then numerically integrated to steady-state with a constant light intensity of 1/4 the daily maximum at the equinox at 45° latitude. All chemical species are removed in first-order processes relative to their water solubility, to simulate precipitation scavenging. Scavenging lifetimes are the following: highly soluble species (HNO_3, H_2O_2, etc.) 10 days; moderately soluble species (O_3, NO_2, aldehydes, etc.) 50 days; sparingly soluble species (CO, NO, NMHC's, etc.) 500 days. When the output of the numerical integration indicates that concentrations have reached constant (equilibrium) values, the source rates are increased and the next point on the isopleth surface is calculated. In the calculations shown in Figure 8, the NMHC source rate was held constant at each value on the horizontal axis and the NO_x source rate was increased sequentially from low to high values. When the maximum NO_x source rate was achieved, the NMHC source was increased one step and the process repeated. In this steady-state formulation, source rates for CO, O_3, and CH_4 were employed (1, 2, and 5×10^5 molec cm^{-3} s^{-1}, respectively) to cause their steady-state concentrations to approximately achieve values observed in unpolluted air. (The ozone source rate corresponds to stratospheric intrusion, the other two source rates correspond to emissions from earth's surface. In fact, a portion of CO emissions are proportional to NMHC emissions, but this facet was not incorporated into these calculations). The fractional distribution of the individual NMHC source rates is as given in Table V, but the NO_x source was 95% NO and 5% NO_2, to correspond to estimated global proportions (58).

No attempt has been made here to exactly match appropriate emission rates for CO, CH_4, and O_3 in order to closely match observed global levels of these three trace gases; more detailed calculations will be presented elsewhere. However, calculations we have performed with other source rates for CO, O_3, and CH_4, as well as with a variety of other NMHC mechanisms, all yield isopleths qualitatively similar to those in Figure 8. The shape is also reproduced when a diurnal light cycle is employed (a computer-time-consuming exercise), rather than the average light intensity employed here. Changes in polluted air mechanisms, or in *natural* emission rates do produce significant changes in the positions of the various species contours.

Isopleth features. The general features of the species contours shown in Figure 8 are similar to the one-day calculations in many respects, but have notable differences. The ozone contours (Figure 8a) have familiar behavior in the high-emissions region, and indicate a maximum ozone contour in NMHC-free air between NO_x source rates of 3 and 8×10^5 molec cm^{-3} s^{-1}. At lower NO_x emissions, ozone declines gradually. This behavior is consistent with the *limiting reagent* role of NO in unpolluted air which has been noted in many other calculations, although the corresponding NO concentration (Figure 8d) of about 50ppt is higher than generally accepted for the remote troposphere. This high NO concentration probably reflects improperly balanced source rates for the three *naturally* emitted species.

At higher NO_x emissions, there is a precipitous drop in ozone concentration. This concentration *cliff* turns diagonally when influenced by NMHC sources rates $>5 \times 10^3$ molec cm^{-3}s^{-1}. This *cliff* is present in most other species concentrations, some suffering a sharp decline and others a increase. The [HO·] contours in Figure 8b indicate the reason for this discontinuity, as [HO·] drops by about an order of magnitude along this feature. Thus, any species primarily removed by HO· will undergo an increase proportionate with the HO· decrease.

The discontinuity predicted by the model has been   found in past

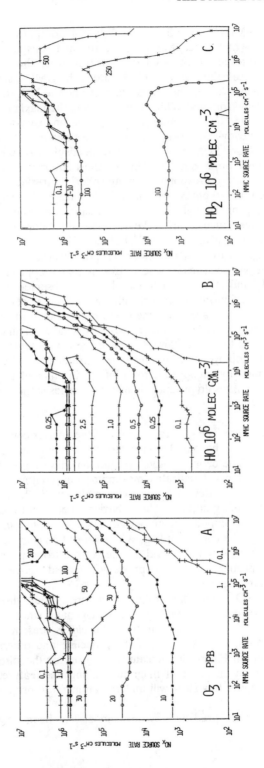

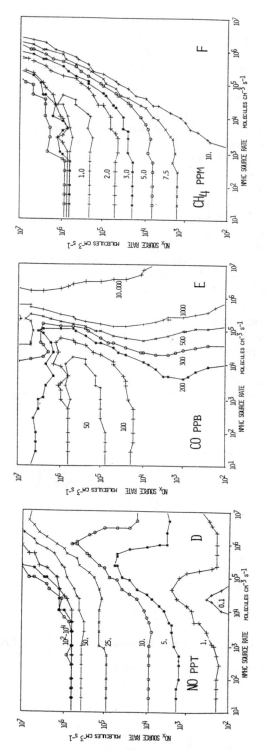

Figure 8. Steady-state isopleths calculated from clean/polluted air chemical mechanism using NMHC and NO_x source rates on axes. Mechanism was integrated to steady-state for each calculation using 1/4 the equinoxial light intensity at 45° latitude. A. $[O_3]$ ppb. B. $[HO \cdot]$ 10^6 molecules cm^{-3}. C. $[HO_2]$ 10^6 molecules cm^{-3}. D. $[NO \cdot]$ ppt. E. [CO] ppb. D. CH_4 ppm.

calculations. White and Dietz (190) used a simpler chemical mechanism lacking NMHC in a zero-dimensional calculation where the NO_x emission rates were varied. They concluded that the atmosphere may be capable of supporting two different steady-state conditions as a function of NO_x emissions, the low [NO_x] high [HO$\cdot$] state below the *cliff*, and a high [NO_x] low [HO$\cdot$] above the *cliff*. These calculations were repeated in a one-dimensional model and a similar discontinuity was calculated. Here we find the effect of NMHC is to increase the level of NO_x emissions required to push tropospheric chemistry *over the cliff* into a situation where water-insoluble trace gases would reach very high tropospheric concentrations compared to those now occurring.

It seems likely that worldwide emissions of NMHC and NO_x will increase in the future (even though the US and other "developed" nations may impose further restrictions) because of the desire of "undeveloped" nations to achieve a higher standard of living. Figure 8 suggests that roughly proportionate future global increases in NMHC and NO_x emissions may lead to a relatively constant hydroxyl radical concentration, with gradually increasing ozone concentration. From an air pollution standpoint, the ozone increase is problematical, given that the U.S. and other country's air quality standards are set at only 2-4 times the *natural* tropospheric background. Increasing tropospheric ozone may have some offsetting effect on stratospheric ozone destruction, although currently only about 10% of the total column ozone resides in the troposphere.

If future increases in NMHC or NO_x emissions are not proportional, then the trajectory in Figure 8 could lead to either an increase or a decrease in [HO$\cdot$], depending upon which species increases faster. Clearly, more detailed calculations of the influence of future NMHC and NO_x emissions on global air quality will be essential in understanding the future of Earth's atmosphere.

Acknowledgments

We are grateful for support from the National Science Foundation (grant ATM-8615163), the National Aeronautics and Space Administration (grant NAG-1-697) and the Environmental Protection Agency (grant R81-3012). We are grateful to T.M. Hard for helpful suggestions on this manuscript.

Literature Cited

1. Solomon, S. *Nature* **1990**, 347, 347.

2. Rodriguez, J.M; Ko, M.K.W.; Sze, D.D. *Geophys. Res. Lett.* **1990**, 17, 255.

3. Khalil, M.; Rasmussen, R. *Tellus* **1990**, 42B, 229-236.

4. Cicerone, R.J.; Oremland, R.S. *Global Biogeochemical Cycles* **1988**, 2, 299-328.

5. Warneck, P., *Academic Press*, **1988**, London, 170-175.

6. Lamb, B.; Guenther, A.; Gay, D.; Westberg, H. *Atmos. Environ.* **1987**, 21, 1695-1706.

7. Hanst, P.L.; Spence, J.W.; Edney, O. *Atmos. Environ.* **1980**, 14, 1077-1088.

8. Seiler, W. *Tellus* **1974**, 26, 117-135.

9. Seiler, W.; Fishman, J. *J. Geophys. Res.* **1981**, 86, 7255-7265.

10. Reichle, H., Jr.; Connors, V.S.; Holland, J.A.; Sherill, R.T.; Wallio, H.A.; Casas, J.C.; Condon, E.P.; Gormsen, B.B.; Seiler, W. *J. Geophys. Res.* **1990**, 95, 9845-9856.

11. Hayakeyama, S.; Izumi, K.; Fukuyama, T.; Akimoto, H.; Washida, N. *J. Geophys. Res.* **1991**, 96, 947-958.

12. Bates, T.; Johnson, J.E.; Quinn, P.K; Goldan, P.D.; Kuster, W.C.; Covert, D.C.; Hahn, C.J. *J. Atmos. Chem.* **1990**, 10, 59-82.

13. Andreae, M.O., In *Trace Gases and the Biosphere*, U. of Arizona Press, Tucson, AZ **1990**.

14. Erickson, D.J. III, Ghan, S.J.; Penner, J.E. *J. Geophys. Res.* **1990**, 95, 7543-7552.

15. Bates, T.S.; Cline, J.D.; Gammon, R.H.; Kelly-Hansen, S.R. *J. Geophys. Res.* **1987**, 92, 2930-2938.

16. Chameides, W.L; Lindsay, R.W.; Richardson, J.; Kiang, C.S. *Science* **1988**, 241, 1473-1475.

17. Dodge, M.C. *In Proceedings of the International Conference on Photochemical Oxidant Pollution and Its Control*; Dimitriades, B., Ed.; EPA-600/3-77-001b; U.S. EPA: Research Triangle Park, N.C., 1977, Vol. II; pp 881-889.

18. Dodge, M.C. *Effect of Selected Parameters on Predictions of a Photochemical Model - EPA-600/3-77-048*; U.S. EPA: Research Triangle Park, N.C., **1977**.

19. Dimitriades, B.; Dodge, M. Eds,; *Proceedings of the Empirical Kinetic Modeling Approach (EKMA) Validation Workshop - EPA-600/9-83-014*, U.S. EPA: Research Triangle Park, N.C., 1983.

20. Levy, H., II. *Science* **1971**, 173, 141-143.

21. Blake, D.R.; Rowland, F.S. *Science* 1988, 239, 1129-1131.

22. Matthews, E.; Fung, I. *Global Biogeochemical Cycles* **1987**, 5, 3-24.

23. Aselmann, I.; Crutzen, P.J. *J. Atmos. Chem.* **1989**, 8, 307-358.

24. Koyama, T., In *Recent Researches in the Fields of Hydrosphere, Atmosphere, and Geochemistry*; Miyake, T; Koyama, T, Eds.; **1964, pp** 143-177.

25. Seiler, W.; Holzapfel-Pschorn, A.; Conrad, R.; Scharffe, D. *J. Atmos. Chem.* **1984**, 1, 171-186.

26. Crutzen, P.J.; Aselmann, I.; Seiler, W. *Tellus* **1986**, 38B, 271-284.

27. Lerner, J.; Matthews, E.; Fung, I. *Global Biogeochem. Cycles* **1988**, 2, 139-156.

28. Zimmerman, P.R.; Greenberg, J.P.; Wandiga, S.O.; Crutzen, P.J. *Science* **1982**, 218, 563-565.

29. Zimmerman, P.R.; Greenberg, J.P. *Nature* **1983**, 302, 354-355.

30. Rasmussen, R.A.; Khalil, M.A.K. *Nature* **1983**, 301, 700-702.

31. Fraser, P.; Rasmussen, R.A.; Creffield, J.W.; French, J.R.; Khalil, M.A.K. *J. Atmos. Chem.* **1986**, 4, 295-310.

32. Fung, I.; John, J.; Lerner, J.; Matthews, E.; Prather, M.; Steele, L.P.; Fraser, P.J. *J. Geophys. Res.* **1991**, 96, 13033-13065.

33. Crutzen, P.J.; Andreae, M.O. *Science* **1990**, 250, 1669-1678.

34. Wang, W.-C.; Yung, Y.L.; Lacis, A.A.; Mo, T.; Hansen, J.E. *Science* **1976**, 194, 685-690.

35. Khalil, M.A.K.; Rasmussen, R.A.; Shearer, M.J. *J. Geophys. Res.* **1989**, 94, 18279-18288.

36. Levine, J.S.; Rinsland, C.P.; Tennille, G.M. *Nature* **1985**, 318, 254-257.

37. Rinsland, C.P.; Levine, J.S.; Miles, T. *Nature* **1985**, 318, 245-248.

38. Blake, D.R.; Rowland, F.S. *J. Atmos. Chem.* **1986**, 4, 43-62.

39. *Climate change: The IPCC Scientific Assessment*; Houghton, J.T.; Jenkins,G.J.; Ephraums, J.J. Eds.; Cambridge University Press, Cambridge U.K. 1990.

40. Khalil, M.A.K.; Rasmussen, R.A. *Atmos. Environ.* **1987**, 21, 2445-2452.

41. Thompson, A.M.; Stewart, R.W.; Owens, M.A.; Herwehe, J.A. *Atmos. Environ.* **1989**, 23, 519-532.

42. Thompson, A.M.; Huntley, M.A.; Stewart, R.W. *J. Geophys. Res.* **1990**, 95, 9829-9844.

43. Siela, R.L.; Lonneman, W.A.; Meeks, S.A. *Determination of C_2 to C_{12} ambient air hydrocarbons in 39 U.S. cities from 1984 through 1986 - EPA-600/3-89-056*, 1989.

44. Altshuller, A.P. *J. Atmos. Chem.* **1991**, 12, 19-61.

45. Atkinson, R. *Chem. Rev.* **1986**, 86, 69.

46. Atkinson, R., *Atmos. Environ.* **1990** 24A, 1-42.

47. Dumdei, B.E.; O'Brien, R.J. *Nature* **1984**, 311, 248-250.

48. Khalil, M.A.K.; Rasmussen, R.A. *Atmos. Env.* **1987**, 21, 2445.

49. Stauffer, B.R.; Neftel, A. In *The Changing Atmosphere*; Rowland, F.S.; Isaken, I.S.A., Eds.; Wiley-Interscience, New York, NY, 1987; 63-77.

50. Ehhalt, D.H. In *The Changing Atmosphere*; Rowland, F.S.; Isaken, I.S.A., Eds.; Wiley-Interscience, New York, NY, **1988**, 25-32.

51. Cicerone, R.J. In *The Changing Atmosphere*; Rowland, F.S.; Isaken, I.S.A., Eds.; Wiley-Interscience, New York, NY, **1988**, pp 49-61.

52. Prinn, R.J. In *The Changing Atmosphere*; Rowland, F.S.; Isaken, I.S.A., Eds.; Wiley-Interscience, New York, NY, **1988**, 33-48.

53. Oeschger, H. and Siegenthaler, U. In *The Changing Atmosphere*; Rowland, F.S.; Isaken, I.S.A.; Eds. Wiley-Interscience, New York, NY, **1988**, 5-23.

54. Logan, J.A. *J. Geophys. Res.* **1983**, 88, 10785-10807.

55. Penner, J.; Atherton, C.; Dignon, J.; Ghan, S.; Walton, J.; Hameed, S. *J. Geophys. Res.* **1991**, 96, 959-990.

56. Liaw, Y.P.; Sisterson, D.L; Miller, N.L. *J. Geophys. Res.* **1990**, 95, 22489-22494.

57. Howard, C.J.; Evenson, K.M. *Geophys. Res. Lett.* **1977**, 4, 437.

58. Logan, J.; Prather, M.J; Wofsy, S.C.; McElroy, M.B. *J. Geophys. Res.* **1981**, 86, 7210-7254.

59. Isaksen, I. S. A. In *The Changing Atmosphere*; Rowland, F.S.; Isaken, I.S.A., Eds.; Wiley-Interscience, New York, NY, **1988**, 149-157.

60. Liu, S.C; Kley, D.; McFarland, M.; Parrish, D.D.; Williams, E.J.; Fahey, D.W.; Hubler, G.; Murphy, P.C. *J. Geophys. Res.* **1987**, 92, 4191-4207.

61. Leighton, P. *Chemical Reactions in the Lower and Upper Atmosphere;* Wiley-Interscience, New York, NY, 1961, pp 1-14.

62. O'Brien, R.J. *Environ. Sci. Technol.* **1974**, 8, 579.

63. Stedman, D.; Jackson, J.O. *Int. J. Chem. Kinet. Symp.* **1975**, *I*, 493.

64. Calvert, J.G. *Envir. Sci. Tech.* **1976**, *10*, 256.

65. George, L.A. *Development of a Direct, Low Pressure, Laser-induced Fluorescence Technique for NO_2,* Ambient Measurements and Urban NO_x, Ph.D. Thesis, Portland State University: Portland, OR, **1991**, 1-135.

66. Parrish, D.D.; Trainer, M.; Williams, E.J.; Fahey, D.W.; Hubler, G.; Eubank, C.S.; Liu, P.C.; Murphy, D.L.; Albritton, D.L.; Fehsenfeld, F.C. *J. Geophys. Res.* **1986**, 91, 5361-5370.

67. Ridley, B.A. *Atmos. Environ.* **1991**, 25A, 1905-1926.

68. Platt, U.; Perner, D.; Winer, A.M.; Harris, G.W.; Pitts, J.N. Jr. *Geophys. Res. Lett.* **1980**, 7, 89-92.

69. Winer, A.M.; Atkinson, R.; Pitts, J.N., Jr. *Science* **1984**, 224, 156-159.

70. Wayne, R.P.; Barnes, I.; Biggs, P.; Burrows, J.P.; Canosa-Mas, C.E.; Hjorth, J.; LeBras, G.; Moortgat, G.K.; Perner, D.; *et al. Atmos. Envir.* **1991**, 25A, 1-203.

71. Hoffman, M.R.; Boyce, S.D. *Adv. Environ. Sci. Tech.* **1983**, 12, 147.

72. Jacob, D.J.; Hoffman, M.R. *J. Geophys. Res.* **1983**, 88C, 6611.

73. Jacob, D. J.; Shair, F.H.; Waldman, J.M.; Munger, J.W.; Hoffman, M.R. *Atmos. Environ.* **1987**, 21, 1305-1314.

74. Toon, O.B.; Kasting, J.F.; Turco, R.P.; Liu, M.S. *J. Geophys. Res.* **1987**, 92, 943-964.

75. Moshiri, E. Computer Modeling of Photochemical Ozone Formation: A Simplified Approach; Ph.D. Thesis Portland State University: Portland, OR, 1984; 1-211.

76. O'Brien, R.J.; Theisen, T.H.; Pan, W.H.; Hard, T.M.; Chan, C.Y.; Mehrabzadeh, A.A. *Preprint Extended Abstract* **1986**, *1986 Spring National ACS Meeting, Denver CO,* 620-625.

77. Haagen-Smit, A.J.; Bradley, C.E.; Fox, M.M. *Indust. Eng. Chem.* **1953**, 45, 2086.

78. Darnall, K.R.; Lloyd, A.C.; Winer, A.M.; Pitts, J.N., Jr. *Environ. Sci. Technol.* **1976**, 10, 692.

79. Crutzen, P.J.; Heidt, L.E.; Krasnec, J.P.; Pollock, W.H.; Seiler, W. *Nature* **1979**, 282, 253-256.

80. Logan, J.; Kirchoff, V.W.J.H. *J. Geophys. Res.* **1986**, 91, 7875-7881.

81. Fishman, J; Larson, J.C. *J. Geophys. Res.* **1987**, 92, 6627-6634.

82. Fishman, J. In *The Changing Atmosphere*; Rowland, F.S.; Isaken, I.S.A., Eds.; Wiley-Interscience, New York, NY, **1988**, pp. 111-123.

83. Fishman, J.; Minnis, P.; Reichle, H.G.,Jr. *J. Geophys. Res.* **1986**, 92, 14451-14465.

84. Fishman, J.; Watson, J.; Larsen, J.; Logan, J*J. Geophys. Res.* **1990**, 95, 3599-3618.

85. Trainer, M; Hsie, E.Y.; McKeen, S.A.; Tallamraju, R.; Parrish, D.D.; Fehsenfeld, F.C.; Liu, S.C. *J. Geophys. Res.* **1987**, 92, 11879-11894.

86. Sillman, S.; Logan, J.A.; Wofsy, S.C. *J. Geophys. Res.* **1990**, 95, 1837-1852.

87. Cardelino, C.A; Chameides, W.L. *J. Geophys. Res.* **1990**, 95, 13971-9.

88. Roselle, S.J.; Pierce, T.E.; Schere, K.L. *J. Geophys. Res.,* **1991**, 96, 7371-7394.

89. Lindsay, R.W.; Richardson, J.L.; Chameides, W.L. *J. Air Poll. Control Assoc.* **1989**, 39, 40-3.

90. Sandberg, J.S.; Basso, M.J.; Okin, B.A. *Science* **1978**, 200, 1051-1053.

91. Levy, H., II. *Planet. Space Sci.* **1972**, 20, 919.

92. Levy. H., II. *J. Geophys. Res.* **1973**, 78, 5325.

93. Weinstock, B. *Nature* **1969**, 166, 224-225.

94. Weinstock, B.; Niki, H. *Science* **1972**, 176, 290.

95. Madronich S.; Calvert, J.G. *J. Geophys. Res.* **1990**, 95, 5697-5715.

96. Saltzman, E.S.; Savoie, D.L.; Zika, R.G.; Prospero, J.M. *J. Geophys. Res.* **1983**, 88, 10897-10902.

97. Clarke, A.D.; Ahlquist, N.C.; Covert, D.S. *J. Geophys. Res.* **1987**, 92, 4179-4190.

98. Charlson, R.J.; Lovelock, J.E.; Andreae,M.O.; Warren, S.G. *Nature* **1987**, 326, 6555-661.

99. World Meteorological Organization (WMO), *Report 20*, Global Ozone Research and Monitoring Project, Geneva, 1990.

100. Spicer, C.W.; Holdren, M.W.; Keigley, G.W. *Atmos. Environ.* **1983**, 17, 1055.

101. DeMore, W.B.; Sander, S.P.; Molina, M.J.; Golden, D.J.; Hampson, R.F.; Kurylo, M.J.; Howard, C.J.; Ravishankara, A.R. *JPL-Publ.* **1988**, 88-62,8.

102. Haagen-Smit, A.J. *Ind. Eng. Chem.* **1952**, 44, 1342 .

103. Atkinson, R. *J. Phys. Chem. Ref. Data Monograph Number*, **1989**, 1, 10268.

104. O'Brien, R.J.; Green, P.J.; Doty, R.A. *J. Phys. Chem.* **1979**, 83, 3302.

105. Wang, C.C.; Davis, L.I.; Wu, C.H.; Japar, S.; Niki, H.; Weinstock, B. *Science* **1975**, 189, 797-800.

106. Davis, L.I.; James, J.V.; Wang, C.C; Guo, C.; Morris, P.T.; Fishman, J.J. *Geophys. Res.* **1987**, 92, 2020-2024.

107. Davis, L.I.; Guo, C.; James, J.V.; Morris, P.T.; Postiff, R. and Wang, C.C. *J. Geophys. Res.* **1985**, 90, 12835-12842.

108. Davis, D.D.; Heaps, W. and McGee, T. *Geophys. Res. Lett.* **1976**, 3, 331-333.

109. Rodgers, M.O.; Bradshaw, J.D.; Sandolm, S.T.; KeSheng, S.; Davis, D.D. *J. Geophys. Res.* **1985**, 90, 12819-12834.

110. Hard, T.M.; O'Brien, R.J.; Chan, C.Y.; Mehrabzadeh, A.A. *Environ. Sci. Technol.* **1984**, 18, 768-777.

111. Hard, T.M.; Chan, C.Y.; Mehrabzadeh, A.A.; Pan, W.H.; O'Brien, R.J. *Nature* **1986**, 322, 618-620.

112. Chan, C.Y.; Hard, T.M.; Mehrabzadeh, A.A.; George, L.A.; O'Brien, R.J. *J. Geophys. Res.* **1990**, 96, 18569-18576.

113. Ortgies, G.; Gericke, K.-H.; Comes, F.J. *Geophys. Res. Lett.* **1980**, 7, 905-908.

114. Hard, T.M.; O'Brien, R.J.; Cook T.B.; Tsongas, G.A. *Applied Optics* **1979**, 18, 3216.

115. Hard, T.M.; O'Brien, R.J.; Cook, T.B. *J. Appl. Phys.* **1980**, 51, 3459.

116. Hard,T.M.; Chan, C.Y.; Mehrabzadeh A.A.; O'Brien, R.J. *Applied Optics* **1989**, 28, 1.

117. Davis, D.D.; Rodgers, M.O.; Fischer, S.D., *Geophys. Res. Lett.* **1981**, 8, 73-76.

118. Davis, D.D.; Rodgers, M.O.; Fischer, S.D.; Asai, K. *Geophys. Res. Lett.* **1981**, 8, 69-72.

119. Shirinzadeh, B.; Wang, C.C.; Deng, D.Q. *Geophys. Res. Lett.* **1987**, 14, 123-126.

120. Smith, G.P.; Crosley, D.R. *J. Geophys. Res.* **1990**, 95, 16427-16442.

121. Beck, S.M., Bendura, R.J.; McDougal, D.S.; Hoell, J.M., Jr.;Gregory, G.L.; Curfman, H.J., Jr.; Davis, D.D.; Bradshaw, J.; Rogers, M.O.; Wang, C.C.; Davis, L.I.; Campbell, M.J.; Torres A.L.; Carroll, M.A.; Ridley, B.A.; Sachse, G.W.; Hill,G.F.; Condon, E.P.; Rasmussen, R.A. *J. Geophys. Res. 1987* 92, 1977-85.

122. Hubler, G.; Perner, D.; Platt, U.; Tonnissen, A.; Ehhalt, D.H. *J. Geophys. Res.* **1984**, 89.

123. Platt, U.; Rateike, M,; Junkermann, W.; Rudolph, J.; Ehhalt, D. H. *J. Geophys. Res.* **1988**, 93, 5196.

124. Platt, U.; Rateike, M.; Junkermann, W.; Hofzumahaus. A.; Ehhalt, D.H. *Free Radical Res. Commun.* **1987**, 3, 165-72.

125. Perner, D.; Platt, U.; Trainer, M.; Hubler, G.; Drummond, J.; Junkermann, W.; Randolph, J.; Schubert, B.; Volz, A.; Ehhalt, D.H. *J. Atmos. Chem.* **1987**, 5, 185.

126. Armerding, W.A.; Herbert, A.; Schindler, T.; Spiekermann, M. and Comes, F.J. *Ber. Bunsenges. Phys. Chem.* **1990**, 4, 775-781.

127. Mihelcic, D.; Volz-Thomas, A.; Paetz, H.W.; Kley, D.; Mihelcic, M. *J. Atmos. Chem.* **1990**, 11, 271-97.

128. Mihelcic, D.; Muesgen, P.; Ehhalt, D. H. *J. Atmos. Chem.* **1985**, 3, 341-61.

129. Weinstock, B.; Chang, T.Y. *Tellus* **1974**, 26, 108.

130. Bates D.R.; Witherspoon, A.E. *Mon. Not. R. Astron. Soc.* **1952**, 112, 101.

131. McConnell, J.C.; McElroy, M.B.; Wofsy, S.C. *Nature* **1971**, 233, 187.

132. Wofsy, S.C.; McConnell, J.C.; McElroy, M.B. *J. Geophys. Res.* **1972**, 77, 4477.

133. Singh, H.W. *Geophys. Res. Let.* **1977**, 4, 101-104.

134. Singh, H.B. *Geo. Phys. Res. Lett.* **1977**, *4*, 453-456.

135. Lovelock, J.E. *Nature* **1977**, *267*, 32.

136. Prinn, R.; Cunnold, D.; Rasmussen, R.; Simmonds, P.; Alyea, F.; Crawford, A.; Fraser, P. and Rosen, R. *Science* **1987**, 238, 945-950.

137. Volz, A.; Ehhalt, D.H. and Derwent, R.G. *J. Geophys. Res.* **1981**, 86, 5163-5171.

138. Khalil, M.A.K; Rasmussen, R.A.; French, J.R.J.; Holt, J.A. *J. Geophys. Res.* **1990**, 95, 3619

139. Calvert, J.G. *Envir. Sci. Technol.* **1976**, 10, 256-262.

140. Singh, H.B.; Martinez, J.R.; Hendry, D.R.; Jaffe, R.J.; Johnson, W.B. *Envir. Sci. Technol.* **1981**, 15, 113-119.

141. Roberts, J.M; Fehsenfeld, F.C.; Liu, S.C.; Bollinger, M.J.; Hahn, C.; Albritton, D.L.; Sievers, R.E. *Atmos. Environ.* **1984**, 18, 2421-2432.

142. McKeen, S.A.; Trainer, M.; Hsie, E.Y.; Tallamraju, R.K.; Liu, S.C. *J. Geophys. Res.* **1990**, 95, 7493-7500.

143. Campbell, M.J.; Sheppard, J.C. and Au, B.F. *Geophys. Res. Lett.* **1979**, 6, 175-178.

144. Campbell, M.J.; Farmer, J.C; Fitzner, C.A.; Henry, M.N.; Sheppard, J. C.; Hardy, R.J.; Hopper, J.F.; Muralidhar, V. *J. Atm. Chem.* **1986**, 4, 413-427.

145. Felton, C. C.; Sheppard, J.C; Campbell, M.J. *Nature* **1988**, 335, 53-55.

146. Eisele, F.I.; Tanner, D.J. *J. Geophys. Res.* **1991**, 96, 9295-9308.

147. Altshuller, A.P. *J. Air Poll. Control Assoc.* **1989**, 39, 704-708.

148. Beck, S.M.; Bendura, R.J.; McDougal, D.S.; Hoell, J.M., Jr. *et al. J. Geophys. Res.* **1987**, 92, 1977-85.

149. Hofzumahaus, A.; Dorn, H.-P,; Callies, J.; Platt, U.; Ehhalt, D.H. *Atmos. Environ.* **1991**, 25A, 2017-2022.

150. Liu, S.C. In *The Changing Atmosphere*; Rowland, F.S.; Isaken, I.S.A., Eds.; Wiley-Interscience, New York, NY, **1988**, 219-232.

151. Lelieveld, J.; Crutzen, P.J. *J. Atmos. Chem.* **1991**, *12*, 229.

152. Greenberg, J.P.; Zimmerman, P.R. *J. Geophys. Res.* **1984**, 89, 4767-4778.

153. Greenberg, J.P.; Zimmerman, P.R.; Haagenson, P. *J. Geophys. Res.* **1990**, 95, 14015-14026.

154. Chameides, W.L.; Davis, D.D.; Bradshaw, J.; Rodgers, M.; Sandholm, S.; Bai, D.B. *J. Geophys. Res.* **1987**, 92, 2153-6.

155. Zellner, R; Weibring, G. *Z. Phys. Chemi* **1989**, 161, 167-188.

156. Donahue, N.M.; Prinn, R.G, *J. Geophys. Res.*, **1990**, 95, 18387-18411.

157. Kasting, J.; Singh, H. *J. Geophys. Res.* **1986**, *91*, 13239-13256.

158. Thompson, A.M.; Cicerone, R.J. *J. Geophys. Res.* **1986**, 91, 10853-10864.

159. Chameides, W.L.; Tan, A. *J. Geophys. Res.* **1981**, 86, 5209-5223.

160. Crutzen, P.J.; Gidel, L.T. *88*, , 6641-6661, 1983.??

161. Hough, A. *J. Geophys. Res.* **1991**, 96, 7325-7362.

162. Spivakovsky, C.M.; Yevich, R.; Logan, J.A; Wofsy, S.C.; McElroy, M.B.; Prather, M.J. *J. Geophys. Res.* **1990**, 95, 18441-18472.

163. Finlayson-Pitts, B.J.; Pitts, J.N., Jr. *Atmospheric Chemistry: Fundamentals and Experimental Techniques*; John Wiley & Sons: New York 1986; 589-600.

164. Leone, J. A.; Seinfeld, J.H. *Atmos. Environ.* **1985**, 19, 437-464.

165. Hough, Adrian M. *J. Geophys. Res.* **1988**, 93, 3789-3813.

166. Jacob, D.J.; Sillman, S.; Logan, J.A.; Wofsy, S.C. *J. Geophys.Res.* **1989**, 94, 8497-8510.

167. Gery, M.W.; Whitten, G.; Killus, J.P.; Dodge, M.C. *J. Geophys. Res.* **1989**, 94, 12925

168. Stockwell, W.R.; Calvert, J.G. *J. Geophys. Res.* **1983**, 88, 6673-6682.

169. Atkinson, R.; Lloyd, A.C.; Winges, L. *Atmos. Environ.* **1982**, 16, 1341-1355.

170. Besemer, A.C.; Nieboer, H. *Atmos. Envir.* **1985**, 19, 507.

171. Carter, W.; Atkinson, R.; Winer, A.M.; Pitts, J.N., Jr. *Atmos. Environ.* **1985**, 19, 345.

172. Carter, W.; Atkinson, R.; Winer, A.M. and Pitts, J.N., Jr. *Int. J. Chem. Kinet.* **1981**, 13, 735.

173. Carter, W.; Atkinson, R.; Winer, A.M. and Pitts, J.N., Jr. *Int. J. Chem. Kinet.* **1982**, 14, 1071.

174. Kelly, N. A.; Olson, K.L. and Wong, C. A. *Environ. Sci. Technol.* **1985**, 17, 177.

175. Jefferies, H.E; Fox, D.L.; Kamens, R. J. *Air Pollut. Control Assoc.* **1976**, 26, 480.

176. Pitts, J.N., Jr.; Darnall, K.; Carter, W.; Winer. A; Atkinson, R. *Rep. EPA-600/3-79-110*, **1979**, U.S. EPA, Research Triangle Park, N.C..

177. Gery, M.W.; Fox, D.L.; Jefferies, H.E.; Stockburger, L.; Weathers W. *Int. J. Chem. Kinet.* **1985**, 17, 931.

178. Gery, M.W.; Fox, D.L.; Kamens, R.M.; Stockburger, L. *Environ. Sci. Tecnol.* **1987**, 21, 339.

179. Thompson, A.M.; Stewart, R.W. *Chemometrics and Int. Lab Sys.* **1991**, 10, 69-79.

180. Thompson, A.M.; Stewart, R.W. *J. Geophys. Res.* **1991**, 96, 13089-13108.

181. Dodge, M.C. *J. Geophys. Res.* **1989**, *94*, 5121.

182. Lurmann, F.W.; Lloyd, A.C.; Atkinson, R. *J. Geophys. Res.* **1986**, 91, 10905-10936.

183. Stockwell, W.R. *Atmos. Environ.* **1986**, 20, 1615-1632.

184. Sakamaki, F; Hatakeyama, S.; Akimoto, J. *Int. J. Chem. Kinet.* **1983**, 15, 1013-1029.

185. Pitts, J.N., Jr., Sanhueza, E.; Atkinson, R.; Carter, W.P.L.; Winer, A.M.; Harris, G.W.; Plum, C.N. *Int. J. Chem. Kinet.* **1984**, 16, 919-939.

186. Seinfeld, J.H. *Science* **1989**, 243, 745-752.

187. O'Brien, R.J; Green, P.J.; Nguyen, N.L.; Dumdei, B.M. *Environ. Sci. Technol.* **1983**, 17, 183-86.

188. Zellner, R.; Exner, M.; Herrmann, H., *J Atmos. Chem.* **1990**, 10, 411.

189. Khalil, M.A.K.; Rasmussen, R.A. *Science* **1984**, 224, 54-56.

190. White, W.; Dietz, D. *Nature* **1984**, 309, 242-244.

RECEIVED September 24, 1991

Chapter 5

Dust in the Environment
Elemental Composition and Sources

Jack E. Fergusson

Department of Chemistry, University of Canterbury, Christchurch, New Zealand

The name "dust", is used in a variety of ways, and with different meanings. These range from the material that accumulates on the earth's surface, such as on streets and in living and working environments, to the particulate material suspended in the atmosphere. In this paper I wish to consider these two materials in terms of their chemical composition, sources and relationship between them. The names used for the two materials will be "surface dust" and "atmospheric dust". The word "aerosol" may also be used for atmospheric dust but it more properly applies to the finer particles of atmospheric dust and includes liquid aerosol (*1*). Both surface and atmospheric dusts are increasingly seen to be a hazard to human beings as they are a source of intake of toxic materials such as heavy metals. For this reason study is important of the composition and sources of the dusts.

Both dusts display a wide spectrum of sizes, and for atmospheric dust the size distribution (with respect to the total mass or volume or number of particles) has a log-normal shape skewed towards the larger size. The diameter of atmospheric dust spans the size range <0.005 µm to >10 µm. The distribution of an urban aerosol (expressed as dM/d(log d) vs log d, where M = particle mass and d the particle diameter) is divided into three distinct log-normal sections giving a tri-modal appearance of the distribution (Fig. 1). Particles 0.005-0.1µm in diameter are primary particles and called Aitken nuclei produced from high temperature combustion processes and gas condensation. The particles within the size range 0.1-1.0 µm are called fine and are the result of the accumulation of smaller particles. Finally particles with diameters >1 µm are called coarse and are the result of mechanical production of the dust (*1-6*). The characteristics of the three modes are summarised in Fig. 1 and Table I. The size distribution for surface dust is more complex to describe as it depends very much on the sampling technique and location. The mass of material generally increases over the size range <2 µm to around 200 µm (*7*). The size of the particles may be described according to the classification of soil particles and cover the range from clay size (<2 µm) to coarse sand (<200 µm).

The contribution of atmospheric dust to surface dust depends on the dust falling to the earth. This occurs either as dry dust fall or wet washout with rain, snow or hail (*1-6, 8-10*). Dry dust fall occurs by sedimentation, impaction, interception or diffusion. Sedimentation, the fall under gravity, may be estimated using Stoke's law which relates the density and diameter of particles to their falling velocity. A particle of density 1.0 g cm^{-3} and diameter around 0.1 µm would fall with a velocity of around 9 x 10^{-5} cm s^{-1}

0097–6156/92/0483–0117$06.00/0

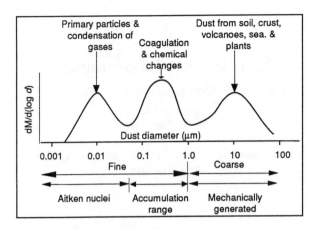

Fig. 1. The size distribution of particles in an urban atmospheric dust showing the three size modes. Based on Whitby, 1977 (*4*).

Table I   Characteristics of the Three Size Modes of Urban Atmospheric Dust

Size μm	Name	Classification	Source
0.005-0.1	Fine	Aitken nuclei, transient lifetime	High temperature combustion processes, condensation from the vapour
0.1-1.0	Fine	Accumulation particles	Coagulation from smaller particles, chemical conversion of gases to solids, some mineral material
>1.0	Coarse	Mechanically produced	From soil, plants, sea salt, volcanoes, wind blown material, abrasion

References: 1-6

(approximately 28 m yr^{-1}), whereas a 20 μm particle would fall with a velocity of 0.13 cm s^{-1}. However, the rate of fall is considerably modified by air movement. Wash out on the other hand is a more complete process for removal of atmospheric dust.

Dust is a source of intake of toxic materials, either by intake of atmospheric dust through the lungs, or by oral ingestion of surface dust. The intake of atmospheric dust into the lungs and the extent of penetration depends on the size of the particles. For diameters >5 μm the particles are deposited in the nasopharyngeal region. Smaller particles, 1-2 μm will deposit in the tracheobronchial region, whereas particles in the range 0.1-1 μm penetrate as far as the alveolar region. Very small particles act as if they are gaseous and can be expelled from the lungs if they do not deposit by impaction (*3, 11-13*). The uptake of heavy metals from the lungs into the blood stream can be very efficient The oral ingestion of surface dust through hand-to-mouth activities is the second major way the components of dust can get into human beings. For young children this is considered a major intake route, more important than aerosol intake through the lungs. Uptake of lead from surface dust has been shown to significantly increase the blood-lead levels of young children, especially around the age of 1-3 years (*12*).

It is clear that both atmospheric and surface dusts are complex materials and not all that easy to describe. A summary is given in Fig. 2 of the sources of atmospheric and surface dusts and their inter-connection. Both natural and anthropogenic sources contribute to both dusts. The inter-connection between the two dusts is wet and dry deposition from the atmosphere to the ground, and the re-entrainment of surface dust through wind and human activity into the atmosphere. Dust is an important global component of our earth, and impinges on the wellbeing of people.

Atmospheric Dust

It is remarkable that, except for local "hot-spots" such as around industrial sites, mining areas and volcanoes, the elemental compositions of atmospheric dust in similar locations, such as remote or rural or urban are relatively constant over the world. This suggests either common sources, or a dominant source, or good mixing and transport of the dust around the globe. In fact all three factors have a role in determining the uniformity. Because of the consistent composition it is possible to estimate the median concentrations of the elements in atmospheric dusts in similar, but widely separated, locations. These estimates are given in columns 2 to 7 in Table II. The concentrations of the elements in the atmospheric dust are expressed as mass per volume of air. For remote locations (columns 2 to 5) the concentrations are in ng m^{-3}, whereas for rural and urban areas (columns 6 and 7) the elemental concentrations are in μg m^{-3}.

Remote atmospheric dust. Four remote dusts have been identified as listed in Table II. The titles "islands" and "continental" refer to remote islands and land masses (often mountainous) respectively. The elemental compositions of the four areas display a close relationship with each other as exhibited by the scatter plots of paired log concentration data. Two examples are shown in Fig. 3 for continental vs Antarctic atmospheric dust, and island vs Arctic atmospheric dust. The plots show a linear and significant relationship (correlation coefficients (r) range from 0.80 to 0.95 (p < 0.001) between the concentrations of the elements common to two different dusts. That is, if the concentration of an element is high in one dust it is likely to be high in the other dust. The relationships are weaker, but still significant, when the major and trace elements are considered separately. This indicates that the high and low concentrations are not biasing the regression line. The concentrations of the majority of the elements in the four remote atmospheric dusts increase in the order Antarctic < Arctic < island < continental. This is illustrated graphically for Al, Ti, Cl, Cd, Cu, Se and Zn in Fig. 4, which also includes rural and urban dusts. The increase from left to right relates to a decrease in remoteness, and an increase in contamination of the dust with anthropogenic material. The concentration ratio, [M]$_{continental}$/[M]$_{Antarctic}$, where M stands for a particular element, has a range from 1 to 10,000, with a median around 100. That is on average, the concentrations of the elements in continental atmospheric dust are around 100 times greater than in Antarctic atmospheric dust.

A common approach for identifying the enriched elements in a material is to calculate the enrichment factor (EF). The EF of an element, M, is obtained by comparing its concentration with that of a reference element, R, such as cerium or

Table II   Concentrations of Elements in Aerosols, Surface Dusts, the Crust and Soils[a]

	Atmospheric Dusts						Surface dusts		Crustal	Soil
	Antarctic ng m^{-3}	Arctic ng m^{-3}	Islands ng m^{-3}	Continental ng m^{-3}	Rural μg m^{-3}	Urban μg m^{-3}	Street μg g^{-1}	House μg g^{-1}	μg g^{-1}	μg g^{-1}
Ag	0.002	0.003	0.004	0.12		0.0002	0.7		0.07	0.05
Al	0.5	15	30	200	0.4	1.5	40000	25000	82000	71000
As	0.02	0.1	0.2	1	0.002	0.006	10	16	1.5	6
Au	5x10^{-5}	0.0005		0.002	0.0006		0.1	0.4	0.001	0.01
Ba	0.02	0.4	0.5	5	0.008	0.04	310		500	500
Bi						0.0006				
Br	0.5	5	10	5	0.02	0.25	60	40	0.37	10
C				800	3	14	10	400000	480	20000
Ca	0.5	20	200	300	0.3	1.5	60000	15000	41000	15000
Cd	0.02	0.04	0.02	1	0.0005	0.005	2	7	0.11	0.35
Ce	0.002	0.03	0.05	0.1	0.0003	0.003	30	25	68	50
Cl	10	100	5000	40	1	2	600	4000	130	100
Co	0.0005	0.007	0.01	0.2	0.0004	0.001	7	9	20	8
Cr	0.01	0.1	0.1	1	0.003	0.03	110	60	100	70
Cs	0.0001	0.006	0.01	0.05	0.0003	0.0006			3	4
Cu	0.05	0.2	0.1	5	0.03	0.06	200	250	50	30
Dy							2		6	5
Eu	2x10^{-5}	0.001	9x10^{-5}	0.2	2x10^{-5}	6x10^{-5}	0.4		2.1	1
F	0.6	3		200					15	200
Fe		20	20	96	0.3	2	35000	10000	41000	40000
Ga		0.07		0.04		0.001	5		18	20
H	6x10^{-5}	6								
Hf			0.001	1	2x10^{-5}	0.0002	4	2	5.3	6
Hg	0.2	0.6	0.005	0.2	8x10^{-5}	0.004	0.09		0.05	0.06
I			2	0.001	1.5x10^{-5}	0.005			0.14	5
In	6x10^{-5}	0.0014	0.02		5x10^{-5}	0.0002	9	8	0.049	1
K	0.6	20	200	150	0.3	1	12500	13000	21000	14000

Element										
La	0.0006	0.01		0.04	0.0005	0.002	15	10	32	40
Li	6×10^{-6}	0.001			0.009	0.004	0.2		0.51	0.4
Lu						1×10^{-6}				
Mg	1	40	300	40	0.2	0.7	7500	6000	23000	5000
Mn	0.011	0.5	1	12	0.015	0.05	500	200	950	1000
Mo		0.1	0.2	0.3					1.5	1.2
Na	5	100	3000	200	1	1.5	15000	12000	23000	5000
Ni		0.13	1	1	0.003	0.02	75	40	80	50
P		1.5							1000	800
Pb	0.7	1	0.1	10	0.1	1	2000	500	14	35
Rb	0.003	0.08	0.1	0.7	0.001	0.005	22		90	150
S	50	100		1000					260	700
Sb	0.001	0.11	0.01	0.6	0.002	0.01	6	10	0.2	1
Sc	0.00014	0.01	0.008	0.05	0.0001	0.00025	5	3	16	7
Se	0.006	0.05	0.15	0.2	0.001	0.003	4		0.05	0.4
Si	2.5	50		500	2	7	160000		277000	330000
Sm	5×10^{-5}	0.002		0.01	6×10^{-5}	0.0003	2	1.2	7.9	4.5
Sn										
Sr	0.1	0.5	3	1	0.003	0.01	350		370	250
Ta	7×10^{-5}		0.001	0.015		0.03			2	2
Tb				0.02		1×10^{-6}	0.4		1.1	0.7
Th	0.0001	0.003	0.005	0.1	0.0001		4	3	12	9
Ti	0.12	1	9	15	0.02	0.00025	2000		5600	5000
Tl				0.1	0.001	0.2			0.6	0.2
U							3.5		2.4	2
V	0.0013	0.3	0.1	5	0.002	0.02	120	30	160	90
W	0.002	0.01		0.01	0.0004	0.0002			1	1.5
Yb					0.0001	0.0002	1		3.3	3
Zn	0.03	1.5	0.5	10	0.05	0.2	600	1200	75	90
Zr							70		190	400

a References: Antarctic, 14-19; Arctic, 20-27; Islands, 1, 28-35; Continental, 25, 36-48; Rural, 5, 23, 27, 32, 33, 47, 49-53; Urban, 1, 23, 27, 32, 47, 49, 52, 54-72; Street and house dusts, 73 and refs. therein; Crustal and soil, 74.

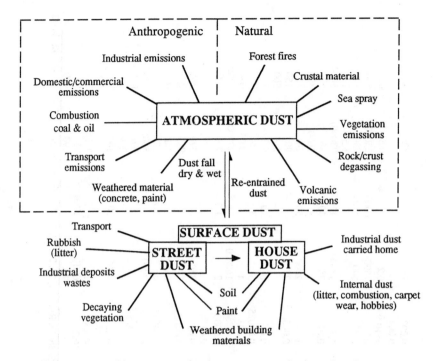

Fig. 2. The sources and inter-connection between atmospheric and surface dusts.

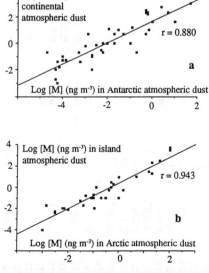

Fig. 3. Relationships between the concentrations of the elements in remote atmospheric
dusts: (a) continental vs Antarctic atmospheric dust, (b) island vs Arctic
atmospheric dust. [M] is the concentration of element M.

aluminium, in a material "x" against their concentrations, in a reference material "r", such as the earth's crust or soil. Hence EF = $[M]_x[R]_r/[M]_r[R]_x$. For all four remote atmospheric dusts (x) compared with crustal or median global soil (r) concentrations (see Table II columns 10 and 11), using cerium as the reference element, the enriched elements (EF > 10) are: Br, S, Cd, Se, Cl, Pb, Au, Ag, As, Sb, Mo, Cu, Zn, In, Hg, and less markedly so W, V, Na, Tl, and C. A typical plot of log EF is given in Fig. 5 for Antarctic atmospheric dust with respect to mean crustal concentrations. The medians of the concentration ratio $[M]_{continental}/[M]_{Antarctic}$ (see above) for the enriched and non-enriched elements are ~40 and ~200 respectively. This suggests that of the two atmospheric dusts the enriched elements have been diluted, presumably with silicate material, in the continental dust. This is reasonable considering the different geological locations of the dusts with respect to sources of silicate material. The order of dilution of the enriched elements in the four atmospheric dusts is; Antarctic < Arctic < island < continental.

A summary is given in Table III of the results of the elucidation of the sources of the elements in remote atmospheric dusts. Four main sources are identified: silicate dust, marine spray, high temperature natural emissions (e.g. volcanic, plant and rock emissions and forest fires) and anthropogenic inputs. It is apparent from the table that the enriched elements are associated with the high temperature emissions and anthropogenic inputs. There has been controversy over the relative contributions of natural high temperature emissions and anthropogenic emissions to remote atmospheric dusts, especially in the Antarctic (*14, 15, 17, 72, 75, 78-83, 86-90*). The problem is confounded by the very low concentrations of many of the elements in Antarctic snow, the material used for estimating atmospheric dust concentrations. In many studies prevention of contamination during sampling and analysis has been inadequate leading to incorrect analytical data (*79, 81, 90*). It appears that the enrichment of many elements in the Antarctica may be due to volcanic activity, with a contribution from high temperature anthropogenic processes. Less problem exists over the contribution of pollution related elements in the other remote aerosols. The concentrations of some elements have not altered greatly in old ice/snow (pre 1900) compared with new ice/snow (present day) in remote places (Table IV). However, for some, particularly lead, their concentrations are elevated at the present time. The lead most likely originates from industrial and automotive sources, as the increase in the lead concentrations in the ice/snow parallels the introduction of these sources (*90*).

Rural and urban atmospheric dusts. The rural and urban atmospheric dusts have higher concentrations of most of the chemical elements in them as indicated by the data in columns 6 and 7 in Table II, and in Fig. 4. (Note the different concentration units used in Table II). The increase in concentrations of the elements from remote to rural and urban atmospheric dusts are around 3 to 4 orders of magnitude (depending on the element). Irrespective of this, linear relationships exist between the concentrations of the elements in the remote and either rural or urban atmospheric dusts, as illustrated by the two scatter plots; urban vs Antarctic dust and rural vs remote continental dust in Fig. 6. Plots for other atmospheric dust pairs are similar, the relation between rural and urban aerosols being particularly strong (r = 0.96, p<0.001). Whereas the absolute concentrations of the elements vary with atmospheric dust type, for the majority of the elements the order of their relative concentrations remains the same. Also the elements found to be enriched in the remote atmospheric dusts (see above) are also the enriched (EF >10) elements in the rural and urban atmospheric dusts (relative to crustal or soil concentrations). There is therefore a distinct group of elements enriched in the various atmospheric dusts over the world. This probably relates, in part, to the higher volatility of the enriched elements (or their compounds). The plot of log EF against melting point (M. Pt., K) (Fig. 7) for a number of elements demonstrates there is a distinct grouping of the enriched elements with low M. Pt's and the non-enriched with higher M. Pt's. This suggests that high temperature processes, both natural (e.g. volcanic) and anthropogenic (e.g. combustion) are the sources of the elements. Overall it appears that the anthropogenic enriched elements are transported from urban into rural then remote

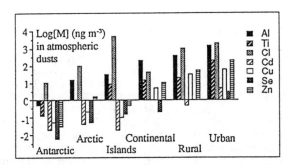

Fig. 4. Concentrations (ng m-3) of the elements Al, Ti, Cl, Cd, Cu, Se and Zn in
atmospheric dusts at various locations. [M] is the concentration of element M.

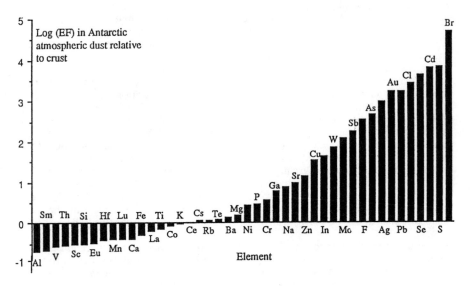

Fig. 5. The log (enrichment factor) for 44 elements in Antarctic atmospheric dust
compared with mean crustal concentrations.

Table III   Proposed Sources of Elements in Remote Aerosols[a]

	Silicate dust	Marine	High temperature processes: volcanic, rock and plant emissions, forest fires	Anthropogenic
Major[b]	Al, Ba, Ca, Fe, K, Mg, Mn, Na, S, Si, Sr, Ti	Ca, Cl, Mg, Na	Br, Cd, Cl, Pb, S, Se	Br, Cd, Cu, Fe, Mn, N, Pb, S, V
Minor[c]	Ag, Cd, Ce, Co, Cr, Cs, Cu, Eu, Ga, Hf, La, Lu, Ni, P, Pb, Rb, Sc, Sm, Ta, Th, V, W, Zn	Br, I, K, Pb, S, Sr	Ag, As, Au, Cr, Cu, Hg, I, In, Mg, Mo, Ni, Sb, V, W, Zn	Ag, As, Au, Cr, H, Hg, In, Mo, Ni, Sb, S, Sr, W, Zn

a References: 14, 16-22, 24, 25, 29-34, 39, 44, 75-97. b Source is the major contributor of the
elements listed. c Source is the minor contributor of the elements listed.

Table IV Median Concentrations in Both Old (pre 1900) and New
Antarctic and Arctic Snow/Ice (ng g^{-1})[a]

	New	Old		New	Old		New	Old
Ag	0.005	0.001	Hg	0.03	0.01	Sb	0.01	0.02
Al	1.5	2.5	K	2	2	Se	0.1	0.01
As	0.01	0.02	Mg	3	2	Si	20	10
Ca	3	3	Mn	0.6	0.3	Ti	0.06	0.06
Cd	0.002	0.001	Na	10	10	U	0.01	0.01
Cl	50	50	Pb	0.06	0.001	V	0.02	0.02
Cu	0.03	0.03	S	0.05	0.04	Zn	0.1	0.05
Fe	7	7						

a References: 15, 16, 18, 21, 75, 77-80, 82, 83, 87-90.

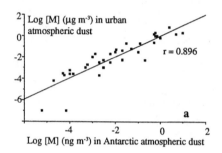
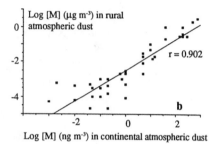

Fig. 6. Relationship between the concentrations of the elements in various atmospheric dusts: (a) urban vs Antarctic atmospheric dust, (b) rural vs continental atmospheric dust. [M] is the concentration of element M.

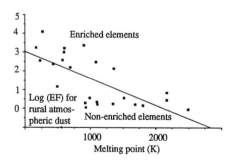

Fig. 7. Relationship between Log (EF) for elements in rural atmospheric dust and the melting point (K) of the elements.

areas, and that the atmospheric dusts have common sources, though these will vary in magnitude with location.

Diverse techniques have been employed to identify the sources of elements in atmospheric dust (and surface dust) (Table V). Some involve considering trends in concentration and others use various statistical methods. The degree of sophistication and detail obtained from the analyses increases from top left to bottom right of the Table. The sources identified as contributing the elements in rural and urban atmospheric dusts are detailed in Table VI. The principal sources are crustal material, soil, coal and oil combustion emissions, incinerated refuse emissions, motor vehicle emissions, marine spray, cement and concrete weathering, mining and metal working emissions. Many elements occur in more than one source, and they are classified in the table as originating from either primary sources or secondary sources.

The contribution of each source to the urban atmospheric dust can be estimated using statistical techniques such as chemical element balance and principal component analysis. Around 40-50% comes from the crust and soil, 10% marine (dependent on the proximity to the ocean), 3-5% fossil fuel, 10-15% transport emissions, and the rest from other sources (33, 42, 66). Assuming that aluminium derives entirely from crustal/soil material the mass concentration ratio [Al]atmospheric dust/[Al]soil is 0.23, 0.42, and 0.56 for remote continental, rural and urban atmospheric dusts respectively. This indicates an increase in the soil contribution to the three atmospheric dusts in the approximate ratios 1:1.8:2.4 respectively. If the concentrations of the elements Fe and Ti are treated in the same way the relative soil contributions are found to be 1:1.8:1.7, and 1:3.7:3.7 respectively. Though the ratios are not exactly the same they are indicative of the importance of crustal/soil material to atmospheric dust and variation with locations.

Surface Dust

Eventually much of the atmospheric dust becomes surface dust either through dry deposit or washed out by precipitation. The rate at which this happens depends on numerous factors including the density of the particle, meteorological factors, coagulation and condensation processes for atmospheric particles. The dust that eventually falls to the earth's surface has been investigated in a number of guises. These include dust on plants, in snow and ice, in peat bogs, in precipitation, in dust fall, on the street and in buildings. These surface dusts will, in most cases, contain contributions from material that had not been airborne, or at least only for a short time, such as weathered building materials, soil, deposited litter and large particles from traffic emissions.

The two surface dusts most studied are street and house dusts. As with atmospheric dust there is a remarkable agreement in the concentrations of the elements in either street or house dusts taken from a wide variety of sources (73). Therefore it is possible to estimate median concentrations for each element in the two dusts. The estimates are listed in columns 8 and 9 in Table II. One feature is that the concentrations of the elements in the two dusts are of the same order of magnitude as in soil (column 11, Table II).

Since the majority of the elements in surface dust arise from deposited aerosol and added soil it is not surprising to find strong linear relationships between the concentrations of the elements in an atmospheric dust and street or house dust. This is illustrated by the two examples given in Fig. 8 for remote house dust vs urban atmospheric dust and street dust vs rural atmospheric dust. As discussed above crustal/soil material is a major component of atmospheric dust and the soil based elements in the atmospheric dust are: Al, Ca, Fe, Mg, Mn, Ni, K, Si and Ti. The elements As, Br, Cd, Cl, Co, Cu, Pb, Rb, Se, V, and Zn are, on the other hand, enriched in atmospheric dust. The same elemental distribution applies to surface dust, but in this case their concentrations (compared on a mass basis) are reduced presumably due to dilution with soil. However, the elements enriched in the atmosphere remain enriched in the surface dusts.

**Table V   Methods of Identifying Sources of Elements in Aerosols
and Surface Dust**

Type	Method	Type	Method
Analysis	Ultra clean analysis	Element ratios	Element ratios
	Comparison of data		Element signatures
Trends	Seasonal variations	Basic statistics	Correlation
	Meteorological factors		Regression analysis
	Variation with time	Advanced statistics	Cluster analysis
	Variation with distance		Dendograms
Chemical	Chemical differences		Chemical element balance
	Isotopes, and isotope ratios		Principal component analysis
Enrichments	Enrichment factor		Factor analysis
	Interference factor		Specific rotation factor analysis
	Mobilization factor		
	Historical factor		

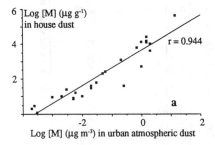

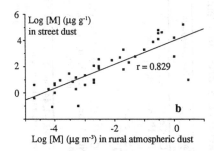

Fig. 8.   Relationship between the concentration of elements in surface and atmospheric
dusts: (a) house dust vs urban atmospheric dust, (b) street dust vs rural
atmospheric dust. [M] is the concentration of element M.

Table VI. Sources of Elements, Anions and Cations in Urban and Rural Aerosols[a]

Significance	Crustal/soil	Coal combustion	Oil combustion	Incineration (refuse)	Motor vehicle	Marine	Cement & concrete	Mining & metal working
Primary contributors[b]	Al, Ba, Ca, Ce, Co, Cs, Eu, Fe, Hf, K, La, Lu, Mg, Mn, Na, Rb, Sc, Si, Sm, Sr, Ta, Tb, Th, Ti	Al, As, Ba, Ce, Fe, La, N, S, Se	Co, Ni, S, Se, V	Cd, Sb, Zn	Br, C, N, Pb, S	Cl, K, Mg, Na	Ca	Cd, Cr, Cu, Fe, Ni, Pb, Sb, Sn, Ti, V, Zn
Secondary contributors[c]	As, Cd, Cr, Cu, Ga, In, Li, Ni, Sb, Se, V, U, Zn	Ca, Cd, Cl, Co, Cr, Cu, H, Hg, I, Na, Rb, Sb, Th, Ti, V	Ba, Cd, Cu, Fe, Mn, Na, Zn	As, Mn, Pb	Ba, Cl, Fe, S, Sb, Zn	Br, Sr	Al, S	Ca, K

a References: 23, 32, 33, 37, 40, 42, 44, 46, 48-51, 53-59, 61-70, 72, 91, 92. b Elements for which the source is a major origin.
c Elements for which the source is a minor origin.

Table VII. Sources of the Elements in Street Dust and House Dust

Street dust[a]

Soil	Combustion (oil, coal, refuse)	Tire wear	Concrete & cement	Salt spray, de-icing salt	Metal corrosion & wear	Motor vehicle	Weathered paint
Al, Ba, Ca, Ce, Cu, Dy, Ga, Hf, K, La, Lu, Mg, Mn, Sc, Si, Sm, Sr, Tb, Th, Ti, U, Yb, Zr	Al, As, Ba, C, Cd, Ce, Co, Hg, Ni, Sb, Se, V, Zn	As, Ba, Cd, Cr, Mn, Zn	Al, Ca, Fe, Si	Cl, I, K,, Mg, Na	Cd, Co, Cr, Fe, Ni, V, Zn	Br, Cu, Cr, Fe, Ni, Pb	C, Pb, Ti, Zn

House dust[b]

Soil	Street dust	Motor vehicle	Metal corrosion & wear	Other external sources	Carpet wear	Paint	Internally produced (combustion, spills etc.)
Al,Ca, Ce, Fe, Hf, K, La, Mg, Mn, Sc, Sm, Th, V	As for soil, Br, Pb, Zn	Br, Pb	Al, Co, Cr, Cu, Fe, Mn, Ni, Zn	As above: tyre wear, salt, concrete	C, Cd, Cu, Pb, Zn	Pb, Ti, Zn	Al, As, Au, C, Ca, Cl, Cu, Fe, I, Na, Sb, V, Zn

a References: 7, 93-101. b References: 93, 97, 100-109

Street dust. For the sixteen elements (Yb, La, Dy, Eu, Ti, Sm, Th, Si, Lu, Mn, Al, Tb, Ce, Ba, Hf and Sc) the concentration ratio [M]street dust/[M]soil has a mean of 0.50 (standard deviation = 0.11) (7, 93). This suggests that soil contributes approximately 50% to the dust and that the dust and soil have a similar constitution. Most of the other elements measured in street dust are enriched with respect to the crust or soil, and include Pb, Se, Au, Ag, Zn, As, Cu, Sb, Cr, Cl, Br, Cd and Ca.

More detailed statistical analyses (chemical element balance, principal component analysis and factor analysis) demonstrate that soil contributes >50% to street dust, iron materials, concrete/cement and tire wear contribute 5-7% each, with smaller contributions from salt spray, de-icing salt and motor vehicle emissions (6, 93-100). A list is given in Table VII of the main sources of the elements which contribute to street dust.

House dust. Houses are enclosed spaces and tend to accumulate dust from the outside. There are also internal sources of house dust. The concentration ratio [M]house dust/[M]soil has a mean of 0.33 (standard deviation = 0.09) for the ten elements Mn, Fe, La, Sm, Hf, Th, V, Al, Sc and Ce suggesting that around 33% of house dust is soil (93). The concentration ratio for the two surface dusts, [M]house dust/[M]street dust, is >1 for the elements Cu, Co, As, Sb, Zn, Cd, Au, Cl and C suggesting these elements also have an internal component. All of these elements, as well as Pb and Br, are enriched in house dust relative to their concentrations in soil. Lead and bromine originate mainly from outside the house, and probably from street dust and motor vehicle emissions and, in the case of lead, from paint. When the concentrations of lead in house dust are very high this generally signifies an internal source of lead paint, especially in older houses.

One of the main contributors of internally produced house dust is carpet wear, and the amounts ($\mu g\ m^{-2}$) of the four metals Cd, Cu, Pb and Zn were found to increase with the amount of carpet wear (107, 108).

Conclusion

In this brief review it has been possible to demonstrate that there are common features contributing to the composition of atmospheric and surface dusts. There are at least three main reasons for this. (a) There are a number of common sources for the different dusts. (b) Transport of the dust throughout the atmosphere provides a mechanism for mixing. (c) The prominent contribution of soil and crustal material to both atmospheric and surface dusts tends to be a levelling factor, and is the main source of the elements; Al, Ba, Ca, Ce, Co, Cr, Cs, Eu, Fe, Ga, Hf, K, La, Li, Lu, Mg, Mn, Na, Rb, Sc, Si, Sm, Sr, Ta, Tb, Th . However, there are natural and anthropogenic high temperature processes that produce significant enrichment of many elements including Br, S, Cd, Se, Cl, Pb, Au, Ag, As, Sb, Mo, Cu, Zn, In and Hg in the atmosphere and surface dusts. In addition there are localised areas (e.g. mining) where specific activity cause enrichment of certain elements.

Literature Cited

1. Cawse, P. A. In: *Environmental Chemistry*. Bowen, H. J. M., Snr. Reporter. London: Roy. Soc. Chem.; **1982**, *2*, 1-69.
2. Jaenicke, R. In: Chemistry of the Unpolluted and Polluted Troposphere, Geogii, H. W. and Jaeschke, W. D., Eds., Reidel Pub. Co., **1982**, 341-373
3. Pauxbaum, H. In: Metals and Their Compounds in the Environment, Merian, E., Ed., VCH, Weinheim, **1991**, 257-286.
4. Whitby, K. T. *Atmos. Environ.*, **1977**, *12*, 135-159
5. Warren, R. S. and Birch, P. *The Sci. Total Environ.*, **1987**, *59*, 253-256.
6. Warneck, P. Chemistry of the Natural Atmosphere, Academic Press, London, **1988**.
7. Fergusson, J. E. and Ryan, D. E. *The Sci. Total Environ.*, **1984**, *34*, 101-116.

8.   McMahan, T. A. and Denison, P. J. *Atmos. Environ.*, **1979**, *13*, 571-585
9.   Sehmel, G. A. *Atmos. Environ.*, **1980**, *14*, 983-1011
10. Lantzy, R. J. and Mackenzie, F. T. *Geochim. et Cosmochim. Acta*, **1979**, *43*, 511-525
11. Fergusson, J. E. Inorganic Chemistry of the Earth, Pergamon Press, Oxford, **1982**.
12. Fergusson, J. E. The Heavy Elements: Chemistry, Environmental Impact and Health Effects, Pergamon Press, Oxford, **1990**.
13. Luckey, T. D. and Venugopel, B. Metal Toxicity in Mammals, Vol. 1, Plenum Press, **1977**.
14. Cunningham, W. C. and Zoller, W. H. *J. Aerosol Sci.*, **1981**, *12*, 367-384.
15. Dick, A. L. In: Trace Elements in the New Zealand Environment, Humans and Animals, Proc. New Zealand Trace Elements Group Conf., McLaren, R. G., Haynes, J. R. and Savage, G. P., Eds. **1989**, 11-23.
16. Dick, A. L. and Peel, D. A. *Ann. Glaciol.*, **1985**, *7*, 61-69.
17. Maenhaut, W., Zoller, W. H., Duce, R. A. and Hoffman, G. L. *J. Geophys. Res.*, **1979**, *84*, *C5*, 2421-2431.
18. Peel, D. A. and Wolff, E. W. *Ann. Glaciol.*, **1982**, *3*, 255-259.
19. Zoller, W. H., Gladney, E. S. and Duce, R. A. *Science*, **1974**, *183*, 198-200.
20. Barrie, L. A. and Hoff, R. M. *Atmos. Environ.*, **1985**, *19*, 1995-2010.
21. Davidson, C. I., Chu, L., Grimm, T. C., Nasta, M. A. and Qamoos, M. P. *Atmos. Environ.*, **1981**, *15*, 1429-1437.
22. Davidson, C. I., Santhanam, S., Fortmann, R. C. and Olson, M. P. *Atmos. Environ.*, **1985**, *19*, 2065-2081.
23. Gordon, G. E. In: Air Pollutants and Their Effects on the Terrestrial Environment. Legge, A. H. and Krupa, S. V., Eds. Wiley, N. Y., **1986**, 137-158.
24. Heidam, N. Z. *Atmos. Environ.*, **1981**, *15*, 1421-1427.
25. Heidam, N. Z. In: Toxic Metals in the Atmosphere. Nriagu, J. O. and Davidson, C. I., Eds. Wiley-Interscience, N. Y., **1986**, 267-294.
26. Maenhaut, W., Cornille, P., Pacyna, J. M. and Vitols, V. *Atmos. Environ.*, **1989**, *23*, 2551-2569.
27. Rahn, K. A., Lowenthal, D. H. Harris, J. M. *Atmos. Environ.*, **1989**, *23*, 2597-2607.
28. Chester, R., Aston, S. R., Stoner, J. H. and Bruty, D. *J. Rech. Atmos.*, **1974**, *8*, 777-789.
29. Duce, R. A., Arimoto, R., Ray, B. J., Unni, C. K. and Harder, P. J. *J. Geophys. Res.*, **1983**, *88*, *C9*, 5321-5342.
30. Duce, R. A., Hoffman, G. L. and Zoller, W. H. *Science*, **1975**, *187*, 59-63.
31. Duce, R. A., Ray, B. J., Hoffman, G. L. and Walsh, P. R. *Geophys. Res. Lett.*, **1976**, *3*, 339-342.
32. Nriagu, J. O. In: The Biogeochemistry of Lead in the Environment. Part A Ecological Cycles. Nriagu, J. O., Ed. Holland: Elsevier/ North Holland, **1978**, 137-184.
33. Peirson, D. H., Cawse, P. A. Salmon, L. and Cambray, R. C. *Nature*, **1973**, *241*, 252-256.
34. Settle, D. M. and Patterson, C. C. *J. Geophys. Res.*, **1982**, *87*, 8857-8869.
35. Wiersma, G. B. and Davidson, C. I. In: Toxic Metals in the Atmosphere. Nriagu, J. O. and Davidson, C. I., Eds., N. Y.: Wiley-Interscience, **1986**, 201-266.
36. Adams, F., Dams, R., Guzman, L. and Winchester, J. W. *Atmos. Environ.*, **1977**, *11*, 629-634.
37. Alkezweeny, A. J., Laulainen, N. S. and Thorp J. M. *Atmos. Environ.*, **1982**, *16*, 2421-2430.
38. Crecelius, E. A., Lepel, E. A., Laul, J. C., Rancitelli, L. A. and Mckeever, R. L. *Environ. Sci. Techn.*, **1980**, *14*, 422-428.
39. Dams, R. and De Jonge, J. *Atmos. Environ.*, **1976**, *10*, 1079-1084.
40. Davidson, C. I., Goold, W. D., Mathison, T. P., Wiersma, G. B., Brown, K. W. and Reilly, M. T. *Environ. Sci. Techn.*, **1985**, *19*, 27-35.

41. Davidson, C. I., Grimm, T. C. and Nasta, M. A. *Science*, **1981**, *214*, 1344-1346.
42. Parehk, P. P. and Husain, L. *Atmos. Environ.*, **1981**, *15*, 1717-1725.
43. Priest, P., Navarre, J-L. and Ronneau, C. *Atmos. Environ.*, **1981**, *15*, 1325-1330.
44. Rojas, C. M., Figueroa, L., Janssens, K. H., Van Espen, P. E. Adams, F. C. and Van Grieben, R. E. *The Sci. Total Environ.*, **1990**, *91*, 251-267.
45. Stevens, G. B., Dzubay, T. G., Shaw, R. W., Maclenny, W. A., Lewis, C. W. and Wilson, W. E. *Environ. Sci. Techn.*, **1980**, *14*, 1491-1498.
46. Stevens, R. K., Dzubay, T. G., Lewis, C. W. and Shaw, R. W. *Atmos. Environ.*, **1984**, *18*, 261-272.
47. Winchester, J. W., Ferek, R. J., Lawson, D. R., Pilotte, J. O. Thiemens, M. H. and Wangen, L. E. *Water, Air, Soil Pollut.*, **1979**, *12*, 431-440.
48. Winchester, J. W., Weixiu, L., Lixin, R., Mingxing, W. and Maenhaut, W. *Atmos. Environ.*, **1981**, *15*, 933-937.
49. Dutkiewicz, V. A., Pareka, P. P. and Husain, L. *Atmos. Environ.*, **1987**, *21*, 1033-1044.
50. Morales, J. A., Hermoso, M., Serrano, J. and Sanhueza, E. *Atmos. Environ.*, **1990**, *24A*, 407-414.
51. Mukai, H., Ambe, Y., Shibata, K., Muku, T., Takeshita, K., Fukuma, T., Takahashi, J. and Mizota, S. *Atmos. Environ.*, **1990**, *24A*, 1379-1390.
52. Nriagu, J. O. In: Cadmium in the Environment. Nriagu, J. O., Ed. Wiley, N.Y., 1980, 71-107.
53. Schneider, B. *Atmos. Environ.*, **1987**, *21*, 1275-1283.
54 Alpert, D J. and Hopke, P. K. *Atmos. Environ.*, **1980**, *14*, 1137-1146.
55. Barratt, R. S. *The Sci. Total Environ.*, **1988**, *72*, 211-215.
56. Bertolaccini, M. A. and Gucci, P. M. B. *The Sci. Total Environ.*, **1986**, *57, 7*-17.
57. Fidalgo, M. R., Mateos, J. and Garmendia, J. *Atmos. Environ.*, **1988**, *22*, 1495-1498.
58. Gaarenstroom, P. D., Perone, S. P. and Moyers, J. L. *Environ. Sci. Tech.*, **1977**, *11*, 795-800.
59. Gomez, M. L. S. and Martín, M. C. R. *Atmos. Environ.*, **1987**, *21*, 1521-1527.
60. Goodman, H. S., Noller, B. N., Pearman, G. I. and Bloom, H. *Clean Air*, 1976, *10*, 38-41.
61. Hopke, P. K., Gladney, E. S., Gordon, G. E. and Zoller, W. H. *Atmos. Environ.*, **1976**, *10*, 1015-1025.
62. Koutrakis, P. and Spengler, J. D. *Atmos. Environ.*, **1987**, *21*, 1511-1519.
63. Kowalczyk, G. S., Choquette, C. E. and Gordon, G. E. *Atmos. Environ.*, **1978**, *12*, 1143-1153.
64. Kowalczyk, G. S. Gordon, G. E. and Rheingrover, S. W. *Environ. Sci. Techn.*, **1982**, *16*, 79-90.
65. Moyers, J. L., Ranweiler, L. E., Hopf, S. B. and Korfe, N. E. *Environ. Sci. Tech.*, **1977**, *11*, 789-795.
66. Negi, B. S., Sadasivan, S. and Mishra, U. C. *Atmos. Environ.*, **1987**, *21*, 1259-1266.
67. Paciga, J. J. and Jervis, R. E. *Environ. Sci. Techn.*, **1976**, *10*, 1124-1128.
68. Parekh, P. P., Ghauri, B., Siddiqi, Z. R. and Husain, L. *Atmos. Environ.*, **1987**, *21*, 1267-1274.
69. Sadasivan, S. and Negi, B. S. *The Sci. Total Environ.*, **1990**, *96*, 269-279.
70. Trier, A. and Silva, C. *Atmos. Environ.*, **1987**, *21*, 977-983.
71. Tripathi, R. M., Khandekar, R. N. and Mishra, U. C. *The Sci. Total Environ.*, 1988, *77*, 237-244.
72. Yost, K. J. In: Cadmium Toxicity, Dekker, Mennear, J. H., Ed. 1979, 181-206.
73. Fergusson, J. E. and Kim, N. D. *The Sci. Total Environ.*, **1991**,*100*, 125-150.
74. Bowen, H. J. M. Environmental Chemistry of the Elements. Academic Press, New York, **1979**.
75. Batifol, F., Boutron, C. and de Angelis, M. *Nature*, **1989**, *327*, 544-546.

76. Boutron, C. F. and Wolff, E. W. *Atmos. Environ.*, **1989**, *23*, 1669-1675
77. Boutron, C. *Geochim. et Cosmochim. Acta*, **1979**, *43*, 1253-1258.
78. Boutron, C. and Martin, S. *J. Geophys. Res.*, **1980**, *85*, *C10*, 5631-5638.
79. Boutron, C. F. In: Toxic Metals in the Atmosphere. Davidson, C. I. and Nriagu, J. O., Eds. Wiley; N.Y., **1986**, 467-506.
80. Boutron, C. F. and Loris, C. *Nature*, **1979**, *277*, 551-554.
81. Boutron, C. F. and Patterson, C. C. *Geochim. et Cosmochim. Acta*, **1983**, *47*, 1355-1368.
82. Boutron, C. F., Leclerc, M. and Risler, N. *Atmos. Environ.*, **1984**, *18*, 1947-1953.
83. Boutron, C. F., Patterson, C. C., Petrov, V. N. and Barkov, N. I. *Atmos. Environ.*, **1987**, *21*, 1197-1202.
84. Heidam, N. Z. *Atmos. Environ.*, **1985**, *19*, 2083-2097.
85. Landy, M. P. and Peel, D. A. *Nature*, **1981**, *291*, 144-146.
86. Ng, A. and Patterson, C. *Geochim. et Cosmochim. Acta*, **1981**, *45*, 2109-2121.
87. Wolff, E. W. and Peel, D. A. *Ann. Glaciol.*, **1985**, *7*, 61-69.
88. Boutron, C. *Atmos. Environ.*, **1982**, *16*, 2451-2459.
89. Boutron, C. *J. Geophys. Res.*, **1980**, *85*, *C12*, 7426-7432.
90. Murozumi, M., Chow, T. C. and Patterson, C. C. *Geochim. et Cosmochim. Acta*, **1969**, *33*, 1247-94.
91. Gatz, D. F. *Atmos. Environ.* **1975**, *9*, 1-18
92. Pio, C. A., Nunes, T. V. Borrego, C. S. and Martins, J. G. *The Sci. Total Environ.*, **1989**, *80*, 279-292.
93. Fergusson, J. E. Forbes, E. A. and Schroeder, R. J. *The Sci. Total Environ.*, **1986**, *50*, 217-222.
94. Batterman, S. A., Dzubay, T. G. and Baumgardner, R. E. *Atmos. Environ.*, **1988**, *22*, 1821-1828.
95. Hopke, P. K., Lamb, R. E. and Natusch, D. F. S. *Environ. Sci. Techn.*, **1980**, *14*, 164-172.
96. Linton, R. W., Natusch, D. F. S., Solomon, R. C. and Evans C. A. *Environ. Sci. Techn.*, **1980**, *14*, 159-164.
97. Culbard, E. B., Thornton, I., Watt, J., Wheatley, M., Moorcroft, S. and Thompson, M. *J. Environ. Qual.*, **1988**, *17*, 226-234.
98. Fergusson, J. E. *Canad. J. Chem.*, **1987**, *65*, 1002-1006.
99. Fergusson, J. E. and Simmonds, P. R. *N. Z. J. Sci.*, **1983**, *26*, 219-228.
100. Johnson, D. L., Fortmann, R. and Thornton, I. *Trace Subst. Environ Health*, **1982**, *16*, 116-123.
101. Sturges, W. T. and Harrison, R. M. *The Sci. Total Environ.*, **1985**, *44*, 225-234.
102. Bornschein, R. L., Succop, P. A., Krafft, K. M. Clark, C. S., Peace, B. and Hammond, P. B. *Trace Subst. Environ. Health*, **1986**, *20*, 322-332.
103. Davies, B., Elwood, P. C., Gallacher, J. and Ginnever, R. C. *Environ. Pollut.*, **1985**, *B9*, 255-266.
104. Diemal, J. A. L. Brunekreef, B., Boleij, J. S. M., Biersteker, K. and Veinstra, S. *J. Environ. Res.*, **1981**, *25*, 449-456.
105. Fergusson, J. E. and Schroeder, R. J. *The Sci. Total Environ.*, **1985**, *46*, 61-72.
106. Harper, M., Sullivan, K. R. and Quinn, M. J. *Environ. Sci. Techn.*, **1987**, *21*, 481-484.
107. Kim, N. D. and Fergusson, J. E. In:Trace Elements in New Zealand Environment, Human and Animal. Proc. New Zealand Trace Elem. Gp. Conf., McLaren, R. G., Haynes, J. R. and Savage, G. P., Eds. **1988**, 193-200.
108. Kim. N. D. and Fergusson, J. E. Unpublished results, **1990**.
109. Thornton, I., Culbard, E., Moorcroft, S., Watt, J., Wheatley, M., Thompson, M. and Thomas, J. F. A. *Environ. Techn. Lett.*, **1985**, *6*, 137-144.

RECEIVED September 27, 1991

Chapter 6

Anthropogenic Contaminants

Atmospheric Transport, Deposition, and Potential Effects on Terrestrial Ecosystems

Thomas J. Moser[1], Jerry R. Barker[1], and David T. Tingey[2]

[1]ManTech Environmental Technology Inc., 200 SW 35th Street, Corvallis, OR 97333
[2]Environmental Research Laboratory, U.S. Environmental Protection Agency, 200 SW 35th Street, Corvallis, OR 97333

Through the processes of atmospheric transport and deposition, many anthropogenic contaminants such as industrial organics, pesticides, and trace metals have become widely distributed around the globe. Due to the phenomenon of long-range atmospheric transport, even the most remote areas of the planet are not out of range of contaminants emitted from distant anthropogenic sources. Many of these airborne contaminants are toxic and persistent, can bioaccumulate, and may remain biologically harmful for long periods of time. Although airborne contaminants are considered primarily a human health problem, there is increasing concern that they may have deleterious ecological consequences. When sensitive terrestrial plants and other biota experience chronic exposure to low concentrations of airborne toxic chemicals, sublethal effects may occur, with subsequent impacts on ecosystem structure and function.

A large variety and quantity of contaminants are being released into the environment from point, area, and mobile anthropogenic sources. Once released, these contaminants may become widely dispersed via the fluid dynamics of surface waters and the atmosphere. The atmosphere is responsible for the long-range dissemination of contaminants over regional, hemispherical and global scales due to its dynamic nature and its ability to move contaminants rapidly. Through the processes of atmospheric transport and deposition, toxic chemicals have found their way to remote environments far from emission sources. Recent data strongly suggest that the enriched concentrations of several contaminants detected in the abiotic and biotic components of rural and remote environments are the result of long-range atmospheric transport from urban-industrial and agricultural sources (1-6). Many of these chemicals are toxic and persistent, can bioaccumulate, and may remain biologically active for long periods of time.

0097–6156/92/0483–0134$06.00/0
© 1992 American Chemical Society

An airborne pollutant can be broadly defined as any chemical occurring in the atmosphere in concentrations and exposure durations that may pose a threat to human health or the environment. This broad definition includes an array of chemicals ranging from the criteria pollutants (e.g., ozone, sulfur dioxide), which have resulted in well-documented biological effects at local and regional scales, to the greenhouse gases (e.g., methane, chlorofluorocarbons), with their implications for global warming and stratospheric ozone depletion. Another group of chemicals, often referred to as 'air toxics' or 'airborne contaminants', include a large number and variety of chemical species broadly categorized as industrial organics, agricultural pesticides, and trace metals and metalloids. These contaminants have strong anthropogenic emission sources and are known to be transported long distances (hundreds to thousands of kilometers) in the troposphere before being deposited into remote environments.

The recent publication of the U.S. Environmental Protection Agency's Toxic Release Inventory (TRI) (7) has heightened the concern over the nation's air quality. Although this concern has been directed primarily at human health effects in urban-industrial areas, there is increasing concern among scientists that adverse ecological impacts may result from the deposition of toxic chemicals into natural ecosystems and the subsequent exposure of plants and other biota. The chronic exposure of vegetation to low concentrations of airborne toxic chemicals may result in sublethal effects, such as decreased plant productivity, vigor, and reproduction. Exposure may culminate in changes in plant community composition and ecosystem structure and function. This paper presents an overview of contaminant emission sources, atmospheric transport and deposition processes, evidence of the long-range transport of contaminants, and the potential effects of contaminants on terrestrial vegetation and ecosystems.

Anthropogenic Emission Sources

Although humans have been responsible for emitting contaminants into the atmosphere for thousands of years, air pollution has increased exponentially, both in quantity and variety, since the industrial revolution. Anthropogenic contaminants emanate from a host of different industrial, urban, and agricultural sources (Figure 1) such as: chemical, metal, plastic, and paper/pulp industries; fossil fuel processing plants; motor vehicles and aircraft; municipal waste incinerators; agricultural practices such as pesticide usage and field burning; and small businesses such as dry cleaners (7-9). Emissions of toxic chemicals into the atmosphere may occur directly, through deliberate or inadvertent release from industrial or urban sources, or indirectly, through volatilization following the deliberate or accidental discharge of chemicals into water or soil. Considerable amounts of toxic chemicals enter the atmosphere from wind drift and volatilization during and following agricultural pesticide applications (10). Glotfelty et al. (11) reported the significance of fog as an atmospheric phenomenon for concentrating and transporting pesticides at levels frequently exceeding 10 μg/L.

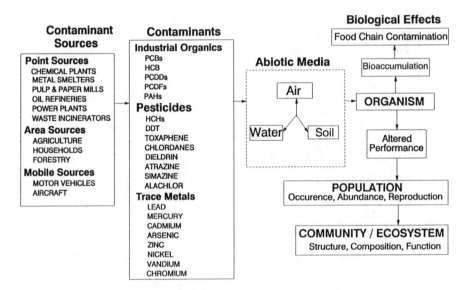

Figure 1. Conceptual model illustrating examples of major anthropogenic contaminant sources and contaminants, their distribution within the abiotic environmental media, their movement into biota with potential food chain contamination, and potential effects at the organismal, population, community and ecosystem level of organization.

Worldwide, over 63,000 chemicals are commonly used (*12*). The world's chemical industry markets an estimated 200 to 1,000 new synthetic chemicals, annually (*13*). Many of these chemicals eventually are emitted into the atmosphere. Industry is probably the major anthropogenic source of airborne toxic chemicals (*7, 14*). According to the TRI estimates, United States industries emitted more than 1×10^9 kg of toxic chemicals into the atmosphere, both in 1987 and 1988 (*7*). The TRI underestimated the actual air emissions as it did not include air emissions from numerous area sources (e.g., agriculture, households), mobile sources (e.g., motor vehicles), some industrial categories such as petroleum tank farms, federal facilities, companies with fewer than 10 employees, and urban businesses (e.g., dry cleaners), nor did the report consider volatilization of toxic chemicals from contaminated soils and water. Another group of environmental contaminants not considered by the TRI are the polycyclic aromatic hydrocarbons (PAHs), which are released into the atmosphere during the combustion of fossil fuels, waste incineration and agricultural burning (*15*).

The application of pesticides to agricultural, forest and household lands is likely a significant source of atmospheric contaminants. Atmospheric loads of pesticide residues can arise as aerosols transported by wind during initial spraying, by volatilization from soil and plant surfaces, or by attachment to airborne soil particles. Agricultural lands account for approximately 75% of the pesticide usage in the United States (*16*). Approximately 4.55×10^6 kg of pesticide active ingredients are used annually on 16% of the total land area of the United States (*16*). The magnitude of pesticide residues entering the atmosphere during and following application is not well known, but is likely significant (*10*). Aside from the obvious atmospheric contaminant loadings that occur during spray applications of pesticides, volatilization of deposited pesticides from soil and plant surfaces can be as large as 90% of the amount applied, even for chemicals with relatively low vapor pressures (*17*). In a regional study, Glotfelty et al. (*18*) reported that atmospheric transport and deposition resulted in low-level but widespread contamination of the Chesapeake Bay. Measurable concentrations of the herbicides, atrazine and simazine existed at all times of the year in the Maryland airshed. These authors estimated that annual pesticide deposition (summer rainfall only) into Chesapeake Bay during the early 1980s ranged from 0.6 to 1.2 metric tons of atrazine, 0.11 to 0.14 metric ton of simazine, 2.4 to 9.8 metric tons of alachlor, and 0.54 to 1.1 metric tons of toxaphene.

Although numerous toxic chemicals are released from anthropogenic sources, organochlorine compounds and several trace metals are of particular concern. Organochlorines are significant environmental contaminants due to their high stability and persistence in the environment, their chronic toxicity, their proven ability for bioaccumulation and biomagnification in food chains, and the large quantities that have been manufactured, used, and released into environmental media (*19-21*). Organochlorines represent a large class of chemicals that includes synthetic industrial organics (and their by-products) such as polychlorinated biphenyls (PCBs), hexachlorobenzene (HCB), polychlorinated dibenzodioxins (PCDD), and polychlorinated dibenzofurans (PCDF), and pesticides such as DDT, hexachlorocyclohexane (HCH) and toxaphene.

Unlike synthetic organic contaminants, airborne trace metals have significant natural sources such as volcanoes, wind-borne soil particles, sea-salt spray, forest fires, and various biogenic sources (22, 23). Global estimates of both natural and anthropogenic trace metal emissions into the atmosphere suggest, however, that urban-industrial sources contribute significantly to atmospheric trace metal inputs. For example, ratios of anthropogenic-to-natural emissions for lead, cadmium, vanadium, zinc, nickel, arsenic and mercury were reported to be approximately 27.7, 5.8, 3.1, 2.9, 1.9, 1.6, and 1.4, respectively (23). All trace metals, even those with essential biochemical functions, have the potential to produce adverse biological effects at excessive levels of exposure. However, trace metals such as mercury, cadmium, lead, and arsenic are of particular environmental concern because they are biologically nonessential and are toxic to most organisms at relatively low concentrations (24). The deposition of persistent synthetic organics and trace metals into terrestrial ecosystems not only results in increasing concentrations of these contaminants in vegetation and soils, but also increases the contamination and risk to organisms at higher trophic levels such as herbivores, detritivores, and carnivores (19, 20, 25, 26).

Atmospheric Transport and Deposition Processes

On a global scale, the atmosphere serves as the major pathway for the transport and deposition of contaminants from emission sources to terrestrial and aquatic ecosystem receptors (22, 27). Once a contaminant is airborne, the processes of atmospheric diffusion, transport, transformation, and deposition act to determine its fate. These processes are complex and the degree to which they influence the fate of a particular contaminant is dependent on its physico-chemical characteristics, the properties and concentrations of coexisting substances, and the prevailing meteorological conditions, including wind, precipitation, humidity, temperature, clouds, fog, and solar irradiation.

The simultaneous atmospheric processes of diffusion and transport are responsible for the dispersion of contaminants after their initial release from emission sources (22). Gaseous and particulate contaminants are dispersed horizontally and vertically through the lower atmosphere by turbulent diffusion, vertical wind shear, and precipitation. Contaminant transport is a result of local, regional, and global air mass circulations. The atmospheric residence times of individual contaminants, along with the factors stated earlier, determine their transport distances. Depending on emission source factors and meteorological conditions, and on the their physical and chemical properties, airborne contaminants may be deposited close to the source or be carried great distances by the wind before being deposited to surface receptors. Atmospheric residence times depend upon such characteristics as mode and rate of emission, atmospheric transformations, physical state (gas, solid, or liquid), particle size, and chemical reactivity (9, 22, 28).

Atmospheric aerosols (suspensions of solid or liquid particles in a gas) contain particles with diameters ranging from approximately $0.002\,\mu m$ to $100\,\mu m$ (*28*). With respect to atmospheric chemistry, the most important particles are in the $0.002\,\mu m$ to $10\,\mu m$ range. Particles with diameters greater than $2.5\,\mu m$ are usually referred to as large or coarse particles, while those with diameters less than $2.5\,\mu m$ are identified as small or fine particles. Because of their relatively large size, coarse particles usually settle out of the atmosphere rapidly due to gravitational sedimentation. The smallest sized fraction (diameters less than $0.08\,\mu m$) of the fine particle grouping, often referred to as Aitken nuclei, have short atmospheric lifetimes due to their rapid coagulation. The mid-sized fraction (diameters ranging between $0.08\,\mu m$ and $2\,\mu m$) of the fine particle grouping, known as the accumulation mode, is considered significant for air pollutants as these particles contain high levels of organic and trace metal contaminants. Because of their small size, accumulation-mode, fine particles do not settle out of the atmosphere rapidly by gravitational sedimentation and are removed more slowly by dry and wet deposition (*27*). Consequently, fine particles in this size range tend to have longer atmospheric residence times, and the potential for long-range transport is greater.

In general, short atmospheric residence times for contaminants correlate with coarse particle size, high reactivity (i.e., likely to be transformed to secondary products), and water solubility. Chemicals that remain as fine particles or that are sparingly water soluble may have atmospheric residence times of several weeks or months. Toxic chemicals that are persistent and have high vapor pressures are more likely to enter the atmosphere and reach remote areas. Many organochlorine compounds are transported over long distances because of their physico-chemical characteristics of relatively high volatility, low water solubility, and high chemical stability.

Although high vapor pressure indicates greater partitioning of the chemical into the atmosphere, this factor alone cannot be used to discount the importance of the atmosphere as the transport mechanism of chemicals with low vapor pressures. For example, synthetic organics with low vapor pressures that also have low water solubilities tend to volatilize from water or moist soil surfaces into the atmosphere, despite their low vapor pressures (*29, 30, 31, 32*). Henry's law coefficients (ratio of vapor pressure to water solubility) is an important indicator of the significance of the atmospheric pathway for toxic organic contaminants (*30, 31*). In addition, many synthetic organics and trace metals are either emitted directly into the atmosphere as fine particles or are adsorbed on atmospheric particles. Retention and long-distance transport of fine particles by the atmosphere is considered significant.

Transformation of parent contaminants into secondary products may occur during the processes of atmospheric diffusion and transport as a result of physical, chemical, and photochemical processes (*22*). Chemical conversion within the atmosphere may also change the physico-chemical characteristics of contaminants, dramatically altering their atmospheric residence times and fates from those of the parent contaminants. The complex reactions within the atmosphere that are driven by chemical processes such as hydroxyl scavenging or solar irradience may result in the formation of products that can be more or less toxic than the parent compounds.

Deposition is the atmospheric removal process by which gaseous and particulate contaminants are transferred from the atmosphere to surface receptors -- soil, vegetation, and surface waters (22, 27, 28, 32). This process has been conveniently separated into two categories -- dry and wet deposition. Dry deposition is a direct transfer process that removes contaminants from the atmosphere without the intervention of precipitation, and therefore may occur continuously. Wet deposition involves the removal of contaminants from the atmosphere in an aqueous form and is therefore dependent on the precipitation events of rain, snow, or fog.

Evidence of Long-Range Atmospheric Transport and Deposition

The transport of airborne contaminants downwind from point sources has received a great deal of attention since the beginning of this century due to the damaging effects of the plumes on vegetation (33). Vegetation damage in areas surrounding pollutant point sources has generally decreased through emission control technologies, but adverse effects resulting from regionally distributed pollutants (e.g., oxidant air pollutants, acid precipitation precursors) still persist. During the last 10 to 20 years, however, the phenomenon of long-range atmospheric transport has drawn more attention and has been implicated in the wide distribution of anthropogenic contaminants on regional to global scales. Synthetic industrial organics, pesticide residues, and trace metals have been detected in the air, water, soil, and biota of rural and remote areas such as the Arctic and Subarctic (34-44), the Antarctic (45-47), high-elevation forests and lakes (48, 49), the Great Lakes (50, 51), peatlands, (52, 53, 54, 55), and open oceans and seas (56, 57, 58).

Perhaps the best evidence of long-range atmospheric transport and deposition of contaminants is the data generated from investigations conducted in peatlands and arctic environments. Ombrotrophic peatland ecosystems are considered ideal for establishing trends in contaminant deposition (59). Ombrotrophic bogs are isolated from surface and ground waters, and thus receive all their hydrologic, nutrient, and mineral inputs from the atmosphere. Secondly, due to the acidity of bogs, microbial activity is low, resulting in reduced transformation and degradation of anthropogenic organic chemicals. Lastly, due to the bog's high organic matter content, hydrophobic contaminants adsorb strongly to peat, minimizing depositional mobility. Because of these attributes, dated peat cores have been used to reconstruct the historical record of environmental exposure of remote areas to atmospherically derived chemicals, such as synthetic organic contaminants, which have not been continuously measured at any site since the beginning of their commercial production and use. Using dated peat cores from ombrotrophic bogs, Rapaport and Eisenreich (53, 55) demonstrated unequivocal evidence for chronic atmospheric deposition of PCBs, DDT, HCHs, HCB, and toxaphene across the mid-latitudes of eastern North America, and correlated their historical accumulation rates with production and use in the United States. Although the production and use of PCBs, DDT, HCHs, and toxaphene have been banned or restricted in the United States, Rapaport and Eisenreich (55) concluded that atmospheric deposition of these organochlorines to peat bogs of eastern North America is still occurring, and that atmospherically derived fluxes of DDT to these peat bogs are approximately 10-20% of the levels that occurred during the peak DDT usage of the 1960s. They postulated that the recent flux of DDT is a result of long-range atmospheric transport from Mexico and Central America, where this pesticide is still used in substantial quantities (52).

Arctic regions have few significant, local anthropogenic sources of contaminants. However, during the last decade, it has become increasingly evident that the Arctic is the receptor of long-range, atmospherically transported chemical contaminants originating from anthropogenic sources located in more southern latitudes. Synthetic industrial organics and pesticides such as PCBs, DDT, toxaphene, chlordane, HCB, HCHs, aldrin, and dieldrin, which are produced and used in urban-industrial and agricultural regions of temperate and subtropical latitudes of North America and Eurasia, have been detected in measurable quantities in the abiotic and biotic components of arctic ecosystems. For example, average air concentrations for two sites in the Canadian high Arctic during sampling periods in 1986, 1987, and 1988 ranged between 183 and 577 pg/m^3 for HCH, 74 and 189 pg/m^3 for HCB, 35 and 44 pg/m^3 for toxaphene, 15 and 38 pg/m^3 for PCBs, 3 and 10 pg/m^3 for chlordane, and 1 and 5 pg/m^3 for DDT (p,p'-DDT + p,p'-DDE) (40, 43, 57). At three sites in the same geographic region, Gregor (42) reported that the annual snowpack concentration for total HCH in 1986 ranged between 650 and 11,106 pg/L. Larsson et al. (21) and Bidleman et al. (60) provide evidence of an atmospheric link for various organochlorine contaminants to arctic terrestrial and marine food chains, respectively.

Environmental Partitioning and Vegetation Exposure

Biota are exposed to toxic chemicals through the environmental media of air, water, and soil (Figure 1). After atmospheric deposition to terrestrial ecosystems, the fate of a contaminant depends on its environmental partitioning, which dictates its potential impact on vegetation and other biota (61). For example, trace metals tend to accumulate on soil surfaces by their adsorption to organic matter and clay particles (25). Trace metal accumulation may reduce plant growth and vigor through the disruption of nutrient uptake by the roots and decreased organic matter decomposition by soil microorganisms. Gaseous chemicals reside in the atmosphere with the potential to disrupt plant-leaf biochemical processes (e.g., photosynthesis, respiration) after absorption through the stomata or cuticle (32). Because of the lipophilic nature of many synthetic organics, the waxy cuticle of plant leaves may accumulate high levels of these substances (26, 62, 63).

Transfer of toxic chemicals among ecosystem compartments often occurs. For example, trace metals may be absorbed by plant roots or deposited onto the leaves and then transferred to the soil through tissue loss and decay (64). Contaminants may also be passed along food chains through herbivory with the potential for biomagnification (19, 25, 63, 64). The deposition of airborne toxic chemicals deposited into agricultural ecosystems may contaminate human food resources (65).

Potential Impacts on Terrestrial Vegetation and Ecosystems

Scientists have recognized that air pollutants such as ozone, sulfur dioxide, fluoride, acid precipitation, and certain trace metals can adversely impact agricultural and natural plant communities (61, 66-68). Emissions of sulfur dioxide, hydrogen fluoride, trace metals, and other toxics from pulp and paper mills, ore smelters, and power plants have severely reduced vegetation cover, biodiversity, and ecosystem integrity downwind from point sources (33, 61, 69, 70). In addition to the localized adverse effects near point sources, atmospheric pollutants have also caused regional damage to agricultural crops and natural plant communities through exposure to chemical oxidants such as ozone and peroxyacetyl nitrates, or acid precipitation (67, 68, 71, 72).

Although the effects on vegetation from most criteria pollutants are well documented in the literature, little is known regarding the effects from airborne contaminants transported and deposited in rural and remote environments. Weinstein and Birk (61) suggest that the "chemical substances that may have the most substantial effect on terrestrial ecosystems over the long term are those that are dispersed over wide regions at concentrations that induce sub-lethal, chronic, physiological stress." These authors also suggest that changes in ecosystem structure and function from such chronic exposures may not be fully manifested for long periods, and once expressed these changes may be irreversible.

The potential biological effects of airborne contaminants on terrestrial vegetation can be mediated through individual plants to the community and ecosystem (61). Although the adverse impacts cannot be specified in detail, as plant species and ecosystem types react differently to stress, chronic exposure to airborne contaminants may lead to a cascading effect in which the following stages may be observed (Figure 1): (1) disruption of biochemical or physiological processes of sensitive plant species resulting in altered performance (73), (2) reduction in growth, reproduction, and abundance of sensitive populations (74), and (3) alteration in the composition, structure, and function of plant communities and terrestrial ecosystems (25, 66, 75). The type and magnitude of these effects depends on the pattern of exposure (e.g., duration, concentration, frequency, season) that individual plants receive, their sensitivity to the contaminant, and the phytotoxicity of the chemical.

This cascading effect may have been best demonstrated from interdisciplinary research addressing the consequences of chronic oxidant air pollution exposure to the mixed conifer forests of the San Bernardino Mountains of Southern California. Miller et al. (76) reported that chronic exposure to oxidant air pollutants resulted in decreased photosynthetic capacity, premature leaf fall, reduced growth and seed production, and lower nutritive content in the living foliage of sensitive pine species. Subsequently, the weakened trees became more susceptible to fungal disease and insect attack. Increased pine defoliation and mortality resulted in increased litter depth, hindering pine seedling establishment; while, encouraging oxidant pollution-tolerant, fire-adapted plant species establishment in the understory. Miller et al. (76) concluded that the gradual destruction of this pine-dominated forest will eventually result in a less desirable, self-perpetuating community of shrub and oak species that will inhibit the natural reestablishment of pine and other conifer species.

After contaminant absorption by the plants through the leaves or roots, biochemical processes are the first affected. If enzymatic degradation detoxifies the pollutant, then no injury will occur. However, if enzymatic action cannot render the pollutant or its metabolites harmless, then alterations in plant metabolism may result in foliar injury, altered carbohydrate and nutrient allocation, and reduced growth and reproductive capability (72). The degree of impact to the plant depends on the toxicity of the pollutant and its exposure pattern. Acute exposures usually cause observable morphological damage, such as leaf lesions, stunted growth, or even death. Plant death resulting from acute exposure is usually localized when it does occur, for example, when an inordinate amount of toxic chemical exposure occurs via an accidental release or pesticide wind drift.

Chronic, sublethal exposures may not induce observable morphological damage; they may, however, alter biochemical pathways, which can result in decreased vigor and productivity, altered phenology, loss of tissue, or reduced reproductive potential. Altered physiological processes cause a loss of vigor and render the plant more susceptible to insect damage or disease (74, 77). With continual exposure, even at sublethal concentrations, sensitive plant populations may decrease in numbers, allowing tolerant species to become dominant. Thus, shifts in plant community structure and composition could result in decreased biological diversity and altered ecosystem functions (74, 77).

Plant damage resulting from acute air toxic exposures are usually limited in time and space as a result of control technology and legislation. However, sublethal, chronic exposure to airborne contaminants may predispose vegetation to other natural stressors and induce damage or mortality (77). Even though airborne contaminant damage may not cause permanent functional loss, the diversion of biochemical resources to repair the injury can inhibit normal plant functions and retard plant growth. Thus, physiological stress induced by airborne contaminants may predispose a plant to other stressors such as frost, drought, insects, or disease (74).

When an airborne toxic chemical is introduced into a plant community, some plants will be more affected than others depending on individual tolerances endowed by their genotype, as well as on their phenology, and various modifying microclimatic variables. The sensitive plants or species that are no longer able to compete adequately with the tolerant plants or species will be partially or completely replaced. Some scientists propose that the widespread forest tree decline is not the result of a single agent but of an interaction among chronic exposures to air pollutants and natural stressors (*78, 79*).

Airborne contaminants may also have indirect effects on vegetation by directly affecting other organisms critically associated with the plants. Soil microorganisms and invertebrates are critical in ecosystems for litter decomposition and nutrient cycling. Accumulation of trace metals within the organic horizon of the soil may limit organic matter decomposition and nutrient availability to plants (*25*). Many plants rely on insects for pollination. Airborne contaminants arising from anthropogenic activities (e.g., agricultural insecticide use, power plant emissions) have been shown to adversely impact beneficial insect populations (*80, 81, 82*), with the potential to result in inadequate flower pollination and subsequent seed and fruit set.

The effects caused by airborne contaminants on vegetation can indirectly affect animals within the system through impacts on food chains and habitat requirements. The best documented effect is biomagnification of contaminants through the food chain (*19, 83, 84*). As vegetation provides substantial depositional surface area, and since plants are the beginning of the terrestrial food chains, contaminants accumulated by plants (either internally or as external foliar contamination) are made available to herbivores. Biomagnification of contaminants occurs when the organisms in the food chain do not have the ability to detoxify or eliminate the chemical from their systems, resulting in increased concentrations within the organism. Radio-ecological investigations of the lichen--caribou--man food chain convincingly demonstrated that radionuclide, particularly cesium-137 and strontium-90, concentrations increased through this relatively simple food chain and that radionuclide adsorption by aerial parts of plants was the most important entry route into the food chain (85, 86). In a study conducted on the Scandinavian peninsula, Larsson et al. (*21*) provides data demonstrating a positive correlation between the atmospheric deposition of PCBs, DDT, and lindane (γHCH) and the concentrations of these persistent contaminants contained in terrestrial herbivores and predators. The authors postulated that the entry route into the food chain was herbivory of contaminated vegetation. Biomagnification of contaminants through food chains has resulted in adverse consequences to animals, particularly carnivores (*19*). For example, the population decline of peregrine falcons in Great Britain during the 1950s and 1960s was caused by the contamination of their food chain by dieldrin (*13*).

Potential impacts of contaminants on habitat are reductions in cover and quality. The loss of preferred habitat may leave animals more susceptible to predation and disease. Loss of reproductive habitat may result in fewer animals reproducing in a given season or exposing the young to increased predation. For some animal populations, then, habitat changes may lead to decreased reproduction, increased mortality, and increased emigration.

Conclusion

Numerous anthropogenic sources and activities are responsible for releasing a large volume of persistent and toxic chemicals into the atmosphere. As supported by scientific evidence, many of these contaminants are transported long distances and deposited in rural and remote locations. The impacts from the chronic deposition of airborne toxic chemicals on various levels of ecosystem organization and their potential interaction with natural stresses to induce antagonistic to synergistic effects are unknown. The fact that many airborne chemicals pose hazards to human health is only one aspect of the problem. The continued deposition of airborne toxic chemicals on a regional to global scale will affect public welfare if it results in adverse impacts on the structure and function of sensitive ecosystems.

Acknowledgments

The research described in this document has been funded wholly by the U.S. Environmental Protection Agency. This manuscript has been subjected to the Agency's peer and administrative review, and it has been approved for publication as an EPA document. Mention of trade names or commercial products does not constitute endorsement or recommendation for use.

Literature Cited

1. Björseth, A.; Lunde, G.; Lindskog, A. *Atmos. Environ.* **1979**, *13*, 45-53.
2. Rahn, K.A. *Atmos. Environ.* **1981**, *15*, 1447-1455.
3. Rahn, K.A.; Lowenthal, D.H. *Science* **1984**, *223*, 132-139.
4. Jones, K.C.; Stratford, J.A.; Tidridge, P.; Waterhouse, K.S.; Johnston, A.E. *Environ. Pollut.* **1989**, *56*, 337-351.
5. Atlas, E.L.; Schauffler, S. In *Long Range Transport of Pesticides*; Kurtz, D.A. Ed.; Lewis Publishers, Inc.: Chelsea, MI, 1990; pp 161-183.
6. Levy, H., II. In *Long Range Transport of Pesticides*; Kurtz, D.A. Ed.; Lewis Publishers, Inc.: Chelsea, MI, 1990; pp 83-95.
7. *Toxics in the Community: National and Local Perspectives;* U.S. Environmental Protection Agency: U.S. Government Printing Office, Washington, D.C., 1990; EPA560/4-90-017.
8. Freedman, B.; Hutchinson, T.C. In *Effect of Heavy Metal Pollution on Plants: Volume 2 Metals in the Environment*; Lepp, N.W. Ed.; Applied Science Publishers: Englewood, NJ, 1981; pp 35-94.
9. Schroeder, W.H.; Dobson, M.; Kane, D.M.; Johnson, N.D. *JAPCA* **1987**, *37*, 1267-1285.
10. Waddel, T.E.; Bower, B.T. *Managing Agricultural Chemicals in the Environment: the Case for a Multimedia Approach*; The Conservation Foundation: Washington, D.C., 1988; pp 42-43.
11. Glotfelty, D.E.; Seiber, J.N.; Liljedahl, L.A. *Nature* **1987**, *325*, 602-605.
12. Maugh, T.H. *Science* **1978**, *199*, 162.

13.   *Ecotoxicology: The Study of Pollutants in Ecosystems*; Moriarty, F., Ed., Academic Press: New York, 1988; p 289.

14.   Nriagu, J.O.; Pacyna, J.M. *Nature* **1988**, *333*, 134- 139.

15.   Edwards, N.T. *J. Environ. Qual.* **1983**, *12*, 427-441.

16.   Pimentel, D.; Levitan, L. *BioScience* **1986**, *36*, 86- 91.

17.   Spencer, W.F.; Cliath, M.M. In *Long Range Transport of Pesticides*; Kurtz, D.A. Ed.; Lewis Publishers, Inc.: Chelsea, MI, 1990; pp 1-16.

18.   Glotfelty, D.E.; Williams, G.H.; Freeman, H.P.; Leech, M.M. In *Long Range Transport of Pesticides*; Kurtz, D.A. Ed.; Lewis Publishers, Inc.: Chelsea, MI, 1990; pp 199-221.

19.   Stickel, W.H. In *Ecological Toxicology Research: Effects of Heavy Metal and Organochlorine Compounds*; McIntyre A.D.; Mills, C.F. Eds.; Plenum Press: New York, 1975; pp 25-74.

20.   Muir, D.C.G.; Norstrom, R.J.; Simon, M. *Environ. Sci. Technol.* **1988**, *22*, 1071-1079.

21.   Larsson, P.; Okla, L.; Woin, P. *Environ. Sci. Technol.* **1990**, *24*, 1559-1601.

22.   Schroeder, W.H.; Lane, D.A. *Environ. Sci. Technol.* **1988**, *22*, 240-246.

23.   Nriagu, J.O. *Nature* **1989**, *338*, 47-49.

24.   Nriagu, J.O. *Environ. Pollut.* **1988**, *50*, 139-161.

25.   Martin, M.H.; Coughtrey, P.J. In *Effect of Heavy Metal Pollution on Plants: Volume 2 Metals in the Environment*; Lepp, N.W. Ed.; Applied Science Publishers: Englewood, NJ, 1981; pp 119-158.

26.   Buckley, E.H. *Science* **1982**, *216*, 520-522.

27.   Bidleman, T.E. *Environ. Sci. Technol.* **1988**, *22*, 361- 367.

28.   Sehmel, G.A. *Atmos. Environ.* **1980**, *14*, 983-1011.

29.   Spencer, W.F.; Cliath, M.M.; Jury, W.A.; Zhang, L. *J. Environ. Qual.* **1988**, *17*, 504-509.

30.   Mackay, D.; Paterson, S.; Schroeder, W.H. *Environ. Sci. Technol.* **1986**, *20*, 810-816.

31.   Canton, R.B.; Schroeder, W.H.; Young, J.W.S. *Int. J. Environ. Studies* **1988**, *31*, 111-127.

32.   Foster, J.R. In *Ecological Exposure and Effects of Airborne Toxic Chemicals: An Overview*; Moser, T.J.; Barker, J.R.; Tingey, D.T. Eds.; U.S. Environmental Protection Agency: Environmental Research Laboratory, Corvallis, 1991; pp 60-89; EPA/600/3-91/001.

33.   Gordon, A.G.; Gorham, E. *Can. J. Bot.* **1963**, *41*, 1063-1078.

34.   Thomas, W. *Water Sci. Technol.* **1986**, *18*, 47-57.

35.   Steinnes, E. In *Lead, Mercury, Cadmium and Arsenic in the Environment*.

36.   Hutchinson, T.C.; Meema, K.M. Eds.; John Wiley & Sons Ltd.: 1987; pp 107-117.

37.   Hargrave, B.T.; Vass, W.P.; Erickson, P.E.; Fowler, B.R. *Tellus* **1988**, *40*, 480-493.

38.   Norstrom, R.J.; Simon, M.; Muir, D.C.G.; Schweinsburg, R.E. *Environ. Sci. Technol.* **1988**, *22*, 1063-1070.

39.   Pacyna, J.M.; Oehme, M. *Atmos. Environ.* **1988**, *22*, 243-257.

40. Patton, G.W.; Hinckley, D.A.; Walla, M.D.; Bidleman, T.F.; Hargrave, B.T. Tellus, **1989**, *41*, 243-245.
41. Steinnes, E. *Toxicol. Environ. Chem.* **1989**, *19*, 139- 145.
42. Gregor, D.J. In *Long Range Transport of Pesticides*; Kurtz, D.A. Ed.; Lewis Publishers, Inc.: Chelsea, MI, 1990; pp 373-386.
43. Patton, G.W.; Walla, M.D.; Bidleman, T.F.; Barrie, L.A. *J. Geophys. Res.* **1991**, *96*, 10,867-10,877.
44. Welch, H.E.; Muir, D.C.G.; Billeck, B.N.; Lockhart, W.L.; Brunskill, G.J.; Kling, J.J.; Olson, M.P.; Lemoine, R.M. *Environ. Sci. Technol.* **1991**, *25*, 280-286.
45. Tanabe, S.; Hidaka, H.; Tatsukawaw, R. *Chemosphere* **1983**, *12*, 277-288.
46. Bacci, E.; Calamair, D.; Gaggi, C.; Fanelli, R.; Focardi, S.; Morosini, M. *Chemosphere* **1986**, *15*, 747- 754.
47. Luke, B.G.; Johnstone, G.W.; Woehler, E.J. *Chemosphere* **1989**, *12*, 2007-2021.
48. Friedland, A.J.; Johnson, A.H.; Siccama, T.G. *Water, Air, Soil Pollut.* **1984**, *21*, 161-170.
49. Heit, M.; Klusek, C.; Baron, J. *Water, Air, Soil Pollut.* **1984**, *22*, 403-416.
50. Eisenreich, S.J. *Environ. Sci. Technol.* **1981**, *15*, 30-38.
51. Swackhamer, D.L.; Hites, R.A. *Environ. Sci. Technol.* **1988**, *22*, 543-548.
52. Rapaport, R.A.; Urban, N.R.; Capel, P.D.; Baker, J.E.; Looney, B.B.; Eisenreich, S.J.; Gorham, E. *Chemosphere* **1985**, *14*, 1167-1173.
53. Rapaport, R.A.; Eisenreich, S.J. *Atmos. Environ.* **1986**, *20*, 2367-2379.
54. Urban, N.R.; Eisenreich, S.J.; Gorham, E. *Can. J. Fish. Aquat. Sci.* **1987**, *44*, 1165-1172.
55. Rapaport, R.A.; Eisenreich, S.J. *Environ. Sci. Technol.* **1988**, *22*, 931-941.
56. Atlas, E.A.; Giam, C.S. *Science* **1981**, *211*, 163-165.
57. Hargrave, B.T.; Vass, W.P.; Erickson, P.E.; Fowler, B.R. *Tellus*, **1988**, *40*, 480-493.
58. Hinckley, D.A.; Bidleman, T.F.; Rice, C.P. *J. Geophys. Res.* **1991**, *96*, 7201-7213.
59. Urban, N.R. In *Ecological Exposure and Effects of Airborne Toxic Chemicals: An Overview*; Moser, T.J.; Barker, J.R.; Tingey, D.T. Eds.; U.S. Environmental Protection Agency: Environmental Research Laboratory, Corvallis, 1991; pp 90-101; EPA/600/3-91/001.
60. Bidleman, T.F.; Patton, G.W.; Walla, M.D.; Hargrave, B.T.; Vass, W.P.; Erickson, P.; Fowler, B.; Scott, V; Gregor, D.J. *Arctic* **1989**, *42*, 307-313.
61. Weinstein, D.A.; Birk, E.M. In *Ecotoxicology: Problems and Approaches*; Levin, S.A.; Harwell, M.A.; Kelly, J.R.; Kimball, K.D., Eds.; Springer-Verlag: New York, NY, 1989; pp 181-212.
62. Travis, C.C.; Hattemer-Frey, H.A. *Chemosphere* **1988**, *17*, 277-283.
63. Reischl, A.; Reissinger, M.; Thoma, H.; Hutzinger, O. *Chemosphere* **1989**, *18*, 561-568.
64. Hughes, M.K. In *Effect of Heavy Metal Pollution on Plants: Volume 2 Metals in the Environment*; Lepp, N.W. Ed.; Applied Science Publishers: Englewood, NJ, 1981; pp 95-118.

65.   Webber, J. In *Effect of Heavy Metal Pollution on Plants: Volume 2 Metals in the Environment*; Lepp, N.W. Ed.; Applied Science Publishers: Englewood, NJ, 1981; pp 159-184.

66.   Bormann, F.H. *BioScience* **1985**, *35*, 434-441.

67.   Tingey, D.T. In *Perspectives in Environmental Botany*; Rao, D.N; Ahmad, K.J.; Yunus, M; Singh, S.N. Eds.; Print House: Luchnow, India, 1985; pp 1-25.

68.   MacKenzie, J.J.; El-Ashry, M.T. In *Air Pollution's Toll on Forests and Crops*, Yale University Press: New Haven, CT, 1989; pp 1-21.

69.   Nash III, T.H. *Bryologist* **1972**, *75*, 315-324.

70.   Freedman, B.; Hutchinson, T.C. *Can. J. Bot.* **1980**, *58*, 2123-2140.

71.   Johnson, A.H.; Siccama, T.G.; Turner, R.S.; Lord, D.G. In *Direct and Indirect Effects of Acidic Deposition on Vegetation*; Linthurst, R.A., Ed.; Butterworth Publishers: Boston, MA, 1984; pp 81-95.

72.   Guderian, R.; Tingey, D.T.; Rabe, R. In *Air Pollution by Photochemical Oxidants: Formation, Transport, Control, and Effects on Plants*; Guderian, R. Ed; Ecological Studies, Vol 52; Springer Verlag: New York, NY, 1985; pp 129-169.

73.   Malhotra, S.S.; Kahn, A.A. In *Biochemical and Physiological Impact of Major Pollutants*; Treshow, M., Ed.; John Wiley & Sons: New York, NY, 1984; pp 113-158.

74.   Guderian, R. *Air Pollution by Photochemical Oxidants*; Guderian, R. Ed.; Ecological Studies; Analysis and Synthesis; Springer-Verlag: New York, NY, 1985; Vol. 52; p 346.

75.   Rapport, D.J.; Regier, H.A.; Hutchinson, T.C. *The American Naturalist* **1985**, *125*, 617-640.

76.   Miller, P.R.; Taylor, O.C.; Wilhour, R.G. U.S. Environmental Protection Agency: Environmental Research Laboratory, Corvallis, OR, 1982; EPA-600/D-82-276.

77.   Huttunen, S. In *Air Pollution and Plant Life*; Treshow, M. Ed.; John Wiley & Sons: New York, NY, 1984; pp 321-356.

78.   Hinrichsen, D. *Ambio* **1986**, *15*, 258-265.

79.   Cowling, E.; Krahl-Urban, B.; Schimansky, C. In *Forest Decline*; Krahl-Urban, B.; Brandt, C.J.; Schimansky, C.S.; Peters, K. Eds.; Assessment Group of Biology, Ecology and Energy of the Jülich Nuclear Research Center: Jülich, FRG, 1988; pp 120-125.

80.   Johansen, C.A. *Ann. Rev. Entomol.* **1977**, *22*, 177-192.

81.   Bromenshenk, J.J.; Carlson, S.R.; Simpson, J.C.; Thomas, J.M. *Science* **1985**, *227*, 632-634.

82.   Anderson, J.F.; Wojtas, M.A. *J. Econ. Entomol.* **1986**, *79*, 1200-1205.

83.   Fangmeier, A.; Steubing, L. In *Atmospheric Pollutants in Forest Areas*; Georgii, H.W. Ed.; Reidel Publishing Company: 1986; pp 223-234.

84.   Wren, C.D. *Environ. Res.* **1986**, *40*, 210-244.

85.   Hanson, W.C. *Am. J. Vet. Res.* **1966**, *27*, 359-366.

86.   Hanson, W.C. *Arch. Environ. Health*, **1968**, *17*, 639-648.

RECEIVED September 4, 1991

Chapter 7

Air Quality in Mexico City

J. Garfias[1,2] and R. González[1]

[1]Subsecretaría de Ecología, Secretaría de Desarrollo Urbano y Ecología, Río Elba 20, México, D.F., CP 06500
[2]Facultad de Química, Universidad Nacional Autónoma de Ciudad Universitaria, México, D.F., CP 04510

In Mexico City, several air quality parameters are measured continuously by an Automated Monitoring Network operated by the Under Secretariat of Ecology. Carbon monoxide, particulate matter, sulfur dioxide, nitrogen oxide, and ozone are the contaminants exceeding Air Quality Standards. Emissions produced by 2.7 million vehicles and 35,000 commercial and industrial outfits are not easily dispersed in a Valley located at 2240 m and surrounded by two mountain chains which hinder air circulation. An Integral Program, recently established to alleviate pollution, is briefly described.

Illustrated writings in the Mendocino Codex indicate that the Aztec pilgrimage of 1327 ended with the founding of Mexico City on an island where an eagle was seen eating a snake atop a cactus tree. At that time, the surface area covered by water in the Valley of Mexico was as large as the land area. Old paintings belonging to the 16th and 17th century depict a valley with three large lakes encircling the city: Xochimilco, Texcoco and Chalco. Mexico City was usually flooded during the rainy season: the worst deluge took place in 1629, lasting five years and decimating the population. It is then not surprising to trace, as early as the 17th century, efforts directed to dry the lakes. To this day, dust storms, ensuing after Texcoco and Chalco Lakes were partially drained, sweep the city in February and March (*1*). Although particulate matter often exceeds the air quality standard, dust has now been reduced by seeding a grass variety resistant to saline soils.

Air at 2240 m is 23% lighter than air at sea level; this fact led Humboldt to observe, at the beginning of the last century, that Mexico City's air was "the most transparent one." Intense industrialization and population growth in the last 40 years, plus adverse geographical and

0097–6156/92/0483–0149$06.00/0

meteorological conditions, have transformed Mexico City to one of the most contaminated metropolises in the world.

Geographical and Meteorological Considerations

Combustion efficiency at Mexico City's elevation is considerably reduced, compared to sea level, and carbon monoxide (CO) and hydrocarbon (HC) emissions enhanced, unless an extra 23% volume of air is fed. Contaminant dispersion is not easily achieved in Mexico City as she lies in a valley flanked by two cordilleras, averting strong wind formation. Average wind velocity is 2.4 m/s. The direction of prevailing winds is NE-SW during the day (see Figure 1). At night, a light mountain wind descends towards the Valley. Thermal inversions occur almost daily during the winter but less often in summer (see Figure 2a). Inversions break at around 9:30 AM in winter (Figure 2b). The average thickness of the inversion layer is less than 200 m in 64% of the days showing an inversion. Particularly adverse conditions may prevail in winter whenever a combined mechanism of high air pressure and thermal inversion occurs. Seasonal rains that fall from June to September help to clear the atmosphere. However, a quasi-static atmosphere associated with high pressures may lead to high ozone levels at any time.

Pollution Inventory

Eighteen and a half percent of Mexico's total population live in the Mexico City Metropolitan Area (MCMA). The MCMA comprises the Federal District and 17 Municipalities from the State of Mexico. The MCMA has an estimated total area of 2,000 square kilometers, of which 34% is urban, 28% forest, 27% agricultural, and 11% arid. Fifteen million people living in the MCMA produce 36% of the Gross National Product, and consume 15% of total fuel.

Mobile, fixed and natural sources contribute 83, 12, and 5% respectively to the 4.9 million metric tons of contaminants yearly emitted into the atmosphere (Table I).

Table I. Sources of Atmospheric Pollution in 1989 (metric tons per year)

Contaminant	Industrial	Vehicular	Natural	Total
Particulates	128,000	41,000	251,000	420,000
Sulfur Oxides	184,000	7,300	-------	191,300
Hydrocarbons	137,500	310,000	-------	447,500
Carbon Monoxide	53,000	3,573,000	-------	3,626,000
Nitrogen Oxides	68,000	111,300	-------	179,300
Total	570,500	4,042,800	251,000	4,864,300

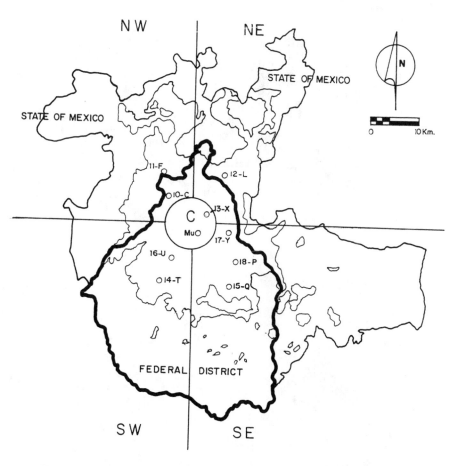

Figure 1. Map of the Mexico City Metropolitan Area showing the location of the following monitoring stations: 10-C Azcapotzalco; 11-F Tlanepantla; 12-L Xalostoc; 13-X Merced; 14-T Pedregal; 15-Q Cerro de la Estrella; 16-U Plateros; 17-Y Hangeras; 18-P UAM-Iztapalapa; Mu Museo.

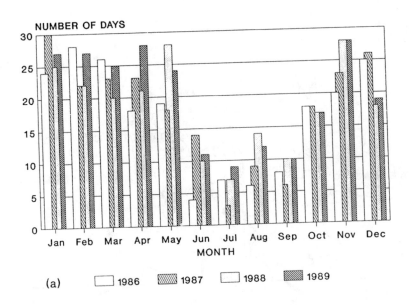

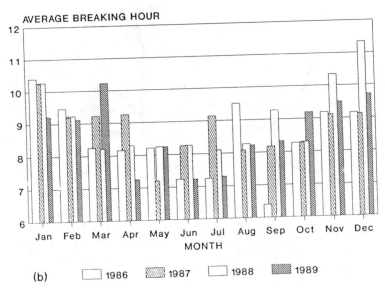

Figure 2. Thermal Inversions. (a) Number of days occurring. (b) Average breaking hour.

Mexico depends mostly on oil and gas (89.8%) as a source of energy. The relative contribution to pollution by different activities at National and MCMA levels may be assessed by comparing fuel consumptions (Table II). With the exception of kerosenes, each fuel has a distinctive usage in Mexico. Consequently, 51.6% of fuel (gasoline and diesel) consumed in the MCMA is used in transportation, 15.2% (L.P.G.) in residential water heating and cooking, and 27% (natural gas and fuel oil) in industrial and power generation enterprises. Furthermore, by remembering that almost one fifth of Mexico's population lives in the MCMA, it can be inferred from inspection of Table II, that there is a substantially lower per capita consumption of diesel, and in particular of fuel oil in the MCMA than in the rest of the country. The proportionally low diesel figure may be explained by the importance of metro transportation in Mexico City; the even lower fuel oil figure may be explained by the establishment of heavy industry in other regions, and by the fact that power generation *in situ* has been largely curtailed in Mexico City to reduce pollution.

Table II. Fuel Consumption in Mexico and in Mexico City Metropolitan Area in 1989 (metric tons per day)

Fuel	Mexico[a]	%	MCMA	%
Natural Gas[b]	27,452	14.6	4,840	17.5
L.P.G.	16,213	8.6	4,224	15.2
Gasoline	46,821	24.9	10,947[c]	39.5
Kerosene	6,078	3.2	1,734	6.2
Diesel	26,273	13.9	3,367	12.1
Fuel Oil	65,510	34.8	2,625	9.5
Total	188,347	100.0	27,737	100.0

[a] Reference 2
[b] Equivalent to fuel oil
[c] 2.5% is unleaded gasoline

Fuel consumption is very sensitive to economic growth, price structure, and ecological policies. After seven years of economic stagnation, a recovery initiated in 1989 led to a 6.2% annual increase in gasoline demand in the MCMA. However, a rise in gasoline prices plus the permanent establishment of a program in the MCMA to keep vehicles out of circulation one day a week, have lowered the gasoline demand growth rate for 1990. On the other hand, unleaded gasoline is expected to reach 7% of total gasoline demand in 1990. It's increased availability is required by the appearance of 1991 models running exclusively on unleaded petrol. An additional daily substitution of 1,590 tons of fuel oil by 1.93 million cubic meters of natural gas in power stations has also changed the consumption pattern for 1990.

There are 35,000 commercial and industrial establishments and 2.5 million vehicles using fuels. Major industries, such as an oil refining (16,000 tons per day, operating until 18 March 1991), two power stations (1,000 total MW), foundries and several chemical and manufacturing plants are located upwind in the northern part of the MCMA.

The average life of a car is 10 years. New car sales amounted to 368,000 units in the MCMA in 1989, compared to 136,000 in 1984. Vehicular transportation accounts for 22.4 million personal journeys a day: 51% are taken to go to work, 24% to school, 8% for shopping, 3% for entertainment, and 14% in other activities. Although 79.4% of personal journeys are made by public transport, those 19.0% related to the use of private cars are sufficient to create traffic jams, low transit speeds and 70.4% of vehicular emissions.

Vehicular Emission Standards

The latest revision of Emission Standards for New Vehicles was issued in September 1988. A summary of past and present emission standards is given in Table III.

Table III. Emission Standards for New Vehicles (g/km)

Model Year	CO	HC	NO_x
Automobiles:			
1976 to 1985	33.0	3.0	-
1986 to 1987	27.0	2.8	2.3
1988 to 1989	22.0	2.0	2.3
1990	18.0	1.8	2.0
1991* and 1992*	7.0	0.7	1.4
1993*	2.11	0.25	0.62
Commercial Trucks:			
1990 and 1991	35.0	3.0	3.5
1992 and 1993	22.0	2.0	2.3
1994	8.75	0.63	1.44

*The standard may be met by emission weighting of a company's car production.

The Emission Standard for New Diesel Vehicles, issued in December 1988, established a maximum of 50 Hartridge Opacity Units. The Ecological Technical Standard of June, 1988, enforced the maximum allowable emissions for circulating cars (Table IV). The Diesel Regulation of November 1988, requires biannual inspections. The maximum allowable opacity in diesel engines is related to nominal gas flow. There are 636 Car Inspection Centers in the Federal District and 250 in the State of Mexico, and 114 Diesel Inspection Centers operated by the Secretaría de Communicaciones y Transportes.

Table IV. Maximum Allowable Emissions for Cars in Circulation

Year Model	CO (%vol)	HC(ppm)
Previous to 1979	6.0	700
1980 to 1986	4.0	500
Later than 1987	3.0	400

Fuel Quality. Petróleos Mexicanos markets two gasoline brands: leaded Nova Plus and unleaded Magna Sin. Nova Plus is specified to have tetraethyl lead (TEL) in the 0.5 to 1 milliliters per gallon range, a minimum Research Octane Number of 81, and a Reid Vapor Pressure (RVP) in the 7 to 9.5 psi range. Magna Sin is similar to American Regular, with a minimum 86 Road Octane Number, a maximum of 0.01 grams of lead per gallon, and the same RVP as Nova Plus. Diesel for combustion engines contains no more than 0.5% sulfur with a minimum 40 octane number. Industrial Fuel Oil is limited to 3% sulfur, but has from 0.2 to 0.7% of compounded nitrogen.

To meet Emission Standards, new 1991 models are designed to run on unleaded petrol, and therefore, new engines working at a higher compression ratio will be from 8 to 10% more efficient than older ones.

Air Quality Monitoring Network. The first systematic effort to measure air quality began in 1966 with the installation of 4 manned monitoring stations. The Mexican Air Quality Standards (MAQS), given in Table V, were promulgated in November 1982. The air monitoring network has been expanded and transformed over the years. At present, the Undersecretariat of Ecology operates an Automated Monitoring Network comprising 25 stations, of which 15 measure sulfur dioxide, 5 nitrogen oxides, 15 carbon monoxide, 3 non-methane hydrocarbons, 10 ozone and 2 hydrogen sulfide. Ten stations measure the meteorological parameters wind velocity, wind direction, relative humidity, and temperature. The information received by telephone in a computer at the Central Office is processed and relayed to officers in charge of emergencies and to the press.

There is an additional Manual Monitoring Network, made up by 16 stations, committed to evaluate total particulate matter, PM10 (suspended particulate matter less than 10 μm in diameter), sulfur dioxide and heavy metals. Two acoustic radars are used to measure the heights of inversion layers. Geopotentials are appraised at 300, 500 and 700 millibar.

Table V. Air Quality Standards*

Contaminant	Averaging Time	Mexican Standard	U.S.A. Standard
Carbon Monoxide	8 h	13 ppm	9 ppm
	1 h	--	35 ppm
Sulfur Dioxide	annual average	--	0.03 ppm
	24 h	0.13 ppm	0.14 ppm
Hydrocarbons (corrected for metane)	3 h (6-9 a.m.)	--	0.24 ppm
Nitrogen Dioxide	annual average	--	0.05 ppm
	1 h	0.21 ppm	--
Ozone	1 h	0.11 ppm	0.12 ppm
Total Particulate Matter	annual geometric mean	--	75 $\mu g/m^3$
	24 h	275 $\mu g/m^3$	260 $\mu g/m^3$

* Standards, other than those based on annual average or annual geometric average, are not to be exceeded more than once a year.

Thermal inversions make winter the most unfavorable season for clean air. Vast differences in air quality are found in the industrialized north, and the residential southwest regions. Particulate matter influences mainly the north, where industries, landfills, and the dried bed of Texcoco Lake are located. Sulfur oxides impinge primarily on the northeast and southwest. High carbon monoxide concentrations are found in heavy traffic areas such as the northwest. Ozone affects predominantly the southwest at any season. We have selected air quality records from data generated by stations registering the higher pollutant levels, as follows:

Carbon Monoxide. The Standard is often exceeded at the Cuitlahuac Station (northwest) during winter, as displayed in Figure 3a. However, a diminishing trend on the number of hours reaching a 26 ppm level can be appreciated in Figure 3b.

Sulfur Dioxide. High concentrations are found at Xalostoc (NE) and Santa Ursula (SW) stations during fall and winter, the former is located close to a power plant, and the latter near an asphalt factor; the Standard was exceeded 5 and 9 days respectively from October 1989 to February 1990.

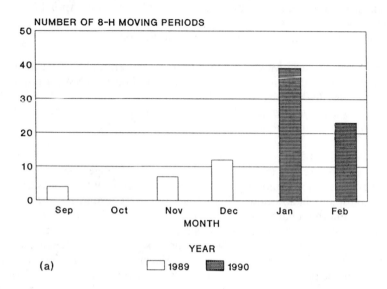

(a)

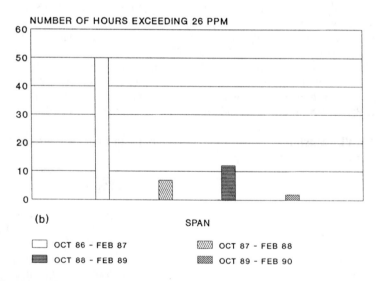

(b)

Figure 3. Carbon Monoxide at Cuitlahuac Station. (a) Number of 8-h moving periods in which the Standard is exceeded. (b) Number of hours in which 26 ppm is exceeded.

Nitrogen Dioxide. At Merced Station, located in the central region, the Standard was exceeded on 19 days from October 1988 to April 1989. In the same period, the Standard was exceeded 12 days at Tlalnepantla Station (northwest), and 3 days at Pedregal Station (southwest).

Particulate Matter. Maximum daily average concentration of particulate matter, smaller than 10 microns, measured at Xalostoc (NW), from July 1989 to July 1990 is exhibited in Figure 4a. The American Standard is 150 μg m^{-3} as a daily average. Maximum PM10 concentrations measured in several stations in June 1990 are presented in Figure 4b.

Lead. Lead in petrol was decreased to 1.2 mL of TEL per gallon in 1983. TEL has been kept in leaded gasoline in the 0.5-1.0 range since 1986. The lead concentration trend in petrol is followed closely by that measured in the atmosphere in downtown Museo Station. Lead concentration at Museo is within International Standards (average 1.5 μg/m^3 in 3 months), however, Xalostoc Station placed in an industrial area shows twice as high lead concentrations as the international standards, pointing to the need for relocating some foundries outside the Valley, and controlling others. Replacement of TEL in gasoline byy 5% methyl-terbutyl ether (MTBE) and the increased use of unleaded petrol will gradually lower lead emissions.

Ozone. High ozone concentrations are confronted in the southwest region, where an air parcel accumulates photochemical contaminants collected and generated after sweeping the north and central regions. The number of days exceeding 0.11 and 0.22 ppm at Pedregal Station are illustrated in Figure 5. The maximum hourly average ozone concentration ever measured was 0.441 ppm at Pedregal Station in December 1986. The maximum hourly ozone concentrations determined in a year at Pedregal and Plateros Stations from 1986 to October 1990 are given in Table VI.

Table VI. Maximum Ozone Concentrations in an hour at Pedregal and Plateros Stations (ppm)

Year	Pedregal	Plateros
1986	0.441	0.398
1987	0.344	0.331
1988	0.405	0.351
1989	0.340	0.310
1990*	0.403	0.375

* Up to October 31st.

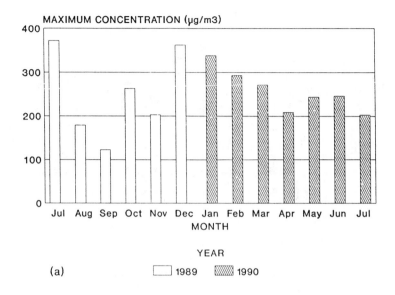

(a)   ☐ 1989   ▨ 1990

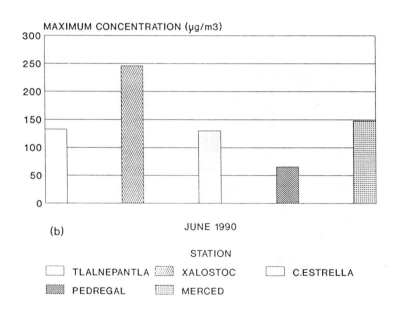

Figure 4. Particulate matter less than 10 microns (PM10). (a) Maximum daily average concentration observed at Xalostoc Station (northwest). (b) Maximum daily average concentration observed at five stations in June 1990.

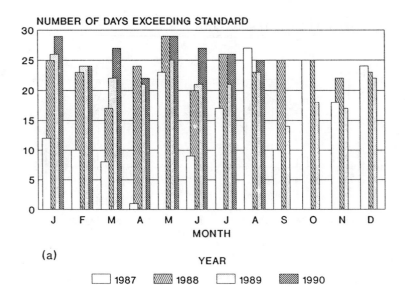

(a)

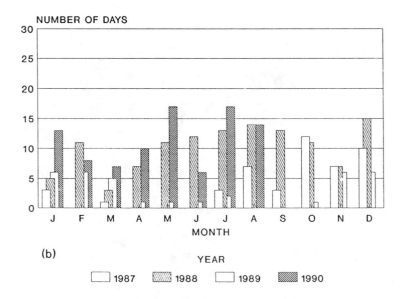

(b)

Figure 5. Ozone at Pedregal Station (southwest). (a) Number of days exceeding the Standard. (b) Number of days exceeding twice the Standard concentration.

Integral Programs to Control Atmospheric Pollution

Some invaluable isolated actions were taken from time to time in the last twenty to twenty five years that prevented air quality from declining at an even faster rate. For example, energy demand was met (electricity and refined oil products) by expanding capacity of plants located outside of the MCMA; a metro was built; the vehicular traffic system was reordered; and new hydrotreating, reforming and catalytic cracking units reduced lead and sulfur in refined products.

Four months after the September 1985 earthquake, a set of wider actions was implemented: 1600 and 320 tons per day of fuel oil were substituted respectively by natural gas at a power station and at Atzcapotzalco Refinery in 1986; a detergent additive was incorporated into gasoline to keep carburetors cleaner in 1986; a far reaching Federal Law on Ecological Ordering and Environmental Protection was enacted in March 1988; Emission Standards for cars in circulation and new cars were legislated in June and September 1988 respectively; and Emission Standards for Industrial Combustion Processes were issued in 1988, among other actions.

In the last two years, the federal and city authorities, with the financial assistance and the expert advice of specialists from Japan, the United States of America, Germany, France, and Great Britain, devised an Integral Program (3) aimed at bettering air quality in the MCMA.

The Integral Program includes fuel quality improvement and reduction of emissions in gasoline distribution; a public transport system more efficient and less contaminating; industrial assimilation of advanced process technology and pollution control systems; reforestation and ecological restoration of barren land and open dumping sites; and the strengthening of ecological research, education and communication activities.

Several actions have already started: 5% MTBE is added to gasoline; two additional metro lines are under construction; the program "No Circulation Today" was commenced in November 1989; and loans have been approved for expanding the Automated Air Quality Network, for initiating air modeling in real time, and for building new plants outside the MAMC to produce MTBE and isomeric gasoline, to hydrotreat diesel (0.1% maximum sulfur) and fuel oil (0.8% maximum sulfur), and to increase reforming capacity.

A long and difficult task will be confronted, in particular to bring ozone within the air quality standards, as the physics and chemistry of ozone formation in the MCMA are not sufficiently understood.

Literature Cited

1. Jauregui, E., *Int. J. Climatology* **1989**, 9, 169-180.
2. *Memoria de Labores 1989*; Petróleos Mexicanos: Mexico City, 1989.
3. *Programa Integral Contra la Contaminación Atmosférica de la Zona Metropolitana de la Ciudad de México*, Departamento del Distrito Federal: Mexico City, 1990.

RECEIVED October 7, 1991

Chapter 8

Global Assessment of Ambient Urban Air Quality

Gerald G. Akland[1], Henk de Koning[2], David T. Mage[3], and Guntis Ozolins[3]

[1]U.S. Environmental Protection Agency, Mail Drop 75,
Research Triangle Park, NC 27711
[2]Pan American Health Organization, World Health Organization,
525 23rd Street, NW, Washington, DC 20037
[3]World Health Organization, Geneva 27, Switzerland

The World Health Organization (WHO) and the United
Nations Environmental Programme (UNEP) have been
collaborating since 1974 on an urban ambient air
monitoring project. Monitoring results indicate that
about 50% of the cities do not exceed the annual WHO SO_2
guideline of 40-60 µg/m3 and only about 20% of the
cities do not exceed the annual suspended particulate
matter guideline of 60-90 µg/m3. Fortunately, progress
in controlling sources is indicated by the downward
trends in levels of SO_2 and particulates measured in
many of the cities. Fewer data are available for
nitrogen dioxide, carbon monoxide and lead. It appears
that emissions are increasing for all five pollutants in
developing countries which will likely result in an
increased risk to the public health of the world's 1.8
billion city dwellers.

Measurements of ambient air quality are necessary for a
realistic appraisal of the risks originating from outdoor sources
and for the design and implementation of strategies to control and
limit these risks. Such measurements are usually based on
measurements of ambient air pollutant concentrations at fixed
sites. Recognizing the need for such measurements on a global
basis, an international program of air quality monitoring was
established by the World Health Organization (WHO) and the United
Nations Environmental Program (UNEP) in 1973. The stated
objectives of the monitoring project are to assist countries in
operational air pollution monitoring, to promote the global
exchange of environmental information, and to provide a global
basis for assessing the impact of air pollution on public health.
Obviously there is a need for this type of information. Air
pollution, which may affect human health, occurs in every country.

In addition to local emissions, pollutants may come from neighboring or distant countries, having been transported through the atmosphere. The common nature of pollution problems as well as the widespread extent of affected regions makes international collaboration the obvious approach towards solution. Shared data and information promote awareness of issues, provides perspective on problems, suggests the need for effective control strategies, and points to progress in achieving a healthier environment.

The Global Environmental Monitoring System (GEMS) air monitoring network was initiated by WHO primarily through the Ministries of Health in the WHO Member States at a time when separate Environmental Protection Agencies (EPAs) or Bureaus (EPBs) did not exist in most of them. As explained below, the stations were either existing stations or new stations often were established and operated by universities within the country set up in representative industrial, commercial and residential areas. In many countries new EPAs and EPBs have now been established to collect air quality data in the same cities where GEMS/AIR data are being collected. Whereas WHO chose the GEMS/AIR station locations to be typical of conditions in the three types of areas, local EPBs which have responsibility for control often site some of their stations at locations which are expected to have maximal values. Consequently, these data and the conclusions reached in this paper should be interpreted conservatively as representing typical or average urban air quality with the understanding that in many of these cities there are locations with significantly higher values.

Global Environment Monitoring Systems (GEMS) Air Monitoring Network

At present, some 50 countries are participating in the GEMS air monitoring network in which data are obtained at approximately 175 sites in 75 cities. In most cities, there are three monitoring stations: one located in each of an industrial, commercial, and residential area chosen to represent each of these three exposure conditions. The geographical coverage of the GEMS network is fairly representative of the world regions as can be seen in Table I. Notice that the highly industrialized countries of the Northern Hemisphere are well represented. However most developing countries are underrepresented, as are the Eastern European countries. (This will likely change in the future.) The network has been relatively stable since about 1980.

The network is implemented by the participating countries through WHO. Sulfur Dioxide (SO_2) and suspended particulate matter (SPM) data are routinely reported from each of the participating countries to WHO for entry into the global data base, which is maintained by the United States Environmental Protection Agency (U.S. EPA) at Research Triangle Park, North Carolina. Methods of collection and analysis varies by country. SPM is reported either as a gravimetric or a photometric (transmittance or reflectance) measurement converted to mass units. Since the accuracy of the conversion of the photometric measurement to mass units is

Table I. Countries Participating in the GEMS/AIR

Monitoring Assessment

Australia	Israel
Austria	Italy
Belgium	Japan
Bulgaria	Kuwait
Canada	Luxembourg
China	Netherlands
Czechoslovakia	New Zealand
Denmark	Norway
Finland	Poland
France	Portugal
Germany (Fed.Rep.)	Romania
Germany (Dem.Rep.)	Spain
Greece	Sweden
Hong Kong	Switzerland
Hungary	Thailand
Iceland	Turkey
India	United Kingdom
Ireland	United States of America
	Yugoslavia

dependent on its physical characteristics, data are reported in tables under the hearing of "SPM" for the gravimetric method and "smoke" for the photometric method. Results of pollutant measurements at monitoring sites in the network are published in biennial data reports (1-4) and interpretive reports have been published (5-7). For the purpose of a more inclusive GEMS/WHO/UNEP appraisal of urban air quality conducted in 1988 (8), additional data were requested for nitrogen dioxide (NO_2), carbon monoxide (CO) and lead (Pb). Ozone was not included for lack of representative data for the time period covered by this assessment.

This assessment concerns urban air quality and trends for contributed SO_2 and SPM collected by GEMS which is supplemented by analyses of NO_2, CO and Pb data which have been obtained from other sources, including national reports, open literature and through the use of a questionnaire submitted to each participating country. These pollutants were selected because they are: (1) ubiquitous with sources common to most urban areas, (2) emitted in large quantities, (3) generally related to specific industries and processes, which have an impact on the environment, and (4) known to cause health effects. (As mentioned previously, ozone was not considered in this assessment for lack of data and it also fails to meet the second criterion.) The results presented here mostly cover the decade 1975-1984. Although this may seem very outdated, in a global monitoring program it is not possible to obtain current data from all participating countries in a timely manner. This is because data from national authorities become available only some time after they have been collected, and additional time is required to compile, validate and analyze the results. Even with this limitation, these data provide a basis for long-term trend assessment on a global scale which can be related to specific country regulatory actions, which have occurred over the 10-year period.

Sources and Effects of Air Pollution

During the forties and fifties, episodes of severe air pollution occurred in a number of urban and industrial areas. They were responsible for ill health and in some cases caused death among the populations concerned. As the scientific and public information base on the adverse effects of urban air pollution increased, so did public demand for control measures. As a result, many industrial countries introduced comprehensive air pollution control laws at various times from the mid-fifties onwards. Industrial response to these laws led to the application of control techniques which effectively reduced the emissions of some pollutants. However there are other sources and factors which can obscure the benefits of these control actions. For example, consider urban growth. In 1980 there were 35 cities with populations over 4 million. By the year 2000 this number will nearly double to 66, and by the 2025, this number will more than double to an estimated 135 (9). In developing countries, from 1980 to the year 2000, it is estimated that twice as many people will live in cities of a total population of 1 million or more in Latin America (101 million to 232 million) and East Asia (132 million to 262 million). Three times as many people will live in cities of 1 million or more in South Asia (106 million to 328 million) and four times as many in Africa (36 million to 155 million) (10). Accompanying this rapid growth are increases in industrial activity and transportation. The resulting deterioration of environmental conditions, including air quality, can already be observed in many large cities, particularly in the developing world.

The unplanned growth of cities is accompanied by increased traffic, energy consumption, industrial activity and pollution. Stationary sources such as power plants, emit most of the SO_2 and some of the SPM and NO_2. Most of the CO and Pb and much of the particulate matter and NO_2 are emitted from mobile sources (cars, trucks, buses, planes, etc.).

One of the most significant indices of air pollution potential is provided by statistics on motor vehicle use. On a global scale the number of vehicles continues to rise although the rate of growth has slowed in North America and Europe as a whole, where vehicle densities are the highest in the world. Since 1979, the most rapid growth has occurred in Asia and South America where vehicle ownership has more than doubled (11). In the developing countries, as well as many others, these vehicles are not equipped with emission control devices.

The other major contributor to air pollution is the role of energy consumption and type of energy trend over the past 20 years by region. Although the energy usage has dropped in North America, it still exceeds the usage in the other regions. In addition, there has been a dramatic increase in usage by the developing countries (12). In developing countries, investment in industrial expansion will often have higher priority than pollution control. This has led to the current situation where emission reductions are being achieved in many industrialized countries while in many cases air quality in the developing world is deteriorating.

The health effects of different pollutants vary according to the intensity and duration of exposures and the health status of the persons exposed. A summary of these effects is provided in Table II, together with the WHO (1979) guideline values for the protection of human health. The WHO European office has reviewed these guidelines, WHO (1987), and has recommended additional values for SO_2 in the presence of particulate matter.

Sulfur Dioxide

Sulfur dioxide is formed primarily from the industrial and domestic combustion of fossil fuels. On a global scale, man-made emissions of SO_2 are currently estimated to be 160-180 million tons per year. These emissions slightly exceed natural emissions, largely from volcanic sources. The northern hemisphere accounts for approximately 90% of the man-made emissions (13-14). Over the past few decades global SO_2 emissions have risen by approximately 4%/year corresponding to the increase in world energy consumption.

Figure 1 shows that many industrialized countries experience declining trends in SO_2 emissions. During 1974-1984, for example, there were decreases of 58% in Sweden, 39% in France, 19% in the

Table II. WHO Air Quality Guideline Values and Health Effects

Pollutant	WHO Guidelines, $\mu g/m^3$		Effects
	Annual Mean	98 Percentile	
SO_2	40-60	100-150	Respiratory Illness
Smoke	40-60	100-150	Pulmonary Effects
SPM	60-90	150-230	Pulmonary Effects
Pb	0.5-1.0	x	Neurobehavioral Effects
		Not to be Exceeded	
CO	x	1-hour 30 mg/m^3	Cardiovascular Effects
		8-hour 10 mg/m^3	Cardiovascular Effects
NO_2	x	1-hour 400	Lung Function
		24-hour 150	Lung Function

Source: Adapted from ref. 16.

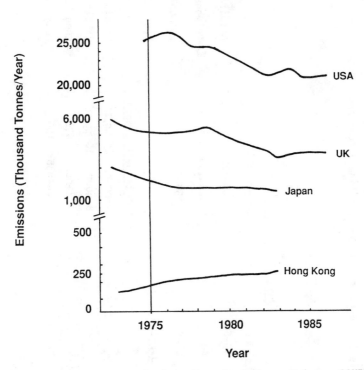

Figure 1. Trends in SO$_2$ emissions in selected countries. SOURCE:
Adapted from Ref. 8.

Netherlands and 18% in the USA. Despite these declines, total emissions in Europe have not diminished between 1972-1982 (15) and global emissions have increased. It can also be seen in Figure 1 that total nationwide emissions unadjusted for population density or area, do not accurately reflect concentration levels measured.

SO_2 Concentrations in Cities

The WHO air pollution network provides a good indication of the current levels of SO_2 in urban areas throughout the world. A summary of the annual average SO_2 levels in 52 cities of the network during 1980-84 is provided in Figure 2. It shows the relative ordering of cities within the network by the average of all sites within the city for each of the years 1980-84. Eighteen of the 54 cities (33%) show data below the WHO annual guideline of 40-60 ug/m3. At the other extreme 4 cities (7%) show data above the guideline for all sites within the city.

An insight into the potential impact on human health of urban SO_2 concentrations may be gained by comparing the data with suggested guidelines for population exposures. The guideline published by WHO (16) specifies a range of 100-150 ug/m3 for the 98 percentile of daily average concentrations, and a range of 40-60 ug/m3 annual mean. Network results show cities both below and above guideline ranges. The summary in Table III gives the number of cities considered to have acceptable air quality conditions (below the guideline range), to be marginal (within the guideline range) or to be unacceptable (above the guideline range). It can be seen that air quality levels exceed the guidelines for SO_2 in many cities. The extent of the risk in terms of either acute or chronic respiratory effects clearly depends on the degree to which the guidelines are exceeded. In some cities the guidelines are exceeded consistently, while in others they are exceeded for some sites in some years, but not all (8).

In order to translate the concentration data into estimates of population exposed, the total 1978 urban population (cities greater than 200,000) of 1.8 billion was used as the global population (17). Results of this calculation can also be seen in Table III. It can be seen that 625 million people are estimated to live in urban areas where average SO_2 levels exceed the WHO guideline and 975 million people live in areas which exceed the short-term level. (8)

Suspended Particulate Matter (SPM)

Particles are emitted into the atmosphere from numerous natural and manmade sources and are also formed upon condensation of gases and vapors. Direct emissions of Suspended Particulate Matter (SPM) arise from a variety of human activities including combustion, industrial and agricultural practices; the remainder is formed from gas-particle conversions (chiefly from SO_2 oxidation to sulfuric acid as sulfate salts). Particles larger than about 10μm in diameter deposit in the vicinity of the sources, but smaller

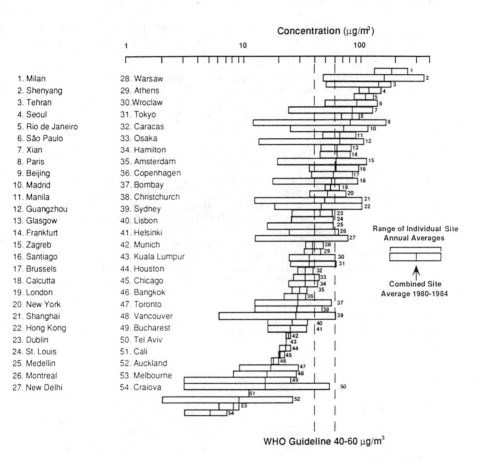

Figure 2.   Summary of the annual SO₂ averages in GEMS/Air cities,
1980-1984.   SOURCE: Adapted from Ref. 8.

Table III. Air Quality Cities with Reference to WHO Guidelines

Pollutant	Air Quality Conditions	Number of Cities		Number of Persons (Millions)	
		Annual Average	P98 Levels	Annual Average	P98 Levels
SO$_2$	Acceptable	27 (50%)	20 (37%)	625	550
	Marginal	11 (20%)	11 (20%)	550	275
	Unacceptable	16 (30%)	23 (43%)	625	975
SPM	Acceptable	7 (17%)	10 (24%)	350	275
	Marginal	10 (24%)	9 (22%)	200	275
	Unacceptable	24 (59%)	22 (59%)	1250	1250
Smoke	Acceptable	8 (50%)	5 (31%)	350	275
	Marginal	3 (19%)	4 (25%)	200	275
	Unacceptable	5 (31%)	7 (44%)	1250	1250

Source: Adapted from ref. 8.

particles may remain airborne for extended periods and be transported long distances. Annual man-made particulate emissions are estimated to be approximately 300 million tons, about half of which are sulfate particles formed from SO_2 conversion (18). In most urban regions particles from human activities account for over half the emissions, but on a global scale, man-made emissions are estimated to be only between 5-50% of total particulate emissions (19).

Figure 3 shows that trends in national particle emissions are mainly downward. For example, it can be seen that decreases of 49% occurred in the U.K. and over 30% occurred in the USA, which indicate positive results from regulatory controls identified before and during this period. A notable exception can also be seen for Poland where emissions are increasing. Furthermore, there are indications of increasing trends in particulate emissions in certain developing countries and in Eastern Europe. In addition to increased industrial activities which account for increased emissions, smoke emissions from diesel engines are increasing. Uncon trolled diesel engines generate about 10 times more respirable particulates than gasoline engines (20).

SPM Concentrations in Cities

The WHO air pollution network provides a good indication of the current levels of SPM in urban areas throughout the world. A summary of the annual SPM averages in 41 cities is shown in Figure 4. It can be seen that in 18 of the 41 cities (44%) the annual averages reported from all sites for 1980-1984 exceeded the WHO guideline of 60-90 μg/m3. Cities with the highest concentrations tend to be in the developing regions. In at least some cases this is partially caused by much higher levels of naturally-occurring dust.

The severity of particulate pollution problems may be judged by comparing the observed air quality concentrations with the WHO health based guidelines. To avoid risks of acute effects from short-term exposures, the guidelines specify a range of 150-230 μg/m3 for SPM as measured by the High Volume Sampler gravimetrically and 100-150 μg/m3 as measured photometrically each being interpreted as the 98 percentile of daily average concentrations. An evaluation of the global situation during the 1980-84 period with respect to the guideline values is also shown in Table III. Cities below the guideline ranges are regarded as having acceptable air quality conditions, those within are said to be marginal and cities exceeding the guidelines are considered as having unacceptable air quality. It can be seen that in about 60% of the cities, air quality levels exceed the guidelines for SPM and about 40% exceed the guidelines for smoke. The proportions of the population in the cities exposed to SPM levels within or above the WHO guideline values were extrapolated to an equivalent global urban population of 1.8 billion.

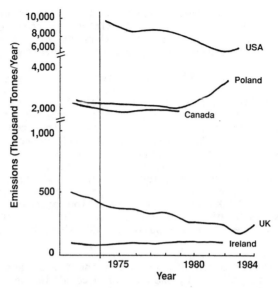

Figure 3. Trends in particulate emissions in selected cuntries. SOURCE: Adapted from Ref. 8.

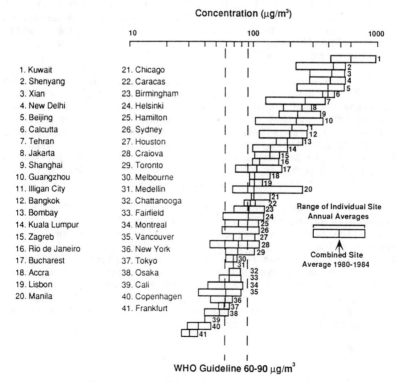

Figure 4. Summary of the annual SPM averages in GEMS/Air cities, 1980-1984. SOURCE: Adapted from Ref. 8.

Over 65% of the global population is living in urban areas where the concentration levels of particles are considered to be unacceptably high. In contrast less than 20% of the people are living in cities considered to have acceptable levels of particles.

Nitrogen Dioxide

Nitrogen Dioxide (NO_2) is a major pollutant originating from natural and man-made sources. It has been estimated that a total of about 150 million tons of NOx are emitted to the atmosphere each year, of which about 50% results from man-made sources (21). In urban areas, man-made emissions dominate, producing elevated ambient levels. Worldwide, fossil-fuel combustion accounts for about 75% of man-made NOx emissions, which is divided equally between stationary sources, such as power plants, and mobile sources. These high temperature combustion processes emit the primary pollutant nitric oxide (NO), which is subsequently transformed to the secondary pollutant NO_2 through photochemical oxidation.

Estimates of urban NOx emissions and trends are generally limited to those provided by the developed countries which have the detailed emission inventories. As in the case of other pollutants, the USA contributes the most on a per-country basis to the global NOx emissions per year. Because of the inaccuracy of the data base used, it is difficult to discern trends in these emissions. However, with new control technologies being implemented for both stationary and mobile sources, downward trends in the developed countries may be more prevalent in the future years. Unfortunately, the opposite trend is likely to occur in the developing countries.

An overview of the NO_2 situation throughout the world can be seen in Figure 5 which describes the national annual averages in urban areas located within 9 industrialized countries for 1980-84. It may be observed that the overall mean NO_2 levels are similar to one another and range between 30 and 50μg/m3. Individual site years are more variable, ranging from about 20-100 μg/m3. Although WHO does not have an annual average guideline value for NO_2, the US standard of 100μg/m3 is shown on the figure, which has not been exceeded by any site-year average for the 5 years of the data base.

Figure 6 shows a cumulative probability plot of both the maximum daily and hourly NO_2 averages in cities for the 1980-84 time period. The plotted values can be directly compared to the WHO guideline values of 150μg/m3 for the maximum 24-hour level and 400μg/m3 for the maximum 1-hour level. In both cases, about 25% of the cities worldwide exceed the guideline values. Based on these proportions of cites with NO_2 concentrations above the short-term guideline values, it is estimated that approximately 15-20 percent of urban residents in North America and Europe are at increased risk to short-term high NO_2 exposures.

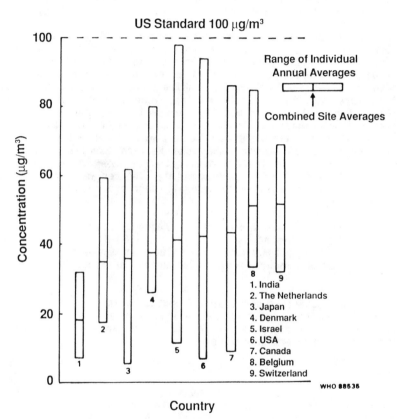

Figure 5. Summary of the national annual NO$_2$ averages in urban areas, 1980-1984. SOURCE: Adapted from Ref. 8.

CARBON MONOXIDE

Carbon monoxide (CO) is one of the most widely distributed air pollutants. It is formed by natural biological and oxidation processes, the incomplete combustion of carbon-containing fuels and various industrial processes. However, the largest individual source of man-made emissions is motor vehicle exhausts which account for virtually all CO emitted in some urban environments. It has been estimated that global man-made emissions range from 300-1600 million tons per year, which is approximately 60% of the total global CO emissions (22-23).

Since man-made emissions of CO are dominated by releases from motor vehicles, it is considered that global emissions have risen along with the rapid growth in vehicle numbers since the 1940s. In the US for example, the number of motor vehicles increased by a factor of 4 between 1940 and 1970 while the CO emissions rose from 73 to more than 100 million tons per year over the same period (24). Since about the mid-70s, control strategies have been initiated which have resulted in reductions in CO emissions. The outcome of these controls has been a gradual decrease of CO emissions in North America and some Western European countries despite increases in traffic density. For example in the USA, emissions have declined by approximately 1.5% per year since 1975, which by 1984 represented an overall decrease of more than 11 million tons.

Figure 7 provides a cumulative frequency distribution of the maximum 8-hour standard in 15 cities in 1980-84. Shown on the graph is the 10 mg/m3 WHO guideline value. It can be seen that the average maximum 8-hour level is exceeded in about 50% of the cities.

A very tentative conclusion from the relatively small sample of cities studied shows that people living in as many as half the cities in the world may be exposed to CO concentrations in excess of the WHO short-term guideline.

LEAD

Lead (Pb) is released to the atmosphere primarily from man-made sources. These sources include both the production and use of lead and its compounds. One global inventory estimates that an annual total of 450 thousand tons are released by human activities (25). The largest source results from the use of alkyl lead as an anti-knock agent in gasoline. Gasoline combustion globally contributes an estimated 60% of the total lead emissions from human activities. In individual countries, this source accounts for 50-90% of national man-made emissions depending on vehicle numbers and effectiveness of lead emission control strategies.

Relatively few countries report annual lead emission estimates. Of those that have, declining trends in lead emissions have occurred, such as in the US where total lead emissions have been reduced by 75% (26).

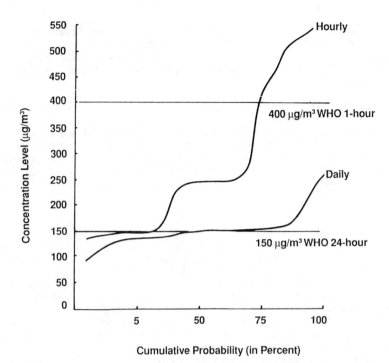

Figure 6. Summary of annual maximum daily and hourly NO$_2$ averages in cities, 1980-1984. SOURCE: Adapted from Ref. 8.

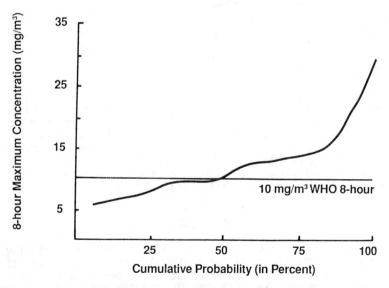

Figure 7. Maximum 8-hourly CO concentrations in cities, 1980-1984. SOURCE: Adapted from Ref 8.

Annual Pb averages in 23 cities are shown on Figure 8. Only 4 of the 23 cities (17%) are shown outside the WHO guideline limit of 0.5-1.0µg/m3. Annual µg mean concentrations of lead range from 0.13 to 2.0µg/m3 with levels at individual sites as low as 0.02µg/m3 and up to 5.3µg/m3.

Extrapolation of the data obtained in this study to the situation world-wide leads to a tentative estimate that people living in about one third of the cities of the world may be exposed to air lead concentrations which are either marginal or unacceptable. The problem is probably most acute in large urban areas in developing countries with dense automobile traffic. This problem could be easily mitigated through a world-wide effort to eliminate lead in fuels.

TRENDS

Trends in levels can be estimated accurately if there are sufficient and representative data for a given urban area for a period of at least five years. Such data are available for 30 cities in the WHO air network for SO_2 and SPM. Figure 9 shows a representation of the trends by regions of the world where there were representative data. This figure shows that, in general, air quality is being improved in more areas than where it is growing worse. Improvements in air quality is more common in the industrialized countries than in developing ones. In Asia there is a higher percentage of stations that report "no change" or a worsening trend than in the European and American regions. For sulfur dioxide levels, for example, the developing countries in Asia, for which trends could be calculated, show an average annual increase in concentrations of the order of 10 percent. The biggest improvements, on the other hand, are seen in Europe and North American cities where over the past 10 years sulfur dioxide levels have been declining at an average rate of approximately 5 percent per year. This decline will plateau in the near future after the full effect of implemented controls have been realized.

More current data than that presented in the previous discussions about levels and trends have been examined to see if there are indications that significant changes are appearing in the 1985-1987 data. Results of this comparison are shown in Table IV for both SO_2 and SPM. It can be seen that the downward trend for SO_2 is continuing at approximately the same percentage of cities in the network. The picture for SPM is also encouraging with fewer cities showing an increase in concentration levels.

CONCLUSION

The wide participation of countries in the WHO air monitoring project ensures that representative distributions of the levels of SO_2 and SPM are obtained for urban areas. In order to assess other pollutants in conjunction with the SO_2 and SPM data, additional information on NO_2, CO and Pb were obtained from national reports,

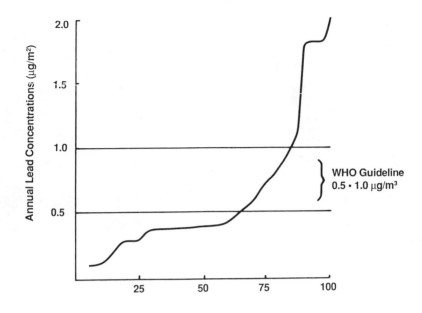

Figure 8. Annual lead averages in cities, 1980-1984. SOURCE: Adapted from Ref. 8.

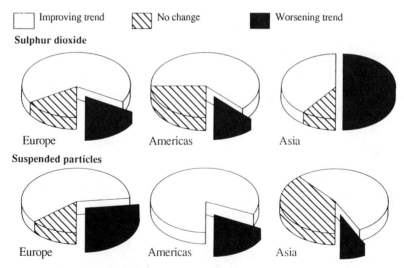

Figure 9. Distribtuion of trends in air quality in GEMS/Air cities, 1973-1984. SOURCE: Adapted from Ref. 8.

scientific literature and through a questionnaire distributed to WHO member countries. Ambient levels were compared with WHO's guidelines on what constitutes acceptable exposure. These results are summarized according to the percentage of cities exceeding the WHO guideline values as shown in Table V.

Table IV. Trends in SO_2 and SPM

	1973-84 Percent with trends			1985-87 Percent with trends		
	Downward	No change	Upward	Downward	No change	Upward
SO_2						
Annual	61	21	18	62	19	19
98 Percentile	64	21	15	73	8	19
Number of Cities		33			37	
SPM						
Annual	51	16	33	28	55	17
98 Percentile	46	16	38	52	41	7
Number of Cities		37			29	

Source: Adapted from ref. 8.

Table V. Cities Reporting Site-Year Averages in Excess
of WHO Guideline Values, in Percent

Cities Exceeding Guideline Value	SO$_2$	SPM	Smoke	NO2	CO	Pb
Long-term	30(54)*	60(41)	30(16)	-	-	20(23)
Short-term	45(54)	55(41)	45(16)	30(28)	55(15)	-

*Number of cities for which data are available

Source: Adapted from ref. 8.

Extrapolating exposure estimates to all urban cities in the world would indicate that as many as 625 million people, mostly in developing countries, are exposed to unacceptable levels of SO2 pollution and about 1.25 billion people live in urban areas where SPM levels exceed acceptable guidelines. This means that less than 20 percent of city dwellers live in environments that can be considered to have acceptable outdoor air quality levels.

Less information is available for the other three pollutants shown in the tables. In industrial countries in North America and Europe air quality monitoring indicates that NO_2 levels may increase risk to 15-20 percent of the residents. Exceedances of the short-term guideline for CO appear relatively common in the reporting cities. Such exposures are likely to occur in locations with high traffic densities. With regard to Pb levels, approximately 20% of the cities have annual average lead concentration levels which exceed the WHO guideline.

In conclusion, based on the information available on urban air pollution, increased risks to public health are likely to occur throughout the world as a direct or indirect result of man-made emissions into the environment. Long-term monitoring of ambient air quality in urban locations throughout the world provides an indicator of the positive results of control actions instituted in developing countries. This provides the example for improvements needed in the developing countries. For example, elimination of lead in gasoline used in developing countries would offer a long-term public health benefit to the children living in the inner areas of the cities. In addition, this global assessment suggests that for the five pollutants considered, a greater benefit would result if particulate controls were installed. Increased attention to the deterioration of the air quality in developing countries will hopefully help mitigate the problem in the not too distant future.

References

1. Air Quality in Selected Urban-Areas, 1982. WHO Internal Document PEP/86.5, Geneva, Switzerland, 1986.

2. Air Quality in Selected Urban Areas, 1981. WHO Internal Document PEP/86.4, Geneva, Switzerland, 1986.

3. Air Quality in Selected Urban Areas, 1979-1980. WHO offset Publication No.76, Geneva, Switzerland, 1983.

4. Air Quality in Selected Urban Areas, 1977-1978. WHO offset Publication No. 57, Geneva, Switzerland, 1980.

5. Urban Air Pollution, 1973-1980. World Health Organization, Geneva Switzerland, 1984.

6. Bennett, B. G., Kretzschmar, J. G., Akland, G. G. and de Koning, H. W. Environ. Sci. Technol. 1985, 19 (4): 298-304.

7. Global Pollution and Health. World Health Organization, Geneva, 1986.

8. Assessment of Urban Air Quality. United Nations Environment Program and World Health Organization, 1988.

9. Estimates and Projections of Urban, Rural and City Populations,1950-2025: The 1982 Assessment. United Nations Department of Economic and Social Affairs, ST/ESA/SER. 4/58 New York City, New York, 1985.

10. The Global Possible Resources, Development and the New Century, Repetto, R. Eds; Yale University Press, New Haven and London, United Kingdom, 1985.

11. National Strategies and Policies for Air Pollution Abatement, United Nations Document, New York City, NY, 1987.

12. World Resources 1986, World Resources Institute 1986. Basic Books; 1985, New York, p. 351.

13. Moller, D., Atm. Env. 1984, 18 (1): 19-27.

14. Vehely:, G., Atm. Env. 1985, 19 (7): 1,029-1,040.

15. Highton, N.H. and Chadwick, N.Y. Ambio 1982, 11: 324-329.

16. Sulphur Oxides and Suspended Particulate Matter. Environmental Health Criteria Document No. 8, Geneva, Switzerland, 1979.

17. Urban, Rural and City Populations, 1950-2000 Assessed in 1978, United Nations Doc ESA/P/WP.66, New York City, New York, 1980.

18. Robinson, E. and Robbins, R.C. In: Air Pollution Control, Strauss, W., Ed., Wiley Interscience, New York City, New York, 1972; Part III. pp 1-93.

19. Air Quality Guidelines for Europe. World Health Organization, European Series No. 23.

20. Wolcoff, M., and Bruetsch, R. Size Specific Total Particulate Emission Factors for Mobile Sources, US EPA Publication EPA-460/3-85-00, Ann Arbor, Michigan, 1985.

21. Atmospheric Chemistry, Goldbert, E.D., Ed.; Springer Verlog, New York City, New York, 1982.

22. Jaffe, L. S., J. Geophys. 1973, Res. 67: 5,293-5,305.

23. Logan, J. A., Prather, M. J., Wofsy, S. C. and McElroy, M. B. J. Geophys. Res. 1981, 86: 7,210-7,254.

24. The National Air Monitoring Program: Air Quality and Emissions Trends, Annual Report, Vol. 1, EPA Publication EPA-450/1-73-001, Research Triangle Park, NC, US, 1973.

25. Nriagu, J. O. Nature, 1979, 279: 409-411.

26. Air Quality Criteria for Lead, EPA Publication EPA- 600/8-83/028/af. Research Triangle Park, NC US, 1986.

RECEIVED October 8, 1991

The Aquatic Component

An Overview

David A. Dunnette

Environmental Science and Resources Program, Portland State University,
P.O. Box 751, Portland, OR 97207

Water is certainly the most wonderful and incredible substance on Earth.
It is the medium through which all life evolved. Its crystals mirror its
molecular geometry and its glaciers preserve a chemical history of our
atmosphere. Water is on a journey with no end, continuously recycling
throughout the pores of the living and non-living Earth, each molecule
having visited every corner of the earth and every species that ever lived.
From dark ocean currents providing life sustaining phosphorus to the global
ocean food chain, from the ancient lagoons of Venice and the depths of the
world's great lakes, water pulses through the global ecosystems composing
the Earth's biosphere in rhythm with life and non-life, with the air, with the
land. Certainly, as anthropologist-naturalist Loren Eisley has stated, if
there is magic in the world, it is in water, a kind of universal common
denominator through which ecosystems are held, often tenuously, in
balance.

Increasingly, the waters of the world are bearing messages disturbing
to the chemistry of life. About twenty years ago, I picked up a fresh copy
of National Geographic magazine, the December, 1970 issue. On the cover
was an oil soaked bird, a Western Grebe, one of thousands of casualties
from the Santa Barbara off-shore oil leak. Twenty years later, in January
of 1990, I picked up another National Geographic: oil soaked bird,
unidentified, Valdez, Alaska. This anecdotal observation is meaningless
except that it is part of a pattern of impacts on the aquatic environment
from human activity which is upsetting ecological balances around the
globe.

Biogeochemical connections - An Illustration: Phosphorus

A better understanding of the interconnections between the various
chemical species in aquatic systems and in the environment is essential in
protecting and conserving the aquatic environment. The cycling of
phosphorus provides a particularly good illustration of this biogeochemical
interrelatedness. For over 25 years phosphorus has been recognized as the

0097–6156/92/0483–0185$06.00/0

element most responsible for limiting primary production of freshwater algae. In the late 1970s it became clear that the degree of eutrophication in water bodies may often be predicted from phosphorus concentration data (1).

On the other hand, when plenty of phosphorus is available in the aquatic environment, nitrogen often becomes the growth-limiting nutrient. This results in a very interesting ecological shift to algal species which fix nitrogen, an example of elemental and ecological coupling between the phosphorus and nitrogen cycles (2).

When phosphorus enters an aquatic system such as the Great Lakes, as discussed by Williams, or the Venice Lagoon, as described by Pavoni *et al.*, additional carbon is extracted from the water by algae. Since most carbon in water is present as bicarbonate, its depletion results in an equilibrium shift,

$$HCO_3^- \rightleftharpoons CO_2 + OH^-$$

where CO_2 is utilized directly by algae in cell production and respiration. The large CO_2 gradient between the atmosphere and water, which results from accelerated production, causes additional CO_2 to be absorbed into the water body. At higher turbulence, more CO_2 enhances conversion of CO_2 to bicarbonate. This example (3) is an illustration of one aspect of the connections between the cycling of phosphorus and carbon in the aquatic environment.

Phosphorus, likewise, has a profound impact on the cycling of various forms of sulfur. In sediments, particularly those in the remote anoxic regions of lakes and seas, sulfate is reduced by certain species of bacteria to hydrogen sulfide. Sulfide, in turn affects the release or deposition of phosphorus in sediments. These examples illustrate primary chemical-ecological concepts which are essential for a global perspective: elemental coupling and uncoupling, feedback, interrelatedness and the importance of both biotic and abiotic factors.

G.E. Hutchinson, world renown aquatic scientist, used a phosphorus example in his early treatise on biogeochemistry over 40 years ago (4) and this has been expanded upon by Botkin (5). Bird guano deposits, a valuable fertilizer from nesting birds, are found on a few small islands near the coasts of Africa and South America. The phosphorus originates from the fish diet of the birds, and in turn from small, free-floating animal life in the water column. The natural upwelling of ocean currents brings the phosphorus- enriched deep water to the surface where it is utilized by algae. The currents in turn are driven by the energy of the winds and ultimately, the sun. When the upwelling fails, as in the case of *El Nino*, the cycle is interrupted, the fishery is depleted, and the rate of guano deposition is reduced. Dust storms which follow desertification contribute significant quantities of phosphorus to ecological systems. Research similar to that conducted by Kauffman *et al.*, as described in this book, has led to the conclusion that phosphorus inputs to the tropical rainforests originate mainly from dust, the topic of Fergusson in the Terrestrial Section.

The Papers

Several examples of imbalances in aquatic systems are presented in the six chapters of this section. El-Sayed's work on the potential impact of ozone depletion on the ocean's food chain is illustrative of the direct connection between the aquatic and atmospheric components of the global environment and indirectly, the terrestrial component. Direct assaults on aquatic systems from human activity are addressed by Pavoni *et al.* and by Levy. Pavoni *et al.* give an account of pollution of the Venice Lagoon and of their work in attempting to reconstruct the impact of human activity on that water body over the last several hundred years. Williams' paper illustrates the impact of human activities on a major freshwater ecosystem-- the Great Lakes of North America--and the positive responses to initiatives involving cooperation of two countries.

Levy discusses a controversial and visible indicator of human activity: oil and plastic contamination of the world's oceans. Impacts of such contamination may be both dramatic and subtle. Finally, Dunnette focuses on water quality of the world's rivers to illustrate some of the technical details involved in assessing the global aquatic environment. The classic case of the Willamette River, Oregon is used as an example of the various approaches available.

The phosphorus example illustrates the need for new ecological perspectives and an interdisciplinary approach to assessing global environmental changes. The reader is encouraged to read the aquatic section chapters in this spirit and to refer to the overview chapters by Tolba and Mar which provide a holistic perspective and guidance in assimilating the variety of papers.

Literature Cited

1. Rast, W. And Lee, G.F. *Summary Analysis of the North American OECD Eutrophication Project: Nutrient Loading-Lake Response Relationships and Trophic State Indices*; USEPA, EPA-600/3-78-008, Corvallis, OR, 1978.
2. Flett, R.J., Schindler, D.W., Hamilton, R.D. and Campbell, N.E., *J. Fish. Aquat. Sci.*, **1980**, *37*, pp. 494-505.
3. Schindler, D.W. in *Some Perspectives of the Major Biogeochemical Cycles*; Likens, G.E., Ed.; 1981, pp. 113- 123.
4. Hutchinson, G.E. *Bull. Amer. Museum Natural History*, **1950**, 96.
5. Botkin, D.B. in *Changing the Global Environment - Perspectives on Human Involvement;* Botkin, D.; Caswell, M.; Orio, A. Eds, Academic Press, San Diego, CA. 1987.

RECEIVED September 13, 1991

Chapter 9

Potential Effects of Increased Ultraviolet Radiation on the Productivity of the Southern Ocean

Sayed Z. El-Sayed[1] and F. Carol Stephens[2]

[1]Department of Oceanography, Texas A&M University, College Station, TX 77843
[2]Naval Oceanographic and Atmosphere Research Laboratory, Stennis Space Center, Bay St. Louis, MS 39529

A month-long study of the effects of ultraviolet radiation (UV) on phytoplankton and ice-algae collected from Arthur Harbor, Anvers Island, Antarctica, was carried out during November-December 1987. The parameters studied included: primary production rates, photosynthetic pigments and the photosynthesis-irradiance (P vs I) relation-ship. The results showed an enhancement of the photosynthetic rates when UV was excluded; conversely, production rates were lower under enhanced UV conditions. Significant changes in phytoplankton pigmentation also occurred as a result of changes in the UV levels. The implications of these findings to our understanding of the trophodynamics of the Southern Ocean and the bearing these have on global marine productivity are discussed.

Composition of Solar Ultraviolet Radiation

Although solar ultraviolet (UV) radiation comprises about 8 percent of the total amount of electromagnetic radiation emitted by the sun, this relatively small amount of radiation plays a significant role in the survival of biological systems. UV radiation is generally defined as radiation of wavelengths between 190 and 400 nanometers (nm). Within this waveband three spectral regions are recognized: UV-A (320-400 nm); UV-B (280-320 nm); and UV-C (200-280 nm). UV-A, which is of lower energy, is not appreciably affected by ozone in the stratosphere and UV-C is completely absorbed before reaching the earth's surface; hence UV-B is the most biologically injurious component of sunlight reaching the earth. Electromagnetic radiation in this wavelength band can cause skin cancer in humans, has been linked to cataracts, and can suppress the immune system. Studies have also shown that UV-B is harmful to many other forms of life, from bacteria (1) to higher plants and crops (2). And recent investigations suggest that aquatic ecosystems may be especially vulnerable (3, 4).

0097–6156/92/0483–0188$06.00/0
© 1992 American Chemical Society

Ozone and Ozone Depletion. Ozone, O_3, a triatomic form of oxygen, is rare in the lower atmosphere. Small but crucial amounts in the stratosphere (altitude between 10 and 50 kilometers above the earth's surface) shield the earth from most solar ultraviolet radiation. Anthropogenic releases of chlorofluorocarbons (CFCs), nitrous oxide, bromine-containing halons, and solvents such as methyl chloroform and carbon tetrachloride are contributing to the decrease in stratospheric ozone (5, 6), resulting in an increase in the level of UV-B radiation reaching the earth's surface (7).   Stratospheric ozone concentration can be viewed as a column of gas 0.32 cm high when standard temperature and pressure are applied.   Recent measurements of the total ozone column from 1979/80 to 1987/88 provide evidence of ozone change over this 8-year period (8), as much as 30-40% decrease over the Antarctic in springtime.   Although the drastic thinning of the ozone layer apparently began about 1976, it was not until May 1985 that scientists with the British Antarctic Survey published the results of the observations they had been making over Hallet Station, Antarctica, since 1957.   It was found that the ozone level over Antarctica decreased drastically each September and October and then gradually replenished itself by the end of November (9).   Scientists monitoring the annual thinning of the ozone layer over Antarctica reported that in October 1987 the ozone reached one of its lowest recorded levels ever, and the decline lasted into December, the longest period ever.   In 1990, the ozone level was even lower than in 1987.   At its maximum, the "hole" was the size of the United States.   More alarmingly, recent data indicate that ozone depletion is occurring on a global scale, although nowhere as extensively as over Antarctica.

Effects of UV wavelengths on biological systems. Since sunlight in the UV range is absorbed by proteins, damage to several basic cellular mechanisms may occur.   The diversity of damaged pathways in plant cells includes damage to the Hill reaction carrier proteins, membrane damage, and damage to DNA.   Although the pathways are different, all have the common property of greater damaging effect as wavelengths decrease.

Consequences of Ozone Depletion. Ozone depletion over Antarctica is causing renewed concern about the consequences of increased levels of UV reaching the earth's biosphere.   One area of concern involves the free-floating microscopic plants, known collectively as phytoplankton (the grass of the sea), which through the process of photosynthesis, fix carbon dioxide into living organic matter. Phytoplankton forms the basis of the marine food chain on which zooplankton (animal plankton) and all other components of the ecosystem depend for their sustenance.

Numerous studies have shown that increased levels of UV affect photosynthetic activity (10-23), growth rate (24), nitrogen metabolism (25), and locomotion (26) of phytoplankton.   Additionally, increases in UV-B are likely to alter community diversity as well as phytoplankton species composition.   Thus, by weakening the base of the food web and altering trophodynamic relationships, UV-induced changes could potentially have far-reaching effects on the entire ecosystem.

Effects of UV Radiation on Antarctic Phytoplankton. Because ozone depletion and UV-B increases are greatest over the Antarctic, biological effects of UV on plankton in that region are particularly important. Although the effects of ultraviolet radiation on marine phytoplankton in temperate and subtropical regions had been studied by several investigators, no such studies had been carried out on Antarctic phytoplankton. In this chapter we will focus on the effects of ultraviolet radiation on Antarctic phytoplankton. We will discuss the results of an investigation which we undertook in late austral spring/early summer 1987 to study the effects of UV on these algal cells. We will then discuss the potential threat to the Antarctic ecosystem as a result of increased UV-B radiation.

Although our original plans were to conduct the field experiments in the open waters of Arthur Harbor, Anvers Island, Antarctica, they were thwarted by unusually heavy sea ice, which covered almost all of the harbor during the entire period of our investigation. It was necessary, therefore, to modify our sampling strategy and to depend, for the most part, on the water pumped from a hole (cut through sea-ice four to five feet thick) to the experimental site. We also experimented with ice-algae collected in the vicinity of Palmer Station's ship dock, and with phytoplankton collected from the open waters at Bonaparte Point (Fig. 1).

The Experimental Set-up

Our investigation was designed to examine the effects of ultraviolet radiation on the rates of carbon fixation as well as on the chlorophyll and carotenoid pigments of the algal cells. Responses of natural phytoplankton and ice-algae communities to ultraviolet radiation were assessed by measuring changes in the photosynthetic rates and pigmentation following incubation in an array of tanks and chambers. Seawater containing natural population of phytoplankton was pumped from the ice-hole into a mixing tank, from which it flowed (by gravity) into a series of 18-liter flow-through chambers. The chambers were situated within the larger treatment tanks (3 per tank), through which seawater was pumped in order to maintain a constant temperature ($\pm 0.5°C$), (Fig. 2). Mixing within the chambers was accomplished with air bubbles. Samples collected from these tanks, from Bonaparte Point, and from the pack-ice were included in plastic bags placed in these chambers for measurements of ^{14}C uptake. These tanks were kept outdoors under natural sunlight conditions and provided the following irradiation conditions:

Treatment 1:	Near ambient light, including UV-A and UV-B
Treatment 2:	Near ambient visible light, excluding both UV-A and UV-B (99.7% UV removed)
Treatment 3:	Near ambient visible and UV-A light, but with reduced levels of solar UV-B (35% UV-B removed)
Treatment 4:	Near ambient light including UV-A and UV-B plus artificially enhanced UV-A and UV-B (approximately 3% enhancement).

Materials and Techniques. The tanks and chambers for treatments 1, 3 and 4 were constructed of 3/16-inch-thick OP-4 Plexiglas; those for treatment 2 were constructed of 1/4-inch-thick OP-2 Plexiglas. Mylar D (thickness 4 mils) was placed over the top of treatment tank 3 to reduce levels of ambient UV-B. Transmission spectra of these materials are shown in Fig. 3. Enhancement of UV-A and UV-B was achieved by placing four FS-20 Westinghouse fluorescent sunlamps underneath treatment tank 4. In order to exclude most of the radiation less than 290 nm wavelength emitted by the lamps, a sheet of 4 mils thick Kodacel (TA 401), which had been preconditioned by exposure to a sunlamp for approximately 100 hours, was placed between the sunlamps and the bottom of the enhanced UV tank.

The effective biological dose (Eε; 18) at local apparent noon for each chamber was estimated by multiplying the relative biological efficiency for photoinhibition [$\varepsilon_{P1}(\lambda)$] by the available spectral irradiance [E(λ)], and integrating with respect to wavelength (λ, 290-400 nm):

$$E\varepsilon = \int(\lambda) \cdot \varepsilon_{P1}(\lambda) \cdot d\lambda.$$

The downward spectral irradiance data [$E_d(\lambda)$, the ambient UV radiation] were generated with the atmospheric model of Frederick and Lubin (27) and ozone levels measured during the course of this study (J.E. Frederick, pers. commun.). The relative degree of UV enhancement (%ENH) for each chamber was calculated as follows:

$$\%ENH = \frac{(E\varepsilon) \text{ exp} - (E\varepsilon) \text{ amb}}{(E\varepsilon) \text{ amb}} \times 100.$$

Photosynthetic rates were measured using the ^{14}C-uptake method (28). For pigment analyses, the chlorophylls and carotenoids were analyzed by high performance liquid chromatography (HPLC) according to the methods outlined by Bidigare et al. (29). Further details of the experimental set-up and methodology used are given in (23).

Effects of UV on Phytoplankton Pigments

Short-term (i.e., 4 hr) exposure of phytoplankton and ice-algae to UV radiation produced no significant changes in the concentrations of chlorophyll *a*, chlorophyll *c* and fucoxanthin. On the other hand, the 24-48 hr exposure of phytoplankton to UV radiation under ambient visible light conditions produced drastic alterations in phytoplankton pigmentation. For seawater samples collected off Bonaparte Point, there was a selective loss of chlorophyll *a* with increasing UV dose; however, concentrations of the other pigments showed little or no change.

In another experiment, seawater was pumped from a sea-ice hole, incubated for 24 and 48 hours, and analyzed for pigment content. Significant changes in pigment concentrations were observed for all the major photosynthetic pigments including, chlorophyll *a*, chlorophyll *c* and fucoxanthin. After a 48-hour incubation period, the highest and lowest pigment concentrations were measured for

A

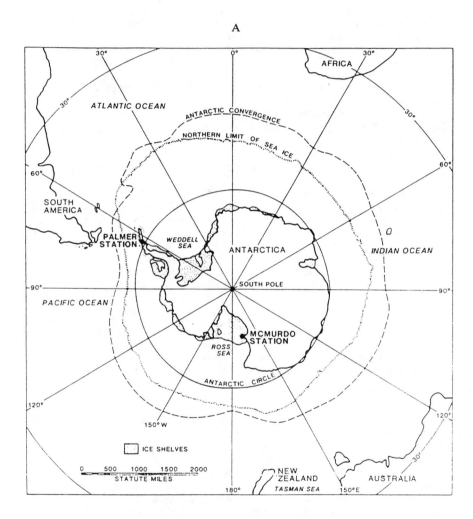

Figure 1A. Map of Arthur Harbor showing location of Palmer Station. (Reproduced with permission from reference 46. Copyright 1991 Cambridge.)

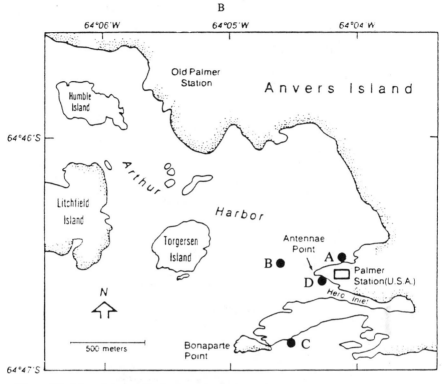

Figure 1B. Map of Arthur Harbor showing location of the four sampling sites (A, B, C, and D). (Reproduced with permission from reference 46. Copyright 1991 Cambridge.)

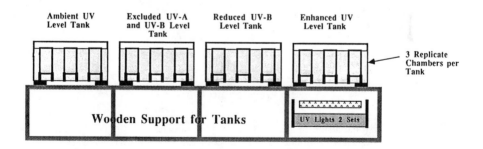

Figure 2. Schematic drawing of the four experimental tanks and chambers used to investigate the effects of UV radiation of Antarctic phytoplankton and ice-algae. (Reproduced with permission from reference 23. Copyright 1990 Springer-Verlag, Berlin.)

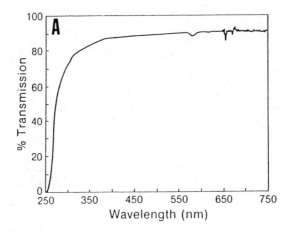

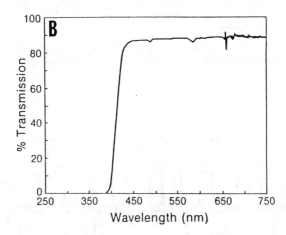

Figure 3. Light transmission properties of (A) OP-4 plexiglas and (B) OP-2 plexiglas. (Reproduced with permission from reference 23. Copyright 1990 Springer-Verlag, Berlin.)

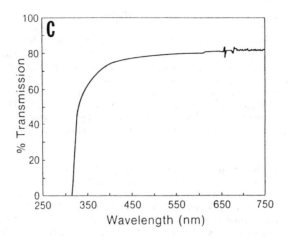

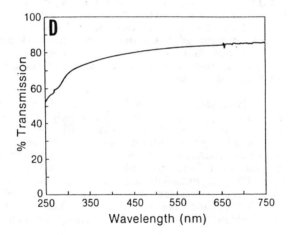

Figure 3. Light transmission properties of (C) OP-4 plexiglas plus Mylar D and (D) the plastic bags (Nasco Company) used in this study for the incubation of Antarctic phytoplankton. (Reproduced with permission from reference 23. Copyright 1990 Springer-Verlag, Berlin.)

treatment 2 (i.e., UV excluded) and treatment 4 (i.e., UV enhanced), respectively. Intermediate pigment concentrations were observed for treatment 1 (ambient UV) and treatment 3 (reduced UV).

Effects of UV on Photosynthetic Rates

The average photosynthetic rates for each of the three experiments performed, increased with UV exclusion and decreased with increased UV exposure (Table I). However, primary production rates of phytoplankton (collected on 17 November and 3 December 1987) measured under near-ambient light conditions were low, but not statistically different from those measured under either UV-reduced or UV-enhanced conditions. Small but statistically significant increases in primary production rates were measured when UV radiation was excluded.

Response by Ice-Algae. In contrast, primary production rates of ice algae (samples collected on 17 November and 3 December 1987) were greater when UV-B radiation was reduced as well as when all UV was excluded. As with phytoplankton, however, production rates of ice-algae were not statistically different between samples incubated under ambient and enhanced UV levels. These results suggested that early in the austral springtime, phytoplankton sampled from beneath the ice or near the ice-edge was susceptible to photo-inhibition by exposure to ambient solar Photosynthetically Active Radiation (PAR). On the other hand, ice algae, which had been exposed to ambient PAR for several days prior to measurement of productivity, may have adapted to solar radiation in such a way that productivity rates were affected more by UV than by visible radiation; in other words, they had become adapted to higher levels of PAR, but not to UV-B.

P vs I Relationships. In our investigation we em-ployed a technique widely used by plant physiologists, namely, the study of rate of photosynthesis (P) as a function of irradiance (I). The results of one experiment in which phytoplankton were kept under the four experimental treatment conditions for 24 hours are shown in Fig. 4. It is clear from this figure that phytoplankton exposed to visible light alone (i.e., when UV was excluded) had the highest photosynthetic rates, and these rates were maintained over a higher range of irradiance levels. On the other hand, the lowest carbon fixation rates occurred when the phytoplankton were exposed to ambient and enhanced levels of UV.

Discussion

Potential Effects of UV on Primary Production. The results of the study carried out at Palmer Station during November-December 1987 provided insight into the potential deleterious effects of enhanced UV radiation. These results showed an enhancement of the photosynthetic rates in the tanks where UV-A and UV-B were excluded. Conversely, rates of production were much lower under ambient and enhanced UV

Table I. Photosynthetic rates (mean ± standard deviation; n=3) for samples taken from three different habitats and incubated for 4 hours under the four experimental conditions described in the text (Amb = ambient UV; Exc = UV excluded; Red = reduced UV; Enh = enhanced UV; and NM = not measured).

Habitat Description and Collection Date	Solar Irradiance (PAR) (μEin m^{-2} s^{-1})	Production Rate (mgC m^{-3} h^{-1})	Treatment Number
Phytoplankton (Open-water from Bonaparte Point; 17 November 1987)	1318	0.08 ± 0.01	1 (Amb)
	1221	0.40 ± 0.10	2 (Exc)
	1260	0.11 ± 0.01	3 (Red)
	1318	0.05 ± 0.04	4 (Enh)
Pre-adapted Ice Algae (21 November 1987)	NM	7.40 ± 1.56	1 (Amb)
	NM	42.08 ± 0.69	2 (Exc)
	NM	17.38 ± 4.05	3 (Red)
	NM	4.98 ± 1.18	4 (Enh)
Phytoplankton (Water Pumped from Sea-ice Hole; 3 December 1987)	1536	0.04 ± 0.02	1 (Amb)
	1423	0.29 ± 0.06	2 (Exc)
	1468	0.11 ± 0.05	3 (Red)
	1536	0.01 ± 0.01	4 (Enh)

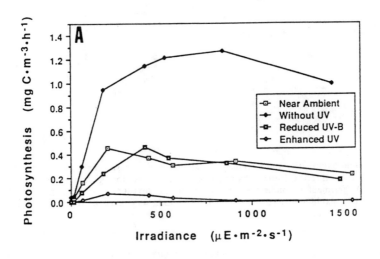

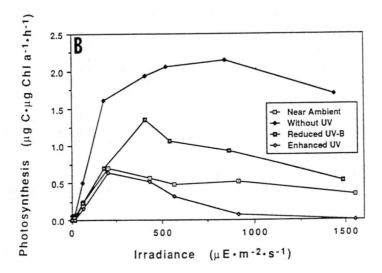

Figure 4. (a) Volume-based and (B) chlorophyll-based photosynthesis–irradiance data for phytoplankton sampled on December 6, 1987 from the experimental chambers (after flow had been stopped for 24 h). Samples were incubated for 4 h under the four treatment conditions described in the text. (Reproduced with permission from reference 23. Copyright 1990 Springer-Verlag, Berlin.)

conditions. This was the case in all our experiments, whether we used the phytoplankton from under the sea-ice, ice-algae, or phytoplankton found in the open waters off Bonaparte Point.

Effects on Pigmentation. As to the phytoplankton pigmentation and how it changed with exposure to varying levels of UV, significant decreases in photosynthetic pigmentation were observed for those phytoplankton samples exposed to enhanced UV radiation. As one might have expected, the magnitude of change varied in relation to the amount and duration of exposure. Reductions in rates of photosynthesis could, in part, be explained by the loss of chlorophyll *a* and accessory pigments.

Effects on Species Composition. Other similar studies have demonstrated that the impact of increased UV radiation on algal cells is not limited to a decrease in rate of photosynthesis, change in pigment concentrations, and production of protective pigments, but also affects the species composition of the algal community. Evidence from laboratory studies by other investigators indicates a differential sensitivity of algal cells to enhanced UV levels (11, 30, 31, 32). Some algal species have been shown to be susceptible even to current levels of UV-B radiation, whereas other species showed little apparent effect even at levels several times the current dose.

The possible shift in the composition of the algal population was also accompanied by change in relative proportions of large and small species. Most easily harmed by enhanced UV were the nanoplankton (organisms less than 20 μm in diameter). Some researchers hypothesize that protozooplankton feeding on Antarctic nanoplankton and picoplankton (organisms less than 2 μm in diameter) form a major link between the primary producers (i.e., phytoplankton) and the herbivorous zooplankton and krill (33) (Fig. 5). Recent studies carried out by the author and others have shown that the nanoplankton and picoplankton make up a substantial proportion (up to 95 percent or more) of the total biomass of phytoplankton and primary production in Antarctic waters (see 34 for review). This finding, plus the possibility that these organisms are especially sensitive to UV-B could have serious implications for the overall community structure and trophic relationships in the Antarctic marine ecosystem.

Effect of UV on Water Column Phytoplankton. So far we discussed only the possible effects of UV-B radiation on surface and near-surface phytoplankton and on ice algae. But what about the phytoplankton that live well below the surface? Photosynthetic organisms are found throughout the water column, down to (and even below) the so-called euphotic depth, i.e., the depth at which only 1 percent of surface light penetrates. Although turbidity of the water may limit the penetration of light into coastal waters, in calm waters of the open ocean, 1 percent of surface UV light can penetrate to greater depths. Thus, UV may still have a damaging effect on a significant portion of the euphotic layer and on the species that move up and down in the water column. In periods of very low mixing (e.g., in calm weather or when the ice melts during the austral summer), the low salinity of the meltwater contributes to the stability of the water column, thus helping to retain phytoplankton in near-surface waters

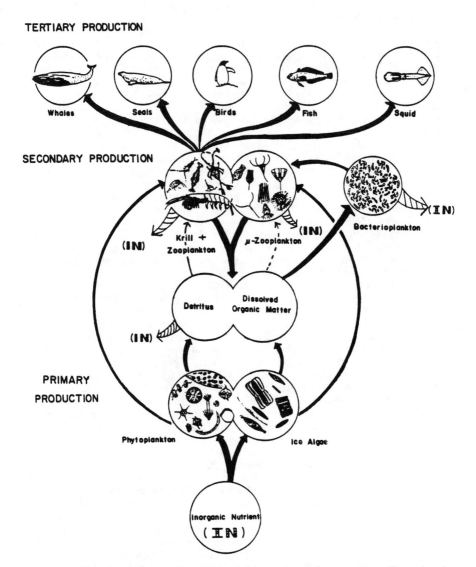

Figure 5. Paradigm of energy flow within the Antarctic marine ecosystem. (Reproduced with permission from reference 33 by the Scientific Committee on Antarctic Research of the International Council of Scientific Unions. Copyright 1987.)

resulting in increased productivity. On the other hand, the low stability of the water prevents the phytoplankton from remaining in the optimal light zone long enough for extensive production, thus contributing to low productivity. Accordingly, the residence time of deeper water organisms in the near-surface layer (and therefore their exposure to UV-B radiation) must be considered when assessing the total effect of UV on plankton production.

Comparison with other Studies. How do the results of our investigation compare with similar studies? Our results corroborate the data provided in a similar study of the effect of UV-B on primary productivity in the southeastern Pacific Ocean (35). In the latter study, it was noted that enhanced UV-B radiation caused significant decreases in the productivity of surface and deep samples. Compared to ambient, primary productivity decreased with increasing doses of UV-B. In another study in which *in situ* experiments using natural Antarctic phytoplankton populations, it was noted that incident solar radiation significantly depressed photosynthetic rates in the upper 10-15 meters of the water column (36). It was also found that the spectral region between 305 and 350 nm was responsible for approximately 75 percent of the overall inhibitory effect.

How do Phytoplankton Cope with Enhanced UV? Several investigators have reported the existence in Antarctic algae of UV-absorbing mycosporine amino acids identical to those of tropical and temperate marine species (37). These compounds absorb in the UV-B region of the spectrum and may act as sunscreens which may provide some measure of protection from damaging UV-B.

Plants (as well as animals), in general, have several mechanisms to repair the genetic damage caused by exposure to UV radiation. It is well known that direct mutagenic and lethal effects of UV exposure occur from damage to DNA. According to some investigators (Karentz, D. Antarctic J., in press) when DNA molecules are exposed to UV radiation, they change their structure. If the DNA molecules are not repaired, mutations in impaired cells may affect the genetic make-up of future generations. There are three known cellular repair mechanisms: photoreactivation, excision repair and recom-bination repair. Of these the former is the primary means of correcting UV-induced DNA damage in bacteria and phytoplankton (Karentz, *ibid.*). While some organisms have only one DNA repair mechanism, others may have two or three. The question now is, how effective are these pathways in Antarctic organisms? Only future research will tell. However, laboratory experiments on one phytoplankton species suggest an inability to adapt to increasing UV-B radiation (Behrenfeld and Hardy, in review).

Effects of UV on Phytoplankton--A Cautionary Note. Despite the preliminary nature of the results of the Palmer Station experiments, there seems to be sufficient evidence to suggest that elevated UV-B radiation can decrease the photosynthetic rates of Antarctic phytoplankton and ice-algae, and bring about a pigmentation change in algal cells (38, 39). However, we do not yet know whether these findings can be applied to the phytoplankton and ice-algae of the whole Southern Ocean. Considerable caution must be exercised in extrapolating the results of these short-term laboratory/field experiments to the real world. In the latter one has to contend with a host of complex, interrelated factors, among which are: the depth at which UV is attenuated; the depth of the water column mixed by the wind; the residence time of the algal cells in the euphotic zone; seasonality of UV exposure; behavioral response of the targeted organisms to solar UV and their ability to repair damaged DNA molecules. As to whether the effect of UV-B on algal populations is short-lived, long-lasting, or reversible, our limited data do not provide a final answer. Here again, only future research will provide the data needed to answer this question.

Effect of UV on Productivity of the Southern Ocean. Has ozone depletion over Antarctica affected the productivity of the Southern Ocean? There is no easy answer. First, one has to take into account the fact that the drastic decrease of ozone over Antarctica has been reported as recently as 1976, a relatively short time in the evolution of the organisms to develop mechanisms to cope with elevated UV. One of the most vexing problems in studying the effects of UV radiation on productivity, is a dearth of historical data on the level of UV. Without these baselines, normal fluctuations could easily be interpreted as decline in productivity. Second, there is a host of biotic and abiotic factors that play significant roles in governing the productivity of the Southern Ocean (40). Ultraviolet radiation is but one more complicating factor to be considered in an already stressful environment.

Effect of UV on Global Productivity. As to the long-term effects of enhanced UV radiation on the Antarctic marine ecosystem, based on the Arthur Harbor findings and given the long residence time of anthropogenic atmospheric pollutants; e.g. chlorofluorocarbons (estimated to be between 20 and 380 years!), the impact of elevated UV-B could be long-lasting and potentially damaging. Since phytoplankton are the basic primary producers in the Antarctic Ocean on which all other components of the ecosystem (zooplankton, krill, fish, squid, winged birds, penguins, seals, and whales) depend for their livelihood (Fig. 6), any substantial decrease in the productivity of these waters, or any change in their community structure, could have far-reaching ecological implications.

Although in this chapter we have focused on the potential effects of increased UV-B radiation on the Antarctic marine ecosystem, our results also have bearing on efforts to describe the effects of UV radiation on global marine productivity. However, here again, considerable uncertainties still remain in assessing the effects of ozone depletion on global production. Several authors have predicted a significant decrease in primary production over a wide latitudinal area in response to predicted increase in UV-B reaching the earth's surface. This decrease would likely affect higher trophic levels and would very likely decrease fisheries yield (41, 42). For instance, it has been estimated that a 5 percent reduction in primary productivity would lead to a 6 to 9 percent reduction in fisheries catch (43). Another far-reaching ecological implication is that any substantial decrease in marine primary production would decrease the ocean's capacity as a sink for anthropogenic CO_2 (44), thus exacerbating the global greenhouse warming.

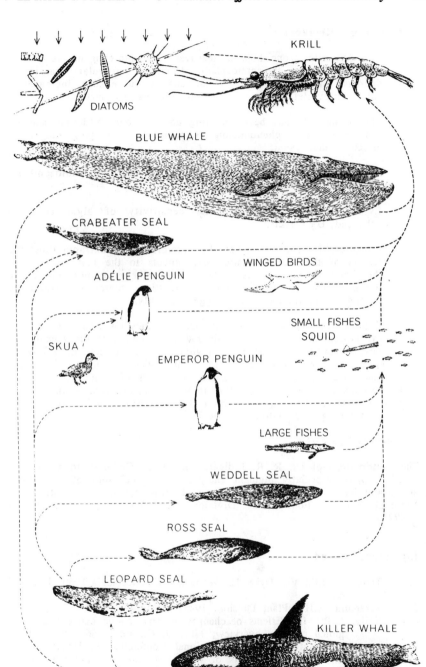

Figure 6. Food web in the Antarctic marine ecosystem showing the key position occupied by krill. (Reproduced with permission from reference 45. Copyright 1962 W. H. Freeman and Company.)

Concluding   Remarks

•   The Antarctic ozone hole is the result of anthropogenic release of trace gases into the atmosphere (CFCs in particular), causing a decrease in stratospheric ozone and a subsequent increase in solar ultraviolet radiation reaching the earth's surface.

•   The ozone hole has been recurring now for over a decade and we can expect this phenomenon to continue in varying magnitude as an annual event.

•   Increased UV-B radiation decreased the rate of photosynthesis and changed pigment concentration.

•   Evidence exists of differential sensitivity of algal cells to enhanced UV levels.

•   Considerable caution must be exercised in extrapolating the results of the Palmer Station experiments to the real world (i.e., the Southern Ocean), as tanks and chambers do not mimic the ocean. The results of our investigation, therefore, should be treated as preliminary and suggestive only.

•   Further research is needed to address questions/issues related to (a) latitudinal effects of UV-B radiation, i.e., will the damage be largely confined to the polar regions?, (b) effects of UV-B on the chemical concentration of vital nutrients such as vitamins and trace metals, (c) what are the effects of lethal and sublethal responses to UV-B and the reasons for differences in species response, (d) quantification UV exposure, and (e) UV-photobiology of individual species.

Acknowledgments

The contributions of Dr. R. R. Bidigare and M. E. Ondrusek to all aspects of the project, especially pigment analyses and calculations of UV doses, are gratefully acknowledged. This work was supported by the U.S. National Science Foundation, Division of Polar Programs (DPP-88-12972).

Literature   Cited

(1)   Thomson, B.E.; Van Dyke, H.; Worrest, R.C. Oceologia 1980, 47:56-60.
(2)   Teramura, A.H.   Plant Physiol., 1983, 58:416-427
(3)   Kelly, J. R. In Effects of changes in stratospheric ozone and global climate, overview; Titus, J. G., Ed. 1986. Proceedings of the UNEP/EPA International Conference on Health and Environmental Effects of Ozone Modification and Climate Change, 237-251
(4)   Worrest, R. C. In Effects of changes in stratospheric ozone and global climate, overview; Titus, J. G., Ed. 1986. Proceedings

of the UNEP/EPA International Conference on Health and Environmental Effects of Ozone Modification and Climate Change, 175-191

(5)   Hoffman, J. S.; Gibbs, M. J. U. S. Environmental Protection Agency, Office of Air and Radiation, EPA 400/1-88/005. 1988, 63 pp.

(6)   Watson, R. Ozone Trends Panel, Executive Summary. NASA, Washington, D.C. 1988, No. 1208, 208 pp.

(7)   Lubin, D.; Frederick, J. E.; Booth, C. R.; Lucas, T.; Neushuler, D. Geophy. Res. Letters, 1989, 16:783-785

(8)   Madronich, S. In Effects of solar ultraviolet radiation on biogeochemical dynamics in aquatic environments; Blough, N. V. and Zepp, R. G., Eds. Woods Hole Oceanogr. Inst. Tech. Rep., WHOI-90-09, 1990, 30-31

(9)   Farman, J. C.; Gardiner, B. G.; Shanklin, J. D. *Nature*, 1985, 315:207-210

(10) Jitts, H. R.; Morel, A.; Saijo, Y. Aust. J. Mar. Freshwater Res. 1976, 27:441-454

(11) Worrest, R. C.; Van Dyke, H.; Thomson, B.E. Photochem, Photobiol., 1978 27:471-478

(12) Worrest, R. C.; Brooker, D. L.; Van Dyke, H. Limnol. Oceanogr., 1980 25:360-364

(13) Worrest, R. C.; Wolniakowski, K. U.; Scott, J. D.; Brooker, D. L.; Thompson, B. E.; Van Dyke, H. Photochem Photobiol., 1981, 33:223-227

(14) Worrest, R. C. In the Role of Solar Ultraviolet Radiation in Marine Ecosystems; Calkins, J., ed., Plenum Press, New York, 1987, 429-457

(15) Lorenzen, C. J. Limnol. Oceanogr. 1979, 24:1117-1120

(16) Calkins, J.; Thordardottir, T. *Nature*, 1980, 283:563-566

(17) Baker, K. S.; Smith, R. C.; Green, A. E. S. In The Role of Solar Ultraviolet Radiation in Marine Ecosystems; Clakins, J., Ed., Plenum Press, New York, New York, 1982, 79-91

(18) Smith, R. C.; Baker, K. S. *Science*, 1980, 208:592-593

(19) Smith, R. C.; Baker, K. S.; Holm-Hansen, O.; Olsen, R. Photochem. Photobiol., 1980, 31:585-592

(20) Smith, R. C.; Baker, K. S. Oceanogr. Mag., 1989, 2:4-10

(21) Smith, R. C. Photochem. Photobiol., 1989, 50:459-468

(22) Maske, H., J. Plankton Res., 1984, 6:351-357

(23) El-Sayed, S. Z.; Stephens, F. C.; Bidigare, R. R.; Ondrusek, M. E. In Antarctic Ecosystems: Ecological Change and Conservation; Kerry, K. R. and Hempel, G. Eds.; Springer-Verlag Berlin, Heidelberg, 1990, 379-385

(24) Jokiel, P. L.; York, J. R. H. Limnol. Oceanogr., 1984, 29:192-199

(25) Döhler, G. Plant Physiol. (Life Sci. Adv.), 1988, 7:79-84

(26) Häder, D. P.; Häder, M. Arch. Microbiol., 1988, 150:20-25

(27) Frederick, J.E.; Lubin, D. J. Geophys. Res. 1988 93:3825-3832

(28) Steemann Nielsen, E. J. Conseil., 1954, 19:309-328.

(29) Bidigare, R. R.; Schofield, O.; Prezelin, B. B. Mar. Ecol. Prog. Ser., 1989, (in press)

(30) Worrest, R.C.; Thompson, B.E.; Van Dyke, H. Photochem. Photobiol., 1981, 33:861-867.

(31) Nachtwey, D.S. In Fourth Conference on CIAP. U.S. Department of Transportation, 1975, 75-86

(32) Van Dyke, H.; Thomson, B.E. In Impacts of Climate Change on the
      Biosphere, Part 1; Nachtwey, D.S., Ed.; U.S. Department of
      Transportation, DOT-TST-75, 55, Washington, D.C., 1975, 5-9,
      10
(33) El-Sayed, S.Z. In Marine Phytoplankton and Productivity; O.
      Holm-Hansen, L. Bolis and R. Giles, Eds., Springer-Verlag,
      New York, 1984, 19-34
(34) Weber, L. H.; El-Sayed, S. Z. J. Plankton Res. 1987, 9:973-994
(35) Behrenfeld, M. M.S. Thesis, Dept. General Sciences, Oregon State
      University, Corvallis, Oregon, 1989, 37 pp.
(36) Holm-Hansen, O.; Mitchell, B. G.; Vernet, M. Antarctic J. of the U.
      S., 1989, 24:177-178
(37) Dunlap, W. C.; Chalker, B. E.; Oliver, J. K. J. Exper. Mar. Biol. and
      Ecol., 1986, 104:239-248
(38) Bidigare, R. R. Photochem. Photobiol., 1989, 50:469-477
(39) Vernet, M; B. G. Mitchell; Holm-Hansen, O. Antarctic J. of the U. S.,
      1989, 24:181-183
(40) El-Sayed, S. Z. In Antarctic Ocean and Resources Variability;
      Sahrhage, D., Ed, Springer-Verlag, Berlin, Heidelberg,
      1988; pp 101-119
(41) Nixon, S. W. Limnol. Oceanogr., 1988, 33:1005-1025
(42) Gucinski, H.; Lackey, R. T.; Spence, B. C. Fisheries, Bull. Amer.
      Fish. Soc., 1990, 15:33-38
(43) Hardy, J.; Gucinski, H. Oceanogr. Mag. 2, 1989, 18-21
(44) Gaudry, A.; Monfray, P.; Polian, G.; Lanabert, G. Tellus, 1987,
      39B:209-213
(45) Murphy, R.C. Scientific American, 1962, 207:187-210

(46) Karentz. Anarct. Sci., 1991, 3:1:3-11

RECEIVED September 4, 1991

Chapter 10

Great Lakes Water Quality

A Case Study

D. J. Williams

Inland Waters Directorate—Ontario Region, Canada Center for Inland Waters, 867 Lakeshore Road, Burlington, Ontario, Canada L7R 4A6

Pollution of the Laurentian Great Lakes exemplifies the serious problems associated with the impact of human activities on a major aquatic ecosystem. Problems have included serious bacteriological contamination, cultural eutrophication and contamination by hundreds of anthropogenic, potentially toxic substances. Management of the Great Lakes is divided between Canada and the United States and involves eleven governments at federal, state and provincial levels. Despite this environmental and institutional complexity, the Great Lakes have responded dramatically to remediation initiatives. Human impacts on the lakes associated with development of the Great Lakes Basin are discussed in the context of the unique binational arrangements agreed to by the two countries to restore and protect this shared, unique global ecosystem.

The Laurentian Great Lakes of North America are unique. Formed in basins left by the receding glaciers some 12,000 years ago, they are the largest body of freshwater in the world containing nearly 20% of the total standing freshwater on the earth's surface. Lake Superior is the world's largest freshwater lake in surface area and third largest in volume (1). The Great Lakes are composed of five interconnected lakes in a single watershed comparable in size to the area of Central Europe (Table I; Figure 1). The international boundary between Canada and the United States passes through the lakes with the result that each lake is shared by both countries with the exception of Lake Michigan which is entirely within the United States. In Canada, the watershed lies almost completely within the Province of Ontario, but in the USA, it is divided among eight states. Thus, not only are the Great Lakes a unique global feature but their management which is the responsibility of eleven governments at federal, state and provincial levels has also presented some unique challenges.

0097–6156/92/0483–0207$06.00/0
© 1992 American Chemical Society

Table I. The Great Lakes Basin -- Physical Features and Population

	Superior	Michigan	Huron	Erie	Ontario	Totals
Elevation (m)	183	176	176	173	74	
Length (km)	563	494	332	388	311	
Max Width (km)	257	190	245	92	85	
Ave Depth (m)	147	85	59	19	86	
Max Depth (m)	405	281	229	64	244	
Volume (km3)	12,100	4,920	3,540	484	1,640	22,684
Area (km2)	82,100	57,800	59,600	25,700	18,960	244,160
Drainage Basin						
Area (km2)	127,700	118,000	134,100	78,000	64,030	521,830
Total Area (km2)	209,800	175,800	193,700	103,700	82,990	765,990
Shoreline						
Length (km)	4,385	2,633	6,157	1,402	1,146	10,210
Retention						
Time (years)	191	99	22	3	6	
Population						
U.S. (1980)	558,100	13,970,000	1,321,000	11,347,500	2,090,300	29,287,800
Canada (1981)	180,440		1,051,119	1,621,106	4,551,875	7,404,540
Totals	738,540	13,970,900	2,372,119	12,968,606	6,642,175	36,692,340

Source: Adapted from ref (2)

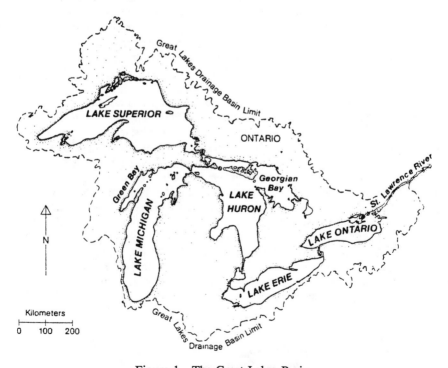

Figure 1. The Great Lakes Basin.

The quality and abundance of Great Lakes basin resources have been the foundation of the region's development since earliest European settlement. Indeed, in a little over a century, the Great Lakes Basin has evolved from a backwoods subsistence economy to a highly geared industrialized society. By way of current example:

- 30% (7.5 million people) of Canada's population and 20% (30 million people) of the United State's population live in the Great Lakes drainage basin;
- Twenty-four million people rely on the Great Lakes for drinking water supply;
- Almost one half and one fifth of Canadian and U.S. manufacturing, respectively, are located in the Great Lakes Basin;
- One half of the $150 billion-a-year Canada/U.S. trade starts and ends in Great Lakes states and province (Ontario);
- Commercial and recreational fisheries total over $160 million and $1 billion per year, respectively, with about 2 million people participating;
- Great Lakes shipping is an important means of transporting bulk goods cheaply (e.g., in 1980, Great Lakes shipping transported 225 million tons of cargo).

The exponential growth in population and technology that has occurred in the Great Lakes Basin has resulted in human activities degrading even these large bodies of water.

It is not surprising that the Great Lakes have been subjected to such degradation. Exploitation of resources for economic gain at the expense of valuable ecosystems is a pattern that has been repeated all too often in every country in the world. Since early settlement, the vastness of the Great Lakes has generated an attitude, which in part remains today, that the lakes have an infinite capacity to absorb human abuse and waste. The chronology of human mismanagement of the lakes and the effects on water quality and use have clearly demonstrated the fragility of this ecosystem. Seen in this light, the uniqueness of the Great Lakes fades. They become simply a microcosm of events as we see them on a global scale.

This paper discusses some of the impacts of development on the Great Lakes. Efforts that have been made to resolve individual problems are also discussed including the unique Canada/U.S. institutional framework for addressing these issues. Emphasis is placed on eutrophication and toxic substances, issues which have been the major focus of concern over the last three decades.

Chronology of Human Impacts on the Great Lakes

The nature of human impacts on the Great Lakes relates closely to historical development and land use in the basin which, in turn, relate closely to the geology and physiography of the watershed. The southern part of the basin consists largely of Palaeozoic sedimentary rocks. Land use consists primarily of intense urban/industrial development and agriculture. The northern part of the basin lies largely within the Precambrian Shield where settlement is more sparse. Impacts are due primarily to forestry and mining with only localized effects related to industrial and urban land use. As a result, both the nature and severity of the resultant human impacts are quite different when comparisons are made between the northern lakes (Superior and Huron) and the southern lakes (Erie and Ontario). The former remain close to pristine conditions, while the latter manifest the signs of degradation related to a variety of human activities.

Early explorers of the Great Lakes Basin found a system in harmony with indigenous native cultures. Major signs of change started coincident with European settlement of the Basin around the 1800s (3-5). Deforestation of the Lake Ontario drainage basin for agricultural purposes caused reduced flows at critical times for fish and made large stretches of streams uninhabitable by reason of increased temperatures and heavy siltation. Moreover, the construction of dams blocked spawning migrations. As a result, Lake Ontario Atlantic salmon were in serious difficulty before 1850 and extinct by 1900 (4). Hartman (6) recorded comparable physical changes for the Lake Erie basin and in addition drew attention to extensive marsh drainage in the early years of settlement. As settlements grew and prospered along the shorelines, human waste discharged into the streams and lakes resulted in contaminated drinking water supplies and serious epidemics of typhoid fever and cholera through the 1930s. Continued industrial growth was accompanied by oil pollution in the 1940s and accelerated eutrophication in the 1960s. By the late 1960s degradation had become so extreme, particularly in the west and central basins of Lake Erie, that headlines such as "Lake Erie is Dead" were appearing in the news (7). In the interim, fisheries of the Great Lakes continued to be impacted by other factors including overfishing and the introduction of exotic species such as the smelt, alewife and sea lamprey. The sea lamprey drastically reduced lake trout stocks, particularly in Lakes Huron and Superior (4). Today, contamination by hundreds of potentially toxic substances via municipal and industrial discharges, land runoff and atmospheric deposition is the major environmental problem in the Great Lakes and will continue to be so for some time into the future (8).

The Institutional Framework

The involvement of eleven governments has presented both unique difficulties and opportunities in managing the Great Lakes. In an effort to cooperatively resolve problems along their common border, Canada (actually the UK) and the United States signed the Boundary Waters Treaty in 1909. This document has as its major premise that neither Party may use the water on its side of the border to the detriment of water, health or property of the other side. The Treaty also established the International Joint Commission (IJC), a unique binational organization, as principal overseer and arbitrator of any disputes that should arise including those related to water and air pollution, lake levels, hydroelectric power generation and other issues of mutual concern.

With the passage of time, a wide array of environmental problems became evident, particularly cultural eutrophication due to excess phosphorus inputs. In

1972, the first Great Lakes Water Quality Agreement (GLWQA) was signed by Canada and the United States to restore and maintain the water quality of the Great Lakes. The 1972 Agreement provided the focus for a co-ordinated effort to control cultural eutrophication by reducing phosphorus inputs. The IJC was also empowered to review and assess progress under the Agreement. In 1978, the Agreement was revised and expanded to recognize the need to effectively manage toxic substance loadings into the Great Lakes. An "ecosystem approach" was also embodied in the 1978 Agreement. This approach recognized the need for a more integrated and holistic perspective to protect water quality and the health of the entire Great Lakes ecosystem (*9*). The 1978 Agreement, with minor modifications incorporated in 1987, is the current cornerstone in the bilateral framework for joint management of the Great Lakes.

   Commitment to the Agreement is largely political and fluctuates depending on political attitudes. Given this, it is, indeed, remarkable that commitment to this document has resulted in a number of successes in combatting Great Lakes problems. How the Agreements and the institutional framework have worked toward remediating some of the major problems related to human activity in the basin is assessed below within the discussion of each issue.

Human Health

It was concern over human health through the occurrence of major outbreaks of typhoid that led the two countries to ask the IJC in 1912 to investigate the "pollution" of the lakes. Table II presents a statistical summary of typhoid mortality between 1913 and 1947 for the St. Clair/Detroit River area of the Great Lakes, the state of Michigan and the province of Ontario (*10*). These statistics clearly show a higher death rate for the Detroit/St. Clair region than for the rest of Michigan or Ontario up to about 1930. Since 1930 the problem has been eradicated although a significant drop had already occurred by 1920. This was accomplished largely through treating drinking water supplies by filtration and disinfection by chlorine and moving drinking water intakes to non-polluted areas.

   It is interesting to note that the Commission's 1918 Report to Governments confirmed that transboundary pollution was, indeed, occurring and that it was "feasible and practicable, without imposing an unreasonable burden upon the offending communities, to prevent or remedy pollution in the boundary waters" (*11*). At the request of the two Governments, the Commission in 1920 drafted a "convention" which would accomplish this purpose. However, with the advent of chlorination of municipal water supplies **and in the general belief that there was an inexhaustible supply of clean, fresh water to dilute all wastes,** the expenditures of large sums of money on waste treatment facilities did not appear to be urgent. The proposed convention was never negotiated to conclusion. It would be almost another 30 years (1946) before the Commission was again approached by governments, this time to examine the pollution problems resulting from the new types and greater volumes of waste discharges by developing industrial complexes and accompanying growth and concentrations of population. Today the problem of human health is again high on the public agenda due to

Table II. Mortality for Typhoid Fever and Death Rates per 100,000 Population

Municipality	1913 No.	1913 Rate	1920 No.	1920 Rate	1930 No.	1930 Rate	1940 No.	1940 Rate	1947 No.	1947 Rate
State of Michigan	538	17.5	399	8.2	89	1.8	11	0.2	5	0.08
Detroit	153	29.4	61	6.1	16	1	5	0.3	0	0
Marine City	4	106.4	1	26.8	0	0	0	0	0	0
Monroe	1	12.1	1	8.6	0	0	0	0	0	0
Port Huron	5	26.6	4	15.4	2	6.4	0	0	0	0
St. Clair	0	0	1	31.2	0	0	0	0	0	0
Wyandotte	7	70.3	17	122.7	0	0	0	0	0	0
Province of Ontario	446	16.7	203	7	76	2.3	26	0.7	6	0.1
Amherstburg					0	0	0	0	0	0
Chatham	7	56.5	3	19.2	1	6.1	0	0	0	0
Sarnia	5	43.5	3	20.5	0	0	0	0	0	0
Wallaceburg					0	0	0	0	0	0
Windsor	2	9.3	3	8.2	3	4.3	0	0	0	0

Source: Adapted from ref (8).

"pollution" associated with pervasive, persistent and highly toxic organic chemicals (see below).

Eutrophication

By the 1960s, problems associated with bacteriological and oil pollution were replaced by those related to cultural eutrophication. Degradation of Lakes Erie and Ontario was particularly severe along with Green Bay in Lake Michigan, Saginaw Bay in Lake Huron and several other embayments around the lakes (eg., Hamilton Harbour). There were massive die-offs of fish (mostly alewife) in Lake Michigan and Lake Ontario. Massive algal blooms were occurring frequently and a number of municipal and industrial areas were devoid of visible aquatic life. Lake Erie had reached a point where decomposing *Cladophora* which washed onto beaches had to be removed by bulldozers. Blue-green algae were causing taste and odour problems in drinking water and the hypolimnion of the central basin became totally anoxic during summer stratification. In response to this catastrophic situation, the IJC was asked by governments to initiate a review of the state of the lower Great Lakes (Erie and Ontario). The results were released in 1969 (*12*) and marked the beginning of official action, unprecedented so far in history, with the objective of stopping further degradation and initiating restoration.

Phosphorus was identified as the key nutrient controlling the eutrophication process and at the same time the only controllable nutrient (*13,14*). Uncontrolled inputs from municipal treatment plant effluents containing household laundry detergents, industrial wastes and agricultural runoff were identified as the principal sources. These three sources were targeted for a major phosphorus reduction management plan in the 1972 Water Quality Agreement. Specific phosphorus target loads and required load reductions were incorporated into the Agreement for each lake (eg., for Lake Erie, total reduction between 1972 and 1976 was set at about fifty percent from 31,200 tons per year to 16,100 tons; for Lake Ontario, from 18,000 to 10,000 tons per year). Implemented programs included limiting the phosphorus content of household laundry detergents and reducing the total phosphorus concentration to 1.0 mg $P.L^{-1}$ in the effluents of municipal water treatment plants discharging more than 3,800 $m^3.d^{-1}$. It was anticipated that implementation of these programs would (a) restore year-round aerobic conditions in the bottom waters of the central basin of Lake Erie; (b) reduce the current levels of algal growth in Lakes Erie and Ontario and the International Section of the St. Lawrence River; and (d) stabilize Lake Superior and Lake Huron in their present oligotrophic state.

Gradual implementation of these programs took several years and was completed in principal between 1973-76. Reductions of phosphorus in laundry detergents were subsequently legislated by all jurisdictions. Since the signing of the 1972 GLWQA, Canada and the U.S. have spent over $7.6 billion to upgrade and construct municipal wastewater treatment plants throughout the basin. Despite the successes of point source control programs, publication of the report from the Pollution from Land Use Activities Reference Group (*15*) indicated that additional programs to control non-point sources of phosphorus were needed on Lakes Ontario and Erie and Lake Huron (Saginaw Bay) if the objectives and target loads were to be achieved. In 1983, a Phosphorus Load Reduction Supplement was incorporated into the 1978 Agreement. This supplement required a further phosphorus reduction of 2,000 t.yr^{-1} for Lake Erie, 430 t.yr^{-1} for Lake Ontario and a maximum load to Saginaw Bay of 440 t.yr^{1}, all to be achieved by the control of non-point sources.

The phosphorus management program in the Great Lakes has had dramatic results. Loadings of municipal phosphorus to Lakes Erie and Ontario have been reduced by almost 80%. Corresponding reductions in the Upper Great Lakes were over 50% (Table III). Phosphorus load reductions are clearly reflected in corresponding open lake concentrations of total phosphorus (TP) and soluble reactive phosphorus (SRP) (17). Figure 2 shows the reductions for Lake Ontario. Significant shifts in algal species composition to that more representative of less eutrophic conditions have also been noted for the open waters of the Great Lakes (18). Perhaps even more convincing is the reduction in phytoplankton biomass from the nearshore areas of the Great Lakes where eutrophication has been historically more advanced (19). Finally, oxygen depletion rates for the central basin of Lake Erie have been decreasing gradually since the early seventies (18). Preliminary data indicate that 1989 was the first year since measurements began, that the hypolimnion of the central basin of Lake Erie has not gone anoxic (Bertram, P., Great Lakes National Programs Office, EPA V, Chicago, personal communication, 1989). The phosphorus control program has been extremely successful, meeting in principle all expectations except for some remaining problems in nearshore areas of the Great Lakes.

Toxic Substances

Today, contamination by anthropogenic toxic substances represents the most pressing environmental problem in the Great Lakes. Some 362 toxic organic and inorganic chemicals have been positively identified in water, sediment or biota of the lakes with another four hundred or so that require further verification (16). Particular concern centers around persistent toxic chemicals (i.e., those that do not readily breakdown but get locked into the tissues of organisms and bioaccumulate up through the food chain). The latter have a number of common characteristics. They are ubiquitous in the environment with a wide-spread geographic distribution. A variety of transport mechanisms (eg., atmospheric transport) ensure that contaminants outside the aquatic ecosystem eventually end up within it. Many of the compounds are only slowly metabolized and biodegraded and as a result bioconcentrate and bioaccumulate in organisms in the ecosystem. All have the potential for deleterious effects which can generally by classified into four classes of toxicity including (a) carcinogenicity; (b) mutagenicity; (c) teratogenicity; and (d) all other effects.

The unique physical characteristics of the Great Lakes also contribute to their sensitivity to toxic substance inputs. The vast surface areas of the lakes makes atmospheric contributions of these chemicals, even at low concentrations, quantitatively significant. The relatively large ratio of the lake surface to drainage basin area, and the fact that the boundary of the drainage basin in some locations

Table III. Municipal Phosphorus Load to the Great Lakes Basin, 1972-1985 (t/yr).

Lake Basin	1972 Load Estimate	1975	1976	1977	1978	1979	1980	1981	1982	1983	1984	1985
Superior		286	293	262	239	207	203	170	179	153	147	147
Michigan		2,325	2,336	1,660	1,314	1,224	1,047	934	885	928	919	894
Huron		624	578	557	495	444	427	475	416	435	448	462
Erie	15,260	6,951	5,840	6,406	5,478	4,234	3,500	2,874	2,449	2,630	2,767	2,449
Ontario	9,860	4,220	3,082	3,089	2,728	2,898	2,512	2,208	2,115	1,911	1,824	1,710

Source: Adapted from ref (14).

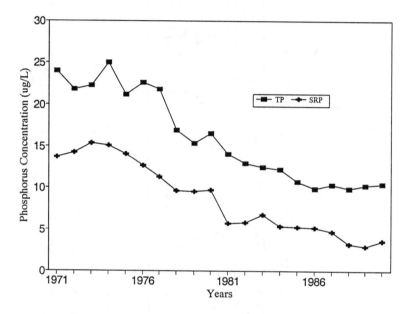

Figure 2. Trends in Phosphorus Concentrations in Lake Ontario.

lies close to the shore of the lakes (eg. south shore of Lake Ontario) means that contaminants deposited in the watershed are transported almost directly to the lakes with little filtering or attenuation as occurs in other basins where the catchment area is generally much larger than the lake surface area. Because of the large depths and volumes, particularly in the Upper Great Lakes, it takes a long time for these substances to be flushed from the system or to settle out with other particulate matter to the bottom. As a result, low level inputs of these substances can bioaccumulate to significant tissue residue concentrations in biological organisms (including humans via drinking water). Active circulation and mixing of the lakes ensures rapid distribution of these chemicals throughout the system.

Sediment cores from throughout the Great Lakes Basin chronicle the history of chemical abuse. Concentrations in cores such as those taken off the Niagara River in Lake Ontario reflect the loadings of these chemicals to the system which, in turn, show remarkable agreement with their industrial production and use within the Basin (*21*). Surficial sediment data also demonstrate widespread geographic distribution in all five lakes (*22*). For some substances such as mercury and mirex, the inputs were generally associated with industrial sources. For others, such as PCBs and lead, the distribution is more pervasive suggesting the importance of more diffuse sources such as the atmosphere. In many cases, such sources are remote from the Great Lakes Basin. This makes control of inputs extremely difficult within any toxic substance management strategy for the Basin.

Concentrations of PCBs in fish from each of the Great Lakes currently exceed the GLWQA objectives for the protection of aquatic life. Similarly, concentrations of some substances (e.g., PCBs, Hg, mirex, toxaphene) in Great Lakes' fish continue to exceed acceptable guidelines for human consumption. Documented effects in the Great Lakes include reproductive failure, congenital abnormalities and induction of tumours in various aquatic, terrestrial and avian species (*23*).

Even this cursory look at the impact of toxic substances in the Great Lakes shows a problem of massive proportions. The approach to management of these substances has been **ad hoc**, particularly when compared to the highly organized and well planned phosphorus control program. Despite this, however, the Great Lakes have been one of the pivotal areas in providing understanding of the overall toxics problem (*25*). Furthermore, the data show that where control programs have been implemented and vigorously enforced, there are signs of success. A few examples illustrate this point.

Elimination of the major source of mercury (chlor-alkali production) in Lake St. Clair in 1970 brought about an almost immediate decline in mercury residues in fish with concentrations declining by 50% between 1970 and 1976 (*25*). Similar declines have were noted in walleye and white bass populations of western Lake Erie (*26*). Production and use of a number of chlorinated organic chemicals including DDT and PCBs were regulated in the early seventies. In response, the historical trends for many of these chemicals in top predator fish exhibited dramatic declines. Figures 3 and 4 show the trends for DDT and PCBs in Lakes Michigan and Ontario. DDT concentrations in some species of Lake Michigan fish declined by as much as 90% between 1969 and 1978 (reference). PCBs declined by 50%

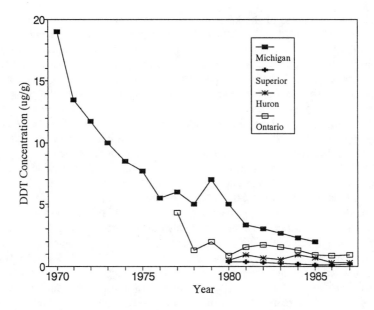

Figure 3. Trends in ΣDDT Concentrations in Lake Trout from the Great Lakes.

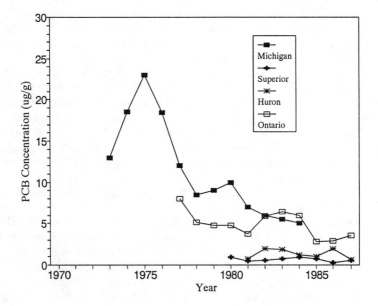

Figure 4. Trends in ΣPCB Concentrations in Lake Trout from the Great lakes.

between 1975 and 1978 (reference). Similarly, reduction in contaminant residue levels have also been observed since the late 70s in herring gull populations in each of the Great Lakes. Figures 5 and 6 show the data for Lake Ontario. Reproductive success of most Great Lakes herring gull populations has also returned to normal (*27*). Data collected since 1983, however, show that the decreasing trend in concentrations for many of these contaminants in both fish and birds appears to have leveled off in some lakes and in some cases, concentrations may be increasing again. It may well be that this is due to the increasing influence of secondary or more diffuse sources (e.g., leaking waste dump sites) which have been more difficult to control (*8,28*). While the present levels are still well below those reported in the mid 1970s, continued careful monitoring will be required to determine with certainty whether or not concentrations will continue to decline.

Other Problems

It is clear that water quality management of the Great Lakes has resulted in a number of successes. However, major problems remain or will arise continually to test the management system and its capability. Some of these issues are summarized briefly below.

Increases in nitrate + nitrite have been well documented in the Great Lakes (*19*). Relative increases over the past twenty years have been between 30 and 200% with the highest increases in the most populated and agriculturally productive basins of Lakes Ontario and Erie (*29*). Currently no adverse impacts due to this increase have been observed and concentrations are well below the 10 mg.L^{-1} maximum acceptable drinking water concentration for the protection of human health. Changing N:P ratios, however, can impact phytoplankton community structure (*30*).

The Great Lakes have suffered the invasion of numerous exotic species of which the smelt, alewife and sea lamprey are probably the best known. More recently, two more species have entered the lakes probably via ballast water from foreign ships. The ruffe (*Gymnocephalus cernuus*), a small percid, feeds on the eggs and larvae of other percids and whitefish. The ruffe is currently considered to be a threat to Lake Superior's $5-$10 million whitefish fishery. The zebra mussel (*Dreissena polymorpha*) was discovered in Lake St. Clair in 1985 (*31*). It has subsequently been discovered at locations throughout the Great Lakes and is of major concern not only environmentally but economically. It has already colonized numerous industrial and domestic water intakes in sufficient numbers to entirely block water flow and is also an intermediate host to parasites which eventually invade fish.

The problem of fluctuating lake levels is currently of major concern. The additional potential effects of climate change on water levels may further exacerbate the problem as will any major diversions of water out of the basin to support developments in the more arid regions of the continent.

As point sources of contaminants become more controlled, the problems associated with more diffuse sources such as the residual effects of contaminated

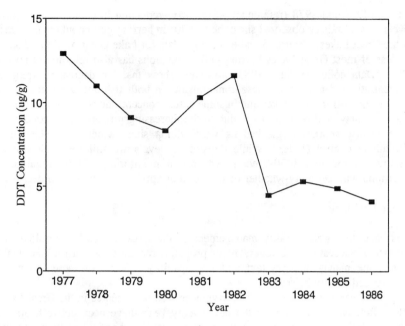

Figure 5. Trends in ΣDDT Concentrations in Herring Gull Eggs from Mugg's Island, Lake Ontario.

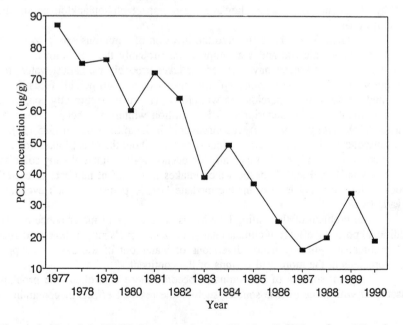

Figure 6. Trends in ΣPCB Concentrations in Herring Gull Eggs from Mugg's Island, Lake Ontario.

sediments, past, present and future waste disposal sites, and contaminated groundwater will become increasingly important. Atmospheric deposition of a number of contaminants is quantitatively significant in the Great Lakes basin. The long-range transport of contaminants from sources outside the basin will become a major problem in any Great Lakes toxic substances control strategy. This problem will require a global strategy for success.

Fish from Lake Erie are generally the least contaminated of all the Great Lakes (*18*). It has been speculated that contaminants in a more advanced eutrophic system become masked or removed by sedimentation within the food chain and have less opportunity to reach higher trophic levels (*24*). The management implications of this interaction between nutrient and contaminants needs to be further elucidated.

Fisheries and water quality management strategies have evolved independently in the Great Lakes. In general, these strategies operate from different ends of the management spectrum -- bottom up (phosphorus control) and top down (massive fish stocking). A more ecologically oriented approach which recognizes the interactions between fisheries and water quality will be required to manage the Great Lakes.

Summary

In many ways, both Canada and the United States continue to be involved in a unique experiment of co-operative management of serious environmental issues which plague a shared international resource. Despite the institutional complexity and the history of abuse that man's activities have wrought on the Great Lakes, the experiment to restore and protect them has had several successes: typhoid and cholera were eradicated; eutrophication problems are now largely under control; and where adequate control programs for toxic chemicals have been implemented and enforced (e.g., mercury, DDT, PCBs), there have been associated declines in concentrations in the lakes. These successes have been due in no small way to the spirit of co-operation that has continued to exist between Canada and the United States and the unique institutional arrangements entered into by the two countries.

It has become increasingly evident, however, that management of Great Lakes resources to provide sustainable benefits cannot be achieved by the co-operative action of governments alone. Despite admirable efforts carried out under the Canada/United States Water Quality Agreements, problems continue to persist and many important resources continue to be depleted both qualitatively and quantitatively. Collective action on the part of **all users** of the lakes will be required if the Great Lakes are to be restored and protected for the benefit of future generations.

Acknowledgments

The author wishes to express appreciation to Ms. Melanie Neilson, Water Quality Branch, Ontario Region, Environment Canada for providing the data for Figure 2.

Appreciation also goes to Messrs. David Dolan and Tim Bartish of the IJC Regional Office, Windsor, Ontario for providing their file data for Figures 3 through 6.

Literature Cited

1.   Beeton, A.M. *J. Great Lakes Research* **1984**, *10(2)*, 106-113.
2.   *The Great Lakes: An Environmental Atlas and Resource Book*; United States Environmental Protection Agency and Environment Canada, 1987, 44p.
3.   Beeton, A.M. In *Eutrophication: Causes, Consequences, Correctives*; Nat. Acad. Sci.; Washington, D.C., 1969, 150-187.
4.   Christie, W.M. *J. Fish. Res. Board Can.* **1974**, *31*, 827-854.
5.   Hartman, W.L., In *Proceedings of the Workshop on the Health of Aquatic Communities*; ASLO, Minneapolis, John Wiley, 1987.
6.   Hartman, W.L. *J. Fish. Res. Board Can.* **1972**, *29*, 899-912.
7.   Burns, N.M. *Erie: The Lake that Survived*, Rowman and Allanheld, Totawa, NJ, 1985.
8.   Williams, D.J. *Environ. Health Rev.* **1984**, *28(3)*, 66-70.
9.   Vallentyne, J.R.; Beeton,A.M. *Environ. Conserv.* **1988**, *15*, 58-62.
10. *Pollution of Boundary Waters*, Report of the International Joint Commission, United States and Canada, International Joint Commission, Washington and Ottawa, 1951, 321p.
11. *Pollution of Boundary Waters*, Report of the International Joint Commission, United States and Canada, Washington and Ottawa, 1970, 105p.
12. *Pollution of Lake Erie, Lake Ontario and the International Section of the St. Lawrence River*, Report to the International Joint Commission by the international Lake Erie and Lake Ontario/St. Lawrence Water Pollution Boards, International Joint Commission, Windsor, Ontario, 1969, Vols. 1,2 and 3.
13. Bruce, J.P. *The Control of Eutrophication*, Technical Bulletin No. 26, Inland Waters Branch, Dep. Energy Mines and Resources, Ottawa, Canada, 1970, 10p.
14. Vallentyne, J.R. *Can. Res. Dev.* **1970**, May-June, 36-43.
15. *Environmental Strategy for the Great Lakes System*, Final Report of the Pollution from Land Use Activities Reference Group to the International Joint Commission, International Joint Commission, Windsor, Ontario, 1978, 116p.
16. *Report on Great Lakes Water Quality*, Report to the International Joint Commission by the Great Lakes Water Quality Board, Windsor, Ontario, 1987, 236p.
17. Hartig, J.H.; Gannon, J.E. *Alternatives* **1986**, *13*, 19-23.
18. Munawar, M.; Munawar, I.F. *Hydrobiologia* **1986**, *138*, 85-115.
19. *State of the Environment Report for Canada*; Bird, P.M.; Rapport, D.J., Eds.; Environment Canada, Ottawa, Ontario, 1986, 263p.

20. *A Review of Trends in Lake Erie Water Quality with Emphasis on the 1978-1979 Intensive Survey*; Rathke, D.E.; Edwards, C.J., Eds.; Report to the Surveillance Work Group, Great Lakes Water Quality Board, International Joint Commission, Windsor, Ontario, 1985, 129p.
21. Durham, R.W.; Oliver, B.G. *J. Great Lakes Res.* **1983**, *9*, 160-168.
22. Thomas, R.L. *Verh. Internat. Verein. Limnol.* **1981**, *21*, 1666-1680.
23. *Literature Review of the Effects of Persistent Toxic Substances on Great Lakes Biota*; Fitchko, J., Ed.; Report to the Great Lakes Science Advisory Board, International Joint Commission, Windsor, Ontario, 1986, 256p.
24. Allan, R.J. *Symp. Biol. Hung.* **1989**, *38*, 217-243.
25. *The Decline in Mercury Concentration in Fish from Lake St. Clair, 1970-1976*, Report No. AQS77-3, Ontario Ministry of the Environment, Toronto, Ontario, 1977, 85p.
26. Kinkead, J.D.; Hamdy, Y. *Trends in the Mercury Content of Western Lake Erie Fish and Sediment, 1970-1977*; Ontario Ministry of the Environment, Toronto, Ontario, 1978, 19p.
27. Mineau, P.; Fox, G.A.; Norstrom, R.J.; Weseloh, D.V.; Hallett, D.J.; Ellenton, J.A. In *Toxic Contaminants in the Great Lakes*; Niriagu, J.O.; Simmons, M.S., Eds.; John Wiley & Sons: Toronto, Ontario 1984; 425-452.
28. Thomas, R.L.; Gannon, J.E.; Hartig, J.H.; Williams, D.J.; Whittle, D.M. In *Toxic Contamination in Large Lakes*; Schmidtke, N.W., Ed.; Proceedings of a technical session of the World Conference on Large Lakes; Lewis Publishers: Chelsea, Michigan, 1988, **Vol.3**; 327-387.
29. Barica, J. *Symp. Biol. Hung.* **1989**, *38*, 43-58.
30. Tilman, D.; Kilham, S.S.; Kilham, P. *Ann. Rev. Ecol. Sys.* **1984**, *13*, 49.
31. Hebert, P.D.N.; Muncaster, B.W.; Mackie, G.L. *Can. J. Fish. Aquat. Sci.* **1989**, *46*, 1587-1571.

RECEIVED September 11, 1991

Chapter 11

Persistent Marine Debris

Petroleum Residues and Plastics in the World's Oceans

E. M. Levy

Physical and Chemical Sciences Branch, Department of Fisheries and
Oceans, Bedford Institute of Oceanography, P.O. Box 1006, Dartmouth,
Novia Scotia, Canada B2Y 4A2

The distribution of persistent marine debris, adrift on world
oceans and stranded on beaches globally, is reviewed and
related to the known inputs and transport by the major surface
currents. Since naturally occurring processes eventually
degrade petroleum in the environment, international measures
to reduce the inputs have been largely successful in alleviating
oil pollution on a global, if not on a local, scale. Many
plastics, however, are so resistant to natural degradation that
merely controlling inputs will be insufficient, and more drastic
and costly measures will be needed to cope with the emerging
global problem posed by these materials.

Persistent debris in the ocean was perhaps first recognized as an
environmental issue in the late 1960's after Heyerdahl drew attention to the
widespread occurrence of petroleum residues in the North Atlantic (1).
Recently, a much more environmentally conscious society has become
increasingly concerned about the deluge of tarry residues and of plastic,
metal and glass rubbish, and other wastes onto seashores worldwide. Long
commonplace on beaches neighboring urban and industrial centers,
persistent marine debris is now common on shorelines in even the most
remote marine regions. Symptomatic of debris adrift in the world ocean,
the ever-increasing amounts of debris stranding on our beaches suggest that
conditions in the open ocean continue to deteriorate. Although the
aesthetic aspects of persistent marine debris are widely recognized, a
common misconception is that its environmental impact is more cosmetic
than real. Yet, more than 50 species of seabirds are known to have
ingested plastic (2) and may suffer from a variety of adverse physiological
effects (3), thousands of seabirds and marine mammals become entangled
in discarded netting and packaging materials (4), and untold numbers of

0097–6156/92/0483–0224$06.00/0

fish are lost to the commercial fishery because of "ghost fishing" (5). While the impact on marine organisms at the population level is virtually unknown, declines in some communities of fur seals in Alaska (4), monk seals in Hawaii (6), and some endangered species of sea turtles in the North Atlantic (7) are, in part, consequences of persistent debris. Public outrage over the potential threat to humans from "medical wastes" which stranded on several New England beaches in 1988 (8), clearly demonstrated that the general public was no longer willing to accept persistent marine debris as an inescapable feature of modern life.

This paper examines the literature on the distribution of persistent marine debris - petroleum residues, plastic debris and other forms of litter in the world ocean and on shorelines globally. It demonstrates that such debris is now common in what have long been considered to be unspoiled environments and appears to have become a marine pollutant of truly global proportions. However, there has not yet been a coordinated international program to quantify such debris and, as a consequence, the information presently available in the literature suffers from not having been collected in a systematic scientific manner and is usually very limited, fragmentary, and often anecdotal. Further, inconsistencies in expressing quantitative results preclude a rigorous overview. Nevertheless, an assessment of the present situation is prerequisite to dealing with this growing environmental issue.

Although the sources and sites of input differ, floating debris is subject to the same oceanographic processes that govern the distribution of oil slicks and floating particulate petroleum residues. Hence, a close relationship exists between these two forms of oceanic pollution and a summary of the global distribution of oil pollution provides a first insight into the distribution of floating debris. Further, measures taken nationally and internationally to abate oil pollution suggest the approach that must be taken to deal with these other forms of persistent debris.

Global Distribution of Floating Petroleum Residues

An international program carried out during the 1970's initiated the study of tar stranded on beaches (9, 10). This program has provided a basic understanding of the global distribution of oil present as visible slicks and particulate residues on the surface of the world's oceans. Subsequently, studies have been carried out in South East Asia, the Arabian Gulf, and the Caribbean area largely under the Regional Seas Program of the United Nations Environmental Program.

Oil Slicks and Floating Tar. About 100,000 visual observations of the sea surface made between 1974 and 1978 (9, 10) demonstrated that oil slicks were closely associated with the tanker routes from the Middle East through the Suez Canal and around the Cape of Good Hope to Europe, from the Middle East to Japan, and to a lesser extent, along the transatlantic and transpacific shipping lanes. Outside these areas, slicks were relatively rare, and there were broad expanses of ocean where they were absent. Slicks were common (>10% of the observations) in the Atlantic along the west coasts of Africa and Europe, throughout the Mediterranean Sea, and in regions to the north and east of South America. The only areas north of 50°N where slicks were common were the Baltic Sea, the North Sea, along the coast of Norway, and near Iceland. In the Pacific, slicks were common along the west coast of North America, in the East China Sea and in the Sea of Japan. In the Indian Ocean, they were prevalent along the east coast of Africa, in the Red Sea and the Arabian Gulf, along the west coast of India, in a band across the Bay of Bengal, and throughout the South China Sea. A subsequent study (11) confirmed the frequent occurrence of slicks near the United Arab Emirates, off the western and southern coasts of India, and in the Strait of Malacca, Gulf of Thailand and South China Sea. Because oil slicks are ephemeral, their presence on the sea surface indicates a recent input nearby. This association of slicks with tanker routes and shipping lanes provides convincing evidence that discharges of oil from tankers and cargo ships were the major source of the slicks.

Some 4,000 surface tows (9, 10) to determine the distribution of tar floating on the sea surface indicated that the highest concentrations of tar in the North Atlantic (20-90 mg m^{-2}) were in the Canary Current (Fig. 1) and off the coast of Northwest Africa. Concentrations in the Gulf Stream were 1-10 mg m^{-2}, while those in the North Atlantic Current were less than 1 mg m^{-2}. With the major inputs of oil along the tanker lanes, the geographical distribution of tar is readily explained in terms of transport by the North Atlantic gyre, and the data suggest that the most refractory residues make several circuits of the North Atlantic before being degraded or stranded. The gyre also tends to accumulate tar in the western Sargasso Sea, while the tar-free waters of the Labrador Current maintain relatively pristine conditions along the Atlantic coasts of Canada and the northeastern United States. In the eastern North Atlantic, a portion of the tar associated with the North Atlantic Current is carried northward along the coast of Norway and eventually enters the Barents Sea.

The role of oceanic processes in controlling the distribution of floating tar is clearly illustrated by data for the Gulf of Mexico where the average concentration in the Loop Current was 2.7 mg m^{-2} while that over the continental shelf from Key West to Louisiana was an order of magnitude lower (12). Of the total tar floating in the Gulf, 10-50% was considered to have been transported into the Gulf from the Caribbean Sea via the Yucatan Straits. Tar associated with the Loop Current is thought to exit through the Strait of Florida and then become entrained in the Gulf Stream. Pelagic tar was distributed throughout the region inshore of the axis of the Gulf Stream between Cape Hatteras and Cape Canaveral (13), but generally at concentrations less than 1.0 mg m^{-2}. The region within 40 km of the coasts of Georgia and Florida was free from tar because of a "dynamic barrier" formed by land runoff (14). Further offshore, concentrations ranged from 0.01-5.6 mg m^{-2} (14) in keeping with previous findings (15).

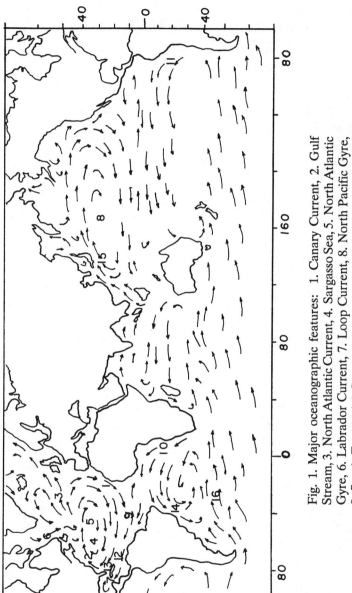

Fig. 1. Major oceanographic features: 1. Canary Current, 2. Gulf Stream, 3. North Atlantic Current, 4. Sargasso Sea, 5. North Atlantic Gyre, 6. Labrador Current, 7. Loop Current, 8. North Pacific Gyre, 9. South Equatorial Current, 10. Benguela Current, 11. Humboldt Current, 12. Antilles Current, 13. Florida Current, 14. Brazil Current, 15. Kuroshio, 16. Antarctic West Wind Drift.

With tanker traffic between the Strait of Malacca and Japan as the major source, the highest concentrations of tar in the Pacific (1-15 mg^{-2}) were in the region south of Japan. The distribution of tar in the Pacific Ocean was accounted for by transport by the North Pacific gyre in a manner similar to that described for the North Atlantic (9, 10). Concentrations along the Pacific coasts of Canada and the United States were generally less than 0.1 mg m^{-2}. There is some evidence to suggest that concentrations of tar in the North Pacific might have decreased slightly between 1976 and 1985 (16).

In the Indian Ocean, concentrations of tar were substantially higher along the west coast of India than along the east coast, and in general, coincided with of the tanker route which passes from the Persian Gulf to the Strait of Malacca *en route* to Japan (9, 10). Recent reports have confirmed a progressive decrease in the concentration of tar from the Gulf of Arabia across the Bay of Bengal to the South China Sea (17). The Bay of Bengal north of the tanker route was relatively free from tar (11).

A circumnavigation of the world's oceans between 1978-1980 (18), further indicated that broad expanses of the Atlantic, Pacific, and Indian Oceans away from major tanker lanes and shipping routes contained little or no tar, whereas tar pollution was prevalent in the Mediterranean, Java Sea and Red Sea, and in western European and Northwest African coastal areas.

Tar Stranded on Beaches. During the late 1960's, tar, believed to have originated largely from tankers which discharged tank washings and ballast water at sea, became a conspicuous nuisance on beaches in many regions. Considered objectionable at concentrations of 10 g m^{-1} of beach face, tar concentrations exceeding 100 g m^{-1} on recreational beaches may result in abandonment by the tourist trade and attendant economic losses. The first systematic study of tar on beaches was carried out in Japan during 1977 and 1978 (9, 10). Substantially greater amounts of tar (in excess of 1000 g m^{-1}) were stranded on the south side of Okinawa during the summer than during the winter (0-200 g m^{-1}), while beaches on the northern side of the island received only one-third as much. This phenomenon was reversed during winter when the prevailing wind was from the opposite direction. Evidently, the source of the tar was the transport by the Kuroshio of water that had been heavily polluted with tar discharged from tankers.

A study of 256 beaches bordering the Indian Ocean, South China Sea, and the Pacific Ocean (19) demonstrated that the highest concentrations of tar were present on shores bordering the Persian Gulf, Red Sea, and South China Sea, while practically none was found on islands of the South Pacific including Australia, New Zealand, Fiji, and Polynesia. Again, the relationship between tar pollution on beaches and oil production or tanker traffic was clear -- the degree of beach contamination increased with the convergence of tanker traffic towards the Middle East (20). Concentrations of tar on the beaches of Oman ranged from 5 to 2325 g m^{-1} (average of

224 g m^{-1}) during 1980, with a definite increase towards the Strait of Hormuz (21). The major source of this pollution was thought to be tankers that discharge ballast water off the coast of Oman before entering the Persian Gulf (21), and this practice is also reflected in the concentrations of hydrocarbons in the surface waters of this region (22). Beaches of Saudi Arabia were particularly polluted with concentrations in 1985 and 1986 commonly exceeding 10 kg m^{-1} and 1 to 10 kg m^{-1} being frequent (23, 24). These amounts were 10 times higher than those of other areas in the Persian Gulf and 100 times those in other regions of the world. Concentrations of tar on the beaches of Kuwait were appreciably lower, and might have decreased since 1979 (25). Any such trend was, however, reversed by the release of large amounts of oil as a consequence of the war in the Persian Gulf (26).

Mean tar concentrations on the Israeli coast of the Mediterranean Sea ranged from 884 to 4388 g m^{-1} in 1975-76 (27). Chemical analyses indicated that 76% of the tar on Israeli beaches was weathered crude, 96% of it from Middle Eastern sources (28). Concentrations of tar on the beaches of Lebanon and Turkey appeared to be much lower than those at Alexandria, Egypt and Paphos, Cyprus, as a consequence of the orientation of these beaches relative to a site in the eastern Mediterranean Sea where dumping of oily sludge was permitted (27).

Beach contamination was serious (mean concentrations exceeded 100 g m^{-1}) in many Caribbean areas with the highest concentrations on beaches in the southern Bay of Campeche, the east coast of Yucatan, the southeast coast of Florida, the Cayman Islands, the area near Kingston Harbor in Jamaica, Curacao, and on the windward sides of Barbados, Grenada, Trinidad, and Tobago (29). Beaches exposed to prevailing southeast trade winds were significantly more contaminated than those on the leeward side of the landmasses. As much as 50% of the tar floating in the Caribbean and stranded on its beaches was thought to enter the region from the North Atlantic gyre with the remainder originating from local discharges of ballast water and tank washings. While the Caribbean coasts of Trinidad and Tobago were almost pristine, pollution of the Atlantic coasts of these islands was similar to that in other areas along major tanker routes (30). The source of the tar on these islands was considered to be residues which were discharged during the cleaning of tanker bilges and transported into the region by the South Equatorial Current.

Concentrations of tar fouling beaches of southeast Florida and the Florida Keys averaged 9.8 g m-2, an order of magnitude greater than the mean for the rest of the state (31). Remarkably, there was no significant increase over the amount observed on Florida beaches 30 years previously (32). Further, there was no evidence that the oil anticipated from the IXTOC-I blowout ever impinged upon the beaches of Florida (14, 33).

A long-term study of tar on beaches of Bermuda indicated that the amount stranded did not differ significantly between 1971-72 and 1978-79 (34). A subsequent study, however, indicated that a significant decrease occurred between 1978-79 and 1982-83, implying that the quantity of tar in the Sargasso Sea had declined during this time (35). This was attributed to reductions in operational discharges from oil tankers and a decrease in the occurrence of maritime oil spills.

To summarize, the inputs of petroleum to the ocean occur primarily along the major tanker routes and shipping lanes, the distributions of slicks and particulate tar are found in the same general oceanographic domains. Immediately following its entry into the ocean, oil is transported by the prevailing surface currents and subjected to an array of naturally occurring physical, chemical, and biological processes that ultimately degrade it. The various chemical components vary widely in their susceptibility to these processes; hence, the ephemeral nature of oil slicks and the very refractory nature of tar. The weathered residues may be transported by oceanic currents far from the point at which the oil entered the ocean. Where these currents impinge on land, contamination of shorelines occurs resulting in aesthetic and, in some areas, serious economic problems. In other instances, surface currents maintain relatively pristine conditions at sea or coastal upwelling prevents the oil from contacting land. Concern about oil pollution of the ocean resulted in several national and international measures to reduce the rate of discharge of oil into the sea. Because of the natural processes of degradation, these measures have brought about a marked improvement in the quality of the global ocean environment insofar as oil pollution is concerned.

The Global Distribution of Plastic Debris

Over the past decade, plastic debris has become a common feature of beaches and coastal waters adjoining populated areas of Europe (36-38), the Mediterranean (39-41), North and Central America (42-44) and New Zealand (45). Plastics are also present in the open ocean both near the major shipping lanes and in the most remote regions of the world; (the Arctic (46), the Benguela Current (47), the Cape Basin area of the South Atlantic (48), the Humboldt Current in the South Pacific (49), and the Antarctic (50, 51).

The first reports of plastic in the North Atlantic indicated the presence of 50-12,000 particles/km^2 in the Sargasso Sea in 1972 (52) and from 0-14.1 particles per m^3 in coastal waters of southern New England (42), where the main source was river-borne effluents from plastic fabrication plants (44). Plastic objects discarded from boats and from recreational activities on beaches were the main sources of debris in Narragansett Bay, being deposited at a rate of 9.6 g m^{-1} of beach front per month (53). During a detailed survey off the southeast coast of the United States (43, 54), fragments of plastic were present in about 70% of the samples collected from the waters of the continental shelf, the continental slope and the Gulf Stream between Florida and Cape Cod, 50% of those from the Caribbean Sea, and 60% of those from the Antilles Current. Since unprocessed plastic was more prevalent in continental shelf waters and fabricated objects were common offshore but rare near land, the authors surmised that the main source of the former was from land-based sources while the latter was the consequence of routine disposal of solid wastes by ships at sea, rather than losses from municipal waste disposal or coastal landfill operations. Inshore of the axis of the Gulf Stream between Cape Hatteras and Cape Canaveral, plastic was present in 14-34% of the samples collected between 1973 and 1975 (13). Since the incidence of plastic was higher in offshore waters and there was no evidence for higher concentrations near industrial areas, the primary source of the material was thought to be entrainment from other regions via ocean currents and shipping traffic. Prior to this, fragments of plastic were only very rarely encountered in the North Atlantic (15).

An "amazing amount of trash", mostly plastic objects, is stranded on the Atlantic coast of Florida during onshore winds, particularly in winter (55). While some of this debris was of United States origin (from local sources or from entrainment in the Florida Current of wastes from shipping), the remainder was of Venezuelan, Columbian, and Jamaican origin. Debris from the easternmost Caribbean and the northern coast of South America could be transported to the Atlantic coast of Florida by the Guiana and Antilles Currents in about four months. Alternatively, debris from the southern or southwestern part of the Caribbean could be carried by the Caribbean Current via the Yucatan Channel and Straits of Florida to the Atlantic coast of Florida in as little as two months.

The Sea Education program (1984-1987) suggested that plastic had become increasingly more prevalent in the western North Atlantic over the last 15 years (68% of 420 neuston tows contained plastic) (56). All tows in the Sargasso Sea contained plastic, the weathered appearance of which implied that it had been in the marine environment for a lengthy period. On the other hand, plastic from the shelf and slope water north of the Gulf Stream appeared relatively fresh. Surveys conducted on beaches of Cape Cod, Bermuda, Bahamas, Florida Keys and the Antilles confirmed the presence of plastic at several sites, particularly in Bermuda and the Bahamas where up to 2,000 pellets m^{-2} were found. A study at Bermuda during 1978 indicated that the number of plastic pellets on beaches varied considerably, but consistently exceeded 5,000 m^{-1} of beach face and in several instances exceeded 10,000 m^{-1}, despite the fact that several of the beaches were cleaned regularly (57). Because of the difference between the methods of expressing the abundance of the plastic, it is not possible to deduce whether there had been any change over this period. Plastic pellets were absent or rare on Nova Scotian beaches and Sable Island, in the early 1980's, although discarded plastic articles were common (57). This region is removed from any major plastic fabrication industry but is subject to the stranding of debris from local sources and discarded from ships at sea. A recent study identified the origins of marine debris on the shores of Halifax Harbor (58) as recreational activities (31.9%), land-based sources (30.2%), sewage outfalls (17.4%), industry (11.4%), fishing (8.1%), shipping (0.8%), and military (0.2%) sources. Plastics comprised 54% of the total.

In the Cape Basin region of the South Atlantic, polyethylene and polypropylene pellets were observed at concentrations of 1333-3600 pellets km^{-2} (48). Since this area is far from any major shipping lane and is dominated oceanographically by the Antarctic West-Wind Drift with possibly some input from the Brazil Current, the source of the floating plastic was thought to be ships transporting the raw material in the South Atlantic (48). The weathered appearance of the pellets indicated that they had been adrift for an extended period and, therefore, carried long distances by the ocean currents.

The distribution of plastic in the subtropical and subarctic North Pacific and the Bering Sea was studied in 1985 (16) and the results were compared with those from similar studies in 1976 (59) and 1984 (60). Objects sufficiently large to be visible from the deck of a ship were twice as abundant south of 39°N latitude than to the north. Plastic particles collected in a neuston net were 26 times more abundant and 400 times more so than in the Bering Sea. Plastic was most abundant in the central subtropical and western North Pacific, suggesting an association with the general shipping traffic in the western Pacific and the "downstream effects" of pollutants entering the ocean near Japan. The abundance of large plastics along 155°W in the Subarctic North Pacific did not differ significantly between 1984 and 1985, while that of small plastics had increased significantly between 1976 and 1985, probably because of increased input and accumulation in the oceans.

The abundance of plastic debris adrift in the North Pacific Ocean north of the subarctic-subtropical boundary is reflected in the amount that strands on beaches of Alaska. Annual surveys of beaches on Amchitka Island from 1972 to 1974 (61) and again in 1982 (62) indicated that the amount of debris had increased from 1972 to 1974 (from 122 to 345 kg km^{-1} of beach) but had then decreased 26% by 1982 (to 255 kg km^{-1}). Most of the debris was from Japanese and Soviet fishing vessels, and the decrease was attributed to a reduction in fishing activity off Alaska. The drift-net fishery in the North Pacific seems to have been a notorious source of plastic debris, as shown by surveys in 1984 and 1985 during which 0.657 pieces of trawl netting were sighted per 1000 km in the western Pacific and up to 3.13 pieces per 1000 km in the eastern Bering Sea (4). This fishery also seems to be the source of the netting on Alaskan shorelines where about 9 fragments of trawl web were deposited per km of beach face per year near Yakutat during 1985-1987 (63). While significantly more fragments were stranded during fall and winter because of the stormy conditions than in spring and summer, the difference between 1985-86 and 1986-87 was not significant. Although movement of trawl web along the beach was uncommon, some fragments were buried in the beach and remained there for at least 19 months before reemerging. In addition to being present on the sea surface and stranded on beaches, fishing debris of Japanese or Korean origin, was present in 33 of 58 benthic trawls from this area (64). Although the floor of the Bering Sea was somewhat less cluttered, even there, 12 benthic trawls in 1975 and 43 out of 106 in 1976 contained man-made debris (metal, synthetic rope, plastic and glass) (65). In addition to the impact of discarded netting on the fishery resource through "ghost fishing", entanglement in synthetic netting and packaging materials discarded by the fishery is thought to be one of the major cause of the decline in the population of northern fur seals on the Pribilof Islands (4).

In the South Pacific, man-made debris was surveyed on 24 islands in the Thousand Island archipelago north of Java in 1985 (66). Polyethylene bags, footwear and polystyrene blocks comprised more than 90% of the 27,600 items. The main source of this debris is the dumping of rubbish and domestic and industrial waste directly into the sea at Jakarta. On New Zealand beaches, plastic litter was widely distributed and predominantly in the form of polyethylene and polypropylene beads. Near Auckland and Wellington concentrations exceeded 10,000 and 40,000 beads m^{-1} of beach, and the unweathered appearance of the beads implied a nearby source (66).

In contrast with the Pacific Ocean, plastics were rarely encountered during a voyage from the Gulf of Oman across the Indian Ocean to Malaysia and hence across the South China Sea in 1980/81 (17). Plastic litter, however, was common on beaches in the Persian Gulf region, being present in amounts ranging from less than 10 to more than 20 pellets per 300 m^{-2} in Kuwait in 1986 (25). Of the total, 96% was polyethylene from the dumping of plastic wastes from factories in the area, and it was suggested that prevailing wind and wave activity from spring to early fall might seasonally rid these beaches of debris. An inspection of beaches along the entire coastline of Saudi Arabia in 1986 revealed the presence of debris, including plastic, at 77% of the sites examined (24).

Polyethylene pellets were "very abundant" on the Mediterranean coast of Spain, particularly near plastics fabrication factories (39, 40). Wastes from these factories and spillage during cargo loading and transport of raw materials were considered to be the major sources. Similarly, wastes from local plastic fabrication factories were thought to be the source of pellets on the beaches of Lebanon (40).

Other Persistent Debris

In addition to tar and plastic, the world's oceans and their bordering shorelines carry an unknown burden of wood, paper, glass and metal rubbish. For example, the concentration of floating rubbish discerned visually over a 22 day period in 1986 at a site in the Mediterranean Sea between Greece and Libya was estimated to be 0.012 g m^{-2} for a total of 3.6 million objects afloat in the Mediterranean (67). Almost a decade earlier, the abundance of debris larger than 1.5 cm in the Mediterranean southwest of Malta was estimated to be 2000 pieces km^{-2} (41) including plastic bags, cups, sheeting, packing material, pieces of wood, rubber, and synthetic rope, large tarballs, glass bottles and paper items and numerous unidentifiable fragments.

A systematic study of floating marine debris in the North Sea (68) demonstrated its presence in 79% of the 1° latitude x 0.5° longitude sectors. Man-made wooden items were most abundant along the main shipping routes and near offshore structures, whereas synthetic netting and rope were associated with fishing areas but were rare elsewhere. Paper and cardboard were widespread in coastal waters, while plastic and polystyrene items were almost uniformly distributed. These geographical trends suggested that the disposal of garbage from ships was the main source of the debris. A year-long survey on Helgoland, where 75% of the items were plastic but 65% of the weight was wood, also indicated that most of the debris originated from the dumping of garbage from ships (69). It has been estimated that the world's merchant fleet of some 71,000 ships (excluding military vessels) is responsible for 6,800,000 metal, 400,000 glass and 600,000 plastic containers being thrown overboard daily (70) and that of the 3-4 billion tons of solid waste generated annually in the United States, some 9 million tons, of which 7.6% may be plastics, are dumped directly into the sea (71).

Persistent Marine Debris: A Global Environmental Concern of the 1980s, a Global Environmental Problem of the '90's?

At the time Hyerdahl drew attention to what he considered to be a deplorable state of pollution of the North Atlantic (1), tar was the only form of floating debris present in quantity. Public outcry precipitated a number of scientific studies which have demonstrated that the distribution of oil in the world's oceans can be accounted for in terms of inputs associated with the major tanker lanes and world shipping routes followed by transport by surface currents which may result in tar being stranded on exposed coastlines often far from the point at which the oil entered the ocean. With the major source of this component of marine debris clearly established, international conventions (International Convention for the Prevention of Pollution from Ships (MARPOL), London Dumping Convention, etc.) have imposed stringent controls on shipping to limit the amounts of oil discharged at sea. As a result of changes in operational procedures and equipment, the amounts of oil discharged during the normal operations of the oil industry have been reduced substantially (72), while improvements in navigational and other equipment have reduced the amounts lost in accidental spills (72). Since many of the components of petroleum are susceptible to natural chemical and biological degradation in the marine environment and, therefore, have a relatively short residence time, from a few months (15) to a year or so (73). Although the residues remaining after the susceptible components have been eliminated may survive for very long periods, perhaps indefinitely, measures to reduce the amount of oil entering the ocean are soon reflected in decreases in the amount of tar present on the surface of the ocean and, subsequently, in the amount being stranded on beaches. Evidence that oil pollution has moderated at least on a regional scale is provided by the reductions noted in the Gulf of St. Lawrence (74), at Bermuda (35) and in the

Mediterranean Sea (75). At the risk of complacency, it can be concluded that this component of the persistent marine debris is reasonably well understood scientifically and is now more or less under control.....except, temporarily, following incidents such as the EXXON VALDEZ spill and the war in the Persian Gulf. Even then, natural processes of degradation will ultimately restore the environment.

The situation regarding the plastics component of persistent marine debris, however, is considerably less encouraging. The polymers from which consumer plastics are manufactured have only been produced in large quantity since World War II, and plastics had not become noticed as marine contaminants until the 1970's. With the phenomenal growth of the plastics industry, however, plastic debris has become an almost ubiquitous feature of the marine environment. Deliberate discharges of pellets from factories and incidental losses associated with their transportation occur mainly in the coastal zone and, from these points of entry may eventually become widely distributed by ocean currents or stranded on shorelines exposed to these currents. These granules are not as aesthetically offensive as tar and other debris, and, consequently, their presence on a beach often escapes casual observation. On the other hand, fabricated plastic objects and most of the other forms of debris at sea originate predominantly from the deliberate dumping of garbage from ships at sea or the disposal of municipal garbage by ocean dumping. Once adrift in the ocean, plastic debris is subject to the same oceanic transfer processes that govern the distribution and stranding of tar. In some coastal areas, debris becomes stranded on beaches near its point of entry into the marine environment. In others, the debris is carried "away" only to be stranded elsewhere. Garbage discharged overboard from merchant ships enters the ocean along the shipping lanes, which coincide with the major surface currents to whatever extent possible. Along with other flotsam, it may be transported great distances by the ocean currents and eventually stranded on exposed shorelines or become entrained in the ocean gyres and remain there for extended periods. In view of the amounts of garbage disposed of at sea, there is little wonder that it is so widely distributed on the world's oceans or that so many beaches today are rendered aesthetically offensive. Because such debris is so visible, the general public is becoming increasingly unwilling to accept it as an inevitable consequence of contemporary life.

Compared with tar, which has a relatively short lifetime in the marine environment, the residence times of plastic, glass and non-corrodible metallic debris are indefinite. Most plastic articles are fabricated from polyethylene, polystyrene or polyvinyl chloride. With molecular weights ranging to over 500,000, the only chemical reactivity of these polymers is derived from any residual unsaturation and, therefore, they are essentially inert chemically and photochemically. Further, since indigenous microflora lack the enzyme systems necessary to degrade most of these polymers, articles manufactured from them are highly resistant or virtually immune to biodegradation. That is, the properties that render plastics so durable and desirable for the manufacture of consumer goods and packaging materials are the very ones that cause them to become an environmental nuisance when discarded. Although the loss of plasticizers which are incorporated to impart pliability and other desired physical properties to fabricated plastic goods, or the addition of substances to render them susceptible to photochemical or biological degradation, eventually causes plastic objects to disintegrate, the polymer, itself, is not degraded. As Duerr (76) so aptly expressed it.

> "Plastic is forever....Whether future archaeologists will find our plastics neatly arranged in dump sites or scattered everywhere across the globe, find them they will. They will still be there long after the wood has rotted, the concrete crumbled and the iron rusted away. This will be known as the Plastic Age".

Is There a Solution?

As was the case in dealing with environmental problems arising from the indiscriminate discharge of oily wastes, the first step in the solution to the plastic component of the persistent marine debris problem must be to reduce the amount of material entering the ocean. Presumably, this can be accomplished by eliminating the dumping of land-produced wastes into the sea and by improving practices for handling shipboard wastes. Since the technology is already available to accomplish these reductions, what is now required is the necessary initiative. On a positive note, some action is already being taken; for example, the United States Plastic Pollution Research and Control Act prohibits dumping of plastic from United States vessels anywhere in the world and bans all other ships from dumping within 200 miles of the United States coast (77). On an international level, Annex V of MARPOL prohibiting the dumping of garbage from ships came into effect on December 31, 1988 (78), and compliance with it will represent a major advance towards reducing the input of garbage into the world's oceans. Since one of the provisions of Annex V is a ban on the dumping into the sea of all plastics, including synthetic ropes and fishing nets, it should greatly benefit the many forms of marine life that now suffer needlessly from entanglement and "ghost fishing". Plastic debris has been highlighted in the 1990 GESAMP (UN Group of Experts on the Scientific Aspects of Marine Pollution) review of the state of the marine environment as a problem of concern, and measures are being taken at national and international levels to assess its impact in the marine environment (79). Yet, national and international regulations cannot succeed without our commitment as individuals to reduce the amount of wastes we generate by replacing our use-it-once/throw-it-away lifestyle with a more environmentally responsible attitude. This can only be accomplished through a convincing, but realistic, educational program. The almost daily reports of recycling and beach clean-ups are encouraging evidence that the general public is not only concerned but is prepared to take some of the necessary corrective measures. Without action at the individual, national and international levels, the input of debris will increase and the problem of persistent marine debris can only continue to worsen. Unlike the case of global petroleum pollution, however, where natural processes of degradation assist by removing some of the existing burden, merely reducing the input of persistent debris will not suffice. Because the lifetimes of other forms of persistent debris in the marine environment are so very long, improved practices at sea cannot be expected to accomplish more than preventing the situation from becoming worse. It seems inevitable, therefore, that a prolonged program to collect and remove persistent debris as it is stranded will also be required.

Literature Cited

1. Heyerdahl, T. The Ra Expeditions; Doubleday and Company, Inc. Garden City, N.Y. 1971.
2. Ryan, P.G. Mar. Environ. Res. 1987, 23, 175-206.
3. Azzarello, M.Y.; Van Vleet, E.S. Mar. Ecol. (Prog. Ser.) 1987, 37, 295-303.
4. Fowler, C.W. Mar. Pollut. Bull. 1987, 18, 326-335.
5. Brothers, G. Unpublished report. Department of Fisheries and Oceans. St. John's, Newfoundland. 1989, 6 pages.
6. Henderson, J.R. In Proceedings of the Workshop on the Fate and Impact of Marine Debris; Editors, Shomura, R.S. and Yoshida, H.O.; U.S. Dept. Commer.: NOAA Techn. Memo. NMFS, NOAA-TM-NMFS-SWFC-54, 1985, pp. 326-335.
7. Carr, A. Mar. Pollut. Bull. 1987, 18, 352-356.
8. Powicki, C.R. J. Water Pollut. Fed. 1989 61, 554-558.
9. Levy, E. M.; Ehrhardt, M.; Kohnke, D.; Sobtchenko, E.; Suzuoki, T.; Tokuhiro, A. Oil Pollution, Results of MAPMOPP, The IGOSS Pilot Project On Marine Pollution (Petroleum) Monitoring; Intergovernmental Oceanographic Commission, Paris. 1981; 35 pp.
10. Levy, E.M. Ambio 1984, 13, 226-235.
11. Sen Gupta, R.; Kureishy, T.W. Mar. Pollut. Bull. 1981, 12, 295-301.
12. van Vleet, E.S.; Sackett, W.M.; Weber, F.F. Jr.; Reinhardt, S.B. Can. J. Fish. Aquat. Sci. 1983, 40 (Suppl. 2), 12-22.
13. van Dolah, R.F.; Burrell, V.G., Jr.; West, S.B. Mar. Pollut. Bull. 1980, 11, 352-356.
14. Cordes, C.; Atkinson, L.; Lee, R.; Blanton, J. Mar. Pollut. Bull. 1980, 11, 315-317.
15. Levy, E.M.; Walton, A. J. Fish. Res. Board Can. 1976,33, 2781-2791.
16. Day, R.H.; Shaw, D. G. Mar. Pollut. Bull. 1987, 18, 311-316.
17. Price, A.R.G.; Nelson-Smith, A. Mar. Pollut. Bull. 1986, 17, 60-62.
18. Holdway, P. Mar. Pollut. Bull. 1986, 8, 374-377.
19. Oostdam, B.L. Mar. Pollut. Bull. 1984, 15, 267-270.
20. Oostdam, B.L. Mar. Pollut. Bull. 1980, 11, 138-144.

21. Burns, K.A.; Villeneuve, J.P.; Anderlin, V.C.; Fowler, S.W. Mar. Pollut. Bull. 1982, 13, 240-247.
22. Emara, H.I. Mar. Pollut. Bull. 1990, 21, 399-401.
23. Coles, S.L.; Gunay, N. Mar. Pollut. Bull. 1989, 20, 214-218.
24. Price, A.R.G.; Wrathall, T.J.; Bernard, S.M. Mar. Pollut. Bull. 1987, 18, 650-651.
25. Shiber, J.G. Environmental. Pollut. 1989, 57, 341-351.
26. Vielvoye, R. Oil and Gas J. 1991, 89, 31.
27. Golik, A. Est. Coastal and Shelf Sci. 1982, 15, 267-276.
28. Shekel, Y.; Ravid, R. Environ. Sci. Tech. 1977, 11, 502-505.
29. Atwood, D.K.; Burton, F.J.; Corredor, J.E.; Harvey, G.R.; Mata-Jimenez, A.J.; Vasquez-Botello, A.; Wade, B.A. Oceanus 1987, 30(4), 25-32.
30. Georges, C.; Oostdam, B.L. Mar. Pollut. Bull. 1983, 14, 170-178.
31. Romero, G.C.; Harvey, G.R.; Atwood, D.K. Mar. Pollut. Bull. 1981, 12, 280-284.
32. Dennis, J.V. Oil Pollution Survey of the United States Atlantic Coast. American Petroleum Institute, Washington, D.C. 1959.
33. van Vleet, E.S.; Sackett, W.M.; Reinhardt, S.B.; Mangini, M.E. Mar. Pollut. Bull. 1984, 15, 106-110.
34. Knap, A.H.; Iliffe, T.M.; Butler, J.N. Mar. Pollut. Bull. 1980, 11, 161-164.
35. Smith, S.R.; Knap, A.H. Mar. Pollut. Bull. 1985, 16, 19-21.
36. Morris, W.W.; Hamilton, E.I. Mar. Pollut. Bull. 1974, 5, 26-27.
37. Kartar, S.; Milne, R.A.; Sainsbury, M. Mar. Pollut. Bull. 1973, 4, 144.
38. Kartar, S.; Abou-Seedo, F.; Sainsbury, M. Mar. Pollut. Bull. 1976, 7.
39. Shiber, J.G. Mar. Pollut. Bull. 1982, 13, 409-412.
40. Shiber, J.G. Mar. Pollut. Bull. 1987, 18, 84-86.
41. Morris, R.J. Mar. Pollut. Bull. 1980, 11, 125.
42. Carpenter, E.J.; Anderson, S.J.; Harvey, G.R.; Miklas, H.P.; Peck, B.B. Science 1972, 178, 749-750.
43. Colton, J.B.; Knapp, F.D.; Burns, B.R. Science 1974, 185, 491-497.
44. Hays, H.; Cormons, G. Mar. Pollut. Bull. 1974, 5, 44-46.
45. Gregory, M.R. Mar. Pollut. Bull. 1977, 8, 82-84.
46. van Franeker, J. Mar. Pollut. Bull. 1985, 16, 367-369.
47. Furness, B.L. Mar. Pollut. Bull. 1983, 14, 307-308.
48. Morris, R.J. Mar. Pollut. Bull. 1980, 11, 164-166.
49. Bourne, W.R.P.; Clark, G.S. Mar. Pollut. Bull. 1984, 15, 343-344.
50. Gregory, M.R.; Kirk, R.M.; Mabin, M.C.G. Antarctic Record 1984, 6, 12-26.
51. van Franeker, J.A.; Bell, P.J. Mar. Pollut. Bull. 1988, 19, 672-674.
52. Carpenter, E.J.; Smith, K.L. Science 1972, 175, 1240-1241.
53. Cundell, A.M. Mar. Pollut. Bull. 1973, 4, 187-188.
54. Colton, J.B., Jr. Oceanus 1974, 18(1), 61-64.
55. Winston, J.E. Mar. Pollut. Bull. 1982, 13, 348-351.
56. Wilber, R.J. Oceanus 1987, 30(3) 61-68.
57. Gregory, M.R. Mar. Environ. Res. 1983, 10, 73-92.

58. Ross, J.B.; Parker, R.; Strickland, M. Pollut. Bull. 1991, 22, 245-248.
59. Shaw, D.G.; Mapes, G.A. Mar. Pollut. Bull. 1979, 10, 160-162.
60. Dahlberg, M.L.; Day, R.H. In Proceedings of the Workshop on the Fate and Impact of Marine Debris; Editors, Shomura, R.S. and Yoshida, H.O.; U.S. Dept. Commer.: NOAA Techn. Memo. NMFS, NOAA-TM-NMFS-SWFC-54, 1985, pp. 198-212.
61. Merrell, T.R. Mar. Environ. Res. 1980, 3, 171-184.
62. Merrell, T.R. Mar. Pollut. Bull. 1984, 15, 378-384.
63. Johnson, S.W. Mar. Pollut. Bull. 1989, 20, 164-168.
64. Jewett, S.C. Mar. Pollut. Bull. 1976, 7, 169.
65. Feder, H.M.; Jewett, S.C.; Hilsinger, J. R. Mar. Pollut. Bull. 1978, 9, 52-53.
66. Willoughby, N.G. Mar. Pollut. Bull. 1986, 17, 224-228.
67. McCoy, F.W. Mar. Pollut. Bull. 1988, 19, 25-28.
68. Dixon, T.J.; Dixon, T.R. Mar. Pollut. Bull. 1983, 14, 145-148.
69. Vauk, G.J.M.; Schrey, E. Mar. Pollut. Bull. 1987, 18, 316-319.
70. Horsman, P.V. Mar. Pollut. Bull. 1982, 13, 167-169.
71. Bean, M.J. Mar. Pollut. Bull. 1987, 18, 357-360.
72. Ambrose, P. Mar. Pollut. Bull. 1991, 22,262.
73. Morris, B.F. and J.N. Butler 1973. In Proc. Conf. Prevention and Control of Oil Spills; American Petroleum Institute: Washington, D.C. pp 521-529.
74. Levy, E.M. Can. J. Fish. Aquat. Sci. 1985, 42, 544-555.
75. Zsolnay, A. Chemosphere 1987, 16, 399-404.
76. Duerr, C. Oceans 1980, 13, 59-60.
77. Anon. J. Water Pollut. Control Fed. 1988, 60, 284.
78. Anon. Mar. Pollut. Bull. 1988, 19, 90-91. 79. McIntyre, A.D. Mar. Pollut. Bull. 1990, 21, 403-404.

RECEIVED October 1, 1991

Chapter 12

Assessing Global River Water Quality

Overview and Data Collection

David A. Dunnette

Environmental Sciences and Resources Program, Portland State University, P.O. Box 751, Portland, OR 97207

Human activities that are transforming the global environment are reflected in the chemical, physical and biological constituents and dynamics of the world's rivers. However, because of the spatial and temporal variability of rivers and the complexity of river dynamics, relatively little is known with much certainty about the water quality of the world's rivers, especially as quality relates to human activities and global change. Shortcomings of current river water quality assessment approaches include inadequate emphasis on river hydrology and how it relates to biogeochemical transformations, uncertainties arising from inter-laboratory variation in methodologies, and the common grab sample "shotgun" or parametric approach often utilized by water quality monitoring agencies.

An alternative to the traditional fixed-station parametric river sampling network is the mechanistic or intensive survey approach in which interrelationships among topography, geology, climatology, ecology, hydrology, biogeochemistry and human activities are utilized in the assessment process. Mechanistic approaches may be classified as quantitative, semi-quantitative and qualitative. These are illustrated with examples from three major problem areas which have developed as a result of human activity: dissolved oxygen depletion, erosion/deposition of soil and potentially toxic trace elements.

Historical Impacts Reflected in River Systems

Ancient civilizations were born in environments which provided the challenge to which humans responded by action and achievements. The optimum conditions necessary for birth of civilizations were provided in the valleys of the world's great rivers, among them, the Nile, the Yellow, the Ganges, the Indus,

0097–6156/92/0483–0240$06.00/0

the Tigris and Euphrates. The importance of rivers derives not from their fractional percentage of total water (0.0001%) or even total freshwater (0.004%) on Earth, but from the important role they have played in cultural development by providing both water and mobility.

Rivers are of interest in a global context because, although the characteristics of rivers reflect predominantly local and regional conditions, they nevertheless are an indicator of the health of the total environment. This is because rivers, like the atmosphere and oceans, are integrative and reflect conditions within their boundaries. Like the winds, rivers are powerful agents of the internationalization of environmental problems. Rainfall into a river drainage basin absorbs gaseous and particulate material, is supplemented by urban and agricultural runoff, melting snow, lakes, swamps and groundwater as well as discharges from municipal and industrial activity. Rainwater flows down land slopes and river beds, dissolving and transporting various chemical and geochemical species and receiving tributaries from adjacent subbasins including substances transported across political boundaries.

Over the course of human history rivers have reflected the impact of human activity. Since the beginnings of the great civilizations 5000 years ago, humankind, in its pursuit of agriculture, exploration and conquest, has exploited and mistreated the environment on a broad scale. Major changes on the face of the earth occurred. Forests were cut, pastures grazed, fields cleared and plowed "... as the landscape was carved to fit the new economic demands of humankind." (*1*). Such changes have been well documented (*2-5*).

Within 1000 years of the development of the great early cities, the huge animal herds of pastoral peoples caused extensive erosion and irreversible aridity in Africa, the Middle East and Asia. Two thousand years later the Mediterranean lands were denuded and despoiled. Within another two thousand years colonial expansion resulted in rapid and disastrous exploitation throughout the Americas (*3,6*). We may be quite certain that all these activities were accurately reflected in river systems as disintegration of basin surface layers led to accelerated transport of soils to the oceans. Then, slowly at first, almost imperceptibly, beginning about 200 years ago and then with lightning-like speed in the geological sense, the chemical and ecological characteristics of rivers in the more rapidly industrializing countries changed as mobilization of trace elements forms and discharges of wastes led to degraded water quality. Today we, as did the golden civilizations of the past, prosper at the expense of the environment. It is therefore critically important that we apply the most effective means possible to utilize the temporally and spatially integrative ability of the worlds rivers to access the terrestrial and aquatic environmental impacts occurring on a global scale.

Global Evidence of Changes in River Quality

Changes in the composition of the atmosphere are perhaps our most valid indicators of the influence of human activities on global systems. The next best barometer may very well be loss of biodiversity due to habitat destruction.

Habitat destruction in turn is reflected in decoupling of elemental cycles and disintegration of surface soil layers due to erosion and overland transport of soil to rivers and ultimately to the oceans. Denudation reduces the ability of soil to absorb water and increases streamflow. As denudation of the landscape has accelerated over the past several decades, a shift in the global water cycle may have resulted in a 3% increased river flow (7). Suspended matter concentration and streamflow may therefore be the most relevant measure of the impact of human activity on land resources and water quality. Average suspended matter in major world rivers has been estimated by Milliman and Meade (8) to vary from 140 mg L^{-1} to 23,000 mg L^{-1} with a discharge-weighted average of 450 mg L^{-1}, although 50 percent of the rivers investigated had suspended matter concentrations of less than 150 mg L^{-1} (9). As sediment is deposited in river basins, reduced river velocity increases opportunities for primary production and the uptake of nutrients by phytoplankton and rooted aquatic plants (10-11). On the other hand plant production in river systems is usually limited by suspended solids and this suggests the potential for reduced primary production. Meybeck (9) has estimated that the transport of nitrogen and phosphorous in rivers has increased significantly. In the USA nitrate increases occurred almost three times more frequently than phosphorus and salinity increases occurred in most drainage basins investigated by Smith and others (12). Milliman and Meade (8) and Meybeck et al. (13) estimated 60% to 99+% reductions in suspended sediment loads due to the influence of reservoirs.

Difficulties in Assessing Global River Quality

The intent of this and the accompanying chapter is not to provide a methodology for assessing river quality of the world as a whole, as admirable a challenge as that might be, or to present the results of such an assessment. Information and data are simply not available to do this and costs would be very great even if suitable methodologies could be found or developed. Rather the goals of the chapters are 1) to provide some basic understanding of the scientific limitations inherent in assessing global river quality 2) to illustrate how different river quality problems require different methodological approaches and 3) to illustrate some of these approaches for three different globally relevant river quality problem areas.

Traditional Approaches to River Quality Assessment

The basis for assessment of river quality is valid data, but the question of data validity is secondary to the fundamental question: What is the purpose of the river quality assessment activity? What questions are being asked? In short the means are determined by the ends. If, for example, the intent of an assessment program is to ascertain compliance with law, then a fixed interval "grab" sampling program could be established at various river system sites selected on the basis of established guidelines which are consistent with the intent of the program. This activity is often referred to as "fixed station ambient monitoring" and can also be appropriate for estimating long-term trends in water quality with some modification in monitoring parameters. Numerous approaches to fixed station monitoring have been described in the literature over the past 15 years *(14-21)*.

Not clearly defining the role of monitoring and assessment can lead to unattained program objectives and reduced cost effectiveness. For Example, faced with the need to meet certain water quality standards on the one hand and identify trends and cause-effect relationships on the other hand, some agencies have tended to simply collect data at numerous station sites. The feeling is that the data will be "accessed" by "users" as the need arises. This data collection strategy has been referred to as the "shotgun" or parametric approach. The number of parameters in a fixed-station sampling program may exceed 40 or 50 often with little solid scientific rationale specified for many of them and with unnecessary redundancy among parameters.

Although a number of papers have commented on the possible deficiencies of ambient fixed-station monitory networks, *(17-19)* more recent papers have recognized the primary difficulty as a failure to identify what questions are being asked that the monitoring and assessment program is supposed to answer *(20-24)*.

River Quality Assessment in the USA

In 1989 the National Academy of Sciences recommended that the US Geological Survey implement a National Water Quality Assessment Program (NAWQA) which was subsequently accomplished in 1991 *(25)*. The river quality assessment component of the study will span a period of 4-5 years at an annual cost of $18-60 million and will include 60 drainage basins throughout the U.S. including the Willamette River basin of Oregon, the model basin discussed in the accompanying chapter. As defined by Hirsch and others *(26)*, the goals of the program are 1) to provide a nationally consistent description of current water-quality conditions for a large part of the Nation's water resources, 2) to define long term trends (or lack of trends) in water quality and 3) to identify, describe, and explain, as possible, the major factors that affect observed water-quality conditions and trends.

At present the program is in a pilot phase that is expected to last 4 or 5 years. The program will focus on regional river quality degradation, primarily that associated with nonpoint sources of pollution and will include a set of 20 trace elements, 6 measures of nitrogen and phosphorous, 7 major constituents, 3 radionuclides, 6 field measurements including acidity, alkalinity, dissolved oxygen, pH, specific conductance and temperature and an unspecified number of organic constituents. Biological measurements will include fecal bacteria, evaluation of potentially toxic substances and their possible effects on abundance and diversity, and other ecological measures. Sampling approaches used will include fixed-station and intensive survey. Sampling frequency will be once a month with additional samples collected at high streamflow for the intensive survey work.

The most recent comprehensive assessment of the quality of rivers in the USA is that of Smith et al. (12). This followed an earlier assessment by Wolman et al. in 1971 (18). The former 1987 assessment was based on 24 water quality measures from 161-383 stations around the country covering the period 1974-1981. Trends observed included major increases in nitrate, phosphorous, sodium, suspended sediment, fecal bacteria, dissolved oxygen deficit, arsenic and selenium. Major decreases were observed with nitrate, suspended sediment, fecal bacteria, dissolved oxygen deficit and lead.

International River Quality.

International agencies such as the United Nations Environment Program (UNEP) based in Kenya and England and the European Organization for Economic Co-operation and Development (OCDE) based in France rely principally on ambient fixed-station networks to assess trends in water quality. The U.N. Global Environmental Monitoring System (GEMS) is intended to provide a rigorous scientific base for environmental management. GEMS attempts to link existing monitoring networks in the areas of climate, transboundary pollution, terrestrial renewable natural resources, oceans, and the health consequences of pollution. The GEMS river quality monitoring network includes 240 stations in 59 countries submitting data on up to 50 water quality parameters (27). Data from the sampling and analysis network are published biannually. A number of large intergovernmental and governmental organizations including the World Conservation Monitoring Center, International Union for the Conservation of Nature and Natural Resources, the Council for Mutual Economic Assistance and the U.S. Environmental Protection Agency provide the data which are incorporated into the GEMS data base.

The uncertainties associated with the data base of an individual river basin are compounded when the intent is to provide a global perspective. This point is made in a recent bound volume of UNEP data in which a number of data interpretation limitations are sited. Quality of data varies from one individual reporting entity to another and the precision of the data is usually not possible to ascertain. Thus direct comparisons between data from one country, or even one laboratory to the next are not always possible. Since uncertainties associated with the data (variability, accuracy, precision, etc.) are often not specified, the significance of the data may be difficult to determine and no valid interpretation of the data may therefore be possible. It comes as no surprise that these and similar data from other data bases are often, if not usually, inadequate to establish cause and effect relationships.

The organization for Economic Co-operation and Development publishes a compendium on environmental data including river monitoring, also on a biannual basis. The most recent edition includes 5 year incremental data from 1970 through 1985 for chromium, copper, lead, cadmium, ammonia, nitrate, phosphorous, dissolved oxygen and biochemical oxygen demand (28).

Numerous precautionary and qualifying statements are given for each parameter listed. The parameters listed are referred to as "water quality indicators" although there is no guidance provided as to what the values actually indicate. In brief the UNEP and OECD data are representative of ambient fixed-station monitoring activity around the world which is not providing the kind of information required to adequately manage land and water resources or provide global perspectives.

River Quality Assessment

River quality assessment is the evaluation of the physical, chemical and biological characteristics of water which determine its suitability for specific beneficial uses. The overall goal of a mechanistic approach to river quality assessment is to provide scientific information that is both adequate and appropriate for water resource management and protection on local, regional and global scales. To accomplish this the conditions and parameters controlling water quality characteristics of concern which are sensitive to growth or economic development must be identified. The most important of these from an assessment standpoint is river hydrology.

Hydrology and River Water Quality. Hydrologic characteristics which control the physical dynamics of rivers also influence the pattern, nature, magnitude and extent of biogeochemical processes. An analysis of river hydrology is therefore a necessary first step in the river quality assessment process. Data obtained in the analysis can provide a measure of background variability in water quality caused by the variability of natural hydrologic processes. This information can then be utilized to better estimate impacts on river water quality resulting from human activities in the river's drainage basin.

River basin hydrology involves complex ecological coupling and interrelationships of topography, geology, climate and vegetation as well as human land and water use (29,30). The assimilation of pollutants from wastewater discharges depends to a significant degree on such hydrologic factors as water temperature, flow rate and river velocity. These in turn influence biogeochemical activity. Low flows, such as those occurring in the middle latitudes in summer, are often particularly critical to water quality. During these periods water quality problems are often exacerbated by increased concentrations of pollutants, low dissolved oxygen and high biological activity both of which are temperature dependent.

Consideration of hydrologic factors in understanding river water quality dynamics is perhaps a first step in the formal recognition that ambient fixed-station monitoring information is of extremely limited usefulness in managing resources. What is required instead is an understanding of the fundamental water-quality-limiting physical, and biogeochemical processes and characteristics of the river and the drainage basin as a whole. Much of the information needed for this phase of an assessment, especially that related to physical processes, is already available for many river systems and much can be obtained relatively inexpensively by visible and IR imagery and a review of river basin history. This information can provide a picture of basic river dynamics, seasonal variation and the potential impact resulting from low and high water conditions.

Mechanistic Approaches. Adequate and appropriate river-quality assessment must provide predictive information on the possible consequences of water and land development. This requires an understanding of the relevant cause and effect relationships and suitable data to develop predictive models for basin management. This understanding may be achieved through qualitative, semi-quantitative or quantitative approaches. When quantitative or semi-quantitative methods are not available the qualitative approach must be applied. *Qualitative assessments* involve knowledge of how basin activities may affect river quality. This requires the use of various descriptive methods. An example of this kind of assessment is laboratory evaluation of the extent to which increases in plant nutrients, temperature or flow may lead to accelerated eutrophication with consequent reduction of water quality.

Examples of *semi-quantitative assessments* include interpretive maps and informational matrices which could be utilized to relate land-use, topography and erosion or other non-point source problems. Remote sensing imagery from low, intermediate and high altitude are applicable to this approach (*29*).

When there is an excellent general understanding of basic processes, a *quantitative assessment* might be possible. Quantitative models provide the most effective approach for assessing problems which can be described mathematically. Although, quantitative assessments provide more definitive (predictive) information than qualitative, rivers are exceedingly complex systems which include processes that may not be practically modeled. Figure 1 is a summary of the state of our knowledge in modeling the impact of human activities on river water quality (*30*). Many river quality problems are not amenable to mathematical modeling. For this reason and because of the high cost of acquiring data, the most practical approach, particularly where resources are severely limited, will be a qualitative technique such as the use of maps or informational matrices which allow some understanding of relations between human activities and environmental impact. The balance of this paper will illustrate three water quality problem areas requiring different mechanistic or intensive survey approaches to river quality assessment: 1) dissolved oxygen for which a quantitative approach has been well developed, 2) erosion and deposition for which semi-quantitative techniques are usually most practical and available, and 3) potentially toxic trace elements for which only qualitative methods are usually feasible. A subsequent chapter will illustrate how the approaches described were applied to a model river, the Willamette River, Oregon, USA.

A Quantitative Approach: Dissolved Oxygen Depletion. The classical primary indicator of the health of a river, especially one receiving oxidizable domestic or industrial wastewater is dissolved oxygen (DO) concentration. Although oxygen concentration in a well-oxygenated river system will normally range between 5 and 15 mg L^{-1} (7.6 and 13.8 parts per million, ppm) at temperatures between 2°C and 30°C, the introduction of oxidizable wastes may result in DO depletion down to 0 mg L^{-1}.

The discharge of oxygen demanding wastewater can lead to a dramatic shift in the ecology of a river system due to both enrichment (carbon, nitrogen, phosphorous, trace elements) and the introduction of suspended and settleable solids which may blanket the substrate to which a wide variety of aquatic organisms are attached. This ecological shift is described by a classical series of diagrams by Bartsh and Ingram (*31*), three of which are reproduced here. Figure 2A depicts shifts in "macro" level aquatic ecology which accompanies changes in downstream concentrations of DO and organic matter. Changes in the aquatic community occur chiefly due to variation in DO needs and alterations of physical substrate on the river bottom. Figure 2B illustrates trophic level shifts in aquatic communities. There is initially an explosion in numbers of heterotrophic bacteria responding to available carbon and nutrients. This community, composed of a variety of organisms biochemically transforming carbonaceous and nitrogenous substances, leads to a higher trophic level community of predators including ciliates, rotifers and crustaceans. Communities of macro-invertebrates develop downstream leading in turn to fish tolerant of polluted water, and further downstream, clean water fish such as trout and salmon.

Figure 2C depicts the biochemical oxygen demand (BOD) imposed on the system largely through the activity of heterotrophic bacteria. As the BOD of the assimilable organic wastes is satisfied, DO drops to a minimum dependent on the magnitude and interaction of the controlling variables. The situation depicted in Figure 2C is one in which the oxygen demanding load is large relative to the self purifying capacity of the water body. In reality the ecological impact of the DO demanding wastes may be greater or less than that illustrated. A number of principal biochemical processes influence the oxygen regime of a river system: oxidation of carbon based substances (BOD), oxidation of reduced nitrogen compounds (nitrification), photosynthesis, and reaeration through contact with the atmosphere. The former three processes consume dissolved oxygen while the latter two are dissolved oxygen sources. Each of these will be discussed briefly in turn.

Carbonaceous Deoxygenation. In this process microorganisms, principally bacteria, enzymatically mediate oxidation of simple and complex organic substances according to first order decay kinetics,

$$\frac{L_t}{L} = 10^{-kt} \qquad (1)$$

where L is the amount of oxidizable organic matter, L_t is the amount of organic matter at time t, and k is a first order rate constant, varying typically

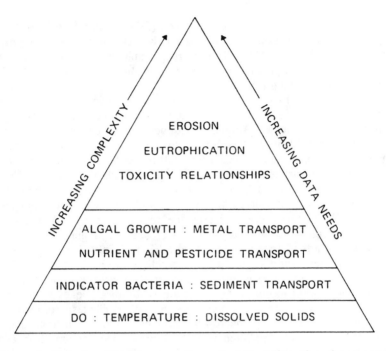

Figure 1. Relative difficulty of mathematical modeling of environmental impact.

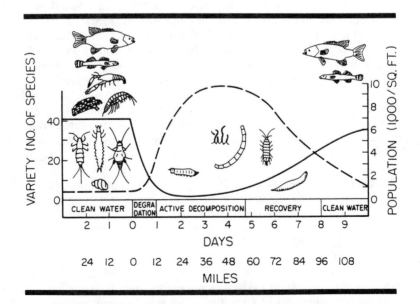

Figure 2A. Impact of domestic wastewater on aquatic macroorganism communities in a hypothetical stream (100 cfs) receiving wastewater from a community of 40,000. Solid line variety; dotted line population.

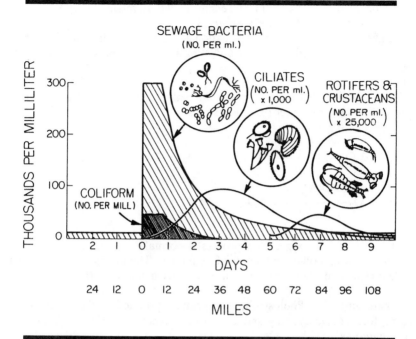

Figure 2B. Impact of domestic wastewater on aquatic microorganism communities in a hypothetical stream (100 cfs) receiving wastewater from a community of 40,000.

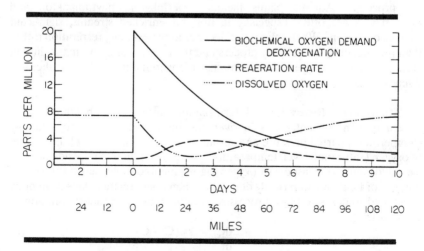

Figure 2C. Impact of domestic wastewater on downstream water quality in a hypothetical stream (100 cfs) receiving wastewater from a community of 40,000.

from 0.02 to 0.2 day^{-1} at 20°C. Technical details related to BOD and its measurement may be found elsewhere (32).

Highest rates of biochemical oxidation are found in shallow, surface active reaches where attached microbiota and interfacial oxygen exchange are at their maxima.

Nitrification. Nitrification refers to biologically mediated oxidation of reduced nitrogen to higher oxidation states:

$$\text{2 NH}_4 + \text{3 O}_2 \xrightarrow{\textit{Nitrosomonas}} \text{4 H}^+ + \text{2 NO}_2^- + \text{2 H}_2\text{O} \tag{2}$$

$$\text{2 NO}_2^- + \text{O}_2 \xrightarrow{\textit{Nitrobacter}} \text{2 NO}_3^- \tag{3}$$

Nitrification as a deoxygenation process is normally significant only in river systems receiving pollutional inputs of ammonia. The kinetics of nitrification are less clear than those for carbonaceous deoxygenation (33).

Photosynthesis. Photosynthesis is primary production, the fundamental driving force of ecosystems and is a critical dynamic in rivers. It may be represented as

$$\text{CO}_2 + \text{H}_2\text{O} \xrightarrow{\textit{Sunlight}} \text{CH}_2\text{O} + \text{O}_2 \tag{4}$$

where CH_2O is an elemental representation of the carbohydrate produced in the process.   Aquatic plants including periphyton, phytoplankton and macrophytes are often, especially in nutrient enriched streams, significant sources of oxygen. When solar input declines in the evening, respiration rather than production is the primary process and the result is often dramatic diurnal variation in river oxygen concentration. Measurement of photosynthesis is discussed elsewhere (34).

Atmospheric Reaeration. Interfacial properties and phenomena that govern oxygen concentrations in river systems include 1) oxygen solubility (temperature, partial pressure and surface dependency), 2) rate of dissolution of oxygen (saturation level, temperature and surface thin film dependency, i.e., ice, wind), and 3) transport of oxygen via mixing and molecular diffusion. A number of field and empirically derived mathematical relationships have been developed to describe these processes and phenomena, the most common of which is (32):

$$\frac{dC}{dt} = k_2 (C_s - C) \tag{5}$$

where C = dissolved oxygen concentration (percent saturation)
C_s = oxygen saturation value at temperature t
C_s - C = DO deficit
k_2 = reaeration coefficient (velocity and depth dependent)

A Semi-quantitative Approach: Erosion and Deposition. Over the centuries the primary impact of human activity has been to deforest the surrounding countryside and increase the rate of erosion and deposition into rivers. This results primarily from the destruction of vegetation cover which stabilizes soil systems on gradient. The ecological impact of erosion has at present reached catastrophic proportions. The magnitude of continental erosion into rivers is illustrated in Figure 3.

Rivers transport suspended sediments derived from the disintegration of basin surface layers. With reduced velocity, sediment is deposited in the river channel. The finest material is carried to the sea. It has been estimated that the average mechanical denudation rate for continents is 0.056 mm year^{-1} *(35)*. This is based on a total suspended load of 13.5 x 10^9 metric tons year^{-1} *(8)*. Presently, about two-thirds of the world's total suspended sediment load derives from Southern Asia and large Pacific Islands. Berner has estimated the increase in sediment loss in the U.S. and world since prehuman times to be approximately 200% *(35)*. Current estimated erosion rate from the major land forms is provided in Table I.   The relatively recent construction of large sediment trapping dams that normally caused sediment to be deposited in river valleys or transported to the ocean has drastically reduced sediment yields in great rivers.

Table I. Global Erosion Rates of Cropland, Grassland and Forest

Land Type	U.S. Area $10^6 km^2$	Erosion Rate tons km^{-2} yr	World Area $10^6 km$	Erosion Rate tons km^{-2} yr
Cropland	1.43	1371	14	530
Grassland	3.08	1316	24	160
Forest	2.38	176	51	53

Sources: *8,9,30*

Cause and effect relationships associated with erosion and river quality can be clearly established for many activities. For example construction activity at a site could be clearly responsible for a resulting landslide into a river. But other activities such as those related to agriculture and forestry may not be so apparent. Spatial and temporal linkages may not be so clearly established.

The methods described here for a semi-quantitative approach to this

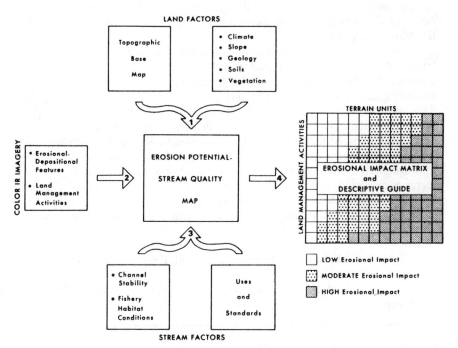

Figure 3. Process for assessing impact of human land use activity on river quality.

problem are matrix/map techniques in which erosional problems are mapped and land characteristics are systematically ranked with respect to erosion potential. The method was developed and applied by the US Geological Survey in the Willamette Basin as is illustrated in Figure 4. Four steps were involved in the approach *(29)*:

- recognizing and mapping erosional and depositional areas referred to as "provinces";
- mapping certain erosion and depositional features using high and low altitude imagery
- land-use activity analysis using color infra-red imagery to arrive at a numerical ranking of land-use impact activities
- construction of a land-use problem matrix using order of magnitude estimates of impact of erosion and deposition as they relate to human activity

In developing and applying the erosional-depositional system, careful consideration was given to the environmental factors which influence the potential for erosion, transport and deposition: climate, topography, geology and soils, as well as human activity.

A Qualitative Approach: Potentially Toxic Trace Elements. Potentially toxic trace elements in rivers result from a combination of man-induced and natural influences. Man-induced inputs originate from direct sources (industrial, commercial, domestic) and indirect sources (e.g., urban runoff, agriculture). Natural inputs result from geochemical characteristics of the drainage basin and biogeochemical processes in the river. Trace elements are of concern for several reasons: they can be toxic to organisms at very low concentrations; they are distributed widely from both natural sources and man's activities; they are persistent in nature; their toxicity and mobility can increase when environmental conditions change; and they can bioaccumulate to toxic levels in organisms when available in certain chemical forms.

Limitations of Commonly Available Data. Traditional ambient monitoring data cannot provide information to adequately evaluate potentially toxic trace elements in water. This is so for several reasons in addition to those already cited for ambient monitoring in general. First, most trace element forms tend to rapidly sorb to sediment particles thus removing them from solution; concentrations of cationic trace metal forms in sediments are generally 3-5 orders of magnitude higher than the metal content in associated water *(36)*. Second, the spatial and temporal variation of trace metals in overlying water are much greater than those of sediments; water data may be useful for assessment of impact only when frequent sampling is conducted to determine the extent of variability. Third, chemical analyses of trace elements in water provides no real measure of toxicity to biota or humans since toxicity is governed by the chemical and physical characteristics of the element in water (usually not determined) and the nature of the organism. Fourth, concentrations of trace elements in aquatic organisms or human tissue (muscle, blood, hair, fingernails) are better indicators of potential stress on the organism

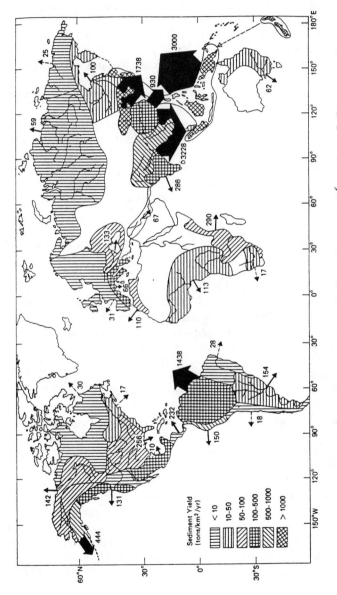

Figure 4. Discharge of suspended sediment from world rivers in 10^6 tons/year. Sediment yield in tons/km^2/year for major drainage basins is shown by pattern (see key).

than concentrations in water because such data provide measures of actual uptake by the organism.

Commonly Used Trace Element Assessment Methods. The complexity of trace elements in water is so great and river quality is so different and variable that it is essentially impossible to determine precisely what will happen to trace elements in water and what their effect on biota and humans will be. Each trace element differs in its chemical properties from other elements and each has its own characteristic spectrum of actual chemical forms. Each chemical form of a single element differs in its ability to exert a toxic effect on humans or aquatic life. Some of these forms are inorganic while others are organic. Some forms are soluble while others are insoluble. For example there are at least six identified soluble forms of copper, each with its own peculiar toxicological characteristics *(37)*. To further complicate matters, other factors such as age, sex, size, and health of the organisms greatly affect toxic response. These and other difficulties can never be entirely overcome but there are several approaches to assessing the toxic or potentially toxic effects of trace elements which have proved successful to some degree.

Toxicity Test (Bioassay). Organisms representative of those to be protected are exposed to the test water under rigorously controlled conditions, usually in a laboratory environment. In this test the organisms, normally fish, are exposed for a standard time period in aquaria to various dilutions of waste or river water while some physiological parameter is carefully monitored to determine fish response. Behavior is also observed.

Tissue Analysis. A toxicological response cannot occur without some level of accumulation of the toxic substances in the organism. Thus, bioaccumulation may be the most direct measure of bioavailability, the extent to which a given chemical substance interacts biochemically with the organism. The tissue of interest is homogenized and the toxic substance is extracted with chemical reagents such as dilute HCl or an organic chelator. The final product is analyzed by appropriate methods, generally atomic absorption spectrophotometry.

Sediment Analysis. Sediment is the most chemically and biologically active component of the aquatic environment. Benthic invertebrate and microbial life concentrate in the sediment, a natural sink for precipitated metal forms, and an excellent sorbent for many metal species. The extent to which potentially toxic trace element forms bind to sediment is determined by the sediment's binding intensity and capacity and various solution parameters, as well as the concentration and nature of the metal forms of interest. Under some conditions sediment analyses can readily indicate sources of discharged trace elements.

Environmental Chemistry. This approach is not independent of the others but is complimentary to them. It involves the careful examination of pertinent chemical data and consideration of fundamental aquatic chemistry principles. For example:

- the concentration of more toxicologically active trace element forms can increase 100 fold as pH is reduced from pH 7 to 6.
- the concentration of cadmium which is toxic to the small crustacean, *Daphni magna*, can be six times greater at a hardness of about 50 than at a hardness of 200 mg L^{-1} *(38)*.
- copper toxicity to rainbow trout can be reduced dramatically when sewage effluent is added to the bioassay chamber due to complexation by organics *(39)*.
- clays and hydrous metal oxides can provide an immense surface area for adsorption of trace element forms in water. Three hundred square meters of absorption surface area can be provided by one gram of hydrous iron or manganese oxide *(40)*.

Mathematical Modeling. An approach which has been used to evaluate the real or potential hazards of chemicals is mathematical modeling. For organic substances such approaches have been very effective in some cases. Although speciation models have been useful for some trace elements, fate and transport model predictions are probably no better than 1 to 5 orders of magnitude *(41)* and the question of ultimate impact on living organisms and humans remains unanswered. Nevertheless, computer model results have permitted first approximation estimates of the effects of dissolved substances on trace element biological availability. Such results indicate that the concentration of free ionic trace element forms may be 4 to 10^{18} times less than what is usually measured as "total recoverable" by "standard" methods *(42)*.

Summary and Conclusions

Global river quality is an important barometer of the impact of human activities on the total environment. Trends in flow rate, suspended solids, oxygen depletion, fecal bacteria, potentially toxic elements and other parameters represent critical indicators of how we are managing our environment. Yet most data generated on the quality of river water is based on the parametric approach to water quality assessment using fixed-station monitoring networks. Data generated from such networks are used primarily for monitoring trends and determining adherence to water quality standards. Difficulties in utilizing currently available data to assess global water quality and evaluate cause and effect relationships include   1) inadequate attention given to integrating understanding from the various water quality sciences (ecology, hydrology, biogeochemistry, geology and climatology) and 2) inherent limitations of grab sampling approaches including large sampling and analysis errors. On-going river quality assessment in the global context has therefore produced disappointing results.

What is needed is a shift of resources to mechanistic water quality assessment utilizing the quantitative, semi-quantitative and qualitative approaches readily available. Global monitoring entities such as the United Nations Global Environmental Monitoring System (GEMS) and the International Geophysical Biophysical Program need to more clearly and formally recognize the opportunities and challenges in mechanistic river water quality assessment and how understanding gained from the world's rivers may be integrated into corresponding studies of the Earth's atmosphere and oceans. International meetings convened to consider biogeochemical aspects of the Earth's environment, should address these issues and develop research priorities and mechanisms for funding.

The following chapter is a case study of how the three problem areas illustrated (dissolved oxygen depletion, erosion/deposition, and potentially toxic trace elements) may be successfully addressed on a major river system using quantitative, semi-quantitative and qualitative approaches respectively.

Literature Cited

1. Southwick, C.H. In *Global Ecology*. Southwick, C.H., Ed., Sinover Associates, Inc: Sunderland, MA, 1983; 205-218.
2. Marsh, G.P. *Man and Nature*; Scribners: NY, 1986.
3. Sauer, C.O. *J. Farm Economy.* **1938**, *20*, 765-775.
4. Sears, P.B. *Deserts on the March*. University of Oklahoma Press: Norman, OK, 1935.
5. Hillel, D.J. *Out of the Earth. Civilization and the Life of the Soil.* Macmillan: NY, 1991.
6. Sauer, C.O. *Land and Life*. A selection from the writings of Carl Ortwin Sauer. Leighly, J. Ed.; University of California Press: Berkeley, CA, 1967.
7. Probst, J.L.; Tardy, Y. *J. of Hydrol.* **1987**, *94*, 289-311.
8. Milliman, J.D.; Meade, R.H. *J. Geology.* **1983**, *91*, 1-21.
9. Meybeck, M. *Am. J. Sci.* **1982**, *282*, 401-450.
10. Lewis, W.M. *Ecology.* **1988**, *69*, 679-692.
11. Schlesinger, W.H. *Biogeochemistry - An Analysis of Global Change.* Academic Press: San Diego, CA, 1991; 226-243.
12. Smith, R.A.; Alexander, R.B.; Wolman, M.G. *Science.* **1987**, *235*, 1607-1615.
13. *Global Freshwater Quality - A First Assessment.* Meybeck, M.; Chapman, D.; Helmer, R. Basil Blackwell, Inc: Oxford, UK, 1989.
14. Ward, R.C.; Nielson, K.S. *Evaluating the Sampling Frequencies of Water Quality Networks.* Environmental Protection Agency, EPA 600-77-78-169, 1978.
15. Whitfield, P.H. *Wat. Resources Bull.* **1989**, *24*, 775-780.
16. Dunnette, D.A. *J. Wat. Pollut. Cont. Fed.* **1980**, *52*, 2807-2811.
17. Howells, D.H. *Water Resources.* Bull. **1971**, *7*, 162-170.
18. Wolman, M.G. *Science,* **1971**, *174*, 905-918.
19. Comptroller General of the General Accounting Office. *Better Monitoring Techniques are Needed to Assess the Quality of Rivers and Streams.* U.S. Government Print Office: Washington, D.C., 1981.

20. Ward, R.C.; Loftis, J.C. *Environ. Man.* **1986**, 10, 291-297.
21. Valiela, D.; Whitfield, P.H. *Wat. Resour. Bull.* **1989**, 25, 63-69.
22. van Belle, G.; Hughes, J.P. *J. Wat. Poll. Cont. Fed.* **1983**, 55, 400-404
23. Ward, R. C.; Loftis, J.C.; McBride, G. B. *Design of Water Quality Monitoring Systems*. Von Nostrand Reinhold: NY, 1990.
24. U.S. General Accounting Office. *The Nation's Water: Key Unanswered Questions about the Quality of Rivers and Streams*, Rep. No. GAO/PE MD-86-6. Washington, D.C., 1986.
25. Leahy, P.P.; Rosenshein, J.S.; and Knopman, D.S. *Implementation for The National Water-Quality Assessment Program*. U.S. Geographical Survey Open-File Report 90-174, U.S. Geological Survey, Federal Center, Denver, CO, 1990, 1-10.
26. Hirsch, R.M.; Alley, W.M.; Wilber, W.G. *Concepts for a National Water Quality Assessment Program*. U.S. Geological Survey Circular 1021, U.S. Geological Survey, Federal Center, Denver, CO, 1988, 1-42.
27. GEMS Monitoring and Assessment Research Center, London, UK, *Environmental Data Report*. United Nations Environmental Program, Blockwell, England, 1989.
28. Organization for Economic Co-operation and Development. Compendium of Environmental Data, 1989. OECD, Paris, France.
29. Rickert, D.A.; and Beach, G.L. *J. Wat. Pollut. Cont. Fed.* **1978**, 50, 2439-2445.
30. Hines, W.G.; Rickert, D.A.; McKenzie, S.W.; Bennett, J.P. *Formulation and Use of Practical Models for River-Quality Assessment*. Geology Survey Circular 715-B, *USGS*, Reston, VA, Washington, D.C., 1975.
31. Bartsch, A.F.; Ingram, W. *Public Works*, 1959, 90 as modified by Christman, et al., The Natural Environment: Wastes and Control, Goodyear Pub. Co: Pacific Palisades, CA, 1974.
32. Velz, C.J. *Applied Stream Sanitation*. John Wiley: NY, 1971, 137-233.
33. Dunnette, D.A.; Avedovech, R.M. *Water Res.* **1983**, 17, 997-1007.
34. Clesceri, L.S.; Greenberg, A.E.; Trussell, R.R. Eds.; *Standard Methods for the Examination of Water and Wastewaters*; 17th Edition, American Public Health Association, American Water Works Assoc., Water Pollution Control Federation, Baltimore, MD. 1989.
35. Berner, E.K.; Berner, R.A. *The Global Water Cycle*. Prentice-Hall: Englewood Cliffs, NJ, 1987, 178.
36. Forstner, V.; Wittmann, G.T. *Metal Pollution in the Aquatic Environment* Springer-Verlag: Berlin, GR; NY,NY, 112, 1979.
37. Mancy, K.H.; Allen, H.E. *A Controlled Bioassay System for Measuring Toxicity of Heavy Metals*. U.S. Environmental Protection Agency: Washington D.C., 1977.
38. U.S. Environmental Protection Agency. *Ambient Water Quality for Cadmium*, EPA 400/5-80-025. U.S. Govn't Print. Off. 1980.
39. Chynoweth, D.P.; Black, J.A.; Mancy, K.H. *In Workshop on Toxicity to*

Biota of metal forms in natural waters. International Joint Commission: Duluth, MN, 1976.
40. Stumm, W.; Morgan, J. *J. Aquatic Chemistry*. Wiley Interscience: NY, 1982.
41. Vaughan, B.E.; *The Sci. of the Tot. Environ.* 1983, *28*, 505.
42. Morel, F. and Morgan, J. *Environ. Sci. and Tech.* 1972, *6*, 58-67.

RECEIVED September 4, 1991

Chapter 13

Assessing Global River Water Quality

Case Study Using Mechanistic Approaches

David A. Dunnette

Environmental Sciences and Resources Program, Portland State University,
P.O. Box 751, Portland, OR 97207

Rivers, like the atmosphere and oceans, are integrative and reflect conditions within their boundaries. Critical to an understanding of the role of human activity in environmental change is an understanding of the impact of human activity on river quality and how river quality may be used as an indicator of environmental change. Current data collection practices, based largely on the traditional parametric or ambient fixed-station network approach, do not generally provide the information necessary to relate human activity to quality of river water or to utilize water quality data as an indicator of global environmental change.

What is needed is an alternative approach which permits development of valid cause and effect relationships. This strategy, one involving intensive surveys, is referred to here as mechanistic. The Willamette River, Oregon, USA, is used as a case study to illustrate quantitative, semi-quantitative and qualitative approaches to mechanistic assessment of river water quality using, respectively, dissolved oxygen depletion, erosion/deposition and potentially toxic trace elements as examples.

The Willamette River Basin, Oregon serves as an excellent case study of river quality assessment for a number of reasons. First, the Willamette River has been cited internationally as a classic example of how water quality can be restored from a previously poor quality waterway (1-3). Second, excellent background data were available, particularly on hydrology. Third, at the time most of these studies were initiated, the Willamette River was the largest river in the U.S. for which all point-source discharges were receiving secondary wastewater treatment.

The Willamette River is the twelfth largest river in the U.S. and has been studied extensively for over sixty years. The early history of the river was

0097–6156/92/0483–0260$07.75/0
© 1992 American Chemical Society

characterized by low dissolved oxygen and high levels of fecal coliform bacteria due to discharges of untreated municipal wastes, pulp and paper effluents and vegetable processing wastes. Public concern over the river's condition quickened in the 1930s and following WWII construction of wastewater treatment plants began in earnest. By the 1960s, conditions in the river had improved to such an extent that for the first time in several decades, fall Chinook salmon returned to the lower river and its tributaries. The experience was one of the first to demonstrate that a major heavily polluted river could be restored to health *(1)*.

The goals of this chapter do not include a "state of the art" literature review which would be appropriate for a more in-depth discussion of one particular problem area. Rather the intent is to illustrate mechanistic approaches to river quality assessment using the three globally relevant water quality problem areas discussed in the previous chapter: dissolved oxygen depletion, erosion/deposition, and potentially toxic trace elements. The information provided does not include all rationale, methology or approaches used in the study as this is beyond the scope of the chapter. Additional general information on application of the intensive river quality assessment approach in the Willamette River basin may be found elsewhere *(4-9, 11-14, 17)*.

Physical Setting

The Willamette River basin (Figure 1) contains Oregon's three largest cities (Portland, Eugene and Salem) and includes more than two-thirds of the states population within a drainage area of 30,000 km^2. About fifty percent of the land is forested. Agriculture is practiced intensively in the valley where irrigation is by sprinkler.
The primary industries are pulp and paper, lumber, electronics, and tourism. The basin supports extensive wildlife and fish habitat. Precipitation varies from 100 cm at the basin floor to more than 300 cm in the Cascade Range and summers are dry and warm with winters cloudy and wet. Daily average temperatures in the basin range from 1.7°C in winter to 28°C in summer. A cross-sectional profile of the basin is shown in Figure 2A. Figure 2B identifies specific morphological reaches of the main stem Willamette River.

Dissolved Oxygen - A Quantitative Investigation

Background. Through the early 1950s, the Willamette River experienced severe water quality problems based primarily on dissolved oxygen (DO) deficits created by a combination of summertime low-flow conditions and oxygen demanding wastes discharged from municipal and industrial sources. The low DOs (0 - 4 mg L^{-1}) resulted in serious impacts on many beneficial uses of the river; fish survival and migration, aesthetic appeal, recreation, industrial use and potential drinking water quality all suffered. Over the course of three decades from 1950 through 1980 water quality was improved

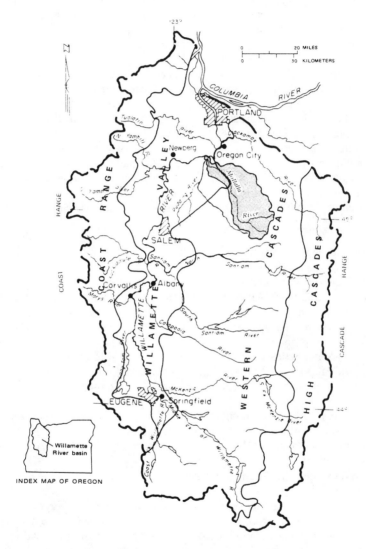

Figure 1. Map of the Willamette River Basin, Oregon, showing major
physiographic divisions and the Molalla River basin (shaded).

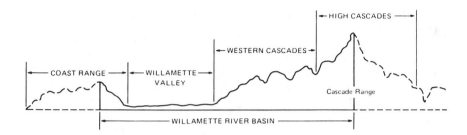

Figure 2A. Cross-sectional profile of the Willamette River Basin showing relief dimensions of major physiographic divisions.

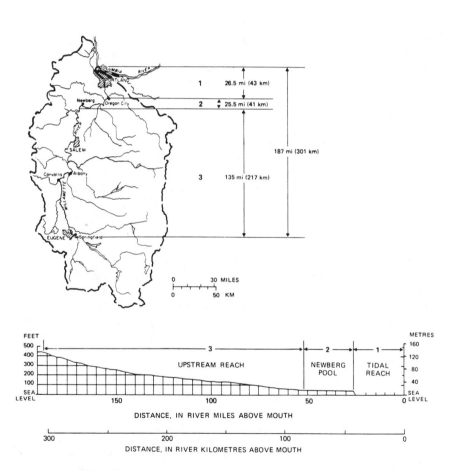

Figure 2B. Willamette River, Oregon showing gradient and morphological reaches.

dramatically due to reduction of waste loading to the river and flow augmentation from headwater reservoirs (see Figure 1). The dissolved oxygen investigations described here had two primary goals: to document the improvement in Willamette River water quality and to develop an understanding of the physical, biochemical and biological dynamics of the DO regime of the Willamette River which could be applied to river basin planning and management.

Methodology. The design of this investigation was based on the philosophy expressed in the previous chapter, i.e., that a mechanistic or intensive survey approach can most effectively provide the understanding which will permit development of reliable basin management control alternatives. Reconnaissance studies were initially carried out to obtain preliminary measurements of DO, biochemical oxygen demand (BOD), nitrification, sedimentary oxygen demand (in Portland reach), photosynthesis and reaeration as well as the magnitude of municipal and industrial oxygen demanding wastes. DO investigations were conducted during the summer low-flow, a period of relative ecological stability. Standardized methods were used and 3 to 6 samples were collected at each site selected. Details of methodology are provided elsewhere *(6-13)*.

Results. Total point and non-point source BOD_{ult} (20 day BOD incubation) loading to the river between river kilometer (RK) 300 and 0 was 77,000 kg d^{-1} with point sources contributing 54% and nonpoint sources 46%. Seventy-six percent of BOD_{ult} loading was exerted in the shallow upstream reach between the RKs 300 and 84. In addition to these carbonaceous based oxygen demands, nitrification accounted for an estimated additional 31,000 kg d^{-1} loss of oxygen, almost all of which occurred between RKs 140 and 89, the most "surface active" reach of the main stem Willamette River. Carbonaceous deoxygenation between RKs 140 and 89 accounted for 40,000 kg d^{-1} of DO loss with sedimentary demand estimated at 12,000 kg d^{-1}. Figure 3 summarizes DO data for an intensive survey conducted during low-flow. The dramatic drop in DO between RKs 194 and 81 was determined to be due mainly to microbially mediated in-stream nitrification of 3,300 - 6,200 kg d^{-1} ammonia N discharged from a pulp and paper plant at RK 140. The increase in DO at RK 47 is due to the combined effects of reaeration at Willamette Falls and a contribution from the highly oxygenated Clackamas River.

    The drop in DO below RK 32 was found to be due largely to sedimentary oxygen demand in the Portland reach where organically enriched material is deposited. Recovery below RK 6.5 was due to a combination of reduced oxygen demanding waste loading and mixing with Columbia River water. Reaeration coefficients calculated from hydrologic data varied from 2.0 in the upper river to a low of 0.003 in the lower river near Portland. A nitrification rate constant of 0.7 day^{-1} for RK 140 - 89 was estimated from changes in nitrate concentrations.

    DO measurements taken during operation and closure a pulp and paper plant indicated a drop in DO of 3-4% saturation 5 KM below the plant. An analysis of dissolved oxygen saturation of the lower river during the period 1973-1979 indicates the 15% increase in DO in the lower Willamette is primarily a result of the elimination of the industrial ammonia discharge at RK 136. Improvement in DO in the Willamette River was due principally to the ammonia source elimination in 1977 (Figure 4).

A DO computer model was developed using the accounting method of Velz and a simple Lagrangian reference system *(9, 12)*. A sensitivity analysis of the model is provided in Table 1 *(12)*. Results indicate that model projections are most sensitive to flow, initial DO, reaeration method calculation, ammonia loading and sedimentary oxygen demand and are relatively insensitive to BOD load variations, BOD rates and nitrification rates. Verification of model projections based on sampling results (diurnally normalized) is summarized in Table 2 *(8)*. Figures 5, 6 and 7 illustrate typical model output which can be translated directly into river basin planning strategies *(12)*.

Conclusions - Dissolved Oxygen. Continued attainment of DO standards in the Willamette Basin in the face of a current regional growth rate of 1% yr^{-1} will require continued augmentation of flow as well as pollution control, particularly with respect to ammonia. Based on model results discussed, there appears to be little justification for the installation of advanced wastewater treatment systems in the basin for the purpose of maintaining acceptable DO levels.

Erosion/Deposition - A Semi-quantitative Investigation

Introduction. Disintegration and erosion of surface layers of the world's soils may be the most severe of the environmental impacts caused by human

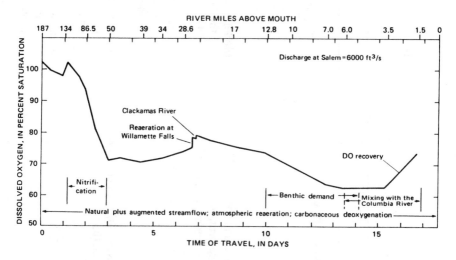

Figure 3. Dissolved oxygen profile of Willamette River, low flow conditions, 1973 with major DO controlling factors.

Table 1. Sensitivity Analysis Summary Of DO Model

Variable tested	Comments
Streamflow	Model is sensitive to flow, particularly at values less than 328 m^3s^{-1} (6,760 ft^3s^{-1}). At 243 m^3s^{-1} (5,000 ft^3s^{-1}), predicted percent DO saturations are as much as 10 percent less than those at 328 m^3s^{-1} (6,760 ft^3s^{-1}). At 158 m^3s^{-1} (6,760 ft^3s^{-1}, estimated natural low flow), predicted values are as much as 30 percent lower than standard conditions. At 437 m^3s^{-1} (9,000 ft^3s^{-1}), predicted values are higher by 6-8 percent saturation.
Percent DO saturation at boundary point (RK 140)	Model is sensitive to changes in initial percent of DO saturation. The major impact is near the boundary point; differences between profiles become smaller with downstream distance.
Water temperature	For the reasonably expected range of summertime water temperatures, the model is insensitive to temperature changes. Maximum predicted deviation from standard conditions is ± 3 percent of DO saturation.
Reaeration calculation method	Model is sensitive to the method used to calculate reaeration. Only the Velz method gave segment-by-segment reaeration inputs which resulted in good agreement of predicted and observed DO profiles.
BOD loading	Model is relatively insensitive to BOD_{ult} load variations. A doubling of loads (from each point source) results in deviations of 5-9 percent DO saturation from the standard profile.

Rate of carbonaceous deoxygenations (k_r)	Model is relatively insensitive to changes in k_r over a three-fold range of 0.02-0.06 day^{-1}. Predicted DO concentrations deviate no more than 6 percent saturation from standard profile.
Ammonia-N loading	Model is sensitive to variations in ammonia-N loading. A doubling of loads (from outfalls in the nitrifying segment) results in as much as a 14 percent reduction in percent DO saturation values from the standard profile. Reducing the ammonia loading by 50 percent increases the predicted DO values by up to 8 percent saturation.
Rate of nitrogenous deoxygenation (k_n)	Model is insensitive to changes in k_n over a range of 0.5-0.9 day^{-1}. Predicted DO concentrations differ from standard profile ($k_n = 0.7$) by less than 3 percent. Note that differences decrease with downstream distance.
Variation in water depth owing to backwater or tidal influences	Model is insensitive to expected range of changes in summertime water depth in the tidal reach. Predicted DO values differ from standard profile by an average of 1 percent saturation.
Benthic demand	The model is sensitive to lower river sediment oxygen demand. If the demand is removed, the predicted DO value at RK 3.1 (RM 5.0) is 8 percent higher than the standard condition.

Source: *(13)*

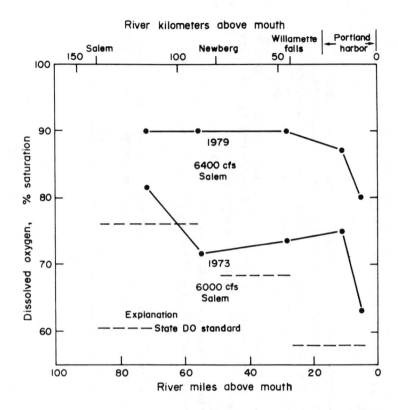

Figure 4. Dissolved oxygen profile of Lower Willamette River, low flow conditions. Data points are means of 4-6 samples, diurnally normalized.

Table 2. Verification of Willamette River DO Model[a]

Location	RK	Model results Projection % sat.	RK	DEQ Results Verification Measured % sat.
Wheatland Ferry	116	89	116	90
Newberg	89	86	78	90
Oregon City	46	88	44	89
Portland	19	87	19	86
Portland	8.1	78	11	79

[a]Mean of 23 weekly grab samples collected during months of July, August and September, mean flow of 184 m^3s^{-1} at Salem. DEQ values have been diurnally normalized. Source: (8)

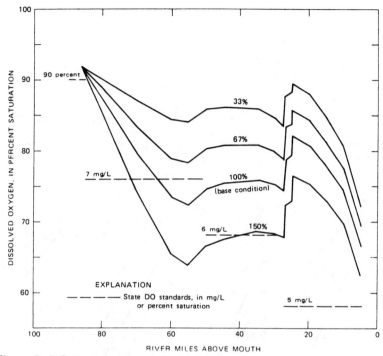

Figure 5. DO levels at River Mile 28.6 for various streamflow, point-source ammonia and BOD loading.

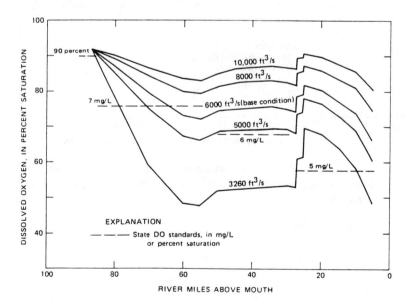

Figure 6. Dissolved oxygen for various streamflows. Point source ammonia and BOD loading constant.

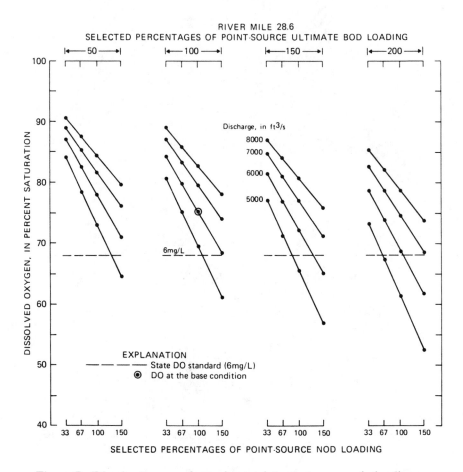

Figure 7. Dissolved oxygen for various point-source ammonia loadings. Flow constant at 6000 ft^{3}s^{-1}. BOD and NPS ammonia loading held constant.

activity. In the Willamette basin the form and character of the land is determined primarily by natural characteristics of the land and rainfall patterns. Over the past 165 years, humans in the Willamette Basin have shifted ecological equilibria with multifaceted land activities, many of which have direct influences on rivers.

The Molalla River basin, a subbasin of the Willamette system (Figure 1) covers about 840 km^2 (325 mi^2) and was used as a model basin to demonstrate use of an erosion/ deposition impact matrix and map. Altitudes in the basin vary from 15 m to 1500 m. The major industries are forestry and agriculture. Precipitation varies from 1000 mm (40 in) in the lowlands to 3000 mm (110 in) in the headwaters with temperatures ranging seasonally from over 38°C to well below 0°C. Average annual runoff varies from less than 500 to over 2500 mm (20 to 100 in) per year. Over two-thirds of the basin has a slope which exceeds 20 percent. The basin is underlain by volcanic rocks in the higher elevations, sedimentary materials in the lowlands and is dominated with conifers of the Douglas Fir variety although alder, oak, shrubs and grasses also occur. Over 80 percent of the higher elevation forest lands have been clear-cut and Figures 8 and 9 illustrate the impact of this particularly destructive form of land use activity in the Molalla River basin. More detailed geologic, climatic and topographic data may be found elsewhere *(14)*.

Erosion/Deposition Impact Matrix and Map. Methods applied in this semi-quantitative assessment involved mapping depositional features using high and low altitude imagery, numerical ranking of land use activity impacts and construction of problem matrixes. The information generated in these first steps were applied to the Universal Soil Loss Equation *(15-16)*.

$$A = RKLSCP \qquad (1)$$

where A = average annual soil loss, in tons acre^{-1}/year^{-1}
B = rainfall coefficient
K = soil erodibility coefficient
L = slope-length coefficient
S = slope-steepness coefficient and
C & P = coefficients related to conservation practices and land use

The rationale for the development and application of the matrix was established 20 to 25 years ago and is discussed elsewhere *(14,17)*. The location and density of land erosion and deposition features were identified through intensive analysis of stereoscopically paired color infra-red images at a scale of 1:130,000. The observations made from the color infra-red analysis were systematically noted and verified through field observation and low altitude imagery *(14)*.

Results. Using the information generated in the analysis, an erosion/deposition impact matrix was developed as shown in Table 3 *(14,15)*. The horizontal axis

Table 3. Matrix for Estimating Interactive Erosional Impact of Land-use Activities with Terrain Properties of Geology Land Slope, Molalla River Basin, Oregon[1]

Slope (percent)	0-3	3-7	7-12		12-20		20-60		>60	
Slope-erosional factor	10^{-2}	10^{-1}	10^{0}		10^{1}		10^{2}		10^{3}	
Geologic group	V_1/V_2	V_2/I_1	C_1	V_2/I_1	C_2	I_2	C_2	I_2	C_2	I_2
Geologic-erosional factor	10^{0}	10^{0}	10^{-1}	10^{0}	10^{-1}	10^{0}	10^{-1}	10^{0}	10^{-1}	10^{0}
Product[2]	10^{-2}	10^{-1}	10^{-1}	10^{0}	10^{0}	10^{1}	10^{1}	10^{2}	10^{2}	10^{3}

Land-use activity	Land-use-erosional factor	Erosional-impact rating[3] (0-3)	Erosional-impact rating[4] (3-7)	(7-12) C_1	V_2/I_1	(12-20) C_2	I_2	(20-60) C_2	I_2	(>60) C_2	I_2
Mature forest	10^{-3}	$<10^{-3}$	$<10^{-3}$	$<10^{-3}$	10^{-3}	10^{-3}	10^{-2}	10^{-2}	10^{-1}	10^{-1}	10^{0}
Managed silviculture or nursery	10^{-3}	$<10^{-3}$	$<10^{-3}$	$<10^{-3}$	10^{-3}	10^{-3}	10^{-2}	10^{-2}	10^{-1}	10^{-1}	10^{0}
Forest regrowth or mixed woods and shrubs	10^{-2}	$<10^{-3}$	10^{-3}	10^{-3}	10^{-2}	10^{-2}	10^{-1}	10^{-1}	10^{0}	10^{0}	10^{1}
Helicopter or balloon logging	10^{-2}	$<10^{-3}$	10^{-3}	10^{-3}	10^{-2}	10^{-2}	10^{-1}	10^{-1}	10^{0}	10^{0}	10^{1}
Metropolitan (developed)	10^{-2}	$<10^{-3}$	10^{-3}	10^{-3}	10^{-2}	10^{-2}	10^{-1}	10^{-1}	10^{0}	10^{0}	10^{1}
Orchard with ground cover	10^{-1}	10^{-3}	10^{-2}	10^{-2}	10^{-1}	10^{-1}	10^{0}	10^{0}	10^{1}	10^{1}	10^{2}
Pasture or grassland (light grazing)	10^{-1}	10^{-3}	10^{-2}	10^{-2}	10^{-1}	10^{-1}	10^{0}	10^{0}	10^{1}	10^{1}	10^{2}
Semirural (developed with light farming)	10^{-1}	10^{-3}	10^{-2}	10^{-2}	10^{-1}	10^{-1}	10^{0}	10^{0}	10^{1}	10^{1}	10^{2}
Paved roads (well maintained)	10^{-1}	10^{-3}	10^{-2}	10^{-2}	10^{-1}	10^{-1}	10^{0}	10^{0}	10^{1}	10^{1}	10^{2}
Cable logging	10^{-1}	10^{-3}	10^{-2}	10^{-2}	10^{-1}	10^{-1}	10^{0}	10^{0}	10^{1}	10^{1}	10^{2}
Powerlines (dirt maintenance road)	10^{-1}	10^{-3}	10^{-2}	10^{-2}	10^{-1}	10^{-1}	10^{0}	10^{0}	10^{1}	10^{1}	10^{2}
Cropland	10^{0}	10^{-2}	10^{-1}	10^{-1}	10^{0}	10^{0}	10^{1}	10^{1}	10^{2}	10^{2}	10^{3}
Orchard without ground cover	10^{0}	10^{-2}	10^{-1}	10^{-1}	10^{0}	10^{0}	10^{1}	10^{1}	10^{2}	10^{2}	10^{3}
Pasture or grassland (heavy grazing)	10^{0}	10^{-2}	10^{-1}	10^{-1}	10^{0}	10^{0}	10^{1}	10^{1}	10^{2}	10^{2}	10^{3}
Gravel roads	10^{0}	10^{-2}	10^{-1}	10^{-1}	10^{0}	10^{0}	10^{1}	10^{1}	10^{2}	10^{2}	10^{3}

Tractor logging ————	10^0	10^{-2}	10^{-1}	10^0	10^1	10^1	10^2	10^2	10^3
Fallow agricultural land ————	10^1	10^{-1}	10^0	10^1	10^2	10^2	10^3	10^3	$>10^3$
Light construction and excavation ————	10^1	10^{-1}	10^0	10^1	10^2	10^2	10^3	10^3	$>10^3$
Temporary dirt roads (poorly maintained) ————	10^2	10^0	10^1	10^2	10^3	10^3	$>10^3$	$>10^3$	$>10^3$
Heavy construction and excavation ————	10^2	10^0	10^1	10^2	10^3	10^3	$>10^3$	$>10^3$	$>10^3$

[1] V-Surficial, weakly coherent, alluvial deposits readily eroded by water. (V_1-≤3 percent slope; V_2-≤12 percent slope). I-Incompetent, or weakly coherent, bedrock such as shales and tuffs readily eroded by water and (or) prone to mass movement on steep slopes (1_1-≤12 percent slope; 1_2->12 percent slope). C-Competent, or strongly coherent, bedrock such as layered lava flow rocks and igneous intrusives not readily eroded by water, nor generally prone to mass movement except for rockslides and rockfalls from very steep slopes and cliffs (C_1-≤12 percent slope).

[2] Product of slope- and geologic-erosional factors.

[3] Ratings are the product of land use-, slope-, and geologic-erosional factors. The ratings roughly approximate the average annual order-of-magnitude sediment production in tons/acre/year.

Source: (13,16)

Figure 8. Clear-cut in the Molalla River Basin showing tractor logging
practice and erosion surfaces.

Figure 9. Massive landslide near headwaters of the Molalla River, Oregon,
a tributary of the Willamette River. The landslide occurred on the
lower slope during the winter following the building of two log roads
associated with clear-cutting activity.

consists of assigned factors related to geology and slope whereas the vertical axis lists impact factors assigned to various land-use activities. The values in the matrix are products of geology, slope and land use and represent semi-quantitative estimates of potential impact given the various conditions of slope, geology and human activities. Values are expressed in terms of tons per acre year.

The results of map generation cannot be expressed effectively with the format available here. However, the State of Oregon utilized the map and matrix techniques in their nonpoint source evaluation and as a basis for designing more intensive survey approaches to assessing the impact of human activity on river quality. In addition to reflecting deposition of sediments, the methods can be applied to transport of pesticides, nutrients and trace elements since many of these substances tend to adsorb to the organic and inorganic fractions of soil.

Potentially Toxic Trace Elements - A Qualitative Approach

Introduction. A number of chemical substances in the aquatic environment have been identified as toxic to living organisms. Such substances include pesticides, herbicides and certain trace elements. Concern for these substances is based on a complex set of factors leading to the public's perception that certain chemical forms in the environment are dangerous. Although many of the substances identified as toxic are essential nutrients including chromium, copper, zinc, and selenium, little attention is often given to Paracelsus' corollary that the dose makes the poison (i.e., that risk is a function of both intrinsic hazard and exposure), that trace elements in the environment occur naturally in soil and rocks, or that all humans ingest these substances continuously in doses ranging from a few micrograms (mercury) to several milligrams (copper, zinc) per day. The question of potential harm to aquatic life or human health from the presence of certain trace elements in rivers is extremely complex and is discussed in the previous chapter. The reader is referred to recent sources which discuss risks related to environmental chemicals *(18-20)*.

The Willamette River basin is bounded on the west by the Coast Range and on the East by the Cascade Range. The volcanics of the Cascade Range consist of basalt and andesite. The Coast Range and its foothills are composed largely of sedimentary material of both volcanic and marine origins including basaltic materials, mudstone, shale, and sandstone. The Willamette valley lowlands are composed of terrace deposits of sand, silt and clay. The basin is not highly industrialized and the major oxygen demanding wastes entering the main stem originate from pulp and paper companies and municipal wastewater treatment plants. There are a number of mineralized areas in the southeastern part of the basin which have produced quantities of copper, gold, silver, lead, mercury and zinc. The goals of the investigation reported here were to determine 1) the concentrations of trace elements in water, fish and other indicator media in the Willamette River system and 2) what evidence or documentation exists which indicates or suggests harm to humans or aquatic life.

Methods. As discussed in the previous chapter, a number of approaches have been used to assess the presence of potentially toxic trace elements in water. The approaches used in this assessment include comparative media evaluation, a human health and aquatic life guidelines assessment, a mass balance evaluation, probability plots, and toxicity bioassays. Concentrations of trace elements were determined by atomic absorption spectrometry according to standard methods *(21,22)* by the Oregon State Department of Environmental Quality and the U.S. Geological Survey.

Sampling sites for water, sediment and fish were distributed along the main stem Willamette. Water data are based on a total of 12 monthly samples for each of the twelve sites (DEQ data) or quarterly samples over a period of 4 years (USGS data). Sediment samples were taken from 44 different sites covering the entire main stem Willamette River. The <20 um fraction was analyzed for trace elements by USGS using atomic absorption spectrophotometry according to Ward et al. *(21)*. Fish data are based on 4-6 fish samples from each of 7 sites in the basin. Fish samples were collected during the low flow months of August-October.

Results

Comparative Media Evaluation. Table 4 is a summary of trace element occurrences for water, sediment, fish and rocks in Oregon as compared with concentrations measured elsewhere in the world. Details of the comparison parameters are provided in the footnotes to Table 4. The table indicates that no excessively high concentrations of potentially toxic trace elements exist in Willamette River water relative to "uncontaminated" sites.

Guidelines Assessment. Table 5 is a summary of maximum water concentrations observed over a two to four year period as they relate to the U.S. Environmental Protection Agency acute and chronic aquatic life guidelines and the guidelines for human health and agriculture. Although some guidelines are exceeded, the 10-100 fold safety factors, as well as the mitigating factors discussed in the preceding chapter indicate that in general, there is little reason to suggest that human health or aquatic life are threatened.

Mass Balance Estimates. Based on National Pollutant Discharge Elimination System monitoring reports, the total daily discharge of trace elements into the main stem Willamette River is of the order of 100 pounds per day. Seventy-five percent of the total is zinc with the bulk of the remainder due to chromium and copper. Table 6 identifies industrial and natural sources of trace elements into the Willamette basin. The table indicates that an average of 97 percent of all trace element loading to the basin is natural in origin. The natural component is due to weathering of soil and rocks in the basin and this

Table 4. Summary of Trace Element Occurrences for Water, Sediment, Fish and Rocks
in Oregon and Elsewhere with Comparisons

| | Concentration in Oregon | | | | Concentrations Elsewhere in World | | | |
	Water[a] $\mu g\ L^{-1}$	Sediment[b] $\mu g\ g^{-1}$	Fish[c] $\mu g\ g^{-1}$	Rocks[d] $\mu g\ g^{-1}$	Water[e] $\mu g\ L^{-1}$	Sediment[f] $\mu g\ g^{-1}$	Fish[g] $\mu g\ g^{-1}$	Rocks[h] $\mu g\ g\text{-}1$
Arsenic								
Max	1.6	20	0.60	6		3.2-200 (69)	2.92	13
Min	<0.1	10	<0.15	2		0.6-11 (5.9)	0.05	1
Mean	0.56	13	0.19	4	5.1 (2.0)	37	0.27	7
Cadmium								
Max	8.0	2.5	0.14	0.3		0.7-4.6 (2.6)	1.04	0.2
Min	<0.1	0.5	<0.04	0.12		0.14-2.5 (1.0)		0.01
Mean	1.4	1.0	0.03	0.21	1.4 (0.07)	1.8	0.7	0.1 1
Chromium								
Max	20	100	0.83	128		42-153 (82)	1.6	1600
Min	<0.1	40	<0.15	78		7-77 (37)	0.02	2
Mean	1.8	57	0.23	103	3.6 (0.5)	60	0.7	800
Copper								
Max	27	95	0.99	46		34-268 (97)	2.7	87
Min	<0.5	30		26		16-44 (26)	0.05	1
Mean	3.7	42	0.36	36	8.9 (1.8)	67	0.6	44
Lead								
Max	22	120	0.44	16		52-400 (180)	4.9	20
Min	<1.0	10	<0.15	9		14-40 (23)	0.1	1
Mean	2.7	38	0.16	13	7.5 (0.2)	102	0.38	11
Mercury								
Max	0.5	0.38	1.7	0.4		0.2-4.5 (1.5)	0.84	0.4
Min	<0.005	0.02	<0.02	0.04		0.004-0.24 (0.12)	0.01	0.004
Mean	0.03	0.16	0.51	0.2	0.14 (0.01)	0.81	0.12	0.2
Zinc								
Max	60	1295	---	73		42-380 (65)	16.1	130
Min	<2	115	---	53		7-124	0.8	16
Mean	12.0	249	---	63	34.1 (10)	139	5.3	73

[a]Based on USGS 0.45 u membrane filtered data 1976-1979. Value in parentheses is based on a DEQ Total Recoverable value multiplied by 0.71, the observed USGS filtered/total recoverable ratio for the data considered in this analysis.
[b]Based on USGS work on Willamette River (Rickert et al.,1977) - Table 21.
[c]Based on DEQ fish tissue data for 1979-1981 + additional mercury data as included in Dunnette,1983, Table 29 (*38*).
[d]Based on concentrations of trace elements in rock types found in Oregon (*38*).
[e]First value given is mean calculated from data of Appendix A, Forstner and Wittmann, 1979, (*23*). Second value (in parentheses) is average world background level (Table 28, Forstner and Wittmann, 1979), (*23*).
[f]Based on core data from 5 lakes in which significant anthropogenic inputs of trace elements were documented. Mean of high values (upper strata) was taken as representative of a "contaminated" environment; mean of low values (lower strata) was taken as representative of "clean" environment. Lakes were: Lake Constance (Forstner and Muller, 1974), (*24*), Lake Michigan (Ruch et al., 1970, (*25*), Shimp et al., 1971, (*26*), Kennedy et al., 1971, (*27*), Frye and Shimp, 1973, (*28*)); Lake Monana, Wisconsin (Syers et al., 1973, (*29*), Shukla et al., 1972 (*30*)); Lake Washington (Barnes and Schell, 1973, (*31*), Crecelius and Piper,1973, (*32*), Schell, 1974, (*33*), Crecelius,1975 (*34*)); and Lake Erie (Walters et al., 1974 (*35*)). Value in parenthesis is mean of range.
[g]Values taken from Appendix B, Forstner and Wittmann, 1979.
[h]Turekian and Wedepohl, 1961 (*36*).

Table 5. Maximum Concentrations of Selected Trace Elements in Oregon
Streams and Related Guidelines and Criteria

Maximum Concentrations[a]
µg/L

Element	DEQ Data[c]	USGS Data[c]
Arsenic	145	6.0
Barium	400	700[b]
Boron	1520	--
Cadmium	14	22
Chromium total	29	320
Chromium III	--	--
Chromium VI	--	--
Copper	12	1100[b]
Fluorine	800	--
Iron	4600	--
Lead	44	200
Manganese	600	--
Mercury	0.8	6.0
Selenium	<5	--
Silver	<1	--
Zinc	39	360[b]

[a] Expressed as "Total Recoverable." See text for explanation
[b] Sample from John Day River - extremely high for several elements
[c] DEQ data based on samples from 80 ambient sites; USGS data from 17 sites

Guidelines µg/L

Element	DEQ[a]	EPA Aquatic Life-Acute[b]	EPA Aquatic Life-Chronic[b]	EPA Human Health/Irrigation[b]
Arsenic	10	440 (As III)	None	0.2-22 (ng/L)
Barium	1000	None	None	1000
Boron	500	None	None	750
Cadmium	3	0.006-0.05	0.006-0.05	10
Chromium total	20	--	--	--
Chromium III	--	1030-9900[c]	21	170
Chromium VI	--	44	0.29	50
Copper	5	6.6-43[c]	5.6	1000
Fluorine	1000	None	None	None
Iron	100	1000	--	300
Lead	50	32-400[c]	0.15-20	50
Manganese	50	None	None	50
Mercury	None	0.0017	0.00057	0.144
Selenium	None	260	36	10
Silver	None	0.35-13[c]	0.12	50
Zinc	10	101-570[c]	47	5000

[a] Department of Environmental Quality Water Quality Guidelines.
[b] Expressed as "Total Recoverable".
[c] Guidelines vary according to hardness. Lowest of range corresponds to 25 mg/L and highest to 200 mg/L CaCO$_3$ hardness.
Source: (38)

Table 6. Trace Element Loading to the Willamette River, Oregon USA

			Estimated Loading lbsd⁻¹, Total Recoverable[d]				
Source	As	Cd	Cr	Cu	Pb	Hg	Zn
Industrial[a]	0.58	0.11	10.09	15.96	7.59	0.25	81.0
Municipal[b]	g	0.04	0.20	0.24	0.13	0.0	2.7
Natural Sources	43.1	184	429	1226	1902	3.05	1839
Percent Due to Natural Sources							
Non-Storm	99	100	98	99	100	92	96
Storm Event[c]	99	78	76	85	65	92	67

[a]Based on industrial monitoring data
[b]Based on literature values (36)
[c]Based on National Urban Runoff Program Report (37), estimated Willamette Basin impervious drainage area at 518 km² (200 mi²) and mean discharge rate of 5.4 ft³/s⁻¹.
[d]Based on USGS quarterly sample means over 4 year period.

point is illustrated in Table 7 which shows mean concentrations of trace elements in Oregon rocks, soil and Willamette River water *(37)*. High correlations between concentrations in rocks and natural water are reflections of the history of the water and its association with rocks, soil and the weathering process.

Probability Plots. To distinguish between background distributions and human activity, trace element data were probability plotted using the method of Velz *(10)*. The plots produce two separate trend lines, the intersection of which distinguishes natural from anthropogenic concentrations. Figure 10 is an illustration of the resulting plots for zinc *(38)*.

The intersection points for the elements investigated were copper, 40 μg g^{-1}, chromium, 60 μg g^{-1}; lead, 50 μg g^{-1}; mercury, 0.04 μg g^{-1}; and zinc, 150 μg g^{-1}. Values in excess of there concentrations are interpreted as anthropogenic contributions. The anthropogenic components of these elements originated from: electroplating and corrosion control (chromium), electroplating and electronics (copper), automobile exhaust (lead), electroplating and coating of steel (zinc) and small concentrations of mercury from unknown sources but which probably are residuals from use of mercury antifungal agents on lumber products 25 to 40 years ago.

Toxicity Bioassay. Ninety-six hour acute toxicity tests were conducted on the effluent streams of major industries. A static renewal procedure was used in which waste waters of various dilutions were renewed at 24 hour intervals over a 96 hour period. Rainbow trout was used as the test organism. Tests were conducted at 13°C in 20 liter aquaria according to standard procedures *(22)*. Results are summarized in Table 8. Chemical and toxicity test results indicate that the trace element quantities identified in Table 8 are not acutely toxic under the prevailing conditions and unlikely to pose an acute threat to aquatic life. In this case a chronic toxicity assessment would require additional research.

Summary

In contrast to traditional ambient fixed station "parametric" approaches to river quality evaluation for trends determination and water quality standards attainment, data from the Willamette River, Oregon, USA were used to demonstrate the value of quantitative, semi-quantitative and qualitative approaches to mechanistic assessment of river water quality.

To illustrate a quantitative approach, the complex dynamics determining the concentration of dissolved oxygen (DO) were investigated and used to develop a DO mathematical model which was subsequently validated. A semi-quantitative matrix and mapping approach was illustrated with data from an investigation of the dynamics controlling erosion and deposition in a sub-basin of the Willamette which is undergoing extensive deforestation. A combination of field survey, low and high altitude imagery and ground truth methods were

Table 7. Comparisons of Trace Element Content in Oregon Soil and Rocks with That in Water

| | Conc in Rocks and Soil $\mu g \, g^{-1}$ | | | Conc. in Oregon Streams, Mean, mg L^{-1} | |
| | | | | Total Recoverable | |
Elements	Crustal Abundance	Mean in Oregon Rock Types	Western Surface Soils	USGS Mean	DEQ Max
Arsenic	1.8	4	6.1	0.76	76
Barium	425	255	560	43	385
Cadmium	0.2	0.9	---	2.0	8
Chromium	100	103	38	4.3	20
Copper	25	36	21	14	9
Lead	12.5	13	18	21	31
Mercury	0.8	0.06	51	3.1	34

Source: (38)

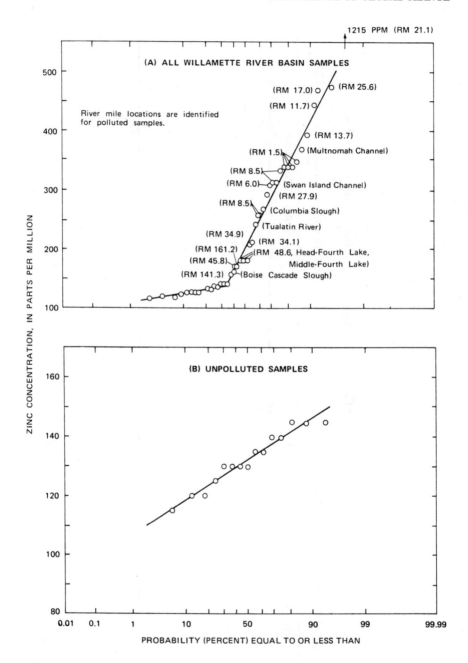

Figure 10. Normal-probability plots of zinc concentrations in 20 um
sediments. A - all Willamette River Basin samples; B -
uncontaminated area samples. B curve is an enlargement of the lower
portion of A curve. Discontinuity is interpreted as concentration limit
of uncontaminated sediments.

Table 8. Industrial Wastewater Toxicity Bioassay Test Results Concentration in Wastewater[a]

	Cr	Cu	Pb	Ni	Zn	NH$_3$	Hard	Alk	pH	Toxicity Results
					Concentration of Waste[b]					
Metal Refiner 1	3	7	11	140	30	5.8	2720	22	7.2	NOT[c]
Pulp and Paper 1	5	27	10	<50	100	1.2	350	68	6.9	LC5O = 19%
Pulp and Paper 2	5	27	10	<50	100	0.12	318	77	7.0	LC5O = 23%
Electronic	<100	1500	---	600	<100	10.0	---	219	8.4	LC5O = 65%
Metal Refiner 2	<2	7	<10	---	<10	0.11	1740	469	7.7	LC5O = 46%
Pulp and Paper 3	5	<2	<10	---	20	0.15	82	60	7.1	NOT[c]
Can Company	5	<2	<10	---	20	0.17	171	152	6.6	NOT[c]
Pulp and Paper 4	<1	3	<10	<50	30	0.13	67	37	6.8	LC5O = 90%

[a]The LC5O refers to the wastewater concentration which results in 50 percent mortality under the test conditions (see text). It is an extrapolated value with varying confidence limits. In the work summarized here confidence limits were quite variable and often could not be calculated due to insufficient data points. Nevertheless the data satisfies the primary intent of the tests as a screening tool.
[b]As <5 mg/L, Cd <1 mg/L, Hg <0.05 mg/L in all samples
[c]NOT: No Observed Toxicity
Source: (38)

used and validated. Finally, a qualitative mechanistic approach to river quality assessment was illustrated by a multi-tiered investigation of potentially toxic trace elements in the main stem Willamette River. Specific methods used in this phase included comparative media evaluation, mass balance, a human health and aquatic life guidelines assessment, probability evaluation and toxicity bioassay.

Acknowledgement

The investigations of the United States Geological Survey, Portland, Oregon have provided the basis for much of the material included in this chapter including a number of figures and tables as indicated. Word processing assistance by Karen McNeil (who typed several drafts including the final manuscript) and Kellie Hanley is gratefully acknowledged.

Literature Cited

1. Council on Environmental Quality. The Fourth Annual Report of the Council on Environmental Quality. Washington, D.C., 1973.
2. Gleeson, G.W. *The Return of a River. The Willamette River, Oregon.* Advisory Committee on Environmental Science and Technology and Water Resources Institute, Oregon State University, 103.
3. Starbird, E.A. *Natl. Geog.* **1972**, *141*, 817-834.
4. Rickert, D.A.; Hines, W.G. *Practical Framework for River-Quality Assessment*. Geological Circular 715-A, USGS, Reston, VA, 1975; 1-17.
5. Hines, D.A.; Rickert, D.A.; McKenzie, S.W; Bennett, J.P. *Formulation and Use of Practical Models for River Quality Assessment.* Geological Survey Circular 715-B, USGS, Reston, VA, 1975; 1-13.
6. Rickert, D.A.; Hines, W.G.; McKenzie, S.W. *Project Development and Data Programs for Assessing the Quality of the Willamette River, Oregon.* Geological Survey Circular 715-C. US6S, Reston, VA, 1976; 1-31.
7. Hines, W.G.; McKenzie, S.W.; Rickert, D.A.; Rinella, F.A. *Dissolved Oxygen Regimen of the Willamette River, Oregon, Under Conditions of Basinwide Secondary Treatment.* Geological Survey Circular 715-I, Reston, VA, 1977; 1-52.
8. Dunnette, D.A.; Avedovech, R.N.; Water Res. **1983**, *17*, 997-1007.
9. McKenzie, S.W.; Hines, W.G.; Rickert, D.A. *Steady State Dissolved - Oxygen Model of the Willamette River, Oregon.* Geological Survey Circular 715-J, Reston, VA, 1979; 1-28.
10. Velz, C.J. *Applied Stream Sanitation*, Wiley Interscience, NY, NY, 1970.
11. Dunnette, D.A. *Effect of an Ammonia Discharge on the Willamette River*, Technical Report. Department of Environmental Quality, Portland, OR 1977; 1-24.
12. McKenzie, S.W.; Hines, W.G.; Rickert, D.A.; Rinella, R. *Steady State Dissolved Oxygen Model of the Willamette River, Oregon.* Geological Survey Circular 715-J, Reston, VA, 1979; 1-28.

13. Rickert, D.A.; Rinella, F.A.; Hines, W.G.; McKenzie, S.W. *Evaluation of Planning Alternatives for Maintaining Desirable Dissolved - Oxygen Concentration in the Willamette River, Oregon.* Geological Survey Circular 715-K, Reston, VA, 1980; 1-30.
14. Brown, W.M.; Hines, W.G.; Rickert, D.A.; Beach, G.L. *A Synoptic Approach for Analyzing Erosion or a Guide to Land Use Planning.* Geological Survey Circular 715-L. US6S, Reston, VA, 1979; 1-45.
15. Musgrave, G.W. *J. Soil and Wat. Conserv.* **1947**, *2*, 133-138.
16. Chow, V.T. *Handbook of Applied Hydrology*, McGraw-Hill: NY, NY, **1964**.
17. Rickert, D.A.; Beach, G.L. *J. Wat Pollut. Cont. Fed.* **1978**, *50*, 2439-2445.
18. Moore, J.W.; Romamoarthy. *Heavy Metals in Natural Waters Applied Monitoring and Impact Assessment.* Springer - Verlog: NY, 1984; 1-268.
19. Dunnette, D. *J. of Community Health.* **1989**, *14*, 169-186.
20. Ames, B.N.; Magaw, J.; Gold, L.S. *Science.* **1987**, *236*, 271-280.
21. Ward, F.N.; Nakagawa, H.M.; Harms, T.F.; Von Sickle, G.H. *Atomic Absorption Methods of Analysis Useful in Geochemical Exploration,* Geological Survey Bulletin 1289, Reston, VA, 1969; 1-45.
22. Clesceri, L.S.; Greenberg, A.E.; Trussell, R.R. *Standard Methods for the Examination of Water and Wastewaters,* 17th Edition; American Public Health Association, American Water Works Assoc., Water Pollution Control Federation, Baltimore, MD. 1989.
23. Forstner, V.; G.T.W. Witmann. *Metal Pollution in the Aquatic Environment.* Springer-Verlag: New York, 1979.
24. Forstner, V.; G. Muller. *Schwermetalle in Flussen und Seen.* Springer: Berlin, 1974.
25. Ruch, R.R.; Kennedy, E.J.; Shimp, N.E. *Distribution of Arsenic in Unconsolidated Sediments from Southern Lake Michigan.* Environ. Geol. 1979; Notes 37, 1-16.
26. Shimp, N.F.; Schlercher, J.S.; Ruch, R.R.; Heck, D.B.; Leland, H.V. *Trace Element and Organic Carbon Accumlation in the Most Recent Sediments of Southern Lake Michigan.* Environ. Geo. 1971; Notes 41, 25.
27. Kennedy, E.J.; Ruch, R.R.; Shimp, N.F. *Distribution of Mercury in Unconsolidated Sediments From Southern Lake Michigan.* Environ. Geo. 1971; Notes 44.
28. Frye, J.C.; Shimp, N.F. *Major, Minor and Trace Elements in Sediments of Late Pleistocene Lake Saline Compared with Those in Lake Michigan S Sediments.* Environ. Geo. 1973; 60, 14 pp.
29. Syers, J.K.; Iskandar, I.K.; Keeney, D.R. *Distribution and Background Levels of Mercury in Sediment Cores from Selected Wisconsin Lakes.* Water Air Soil Pollut. 1973; 2, 105-118.
30. Shukla, S.S.; Kyers, J.K.; Armstrong, D.E. *Arsenic Interference in the Determination of Inorganic Phosphate in Lake Sediments. J. Environ. Quality,* **1972**, 1, 292-295.
31. Barnes, R.S.; Schell, W.R. *Physical Transport of Trace Metals in the Lake Washington Watershed.* In: Cycling and Control of Metals, Proc. of an

Environ. Resources Cong. Curry, M.G.; Gigliotti, G.M., compilers; Nat. Environ. Res. Center, U.S. EPA, Cincinnati, Ohio, 1973; 45-53

32. Crecelius, E.A.; Piper, D.Z., *Particulate Lead Concentration Recorded in Sedimentary Cases from Lake Washington, Seattle.* Environ. Sci. Tech. 1973; 1, 1053-1055.

33. Schell, W.R. *Sedimentation Rates and Mean Residence Times of Pb and ^{210}Pb in Lake Washington, Puget Sound Estuaries and a Coastal Region.* Abstr. Meet. Am. Soc. Limnol. Oceanogr, 1974.

34. Crecelius, E.A., Liminol. Oceanogr., 1975: 20, 441-451.

35. Walters, L.J.; Wolery., T.J.; Myser., R.D. *Occurrence of As, Cd, Co, Cr, Cu, Fe, Hg, Ni, Sb, Zn in Lake Erie Sediments.* Proc. 17th Conf. Great Lakes Res. 1974; 219-234.

36. Turkian, K.K.; Wedepohl, K. H. *Distribution of the Elements in Some Major Units of the Earth's Crust.* Bull. Geol. Soc. Am., 1961; 72, 175-192.

37. Richert, D.A.; Kennedy, B.C.; McKenzie, S.W.; Hines, W.G. *A Synoptic Survey of Trace Elements in Bottom Sediments of the Willamette River, Oregon.* Geol. Survey Circ. 715F, USGS, Reston VA, 1977; 1-27.

38. Dunnette, D.A. *Trace Elements in Oregon Waters - An Environmental Assessment.* Oregon Dept. of Environ. Qual., 1983; 1-93.

RECEIVED September 4, 1991

Chapter 14

Changes in an Estuarine Ecosystem

The Lagoon of Venice as a Case Study

Bruno Pavoni, Antonio Marcomini, Adriano Sfriso, Romano Donazzolo, and Angel A. Orio

Department of Environmental Sciences, University of Venice, Calle Larga S. Marta 2137, 30123 Venice, Italy

Metal and hydrocarbon pollution and eutrophication that have occurred in the Lagoon of Venice in this century are discussed. The evolution of pollutant concentrations and fluxes has been determined by analyzing sections of radioisotopically-dated sediment cores. Metal loads in the superficial sediments and concentrations of metals and hydrocarbons in various organisms are reported. The eutrophication increase has been monitored both by analyzing changes occurring in algal and animal associations, and by comparing nutrient concentrations obtained during different periods using the same methodologies. An evaluation of present Lagoon conditions is presented in conjunction with some possible interventions that would improve future Lagoon quality.

Morphological Evolution of the Venice Lagoon

The Lagoon of Venice represents a peculiar example of an ecosystem whose natural evolution has been deeply modified by human interferences with the aim of preserving the Lagoon's original shape. The Lagoon originated about 12,000 years ago by the action of marine currents on river-borne sediments. Sand banks emerged as a chain of islands as sea level lowered during the Würm glaciation. The Venice Lagoon reached its current configuration about 1000 years ago. The Governments of the *Serenissima Repubblica di Venezia*, the oligarchic council that ruled the city-state of Venice between the 10th and 18th centuries, devoted great care to preserving the integrity of the Lagoon, that was considered a powerful natural defence, and a rich sustenance source.

Rivers flowing into the Lagoon (the Brenta, Bacchiglione, Dese, Sile, and Piave) were progressively silting up large areas. At the same time, the

0097–6156/92/0483–0287$06.00/0

shoreline was undergoing strong erosion by waves and coastal currents. Therefore the most important works carried out by the Republic of Venice starting in 1324 were aimed at diverting the major streams from one side of the Lagoon directly into the sea, and at constructing barriers on the opposite Lagoon shoreline.

During the eighteenth and nineteenth centuries, 2.5 km^2 of Lagoon were filled up by debris or dredged materials and transformed into land mainly for commercial, agricultural and urban uses. In addition, 69.1 km^2 of tidal land was reclaimed in this century, mostly after 1930, for the same purposes and for developing port and industrial activities in Marghera (1). A large number of *valli da pesca*, fishing ponds, are located along the southern and northern inland borders and occupy 85.3 km^2. As a final result, about 30% of the entire Lagoon area (at present 550 km^2) is isolated from tidal purging. At the same time, about 85 million m^3 of sediments were dredged to maintain the normal navigability of channels, but mainly to create the industrial port in Marghera and the commercial canals Vittorio Emanuele and Malamocco-Marghera, dug in 1919-1930 and 1961-1969, respectively.

Reduction of the lagoon water surface and widening of the canals, allowing a faster propagation of the tide, are considered among the major factors that cause an increased number of exceptionally high tides and stronger sediment erosion in most lagoon areas as observed in recent decades (2,3). These tides now flood the historical center of Venice, locally called *Acqua alta*. At present, 1.6-5.2 10^8 m^3 of water are exchanged through the three entrance channels during a half tide cycle (4). The railway bridge across the Lagoon was completed in 1846. In 1931-1934 it was enlarged to allow motor-car traffic. The construction of this bridge has considerably limited water movements across this part of the Lagoon and almost isolated the northern section near the airport. A map of the present Lagoon is shown in Figure 1.

Environmental Changes

Contamination of lagoon water and sediments began in 1920, after the first world war, when the first industrial district of Porto Marghera was installed on the inner border of the Lagoon. Industrial development accelerated following World War I, mainly after 1933, and especially following World War II. Until the 1970's, Porto Marghera was one of the most important industrial districts of Italy, with important plants for the production of chloralkalis, sulphuric acid, ammonia, fibers, fertilizers from phosphorites, glass, paints, detergents and fire bricks; for the recovery of zinc and cadmium from sphalerites, and for electrochemical production of aluminum. Unfortunately, large amounts of eutrophicating and polluting substances were discharged into the Lagoon, which was used for a long time as a dumping site. In addition, industries formerly pumped water from the underground aquifer. The contribution of this activity to the sinking of Venice, and therefore to the *Acqua alta*, was very serious: in 1968-69 the

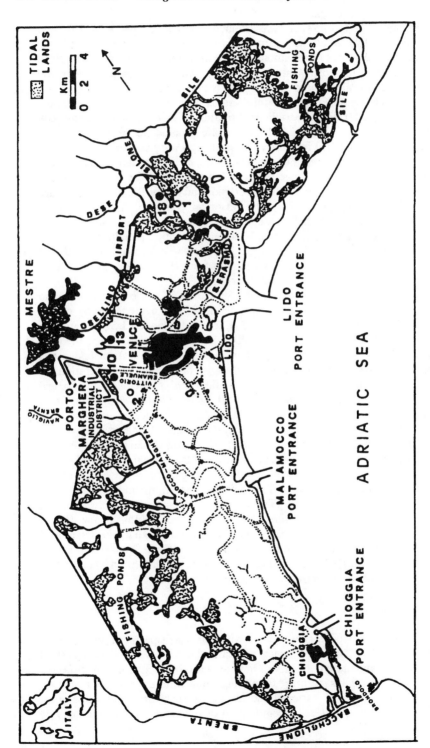

Fig. 1. The Lagoon of Venice at present. The sites of cores 1 and 2. The most eutrophicated stations resulted of the 1987-88 survey.

peak rate of 12-14 mm year^{-1} was attained. Sinking declined since 1970 and stopped in 1975, when the waterworks from the river Sile were completed. According to recent observations, the ground sinking rate has returned to the natural values of 0.4 mm year^{-1} (5,6). On the other hand, with the entire basin draining into the Lagoon (some 2000 km^2), agriculture has radically changed. From a "natural" agriculture using fertilizers of animal origin and performing the traditional rotation of cultivation, there has been extensive mechanization. Cultivations are planted according to market demand and chemical fertilizers and pesticides are extensively used.

In addition, a number of small factories, including tanneries, paint and electroplating facilities, have been settled all around the inland territory. The number of residents in the hinterlands and of tourists in all the Venice area has grown constantly. The historical center of Venice (110,000 residents) still has no adequate sewage system and the connections to treatment plants have been completed only recently in the inland territory (>350,000 inhabitants). The central lagoon, where Venice is located, and the most important fresh water channels from the interior, still receive a heavy load of eutrophicating substances.

Furthermore, excavations of the canals Vittorio Emanuele and Malamocco-Marghera, have deeply modified the hydrogeography of the central lagoon by isolating parts of it, formerly flooded by a strong tide rising from the Adriatic. As a result, in large inner areas, where the tidal water renewal is lacking, eutrophic conditions were established every spring-summer for the last decade. Because of the high concentrations of nutrient elements (N, P, C, Si) microalgal and particularly macroalgal blooms take place. Biomass up to 20 kg m^{-2} (fresh weight) has been observed. Fronds grow by photosynthesis, producing oxygen, and decompose by consuming it. The oxygen balance remains positive and production proceeds, as long as the nutrient supply--particularly the N/P ratio--is adequate, and fronds can be reached by sunlight. Then, when the water column is filled up with fronds allowing no more space for others and/or the nutrient supply is insufficient, production suddenly stops and rapid decomposition occurs. The water becomes anoxic, dissolved oxygen drops to zero, algal and animal life are impeded. Within a few days, a thousand tons of macroalgae decompose, releasing high concentrations of assimilated nutrients, producing hydrogen sulphide and causing fish mortality. (7-10). The occurrence of such conditions in the Lagoon severely hinders city activities, in particular tourism.

Discussion

A number of studies have dealt with various aspects of the Lagoon environment. A literature review was carried out in 1985 by the Magistrato alle Acque and more publications have appeared subsequently. A thorough inspection of all this literature found substantial differences in the analytical procedures used in various studies. It is therefore very difficult to reconstruct the progressive degradation of sediment and water quality by comparing pollutant concentrations measured during different periods. A different approach to the same goal involves analysis of radioisotopically-dated sediment cores.

Radiometric Dating of Cores. A number of sediment cores were obtained in parts of the Lagoon representing positive sedimentation or peculiar situations. All were sectioned, lyophilized, and the ^{210}Pb activity was measured. This isotope has a half-life period of 22.26 years and enables reliable dating for the last 100 years. For two cores an interpretable time-to-depth profile was determined. These cores were sampled at the stations shown in Figure 1. Core 1 was taken in September, 1979, close to the mouth of the canal Silone, that receives waters from derivations of the rivers Dese and Sile. Core 2 was taken in July, 1982, close to the industrial district of Porto Marghera. These zones are among the most contaminated in the Lagoon, as they receive pollution from the inland territory as well as from the industrial zone.

Radioisotopic determinations were performed at the Scripps Institution of Oceanography, La Jolla, California (core 1) and at the Istituto di Chimica e Tecnologia dei Radioelementi in Padova (core 2). The profiles were drawn by measuring the 'non supported' ^{210}Pb activity and subtracting the 'supported' ^{210}Pb activity. Calculations were made assuming a constant rate of supply of unsupported ^{210}Pb to the sediment (*crs model*, Appleby & Oldfield, 11,12). An average sedimentation rate of 0.59 cm year^{-1} was calculated for core 1. For the second core, an independent check was made by measuring the activity of ^{137}Cs from fall-out and interpreting the data according to the same *crs* model. The radiodating of this core was judged reliable down to the ninth section i.e. 93 years from the sampling date. An average sedimentation rate of 0.31 cm year^{-1} was computed. The complete radioisotopic dating methodology is reported by Battiston et al. (13,14) including references therein.

Sediment pollution. The concentrations of pollutants in the dated sediment cores have been determined in our laboratory by atomic absorption spectrophotometry (AAS). Donazzolo et al. (15) and Pavoni et al. (16) reported mainly heavy metal concentrations. Marcomini et al. (17) and Pavoni et al. (18) discussed the concentration profiles of organic pollutants such as chlorinated hydrocarbons and polycyclic aromatic hydrocarbons.

Heavy metals. The profiles of sediment and pollutant depositions and the relationships of concentrations with time have been reconstructed. For most metals the highest accumulations took place between the fifties and the sixties, when the fastest industrial development of Porto Marghera took place. In Figure 2 the concentration profiles of three of the most interesting metals (Hg, Pb, Cd) are plotted vs. depth. Data were "normalized" (i.e. divided) by the background levels, as metals have different natural presence in the environment. This leads to accumulation factors, referred to pre-industrial background values. Any derived data tell

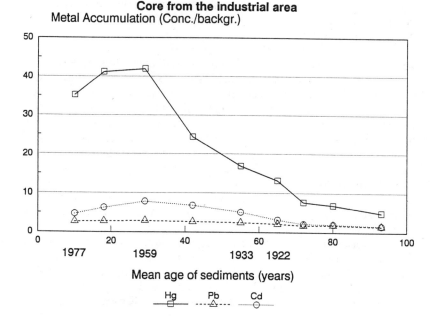

Fig. 2.   Accumulation of Hg, Cd, Pb in core 2.

how many times the concentration of a metal in a given sample is higher than the reference value. The background values have been derived from metal concentrations found in the deepest strata of the cores and from reference values reported in the literature for non-polluted sediments (see reference 16 and references therein). The background values we used are the following (mg kg^{-1}, dry weight, d.w.): Hg 0.1; Pb 25; Cd 1; Ni 20; Co 15; Zn 70; Cr 20; Cu 20; Fe 20000. Whitehead et al. (19) proposed the following values for the whole Mediterranean area: Cr 15; Cu 15; Zn 50; Cd 0.15; and Pb 25. These values are fairly in agreement with ours, except for cadmium. The difference might be due to some differences in the mineralogical composition of samples and/or in the analytical procedure adopted.

In the profiles of the core from the industrial area, mercury displays the highest accumulation. Mercury in this area, close to the industrial district, has probably derived from a large chloralkali plant which has employed mercury cathodes since the fifties. Whereas, at present, very severe measures are taken to prevent mercury spills into the Lagoon, in the past, polluted waters and solid materials were discharged almost untreated. In the most superficial strata a marked decrease in the accumulations is, in fact, recorded. Lead and Cd accumulations are lower here by a factor of 5-10. The presence of cadmium in the sediments of the Lagoon has been referred to sphalerite (ZnS) processing on the basis of a strict concomitant occurrence of Zn and Cd concentrations (high linear correlation). This correlation was found in a significant number of surface Lagoon sediments and is attributed to similar chemical characteristics and a common origin for the two metals (20). Lead, also present in sphalerites in a remarkable amount (up to 2%), but non-correlated with Cd and Zn concentrations, was postulated to derive in large part from atmospheric fall-out of gasoline combustion particles.

Accumulation of metals in the core sampled in the northern Lagoon, relative to the industrial core, are about 5 times lower for mercury and comparable for the other two metals. Metals reaching this area of the Lagoon are carried by fresh water streams from the basin. A very high number of small productions, whose environmental impact has not yet been adequately evaluated, contribute to this pollution.

The concentrations of metals in the surface sediments of the Lagoon have been determined in 163 samples distributed all over the Lagoon. From the lagoon concentrations of metals, a rough estimation of metal load in the 10 cm surface sediments of the Lagoon has been attempted, assuming an average density of 1.2 g of dry sediment per cubic centimeter of natural sediment. The following values have been calculated (in metric tons): Hg 35; Cd 200; Pb 1300; Cu 1600; Zn 16500; Fe 600000; Ni 240; Co 550; and Cr 480.

Eleven samples of surface sediments located in the Valle di Brenta, south of Chioggia, have also been analyzed by Campesan et al. (21), using atomic absorption spectrophotometry. They determined As, Cd, Cr, Cu, Hg, Mn, Pb, and Zn, and attributed the presence of metals to a connection of the Lagoon with the mouth of the rivers Brenta, Bacchiglione and Gorzone. Data are also available on Pb speciation in the Lagoon waters. Capodaglio et al. (22,23), by anodic stripping voltametry, found total Pb concentrations in the range 0.15-0.57 nmol l^{-1}. The Pb ionic or weakly complexed fraction was about 20% of the total.

More data are available on concentrations of metals in organisms (24,25). These two 1980 studies analyzed extracts using AAS and found the following ranges in mussels *Mytilus galloprovincialis* sampled at stations distributed throughout the Lagoon: Hg 0.06-0.12 (average = 0.085); Cd 0.18-0.89 (0.41); Pb 0.83-1.83 (1.5); Cr 0.17-0.53 (0.3); Mn 1.8-3.17 (2.58); all values in mg kg^{-1}. For these mollusks to be marketed, Italian law states the sanitary limits of 0.7 and 2 mg kg^{-1} for Hg and Cd respectively. All monitored samples were below these limits.

Heavy metal concentrations have been determined in 156 sediment samples disseminated in the Gulf of Venice. The presence of metals has been related to a number of factors (26-31):

- transport of contaminated sediments from the Lagoon to the open sea by resuspension-redeposition;

- direct disposal of sediments dredged from the canals of the Lagoon for maintaining them navigable;

- dumping of industrial tailings directly into the sea; and

- contaminated sediment transport by the rivers Piave, Tagliamento, Brenta, Bacchiglione, and Adige.

This last mechanism has been considered very important for chromium. High concentrations of chromium (>120 μg g^{-1} in one sample) were found in the sediments of the sea area facing Chioggia and in the mouths of the rivers Brenta-Bacchiglione and Adige (30). These rivers drain an intensively industrialized area, where numerous tanneries are settled and chromium salts are used to tan hides. Most refuse waters are now conveyed to a treatment plant, but in the past, no treatment was operating and direct dumping was usual. Even today, a portion probably is released without treatment. As some of these industries are very small workshops, frequently family managed, complete control is very difficult and illegal disposals are possible. For this element, relatively higher concentrations have been detected in the southernmost area of the lagoon close to Chioggia, where concentrations of other metals average lower than in the central and northern lagoon. On the basis of these observations, it has been hypothesized that chromium contamination of the southern lagoon has an origin related to the sediments transported by the rivers. This is possible through a sea-lagoon sediment exchange by tidal movements, or by a direct connection between the river Brenta-Bacchiglione and the lagoon through the navigable canal of Brondolo, in the southernmost corner of the Lagoon (Figure 1).

Hydrocarbons. In other publications the historical trend of organic pollutant concentrations, namely polychlorinated biphenys (PCBs), chlorinated pesticides DDT and metabolites DDE, DDD, and polycyclic aromatic hydrocarbons (PAHs), have been reconstructed. For this purpose the sediments of the core sampled in the Lagoon area close to the industrial district were employed (16,17).

In this core, concentrations of PCBs (determined as Aroclor 1254 and 1260, by high resolution gas chromatography, electron capture detection and high resolution gas chromatography-low resolution mass spectrometry) were <30 ng g^{-1} and those of total DDT (p,p'DDT + p,p'DDD + p,p'DDE) <5 ng g^{-1}. Campesan et al. (21) in 11 sediment samples from Valle di Brenta, determined by GC-ECD the following mean concentrations (ng g^{-1}, d.w.):

- HCB (hexachlorobenzene) 0.1 (s.d. 0.05);
- total HCH (hexachlorocyclohexane) 0.28 (s.d. 0.13);
- total DDT 0.74 (s.d. 0.40); and
- PCB 3.76 (s.d. 1.61).

In 25 sediment samples from canals inside the city of Venice, were found concentrations (in ng g^{-1} d.w.) up to 120 of total DDT, up to 744 of PCB, and up to 2.1 of total HCH (32). In sediments sampled in the Venice Gulf (n=155) concentrations (ng g^{-1} d.w.) from 0.4 to 66.6 (average=12.9) for total DDT and from 1 to 185 (31) for PCB were determined by GC-ECD

(28). For the halocarbon contamination of sediments in the Gulf, the same mechanisms as for metals were discussed by the authors. Fossato and Craboledda (33) and Nasci and Fossato (34) determined by GC-ECD the halogenated hydrocarbon concentrations in mussels and Fossato (34) determined them in specimens of predators *Anguilla anguilla, Zosterisessor ophiocephalus,* of Crustaceans *Carcinus mediterraneus, Crangon crangon, Amphipoda Gammaridae* and *Leander sp.*, of mollusks *Haminea navicula,* of algae *Gracilaria confervoides* and *Ulv sp.*, taken in two stations of the Lagoon of Venice, one close to the industrial area and the second in the southern Lagoon fairly far from contamination sources. Concentrations clearly reflected the site characteristics. The obtained concentrations are reported in the following table.

Table I. Concentrations of halogenated hydrocarbons in organisms. (ng g^{-1} d.w.). The first number represents samples from the non-polluted site, the second from polluted site

	Total HCH	Total DDT	Total PCB
Anguilla anguilla:	18 - 86	68 - 170	383 - 4870
Zosterisessor ophiocephalus:	3.5 - 3.0	12 - 15	93-259
Carcinus mediterraneus:	2.0 - 3.6	10 - 11	72-451
Crangon crangon:	1.6 - 2.3	19 - 38	71-329
Amphipoda:	2.9 - 4.0	6 - 16	35-240
Leande sp.:	3.2 - 1.9	11 - 20	85 -402
Haminea navicula:	2.7 - 5.9	12 - 19	62 -179
Gracilaria confervoides:	1.8 - 2.2	9 - 8	17 - 24
Ulva sp.:	1.8 - 1.8	9 - 8	23 - 26

Pavoni et al. (35) in young *Ulva rigida* fronds, sampled in the central eutrophicated Lagoon, found the following concentrations of PCB (ng g^{-1} d.w.) in young and old fronds respectively: 27 (s.d. 12) and 121 (s.d. 4).

Figure 3 depicts profiles of Total PAH fluxes vs. time (36). The following polycyclic hydrocarbons have been determined by high performance liquid chromatography, variable wavelength absorption detection: Naphthalene, acenaphthylene, 7,12-dimethylbenzanthracene, 2-methylnaphtalene, fluorene, acenaphtene, phenanthrene, 2,3-dimethylnaphtalene, anthracene, fluoranthene, 1-methylphenanthrene, pyrene, 2,3-benzofluorene, triphenylene, benz(a)anthracene, chrysene, benzo(b)fluoranthene, benzo(k)fluoranthene, perylene, benzo(e)pyrene, 1,2,3,4-dibenzanthracene, benzo(a)pyrene, and 1,2,5,6-dibenzanthracene.

For any section of the core, being known the *in situ* density and the sedimentation rate calculated from the radioisotope profiles, the pollutant fluxes through the sediment surface, or the average yearly load, have been calculated by the following formula:

Flux rate (ng cm^{-2} year^{-1}) =
        sedimentation rate(cm y^{-1}) x in situ density(g cm^{-3}) x
           hydrocarbon concentration(ng g^{-1}, d.w.).

    The environmental occurrence of polycyclic aromatic hydrocarbons is mainly associated with dispersion of oil products and with various types of combustion. For these chemicals a kind of pre-industrial background exists, due to forest fires or to domestic wood burning. The sediments of the deepest strata were certainly deposited in the nineteenth century, when no significant industrial activities had been initiated. The ratio between PAH concentrations found in the sediments dated to this century, and the deepest ones, vary from 1.7 to 30, increasing from the beginning of the

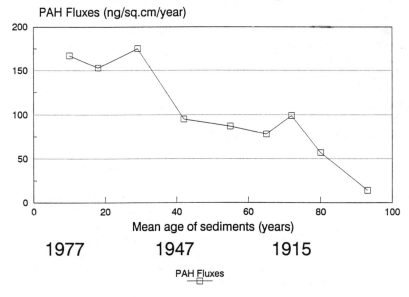

Fig. 3.   Time trend of Tot. PAH fluxes form core 2.

century. Almost all profiles and calculated fluxes of PAH's (except perylene) have similar trends, therefore, in Figure 3, the profile of total PAH flux has been drawn. The time trend of fluxes resembles fairly closely the industrial and urban development in the Venice area. Actually, a rapid increase is observed from the beginning of the century to the first world war, then a drop which corresponds to the war period, a slow rise in the inter-war period, a new fast increment in the period after the second world war, then a flattening or a slight decrease in the last 20 years.

Since the use of fossil fuels in the Porto Marghera area has constantly increased, as indicated by the amounts of coal and oil unloaded in the Port (Figure 4), it is likely that the decrease of PAH load in the most recent sediments can be attributed to the effects of pollution control. These include the advent of stricter regulations on stack emissions, the availability of better technologies for oil transport and discharge and finally to a growing environmental concern among the public and the local authorities, who exert a close control on all industrial activities. This reduction in the surface sediments has been observed also by other authors (37-39), who suggest that the observed decrease in the most recent strata could reflect the transition from coal to oil and gas for house heating purposes, as coal burning usually produces more PAH than the other fuels. A contribution from this factor may be appropriate also in our case. No bioassay experiments have been conducted yet to evaluate the toxicity of lagoon or sea sediments contaminated by metals or hydrocarbons.

Eutrophication

A more difficult task is the reconstruction of the eutrophication growth in the Lagoon of Venice. Sediments could be dated for phosphorus, which was done for the core sampled in the area close to the industrial district. Also, total phosphorus concentrations were determined. These have increased constantly from the beginning of this century up to 170% above the background value fixed at 13 mmol kg^{-1} (d.w.). The effects of increasing eutrophication have been particularly evident in the biological component of the lagoon environment during the seventies. In fact, the progressive alteration of chemical-physical parameters of waters and sediments and the boosted availability of nutrient substances has triggered a marked selection among algal and animal species that populate the Lagoon. The composition and variation of benthic populations in the past were extensively studied by Vatova (40) and by Giordani Soika and Perin (42,43). Subsequently, no further studies have been published. More recently, some publications have documented the evolution of the aquatic lagoon vegetation toward species more resistant to environmental degradation such as *Ulvaceae* (44), and the massive proliferation of *Chironomid* mosquitoes (45). The typology and the vertical distribution of macroalgae associations have fundamentally changed. Nitrophile algae such as *Ulva rigida*, *Enteromorpha spp.*, and *Cladophora spp.* have progressively replaced other species more sensitive to eutrophic conditions. Rhizophytes,

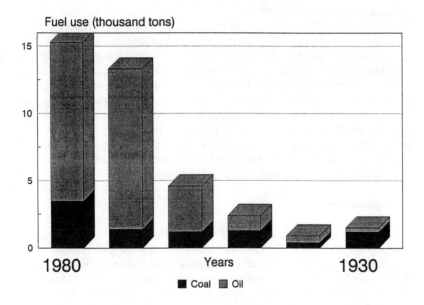

Fig. 4.   Time trend of fossil fuels unloaded in Porto Marghera.

that in the past used to cover a large part of the bottoms around Venice, are now limited to the northern and southern areas of the Lagoon, where no distrophic conditions have yet occurred (44). In addition, the number of sampled species has declined: from 141 in 1940 (40), to 104 in 1962 (46), to 95 in 1987 (44). At the same time, the lagoon surface is populated by monospecific algae populations, that as pleustophitic species, completely fill the shallow lagoon areas both vertically and horizontally.

The entire central lagoon area was sampled in a survey conducted in June, 1987 (47). It was estimated that macroalgae (mostly *Ulva*) were occupying some 85 km^2 (65% of the central lagoon), with a standing crop of 546,900 ton (fresh wight) and densities from 0 to 20 kg m^{-2}. The disappearance of rhyzophytes and the increasingly frequent occurrence of distrophic conditions has caused in the central lagoon a dramatic selection of benthic species, by favoring those that better withstand the frequent and drastic fluctuations of dissolved oxygen. Some species of insects have been selectively favored. As an example, some Diptera (*e.g. Chironomus salinarius* Kieff.) can survive for long periods in anaerobic conditions, whereas all the natural predators are removed. These insects have spread rapidly (up to 25,000 larvae m^{-2}), especially in areas of poor water circulation, namely those located between Lido Island and the city of Venice and in the inner Lagoon area close to Campalto and the airport (Figure 1). In summer during the eighties, swarms of such mosquitoes have invaded the city, the hinterlands, the railway station and the airport, causing severe problems with normal activities. In the most recent years they have been fought by spreading pyrethrum-like insecticides.

Comparison of nutrient concentrations determined in different periods in the waters of the Lagoon does not appear particularly significant for reconstructing the continual degradation. Even if we consider data acquired only 10 years ago, the differences in accuracy and precision of procedures adopted, the frequent lack of other chemical-physical parameters and information regarding sampling, pre-treatment steps (e.g. water samples filtrated or not), tide conditions and so on, render the comparison questionable. A reliable comparison is only possible when data have been obtained by the same laboratory with the same analytical methods. In 7 common stations located around the city of Venice, four seasonal campaigns were conducted in 1984-85 and 1987-88, taking samples at low and high tide (48). Comparison of average concentrations of ammonia and phosphorus show a correlated decrease for both parameters in the more recent samples. The importance of this trend can be questioned, as the period considered is relatively short. However, it could be a sign that the efforts conducted up to now to convey the refuse waters of the inland territory to treatment plants, and to limit the presence of phosphorus in commercial formulations, have had an effect. The percentage of phosphorus allowed in detergents marketed in Venice and the close hinterlands has been reduced from 6.5 % in 1982, to 5 % in 1983, to 2.5 % in 1985, to 1 % in 1986 and to 0 % in 1989. However these efforts are still inadequate since nutrient concentrations remain very high and able to support eutrophication phenomena. In a recent publication, Pavoni et al. (49), focused on the central lagoon and compared the relative importance of nutrients carried by fresh water streams from the inland territory and from the city of Venice. Four sampling sessions were conducted in different seasons of 1987 in eighteen stations located around Venice. In addition to nutrient concentrations (N-ammonia, N-nitrite, N-nitrate, P-phosphate, P-total, total dissolved carbon), some chemical-physical parameters (pH, redox potential, temperature), salinity and total coliform bacteria have been determined. The ranges of mean values obtained in area A, close to the entrance channel of Lido and D, close to the inner border of the Lagoon in low and high tide are reported in the following table. In high tide conditions, and in area A, waters entering from the sea effectively dilute nutrient concentrations of Lagoon waters.

Table II. Mean concentration ranges in the central Lagoon waters (min - max; 4 seasonal samplings, μmol l^{-1}). Area A is represented by 6 stations, area D by 4.

	NH_3		NO_3^-		PO_4^{-3}	
	Hi.Tide	Lo.Tide	Hi.Tide	Lo.Tide	Hi.Tide	Lo.Tide
A.	2.4-9.6	2.7-14.5	5.6-21.7	7.3-66.9	0.3-0.5	0.8-1.5
D.	1.4-9.6	2.7-18.9	2.4-49.8	7.8-106.4	0.4-2.7	1.7-5.9

In this study, salinity has been used as a leading parameter to estimate the hydrographic distance of stations from the sea. A significant negative correlation has been discovered between salinity and nutrient concentrations. The Lagoon is a transitional environment and its brackish water derives from a mixture of freshwaters entering through some twenty input points--small rivers, canals, pumping stations--and of salt water entering from the sea through tidal movements. By means of a simple system of two equations it is possible to estimate the percentage of freshwater in a sample of Lagoon water.

$$X \ Sfw + Y \ Ssw = Sm. \qquad\qquad X + Y = 100$$

[Sfw = salinity of freshwater, 0.1 % mean value monitored in freshwater streams entering the Lagoon; Ssw = salinity of salt water determined at the station close to the Lagoon entrance channel during the same sampling campaign; Sm = actual salinity in the sample; X = percentage of freshwater in the sample; Y = percentage of salt water in the sample.]

If, instead of the salinity, the percentage of fresh water is used in the regression analyses, a equally-significant correlation with nutrient concentrations is obtained. Therefore, on an average, the higher the percentage of fresh water, the higher is the content of eutrophicating compounds. There is no doubt that these substances enter the Lagoon with the fresh waters coming from the hinterlands and the city of Venice (the historical centre and the other Lagoon islands, i.e. Murano, Burano, etc). To attempt an estimation of the amounts of nutrients entering the Lagoon from inland, for want of more recent published results, the data from Bernardi et al. (50) were used. These authors monitored the flow rates of the most important freshwater tributaries of the Lagoon and measured the concentrations of nitrogen and phosphorus compounds. In particular, the canals Osellino and the Naviglio del Brenta, were studied. The first drains waters from Mestre, partially treated in the plant at Campalto, which enter the Lagoon North of the trans-Lagoon bridge, close to the airport. The second, in addition to urban sewage, contains agricultural run-off. By using the mean yearly concentrations reported by these authors (TIN, total inorganic nitrogen, i.e. the sum of nitrate, nitrite and ammonia: 2.5. mg-N l^{-1}; P-phosphate: 0.5 mgP l^{-1}) and the mean flow of the Osellino canal (1.7 m^3 s^{-1}), we can roughly estimate some 134 t of nitrogen and 27 t of phosphorus per year enter the Lagoon through this stream. An analogous estimation for the Naviglio del Brenta, (mean flow: 3.9 m^3 s^{-1}; nutrient concentrations: 2.6 mg-N l^{-1}; 0.3 mg-P l^{-1}), gives 320 t of nitrogen and 37 t of phosphorus entering the Lagoon per year. These values are certainly underestimates, as organic and particulate fractions are not included.

The amounts of nutrients entering the Lagoon from the city of Venice can be estimated on the basis of the amounts of phosphorus and nitrogen discharged per person per day (12.3 g-N, (51); 2.2 g-P (52), in December 1986. Although more recent data are available, comparison with the data of Bernardi et al. (50) should be maintained. The residential population of the historical centre of Venice, including the islands of Murano and Burano, was 110,913; during 1986, 2,458,000 tourists spent a mean period of 2.2 days in Venice (53), equivalent to 14,815 annual residents. From these data, it can be calculated that ~564 t of nitrogen and ~101 t of phosphorus entered the Lagoon through this source annually. In conclusion, the obtained figures of eutrophicating substance loads from the two different sources state that these contributions are both important and fairly comparable.

In 1987-88 a study was carried out with eighteen sampling campaigns, one every 20 days, four samplings per campaign, two in low and two in high tide, at 26 stations disseminated all over the Lagoon, in the most hydrographically representative sites. An additional site in the open sea was taken as referece (54). The monitored parameters were: water and air temperature, salinity, dissolved oxygen, N-ammonia, N-NO$_x$ (nitrite+nitrate), TKN (total Kieldahl nitrogen), Si-silicate, P-phosphate, P-total, Zn, chlorophyll A, and total coliform bacteria. Sampling was almost simultaneous at the different stations. Therefore the data collected during one campaign really give a synoptic picture of the Lagoon situation at that period of time. A statistical analysis of this study's results yields a number of interesting observations about the present environmental situation in the Lagoon.

First of all, the study confirms a significant negative correlation of nutrient concentrations with salinity, and positive correlation with the percentage of fresh water. This correlation is based upon a large number of observations (18 campaigns x 4 samplings per campaign x 27 stations = 1944 samples). This means that the observation, above reported for the central Lagoon, holds valid also for the entire Lagoon: the main eutrophicating load enters the Lagoon through fresh waters of mainly urban origin.

A significant decreasing trend was observed for the important parameter total phosphorus. The mean concentration obtained over all the Lagoon stations dropped significantly from the first to the last sample in the campaign. The same observation was made for P-PO$_4$; in this case an oscillating, decreasing trend was recorded. Therefore, both in the short (1 year) and in the medium (3-4 year) periods, the phosphorus decrease was significant. Three stations were most contaminated compared to the others. Two are located close to the industrial area and to the canal Osellino (stations 10 and 13) the third is located close to the mouth of the river Dese and the canal Silone (station 18, very close to the site of core 1, Figure 1). Only in the areas of the Lagoon directly flooded by the sea tide were relatively low concentrations of eutrophicating substances found.

CONCLUSIONS

On the basis of the observations so far expressed, it can be stated that in recent years some important steps forward have been made to stop the degradation of the Lagoon of Venice. In fact, a better sensitiveness toward environmental problems has favoured a marked reduction in the amounts of polluting and eutrophicating substances discharged into the Lagoon. Still, the concentration of eutrophicating substances present in the Lagoon waters remains very high. Further, it must be pointed out that the damage so far done, especially for the amounts of pollutants stored in the sediments, will require many years to be repaired. At present there is no way to remove the stored pollutants other than complete removal of the sediments. However, due to the huge amounts of materials to be handled, this is probably unfeasible. The sediment removal should be limited to the normal operations carried out to keep the canals navigable, and dredged materials should undergo selective disposal. The most contaminated sediment should be discharged in controlled sites or decontaminated; the least contaminated can be transported to the sea, 20 miles offshore. The other Lagoon areas should be left to recover naturally. In the areas of positive sedimentation, the contaminated sediments are gradually buried. In the others, where erosion occurs, superficial sediments are progressively dispersed and transported to sea.

The efforts so far made by the local administrations to convey refuse waters to treatment plants and to lower the percentage of phosphorus in detergent formulation (as required by law) have really caused a decrease in nitrogen and phosphorus concentrations in the waters of the Lagoon of Venice. Nevertheless, actions to date remain insufficient since distrophic conditions keep showing up every year in the areas of the central Lagoon at low water circulation. Furthermore, these conditions are observed on a limited scale in lagoon zones so far not contaminated. The diversity of animal and algal benthic populations is very reduced, especially in the central Lagoon. Nitrophile species such as *Ulva rigida* expand their domain every year, superseding other species more sensitive to eutrophication. More interventions should be carried out to improve water circulation, where it is insufficient to prevent anoxias, and to reduce nutrient input from the hinterlands. In particular, the efficiency of treatment plants in reducing nitrogen and phosphorus concentrations in the effluents should be improved and concurrently the amount of treated sewages should be increased to 100%. The course of canals from inland could be diverted into closed ponds suitable for the cultivation of aquatic plants (Rhizophytes), or into peripheral lagoon areas, where macroalgae could be harvested for the production of composts or the extraction of polysaccarides. The lagoon channels, that were the main courses of the tide through which the central areas of the Lagoon were flooded, should be deepened and enlarged. An adequate sewage system for the city of Venice and the main islands must be constructed. Without such interventions, the central Lagoon will progressively become a lagoon system in which only a very limited number of vegetal and animal species can survive seasonally, withstanding very selective conditions.

Literature Cited

1. Rosa Salva P. *Rivista Urbanistica*, n. 62 **1974** (In italian).
2. Pirazzoli P. Inundations and sea levels in Venice. Geomorphology Laboratory of High Studies, Paris University, 1973; Report no. 22. (in French).
3. Pirazzoli P. Bologna Academy of Sciences, 1975; Vol. II, Reports series XIII. (in Italian).
4. Ministry of Public Works, *The tide currents in the Lagoon of Venice* (in Italian). Istituto di Idraulica di Padova, Padova, 1975. 95 pp.
5. Carbognin, L., Gatto, P. *An overview of the subsidence of Venice.* I.A.H.S. Pub., #151, 1985; pp. 321-329.
6. Carbognin, L., 1991. Personal communication.
7. Sfriso, A., Marcomini, A., Pavoni, B., *Mar. Envir. Research* **1987**, **22**, p. 297.
8. Sfriso, A., Pavoni, B., Marcomini, A., Orio A. A., *Mar. Poll. Bull.* **1988**, *19*, 2.
9. Sfriso, A., Marcomini, A., Pavoni, B. and Orio, A.A., *Ingegn. Sanit.* **1988**, *5*, pp. 255-266.
10. Sfriso, A., Pavoni, B., Marcomini, A., *Sci. Tot. Envir.*, **1989**, *80*, pp. 139-150.

11. Appleby, P.G. & Oldfield, F. *CATENA* **1978**, *5*, pp. 1-8.
12. Appleby, P.G. Oldfield, F., Thomsom, R., Huuttunen, P. and Tolonen, K. (1979). *Nature*, **1979**, *280*, pp. 53-55.
13. Battiston, G.A., Croatto, U., Degetto, S., Sbrignadello, G. & Tositti, L. (1985). *Inquinamento*, **1985**, *6*, pp. 49-59.
14. Battiston, G.A., Degetto, S., Gerbasi, R., Sbrignadello, G. (1989). *Mar. Chem.*, **1989**, *26*, pp. 91-100.
15. Donazzolo, R., Orio, A.A. & Pavoni, B. *Oceanologica Acta*, **1982** N° SP, pp. 101-106.
16. Pavoni, B., Donazzolo, R., Marcomini, R., Degobbis, D., & Orio, A.A., *Mar. Poll. Bull.*, **1987**. *18*, pp. 17-24.
17. Marcomini, A., Sfriso, A., Pavoni, B., *Mar. Chem.*, **1987**, *21*, pp. 15-23.
18. Pavoni, B., Sfriso, A. & Marcomini, A., *Mar. Chem.* **1987**, *21*, pp. 25-35.
19. Whitehead, N.E., Oregioni, B., Fukai, R. *VII Journées Etudes Pollution Mer Mediterranée*, Lucerne, CIESM, 1984, pp. 233-240.
20. Pavoni, B., Marcomini, A., Sfriso, A. & Orio, A.A., *Sci. Tot. Environ.*, **1988**, *77*, pp. 189-202.
21. Campesan, G., Fossato, V.U., Barillari, A., Dolci, F., Stocco, G. *Istituto Veneto di Scienze, Lettere e Arti, Rapporti e Studi*, **1987**, *10*, pp. 21-28.
22. Capodaglio, G., Scarponi, G., P. Cescon. Lead contamination of seawaters with different anthropic influence. III International Conference "Environmental Contamination", Venice, Sept. 1988, pp. 505-407.
23. Capodaglio, G., Scarponi, G., K.H. Coole, K.W. Bruland. Lead Speciation in surface seawaters. *X Int. Symp. Chemistry of the Mediterranean*, Primosten, Yugoslavia, 4-12 May 1988.
24. Campesan, G., Cappelli, R., Pagotto, G., Stocco, G., Zanicchi, G. *V^es Journées Etudes Pollutions Cagliari*, 1980, CIESM.
25. Campesan, G., Fossato, V.U., Stocco, G. Heavy metals in Mussels (Mytilus sp) from the lagoon of Venice (In Italian). *Istituto Veneto di Scienze, Lettere e Arti, Rapporti e Studi*, **1981**, *8*, pp. 141-152.
26. Donazzolo, R., Hieke Merlin, O., Menegazzo Vitturi, L., Orio, A.A., Pavoni, B., Perin, G., Rabitti, S., *Mar. Poll. Bull.*, **1981**, *12*, pp. 417-425.
27. Donazzolo, R., Orio, A.A. & Pavoni, B. (1982). *Oceanologica Acta*, **1982**, N° SP, pp. 101-106.
28. Donazzolo, R., Hieke Merlin, O., Menegazzo Vitturi, L., Orio, A.A., Pavoni, B., Rabitti, S., *Thalassia Yugosl.*, **1983**, *19*, pp. 111-119.
29. Donazzolo, R., Menegazzo Vitturi, L., Orio, A.A., Pavoni, B. *Envir. Techn. Lett.*, **1983**, *4*, pp. 451-462.
30. Donazzolo, R., Orio, A.A., Pavoni, B., Perin, G., *Oceanol. Acta*, **1984**, *7*, pp. 25-32.
31. Donazzolo, R., Hieke Merlin, O., Menegazzo Vitturi, L., B. Pavoni, (1984). *Mar. Poll. Bull.*, **1984**, *15*, pp. 93-101.
32. Fossato, U.V., Van Vleet, E.S., Dolci, F. *Archivio di Oceanografia e Limnologia*, **1988**, *21*, pp. 151-161.

33. Fossato V.U., Craboledda, *Laguna Veneta*. *Archivio di Oceanografia e Limnologia*, **1979**, *19*, pp. 169-178.
34. Nasci, C., Fossato, V.U., *Envir. Technol. Lett.*, **1982**, *3*, pp. 273-280.
35. Pavoni, B., Calvo, C., Sfriso, A., Orio, A.A., *Sci. Tot. Environ.*, **1990**, *91*, pp. 13-21.
36. Pavoni, B., Sfriso, A. & Marcomini, A., *Marine Chemistry*, **1987**, *21*, pp. 25-35.
37. Grimmer, G. and Böhnke, H., *Z. Naturforsch.*, **1977**, teil C, *32*, pp. 703-711.
38. Hites, R.A., Laflamme, R.E., Windsor Jr., J.G., Farrington, J.W., and Deuser, W.G., *Geochim. Cosmochim. Acta*, **1980**, *44*, pp. 873-878.
39. Gschwend, P.M., and Hites, R.A., *Geochim. Cosmochim. Acta*, **1981**, *45*, pp. 2359-2367.
40. Vatova, A., *Istituto Italo-Germanico di Biologia Marina*, **1940**, *3*, pp. 1-25.
41. Giordani Soika, A., Perin, G. The pollution of the Venice lagoon: study of chemical changes and population variations in the lagoon sediments in the last twenty years (in Italian) [29 Charts of the Venice lagoon], **1974**.
42. Giordani Soika, A., Perin, G., *Atti XI Convegno. A.N.L.S.B.*, Venezia, **1970**, pp. 135-139.
43. Giordani Soika, A., Perin, G., *Bollettino Museo Civico di Storia Natuarle*, Venezia, **1974**, *26 (1)*, pp. 25-68.
44. Sfriso A., *Giornale Botanico Italiano*, **1987**, *121*, pp. 65-85.
45. Ceretti G., Ferrarese, U., Scattolin, M., *Arsenale Editrice*, Venezia, **1985**, *59*.
46. Pignatti, S., *Memorie Istituto Veneto Scienze Lettere e Arti*, **1962**, *32*, pp. 1-34.
47. Sfriso, A., Pavoni, B., Marcomini, A., *Sci. Tot. Envir.*, **1989**, *80*, pp. 139-150.
48. Orio, A.A., Unpublished results, **1991**.
49. Pavoni, B., Donazzolo, R., Sfriso, A. and Orio, A.A., *The Sci. Tot. Environ.*, **1990**, *96*, pp. 235-252.
50. Bernardi, S., Cecchi, R., Costa, F., Ghermandi, G. e Vazzoler, S., *Inquinamento*, **1986**, *1/2*, pp. 187.
51. Progetto Venezia, The available knowledge of the Venice lagoon pollution (in Italian). Edited by Cossu, R. and De Fraja Frangipane for Ministero dei Lavori Pubblici, Magistrato alle acque, Consorzio Venezia Nuova. 4 Vol., **1985**.
52. Marchetti, R., A degenerative process of waters (in Italian). *Franco Angeli Editore*, Milano, Italy, **1987**, 315 pp.
53. Azienda di Promozione Turistica di Venezia, Ufficio Statistica: Touristic Movement in the Venice Municipality in 1986 (in Italian), **1987**.
54. Consorzio Venezia Nuova, Unpublished results, **1991**.

RECEIVED September 25, 1991

The Terrestrial Component

An Overview

Walter G. Whitford

Department of Biology, New Mexico State University,
Las Cruces, NM 88003

The underlying and recurrent theme of the chapters in this section are the direct and indirect effects of an exponentially increasing population of humans on the natural resources and biogeochemical processes of a finite land area. A rapid increase in numbers of humans increases the demand for food, fiber, living space and amenities that ease the stresses of overcrowding. In industrialized societies the demand for more "goods" imposes costs on the environment that are only beginning to be assessed. The chapters in this section document in detail the magnitude of these effects and many of the feedbacks. The topics included address basic issues such as food production for the expanding populations and losses of productivity from marginal lands such as arid and montane environments. All are connected by feedbacks to biogeochemical process that affect productivity of vegetation and global climate stability.

An aspect of the state of the human condition in this last decade of the 20th century is a cost-benefit analysis of technological progress. Most of the chapters in this section address the "costs" associated with the better known benefits of industrialized food production, use of fossil fuels to power our industries, modify the "climate" of our living space and provide freedom of movement plus the use of virtually every element in the planetary crust to produce the array of goods that powers our economic systems.

In the food production arena, our capability of producing biocides has made cosmetic improvements in fruit and vegetables possible but with little gain in net productivity. Pimentel documents just how little improvement in net agricultural productivity has accrued from the use of biocides and the costs associated with widespread use of these materials in terms of losses in human lives, health, wildlife and fisheries, etc. Another aspect of the way in which we conduct the basic enterprise of food and fiber production is addressed by an analysis of costs and benefits of energy

0097–6156/92/0483–0307$06.00/0

inputs or subsidies to agricultural production. Increased energy inputs have resulted in more production per unit area but these energy inputs have reached a point of diminishing returns as documented by Hall.

Chapters in this section and the next address the question of feedbacks from human activities on global systems and natural resources such as forests. The exponential increases in fossil fuels use, forest harvests, forest clearing and farming of marginal lands, all affect global carbon cycles with concomitant effects on climate and basic nutrient cycling processes in virtually all natural ecosystems. In the next section Kaufman et al. (see section on global carbon cycle) discuss the impact of cutting and burning of the world's forests on biogeochemical cycles and the resultant alteration of microclimates and hydrologic and nutrient cycles. The dynamics of the processes discussed by Kaufman et al. are similar to those discussed by Whitford in the context of desertification. In both cases rainfall and productivity are uncoupled and mineralization dynamics are drastically altered.

As noted by Mar in his overview, the significance of microbially mediated methane production, discussed by Chynoweth, is truly global. It represents a potential major energy source, is a significant substance in biogeochemical cycling, and has been increasingly recognized as a important contributor to the build-up of greenhouse gases in the atmosphere.

Inherent in discussions of these kinds of processes is the difficulty of assigning costs and benefits. As human activity changes global element cycles, the chemistry of rainfall, and the rates of efflux of radiatively active gasses, the potential for global change in climate arises. It is this potential that is of concern. We can only examine global change as a probability based on imperfect models. While we cannot prove what the rate of changes will be, nor with accuracy what areas of the planet will be affected, we (humans) are conducting the experiment. The chapters in these sections, while not addressing the global carbon cycle directly, nevertheless describe a variety of sources of radiatively active gasses from biomethanogenesis to nitrous oxides from desertified land areas.

It is not only the potential for climate change resulting from atmospheric additives that must be addressed. Aerosols that react with water vapor in the atmosphere, thereby changing the chemistry of clouds and rainfall, can directly affect plants and aquatic ecosystems. This is dealt with by Kline, who identifies acid deposition as only one of several possible contributing factors to forest decline in the northeastern U.S.

Taken together, these chapters provide a picture of the large costs, generally ignored until recently, that are associated with industrialization and the growth of human populations. No areas of the planet are immune from these costs, which are distributed to all environments on the planet. These chapters, while not a comprehensive treatment of environmental costs, do provide excellent examples of the scope of the problems humankind must face in the coming century.

RECEIVED September 24, 1991

Chapter 15

Pesticides and World Food Supply

David Pimentel

Section of Ecology and Systematics, Department of Entomology,
Cornell University, Ithaca, NY 14853

Despite the use of 2.5 million tons of pesticide
worldwide, approximately 35% of potential crop production
is lost to pests. An additional 20% is lost to pests
that attack the food post-harvest. Thus, nearly one-half
of all potential world food supply is lost to pests
despite human efforts to prevent this loss. Pesticides,
in addition to saving about 10% of world food supply,
cause serious environmental and public health problems.
These problems include: human pesticide poisonings; fish
and bird kills; destruction of beneficial natural
enemies; pesticide resistance; contamination of food and
water with pesticide residues; and inadvertent
destruction of some crops.

The current world population stands at 5.3 billion and is growing
rapidly (1). Demographers project that the world population will
reach 6.1 billion by the turn of the century, approach 8.2 billion
by 2025, and probably reach 15 billion by 2100 (2). Never before
in history have humans, by their sheer numbers, so dominated the
earth and its resources. What is equally alarming is the 1.8%
annual population growth rate -- a rate 1800-times greater than
that during the first million years of human existence. At this
growth rate about one quarter million people are added to the world
population every day.
    Although more people are being fed than ever before, there are
also more malnourished humans than ever before. Thus, more than
1.6 billion of the 5.3 billion people living today are malnourished
and do not have access to adequate supplies of food (3). Clearly,
a malnourished person cannot lead a fully productive life. The
plight of these people is more serious than just a lack of adequate
food, for many are ill with disease and/or carry heavy loads of
parasites. For example, a survey of school children in Kwale
District, Kenya showed that 96% were infected with hookworms, 50%
with roundworms, 95% with whipworms, and 40% with schistosomiasis

0097–6156/92/0483–0309$06.00/0
© 1992 American Chemical Society

(4). Considered together these problems disable people, diminish their productivity and make their lives extremely stressful. Worse still, the outlook for improvement, given the continued rapid growth in the world population, is bleak.

Worldwide the food situation is worsening. Only five nations (Argentina, Australia, Canada, France, and the United States) export substantial quantities of grains. Further, during recent years grain deficits have escalated in Africa, Asia, and the Middle East *(5)*.

About 98% of the world food supply comes from agricultural land or the terrestrial ecosystem *(6)*; meanwhile the small portion from the aquatic ecosystem continues to shrink because of overfishing and pollution. The adequacy of the supply of agricultural land is of concern. Most of the arable land is already in production and millions of hectares of marginal land have had to be brought into crop production *(7)*. In addition, each year soil degradation is causing the abandonment of about 6 million hectares of land, which is being replaced with cleared forest land to keep agricultural yields adequate *(8, 9)*. All these factors are stressing agricultural productivity.

Furthermore, significant amounts of food are lost to pests. Worldwide preharvest crop losses to pests (insects, diseases, and weeds) are estimated to be about 35% each year *(10)*. These major pest losses are occurring despite the application of about 2.5 million metric tons of pesticide, at an annual cost of $18 billion *(11)*. Even after crops are harvested, an additional 20% of the food is lost to pests *(12)*. Overall about 48% of all potential world food supply for humans is lost to pests despite all efforts to protect it.

In this chapter, the agricultural, economic, and environmental impacts of pesticide use in world and U.S. food production are analyzed. In addition, an assessment is made of the potential that substituting nonchemical controls for some pesticide use would have in reducing chemicals and providing adequate pest controls.

Extent of Pesticide Use Worldwide

The total amount of pesticide applied worldwide, as mentioned, is estimated to be 2.5 million tons. Of this 50 to 60% are herbicides, 20 to 30% are insecticides, and 10 to 20% are fungicides. Interestingly, less than one-third of all the agricultural cropland in the world is treated with some kind of pesticide. This illustrates the fact that a significant portion of crops receive no pesticide and, therefore, are protected to some extent by nonchemical biological controls.

The application of pesticides for pest control is not evenly distributed among all crops. For example, the most pesticide is used on high value crops like cotton, fruits, vegetables, and rice. Little pesticide is used on forage crops and most of the grain crops. Although large quantities of pesticides are applied to crops, only a small percentage of these chemicals actually reach the target pests. This is estimated to be less than 0.1% *(13)*. The result is that more than 99.9% of the applied pesticide drifts off into the environment where it adversely affects nontarget

sectors of the ecosystem, including soil, water, and the
atmosphere, as well as beneficial biota.
    One reason for the rapid growth in the use of pesticides
worldwide has been the "Green Revolution" *(5)*. Although there have
been some benefits from pesticide use in agriculture, they also
cause significant environmental and public health problems. The
same is true in public health where insecticides have been used to
control malaria. However, today increased resistance to
insecticides in mosquitoes and increased resistance to drugs by the
malarial parasite are resulting in an explosive increase of malaria
worldwide *(5)*.

Crop Losses to Pests and Changes in Agricultural Technologies

Since 1945 the use of synthetic pesticides in the United States has
grown 33-fold. The amounts of herbicides, insecticides,
and fungicides used have changed with time due, in large part, to
changes in agricultural practices and cosmetic standards *(14, 15)*.
At the same time, the toxicity and biological effectiveness of
these pesticides have increased at least 10-fold *(15)*. For
example, in 1945 DDT was applied at a rate of about 2 kg/ha. With
the more potent insecticides available now, similar effective
insect control is achieved with pyrethroids and aldicarb applied at
0.1 kg/ha and 0.05 kg/ha, respectively.
    Annually, an estimated 37% of all crops in the United States
is lost to pests (13% to insects, 12% to plant pathogens, and 12%
to weeds) in spite of the use of pesticides and various nonchemical
controls *(16)*. Although pesticide use has increased over the past
4 decades, crop losses have not shown a concurrent decline.
According to survey data collected from 1942 to the present, losses
from weeds have fluctuated but slowly declined from 13.8% to 12%
(Table 1). A combination of improved chemical, mechanical, and
cultural weed control practices is responsible for this. Over that
same period, losses from plant pathogens, including nematodes, have
increased slightly, from 10.5% to about 12% (Table 1). This has
resulted in part because crop rotations were abandoned, field
sanitation was reduced, and higher cosmetic standards for fruit
and vegetable products have been legalized.
    Furthermore, the share of crops lost to insects has nearly
doubled during the last 40 years (Table 1), despite a more than
10-fold increase in both the amount and toxicity of synthetic
insecticide used *(17-19)*. Up to the present time the increased
insect losses, in terms of yields per hectare, have been offset by
increased crop yields obtained through the use of higher yielding
varieties and greater use of fertilizers and other energy-based
inputs *(20, 21)*.
    The paradox facing agriculturalists is that 35% of all
potential food is lost to pests even as the use of pesticides and
all other types of pest controls are increasing. Analyses of U.S.
agriculture illustrate the major changes that have taken place in
agricultural technologies and how these have influenced the
magnitude of crop losses to pests. These include: 1) the planting
of some crop varieties that are more susceptible to insect pests
than former varieties, 2) the reduction in crop rotations, which

Table I. Comparison of annual pest losses (dollars[*]) in the USA for the periods 1904, 1910-1935, 1942-1951, 1951-1960, 1974, and 1989 *(15)*.

| Period | Percentage of Pest Losses in Crops | | | | Crop value |
	Insects	Diseases	Weeds	Total	$ x 10^9
1989	13.0	12.0	12.0	37.0	150
1974	13.0	12.0	8.0	33.0	77
1951-1960	12.9	12.2	8.5	33.6	30
1942-1951	7.1	10.5	13.8	31.4	27
1910-1935	10.5	NA**	NA	NA	6
1904	9.8	NA	NA	NA	4

*Not adjusted
**Not available

help prevent further growth in pest populations, 3) the increase in monocultures and reduced crop diversity *(22, 23)*, 4) the reduction in field sanitation, including less attention to the destruction of infected fruit and crop residues *(16)*, 5) reduced tillage, with more crop residues left on the land surface, 6) the culturing of crops in climatic regions where they are more susceptible to insect attack, 7) the insecticide destruction of natural enemies of certain pests, thereby creating the need for additional pesticide treatments *(24)*, 8) the pests becoming resistant to pesticides *(25)*, 9) the use of herbicides that alter the physiology of crop plants, making them more vulnerable to insect attack *(26)*, 10) the lowering of FDA tolerance for insects and insect parts in foods, and the enforcement of more stringent "cosmetic standards" by fruit and vegetable processors and retailers *(14)*, and 11) the increased use of aircraft application technology. The impact of these factors will be explored further in the discussion of alternative biological and cultural controls to pesticide controls.

Integrated Pest Management (IPM)

Although integrated pest management (IPM) entails the combined use of a wide array of pest control practices including the use of pesticides *(16, 27)*, in practice IPM has come to mean monitoring pest populations to determine "when-to-treat." Clearly, this strategy has been a tremendous advancement because previously most pesticide treatments were made on a routine basis whether the pesticide was needed or not. Worldwide, however, most pesticide is applied with little attention given to monitoring the status of pest populations. In part, this is due to a lack of information on pest-economic-thresholds and pest monitoring technologies.

The development of criteria for sound economic thresholds in order to determine when-to-treat is highly complex. Establishing the guidelines for an effective economic threshold for a single pest must take into account the following interacting factors: 1) density of the pest, 2) densities of its parasites and predators, 3) temperature and moisture levels and their impact on the crop, pest, and its natural enemies, 4) level of soil nutrients available to the crop, 5) the growth characteristics of the particular crop variety, 6) crop(s) grown on the land the previous year.

Another important aspect of reducing pesticide use is to enhance application methods to better target the pesticide on the pest and minimize its spread in the environment. Considering that less than an average of only 0.01% of applied pesticide actually reaches the target pests, its obvious that enormous quantities of pesticides are not only being wasted, but dispersed to contaminate the environment *(13)*. This problem is well illustrated by what happens during application of pesticides by aircraft. Under ideal conditions only about half of the pesticide applied by aircraft reaches the target hectare *(13, 28, 29)*. Unfortunately the newest, ultra low volume, (ULV) application technology now being adopted by many aerial applicators places only 25% of the pesticide on the target hectare *(30)*.

However, several application techniques are available that will place more pesticide in the target area and on the target

pests than the presently used aerial methods. For example, a
carefully adjusted boom sprayer will place up to 90% of the
pesticide in the target area. Granular pesticides, where
appropriate for use, place nearly 99% in the target area. Also,
the use of the rope-wick applicator for herbicides is successful in
placing 90% of the pesticide on the target weeds (31, 32).
      Another important methodology that reduces the amount of
pesticide applied to a crop is "spot treatment." That is, only
those areas of the fields where the pest problem is serious are
treated, and those areas where there are few or no pests on the
crop are left untreated.

Biological and Cultural Control Alternatives for Pesticides

The nonchemical biological and cultural controls discussed in this
paper are used broadly, and the focus is only on those management
practices in which humans are able to manipulate the environment to
achieve pest control. Although pesticides receive most of the
publicity worldwide, biological and cultural controls actually are
the dominant methods of pest control. Even in the United States
where pesticide use is extremely heavy (about 500 million kg/year),
biological controls are the dominant techniques used for pest
control (19). For example, nearly all crops planted in the U.S.
have some degree of host plant resistance bred into them to control
plant pathogens (Kelman, A., University of Wisconsin, personal
communication, 1980). This undoubtedly accounts for the fact that
only 1% of the U.S. crop acreage is treated with fungicides (13).
Some acreage receives both herbicide and mechanical weed control.
      To control weeds, approximately 90% of U.S. agricultural
acreage is treated with nonchemical, mechanical weed controls, such
as mechanical cultivation and rotary hoes (15), whereas only about
25% receives treatment with herbicides (13).
      Although natural parasite and predator controls are extremely
helpful in controlling pest insects, their action is not included
in this assessment because they are not manipulated, but rather
function as a part of natural ecosystems. Manipulated insect
biological and cultural controls, however, provide protection on
nearly 10% of the U.S. agricultural land (33, 34). Insecticides
are applied on about a similar percentage of the agricultural land
(13). Nonchemical biological and cultural controls that dominate
pest control throughout the world are discussed below.

Host Plant Resistance. Farmers from the beginning of agriculture,
about 10,000 years ago, have relied on plant breeding to increase a
crop plant's resistance to common pests. At first by selecting
from seeds of the healthiest and most productive individual plants
for planting next year's crop, the early farmer incorporated some
resistant genes in his crop plants. Over time, more scientific
methods have enabled plant breeders to speed the process, and this
improved a plant's capacity to resist the attack of plant pathogens
and pest insects and also to successfully compete with weeds. New
developments in genetic engineering hold promise to further speed
up the process of plant breeding as well as enabling beneficial
genetic material obtained from one plant species to be incorporated
into another.

In addition, naturally growing plants resist plant pathogen
and insect attack because resistance develops over time via natural
selection *(35)*. Also, most natural and crop plants have, as a part
of their basic physical and chemical makeup, a wide array of
mechanisms that help them resist pest attack. These include
chemical toxicants, repellents, altered plant nutrients, hairiness,
thorns, and diverse combinations of these *(35)*.

Crop Rotations and Diversification. For thousands of years farmers
have known that planting their crops in a new location about every
2 years helped reduce insect, disease, and weed problems. Indeed,
crop rotations are effective in reducing many pest problems and are
often highly cost effective *(15, 16)*. Unfortunately for many
crops, the trend has been toward abandonment of rotations and
increased monocultures. Where rotations are not practiced, certain
pests tend to multiply as the crops are cultured on the same land
year after year *(23)*. As a result, the density of pest populations
increases to levels that necessitate heavy pesticide applications.

A practice somewhat related to crop rotation is crop
diversification or polyculture *(36)*. This approach involves
planting selected combinations of crops, like corn and beans.
Insect and plant pathogen attacks are reduced because 1) natural
enemies of the pests are increased in the polyculture ecosystem
because the array of hosts for the natural enemies is increased, 2)
and the movement of pests from one host plant to another is
interrupted by the presence of a different host plant growing
nearby *(36)*. In this way overall pest damage is substantially
reduced.

Sanitation and Burning. Crop remains frequently harbor insect
pests and plant pathogens. Therefore, destroying crop remains
including fruits, before planting the next crop helps eliminate
residual insect pests and plant pathogens *(33)*. In part, early
season tillage helps accomplish this same goal by burying surviving
pests along with crop residues.

In a few circumstances, burning crop residues can accomplish
the same thing as burying crop residues. However, major
disadvantages are associated with the practice of burning crop
residues. In particular, essential nitrogen and valuable organic
matter are lost when crop residues are burned. The loss of these
vital crop nutrient resources will reduce crop productivity. At
the same time the burning of crop residues will add CO_2 to the
atmosphere, thus adding to the "greenhouse gases" and global
warming. Increased CO_2 in the atmosphere may alter the nutritional
make up of plants, making them, in some cases, more susceptible to
pest attack, whereas in other cases more resistant to pest attack
(Pimentel, D., in manuscript).

Tillage. Early farmers cleared the land of unwanted vegetation by
cutting and burning. This practice not only rid the crop area of
weedy vegetation, but the ashes that remained added some nutrients
to the soil. However, as mentioned (see #3), because nitrogen and
organic matter are lost with burning, this technique is not

advisable under most circumstances. In addition to burning, farmers tilled the soil just before planting their crop to rid the plot of any other weeds. This tended to give the crop a decided advantage by getting a head start before the weeds began to crowd them and diminish their growth. Another method that gives crop plants an advantage that is used today is to transplant young seedlings rather than place seeds in the newly tilled soil. Rice and cabbage growers use this technology.

Even with the advantage of being planted in tilled soil, all crops have to be protected from weed competition throughout the growing season. This is done by cultivating the soil at intervals with hoes or tractors. At present, in the United States more than 90% of all cropland is also tilled and cultivated for weed control (15), even though a large percentage of the land is also treated with herbicides.

Planting Time. Selecting the time to plant a crop that will give it the best chance to become established, gives the plant an advantage over weeds, insects, and plant pathogens (33). This relatively simple technique continues to be highly effective in controlling pests throughout the world. In the United States, for instance, planting time is relied on for control of the Hessian fly and boll weevil (10, 33, 37).

Crop Density. Planting crops at a sufficiently high density can help limit the damage inflicted by weeds, insects, and plant pathogens. Some control is provided because the invading pests from outside areas cannot easily overwhelm the dense planting compared with a sparse planting of the same crop. This was demonstrated in a field with collards (38). In this experiment, planting collards at a high density reduced pest insect populations about one-half compared with regular sparse plantings based on the number of insects per unit leaf surface area. This simple technique is being used with other crops. For instance, corn is now planted at twice the density per hectare than it was in 1950. Not only does this strategy help reduce pests, it makes more efficient use of the land, machinery, labor, and other inputs.

Fertilizer and Nutrient Management. Insufficient attention has been given to the possible benefits of managing fertilizer nutrients to assist in pest control. For example, the appropriate timing of fertilizer applications can stimulate the vigorous growth of plants, which enables the crop to overcome some weed problems. However, the use of high levels of nitrogen and other fertilizer nutrients has been found to increase the outbreak of some insects and plant pathogens because the crops are made more nutritious for the pest populations (39). For instance, high nitrogen levels in corn and other crops are reported to increase the outbreaks of certain insects and plant pathogens (26). Therefore, a careful analysis of both the plant and its pest must be done prior to using fertilizers to assist in pest control.

Water Management. For some crops water management directly and indirectly helps control weeds, insects, and plant pathogens. With

rice production, for instance, flooding of paddies helps control
weeds and insects by drowning and burying the pests *(40-42)*.
Appropriate irrigation water applications tailored to the
specific crops and major pests helps reduce plant pathogens and the
attack of microbes on some insects *(33)*. For example, the use of
drip irrigation reduces plant pathogens in contrast to the use of
sprinkle irrigation that tends to wet the upper vegetation, making
it more favorable for plant pathogens. However, with some insect
pests like aphids that feed on crops, wetting the vegetation
stimulates outbreaks of fungal pathogens in the aphid population,
thereby helping control the aphid.

Biological and Natural Controls. Parasites and predators are
effective in limiting the numbers of pest insects and plant
pathogens both in nature and for crops *(35)*. This basic fact led
to the development of biological controls. For example, the
vedalia beetle, which was introduced for control of cottony cushion
scale on citrus in California, has provided continuous effective
control of this pest for many decades. Worldwide only
approximately 1% of the pests have been effectively controlled by
introduced biological control agents *(43)*.

However, not all natural enemies are fully effective. For
example, the gypsy moth has approximately 100 parasites and
predators attacking it but the pest reaches outbreak levels
periodically *(35)*. Nearly 40 biological control agents were
introduced from Europe and Asia to control the moth and 11 of these
became established *(44)*. Yet not one of the 11 biocontrol agents
is providing fully effective control, although each contributes to
some limitation of this pest.

More can be done to control pests with biological control,
especially through the improved methods of selecting biological
control agents *(45)*. This technology takes advantage of the new
association between the biocontrol agent and pest. In particular,
because 60% to 80% of the pests in crops are native species that
move from feeding on natural vegetation, this technology of using
new associations now makes it possible to use biological control in
agriculture, which was not possible with previous biocontrol
technology.

Genetic Control. Some insect pests have been successfully
controlled by releasing sterile insect males in sufficient quantity
so that the pest population cannot reproduce. This has proven
particularly effective in the control of the screwworm fly, a major
pest of cattle *(33)*. Genetic engineers may be able to provide
other genetic techniques that will enhance the control of crop
pests *(34)*.

Behavioral and Hormonal Chemicals. Sex pheromones, which attract
pests to traps, are used effectively to control some insect pests,
like the grape berry moth *(46)* and cabbage looper. With other
insect pests, sex pheromones have been effectively used to monitor
the size of pest insect populations to determine when pesticide
treatments should be made.

Basically growth hormones alter the normal growth of some insect species. The juvenile growth hormone worked effectively to kill some insects in the laboratory, but when applied in the field for pest control, the hormone was not effective. Its problems centered on its high cost, rapid rate of breakdown after application, and its broad spectrum effects. For example, the hormone was found to kill beneficial species as well as pest species, much like insecticides. Thus far, it has not proven to be a useful technology for pest control *(42)*.

Cosmetic Standards. Over the last two decades, the U.S. Food and Drug Administration (FDA) has been lowering the tolerance levels for insects and insect parts allowed in and on fresh and processed foods *(14)*. Concurrently consumers have sought "more perfect," pest-free produce. To achieve this, farmers have increased the quantities of pesticide they applied to crops. Although the presence of small amounts of insect parts in such products as catsup and apple sauce, or blemishes on oranges pose no health risk, these stringent standards have stood for many years. However, the American consumer now seems ready to accept some reduction in cosmetic standards, provided pesticide use is diminished *(47)*. Their concern about pesticide use is confirmed by the growing popularity of organic food stores and supermarkets that guarantee pesticide-free produce *(48)*. Also, the "Big Green" initiative in California, although it didn't pass, signals that consumers are alarmed about pesticide use and are willing to take political action to make their views known.

Economics of Pest Control

Each year the use of pesticides in U.S. agriculture costs the nation about $4.1 billion *(15)*. This cost includes the cost of the chemical plus that of application. Approximately $16 billion worth of crops is saved through the application of pesticides. Thus, for every dollar invested in pesticides about $4 is returned in protected crops.

Most biological and cultural pest controls return greater profits than pesticides. For example, biological pest controls are reported to return from $30 to $300 per dollar invested in control *(16)*. Various cultural controls like host plant resistance, crop rotations, and tillage, also return $30 to $300 per dollar invested in pest control *(16)*.

To date, insufficient attention has been given to the economics of pest control. Most reports dealing with pest control include no data on the economics of the methods used. Complete and accurate information about the economics of pest control is needed to guide future research projects and advance the technologies of pest control.

Environmental and Public Health Problems

Having pesticides as a powerful weapon against a wide array of pests that diminish the yields of food and fiber crops is and will continue to be a valuable asset to agricultural production. Yet

associated with this benefit are the risks that need to be
considered and balanced against pesticide use.

Efforts to protect U.S. public health from pesticide exposure
is a relatively recent event. For example, in the 1930s and 1940s
some in the U.S. Congress were extremely defensive of the use of
pesticides by farmers and ignored possible risks. Representative
Clarence Cannon (D, Mo.), chair of the House Subcommittee on
Agricultural Appropriations, reported that an apple grower
"believed" that "lead arsenate on apples never harmed a man, woman,
or child" *(49)*. Cannon's perspective of pesticides was that "If
it don't kill you immediately it isn't dangerous" *(49)*. Attention
to the extent and seriousness of risks has been slow in coming
throughout the world.

Available records indicate that worldwide each year, there are
about 1,000,000 accidental human poisonings and about 20,000 human
deaths *(50)*. In the U.S. there are 20,000 reported human pesticide
poisonings and about 35 reported fatalities each year (Blondell,
J., U.S. Environmental Protection Agency, personal communication,
1989). The United States has fewer recorded pesticide poisonings
per unit weight of applied pesticide than in other countries. For
instance, the U.S. has only about 1/50th the number of world
poisonings but uses about one-fifth of all the pesticide used in
the world. Thus, it appears that the U.S. program to regulate the
use of pesticides is more effective than in most parts of the
world.

In addition to poisoning humans, pesticides affect
agricultural ecosystems and spread beyond into surrounding
terrestrial and aquatic ecosystems. As a result, detrimental
environmental effects follow pesticide use in the United States.
Some of these are delineated below:

1) A large number of domestic animals are poisoned each year
by pesticides and must be destroyed. Additionally, significant
amounts of meat and milk are contaminated with pesticides and must
be removed from the market place *(51)*. The yearly cost of these
losses is estimated to be at least $30 million.

2) When pesticides are applied to crops, many natural enemies
that help control pests are destroyed *(37)*. This causes pest
outbreaks that subsequently are controlled with additional
pesticide applications. The control of such pest outbreaks is
estimated to cost at least $520 million each year.

3) Since the mid 1940s, pest populations have been developing
resistance to synthetic pesticides. To overcome this resistance,
additional pesticide treatments and more costly controls have been
required to achieve desired levels of pest control. This costs
farmers about $1 billion each year (Pimentel, D., in manuscript).

4) As pesticides are applied, large numbers of honey bees and
wild bees are poisoned resulting in not only a diminished honey
crop, but perhaps more important, reduced crop pollination that is
vital to agricultural production *(51)*. The estimated yearly cost
of reduced pollination and reduced honey production is about $230
million (Pimentel, D., in manuscript).

5) Some pesticides, especially when applied by aircraft, drift
into adjacent agricultural lands where they may damage crops. This
type of destruction is estimated to cost at least $900 million

annually in crops and forest resources (Pimentel, D., in manuscript).

6) A conservative estimate of fishery and wildlife losses amounts to at least $24 million per year (Pimentel, D., in manuscript).

7) The government program, which attempts to regulate and limit pesticide pollution, costs at least $200 million each year in administrative costs (Pimentel, D., in manuscript).

8) About $1.3 billion is projected to be spent monitoring pesticides in wells and groundwater resources if an effective program were initiated (Pimentel, D., in manuscript).

The above analysis is somewhat oversimplified and is considered an incomplete assessment of the existing environmental problems caused by pesticides. Again, it must be emphasized that there is no completely satisfactory way to summarize all of the environmental and social costs in terms of dollars. For example, it is impossible, if not unethical to place a monetary value on human lives either lost, diseased, or disabled because of pesticide use. It is equally difficult to place a monetary value on total wildlife losses. Good health, and indeed life itself have no price tag.

Clearly, the $8 billion attributed to environmental and social costs represents only a small portion of the actual costs. A more complete accounting of the indirect costs also should include costs like: the unrecorded losses of fish, wildlife, crops, and trees; losses resulting from the destruction of soil invertebrates, microflora, and microfauna; true costs of human poisonings; chronic health problems like cancer; groundwater contamination; and contamination of the food we eat *(51)*. If the full environmental and social costs could be more accurately assessed, the total yearly cost is estimated to be approximately $8 billion; if the $1.3 billion for monitoring pesticides in wells and groundwater is included.

Conclusion

From this analysis it is clear that in addition to their benefits, the use of pesticides in food production not only causes serious public health problems but also considerable damage to vital agricultural and natural ecosystems in the United States and world. A conservative estimate suggests that the environmental and social costs of pesticide use in the United States total about $4 billion each year. Worldwide the yearly environmental and public health costs are probably at least $100 billion. This is several times the $18 billion/yr spent on pesticides in the world.

This analysis has demonstrated that pesticide use in the world could be reduced by approximately 50% without any reduction in crop yields (in some cases increased yields) or the food supply. This effort would require applying pesticides only-when-necessary plus using various combinations of the nonchemical control alternatives currently available *(34)*. Although food production costs might increase slightly (0.5% to 1%), the added costs would be more than offset by the positive benefits to public health and the environment *(15)*.

Future studies must focus on those specific agricultural technologies that have contributed to the increased use of pesticides during the past 40 years, and why crop losses to pests continue to increase. Research needs not only to identify the detrimental technologies, but, more important, develop ecologically sound practices that farmers can use as profitable substitutes *(15)*.

All our natural resources must be used carefully to maximize their contributions, not only to sustain the current productivity of world agriculture, but to be able to augment its yields. Both our vast agricultural system and the broader ecosystem must receive greater protection than ever before from all pollutants including pesticides. Certainly this is possible to achieve, if humans work together for the good of society.

If the world is concerned about pesticides contaminating their food and environment, then are the small economic costs necessary to reduce pesticide use worth denying the ecological and public health benefits? There is need for governments to investigate the ecology, economics, and ethics of pesticide reduction in agriculture. Careful assessments of the benefits and risks of both pesticides and the nonchemical alternatives will have to be evaluated in order to protect public health, society, food supply, and the environment, now and in the future. Once this information is gathered, government officials and the public can work cooperatively to ensure adequate, safe food supplies.

Literature Cited

1. *World Population Data Sheet*; Population Reference Bureau: Washington, DC, 1990.
2. Population Crisis Committee; Washington, DC, 1 page memo.
3. Kates, R. W.; Chen, R. S.; Downing, T. E.; Kasperson, J. X.; Messer, E.; Millman, S. R. *The Hunger Report: Update 1989*; Alan Shawn Feinstein World Hunger Program, Brown University: Providence, R.I., 1989.
4. Stephenson, L. S.; Latham, M. C.; Kurz, K. M.; Kinoti, S. N.; Brigham, H. *Am. J. Trop. Med. Hyg.* **1989**, *41*, 78-87.
5. Brown, L. R.; Durning, A.; Flavin, C.; French, H.; Jacobson, J.; Lowe, M.; Postel, S.; Renner, M.; Starke, L.; Young, J. *State of the World*; Worldwatch Institute: Washington, DC, 1990.
6. Pimentel, D.; Hall, C. W. Eds.; *Food and Natural Resources*; Academic Press: San Diego, 1989.
7. Buringh, P. In *Food and Natural Resources*; Pimentel, D., Hall, C. W., Eds.; Academic Press: San Diego, CA, 1989; pp. 69-83.
8. Pimentel, D.; Wen, D., Eigenbrode, S.; Lang, H.; Emerson, D.; Karasik, M. *Oikos* **1986**, *46*, 404-412.
9. Lal, R. In *World Soil Erosion and Conservation*; Pimentel, D., Ed.; Cambridge University Press: Cambridge, UK, 1991.
10. Pimentel, D. In *Biotechnology and Sustainable Agriculture: Policy Alternatives*; Fessenden MacDonald, J., Ed.; National Agricultural Biotechnology Council: Boyce Thompson Institute, Ithaca, NY, 1989; pp. 69-74.
11. Helsel, Z. R. In *Energy in World Agriculture*; Stout, B. A., Ed.; Elsevier: New York, NY, 1987; pp. 179-195.

12. Parpia, H. A. B. Food loss prevention: a means of socioeconomic transformation; Presentation at the 16th Intl. Conf. on the Unity of the Sciences.
13. Pimentel, D.; Levitan, L. *Bioscience* **1986**, *36*, 86-91.
14. Pimentel, D.; Terhune, E. C.; Dritschilo, W.; Gallahan, D.; Kinner, N.; Nafus, D.; Peterson, R.; Zareh, N.; Misiti, J.; Haber-Schaim, O. *BioScience* **1977**, *27*, 178-185.
15. Pimentel, D.; McLaughlin, L.; Zepp, A.; Lakitan, B.; Kraus, T.; Kleinman, P.; Vancini, F.; Roach, W. J.; Graap, E.; Keeton, W. S.; Selig, G. In *Handbook of Pest Management in Agriculture*; Pimentel, D., Ed.; CRC Press: Boca Raton, FL, 1991, pp. 679-718.
16. Pimentel, D. In *Ecological Theory and Integrated Pest Management Practice*; Kogan, M., Ed.; John Wiley & Sons: New York, NY, 1986; pp. 299-319.
17. Arrington, L. G. *World Survey of Pest Control Products*; US Department of Commerce; Washington, DC: US Government Printing Office, 1956.
18. *Statistical Abstract of the United States 1970*; US Department of Commerce; US Bureau of the Census: Washington, DC, 1971.
19. *Statistical Abstract of the United States 1990*; US Department of Commerce, US Bureau of the Census: Washington, DC, 1990.
20. *Agricultural Statistics 1989*; US Department of Agriculture: Washington, DC, 1989.
21. Pimentel, D.; Wen, D. In *Agroecology*; Carroll, C. R.; Vandermeer, J. H.; Rosset, P. M., Eds.; McGraw Hill: New York, NY, 1990; pp. 147-164.
22. Pimentel, D. *Ann. Entomol. Soc. Am.* **1961**, *54*, 76-86.
23. Pimentel, D.; Shoemaker, C.; LaDue, E. L.; Rovinsky, R. B.; Russell, N. P. *Alternatives for Reducing Insecticides on Cotton and Corn: Economic and Environmental Impact*; Environ. Res. Lab., Off. Res. Develop., EPA: Athens, GA, 1979.
24. Van den Bosch, R.; Messenger, P. S. *Biological Control*; Intext Educational Pub.: New York, NY, 1973.
25. Roush, R. T.; McKenzie, J. A. *Annu Rev. Entomol.* **1987**, *32*, 361-380.
26. Oka, I. N.; Pimentel, D. *Science* **1976**, *193*, 239-240.
27. Pimentel, D. *Crop Protect.* **1982**, *1*, 5-26.
28. ICAITI. *An Environmental and Economic Study of the Consequences of Pesticide Use in Central American Cotton Production*; Final Report, Central American Research Institute for Industry, United Nations Environment Programme: Guatemala, 1977.
29. Akesson, N. B.; Yates, W. E. In *Chemical and Biological Controls in Forestry*; Garner, W. Y.; Harvey, J., Eds.; Am. Chem. Soc. Ser. 238: Washington, DC, 1984; pp. 95-115.
30. Mazariegos, F. *UNEP Industry and Environment 1985*, July/August/September, pp. 5-8.
31. Dale, J. E. *Proc. South. Weed Sci. Soc.* **1978**, *31*, 332.
32. Dale, J. *Weeds Today* **1980**, *11(2)*, 3-4.
33. *Restoring the Quality of the Environment*; President's Science Advisory Council: Washington, DC, 1965.
34. Pimentel, D.; Hunter, M. S.; LaGro, J. A.; Efroymson, R. A.; Landers, J. C.; Mervis, F. T.; McCarthy, C. A.; Boyd, A. E. *BioScience* **1989**, *39*, 606-614.
35. Pimentel, D. *Oikos* **1988**, *53*, 289-302.

36. Cromartie, W. J.   In *Handbook of Pest Management in Agriculture*; Pimentel, D., Ed.; CRC Press: Boca Raton, FL, 1991, Vol. 1; pp. 183-216.
37. *Pest Management Strategies. Working Papers*; Office of Technology Assessment, US Government Printing Office: Washington, DC, 1979; Vol. II, pp. 1-169.
38. Pimentel, D. *Ann. Entomol. Soc. Amer.* **1961,** *54*, 61-69.
39. Painter, R. H. *Insect Resistance in Crops*; The University Press of Kansas: Lawrence, KS, 1951.
40. *Integrated Pest Management for Rice*; Div. Agr. Sci. Publ. 3280; University of California: Berkeley, CA, 1983.
41. Moody, K.   In *Handbook of Pest Management in Agriculture*; Pimentel, D., Ed.; CRC Press: Boca Raton, FL, 1991, Vol. 3; pp. 301-328.
42. National Academy of Sciences. *Alternative Agriculture*; National Academy Press: Washington, DC, 1989.
43. Hokkanen, H. M. T.; Pimentel, D. *Canad. Entomol.* **1989,** *121*, 829-840.
44. Dowden, P. B. *Parasites and Predators of Forest Insects Liberated in the United States through 1960*; U.S. Dep. Agr., *Agr. Handbk.* 226.
45. Pimentel, D.; Hokkanen, H.   In *Potential for Biological Control of Dendroctonus and Ips Bark Beetles*; Kulhavy, E. L.; Miller, M. C., Eds.; Center for Applied Studies, School of Forestry, Stephen F. Austin State University: Nacogdoches, Texas, 1989.
46. Dennehy, T. J.; Hoffman, C. J.; Nyrop, J. P.; Saunders, M. C. In *Monitoring and Integrated Management of Arthropod Pests of Small Fruit Crops*, Intercept: London, 1990; pp. 261-282.
47. Healy, M. *USA Today*, **1989,** *March 20*; pp. 6.
48. Hammit, J. K. *Estimating Consumer Willingness to Pay to Reduce Food-Borne Risk*; Rand Corporation: Santa Monica, CA, 1986.
49. Bosso, C. J. *Pesticides and Politics: The Life Cycle of a Public Issue*; University of Pittsburgh Press: Pittsburgh, PA, 1987.
50. *Public Health Impact of Pesticides Used in Agriculture*; Report of a WHO/UNEP Working Group; World Health Organization: Geneva, Switzerland, United Nations Environment Programme: Nairobi, Kenya.
51. Blume, E. *Nutr. Act. News Let.* **1987,** *Oct.,* 8-9.

RECEIVED September 4, 1991

Chapter 16

Energy for Food Production and Processing

Carl W. Hall

Engineering Information Services, Arlington, VA 22207–1033

About 16% of the U. S. commercial energy use is in agriculture
for food production and processing. The processing of food
requires nearly twice as much energy as for production. As commercial energy has replaced animal power and human effort in
farming and has helped provide fertilizer and chemicals for plant
production, production has increased by two orders of magnitude
over the past 100 years. There has been a rapid shift of processing off-the-farm to commercial enterprises. The possibilities of
using the products of agriculture to meet energy needs particularly
by substituting biomass products for commercial energy are discussed.

Farming, the production side of food, is one of the few enterprises that
provides a way of capturing the solar energy through photosynthesis, thus
producing a product with more energy than provided by known inputs.
The total chemical input of energy in terms of nutrients and human
effort is enhanced by utilizing solar energy and incorporating that energy
in the product. After the food is produced, energy is added for the purpose of harvesting, handling, storage, processing, preserving, merchandis-
ing, and cooking. Most of the energy for these activities comes from
human effort, fossil fuel, and electricity rather than directly from the solar
source.

Most of the research on energy conservation, energy alternatives, and
energy from agriculture and forestry was done in the seventies, with the
eighties being a decade in which there was a major lack of government
concern. Thus, most of the references on the subject go back to the earlier years.

0097–6156/92/0483–0324$06.00/0

Energy Availability

Energy, in terms of kilocalories (kcal) [or often stated in other units, i. e., kilojoules (kJ) or British thermal units (Btu)] provides a basis for comparing inputs and outputs in food production and processing. The energy in fuel is quite often expressed in terms of kJ or Btu; the energy in food is usually expressed in terms of kcal. The thermal efficiency is defined as the output divided by input, multiplied by 100 to put in percent. However, in comparing and using values for energy and efficiency, one must be aware of the wide difference in the economic value of the kcal or Btu. Some energy forms are readily available for the intended use, so are quite valuable, economically; whereas other energy forms require considerable effort or work to put into a usable form. We refer to these relationships as the "availability" of energy. The energy in shale for example is quite plentiful, but requires considerable input of energy to put the energy in the form of a liquid fuel for automotive engines; the energy in electricity is readily available for lighting and heating and driving motors, but not for food.

Evolution of Farming

Farming was formerly a nomadic enterprise in which people roamed the land to find soil and water to grow food. Little external inputs were provided, except that considerable manual work was required. People had little time to do anything else except to raise and prepare and store their food. One reads of the early practice by the American Indians to put a fish with seeds as they were planted to increase the yield through fertilization. After the crops were grown their products were eaten, stored, or spoiled. Little energy was exerted in processing the grains, fruits, vegetables, nuts as these were produced. The major input to produce the crop was solar energy, and the major labor was to plant the seed, cultivate the crops, and harvest the produce. Fish was obtained from streams, lakes, and oceans. Meat was obtained by hunting wild animals. Eventually these animals were domesticated and raised for meat, milk, fiber, and used as beast of burden. Crops were then raised specifically to provide feed for animals, referred to as livestock. The word 'feed' is used to represent 'food' for livestock. As the crops were fed to livestock some energy of the crop was lost, some of which was gained by the livestock in a different form.

As farming evolved as an enterprise, along with the industrial revolution, when it was necessary to have workers released from farming to sustain the industrial revolution, energy external to farming other than solar energy, called cultural energy, was used to increase production of crops and animals. The commercial or cultural energy was used both to increase the production and productivity of feed and food. Sixty million acres of land were released for potential production of food when 25 million horses were replaced by 5 million tractors using fossil fuel (*1*). The role of solar energy was not decreased, its function remained the same. The use of commercial or cultural energy primarily from fossil fuels for fertilizer, weed control, and substitution for labor increased dramatically. The dramatic increase in the use of commercial energy greatly increased yields while reducing labor. The information that follows describes these relationships.

Fossil Fuels

Natural gas, oil and coal are fossil fuels that were derived from biological plants and animals formerly produced from solar energy. The biological materials were subjected to appropriate pressure, temperature, and moisture over thousands or millions of years to produce fossil fuels-gas, oil, and coal or related materials, with gas being produced in the shortest time and coal over the longest time. Some writers do not include natural gas as a fossil fuel because it can be quite young in age as compared to coal, although most oil and coal deposits include natural gas. A relatively small amount of energy is required to convert these fossil energy sources to useful fuel as compared to converting those original biological products directly to one of the fuels in use today. The biological plants are primarily carbohydrate and lignocellulose materials that are converted to hydrocarbons to make fuel. The procedure in manufacturing to convert carbohydrate and lignocellulose materials to hydrocarbons is to duplicate the thousands of years used by nature with a rapid conversion process, a process that requires energy input. Until the reserves of fossil fuels become depleted, or are less available, or are much more costly to utilize, so that the cost of fuels becomes considerably higher than at present (1991), the raising of crops and converting these crops to replace fossil fuel will not be economically competitive. Ethanol, an alcohol from grains, makes up 10 percent of the volume of gasoline motor fuels available in some regions of the U. S. These fuel mixtures operate innocuously, provide an additional market for grain, and reduce certain pollutants. Each gallon of ethanol requires 10.5 kg (23 lb) of corn and costs $1.93 per gal to produce, to which must be added the cost of subsidies of about 60 cents per gallon (2). The change in our economy from a fossil fuel base to a biological fuel base will not occur as a step function, but will happen gradually. Readily available and easily converted biological products, usually as byproducts of existing operations, are presently economical sources of energy, particularly for heating operations. These biological products also provide a raw material for fermentation processes to provide liquid fuel and for decomposition to provide methane gas as an equivalent or replacement to natural gas.

Some people claim that a large source of abiotic natural gas is trapped in the earth's crust probably much deeper than conventional sources, untapped to date. The conjecture is that the mass that became the earth was surrounded by methane and as the earth formed a large quantity of methane was incorporated.

Food From Lignocellulosic Crops

Crops produced for human consumption cannot be used entirely for food. Thus, only a portion of the energy in a cereal grain plant is for food. The remainder is a lignocellulosic material that is not digestible by humans without further treatment. Recent studies on nutrition and diet confirm the value of "roughage" or fiber in the diet for good health, not necessarily on the basis of energy. The amount of energy in leafy vegetables, for example, is low as compared to other foods, but leafy vegetables are extremely valuable to the individual's health not only as a roughage but as a source of vitamins and minerals. Similarly, although controversy continues regarding the details and mechanisms, it is generally agreed that plant fats are low in saturated fats and do not contain cholesterol, providing a better diet. Animal fats are high in saturated fats and contain cholesterol, which if eaten in excess is undesirable. The energy in two sources of food could be the same in terms of kilocalories but that value could be misleading in terms of dietary contents.

Some of the components of crop production are more appropriate for animal feed than human food. The animal can serve as being a converter of less available (as a food) crop components, like stems, branches, leaves, and husks, for feed to more available components for food. The ruminant animal has an unique role in this process. Ruminant animals such as cows, sheep, and goats are excellent converters of cellulosic feed materials to milk, meat, and fiber. The notion that the world's population should live on plants exclusive of animal energy for more efficient utilization of crop energy overlooks the important role that animals play in converting grass and forages, and cellulosic plants to food. The balance or ratio of plant to animal calories in human nutrition, and the relation of fat and cholesterol content is a difficult issue without definitive answers, although it is generally agreed that many people in the U. S. consume too much animal fat and cholesterol in their diet. Presently, about 40% of the energy in the diet is supplied from animal sources and it is variously suggested that this figure should be 20 to 30%.

Reducing Losses

A method of increasing the availability of food is to prevent losses of crops and their products and of animal products. Losses of crops vary considerably depending on the crop, season, weather and handling but is estimated to be 35 to 40% for fruits and vegetables, 25 to 30% for forage crops, and 10 to 15% for cereal grains and beans. The losses for livestock meat and milk before consumption range from 5 to 25%. Although it might seem appropriate to stop all losses and wastes in the food system, it is not economical to do so. When it costs more, or requires more energy, to prevent a loss than the value of the product saved, there is little incentive for preventing a loss. From an ethical viewpoint of preventing starvation, it is desirable to use what might be considered losses here to meet a nutrition need elsewhere in the world, but the cost and energy of getting the food to the consumer have to be considered.

Canning, drying, freezing and fermenting formerly were carried out as farm enterprises requiring considerable labor and utilizing available natural resources, such as wood, rather than fossil fuels for heating for cooking. The drudgery and difficult tasks began to be replaced by using natural gas, manufactured gas, and electricity, most of which was produced from fossil fuels-natural gas, oil, and coal.

Energy for Food

This chapter emphasizes the energy use to provide food. That energy can be considered on the basis of production and processing of food. It is not easy to determine the energy needs. The primary needs are easiest to obtain, e. g., the amount of energy in the fuel for an engine. The secondary energy, such as the amount of energy to manufacture an engine, or the tertiary energy, the amount of energy in training and educating the people who build the engine, are difficult to apportion to a particular operation. Writers often don't make clear how the energy figures they are using have been obtained.

In the early years when crops and animals were produced on the farm, and principally consumed on the farm, the production of food and fiber was nearly synonymous with agriculture. In 1900, 40% of the U. S. population lived on the land as compared with 2% in 1990. Today, farming is considered as the production aspect and most off-farm activities prepare the product for food for others to consume and are the processing aspects. Many foods are produced through the feed route by feeding livestock to supply meat for consumption. Today the term agriculture encompasses production and processing as before but the location, specialization and magnitude of the activities are different. The number of people involved in the total enterprise of the food system from planting the seed to providing the food to the consumer is approximately the same as 50 years ago.

Energy for Crop Production

As we moved away from natural and manual inputs to produce crops, other inputs of machinery, fertilizer, pesticides, herbicides and fuel, many of a chemical nature, commercial or cultural energy was used as a replacement. The commercial or cultural energy has come primarily from a fossil fuel base. The approximate amount of energy to provide for these inputs is given in Table I.

Table I. Energy to Provide Inputs to Food Production (*3*)

To Provide	Requires
1 kg herbicide	57,000 kilocalories
1 kg insecticide	44,000 kilocalories
1 kg seed	25,000 kilocalories
1 kg fungicide	22,000 kilocalories
1 kg equipment	21,000 kilocalories
1 kg nitrogen fertilizer	14,700 kilocalories
1 liter of fuel	10,000 kilocalories
1 kg phosphorous fertilizer	3,000 kilocalories
1 kg potassium fertilizer	1,600 kilocalories
1 kg irrigation water	2 kilocalories
1 kg freezing food	7,980 kilocalories
1 kg canned food, heat processing	6,560 kilocalories
1 kg can capacity (for canning)	2,210 kilocalories
1 kg sweet corn, heat processing	575 kilocalories
1 kg frozen food maintenance, monthly	265 kilocalories

$$1kg = 2.205 \text{ lb}$$
$$1Cal = 1kcal = 4.1855J$$
$$1Btu = 1.055kJ$$
$$1Btu/lb = 2.326kJ/kg$$

The use of nitrogen is one of the major methods for increasing production. As nitrogen is increased, production increases until some other limiting factor such as water, seed capability, or lack of another fertilizer nutrient is encountered. As an example, for corn in general nitrogen is used to increase production as represented by energy in kilocalories. For 100 lb/A of nitrogen, will get 1.5 kcal per kcal input; 200 lb/A, 2.5; and 300 lb/A, a decrease to 2.0. (1 lb/A = 1.1 kg/ha) Many other variables are involved such as water, weather, soil, availability of other elements and pests.

Another method of comparison of energy use for production of food is the fossil energy used per unit of protein produced. In intensive livestock operations, such as egg production and animal feed lot operations, 25,000-50,000 kcal of energy are required to produce 1 kg of protein. In contrast, for wheat, rice, potato, and peanut production in the U. S. A., 3,000-10,000 kcal are required to produce 1 kg of protein. Rice production in southeast Asia requires 250-1000 kcal of fossil fuel to produce 1 kg of protein (*3*). In developed countries like the U. S. commercial energy requirements are generally the largest for providing fertilizer followed by fuel for field operations, irrigation, drying, and pesticides. The amount of commercial energy, kcal, to produce 1 kcal of food energy is:

for feedlot beef production, 10-20; grass fed beef, 3-5; modern milking, 1-1.5; corn intensive, 0.3-0.5; and rice, intensive, 0.12-0.2 (7).

Productivity

Productivity is a term used to relate output divided by input, a measure of efficiency, often without regard to the quality factors involved. The efficiency of production of energy relating energy output to the energy input does not consider the increased food value of the energy in the protein output, for example. In food production one needs to consider productivity in terms of both the land and the labor for crops and for livestock (land would not usually be included for confined livestock). Thus, we talk of productivity in terms of weight of crop grown per acre (or hectare) and the weight of crop produced per hour of labor. Or for animal productivity, we consider the milk produced per animal usually on an annual basis and the milk produced per hour of work.

Food productivity and hence food production has increased by one or two orders of magnitude since the domestication of plants and animals, most of which has taken place in the last 100 yr. Whereas 15 eggs per year per hen were produced previously, today one laying hen will average 220 eggs per year. Milk production was 600 pounds per year and now averages 9000 pounds per year. Plant productivity increases are similar. Whereas 15-20 bushels per acre of wheat were obtained, yields of 100 bushels per acre are now common. One bushel (60 lb/bu) per acre of wheat is equivalent to 67 kg per hectare (1.0 kg/ha equals 0.89 lb/a). Corn (56 lb/bu) yields of 150 bushels per acre are now obtained compared to 25 bushels per acre before hybrid varieties were developed. Many of the new varieties increased the capability to provide higher yields with appropriate inputs. Commercial energy or cultural energy has been used to replace the oxen, horses and mules (and humans) and to provide the fertilizer nutrients to increase growth and the insecticides and herbicides to protect the plants and products. As an example, the addition of nitrogen, or other fertilizer component, such as phosphorus and potassium, provides the possibility of increasing the crop production on the same area of land. As nitrogen is increased, water could well become a limiting factor, and until additional water is provided there will not be an increase in yield with additional nitrogen. One has to determine whether the addition of water is cost effective based on cost of providing water and the value of product, while considering other factors such as environmental impacts, effect on the land, drainage, and water quality. Overall in the U. S., it has been found that we've reached the economically practical limit for the addition of nitrogen to increase the yield of cereal grains at this time. Areas need to be selected with care to improve productivity by increased use of nitrogen.

Labor productivity is increased by using better working methods, equipment to magnify the efforts of humans, and power units to operate larger devices. Again there is an economical limit to the size of power unit, as the cost could become prohibitive for a larger power unit and associated equipment; and a large power unit and associated equipment could damage the soil by compaction, thus reducing productivity. And to justify the increased investments for larger equipment there is also a trend to go to larger operations, such as more land and larger herds and flocks.

Energy for Food Processing

Nearly twice as much commercial energy is used for processing than for production of food. About 4.8% of the total U. S. energy consumption is used for processing crops and animals into food (1976), as compared to 2.9% for production of that food (Table II).

Table II. Approximate U. S. Energy Utilization for Food (*4*)

Commercial Energy Use	Percentage
For farm production	2.9
For processing, off the farm	4.8
For in-home preparation	4.3
For out-of-the-home preparation	2.8
For wholesale trade	0.5
For retail trade	0.8
Total	16.1

The ten leading energy consumers in the food industry use about one-half of the energy of the total food processing industry. About 50% of the end use energy is from natural gas, 15% is from petroleum, and 15% is from from purchased electricity. Some of the electricity is produced from natural gas and petroleum so the source use would be higher for gas and petroleum. There have been improvements in efficiencies in most of these industries but the relationships of industries still hold.

The ten leading food industries in end use of energy, percent, are listed in Table III (*5, 6*) :

Food industries have inaugurated many programs to decrease water usage and commercial energy utilization. Byproducts are now being used extensively to supply heat, a major need in the processing industries. These byproducts are biological, are already collected at the site of use, may have to be dried, but can replace coal, petroleum, and gas, and in some cases is used to produce electricity for the processing operations and space heating.

Table III. End Use of Energy by
Ten Leading Food Industries, Percent (5,6)

Food Industry	BTU, trillion	Natural Gas	Electricity	Oil	Coal
Meat packing	99.3	46	31	14	9
Prepared animal foods	86.5	51	38	10	21
Wet corn milling	83.7	43	14	7	36
Fluid milk	78.5	33	47	17	3
Beet sugar	76.6	65	1	5	25
Malt beverages	74.5	38	37	18	7
Bread and related prod	68.6	34	28	38	0
Frozen fruits and vegetables	62.2	41	50	5	4
Soybean oil	56.4	47	28	9	16
Canned fruits and vegetables	52.5	66	16	15	3

Conversion relationships: 1 Btu = 1.055 kJ = 0.2520 kcal

Energy for the Food System

Early in the century the amount of energy output in the form of food was about equal to the commercial energy input to the crop and livestock. That was before electricity, natural gas, and petroleum products were available to the farm. Now at least 10 kcal of commercial energy is used for each kcal of food energy produced. This change has occurred as a result of mechanization, irrigation, and consumer demand for low fat foods and for precooked and prepared foods.

Commercial energy use in the U. S. for the food system production, processing, and marketing uses about 3230×10^{12} kcal annually (7). To place this amount of energy in perspective, it is equivalent to 12.8×10^{15} Btu or 12.8 quads. (The annual use in the U. S. is 75 quads equivalent.) This energy is used about one-fourth for production (24%), three-eighths for processing (39%), and three-eighths (37%) for transportation, distribution, marketing, and preparation. The food energy consumed based on population and calorie consumption was $145\text{-}150 \times 10^{12}$ kcal in 1947 and 200×10^{12} kcal in 1968 (without regard to whether these calories were provided by fats, proteins, carbohydrates), a period in which the commercial energy expended in the food system doubled. In 1968 the energy used to drive the food system was 2000 x 10-12 kcal, which did not include the indirect energy devoted to the system such as highways, education and research, retail transportation, or garbage collection and disposal (7). The data were not adjusted for the export of food, which in that period was only about 10% of the production, and could be considered to balance the additional energy in the infrastructure to support the food system and import of food. For the production, not including processing, of potatoes, cereals, beans and sugar beets the energy available in the product exceeds the commercial energy used for production. Considering only the energy ratios, the digestible energy produced per unit of commercial energy is five to seven times greater with manual operations as compared to modern methods, but the amount of food produced per work unit (hour) may be 200 to 300 times greater using modern industrialized methods.

If the objective were to maximize energy production in producing food, all efforts would go toward grain and bean production where five times the energy is produced as is used, or to the extreme, do all the tasks manually in which 30 to 40 times the energy is produced as used. In the later case, all the able-bodied men, women, and children would be needed to produce the food now available. In that scenario we would also deny our diet of the variety of leafy vegetables, fruits and nuts for fiber and vitamins, and animal and fish products for a variety of proteins.

As a part of providing a safe and protected product to the consumer, often precooked, packing in aluminum, glass, steel, plastic, and paper are used, all requiring considerable energy. The amount of energy expended in packaging is greater than the energy in the food itself, estimated to be 20% of the total energy to supply the food (8). A 1/2 gal plastic container has the thermal content of 2159 kcal (energy in food consumed in one day of a person in a developing country) as compared to the milk it contains of 1268 kcal. A 12 oz. TV dinner has a thermal content of 800 kcal, compared to the aluminum package that contains the dinner of 1496 kcal. The energy content itself is not adequate information to judge the merits of expending energy to provide a product to the consumer.

Mechanization

The use of tractors and machines increases our ability to win the race with the weather in agricultural production, whether it is preparing the land (for best seedbed and best rootbed), precision planting (for optimum depth and location of seed and fertilizer), timely seeding (for adequate number of growing days), appropriate cultivation (to reduce competition with weeds), and timely harvest (to avoid unnecessary losses from shattering, exposure to animals, insects and disease, and bleaching from the sun). Likewise, the use in agriculture of the latest technologies available in the industry sector such as an air conditioned work environment, safe working conditions, communications systems, elimination of back breaking tasks, all of which can affect the health and safety, now puts the farmer on an equal basis with those in the industrial sector regarding worker conditions. These additional work place developments become a part of input labor and input cost. Although mechanization requires an input of commercial energy, with more precise and timely operations, both productivity and production can be maintained or increased.

Substitute for External Commercial Energy

A noble objective for food production and processing is to reduce the dependence on external commercial fuel sources, particularly fossil fuels. As a country an objective is to reduce the dependence on imported fuel. A natural suggestion is that the production of agriculture, particularly farming and forestry, be used to produce the energy to meet those fuel needs. However, to convert the energy products of agriculture, primarily lignocellulosic materials requires considerable energy. After collecting, compacting, and treating the dispersed products of farming and forestry there often isn't enough energy remaining to make the process economical. However, for agricultural production and processing efforts should be made as a first step to use the collected products, byproducts, refuse, and waste of the the system to decrease the dependence on external commercial energy, whether domestic or foreign. Most of these agricultural products are high in moisture and need to be dried requiring energy. Some of the wet products such as animal wastes and food processing wastes are well suited for fermentation and can be used to produce methane as a substitute for natural gas or alcohol as a substitute for gasoline.

Some oil crops can be grown to provide a substitute for petroleum.

Rapeseed, cottonseed, sunflower seed, and linseed provide oils that can be used for lubrication and fuel. High carbohydrate crops can be grown specifically as a source of fuel. Sugar cane in Brazil and wheat and corn in the United States are being used to produce ethanol to supplement or replace fossil based gasoline for vehicles. In both cases the production of these fuels require subsidies, relief from taxes, or some other incentive in order to compete with fossil based fuels on a cost per unit energy basis. Many aspects are involved in developing a public policy regarding production of fuel from biological materials-trade relationships, future needs, climate, availability of food, modification of vehicles to use the fuel, environmental impacts, subsidies, etc.

The various routes from agricultural production to fuel are shown in Figure 1. Products of agricultural production can be converted to a more available energy form as electricity and natural gas as shown in Figure 2.

Global Perspectives

The purpose of providing food is to feed the population. Previous concerns for world starvation have been abated in view of recent trends, albeit that pockets of starvation and inadequate nutrition exist. Increasing population without increasing food availability can lead to starvation or inadequate nutrition.

Over the past 30 years, the world food production has grown faster than the population, the major basis of consumption. The world food production increased at an annual rate of 2.4% (grain production increased at 2.7%), while the world population increase is now less than 2% (9). Research and improved technologies have contributed to an increase in food availability, which will continue if an appropriate political, social, and economic environment exists. The world population, now at 5.5 billion, is predicted to be 10 billion in the last quarter of the next century (9) and will place greater demands on the production and processing of food.

The nutrition needs of the future will be met with more limitations than in the past on the use of energy and restrictions on contamination of the environment. The maintenance of natural resources will receive much more attention than in the past. Concerns will increase regarding desertification, deforestation, urbanization, salinification, soil and water degradation, and atmospheric pollution. There is considerable difficulty in delineating these limitations, particularly as one considers the responsibilities and interests of developed and developing countries. The role of economics offers an additional challenge in working out these relationships.

Greater attention will be given to reducing the use of external energy, principally of chemicals, using biologically-based energy to replace fossil fuels, and saving that food which is produced for providing nutrition.

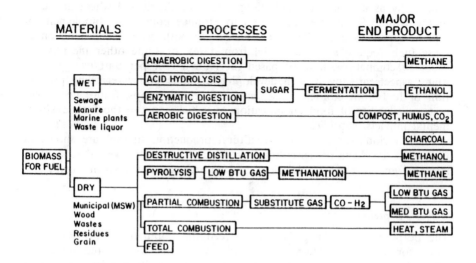

Figure 1. Major processes for conversion of biomass for fuel (8)

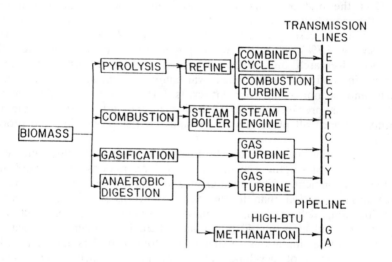

Figure 2. Biomass conversion for electricity and gas production (9)

Summary

The commercial energy input to the food system has increased as the intensity of crop and animal production has increased, and as the commercial processing of the food, precooked and prepared, along with refrigeration to hold raw and processed products have increased. The amount of commercial energy used for crop production has reached a point of "diminishing returns"; the greatest use of commercial energy for the food system is for the processing of crops to produce foods, and that energy has increased since the 1940s and will probably continue to do so, as more affluent consumers, more working families will demand and pay for additional processing to provide food ready for eating with little preparation. Although energy is an important quality of food, other factors such as protein, fat, vitamins, minerals, and fiber content are important dietary aspects. Since the 1960s, the annual increase in world food availability has been 2.4%, outpacing population increase, now at about 2%.

Literature Cited

1. Horsfall, J. G., Chairman. *Agricultural Production Efficiency.* National Research Council, National Academy of Sciences, Washington, DC. 1975. 199 pp.
2. Pimentel, D. Environmental and Social Implications of Waste in the U. S. Agriculture and Food System. *J. Agricultural Ethics* **1990**, vol.*3*(1) , pp 5-20.
3. Pimentel, D., and Hall, Carl W. *Food and Energy Resources.* Academic Press, San Diego, CA. 1984. 269 pp.
4. Singh, R. P. Energy in Food Processing. In *Energy in World Agriculture*, Stout, B. A., Editor. Elsevier Science Publishers, Amsterdam, The Netherlands. 1986. 375 pp.
5. Unger, S. G. Energy Utilization in the Leading Energy Consuming Food Processing Industries. *Food Technology* **1975**, vol*29*(12), pp 33-45.
6. Stout, B. A. *Energy for World Agriculture.* Food and Agriculture Organization, Rome, Italy 1979, 286 pp.
7. Steinhart, J. S., and Steinhart, C. E. Energy Use in the U. S. Food System. *Science* **1974**, vol *184* (4134), pp 307-316. 19 April.
8. Pimentel, D., and Pimentel, M. *Food, Energy and Society.* Edward Arnold Publishers, Ltd., London, England. 1979.
9. Crosson, P.R. and Rosenberg, N.J. Strategies for Agriculture. *Scientific American* **1989** vol 261 (3), pp. 128-135.
10. Milnes, T. A., Connolly, J. S., Inman, R. E., Reed, T. B., and Seibert, M. Research Overview of Biological and Chemical Methods and Identification of Key Research Areas. SERI/TR-33-067, Solar Energy and Research Institute, Golden, CO. 1978. 61 p.
11. Hall, Carl W. *Biomass as an Alternative Fuel.* Government Institutes, Inc., Rockville, MD. 1981. 267 pp.

RECEIVED September 4, 1991

Chapter 17

Global Significance of Biomethanogenesis

D. P. Chynoweth

Agricultural Engineering Department, University of Florida,
Gainesville, FL 32611

Biological formation of methane is the process by which bacteria decompose organic matter using carbon dioxide as an electron acceptor in absence of dioxygen or other electron acceptors. This microbial activity is responsible for carbon recycling in anaerobic environments, including wetlands, rice paddies, intestines of animals, aquatic sediments, and manures. The mixed consortium of microorganisms involved includes a unique group of bacteria, the methanogens, which may be considered to be in a separate kingdom based on genetic and phylogenetic variance from all other life forms. Because methane is a greenhouse gas that is increasing in concentration, its fluxes from various sources are of concern. Biomethanogenesis may be harnessed for conversion of renewable resources to significant quantities of substitute natural gas and to reduce levels of atmospheric carbon dioxide.

In the United States, methane is a major energy source used in many homes for cooking and heating of water and indoor air and water. It is commonly known that some power plants and industries use natural gas as a source of energy for generation of electricity and process heat and that this methane is a fossil fuel obtained from gas wells and transmitted throughout the country by gas pipelines. Most people also know that methane bubbles up from polluted swamps where sedimented plant matter is undergoing decomposition. Because of odors from swamps, and the odor due to natural gas additives, methane is incorrectly considered malodorous.

It is less commonly known that methane was one of the original atmospheric gases and is a normal product of the microbial decomposition of organic matter under anaerobic conditions. Bacteria involved in production of methane are unique in their metabolism and other properties. The balanced

0097–6156/92/0483–0338$06.00/0

cycling of carbon is obligately dependent upon the activity of these organisms in the intestines of animals as well as in large anaerobic pools of organic matter, including sediments and flooded soils. Atmospheric methane is of major concern as a greenhouse gas that is increasing in concentration as a result of man's activities and is a potential cause of future global warming. Biomethanogenesis can be harnessed in the process known as anaerobic digestion to treat organic wastes in a manner that reduces their environmental impact and generates renewable energy. It can also be used to produce substitute natural gas from a variety of energy crops. This renewable methane would not only replace use of fossil fuels, but would also represent a balanced carbon cycle, and therefore not contribute to increases in atmospheric carbon dioxide. These less-known aspects of methane are discussed in this paper.

Methane

Some properties of methane are outlined in Table I. Methane is a colorless and odorless hydrocarbon that is a gas at ambient temperatures and has a critical temperature of -82.2°C and a critical pressure of 45.8 atm. It is combustible when the oxygen:methane ratio exceeds 2.0 (air:methane = 10.0) producing carbon dioxide and water; the heating value is 2350 J g^{-1}. Because of its abundance and high energy content, methane is widely used as a fuel, representing about 20% of the U.S. energy supply in 1988 (2,3). Currently, readily accessible deposits and reserves in the U.S. are estimated at 500-600 trillion cubic feet or a 35-40 year supply at current projected use rates. These estimates exclude a new technology increment estimated at 11 trillion cubic meters (3). Compared to oil and coal, methane is attractive as an energy source because it burns without production of oxides of sulfur and nitrogen and incomplete combustion products such as hydrocarbons. Methane combustion does however contribute to increased concentrations of the greenhouse gas carbon dioxide when derived from fossil resources. One limitation of methane is that it is difficult to liquify and thus can't be easily transported in large quantities as a fuel in vehicles unless maintained at high pressures and/or low temperatures.

The concentration of atmospheric methane increased from 0.70 ppm to 1.68 ppm from 1787 to 1987 and is increasing by about 1.0% per year (4). This trend is based on direct measurements since 1978, prior infrared spectra, and recent analyses of air trapped in polar ice. This increase is of great concern because methane is considered a significant greenhouse gas. It not only absorbs infrared light directly, but also reacts photochemically to produce other greenhouse gases, including ozone, carbon dioxide and water vapor (5). Based on the current atmospheric concentration and rate of increase, the relative contribution of methane to the greenhouse effect (parts per billion volume basis) is estimated at 15% compared to 60% for carbon dioxide. Other gases

Table I. Properties of Methane

molecular formula	CH_4
heating value	2350 J g^{-1}
ratio of O_2:CH_4 required for combustion	2.0
boiling point	$-162°C$
critical temperature	$-82.25°C$
critical pressure	45.8 atm
solubility in water at 35 C	17 mg L^{-1}
combustion products	CO_2, H_2O

SOURCE: Adapted from ref. 1.

with significant effects include nitrous oxide, tropospheric ozone, CFC-11, and CFC-12. The significance of methane is influenced by the facts that the direct effect of methane is 25-fold greater than that of carbon dioxide on a molar basis and the decay time for methane is 10 years compared to 120 years for carbon dioxide (5). When corrected for decay time and indirect effects, the relative contribution of methane compared to carbon dioxide is 15:1. Compared to other greenhouse gases, methane is an excellent candidate for control. Because of its short atmospheric lifetime, emissions must only be reduced by 10% to stop the yearly increase (6). In contrast, reductions of 50 to 100 percent would be required to prevent increases in other greenhouse gases. Furthermore, the value of reducing methane would be realized in the near term compared to centuries for other gases. For example, a 10% reduction in methane emissions is equivalent to a 10% reduction in carbon dioxide emissions, even though the concentration of carbon dioxide is vastly higher.

An estimate of the annual methane flux into the atmosphere can be calculated by adding the sinks and the annual increase. These data (Table II) indicate that a flux of 375-475 trillion tons(Tg) per year would be required to account for an annual increase of 50-60 trillion tons (7). Estimates of sources of atmospheric methane indicate that up to 83% is biogenic in origin (8). The other abiogenic

Table II. Global Losses and Production of Methane

	Methane Tg^{-1}
Sinks	
tropospheric reactions	290-350
stratospheric reactions	25-35
uptake on aerobic soils	10-30
Annual Increase (about 1%)	50-60
Total Production to Account for Increase	375-475

SOURCE: Adapted from ref. 7.

sources include fossil natural gas leaks, coal mine leaks, and methane from incomplete combustion during biomass burns.

Biomethanogenesis

Microbial methanogenesis is a natural process occurring in anaerobic environments, such as ocean and lake sediments and animal digestive tracts, where organic matter has accumulated. In these environments, electron acceptors such as dioxygen, nitrate, and sulfate are depleted and replaced by carbon dioxide resulting in formation of methane (9). Biomethanogenesis is a process occurring only under strict anaerobic conditions where several populations of bacteria react in concert to decompose organic matter to methane and carbon dioxide. An overall scheme of biomethanogenesis, shown in Figure 1, indicates that the principal substrates of methanogenic bacteria are acetate and hydrogen/carbon dioxide (or formate). The relative importance of formate versus hydrogen/carbon dioxide in the methane fermentation is not well documented because of exchanges which occur between these substrates. A different physiological population, the hydrolytic bacteria, are responsible for depolymerization of organic polymers and fermentation to products, including organic acids, alcohols, and the methanogenic substrates. Organisms that convert fermentation products, such as propionate, butyrate, lactate, and ethanol generally exhibit obligate proton-reducing metabolism, i.e. they produce dihydrogen as a fermentation product and this reaction is obligately dependent

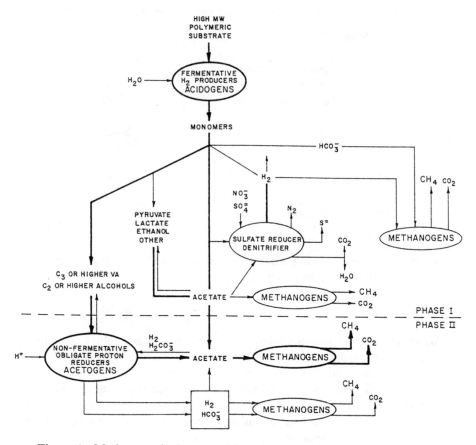

Figure 1. Methanogenic decomposition of compounds in nature (Adapted from ref. 46)

on hydrogen removal by methanogenic or other hydrogen-using bacteria (*10*). In addition, there are organisms present which form acetate and other C-3 or higher volatile acids via back reactions with dihydrogen and carbon dioxide (*10*). The fermentation is dependent upon a delicate balance between activities of bacteria that form acids, carbon dioxide, and dihydrogen (or formate) and methanogenic bacteria which utilize these substrates. Overproduction of electrons resulting from overfeeding or underutilization of electrons by methanogenic bacteria results in the accumulation of fermentation products to inhibitory levels, leading to cessation of decomposition.

During the past 10 years, literature on the microbiology and biochemistry of methanogenic bacteria has increased exponentially with isolation of several new species and development of more rapid techniques for identification. Beginning with the discovery of interspecies hydrogen transfer in 1967 (*11*), several species of hydrogen-producing acetogenic bacteria have been isolated. Although the overall niches of these microbial groups are beginning to be unveiled, it is important to realize that knowledge of the physiology, metabolism and genetics of these organisms is in its infancy. Hydrolytic bacteria are the least studied organisms in the methane fermentation even though hydrolysis is apparently the overall rate-limiting step in many of the methanogenic environments. With the exception of the rumen (*12,13*), knowledge of the microbial ecology of methanogenesis in anaerobic environments, including anaerobic digesters, is at best superficial (*9,14,15*).

The methane bacteria are such a unique group of organisms that they have been placed into a new evolutionary group (separate from eucaryotic plants and animals and procaryotic bacteria) referred to as Archaebacteria (*16*). Archaebacteria also include a few other species of extreme halophilic and thermophilic bacteria. Placement into a separate taxonomic group is related to the variance of their genetic makeup from that of other living organisms, including bacteria. This difference is illustrated in the diagram shown in Figure 2 which is based on analysis of ribosomal RNA of numerous organisms, including most of the available pure cultures of methanogenic bacteria. These genotypic differences are reflected in numerous phenotypic characteristic s unique to this group, including metabolism, coenzymes, and cell membrane lipids. Methanogenic bacteria produce methane from acetate, methanol, dihydrogen/carbon dioxide, formate and mono-, di-, and tri-methylamines (Figure 3). Methane production from acetate, formate, and dihydrogen/carbon dioxide are the most important reactions in nature. These organisms have unique coenzymes for electron transfer, CoM and F_{420} (*17*). The fluorescence property of F_{420} has been used to locate methanogenic colonies and enumerate methanogens in mixed culture (*18,19*). The property of possessing ether-linked instead of ester-linked lipids in their cell membranes (*20*) has been proposed as a method to distinguish methanogens from other microorganisms in the environment.

Biomethanogenesis plays a major role in the cycling of carbon in nature. It has been reported in a broad variety of environments where organic decomposition

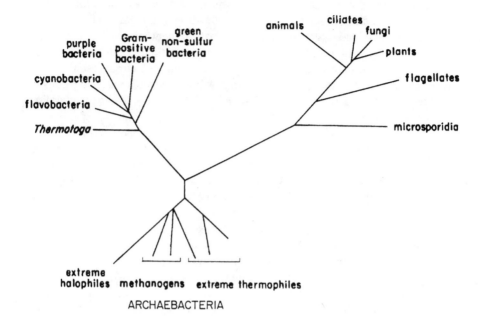

Figure 2.   Universal phylogenetic tree determined from rRNA sequence comparisons. A matrix of evolutionary distances (99) was calculated from an alignment (260) of representative 16S RRNA sequences from each of the three urkingdoms. The length of the lines is proportional to the phylogenetic difference. (Reproduced with permission from ref. 16. Copyright 1987. American Society for Microbiology.)

1. Hydrogen
   $4 H_2 + CO_2 \longrightarrow CH_4 + 2 H_2O$

2. Acetate
   $CH_3COOH \longrightarrow CH_4 + CO_2$

3. Formate
   $4 HCOOH \longrightarrow CH_4 + 3 CO_2 + 2 H_2O$

4. Methanol
   $4 CH_3OH \longrightarrow 3 CH_4 + CO_2 + 2 H_2O$

5. Trimethylamine
   $4 (CH_3)_3N + 6 H_2O \longrightarrow 9 CH_4 + 3 CO_2 + 4 NH_3$

6 Dimethylamine
   $2 (CH_3)_2NH + 2 H_2O \longrightarrow 3 CH_4 + CO_2 + 2 NH_3$

7. Monomethylamine
   $4 (CH_3)NH_2 + 2 H_2O \longrightarrow 3 CH_4 + CO_2 + 4 NH_3$

Figure 3.   Reactions of methanogenic bacteria. (Adapted from ref. 47)

has depleted oxygen and other inorganic electron acceptors, including aquatic sediments and the intestines of many varieties of animals, including ruminants, non-ruminant mammals, reptiles, and insects (21-26). In non-animal environments, decomposition would cease in the absence of methanogenesis due to buildup of inhibitory fatty acids and other fermentation products. Methanogenesis insures removal of electrons and continued degradation of the biodegradable fraction of organic residues releasing the carbon and electrons back into the biosphere. The other fraction of organic matter (about 25-30%), including lignin and other compounds, is refractory to anaerobic catabolism and therefore becomes sequestered in anaerobic sediments (27). This fraction represents the origin of peat, oil, coal, and natural gas. Without biomethanogenesis there would be a rapid accumulation of biomass sequestered in acidic, odorous sediments resulting in an imbalance in the carbon cycle and cycling of other elements such as N, P, and S contained in organic matter.

Many animals are dependent on methanogenesis for their nutrition. In ruminants and certain wood-eating insects such as termites, effective digestion and fermentation of lignocellulosic matter is dependent upon an efficient methane fermentation for depolymerization and hydrogen/formate metabolism. In such animals, nutrition is obtained from low molecular weight bacterial metabolic products (12,13). Although methanogenesis has been reported in man and other mammals with simpler diets, its role in these environments is not known and is not considered significant. The absence of an extensive methane fermentation in these animals may be attributed to washout caused by the short intestinal retention time and the long generation time of methane bacteria.

Concerns over atmospheric methane as a greenhouse gas and the large contribution of biomethanogenesis as a source of this gas make it important to determine the relative significance of various components of this activity. A recent paper (8) summarized estimates (28-30) of source fluxes of atmospheric methane based on several carbon isotopic studies and presented new data on natural sources and biomass burning. These data (Table III) show that of a total flux of 594 million tons (Tg) per year, 83% is produced via biomethanogenesis from a combination of natural (42%) and anthropogenic (41%) sources.

The principal anthropogenic sources of atmospheric methane are rice paddies, cattle and other ruminants, and organic waste processing. The significance of wood-degrading termites may be significant and is debatable (24-26). Flooding of soils rich in organic matter leads to anaerobiosis and methane production. Methane is released directly and transported through plants such as rice to the atmosphere. Increased demands for rice by exploding populations will result in increasing fluxes from this source. Cattle and other ruminants numbering 1.3 billion generate about 13% of the global methane flux from their digestive tracts. These animals generate wastes which contribute further to the methane pool. Most of the organic wastes associated with man's activities are deposited in landfills where decomposition via a methane fermentation releases about 8% of the methane

Table III. Source Fluxes of Atmospheric Methane

Source	Tg y^{-1}	% of total
Natural Sources (tundra, bogs, swamps)	246 ±86	42
Anthropogenic Sources		
rice paddies	120 ±50	20
livestock	78 ± 12	13
biomass burning	45 ± 14	8
landfills, organic waste	50 ±20	8
oil and natural gas		
processing	35 ±?	6
coal mining	20 ± 10	3
Total Flux	594 ±192	100

SOURCE: Adapted from ref. 8.

emission pool. Considerable reduction in these fluxes might be realized through improved rice and animal production practices, and waste handling techniques to capture the methane for use as fuel. These reductions, however, are likely to be offset by increased production in each category resulting from demands of our exploding population and its continued development. Other activities of man resulting in non-biological methane release include coal mining, natural gas mining and transmission leaks, and biomass burning; these sources contribute 17% of the emission pool (*8*).

Applications of Biomethanogenesis

Biomethanogenesis has been harnessed in the process known as anaerobic digestion in which this microbial process is optimized for conversion of organic wastes and energy crops to methane, carbon dioxide, and compost. The earliest use of this process was the treatment of domestic and animal wastes (*31*). It was mostly used in the United States and other developed countries for domestic sludge treatment. Less developed countries like China and India have employed small-scale digesters for treatment of sewage and animal wastes (*32,33*). In these applications the methane produced is used for cooking, lighting, and operation of small engines, and the residues are applied in agriculture as a compost.

     As greater cost and impending depletion of fossil fuels became apparent in the 1970's and early 1980's, the search for renewable alternative fuels resulted in an expanded interest in anaerobic digestion to include industrial wastes, municipal solid waste, and biomass energy crops as feedstocks. During this period several novel high-rate digester designs were commercialized for industrial wastes, predominantly in the food industry (*34,35*). These industries realized the benefits of treating their wastes by a process that eliminates the costly aeration requirement and generates a fuel that can off-set a portion of the energy requirements of their operations. Although a few animal waste digesters were placed into operation in the U.S. and other developed countries, the absence of strict environmental regulations for these wastes and prevailing low energy prices stifled their development. Research on anaerobic digestion of municipal solid waste also blossomed, resulting in new digester designs for high solids feedstocks. Two of these designs are barely commercial in Europe (*36,37*). Low tipping fees and plunging energy prices have stifled commercialization. Several research programs investigated energy crops coupled with anaerobic digestion for generation of renewable substitute natural gas, including marine algae (*38*), grasses (*39*), and woods (*40,41*). These programs have integrated research on crop production and harvesting, conversion by anaerobic digestion, and systems analysis. Resource potential estimates for these feedstocks (Table IV) have been reported at 7 EJ (10^{18} joules or about 10^{15} Btu) for wastes and 30 EJ for terrestrial biomass (*42*). The potential for marine biomass is about 100 EJ (*43*). However, that value has many uncertainties which are related primarily to design of offshore farms. The cost of methane from these renewable energy systems was significantly higher than fossil-derived energy and interest in their continued funding dwindled with a continuation of energy gluts and depressed prices in the late 1980's.

Several factors have recently stimulated a new interest in renewable energy resources and their conversion to methane via biomethanogenesis. Heading the list is the threat of global warming resulting from accumulation of greenhouse gases. The major greenhouse gas is carbon dioxide which is increasing as a direct result of combustion of fossil fuels. Combustion of coal and oil also results in acid rain, urban smog, and stratospheric ozone depletion caused by emissions of oxides of sulfur and nitrogen. Methane produced from anaerobic digestion of renewable energy crops and organic wastes could replace a major fraction of fossil fuels resulting in a direct decrease in the rate of increase of carbon dioxide (*15,44*). Although combustion of biomethane would also release carbon dioxide, an equivalent amount would be fixed by the plants from which it was produced. Furthermore, about 30% of the biomass feedstock is not converted and can be returned to the soil where it remains sequestered as refractory carbon.

Because of biomethanogenesis decomposes organic matter with production of a useful energy product, anaerobic digestion of organic wastes is receiving increased attention. With increased levels of waste production, limited area for landfilling or application, and increased awareness of environmental impact, alternative methods for treatment of solid and agricultural wastes are being sought. An attractive option for treatment of the organic fraction of these wastes is to separately treat

Table IV. Energy Potential From Biomass and Wastes in the
United States

Resource	EJ y^{-1}
municipal solid waste	1.5
sewage sludge and sewage-grown biomass	0.8
biodegradable industrial wastes	0.4
crop residues	4.1
logging residues	0.3
animal manures	0.4
energy crops	
payment-in-kind (PIK) land	
(32 Hectares)	11.0
equivalent to PIK area devoted to	
energy crops	11.0
marine biomass (e.g. macroalgae)	100.
Total (excluding marine)	29.5

SOURCE: refs. 42,43

this fraction by composting and apply the stabilized residues on land as a soil amendment. The residues would reduce water needs and prevent erosion. This scheme, however, requires effective separation of undesired components such as metals, glass, plastics, and toxic compounds which affect the quality of residues more than the conversion process. Although aerobic composting is a more popular process for stabilization of these wastes, anaerobic composting has the advantages of methane production and lack of need for aeration or mixing (45). Currently these wastes release undesired methane into the atmosphere due to anaerobic conversion in landfills, lagoons, or stock piles. Treatment and recovery of this gas in reactors would reduce this source of atmospheric methane.

Conclusion

In spite of the significance of biomethanogenesis to the carbon cycle, as a source of a major greenhouse gas, and as a process for deriving substitute natural gas from renewable resources, the microbiology and ecology of methanogenesis are poorly understood and application of the process for derivation of renewable energy is poorly developed. The principal bacteria involved have not been isolated in total from a single methanogenic fermentation. A limited understanding of the behavior of the overall reactions and factors influencing them has permitted design and optimization of anaerobic digesters for conversion of a number of different feedstocks. Application of this process has been stifled by the perceived instability of the fermentation and high costs of producing methane from renewable sources compared to those of competing fossil fuels. A concentrated effort to understand the fundamentals of the process should lead to the development of methods to improve process stability. As fossil fuels become depleted and their use curtailed because of their contribution to increased atmospheric carbon dioxide, incentives to turn to renewable methane should be increased. Attention should be directed toward development of better estimates of source fluxes of atmospheric methane and methods to reduce these fluxes. In particular, those fluxes related to man's activity should be addressed.

Acknowledgments

The author greatfully acknowledges Dr. Ann Wilke for her thorough review of this chapter and several valuable suggestions for its improvement.

Literature Cited

1. *The Merck Index*; Merck and Co., Inc.: Rahway, NJ, 1983; pp 852-853,
2. Woods, T. J., "The Long-Term Trends in U.S. Gas Supply and Prices: The 1989 GRI Baseline Projection of U.S. Energy Supply and Demand to 2010," *Gas Research Insights (GRI Publ.)*, Gas Research Institute: Chicago, IL, 1990.
3. Kerr, R. A. *Science* **1989**, *245*, 1330-1331.
4. Blake, D. R.; Rowland, F. W. *Science* **1988**, *239*, 1129-1131.
5. Rodhe, H. *Science* **1990**, *248*, 1217-1219.
6. Gibbs, M. J.; Hogan, K. *EPA Journal* **1990**, *16(2)*, 23-25.
7. Bingemer, H. G.; Crutzen, P. J. *J. Geophys. Res.* **1987**, *92*, 2181-2187.
8. Stevens, C. M.; Engelkemeir *J. Geophys. Res.* **1988**, *93*, 725-733.
9. *Anaerobic Digestion of Biomass*; Chynoweth, D. P.; Isaacson, R.; Eds; Elsevier Applied Science: London, 1987.
10. Boone, D.; Mah, R.; In *Anaerobic Digestion of Biomass*; Chynoweth, D. P.; Isaacson, R.; Eds.; Elsevier Applied Science: London, 1987; pp 35-48.
11. Bryant, M. P.; Wolin, E. A.; Wolin, M. J.; Wolfe, R. S. *Arch. Mikrobiol.* **1967**, *59*, 20-31.
12. Hungate, R. *The Rumen and Its Microbes*; Academic Press: New York and London, 1966.
13. *The Rumen Ecosystem;* Hobson, P. N., Ed.; Elsevier Applied Science: London and New York, 1988.

14. Smith, P. H.; Bordeaux, F. M.; Wilkie, A.; Yang, J.; Boone, D.; Mah, R. A.; Chynoweth, D.; Jerger, D.; In *Methane From Biomass: A systems Approach*; Smith, W. H.; Frank, J. R., Eds., Elsevier Applied Science Publishers: London, 1988, pp 335-353.

15. Smith, P. H.; Bordeaux, F. M.; Goto, M.; Shiralipour, A.; Wilkie, A.; Andrews, J. F.; Ide, S.; Barnette, M. W.; In *Methane From Biomass: A systems Approach*; Smith, W. H.; Frank, J. R.; Eds.; Elsevier Applied Science Publishers: London, 1988, pp 291-334.

16. Woese, D. R. *Microbiol. Rev.* **1987**, *51*, 221-271.

17. Daniels, L.; Sparling, R.; Sprott, G. D. *Biochemica et Biophysica Acta* **1984**, *768*, 113-163.

18. Peck, M. W.; Archer, D. B. *Internat. Indust. Biotechnol.* **1989**, *9(3)*, 5-12.

19. Peck, M. W.; Chynoweth, D. P. *Biotechnol. Letts.* **1990**, *12*, 17-22.

20. deRosa, M.; Gambacorta, A.; Gliozzi, A. *Microbiol. Rev.* **1986**, *50*, 70-80.

21. Zeikus, J. C.; *Bacteriol. Rev.*, **1977**, *41*, 514-541.

22. Zehnder, A. J. B.; Ingvorsen, K.; Marti, T.; In *Anaerobic Digestion 1981*; Hughes, D. E.; Stafford, D. A.; Wheatley, B. I.; Baader, W.; Lettinga, G.; Nyns, E. J.; Verstraete, W.; Wentworth, R. L.; Eds.; Elsevier Biomedical Press: Amsterdam, 1982; pp 3-22.

23. Breznak, J. A.; *Symbiosis* **1975**, *24*, 559-580.

24. Zimmerman, P. R.; Greenberg, J. P.; Wandiga, S. O.; Crutzen, P. J. *Science*, **1982**, *218*, 563-565.

25. Rasmussen, R. A.; Khalil, M. A. K. *Nature* **1983**, *301*, 700-703.

26. Collins, N. M.; Wood, T. G. *Science* **1984**, *224*, 84-86.

27. Kelly C. A.; Chynoweth, D. P.; In *Native Aquatic Bacteria: Enumeration Activity, and Ecology, ASTM 695*; Costerton, J. W.; Colwell, R. R., Eds.; American Society for Testing and Materials: Philadelphia, PA, 1979; pp 164-179.

28. Holzapfel-Pschorn, A.; Seiler, W. *J. Geophys. Res.* **1986**, *91*, 11803-11814.

29. Crutzen, P. J.; Aselmann, I.; Seiler, W. *Tellus* **1986**, *38B*, 271-284.

30. Hitchcock, D. R.; Wechsler, A. E.; *Biological Cycling of Atmospheric Trace Gases*; Final Report; NASA Contract NASA-CR-126663; 1972; pp 117-154.

31. McCarty, P. L., In *Anaerobic Digestion 1981*; Hughes, D. E. et al.; Eds.; Elsevier Biomedical Press: Amsterdam, 1982; pp 3-22.

32. Ke-yun, D.; Yi-zhang, Z; Li-bin, W.; In *Anaerobic Digestion 1988*; Hall, E. R.; Hobson, P. N.; Eds.; Pergamon Press: Oxford, 1988; pp 295-302.

33. Ward, R.; In *Anaerobic Digestion 1981*; Hughes, D. E. et al.; Eds.; Elsevier Biomedical Press: Amsterdam, 1982, pp 315-344.

34. Pohland, F. G.; Harper, S. R.; In *Anaerobic Digestion 1985*; Quangzhou China, China State Biogas Association, 1985; pp 41-82.

35. Wilke, A.; Colleran, E.; In *International Biosystems III*; Wise, D. L.; Ed.; CRC Press: Boca Raton, FL, 1989; pp 183-226.

36. DeBaere, L.; Van Meenen, P.; Deboosere, P.; Verstraete, W. *Resources and Conservation* **1987**, *14*, 295-308.

37. Bonhomme, M.; In *Energy From Biomass and Wastes, XI*; Klass, D.; Ed.; Institute of Gas Technology; 1988; pp 721-730.
38. *Seaweed Cultivation for Renewable Resources*; Bird, K. T.; Benson, P. H.; Eds.; Elsevier: Amsterdam, 1987.
39. *Methane From Biomass: A Systems Approach*; Smith, W. H.; Frank, J. R.; Eds.; Elsevier Applied Science Publishers: London, 1988.
40. Kenney, W. A.; Sennerby-Forsse, L.; Layton., P. *Biomass* 1990, *21*, 163-188.
41. Turick, C. E.; Peck, M. W.; Chynoweth, D. P.; Jerger, D. E.; White, E. H.; Zsuffa, L.; Kenney, W. A. *Biomass*, in press, 1991.
42. Legrand, R.; Warren, C. S.; "Biogas generation from community-derived wastes and biomass in the U.S.;" Paper presented at the Tenth Annual Energy-Sources Technology Conf. and Exhib.; ASME; Dallas, TX, 1987.
43. Chynoweth, D. P.; Fannin, K. F.; Srivastava, V.; In *Seaweed Cultivation for Renewable Resources*; Bird, K. T.; Benson, P. H.; Eds.; Elsevier: Amsterdam, 1987; pp 285-303.
44. Wilkie, A. C.; Smith, P. H.; In *Microbiology of Extreme Environments and Its Potential for Biotechnology*; da Costa, M. S.; Duarte, J. C.; Williams, R. A. D.; Eds; Elsevier Science Publishers: London, 1989; pp 237-252.
45. Chynoweth, D. P.; Bosch, G.; Earle, J. F. K.; Legrand, R.; Liu, K. *Applied Biochemistry and Biotechnology* 1991, *28/29*, 421-432.
46. Ghosh, S.; "Microbial Production of Energy: Gaseous Fuels;" Lecture presented at the Seventh International Biotechnology Symposium; New Delhi, India, February 1984.
47. Ferguson, T.; Mah, R.; In *Anaerobic Digestion of Biomass*; Chynoweth, D. P.; Isaacson R.; Eds.; Elsevier Applied Science: London, 1987; pp 49-64.

RECEIVED July 23, 1991

Chapter 18

Biogeochemical Consequences of Desertification

Walter G. Whitford

Department of Biology, New Mexico State University,
Las Cruces, NM 88003

Processes that reduce the productivity of arid and semi-arid lands, collectively known as desertification, affect more than 3 billion hectares or more than 80% of such lands. The degradation process results in redistribution of water and nutrients, loss of find soil fractions and replacement of palatable plants with undesirable plants. These changes frequently uncouple rainfall and productivity on a temporal scale. This uncoupling is probably due to modification of the nitrogen cycle as a result of the desertification processes. Changes in vegetation can produce changes in fluxes of radiatively active gasses and a variety of organic volatiles to the atmosphere. Redistribution of soil and water may produce "hot" spots for denitrification and for ammonia volatilization that differ in extent both spatially and temporally from undesertified ecosystems. Dust from desertified areas can modify the chemistry of rainfall in areas distant from the dust source.

Desertification has been defined as the diminution or destruction of the biological potential of the land leading to desert like conditions (1). There are many symptoms of desertification. These include reduced productivity of desirable plants and increases in undesirable plants; loss of most perennial vegetation; soil loss and deterioration and marked reduction in human habitability. Human activities such as tree harvesting, overgrazing and cultivation in marginal lands with limited and variable precipitation are directly responsible for desertification (2). More than 80% of the lands classified as arid or semi-arid have been affected by desertification. More than 3 billion hectares of rangeland have been subjected to degradation

0097–6156/92/0483–0352$06.00/0
© 1992 American Chemical Society

ranging from moderate to very severe desertification (3). Despite efforts by many national and international agencies to halt and/or reverse the trend toward more severe desertification, the degradation continues at an ever accelerating pace. Desertification is a global problem affecting not only the human populations that live in impacted areas, but also affecting environments of areas at great distances from the desert regions.

Desertification has an effect on most, if not all, ecosystem processes because of changes in the biotic structure of the system. These structural differences change the trajectories of the ecosystems of a region through time. As an example, the changes in vegetation from the perennial grasslands that dominated the Southwestern United States rangelands in the 1850's to the desert shrublands that currently occupy most of that region is well documented (4-7). These shrublands respond to climatic variability much differently than grasslands; hence, over time exhibit much different trajectories than grasslands.

System Heterogeneity

Schlesinger et al. (8), hypothesized that in the process of desertification, the shift from grassland to shrubland altered what was a relatively uniform distribution of water and nutrients in space and over time to a temporally and spatially heterogeneous system. The loss of perennial grasses and replacement with scattered woody shrubs changed the key biogeochemical processes that allowed the original grassland to persist in an area with low unpredictable rainfall. The shrubs have become focal points for water infiltration and nutrients resulting in what has become known as "islands of fertility" (9-14). Table I summarizes characteristics of soil and annual vegetation under canopy and in intershrub spaces. During the shift from grassland to shrubland, there is loss of fine soil fractions by wind erosion and changes in surface hydrology that produces deep erosional soil cutting and overland sheet flow of water, soil and organic matter. These processes rapidly change the spatial distribution of organic matter and the rainfall-water availability patterns. Shrubs trap fine airborne particles that produces aeolian dunes around shrubs further exacerbating the spatial variability in mineral resources. Because the shrublands are poor quality for grazing, numerous efforts have been made to eliminate the shrubs and return shrub dominated areas to a grassland. These efforts have generally been unsuccessful.   The persistence of established shrublands, despite efforts to eliminate shrubs by chemical and mechanical means, is probably a function of the concentration of water and nutrients in the remnant "resource islands" after shrubs have been killed. The "islands" are quickly reoccupied by shrubs. In many cases, part of the deep root systems of the shrubs remain alive and shrub regeneration occurs at the same location by crown or root sprouting.

The changes in spatial distribution of mineral resources and the morphological and physiological characteristics of the dominant plants have an effect on key ecosystem processes by affecting the timing of growth and species composition of the vegetation. Several studies (12, 27-29) have shown that most annual herbaceous plants are concentrated under the canopies of shrubs, (Table I). Successive "wet" years are characterized by vast differences in the productivity of desert annuals (15). These differences are attributable to temporal patterns of nitrogen availability (16). Temporal patterns of nitrogen availability affect not only annual herbs, but also affects productivity of some shrubs (17,18). Thus, in desertified shrubland landscapes, net primary productivity does not exhibit a close linkage with precipitation. Indeed "wet" years may have lower productivity than relatively "dry" or average rainfall years. However, desert perennial grassland ecosystems exhibit a much closer linkage between water inputs and productivity and some species of perennial grasses exhibit little response to nitrogen fertilization (19).

Nutrient Balances

The uncoupling of rainfall and productivity in desertified shrublands probably results from shifts in the balance between mineralization and immobilization of nitrogen. Mineralization occurs when ions or molecules that can be absorbed by plant roots are released from the decomposing cells of microbes or excreted by soil organisms that graze on the microflora. This process is especially important for elements that are needed in relatively large quantities for plant growth such as nitrogen and phosphorus. The soil microflora, especially some fungi, can grow and utilize the energy of dead plant material even when soils are dry (20). Fungi that grow on substrates which have a high carbon to nitrogen ratio can increase their growth rates rapidly when water becomes available and can outcompete plant roots for mineral nitrogen. Fungal hyphae grow out into the soil around a dead root and take up mineral N from the soil. The mineral nitrogen incorporated into fungal biomass is thus immobilized and is not available to plants until the fungal biomass dies or is consumed by soil microfauna. In arid ecosystems where nitrogen availability frequently limits net primary production, the balance between mineralization and immobilization can be the critical determinant of the response of that ecosystem to rainfall. The key biogeochemical processes in mineralization-immobilization are given in Figure 1.

In desert ecosystems, soil microbes are limited by the availability of substrates. Rainfall produces dense stands of annual herbs under the canopies of shrubs. When those annuals die, the dead roots are a large pulse of suitable substrate for soil fungi. Since annual herb roots have very high carbon to nitrogen ratios, the rapidly growing fungi incorporate the available mineral nitrogen into fungal biomass. Rapidly growing fungal hyphae outcompete roots for the available nitrogen. This immobilization of nitrogen into fungal biomass therefore inhibits growth of the shrubs or another population of annual herbs because of nitrogen limitations (Fig. 1).

In a perennial grassland there is a relatively constant rate of root turnover (21). A low level relatively constant input of substrate allows

Table I. Characteristics of soil and annual plant vegetation under shrub canopies and in intershrub spaces. Data from references 12, 27, 28, and 29.

	Under Canopy	Intershrub space
Total N% upper 5 cm Larrea tridentata (27)	0.13	0.022
Total N% upper 5 cm Prosopis glandulosa (28)	0.06-0.1	0.02-0.03
Organic C g.bg-1 upper 5 cm Prosopis glandulosa (28)	8.0	3.0
Bulk density (28) mg.m-3	1.35	1.57
Total N% upper 5 cm Larrea tridentata (12)	0.40	0.33
Density of spring ephemeral plants g.m-2 (12)	24±10	4±1
Infiltration rate time to run-off min (29)	26.93	4.56

Mineralization

$$n\ R\text{-}\underset{\underset{HO}{|}}{\underset{|}{C}}\text{-}\underset{\underset{H}{|}}{\underset{|}{C}}\text{-}\overset{\overset{NH_2}{||}}{\overset{|}{C}}\text{-}OH \xrightarrow[\text{enzymes}]{\text{deaminase}} n(NH_4^+) + n(CO_2) + n(H_2O)$$

$$NH_4^+ \xrightarrow[\text{nitrification}]{\text{microbial}} NO_3^- + H_2O$$

Immobilization

$$NH_4^+ + NO_3^- \xrightarrow[\text{assimilation}]{\text{microbial}} \text{incorporation into fungal biomass}$$

Figure 1. The key biogeochemical processes in mineralization-immobilization.

microbial death and nutrient mineralization to keep up with, or exceed the rate of immobilization (Fig. 1). The root systems of perennial grasses differ from shrub root systems in several important characteristics: grass roots are dense, mat-like, shallow and produce mucigels; shrub roots are sparse, deep and do not produce mucigels. According to this model, (Fig. 1), perennial grassland should respond to rainfall by proportionate increase in growth. This model is supported by the limited available experimental data (19). The perennial grass, Bouteloua eriopoda, which formerly dominated vast areas of what is now desert shrubland, responded to irrigation but not to fertilization with ammonium nitrate. The lack of response to fertilization with NH_4NO_3 is evidence that this perennial grass obtains sufficient N for its growth from mineralization in the root mat or from atmospheric N fixation by non-symbiotic N fixers associated with the grass roots. Mucigels secreted from perennial grass roots provide a concentrated energy source needed by non-symbiotic N fixing bacteria.

The exposure of calcium carbonate soils by erosion in early stages of desertification may contribute to the paucity of available nitrogen by ammonium volatilization. In soils of high pH, ammonium is converted to NH_3 which is lost to the atmosphere by:

$$NH_4^+ + OH^- \text{-------}> NH_3 + H_2O.$$

This represents not only a loss of an essential nutrient for plant growth, but the ammonia is capable of generating alkalinity in rainfall (8). Because of the low rainfall in arid regions, this ammonia is likely to be transported for long distances before affecting the pH of the rainfall (8).

Loss of plant cover during desertification produces conditions for increased energy of storm run-off and transport of organic materials plus clay and silt as suspended materials. These materials are deposited in basins where the accumulation of fine textured soils promote anaerobic soil conditions for long periods after a rainfall. Anaerobic conditions plus the concentration of organic matter undergoing decomposition promote conditions for denitrification. It has been suggested that one-third of the gaseous losses of N from terrestrial ecosystems to the atmosphere occurs in desert regions (21). The fraction of this nitrogen that is N_2O can contribute to greenhouse warming and ozone destruction (8).

Shrubs and Volatile Compounds

One consequence of the shift from grassland to shrubland is the potential for significant increases in volatile hydrocarbons added to the atmosphere. The leaves of creosotebush, Larrea tridentata, yielded 0.1 to 0.2 percent of a complex mixture of volatile compounds. That mixture contains several hundred compounds of which 100 accounted for more than 90% of the total volatiles (23). The volatiles that were identified included four monoterpene hydrocarbons, four oxygenated monoterpenes, six sesquiterpene hydrocarbons, eight aromatics like benzyl acetate and ethyl benzoate, plus eighteen miscellaneous compounds. Larrea tridentata now occupies many hundreds of thousands of hectares of land in the southwestern United States and in Mexico that were grasslands in the 1850's. Although each gram of leaf material contains a very small fraction of volatiles, the vast area covered by these plants suggests that the quantities of volatile hydrocarbons entering the atmosphere could contribute to atmospheric reactions.

There are no data on the flux rates of leaf volatiles into the atmosphere. In the L. tridentata shrublands of North America and in areas in Australia where unpalatable, woody shrubs have replaced grasses, the presence of volatile hydrocarbons in the air is detectable by the human nose. The distinct odors of these hydrocarbons is especially noticeable after a rain. It has been suggested that these compounds may undergo atmospheric reactions that produce ozone and other oxidizing substances (8). However, there are no data on these atmospheric reactions.

Erosional Processes

The shift from grassland to sparse shrubland results in increased area of exposed bare soil in the intershrub spaces. Increased bare soil causes higher soil surface and air temperatures resulting from the reduction in loss of latent heat due to evapotranspiration. The increased temperature of the soils reduces the rate of organic nitrogen accumulation in the soil (8). However, the most significant aspect of increased area of bare soil is long distant transport of soil particles as a result of wind erosion (24, 25). Wind erosion increases exponentially as vegetative cover is reduced. Thus, as desertification becomes more severe, wind erosion is more significant (24).

Wind and dust devils or whirlwinds (cloudless micro-tornadoes) have been calculated to produce 10.5×10^6 tonnes of dust per year for the contiguous U.S. with virtually all of that material coming from recently desertified areas (25). That dust contained an average mass of 345×10^3 kilograms of Ca^{+2}, 900×10^3 kg of Mg^{+2} and 114×10^3 kg of Na^+. Dust transport can have significant effects on global element cycles. Dust that originates from areas of gypsum rich soils can contribute to the SO_4^{-2} concentration of rainfall (8). Most of the arid region soils are rich in calcium carbonate. Soil loss in early stages of desertification exposes calcium carbonate rich layers to wind erosion.

Dust from calcium carbonate rich soils can contribute to neutralization of acidic compounds in the atmosphere by reactions such as:

$$CaCO_3 + H_2SO_4 \longrightarrow CaSO_4 + H_2O + CO_2.$$

Atmospheric dust of desert origin can have important effects on the pH of rainfall. In a study in Northern Israel, cloud droplets with pH as low as 2.5 changed in pH as they grew by condensation into raindrops to pH as high as 8.2 (26). The condensing raindrops had apparently scavenged dust particles containing calcium carbonate that originated in desert dust aerosols from North Africa. Dust from deserts not only affects the pH of rainfall, but it can serve as a source of critical nutrients to severely nutrient limited systems such as mid-ocean waters. The P and Fe in dust from deserts may be especially important for the limited primary productivity of these areas (8).

More than one-third of the land area on earth is desert or subject to desertification. While the loss of harvestable productivity is of great concern because of the increasing need for food production for the rapidly growing human population, the consequences of desertification effect biogeochemical and atmospheric processes far beyond the borders of the arid and semi- arid regions. Our knowledge of many of these processes is fragmentary or even anecdotal. However, there is sufficient evidence to suggest that desertification is a process that we need to understand in order to deal with the many consequences of that process.

Acknowledgments

This chapter is a contribution of the Jornada Long-Term Ecological Research Program II supported by the National Science Foundation Grant BSR 88-11160.

Literature Cited

1. United Nations. 1978. United Nations Conference on Desertification Roundup: Plan of Action and Resolutions. United Nations. New York.

2. Dregne, H.E. In: Editors D.J. McLaren and P.J. Skinner. Resources and World Development John Wiley and Sons, Ltd. 1987. pp 697-710.

3. Dregne, H.E. Desertification of Arid Lands. Harwood Academic Publishers. New York. 1983.

4. Buffington, L.C.; C.H. Herbel. Ecological Monographs **1965**, 35:139-164.

5. York, J.C. and W.A. Dick-Peddie. In: Arid Lands in Perspective, W.G. McGinnies and B.J. Goldman (eds.). University of Arizona Press, Tucson, AZ, 1969 pp. 157-166.

6. Gibbens, R.P. and R.F. Beck. J. Range Mgmt. **1987**, 40:136-139.

7. Gibbens, R.P. and R.F. Beck. J. Range Mgmt. **1988**, 41:186-192.

8. Schlesinger, W.H., J.F. Reynolds, G.L. Cunningham, L.F. Huenneke, W.M. Jarrell, R.A. Virginia and W.G. Whitford. Science **1990**, 247:1043-1048.

9. Garcia-Moya, E. and C.M. McKell. Ecology **1970**, 51:81-88.

10. Charley, J.L. and N.E. West. J. Ecol. **1975**, 63:945- 964.

11. Charley, J.L. and N.W. West. Soil Biol. Biochem **1977**, 9:357-365.

12. Parker, L.W., H.G. Fowler, G. Ettershank and W.G. Whitford. J. Arid Environ. **1982**, 5:53-59.

13. Virginia, R.A. and W.M. Jarrell. Soil Sci. Soc. Am. J. **1983**, 47:138-144.
14. Lajtha, K. and W.H. Schlesinger. Biogeochem. **1986**, 2:29-37.
15. Gutierrez, J.R. and W.G. Whitford. J. Arid Environ. **1987**, 12:127-134.
16. Gutierrez, J.R. and W.G. Whitford. Ecology **1987**, 68:2032-2045.
17. Ludwig, J.A. and P. Flavill. In: E.C. Lopez, T.J. Mabry and S.F. Tavizon (eds.). Larrea, Centro de Investigacion en Quimica Aplicada, Saltillo, Mexico. 1979. 411 pp.
18. Fisher, F.M., J.C. Zak, G.L. Cunningham and W.G. Whitford. J. Range Mgmt. **1989**, 41:387-391.
19. Stevens, G.A. M.S. Thesis, Biology Department, New Mexico State University, 1989.
20. Whitford, W.G. Biol. Fert. Soils **1989**, 8:1-6.
21. Dickinson, N.M. Rev. Ecol. Biol. Sol. **1982**, 19:307- 314.
22. Bowden, W.B. Biogeochem., **1986**, 2:249-279.
23. Mabry, T.J., D.R. DiFeo, Jr., M. Sakakibara, C.F. Bohnstedt, Jr. and D. Seigler. In: Editors Mabry, T.J., J.H. Hunziker and D.R. DiFeo, Jr. Creosotebush: Biology and Chemistry of Larrea in New World Deserts.   Dowden, Hutchinson and Ross, Inc. Stroudsburg, PA. 1977. pp.115-134.
24. Morales, C. Climatic Change **1986**, 9:219-241.
25. Gillette, D.A. and P.C. Sinclair. Atmos. Environ. **1990**, 24A:1135-1142.
26. Levin, Z., c. Price and E. Ganor. Atmos. Environ. **1990**, 24A:1143-1151.
27. Nishita, N. and R.M. Haug. Soil Sci. **1973**, 116:51- 58.
28. Tiedmann, A.R. and S.O. Klemmendson. Soil Sci. Soc. Am. J. **1986**, 50:472-475.
29. Elkins, N.Z., G.V. Sabol, T.J. Ward and W.G. Whitford. Oecologia **1986**, 68:521-528.

RECEIVED September 4, 1991

Chapter 19

Long-Term Fates of Declining Forests

Richard M. Klein and Timothy D. Perkins

Forest Decline Program, Botany Department, University of Vermont, Burlington, VT 05405

Contemporary forest declines were initiated about 1950-1960, virtually simultaneously throughout the industrial world at the same time as damage to aquatic systems and structures became apparent. A broad array of natural and anthropogenic stresses have been identified as components of a complex web of primary causal factors that vary in time and space, interact among each other, affect various plant growth and development systems and may result in the death of trees in mountainous ecosystems. As these ecosystems decline, the alterations in forest ecology, independent of the initial causal complex, become themselves additional stress factor complexes leading to further alterations.

In 1968, reports from Sweden, subsequently confirmed in other industrial countries, noted that shallow lakes with low concentrations of divalent cations were becoming more acidic with consequent decreases in aquatic plants and animals. In severely affected lakes and ponds, only acidophilic algae survived. Increased acidity and the runoff of solubilized aluminum and other metal ions from surrounding watersheds are now known to be primarily responsible for formation of these almost sterile bodies of water.

Shortly thereafter, reports appeared in European forestry journals that plantation-grown silver fir and Norway spruce were exhibiting a decline syndrome characterized by loss of foliage, reduced growth and susceptibility to other stresses (1). Termed *Waldsterben* in Germany, by the late 1970's the phenomenon was evident in montane coniferous forests of upper New England, New York and adjacent Canadian Provinces. The most severely affected tree species was, and still is, the red spruce, a previously dominant tree in upper elevation forests of affected areas of New England and down the Appalachian mountain chain to North Carolina. The other dominant conifer, balsam fir, was not affected, but mature heart-leaved white birch showed decline symptoms and, in hardwood areas of lower mountain slopes, maple species, American beech and other trees seemed to be declining.

0097–6156/92/0483–0360$06.00/0
© 1992 American Chemical Society

Research on Camels Hump

In 1979, the Forest Decline Laboratory of the Botany Department of the University of Vermont conducted a quantitative evaluation of forest health of ecosystems on Camels Hump mountain in Vermont's Green Mountains. Camels Hump is a major summit in the Green Mountains, peaking at a bit over 1200 meters. The lower slopes from 550 to 730 meters are a typical New England sugar maple-beech-yellow birch association. Above a narrow transition zone, the upper elevations from 850 to about 1100 meters are forested with red spruce-balsam fir-white birch above which the forest is almost entirely balsam fir. A small arctic alpine tundra area above tree line is a relict of the last Ice Age, containing plants now found in upper Canada. Cutting and fire damage occurred up to 1950 in the hardwood zone, but the conifer areas have been relatively undisturbed by human activity. Our study area is on the west-facing slope of the mountain along the three-mile long Burrows Trail (Figure 1). Rectangles represent permanently marked survey plots along each of the 60 meter elevational transects.

We have studied Camels Hump since 1963 when a doctoral candidate conducted a comprehensive ecological study including quantitative and qualitative identification of all plant species, their location, density and growth plus data on weather patterns, soils and geology. The 1979 survey results confirmed our suspicions; severe declines in numbers and vigor of deciduous and coniferous tree species in both hardwood and conifer areas had occurred since 1965. We resurveyed in 1983, 1986 and 1990 to complete a full 25 year record of forest decline, now one of the most comprehensive vegetation data bases in the United States (Figures 2 and 3). Although balsam fir was not affected up to 1983, it had begun to decline in 1986. Red spruce has continued to be the most seriously affected tree. Several species of maple are declining as is beech and mountain ash. Declines are not the result of the natural death of older trees; all age classes are affected. Forest decline is real and devastating.

In most particulars, the symptomology of red spruce decline on Camels Hump corresponds to the pattern seen in eastern Canada, in New England and New York and down the Appalachian Mountain chain to the Carolinas. It also matches the pattern of decline of Norway spruce in Europe (*2*). Whether the pattern exists in our western mountains is still controversial. Tree ring analyses and other studies suggest that initiation of forest decline in the northeastern United States, adjacent Canada, and central Europe all date to about 1950 - 1960. Examination of lake sediments also gives the same date range for the damage to both European and North American fresh waters. While making correlations is a dangerous game, this was the same period when alkaline fly ash was eliminated, when construction of tall stacks on power plants allowed pollutions to be widely dispersed, when the high-compression automobile engine resulted in increases in nitrogen oxide emissions, when leaded gasolene became common, and when smelting and refining operations were greatly expanded (*3, 4*).

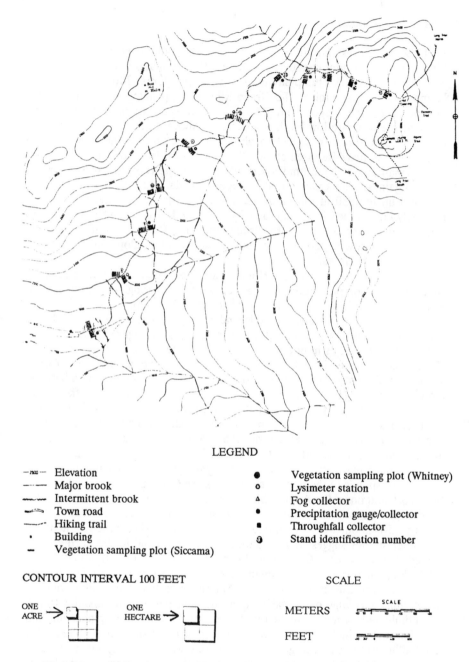

LEGEND

—₁₅₀₀—	Elevation	●	Vegetation sampling plot (Whitney)
—··——	Major brook	○	Lysimeter station
⌇⌇⌇	Intermittent brook	Δ	Fog collector
⥤	Town road	●	Precipitation gauge/collector
——··	Hiking trail	▪	Throughfall collector
•	Building	❸	Stand identification number
—	Vegetation sampling plot (Siccama)		

CONTOUR INTERVAL 100 FEET   SCALE

ONE ACRE ⟶ [diagram]   ONE HECTARE ⟶ [diagram]   METERS [scale bar]

FEET [scale bar]

Figure 1.   Map of the Burrows Trail on the southwest-facing slope of Camels Hump mountain showing location of permanently-marked study plots.

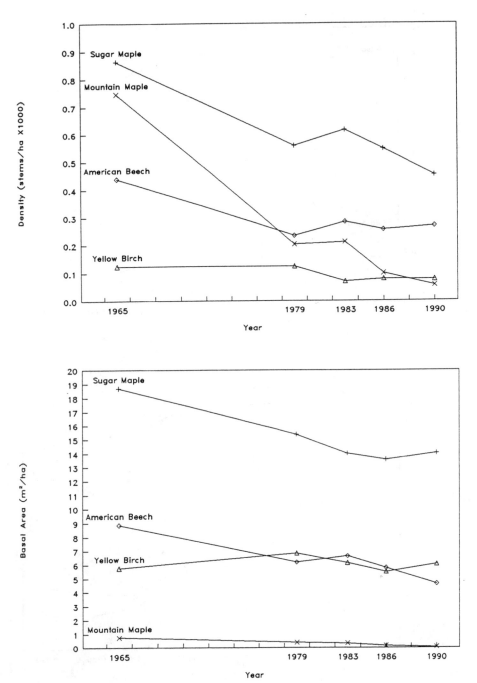

Figure 2. Changes in dominant species of trees in the lower elevation, hardwood ecosystem of Camels Hump based on density (upper graph) and on basal area (lower graph).

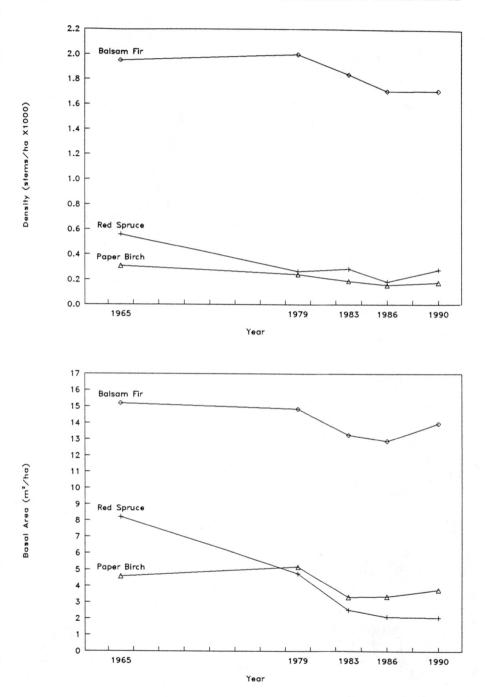

Figure 3.   Changes in dominant species of trees in the upper elevation, coniferous ecosystem of Camels Hump based on density (upper graph) and on basal area (lower graph).

The facts that contemporary forest declines a) were initiated simultaneously throughout the industrial world; b) that they simultaneously affect a number of tree species rather than a single species; c) that forested lands in North America, Europe and Asia are declining; d) that the declines of forests parallel in time and space to the well-documented damage to aquatic ecosystems and to structures; e) that they are found in association with a large number of other damaging alterations in many components of affected ecosystems; and f) that they can be correlated in time and space with changes in human life styles and industrial activities are each cogent arguments that anthropogenic causal factor complexes must be involved in forest decline (*4*).

Primary Causes of Forest Decline

Obviously, one looks for causes. That declines in one or another species have natural factor etiologies is unequivocal. The demise of American elms and of the chestnut were due to natural factors. Insect infestations, bacterial and fungal diseases, hurricanes, floods, freezes, droughts and many other stresses can cause extensive tree death (*5*). But in such declines typically only a single species is affected or climatic events caused decline in a delimited area. In almost all declines caused by natural events, the causal factors can be identified; we know their precise etiologies. Natural events are always part of the natural environment and must be factored in when evaluating forest declines (Table I).

Table I. Natural events and factors that stress forest trees (cf. *4, 6, 7*).

CLIMATIC EVENTS	ROLE IN FOREST DECLINE
Drought	Low in mountains
Flooding	Low in mountains
Soil erosion	Low to moderate
High temperature stress	Low in mountains
Low temperature stress	High for red spruce
High winds	Moderate to high
Global warming	Unknown
Increased UV-B radiation	Unknown
BIOTIC FACTORS	
Viruses/bacteria	Unknown to low
Fungal disease	Usually moderate
Insect infestation	Moderate as co-stresses
Mineral recycling	Moderate as co-stresses
Indigenous metals	Low without acid input

Some of the chemical and biological anthropogenic causal factors that have, individually and in concert, been demonstrated in both field and laboratory to damage tree growth, development and survival are given in Table II. They may interact synergistically or additively, interface with natural causal factor complexes, are strongly affected by site characteristics, weather conditions. They, and the natural factors, vary in time and space with one factor predominating today and, with a change in the weather or shifts in the wind direction, another factor being dominant tomorrow. There is no possibility that we will ever be able to pin down _THE_ or even _A_ cause of forest decline (4, 8). Using what little epidemological evidence is now available on declines, the probability that anthropogenic factors are deeply involved is very high (12). The consensus is that a large share of the factors that cause forest decline are anthropogenic is very high (4, 7). Contemporary forest declines are getting worse and have a bewildering and complex of natural and anthropogenic causal factors (3, 4, 12, 13, 14).

Upper elevation coniferous forest trees live on the edge of disaster under continuous natural biotic and abiotic stresses. Soils are shallow to bedrock, nutritionally poor and wet, wind speed has been measured at close to 100 miles per hour, and winters are usually severe. These forests are immersed in clouds for many days each year. Droplets of this cloud water condense on foliage and drop to the ground. Indeed, this cloud water or fog accounts for up to 70% of the water received by montane coniferous ecosystems. It is many times more acidic than rain or snow with average annual weighted pH values of 3.6 -3.7 compared to the 4.1 - 4.2 of precipitation (15). These acidity levels are sufficiently great to cause direct damage to foliage, cause leaching of cations, sugars, amino acids and proteins from foliage (16) that affect photosynthesis. Cloud water also contains higher concentrations of metal ions than precipitation.

Consequences of Primary Forest Decline

Using a physiological-ecological perspective, we analysed alterations in forest communities occurring as a result of forest decline. Since there are neither roads nor electric power lines on Camels Hump, all monitoring equipment runs on DC batteries recharged by solar panels (Figure 4). Real time data are collected on light flux, soil and air temperatures, wind speed and direction, soil moisture, relative humidity, precipitation, cloud water and ozone from both gap and canopied sites for computer analyses (16). We have found that gap formation has resulted in increased insolation with attendent increases in air and soil temperature, as well as changes in relative humidity. Wind patterns are shifting, there are alterations in competition among plant species, and there are many other modifications of the initial micro and macro environment. These environmental parameters are compared and correlated with quantitative measurements of changes in the vegetation.

The initial causes of forest decline - natural and anthropogenic - have resulted in a forest decline syndrome that is, _per se_, a new series of causal factors whose consequences are themselves new causes for ecosystem alteration.

Table II.   Anthropogenic factors known from laboratory and field studies to cause stresses in forest trees (cf. *3, 4, 9, 10, 11, 12, 13, 14*).

FACTOR	STRESS AND CONSEQUENCES
ACIDITY (H_2SO_4/HNO_3)	
Foliage	Damage to epicuticular waxes
	Altered photosynthesis
	Increased water loss
	Accumulation of acidic anions
	Leaching of ions, sugars, etc.
	Mineral imbalances
	Altered metabolism
	Increased susceptibility to
	winter freezing injury
Root systems	Death of fine roots
	Destabilization of trees
	Reduced water/mineral uptake
	Reduced water uptake
Soils	Cations leached below roots
	Accumulation of acidic anions
	Altered structure/texture
	Altered microflora
	Reduced litter decomposition
	Altered N transformations
	Solubilization of metal ions
METAL IONS	
Soils	Accumulation in soil solutions
	Altered microflora
	Reduced litter decomposion
Roots	Metal ions accumulate
	Reduced water/mineral uptake
	Reduction in mycorrhizae
	Reduced vigor/resistance
GASEOUS POLLUTANTS	
O_3	Altered photosynthesis
	Altered cell metabolism
	Damage to foliage cuticles
	Damage to epicuticular waxes
SO_2 and NO_x	Many foliage effects
	Altered reproductive patterns
Organics (PAN, etc.)	Poorly investigated

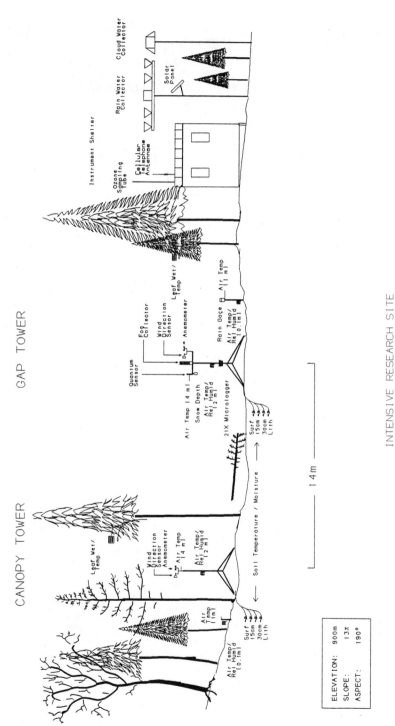

Figure 4. Diagramatic representation of the environmental monitoring units installed in gaps and adjacent canopied sites of the montane coniferous ecosystem of Camels Hump.

There is, then, a complex cascade of causes and consequences whose end is not yet in sight. Let me illustrate this with examples from our research.

Field surveys showed that very few red spruce seedlings are present in the declining ecosystems (*16*). One factor is, of course, that there are very few remaining mature red spruce trees to provide seed. Additionally, germination and seedling development of red spruce seed from Camels Hump are low (*17*). These limitations on natural regeneration are, of course, primary effects of the conditions that result in forest decline. But there are other considerations. Litter on the forest floor is not being degraded because of precipitation acidity, metal toxicity and death of those insects that normally chew litter into small fragments - also primary consequences of forest degradation. The increased depth of litter and forest duff suppresses red spruce seedling root growth down to mineral soil, a secondary effect. Litter and forest duff contain allelopathic substances extractable with synthetic precipitation that inhibit red spruce seed germination and repress red spruce seedling growth (*19*). The gaps formed by tree death become ideal habitats for ferns whose fronds contain allelopathic substances that interfere with seed germination and seedling growth of red spruce, but not balsam fir; this, too, is a secondary effect that will have tertiary effects and consequences. Based on all these findings, one can speculate that even were all pollution taps turned off today, the chances of red spruce again becoming a dominant member of the coniferous forest is minimal, at least for the forseeable future.

Although seen only occasional during the first half of this century, winter injury of first-year red spruce needles has become an annual event in the coniferous montane forest area, resulting in the formation of red-brown first year needles that subsequently desiccate and are shed (*20, 21*). The loss of foliage reduces photosynthesis and the obligatory accumulation of carbohydrate in the twigs and root systems. There is some evidence that this phenomenon involves both natural and anthropogenic causal factors.

Another gap invader is seedling birch (*22*). We are using these thickets to estimate how rapidly gaps are increasing in area as trees on gap edges die. The gaps are, indeed, increasing in size at rates averaging over one m per year. Since the birch in these gaps is a short-lived species, their more permanent replacement is still in doubt, but the birch invasion will undoubtedly set into motion another whole series of causes and consequences.

The changed wind patterns in gaps is causing flagging of the tree tops of surrounding balsam firs. Flagging, easily recognized as an assymetry of the crown due to branch breakage and loss of foliage on the upwind side of the tree, is the one of the first signs of fir decline and has become increasingly evident in the past five years (*23*). Clearly, fir decline is not a primary response to the natural and anthropogenic factors that caused initial forest decline. It is a secondary consequence that will initiate another cascade.

We must also consider the consequences of forty years of ecosystem pollution loading. Compared with soil analyses of heavy metal concentrations made in 1965, cadmium, copper, lead and zinc levels are now elevated (*24*) to the point where laboratory studies have shown that red spruce root and shoot growth is reduced, growth of obligatory mycorrhizal fungi is repressed and

a

Figure 5. Photographs of Camels Hump Mountain montane coniferous zone taken in (a) 1963 and (b) 1983 showing changes in forest composition.

nutrient recycling is inhibited. Since the residence time of these metals is measured in decades, they will continue to exert their influence for many years to come. Acidic deposition has also caused the accumulation of sulfate in soils to possibly repressive levels and has facilitated the leaching of calcium and other divalent cations to below the rooting zone of the trees. As Ca^{+2} decreases, and Al^{+3} increases, the molar Ca/Al ratio falls below 1.0 in the soil solution, a ratio shown *in vitro* to severely repress root growth and transport of nutrients into stems (25). Soil solution K^+ and NH_4^+ are also elevated, causing imbalances in mineral nutrition of plants. Such alterations in mineral metabolism are additional stresses and take long periods of time to correct.

Other studies are designed to evaluate possible changes in the herbaceous flora on the forest floor. There is, in gaps, a shift away from shade-requiring to sun-tolerant or sun-requiring plants. The herbs in the sunlit gaps have not only a different species ratio than in the still canopied plots, but the phenological relationships as shown by time of appearance, time relations of development and decline of seasonal flowers are different between sunlit gaps and shaded areas (26). To date, we have not seen the invasion of any new species of herbs or trees into these gaps. But as the gaps continue to enlarge, seeding in of weedy and aggressive species is possible.

National initiatives in North America and Europe are designed to reduce pollution emissions from both stationary and mobile sources. Independently of whether they succeed in reducing pollutant loadings, the available evidence indicates that alterations in affected forests will continue. Obviously, no one knows what affected forests will be like in 50 years. There is little doubt that they will be different. And the sooner the anthropogenic causal factors - all of them - are reduced qualitatively and quantitatively, the better are the chances of retaining or regenerating forests that will have meaning and value for those who will want to use them.

Acknowledgments. Research and preparation of this manuscript supported by the R. K. Mellon Foundation and the Vermont Agricultural Experiment Station. Data obtained from research of Forest Decline Project participants, including Gregory Adams, Mark Easter, Maureen Jennings, Mark Hemmerlein and Heiko Liedeker.

Literature Cited
1. Cowling, E.B., *Env. Sci. Tech.* **1982**, 16, 110-123.
2. Liedeker, H.; Schütt. P.; Klein, R.M. *Eur. J. For. Path.* **1988**, 18, 13-24.
3. Hinricksen, D., *BioScience* **1987**, 37, 542-546.
4. Klein, R.M.; Perkins, T.D. *Bot. Rev.* **1988**, 54, 2-43.
5. *Response of Plants to Multiple Stresses*. Mooney, H.A.; Winner, W.E.; Pell, E.J. Eds. Academic Press: San Diego, CA, **1991**.
6. *Tree Disease Concepts. 2nd Ed.* Manion, P.D. Prentice-Hall: Englewood Cliffs, NJ, **1991**.
7. *Air Pollution and Forests. 2nd Ed.* Smith, W.H. Springer-Verlag: NY, **1990**.
8. *Air Pollutants and their Effects on Terrestrial Ecosystems*. Legge, A.H.; Krupa, S.V. Eds., John Wiley & Sons: NY, **1986**.

9. *Forest Decline and Air Pollution: A Study of Spruce (Picea abies) on Acid Soils.* Schulze, E.D.; Lange, O.L.; Oren, R. Eds., Springer-Verlag: Berlin. **1989**.

10. *Atmospheric Deposition of Heavy Metals and Forest Health.* Smith, W.H. Virginia Polytechnic Institute: Blacksburg, VA, **1989**.

11. *Soil Acidity.* Ulrich, B.; Sumner, M.E. Eds. Springer-Verlag: Berlin. **1991**.

12. *Mechanisms of Forest Response to Acidic Deposition.* Lucier, A. A. Ed., Springer-Verlag: NY, **1990**.

13. McLaughlin, S.B. *J. Air Pollution Cont. Assoc.* **1985**, 35, 512-534.

14. Manion, P.D. In: *Effect of Atmospheric Pollutants on Forests, Wetlands, and Agricultural Ecosystems.* Hutchinson, T.C.; Meema, K.M. Eds., Springer-Verlag, NY, **1987**, pp. 267-275.

15. Scherbatskoy, T.; Bliss, M. In: *The Meteorology of Acid Deposition.* Sampson, P.J. Ed., Trans. Amer. Poll. Cont. Assoc. Pittsburgh, PA, **1983**. pp. 449-463.

16. Perkins, T.D.; Klein, R.M.; Easter, M.J.; Hemmerlein, M.T. Badger, G.J.; Vogelmann, H.W. Vermont Agric. Exp. Stat. Res. Rpt. 62, Burlington, VT, **1991**.

17. Scherbatskoy, T.; Klein, R.M. *J. Envir. Qual.* **1983**, 126, 189-195.

18. Whitney, H.E. Ph.D. Dissertation, Botany Department, University of Vermont, **1988**.

19. Klein, R.M.; Perkins, T.D.; Tricou, J.; Oates, A.; Cutler, *Amer.J. Bot.* **1991**. (in press).

20. Adams, G.T.; Perkins, T.D.; Klein, R.M. *Amer. J. Bot.* **1991**. (in press).

21. Perkins, T.D.; Adams, G.T.; Klein, R.M. *Amer. J. Bot.* **1991**. (in press).

22. Perkins, T.D.; Klein, R.M.; Vogelmann, H.W.; Badger, G.J. *Eur. J. For. Path.* **1988**, 18, 250-252.

23. Perkins, T.D. Ph. D. Dissertation, Botany Department, University of Vermont, **1991**.

24. Friedland, A.J.; Johnson, A.H.; Mader, D.L., *J. Soil Sci. Soc. Amer.* **1984**, 48, 422-425.

25. Hüttermann, A. *Experientia* **1985**, 41, 584-590.

26. Easter. M.J. M.S. Dissertation, Botany Department, University of Vermont, **1991**.

RECEIVED July 23, 1991

Global Carbon Cycle and Climate Change

An Overview

Robert K. Dixon

Environmental Research Laboratory, U.S. Environmental Protection
Agency, 200 SW 35th Street, Corvallis, OR 97333

The production of greenhouse gases by anthropogenic activities
may have begun to change the global climate. Although the
global carbon cycle plays a significant role in projected climate
change, considerable uncertainty exists regarding pools and
fluxes within this cycle. Given our present understanding of
global carbon sources and sinks, feedbacks from the biosphere
will influence the process of climate change. Opportunities may
exist to manage the biosphere and reduce the accumulation of
greenhouse gases in the atmosphere. The four chapters in this
section survey the role of the global carbon cycle in projected
climate change.

Moran examines the evidence suggesting that the accumulation of
greenhouse gases (e.g., CO_2, CH_4, CFCs, NO_x) in the atmosphere from
anthropogenic activities may have begun to change the global climate.
Carbon dioxide concentrations in the pre-industrial atmosphere have
been estimated to be 280 ppm, increasing to approximately 355 ppm by
1989 (1). If the rise continues unchecked, by the year 2020 global
mean temperature may rise 1.3°C above pre-industrial levels, with a
probable range between 1.3 and 2.5°C (2,3,4). Terrestrial
ecosystems will be affected by greenhouse gases and a changing
climate (4). Feedbacks from terrestrial systems to global climate change
processes will be significant and may affect the rate of climate change
as well as the levels at which dynamic equilibria are attained
(5,6,7,8).

   Post et al.. review components of the global carbon cycle that
encompass biogeochemical processes affecting the movement of carbon
between the atmosphere, terrestrial biosphere and oceans (9,10).
The general outline of the cycle is well known, but major uncertainties sill
exist in the magnitude of carbon pools and in the direction of fluxes.

Oceans store by far the largest fraction of carbon on the globe, approximately 38,500 gigatons (Gt) C. However, the accessible fraction for rapid exchange (scale of decades to a century) is probably similar in magnitude to that of the atmosphere and biosphere. Fossil fuels in the earth's crust are the next largest reserve (5000 - 10,000 Gt C), and it is man's activity that has accelerated this rate of exchange (3,4). Soils contain several times as much carbon as terrestrial vegetation or the atmosphere with estimates ranging from 700 -3000 Gt organic C (11).

Simpson and Botkin review the role of vegetation in the global carbon cycle and assert that estimates of terrestrial biomass carbon storage (above- and below-ground) are highly uncertain, differing by about 50% (3,12,13,14,15,16). Photosynthesis of terrestrial plants removes approximately 110 Gt of carbon from the atmosphere annually. A similar amount of carbon is returned to the atmosphere through plant respiration and decay of organic matter (17). Although vegetation processes significantly influence CO_2 concentrations in the atmosphere, the potential response of vegetation in terrestrial ecosystems to CO_2 enrichment and the associated climate change is known chiefly at the plant level, with few data on ecosystem responses (6). Forests, which may account for up to 64% of terrestrial and 43% of global net primary production (12), contain approximately 90% of all terrestrial biomass carbon and 40% of all soil organic carbon (18).

Annual carbon flux between the atmosphere and the biosphere is approximately equal to that between the atmosphere and the oceans. On a per area basis, however, terrestrial flux is much greater than oceanic flux. Recent data suggest that the flux into and out of the atmosphere may in fact not be balanced. Kaufman et al. indicate the atmosphere is gaining 3 gigatons of carbon per year, and this imbalance appears to be changing with time (1). The two major additions to atmospheric CO_2 are fossil fuel combustion (3,19) and deforestation (9,10,20). The combined total emission from these anthropogenic activities is approximately 6 Gt/year, of which about half remains in the atmosphere.

All four chapters suggest estimates of global carbon pools and flux are uncertain and reveal a critical question regarding the carbon budget: Where is the remaining carbon from deforestation and fossil fuel combustion assimilated? The two obvious possibilities are the oceans and the terrestrial biosphere. Recent estimates suggest that the terrestrial biosphere at temperate latitudes is a greater sink for the remaining carbon than previously thought (21). These estimates rely on a number of as yet unverified assumptions, while carbon isotope ratio information suggests possible increases of biospheric and/or deforestation-caused releases at high northern latitudes (1).

Kaufman et al. and Post et al. outline other uncertainties regarding the global carbon budget and the carbon released through deforestation and fossil fuel emissions. For example, current estimates of carbon emission vary by a factor of 2-3 because of uncertainties in rates of deforestation, amount of carbon in cleared forests, and the amount of regrowth after deforestation (9,10,19,22). Recent estimates of boreal forest biomass may be five times less than earlier assumed.

A variety of anthropogenic activities have the potential for affecting carbon flux between the biosphere and the atmosphere. A reduction in combustion of fossil fuels could significantly slow the accumulation of greenhouse gases in the atmosphere.   Moreover, the terrestrial biosphere could be managed to conserve and sequester carbon. Reforestation, slowing deforestation and desertification, and sustainable agriculture could conserve several Gt of carbon annually (Dixon R.K., Turner D.P., *Envir. Management,* in press). Social, economic and political factors currently hinder the opportunity to employ these options to mitigate the accumulation of greenhouse gases in the atmosphere (18,23).

Literature Cited

1. Keeling, C.D.; Bacastow, R.B.; Carter, A.F.; Piper, S.C.; Whorf, T.P.; Heimann, M.; Mook, W.G.; Roeloffzen, H. *Geophys. Monogr.* **1989**, 55, pp. 165-236.

2. Intergovernmental Panel on Climate Change (IPCC). 1990. Report for WGI Plenary Meeting, UN, New York, NY.

3. Schneider, S.H. *Sci. Amer.* **1989**, 261, pp. 70-79.

4. *The Effects of Climate Change on the U.S.* Tirpak, D.R.; Smith, J., Eds.; U.S. EPA, Washington, DC, 1989.

5. Houghton, R.A. *BioScience.* **1987**, 37, pp. 672-678.

6. Mooney, H.A.; Drake, B.G.; Luxmore, R.J.; Oechel, W.C.; Pitelka, L.F. *BioScience.* 1991.

7. Lashof, D.A. *Climatic Change.* **1989**, 14, pp. 213-242.

8. Harvey, L.D. *Climatic Change.* **1989**, 15, pp. 15-30.

9. Detwiler, R.P.; Hall, C.S. *Science* **1988**, 239, pp 42-46.

10. Woodwell, G.M.; Hobbie, J.E.; Houghton, R.A.; Melillo, J.M.; Moore, B.; Peterson, B.J.; Shaver, G.R. *Science* **1983**, 222, pp. 1081-1086.

11. Schlesinger, W.H. *In The Changing Carbon Cycle*; Trabalka, J.R., Ed.; Reichle, D.E., Ed.; Springer-Verlag: New York, NY, 1986, pp. 194-220.

12. Whittaker, R.H.; Likens, G.E.   In *Carbon and the Biosphere*; Woodwell, G.M., Ed.; Pecan, E.V., Ed.   Symposium Series 30; U.S. Atomic Energy Commission: Washington, DC, 1973; pp. 281-302.

13. Post, W.M.; Emanuel, W.R.; Zinke, P.J.; Stangenberger, A.G. *Nature.* **1982**, 298, pp. 156-159.

14. Atjay, G.L.; Ketner, P.; Duvigneaud, P. In *The Global Carbon Cycle*; Botkin, B., Ed.; John Wiley: Chichester, U.K. pp 129-182.

15. Olson, J.S.; Watts, J.A.; Allison, L.J.   Carbon in Live Vegetation of Major World Ecosystems. ORNL - 5862, Oak Ridge National Laboratory, Oak Ridge, TN. pp. 180.

16. Mooney, H.A.; Vitousek, P.M.; Matson, P.A. *Science* **1987**, 238, pp. 926-932.

17. *Soils and the Greenhouse Effect.* Bouwman, Ed., John Wiley: New York, NY.

18. Waring, R.H.; Schlesinger, W.H. *Forest Ecosystems: Concepts and Management*; Academic Press: Orlando, FL, 1985, pp. 340.

19. National Academy of Science. 1991. Policy Implications of Greenhouse Warming, National Academy Press: Washington, DC. p. 127

20. Houghton, R.A. *Environ. Sci. Tech.* **1990**, 24, pp. 414-422.

21. Tans, P.R.; Fung, I.Y.; Takahashi, T. *Science* 1990.

22. Houghton, R.A.; Boone, R.D.; Fruci, J.R.; Hobbie, J.E.; Melillo, J.M.; Palm, C.A.; Peterson, B.J.; Shaver, G.R.; Woodwell, G.M. *Tellus* **1987**, 39B, pp. 122-139.

23. Brown, L.R.; Durning, A.; Flavin, C.; Hesse, L.; Jacobson, J.; Postel, S.; Renner, M.; Pollock-Shea, C.; Starke, L. *A Worldwatch Institute Report on Progress Toward a Sustainable Society.* Norton: New York, NY, 1989; pp. 256.

RECEIVED October 1, 1991

Chapter 20

The Climatic Future and Lessons of the Climatic Past

Joseph M. Moran

Natural and Applied Sciences, University of Wisconsin—Green Bay,
Green Bay, WI 54311

This paper reviews some lessons of the climatic past that
are useful in evaluating forecasts of the climatic future.
Researchers have employed numerical models of the earth-
atmosphere system in experiments designed to predict
temperature and moisture anomaly patterns that might
accompany continued increases in concentrations of greenhouse gases. It is instructive to consider the well-publicized
results of those experiments in view of what is understood
about climatic behavior based on instrument-derived and
reconstructed climatic records. Such analyses indicate that
climate is inherently variable over a broad range of time
scales, climatic change is geographically non-uniform in
both direction and magnitude, climatic fluctuations may
involve changes in frequency of extreme episodes as well
as trends in mean values, and climate is shaped by a host of
interacting factors. Thus, the lessons of the climatic past
enable us to set boundary conditions and make realistic demands on climate predictions based on numerical models.

Today, considerable interest is directed at the potential global climatic consequences of changes in certain of the planet's biogeochemical cycles. Specifically,
increasing concentrations of infrared-absorbing atmospheric trace gases may
enhance the natural greenhouse effect and, if uncompensated, likely will cause
global warming. Some scientists warn that warming could be at a rate and
magnitude unprecedented in the 10,000 years of civilization and disrupt agricultural
and socioeconomic systems worldwide (1-4). While not all atmospheric scientists
agree with this scenario (5-6), even the possibility of such a future underscores the
need for a better understanding of the climatic system. The purpose of this paper
is to summarize some of the fundamental characteristics of climatic behavior based
on the climatic record.

0097–6156/92/0483–0379$06.00/0
© 1992 American Chemical Society

The Greenhouse Effect

The greenhouse effect is a natural phenomenon whereby the earth's atmosphere is more transparent to solar radiation than terrestrial infrared radiation (emitted by the earth's surface and atmosphere). Consequently, the planet's mean surface temperature is about $33\ K$ higher than the planet's radiative equilibrium temperature (the temperature at which the earth comes into equilibrium with the energy received from the sun).

Water vapor is the atmosphere's principal greenhouse gas. Although water vapor concentration exhibits considerable temporal and spatial variability, its contribution to the greenhouse effect at the global-scale is generally assumed to be fixed. Concern is directed primarily at rising levels of the IR-absorbing trace gases, CO_2 , O_3, CH_4 , N_2O, and CFCs. The latter three are particularly troublesome because they absorb in the so-called atmospheric windows, narrow infrared wavelength bands in which there is very little absorption by the main greenhouse gases, water vapor and carbon dioxide. In fact, absorption within atmospheric windows is directly proportional to concentration, so that doubling the concentration doubles the absorption.

Investigators employ numerical models of the earth-atmosphere system in experiments designed to predict temperature and moisture anomaly patterns that could accompany continued increases in the concentrations of greenhouse gases. Models vary in dimension and spatial resolution, with the most complicated being the 3-dimensional general circulation models (GCMs). The usual approach is to assume global radiative equilibrium initially and then to test the sensitivity of the model by elevating the concentration of one or more greenhouse gases. (The concentration of CO_2, for example, typically is doubled since, at its current growth rate, that concentration would be realized by late in the next century.) The model then shifts to a new equilibrium and generates new global or hemispheric patterns of temperature and moisture.

While step-function tuning of equilibrium models is the traditional approach in climate forecasting (7), there is reason to believe that a time-dependent climate model that responds to the more realistic case of a gradual growth in greenhouse gases (a transient simulation) may provide more reliable predictions. Nonetheless, it is useful to evaluate the well-publicized results of equilibrium-model simulations of future climate in light of what is understood about climatic behavior based on study of long-term instrument-derived and reconstructed climatic time series. In this way, we are able to identify paradigms that set boundary conditions on numerical climate prediction. This paper describes four of the most apparent lessons of the climatic past.

The Inherent Variability of Climate

Instrument-based and reconstructed climatic records indicate that climate is inherently variable over a broad spectrum of time scales, ranging from years to millennia.

Although in some places instrument-based climatic records go back about

300 years, reliable observations are limited to only the past 100 years or so. It was not until the late 1800s that weather observations were made under standardized conditions. Earlier records suffer from interruptions and variable instrument quality and exposure. For one, widespread use of instrument shelters in North America date only to the 1870s even at official weather stations (8). In fact, it was not uncommon during the early to mid 1800s for thermometers to be mounted in direct sunshine (9).

Even climatic records of the past 100 years may be biased by changes in sophistication of weather instruments through the period of record, relocation of instruments at most long-term weather stations, urbanization and expansion of associated heat islands, and huge gaps in monitoring networks, especially over the oceans. In semiarid regions of the world, widespread desertification (often due to overgrazing) may alter the local radiation budget and hence, bias temperature readings (10).

Potential problems with record integrity call into question the reality of the much publicized 20th century global warming trend. Jones and Wigley (11) attempted to remove biases in temperature records from both land and sea by carefully screening and systematically correcting the data. They concluded that although cooling prevailed from about 1940 into the 1970s, the global mean temperature increased about 0.5 C° over the past 100 years.

An instrument record that is limited to only 100 years or so may not encompass the full range of climatic variability and hence, not include all possible analogs for future climates. For example, global warming predicted to accompany the increase in atmospheric carbon dioxide over the next 100 years (1.5 to 4.5 C°) is three to nine times greater than the global warming of the past 100 years (about 0.5 C°). Hence, scientists from a variety of disciplines have attempted to lengthen the climatic record by reconstructing past climates.

Paleoclimatologists reconstruct the climatic past by extracting and synthesizing the climatic implications of a wide variety of biological and geological sensors (12). For example, much of what we know about climatic variations since the last glacial maximum, 18,000 years ago, is based on studies of fossil pollen, tree growth-rings, deep-sea sediments, and shoreline reconstructions. Unfortunately, as we journey back in time, available climatic evidence becomes more fragmentary and unreliable, time control becomes more suspect, and climatic reconstructions become increasingly generalized.

In spite of uncertainties, paleoclimatic research provides insight on the workings of the climatic system (13). It appears, for example, that over the past 570 million years, fluctuations in atmospheric CO_2 tended to parallel changes in global temperature, being lower during cool episodes and higher during mild episodes (14). However, it is not at all clear which was the cause and which was the effect, that is, whether changes in atmospheric CO_2 contributed to climatic change or vice versa.

The paleoclimatic record is the focus of a search for regional response analogs for future greenhouse warming. Proposed analogs include the relatively warm episodes of the mid-Holocene (8500 to 5000 years ago) and the last interglacial (about 120,000 years ago). Crowley (15), however, argues that those and other proposed analogs (e.g. Pliocene, Eocene, and mid-Cretaceous warm intervals) may not be appropriate. He notes that the mid-Holocene and last interglacial warming affected seasonal temperatures primarily with only a slight rise in global mean temperature. Furthermore, the warming was not globally synchronous. Bryson (16) also discredits the mid-Holocene analog by pointing out that at that time sea level was lower and ice sheets more extensive, and the dates of perihelion and aphelion were different than they will be over the next several centuries. Crowley dismisses pre-Pleistocene analogs because of the absence of ice sheets and significant differences in topography and land-sea distribution.

Paleoclimatic data can be useful in validating GCM climate simulations (7,17). GCM portrayals of paleoclimates are checked against reconstructions based on paleoclimatic data. Such comparisons help to assess the model's ability to predict future climates.

Both instrument-based and reconstructed climatic records indicate that change is an inherent characteristic of climate. It is not surprising then that climatic time series have long been the target of painstaking searches for regular rhythms. A formidable challenge in this search is to separate the climatic signal from a record that is often excessively noisy. Some climatic elements are so variable (noise) with time that detection of cycles or trends (signal) is a major challenge. An example of a particularly noisy climatic variable (and one that is cited as likely to change during global warming) is length of growing season (18).

Electronic computers programmed with sophisticated statistical routines (e.g. variance spectral analysis) facilitate the search for climatic rhythms. The motivation behind this effort is obvious: Isolation of real periodicities in climate would be a powerful tool in climate forecasting. However, climatologists have identified only a few statistically significant cycles that are useful for climate forecasting over decades.

Cycles established as statistically real are the familiar annual and diurnal radiation/temperature cycles, a quasibiennial (about every 2 years) fluctuation in various climatic elements, and the interannual variability of June rainfall in northern India. The first merely means that winters are cooler than summers and nights are cooler than days. Examples of the second cycle include Midwestern rainfall, a lengthy temperature record from central England, and winds over the western Pacific and eastern Indian Ocean. According to Campbell et al (19), the third cycle may be a response to the monthly solar-lunar tide and its influence on the monsoon circulation.

Trends may appear in the climatic record, but unless that trend is part of a statistically significant cycle, there is no guarantee that the trend will not abruptly end or reverse direction at any time. Some atmospheric scientists are quick to point to recent trends in climate that are consistent with changes that would attend greenhouse warming as predicted by GCMs. These include the purported global warming trend, occurrence of the seven warmest years since 1980 in a 100-year global land-station record, and recent cooling of the lower stratosphere. These and other observations have been used to bolster the argument that greenhouse warming has begun and give new urgency to strategies that might lessen the warming.

Although much has been written in the popular and scientific press regarding a pending greenhouse warming, the climatic record warns against assuming that weather extremes (e.g. the record hot and dry summer of 1988) signal a long-term climatic change; extreme episodes may well prove to be short-lived. Indeed, the climatic record indicates that events of a single year or even several successive years do not necessarily signal the beginnings of a trend.

The Geographic Non-Uniformity of Climatic Change

The inherent temporal variability of climate thus obscures the search for long-term climatic signals. In addition, the search is plagued by the great spatial variability of climatic change.

Assuming that all other controls of climate are constant, continued increases in concentrations of greenhouse gases likely will elevate the global mean surface temperature. A formidable challenge for the climate forecaster is to predict the regional response, that is, how global-scale climate change translates into temperature and moisture changes during specific meteorological seasons and at specific locations within the earth-atmosphere-ocean system. Indeed, the climatic record shows that anomalies and trends in climate exhibit considerable spatial variability in both sign (direction) and magnitude.

Routine comparison of the weather of a specific week, month, or year over a large geographical area against long-term climatic averages produces complex anomaly patterns. For a given month, for example, departures from monthly mean temperatures and precipitation never have the same sign or magnitude everywhere over the United States. Outside of the Tropics, the prevailing pattern of the planetary westerlies governs the spatial variability of climatic anomalies. This linkage is particularly well-illustrated by Trenberth's analysis of northern hemispheric temperature anomalies and circulation changes during 1977-1988 (20). He found that during that 10-year period, the Aleutian low was deeper and shifted farther eastward than usual. Consequently, the circulation about the system brought anomalous warmth to Alaska and anomalous cold over the North Pacific Ocean.

Some combination of local radiational conditions plus air mass advection controls air temperature at a particular location. In mid-latitudes, air mass advection, in turn, depends on the dominant westerly flow pattern. Hence, mean winter temperatures are below average wherever the prevailing westerly pattern favors more than the usual cold air advection. Prevailing planetary winds also determine the location of weather extremes such as drought or excessive cold. In view of the usual range in westerly wave number and wavelength, a single weather extreme never grips the entire nation at the same time. Also, temperature anomaly patterns are usually less complex than those of precipitation. The greater spatial variability in rainfall arises from shifts in storm tracks, topographic influences, and the almost random distribution of warm-season convective showers.

The geographic nonuniformity of climatic anomalies has important implications for agricultural productivity since some compensation is implied. That is, during a given growing season, good weather and higher crop yields in one area may compensate to some extent for poor weather and consequent lower crop yields in other areas. Hence, the impact of a large-scale climatic change on crop productivity is not likely to be the same everywhere over areas as large as the United States or Canada. All crops are not equally sensitive to the same climatic fluctuation nor are all arable regions equally sensitive to large-scale climatic shifts.

Geographic nonuniformity also characterizes trends in climate. Hence, a global trend in average annual temperature is not necessarily representative either in sign or magnitude of all localities. During the same period, some locations experience cooling trends, while others experience warming trends, regardless of the direction of the global temperature trend. This means, for example, that a persistent cooling trend in some region does not necessarily argue against global warming.

The geographic nonuniformity of climatic change thus complicates the search for a greenhouse signal. So far, global warming has not been spatially uniform nor is it likely to be in the future. Should greenhouse gases force global warming, we should not anticipate warming everywhere at the same rate. In fact, attendant changes in the atmospheric (and oceanic) circulation may mean that some areas exhibit no change in mean temperature or actually cool for a lengthy period.

Not only is it misleading to assume that the direction of large-scale climatic trends applies to all localities, it is also erroneous to assume that the magnitude of climatic trends is the same everywhere. In fact, a small change in the average hemispheric temperature typically translates into greater change in some areas and to little or no change in other areas. Diaz and Quayle (21), for example, show how trends in mean winter (December through February) temperature varied across major climatic subdivisions of the United States from the late 1800s into the mid-1970s. In summary, the trend line varied from essentially flat (no change) in the Pacific Northwest to a cooling of 2.8 C° in New England.

A popular notion holds that sensitivity to large-scale climatic trends increases with latitude. Usually, this is taken to imply that greenhouse warming--if it actually occurs--will be amplified in polar regions where it may trigger wastage of the ice caps and, coupled with thermal expansion of seawater, may cause a destructive rise in sea level. Indeed, most numerical models predict that greenhouse warming will be maximum at high latitudes in winter and will be 1.5 to 3 times the global average warming (1). Paleoclimatic reconstructions point to polar amplification of hemispheric temperature trends during the Ice Age, but Ice Age temperature patterns are necessarily tentative since they are derived from sparse and reconstructed data. The generalized nature of such climatic reconstructions seriously limits our ability to resolve climatic trends both spatially and temporally. It is likely that geographic sensitivity to global-scale climatic change is more complex than a simple dependence on latitude.

How well do GCMs simulate the spatial variability of climatic change? Today's GCMs utilize data grids that partition the atmosphere into cells, each covering an area about the size of Colorado. A mean state of the atmosphere (temperature, humidity, cloud cover, for example) is computed for each cell. Consequently, any output statistics (the prediction) has a lower spatial resolution (more generalized, less detailed) than the real atmosphere is likely to manifest.

That is, existing models do not do well in predicting regional and even continental-scale climate change.

One way of testing the validity of GCMs is to use them to simulate present day climate by inputing modern boundary conditions (*22*). On the whole, the major models do well in portraying the large-scale seasonal patterns of air pressure, temperature, wind and precipitation. Significant errors arise at the regional scale, however. Depending on the specific model, mean surface air temperature errors are from 2 to 3 C° and mean errors of average rainfall range from 20 to 50%. Limited-area models (LAMs) promise to give better results. As Cohen (*23*) notes, LAMs are embedded in a general circulation model and achieve relatively high resolution over small areas.

In evaluating global climate predictions, we also should be aware of possible teleconnections, that is, linkages between climatic anomalies occurring simultaneously in widely separated regions of the globe. One extensively studied teleconnection is the strong correlation between a broad area of anomalously high sea-surface temperatures in the eastern tropical Pacific and various weather extremes in the Tropics and mid-latitudes (the so-called ENSO phenomenon). In 1982-1983, such an event was linked to Australia's worst drought in 200 years (*24*). Another proposed teleconnection links summer rainfall in the Western Sahel of North Africa and the intensity of hurricane activity in the Caribbean (*25*). Teleconnections are one consequence of the basic continuity of the atmosphere and the integrity of the planetary circulation such that a change in one region may propagate to other regions.

Means and Extremes in Climatic Change

Climatic change may occur as fluctuations in means and/or extremes of climatic variables. Most studies of climatic change, however, focus almost exclusively on trends in mean values of climatic variables (usually temperature). In fact, a climatic shift also may be manifest as an increase or decrease in the frequency of occurrence of extremes. That is, episodes of drought or excessive rainfall or record high or low temperatures may become more or less frequent. Changes in frequency of extremes may occur with little or no concurrent change in means.

Consider as an illustration a study of the occurrence frequency of new record low temperatures during winter (December through February) at 20 Upper Midwestern stations (*26*). Intuitively, we expect that the probability of setting a new record low temperature on any day will decline with length of station record (*27*). But in the Upper Midwest, the cumulative number of new record low temperatures sharply increased from the 1940s through the 1970s. During this same period, the region experienced only a slight cooling trend in mean winter temperature.

The possibility that the climatic future might feature a change in frequency of weather extremes underscores the desirability for climate models capable of predicting the future spectrum of prevailing circulation patterns. Weather extremes such as drought or excessive cold are the products of certain persistent (blocking) planetary wave patterns. In fact, it is reasonable to assume that past climatic regimes differed from one another not so much in type of circulation patterns but rather in the frequency of occurrence of individual patterns. Thus the winter of 1976-1977 was one of the coldest on record in the Midwest not because the prevailing circulation pattern was unusual--the same circulation pattern occurs every winter--but because that circulation pattern persisted for an anomalously long period (from mid-October through mid-February).

Multivariate Controls of Climate

Climate is controlled by complex interactions involving many variables operating both within and outside of the earth-atmosphere-ocean system (Figure 1). Indeed, some combination of volcanic activity, short-term fluctuations in solar irradiance, and CO_2 increase, could well account for much of the variance in northern hemispheric mean annual temperature over the past century (28). It is reasonable to assume that the climatic future will be similarly shaped by the interaction of many variables. Furthermore, internal feedback mechanisms may complicate matters by amplifying or dampening climatic changes. Nonetheless, the typical approach in numerical climate forecasting is to manipulate one variable while holding all other controls constant.

The concept of global radiative equilibrium is useful in identifying the various factors that govern climatic variability. At radiative equilibrium, the flux of solar radiation absorbed by the planet equals the flux of infrared radiation to space. That is,

$$S_o(1 - \alpha)\pi R^2 = \varepsilon \sigma T^4 (4\pi R^2)$$

where

> S_o = the solar constant, that is, the flux of solar radiation received at the top of the atmosphere,
> α = the planetary albedo, the fraction of solar radiation reflected or scattered to space,
> R = radius of the earth
> ε = effective emissivity
> σ = Stefan-Boltzmann constant
> T = radiative equilibrium temperature.

Solving for T, the planet's temperature at radiative equilibrium,

$$T = [S_o(1 - \alpha)/4\varepsilon \sigma]^{1/4}$$

Hence, the radiative equilibrium temperature is sensitive to changes in the solar constant, planetary albedo, and the radiative properties of the earth-atmosphere-ocean system. In addition, changes internal to the earth-atmosphere-ocean system may alter the climate. Table I is an incomplete list of phenomena that individually or in concert could alter climate.

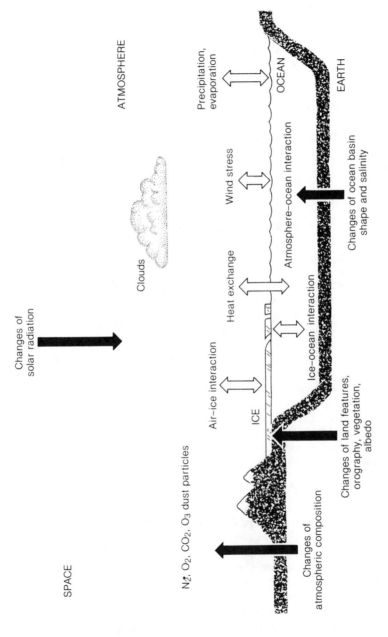

Figure 1. Both internal (white arrows) and external (black arrows) processes influence climatic variability. (Reproduced with permission from ref. 30. Copyright 1975 National Academy Press, National Academy of Sciences.)

In evaluating the influence of individual climate controls, we have three major concerns: the time frame over which the control operates, the potential magnitude of the control's influence on climate, and whether a strong correlation between some forcing phenomenon and climatic response actually indicates a cause-effect relationship.

Individual violent volcanic eruptions, for example, may affect large-scale climate for one or two years whereas Milankovitch cycles affect climate over

---

Table I. Some Possible Causes of Climatic Variability

Solar Constant	Planetary Albedo	Internal
solar irrad- iance	cloud cover	greenhouse gases
sunspots	cloud thickness	plate tectonics
Milankovitch cycles	volcanic emissions	land albedo
interplanetary dust	atmospheric turbidity	ocean circulation

---

periods of thousands to hundreds of thousands of years. By injecting aerosols into the lower stratosphere, a large volcanic eruption may temporarily elevate the planetary albedo and cool the earth's surface. Several historical studies of the volcano-climate relationship (e.g. Krakatoa, 1883; Agung, 1963) suggest that the global mean temperature may fall 0.1 to 0.5 C°. Milankovitch cycles consist of long-term variations in the earth's orbital parameters: tilt and precession of the spin axis, and orbital eccentricity (29). These cycles are thought to be the principal forcing of the major glacial-interglacial climatic shifts of the Ice Age.

Prolonged episodes of low sunspot activity as observed in Europe and China during 1450-1550 and again from 1645 to 1715 closely correlate with relatively cool periods (at least in Europe). The question is whether the correlation is a cause-effect relationship or merely coincidental. Perhaps the estimated 0.2 to 0.6% decline in solar irradiance that accompanied low sunspot activity may have contributed to the cooling. In another example of a possible climate cause-effect relationship, analysis of ancient air bubbles trapped in the Vostok (Antarctica) glacial ice core has enabled researchers to reconstruct long-term changes in atmospheric CO_2 levels over the past 160,000 years. Indications are that CO_2 concentrations fluctuated between about 190 ppm during glacial climatic episodes and about 280 ppm during interglacial climatic episodes. However, as noted earlier, Milankovitch cycles are likely the primary controls of major Ice Age climatic fluctuations. And, it is unclear whether changes in atmospheric CO_2 contributed to or were the consequence of glacial-interglacial climatic shifts.

Individual climate controls do not function in isolation from one another; rather, many factors link together in complex cause-effect chains (Figure 2). Factor interactions may involve feedback loops that at one extreme amplify

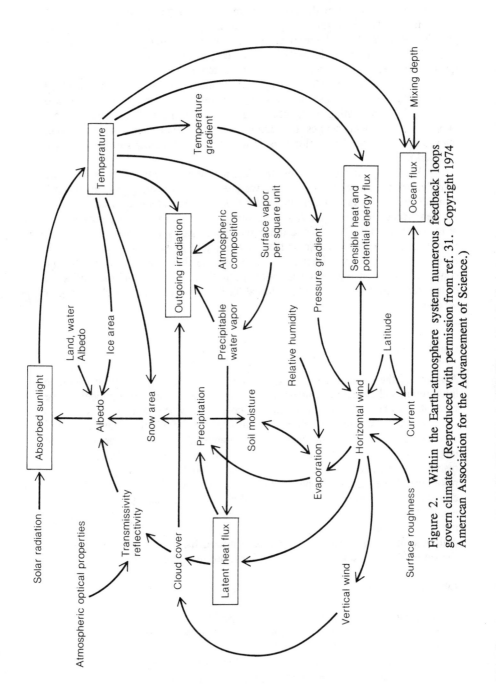

Figure 2. Within the Earth-atmosphere system numerous feedback loops govern climate. (Reproduced with permission from ref. 31. Copyright 1974 American Association for the Advancement of Science.)

(positive feedback) and at the other extreme offset (negative feedback) climatic fluctuations. If, for example, global warming accompanies the buildup in greenhouse gases, the pack ice cover in polar regions will likely shrink. Less pack ice, in turn, lowers the reflectivity of polar seas, further warming the atmosphere (positive feedback). On the other hand, higher temperatures at the earth's surface mean more evaporation, which may result in thicker and more persistent cloud cover. While clouds cause both cooling (by reflecting sunlight to space) and warming (by contributing to the greenhouse effect) at the earth's surface, recent satellite measurements suggest that cooling dominates on a global scale. Hence, thicker and more persistent cloud cover would cool the earth's surface (negative feedback).

We are reminded of the multivariate nature of climatic controls when we consider that the global warming trend was interrupted by cooling from about 1940 into the 1970s. (In fact, during the 1970s there was considerable speculation that we were headed for a new Ice Age!). Cooling occurred in spite of a persistent rise in the concentrations of CO_2 and other greenhouse gases throughout the century. Hence, it is reasonable to assume that the buildup of greenhouse gases is but one of many influences on climate. It could well be that thus far, other climatic controls have lessened greenhouse warming. In the future, the combined influence of the many climatic controls plus internal feedback mechanisms could enhance or offset greenhouse warming.

Conclusions

Analysis of the climatic record yields some observations that may be useful in interpreting and evaluating climate forecasts generated by numerical models of the earth-atmosphere system. The limited instrument-based climatic record plus reconstructed paleoclimates indicate that the change is an inherent characteristic of climate. However, climatic change is geographically variable in both sign and magnitude making it difficult to detect a long-term global warming trend in response to the buildup of greenhouse gases. Models must have greater spatial resolution if they are to properly portray the considerable spatial variability of climatic change. Furthermore, we should be aware that climate change may be manifest as a change in extremes as well as means of climatic variables. Finally, it is well to bear in mind that climate is a complex system that is influenced by a multitude of factors. Hence, the climatic future, like the climatic past, will be shaped by the interaction of many variables, not just greenhouse gases.

Literature Cited

1. Ramanathan, V. *Science*. 1988, *240*, pp. 293-299.
2. Schneider, S.H. *Global Warming*; Sierra Club Books: San Francisco, CA, 1989, 317 p.
3. Schneider, S.H. *Bull. Amer. Meteor. Soc.* 1990, *71*, pp. 1292-1304.
4. White, R.M. *Sci. Amer.* 1990, *263*, No. 1, pp. 36-43.

5. Lindzen, R.S. *Bull. Amer. Meteor. Soc.* 1990, *71*, pp. 288-299.
6. *Scientific Perspectives on the Greenhouse Problem*; The George C. Marshall Institute: Washington, DC, 1989; 37 p.
7. Schneider, S.H. *Sci. Amer.* 1987, *256*, No. *5*, pp. 72-80.
8. Middleton, W.E.K. *History of the Thermometer and Its Use in Meteorology*; The Johns Hopkins Press: Baltimore, MD, 1966.
9. Moran, J.M.; Somerville, E.L. *Trans. Wisc. Acad. of Sci., Arts, and Letters.* 1987, *75*, pp. 79-89.
10. Balling, R.C. Jr. *Bull. Amer. Meteor. Soc.* 1991, *72*, pp. 232-234.
11. Jones, P.D.; Wigley, T.M.L. *Sci. Amer.* 1990, *263, No. 2*, pp. 84-91.
12. Bradley, R.S. *Quaternary Paleoclimatology*; Allen and Unwin: Boston, MA, 1985.
13. Webb, T. III; Wigley, T.M.L. In *Projecting the Climatic Effects of Increasing Carbon Dioxide*; MacCracken, M.C. and Luther, F.M., Ed.; U.S. Dept. of Energy, ER-0235; DOE: Washington, DC, 1985; pp 238-257.
14. Berner, R.A. *Science* 1990, *249*, pp. 1382-1386.
15. Crowley, T.J. *J. Climate* 1990, *3*, pp. 1282-1292.
16. Bryson, R.A. *Quaternary Res.* 1985, *23*, pp. 275-286.
17. COHMAP, *Science*, 1988, *241*, pp. 1043-1052.
18. Moran, J.M.: Morgan, M.D. *Agric. Meteor.* 1977, *18*, pp. 1-8.
19. Campbell, W.H.; Blechman, J.B.; Bryson, R.A. *J. Climate and Appl. Meteor.* 1983, *22*, pp. 287-296.
20. Trenberth, K.E. *Bull. Amer. Meteor. Soc.* 1990, *71*, pp. 988-993.
21. Diaz, H.F.; Quayle, R.G. *Mon. Wea. Rev.* 1978, *106*, pp. 1402-1405.
22. Gates, W.L.; Rowntree, P.R.; Zeng, Q.C. In *Climate Change, The IPCC Scientific Assessment*; Houghton, J.T., Jenkins, G.J., and Ephraums, J.J., Ed.; Cambridge University Press: New York, NY, 1990, pp. 93-130.
23. Cohen, S.J. *Bull. Amer. Meteor. Soc.* 1990, *71*, pp. 520-526.
24. Ramage, C.S. *Sci. Amer.* 1986, *254, No. 6*, pp. 77-83.
25. Gray, W.M. *Science*, 1990, *249*, pp. 1251-1256.
26. Moran, J.M.; Reitan, C.H. *Bull. Amer. Meteor. Soc.* 1980, *61*, p. 423.
27. Reitan, C.H.; Moran, J.M. *Month. Weather Rev.* 1977, *105*, pp. 1442-1446.
28. Revelle, R. *Sci. Amer.* 1982, *247, No. 2*, p. 41.
29. Covey, C. *Sci. Amer.* 1984, *250, No. 2*, pp. 58-66.
30. Gates, W.L.; Mintz, Y. *Understanding Climatic Change*; National Academy Press: Washington, DC, 1975
31. Kellogg, W.W.; Schneider, S.H. *Science*, 1974, *186*, p. 1164.

RECEIVED July 23, 1991

Chapter 21

Climatic Feedbacks in the Global Carbon Cycle

W. M. Post,[1] F. Chavez,[2] P. J. Mulholland,[1] J. Pastor,[3] T.-H. Peng,[1] K. Prentice,[4] and T. Webb III[5]

[1]Environmental Sciences Division, Oak Ridge National Laboratory, P.O. Box 2008, Oak Ridge, TN 37831−6335
[2]Monterey Bay Aquarium Research Institute, 160 Central Avenue, Pacific Grove, CA 93950−0020
[3]Natural Resources Research Institute, University of Minnesota, Duluth, MN 55811
[4]Institute for Space Studies, National Aeronautics and Space Administration Goddard Space Flight Center, 2880 Broadway, New York, NY 10025
[5]Department of Geological Sciences, Brown University, Providence, RI 02912−1846

Increasing atmospheric CO_2 is likely to produce chronic changes in global climate, as it may have done in the geologic past. Future CO_2-induced changes in temperature and precipitation distribution changes could equal or exceed the changes which have occurred over the past 160,000 years and have affected the global carbon cycle. We consider ocean and terrestrial processes that could involve large changes in carbon fluxes (>2 Pg C·yr^{-1}) or changes in storage in large carbon pools (>200 Pg C) resulting from CO_2-induced climate changes. These include (1) air-sea exchange of CO_2 in response to changes in temperature and salinity; (2) climate-induced changes in ocean circulation; (3) changes in oceanic new production and regeneration of organic debris caused directly by climate change; (4) altered oceanic nutrient supply needed to support new production due to climate-induced alteration of ocean circulation and river discharge; (5) $CaCO_3$ compensation in sea water; (6) altered river nutrient flux and effects on coastal organic matter production and sediment accumulation; (7) seasonal balance between GPP and decomposition-respiration in terrestrial ecosystems in response to changes in temperature and precipitation; (8) successional processes in terrestrial ecosystems and formation of new plant associations in response to climatic change; (9) effects on soil nutrient availability, which amplifies ecosystem responses to climate change; (10) and responses of northern forests, tundra, and peatlands which have, until recently, been a sink for CO_2. The potential effect of these processes

0097−6156/92/0483−0392$06.25/0

on the rate of atmospheric CO_2 concentration changes are estimated where possible, but not much quantitative information at a global scale is known, so uncertainty in these estimates is high. Each of these secondary feedbacks, however, has the potential of changing atmospheric CO_2 concentration in magnitude similar to the effects of the direct human processes (fossil fuel burning and land clearing) responsible for the concern about global warming in the first place. It is therefore urgent that these uncertainties be resolved. Lines of research to accomplish this are suggested.

Over long time-scales (millions of years), geological processes determine the range of variation in rates of global carbon cycle fluxes (1). At shorter time-scales (decades and centuries), the rates of rock formation and weathering are too slow, and the exchanges of CO_2 between the relatively active reservoirs of carbon in the atmosphere and terrestrial ecosystems and ocean surface waters are responsible for fluctuations in atmospheric CO_2 concentration. The flux rates of CO_2 between the atmosphere, land, and ocean are determined by a complex and interactive array of chemical, biological, and physical processes (Figure 1). For at least the last 160,000 years, a balance between these faster carbon cycle processes may have been responsible for the atmospheric CO_2 concentrations remaining in the relatively narrow range of 200 to 300 $\mu L \cdot L^{-1}$ (Figure 2a). Fossil fuel burning is resulting in an unprecedented rate of increase in atmospheric CO_2 (Figure 2b). This increase could shift the carbon cycle to a new mode of operation (8, 9). In the future, increasing atmospheric CO_2 levels may significantly reduce or eliminate some negative feedbacks (interactions between carbon cycle components that tend to restore or maintain atmospheric CO_2 levels), enhance existing positive feedbacks (interactions that tend to amplify small deviations from existing CO_2 levels), or introduce new positive or negative feedbacks in the global carbon cycle.

Feedbacks may be affected directly by atmospheric CO_2, as in the case of possible CO_2 fertilization of terrestrial production, or indirectly through the effects of atmospheric CO_2 on climate. Furthermore, feedbacks between the carbon cycle and other anthropogenically altered biogeochemical cycles (e.g., nitrogen, phosphorus, and sulfur) may affect atmospheric CO_2. If the creation or alteration of feedbacks have strong effects on the magnitudes of carbon cycle fluxes, then projections, made without consideration of these feedbacks and their potential for changing carbon cycle processes, will produce incorrect estimates of future concentrations of atmospheric CO_2.

Climate-Ocean CO_2 Feedbacks

Presently, it is not known whether the feedback of oceanic CO_2 in response to the CO_2-induced climatic warming will, on the whole, be positive or negative. The rate of exchange between the oceans and the atmosphere is regulated by the following processes: (a) exchange of CO_2 gas between the atmosphere and the surface layers of the oceans, (b) exchange of water between the upper and the deep layers of the ocean (mixing, upwelling, and deep-water formation) and (c) photosynthetic utilization of CO_2 and nutrients in the surface photic zone and the subsequent gravitational settling of the biogenic debris to the deep ocean. Each of these processes is affected by climatic changes, including temperature, evaporation, precipitation, wind, ice formation, and cloudiness. The feedback responses of each of these processes are discussed below.

Climate Change and Air-Sea Exchange of CO_2. The air-sea exchange flux of CO_2 is governed by the gas exchange rate and by the difference between the partial pressure of CO_2 (pCO_2) in the surface ocean water and that in the atmosphere, as expressed by

$$F = E[(pCO_2)_{air} - (pCO_2)_{seawater}], \qquad (1)$$

where F is the net CO_2 flux from the air to the surface ocean water and E is the gas transfer coefficient for CO_2.

The value of E is insensitive to small changes in ocean temperature but is quite sensitive to wind speed over the sea surface (boundary layer thickness, wave action, and bubble formation are functions of wind speed). Therefore changes in surface wind speed accompanying a climate change could affect rates of air-sea CO_2 exchange.

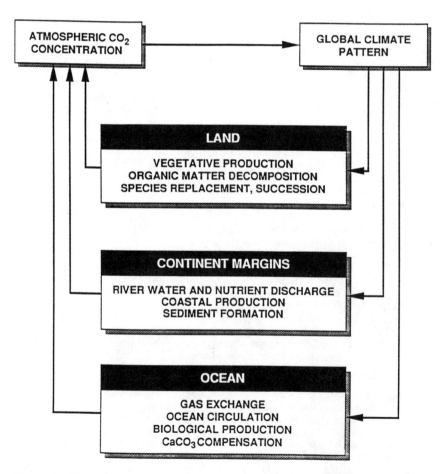

Figure 1. Changes in global climate due to increased atmospheric CO_2 will alter carbon cycle processes in land, continent margins, and oceans, which will in turn effect the atmospheric CO_2concentration. Processes that may have effects large enough to alter future projections of atmospheric CO_2 are listed under their geographic region.

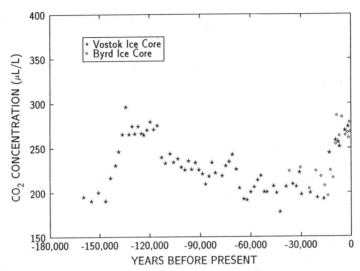

Figure 2a. Carbon dioxide concentrations in the atmosphere have varied over the glacial cycles of the earth's history, with high values at of around 300 $\mu L \cdot L^{-1}$ during the interglacial period approximately 130,000 years ago and reaching that level again at the end of the last glaciation. This graph shows CO_2 measurement from air bubbles trapped in Antarctic ice sampled at Vostok and Byrd stations (*2, 3*).

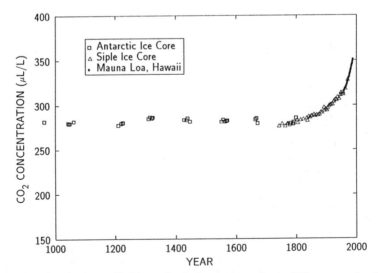

Figure 2b. Since the end of last glaciation, atmospheric CO_2 concentration has remained around 280 $\mu L \cdot L^{-1}$ until it began rising in the 18th century. Direct measurements made at Mauna Loa since 1958 (*4*) indicate that the rate of increase in atmospheric CO_2 is increasing. In 1988, the atmospheric carbon reservoir was estimated at 351 $\mu L \cdot L^{-1}$ and larger than at any time during the past 160,000 years. The South Pole and Siple ice-core data are from (*5–7*).

The $(pCO_2)_{seawater}$ is a function of temperature, salinity, total CO_2, and alkalinity. Increase in seawater temperature will result in greater seawater pCO_2 hence reducing oceanic uptake of CO_2. The seawater pCO_2, will increase by 4.3% as the temperature increases each degree Celsius. The effect of salinity on $(pCO_2)_{seawater}$ is small. On the average, pCO_2 in seawater will increase by 0.94% for a 1% increase in salinity.

The effect of total seawater CO_2 on $(pCO_2)_{seawater}$ is expressed as the Revelle factor, which is defined as a ratio of $(pCO_2)_{seawater}$ to total seawater CO_2 changes. The mean Revelle factor is 8 for warm surface water and 14 for cold surface water. A global mean value is ~ 10. This means that a 1% increase in total CO_2 in the ocean surface water causes a 10% increase in seawater pCO_2 at equilibrium. The Revelle factor increases rapidly with increasing total CO_2 in the ocean water that has a constant alkalinity (10). A 10% increase in total seawater CO_2 would increase the Revelle factor from 10 to 18. Thus, seawater would take up less CO_2 for a given increase in atmospheric pCO_2, weakening the negative feedback of oceans on atmospheric CO_2 levels. In other words, the more CO_2 the oceans take up, the slower they will become at taking up additional CO_2.

An increase in seawater alkalinity (for example, by the dissolution of $CaCO_3$) would decrease pCO_2 in seawater and decrease the Revelle factor (10). Thus $CaCO_3$ dissolution would provide a a strong negative feedback in response to an increased level of CO_2 in the atmosphere and ocean. However, the surface water of temperate and tropical oceans is supersaturated with respect to $CaCO_3$ by several fold. It is not likely that the dissolution of $CaCO_3$ would provide a negative feedback to the air-sea CO_2 transfer process in the near future.

Our existing knowledge of the relationships between pCO_2 in seawater and other parameters, such as temperature, salinity, total CO_2, and alkalinity, allows us to compute precisely the pCO_2 of a given parcel of seawater. Climate change will have the following effects on surface seawater chemistry: colder or wetter climate will favor the uptake of more CO_2 from the atmosphere by the oceans, whereas warmer or dryer climate will decrease the uptake of CO_2 by the oceans. What is not currently known with enough certainty is how the gas exchange rate will vary with changes in surface winds under altered climate. Quantifying the relationship between wind speed and gas exchange rates, particularly at high wind speeds, is necessary for determining oceanic uptake of CO_2 that accompanies CO_2-induced climate change.

Climate Change and Ocean Circulation. The earth's climate is a nonlinear system and responds both gradually and abruptly to perturbations. The climate record obtained from Greenland ice cores reveals several brief regional climate oscillations during glacial time. The most recent of these oscillations, (the "Younger Dryas" cold period), also found in a number of continental pollen records, had a great impact in the climatic regions under the meteorological influence of the northern Atlantic. Atmospheric CO_2 rose quickly by 80 $\mu L \cdot L^{-1}$ following the transition from cold to warm conditions at the end of the Younger Dryas period 11,000 years ago. The only feasible mechanisms to explain rapid changes in the atmospheric CO_2 content involve modifications in patterns and intensity of ocean circulation. Broecker et al. (11) suggest that a rapid shutdown of North Atlantic deep water formation thereby slowing general ocean circulation during glacial time, could result in this dramatic change in atmospheric CO_2 concentration. Broecker et al. (11) demonstrate that this Younger Dryas event occurred between two periods during which the glacial meltwater flooded down the Mississippi River to the Gulf of Mexico. They argue that between these two events, meltwater was diverted to the far north and upset the density stratification of the North Atlantic. Model studies show that if the ocean circulation rate during glacial times was half as fast as the current circulation rate and if $CaCO_3$ compensation (see $CaCO_3$ compensation section), was effective, then the atmospheric CO_2 concentration could increase from 219 $\mu L \cdot L^{-1}$ to 281 $\mu L \cdot L^{-1}$ when ocean circulation increased rapidly to present rates (*12*). Extrapolation of this model calculation to the future climate warming suggests that an amplification of the current rate of increase in atmospheric CO_2 content could result from climate-induced changes in ocean circulation rates.

Fairbanks (*13*), using information provided by oxygen and carbon isotope concentrations recorded in coral reefs, showed that the input of glacial melt water input into the oceans was much reduced during the Younger Dryas event; thus he casts doubt on Broecker et al.'s (*11*) hypothesis. A full explanation of the Younger Dryas, therefore, remains a key research goal (*14*). The climate period is an attractive one to study because rapid climate changes may be involved. An understanding of the Younger Dryas may help in predicting how climate and CO_2 may change during the "super-interglacial conditions" projected by current climate models for atmospheres with greater amounts of CO_2.

Studies in the areas of paleoceanography and paleoclimatology to understand past modifications in ocean circulation patterns are needed to extrapolate future patterns of ocean circulation and levels of atmospheric CO_2. Research in the reconstruction of glacial ocean circulation patterns on the basis of polar ice records and deep sea sediment records may shed some light on how such changes may take place and on the magnitude of the changes. Further development of tracer-style ocean models (box models) and ocean general circulation models, especially ones coupled to atmospheric general circulation models will be essential for analyzing paleoclimatic data and in generating and testing hypotheses.

Climate Change and Ocean Biological Processes. The partitioning of CO_2 between the ocean and the atmosphere is affected by the pelagic food web of the upper ocean. Photosynthesis, carried out primarily by small microscopic plants (phytoplankton) in the shallow, well-lit layer of the ocean (the euphotic zone), converts dissolved inorganic carbon dioxide into organic matter. A major portion of this primary production is recycled within the food web above the thermocline. The remaining fraction escapes from the upper ocean to the thermocline and below, where most of it is recycled and only a minor fraction is deposited in the sediments. It is this escaping fraction that effectively lowers the concentration of dissolved inorganic carbon in the upper ocean. Since this layer is in contact with the atmosphere the concentration of dissolved inorganic carbon, and therefore carbon dioxide, has important consequences for the global carbon cycle and climate change. Ocean carbon cycle models show that changes in the quantity of organic carbon leaving the upper ocean to the thermocline and below coupled with changes in oceanic circulation, can have rapid and significant impact on atmospheric CO_2 (*15, 16*). In the absence of ocean primary production, surface ocean total CO_2 would be 20% higher, and at equilibrium with such a surface ocean, the atmosphere would have a CO_2 concentration close to double present levels (*17*).

The quantity of primary production that is exported from the upper ocean is said to be equivalent to "new production" (*18, 19*). New primary production is that associated with allochthonous nutrients (i.e., those upwelled or mixed into the euphotic zone or input via rivers and rain). In order for steady state to be maintained, an equivalent flux out of the euphotic zone is required. Earlier studies (*19*) suggested that sediment-trap measurements of particulate organic carbon (POC) flux were equivalent to new primary production; however, recently it has become clear that these measurements probably represent only a fraction of the primary production removed from the upper ocean. Small suspended particles (20) and dissolved organic matter (21) have been suggested as important agents in the removal of primary production from the upper ocean. There are several direct and indirect methods of estimating removal of organic carbon from the surface ocean. These include sediment-trap measurements (22), estimates from total production (19, 23), estimates from upwelling models (24), and estimates of recycling rates in the thermocline and below (25). Previous global estimates of new production have been on the order of 2–4 Pg C·yr^{-1} (19,26). Recent sediment trap estimates suggest that the POC removed from the surface ocean (upper 100 m) is between 7–8 Pg C·yr^{-1} (22) and that new production could be as high as 15–22 Pg C·yr^{-1} (27, 28). These estimates (Table I.) show that global new production is a large term in the ocean carbon cycle, and changes in this flux quantity may significantly alter current rates of accumulation of CO_2 in the atmosphere.

Since most of the new production in the ocean is supported, primarily, by upwelling of limiting nutrients from below, one way to estimate the upper limit of new production is to estimate the nutrient flux into the euphotic zone. There are well-defined regions where significant quantities of nutrients are upwelled or mixed into the euphotic zone. These include the equatorial divergences, regions of coastal upwelling, and high-latitude oceans. Although the combined total primary productivity of these regions is probably less than that of the dystrophic open ocean, their proportion of new to total production (the f-ratio) is much higher so that these areas contribute a disproportionate fraction of global new production relative to their area.

Changes in the nutrient supply in the upwelling and polar regions can therefore significantly alter global new production. Using models to calculate nutrient supply requires knowledge of (a) the volume of water upwelled and of the concentration of nutrients in the upwelled water (29) or (b) mixed-layer depth and vertical distribution of nutrients (30). New production can then be estimated by using a Redfield ratio conversion from nutrient to carbon. In the following paragraphs we describe an example of a feedback loop between climate, ocean circulation, and ocean biology. We show how changes in climate and ocean circulation affect nutrient supply, which in turn alters new production, which in turn alters atmospheric CO_2, and which in turn can alter climate, completing the loop.

Rates of coastal and equatorial upwelling rates are directly dependent on ocean-atmosphere dynamics. Greenhouse effects will first be noticeable in the atmosphere and may significantly alter pressure fields. GCM simulation of the changes in global wind fields as a result of increasing CO_2 levels can therefore be used to estimate changes in upwelling rates. For example, a simulated wind field could be used to drive a numerical model of the equatorial Pacific (31). Thus there is a theoretical framework for estimating equatorial new production for the present climate and for future climates with increased atmospheric CO_2. If deep-water formation and high-latitude mixing can also be adequately modeled, the oceanic new production at high latitudes can also be estimated.

A second feedback mechanism involving increasing atmospheric CO_2 and new production can result from predicted changes in upper ocean temperatures and increased ice melting. High-latitude primary production may be temperature limited during the summer months but is enhanced by the increased water column stability provided by melting ice (32). Under the assumption that the rate of nutrient supply in high latitudes remains constant, then an increase in upper-ocean temperatures and increased ice melting could lead to an increased POC flux at high latitudes.

Table I. Summary of ocean biological productivity (from 27)

Type of Water	Primary Production (mg C·m⁻²·day⁻¹)		Annual Production for Each Type of Water (10¹⁵ g C·yr⁻¹)		% New Production	New Production² (10¹⁵ g C·yr⁻¹)
	E&P¹	C&B²	E&P¹	C&B²		
Oligotrophic waters of the central parts of subtropical halistatic areas	70	356	3.79	19.3	LOW (6–14)	1.2–2.7
Transitional waters between subtropical and subpolar zones; extremity of the areas of equatorial divergences	140	336	4.22	10.1	LOW (13–?)	1.3–?
Water of equatorial divergences and oceanic regions of polar zones	200	482	6.31	15.2	HIGH (50–80?)	7.6–12.1
Inshore waters	340	685	4.80	9.7	INTERMED. (30)	2.9
Neritic waters	1000	1000	3.90	3.9	HIGH (50–80)	2.0–3.1
Total, all waters			23	58		15.0–22.1+

[1]Estimates based on information summarized by Eppley and Peterson (19).
[2]Estimates of Chavez and Barber (24).

An important uncertainty associated with oceanic POC fluxes is the rate of regeneration of POC and its relationship to the regeneration of particulate organic N and P. Martin et al. (22) have found that 50% of the organic carbon removed from the surface is mineralized or regenerated at depths <300 m; 75% is regenerated by 500 m, and 90% by 1500 m. A second finding of Martin et al. (22) is that N and P are regenerated from sinking particles much more rapidly than C and H. Deviations from the Redfield ratio in upwelling of inorganic nutrients versus organic export can lead to a net export of up to 1 Pg C by low-latitude and thermohaline upwelling (33).

The study of POC fluxes and mineralization rates that result in development of the vertical distribution of carbon in the oceans needs additional quantification in all parts of the world's oceans. Current biological data largely pertain to isolated points or small regions in the oceans. It will be important for carbon cycle research to develop methods for extrapolating this type of information to determine the entire ocean response. A good example of this type of research is the development of relationships between nutrient concentrations (indicators of productivity) and temperature, upwelling rates, deep water formation, and high-latitude mixing rates. Special attention should also be placed on studies of possible increased high-latitude sea-ice melting and increased POC flux in adjacent oceans.

$CaCO_3$ **Compensation.** The increase in atmospheric CO_2 concentration of about 80 $\mu L \cdot L^{-1}$ from glacial to interglacial time (Figure 2a) is a good example of the changes in atmospheric CO_2 content due to climate change. Four mechanisms have been hypothesized to explain such changes. These mechanisms have one thing in common: they all call upon a greater biological depletion in the content of total CO_2 of the ocean's surface waters during glacial time than during interglacial time. The first mechanism, part of a nutrient inventory effect, involves a reduction in the phosphate and nitrate contents of the ocean at the close of glacial time. With more nutrients in the glacial ocean, the biological cycles in the sea were enhanced, increasing the extent to which surface waters were depleted in total CO_2 and hence lowering the atmospheric CO_2 content. The same thing could be accomplished by an increase in the ratios of C to N and C to P in the organic debris falling from the surface to the deep sea. The third mechanism, a nutrient residence time effect, would result when there is a reduction in the time constant for biological removal of nutrients from high-latitude surface waters. The last mechanism is a ventilation rate effect: reduction in the rates of mixing with adjacent waters would cause an increase in the residence time of cold water in the high-latitude surface reservoir allowing time for biological production to make maximal use of nutrients in converting inorganic carbon into organic matter, resulting in decreased surface pCO_2.

The formation and dissolution of $CaCO_3$ in the ocean plays a significant role in all of these effects (34). $CaCO_3$ is produced by marine organisms at a rate several times the supply rate of $CaCO_3$ to the sea from rivers. Thus, for the loss of $CaCO_3$ to sediments to match the supply from rivers, most of the $CaCO_3$ formed must be redissolved. The balance is maintained through changes in the $[CO_3]^{2-}$ content of the deep sea. A lowering of the CO_2 concentration of the atmosphere and ocean, for example by increased new production, raises the $[CO_3]^{2-}$ ion content of sea water. This in turn creates a mismatch between $CaCO_3$ burial and $CaCO_3$ supply. $CaCO_3$ accumulates faster than it is supplied to the sea. This burial of excess $CaCO_3$ in marine sediments draws down the $[CO_3]^{2-}$ concentration of sea water toward the value required for balance between $CaCO_3$ loss and gain. In this way, the ocean "compensates" for organic removal. As a consequence of this compensation process, the CO_2 content of the atmosphere would rise back toward its initial value.

All four possible hypothesized mechanisms for explanation of the 80 $\mu L \cdot L^{-1}$ glacial to interglacial jump in atmospheric CO_2 concentration would produce changes in the $[CO_3]^{2-}$ ion concentration in the deep sea. The subsequent readjustment of the deep sea $[CO_3]^{2-}$ ion content to that value required for steady state throughput of the ingredients of $CaCO_3$ leads to a large enhancement of the change in atmospheric CO_2 content created by a nutrient cycle change. This enhancement is essentially a positive feedback indirectly caused by the climate change. This readjustment requires several thousand years to occur, so there would be a delay in the positive feedback of atmospheric CO_2 concentration back to the atmosphere through these mechanisms.

The estimated response time of $CaCO_3$ compensation, on the order of a few thousand years, is a serious problem because the ice core data do not show such a long delay in atmospheric CO_2 changes with respect to temperature changes. Such a long delay may preclude $CaCO_3$ compensation as an important process in predicting atmospheric CO_2 in the next few centuries.

Additional model studies are needed to explore the effects of $CaCO_3$ compensation. Examination of the extent of the $CaCO_3$ preservation in deep-sea sediments is needed to verify model predictions of how the $[CO_3]^{2-}$ ion content of deep-sea water has changed with time.

River Nutrient Flux and Coastal Production and Accumulation. The 1–2 Pg $C \cdot yr^{-1}$ of new production estimated for the coastal oceans (*22*) largely results from the flux of river nutrients into these regions. River nutrient flux is highly dependent on river discharge rate because nutrient concentrations and total nutrient amounts in rivers are usually positively related to discharge rate. Increases in river discharge due to climate changes that increase continental precipitation could increase coastal net primary production (NPP). Increases in coastal NPP should in turn result in increased accumulations of organic matter and increased net CO_2 uptake from the atmosphere. However, it is unclear whether the estimated new production in coastal oceans accumulates as organic matter or whether remineralization is largely complete with little net removal of atmospheric CO_2. The negative feedback effect of increased river discharge is therefore dependent on an accumulation of most, if not all, of the coastal new production in long-term deposits. Such accumulations are currently undocumented.

The magnitude and fate of coastal-zone biological production is a major unknown in the global carbon cycle. Since river nutrient flux into these regions may be altered with CO_2-induced climate change, it is important that generation and fate of coastal-zone production be better understood.

Climate–Terrestrial Biota CO_2 Feedbacks

Terrestrial vegetation is a large, dynamic pool of carbon in direct exchange with the atmosphere. This pool is sensitive to climate, and projected CO_2-induced climate changes are large enough to cause significant responses from vegetation at seasonal, interannual, decadal, and longer time-scales. Terrestrial vegetation poses the further complication that global feedback between CO_2 levels and vegetation is the sum of the response from many heterogeneous sites or vegetation types that have their own characteristic response patterns.

Predicting the effect of the terrestrial vegetation response to CO_2-induced climate change for a particular site involves explicit treatment of feedbacks. These are diagramed in Figure 3. The balance between decomposition + autotrophic respiration and gross primary production (GPP) determines the net storage and release of carbon to atmosphere. Climate affects each of these

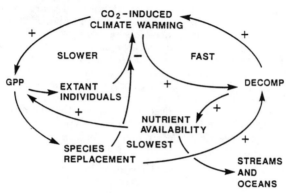

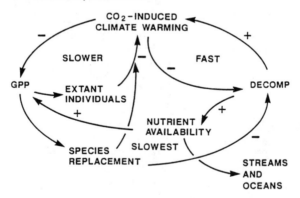

Figure 3. Feedbacks in terrestrial ecosystem responses to CO_2-induced climate change. Arrows with plus signs (+) indicate processes that have positive effects or that increase the rates of other processes. Arrows with minus signs (−) indicate processes that have the opposite effects.

processes in different ways, and each process has a unique response time; consequently, GPP, decomposition, and autotrophic respiration will tend to respond independently to climate perturbations. As a result, for most temporal and spatial scales, they must be considered separately and not combined in a net accounting procedure. Decomposition has a secondary effect of releasing nutrients. This enhances GPP and strengthens the feedback involving GPP, providing direct linkages between decomposition and GPP. Increasing CO_2 will generally warm the climate, increasing the rate of decomposition and releasing additional CO_2 to the atmosphere. This is a positive feedback process that may have a large influence on the atmospheric CO_2 concentration if ecosystems with large pools of dead organic matter (boreal forests, wetlands, and peatlands) are affected by climate warming. If, however, available moisture declines to very low levels as a result of climate warming, then decomposition will be inhibited and the feedback through decomposition will be negative. Moisture declines will also lower GPP so the net effect of warmer, dryer climate will depend on the relative strengths of these two feedback paths through decomposition.

The GPP effect on atmospheric CO_2 is negative, so enhancement of GPP will result in a negative feedback between vegetation and atmospheric carbon. Again, if an insufficiency of available moisture results from increased atmospheric CO_2, this will weaken the negative feedback, resulting in higher atmospheric CO_2 levels. Longer-term changes in climate introduce successional processes that result in species replacement. Because species composition has a strong effect on nutrient cycling, it introduces a feedback at decadal time-scales that again depends on the presence or absence of drought and other climate changes.

The ability to incorporate spatially explicit information that will couple these site-specific responses to global climate change is critical to summarizing the impact these site-specific feedbacks to global-scale feedbacks.

Seasonal, and Interannual Vegetation Response to Climate Change. Approximately 100–120 Pg C are exchanged between the biosphere and atmosphere each year; small imbalances in the annual exchange rates can have large impacts on the atmospheric CO_2 levels. Such an imbalance, on a seasonal time-scale, is seen in the annual oscillations of the Mauna Loa CO_2 data. The seasonal amplitude of the Mauna Loa CO_2 record has been increasing at 0.66% per year since 1975 (*35*). While this increase in seasonal amplitude suggests faster seasonal cycling of CO_2, it may also indicate changes in biospheric storage of carbon (*36*).

The shape of the rising limb of the seasonal CO_2 curve is determined primarily by the amount of carbon released during decomposition of dead organic matter and autotrophic respiration in excess of the amount taken up by photosynthesis. The combination of decomposition and autotrophic respiration will be referred to as "ecosystem respiration." The shape and magnitude of the descending limb of the CO_2 curve depends primarily on global GPP. Both ecosystem respiration and GPP are strongly regulated by climate, but the various GPP and ecosystem respiration processes react differently to changes in climate. Changes in the duration and timing of growing and decay seasons will alter the annual CO_2 curve. Because of the many possible responses of different ecosystem types to climate change, we cannot currently predict the direction or the magnitude of the seasonal amplitude changes and its impact on the long-term net changes in carbon storage in terrestrial ecosystems with possible future climates.

Periodic climatic events such as the El Niño/Southern Oscillation events produce detectable changes in both vegetation dynamics and in atmospheric CO_2 concentration (*37, 38*). Evidence from $^{13}C:^{14}C$ ratios in atmospheric CO_2

(*39*) relate the interannual variations of the seasonal amplitude in the northern hemisphere to biospheric activity. Understanding these interannual changes in atmosphere-biosphere exchanges provides a basis for extrapolating terrestrial vegetation responses to longer-term climate changes (*40*).

Our understanding of seasonal and interannual variation in global terrestrial vegetation dynamics is, however, very sketchy at present. Ecosystem respiration measurements have been made for various soil-vegetation types for variable lengths of time (*41*). Relationships between ecosystem respiration and weather data have been derived from these data for four major biomes (*38*). However, additional systematic collection of field respiration measurements would be necessary for placing much confidence in such a relationship.

The relationship between GPP and weather can be explored through the use of satellite data and field measurements of GPP, combined with corresponding climate data. Some details of potentially useful data are described here.

The Advanced-Very-High-Resolution Radiometer (AVHRR) carried on board the NOAA-7 satellite has been collecting radiance data from the earth's surface since 1978. The polar-orbiting satellite records global data on a near-daily basis. The 4-kilometer data have been remapped by NOAA into monthly composites. The data are collected in 2 bands—one visible (VIS), the other near infrared (NIR). The Normalized Difference Vegetation Index, or NDVI, defined as

$$NDVI = \frac{NIR - VIS}{NIR + VIS}, \qquad (2)$$

has been used to monitor the dynamics of global vegetation. Although we do not know the exact meaning of the NDVI in terms of vegetation dynamics, it seems to be closely related to photosynthetic capacity. The NDVI has been related to field measurements of GPP of grasslands in the Sahel (*42*), to GPP of North American Biomes (*43*), to the amount of photosynthetically active radiation intercepted by vegetation, another useful index of GPP (*44*), and to the seasonal drawdown of atmospheric CO_2 (*45*).

Because of the difficulty and expense of directly measuring GPP, few field measurements are made throughout the growing season. Thus, it will be necessary to obtain additional field measurements of GPP on a seasonal basis for calibration and comparison to satellite and model information.

Monthly temperature and precipitation data recorded at the World Meteorological Organization monitoring stations throughout the world during the 8 years of the AVHRR satellite coverage can assist in deriving necessary relationships between GPP, NDVI, and weather for potential use in aggregating GPP and ecosystem respiration field data to global scale. The GPP-weather and ecosystem respiration–weather relationships can be tested by using weather data independent of the above analyses (e.g., most recent or future data) to predict NDVI or the seasonal CO_2 cycle observed in the atmosphere and then compare observed patterns with predicted ones.

The major problems that will cause large uncertainties with this analysis are as follows:

- paucity in GPP measurements used to calibrate NDVI;
- poor accuracy of precipitation data which must be extrapolated to grid scales comparable to the resolution of the satellite data;
- uncertainties about meaning of NDVI;
- the impact of other processes such as fires on seasonal amplitudes;

- no available data for validation of ecosystem respiration–weather relationships; and
- current inability to remotely sense ecosystem respiration.

Creative analyses of the currently scanty GPP, NPP, and ecosystem respiration data should be continued. Additional primary measurements will also be necessary. New data aquisition projects should be designed to allow extrapolation of small-scale vegetation responses and processes to large regions. Recent developments in extrapolating small-scale vegetation responses through the use of remote sensing technology should be furthered. This important technique should be coordinated with new field measurements of ecosystems.

Species Replacement and Feedbacks Influencing the Carbon Cycle. Current estimates for the magnitude of CO_2-induced climate change are large enough that, over a 20- to 100-year period of climate change the individualistic responses among plant taxa would lead to new plant associations at most spatial scales. Many of these associations may have no close modern counterparts in terms of composition, structure, growth rates of component taxa, or carbon stored in the biomass (*46*) and soil (*47*). These changes are on the temporal and spatial scales of current resource management, such as the timber industry. Therefore, species replacements are important not only for feedbacks to atmospheric CO_2, but also for resource use. These successional changes may also cause long term shifts in the magnitudes of negative and positive feedbacks to atmospheric CO_2.

The negative feedback of sequestering atmospheric CO_2 in biomass will occur to the extent that climatic warming without increased drought enhances growth of extant individuals. This feedback will also be enhanced to the degree that taxa with slow growth rates and small size are replaced by those with more rapid growth rates and larger size (*46*). A further negative feedback could arise from the effect of such changes on soil nutrient availability. If the replacing taxa enhance soil nutrient availability by shedding more easily decomposable litter, then nutrient limitations on productivity are decreased and productivity is enhanced (*48–51*).

A positive feedback between vegetation and atmospheric CO_2 will occur if biomass declines. This will happen to the extent that climatic warming causes increased water stress, either through decreased precipitation or increased evapotransporation, particularly on soils of low water-holding capacity. Decreases in soil nutrient availability, either directly caused by drought or indirectly caused by replacement with taxa with more recalcitrant litter, may further decrease the net release of carbon from the biosphere to the atmosphere. Positive feedback will also arise if the current standing biomass of trees is replaced by small trees, shrubs, and herbs that store less carbon.

It seems unlikely that feedbacks due to species replacement have begun since the beginning of the Mauna Loa record because compositional changes due to climate change will take decades and have not yet been documented on a wide scale. However, this fact increases the importance of such feedbacks to future trends in atmospheric CO_2: when these feedbacks become important it is highly unlikely that positive and negative feedbacks will exactly cancel each other and more likely that one or the other will prevail and cause deviations from current trends in atmospheric CO_2.

Several problems arise concerning current approaches to modeling vegetation response to altered climate. Current models that predict movements of whole biomes in response to climate (*52–54*) do not allow for different assemblages of species that have occurred under past climates (*55*) and that will probably occur under future climates (*46*). Furthermore, these models are equilibrium models with long implicit time-scales for biome conversion. Current species-based forest models (*46, 50, 56, 57*) parameterize species responses to climate on the basis of data only from the edges of species ranges rather than through the full geographic range. However, species-climate response relationships throughout a species range can be derived with current forest inventories and climate data or with current pollen distribution and climate data (*58*). Vegetation changes due to future climate changes can then be predicted on the basis of these response surfaces (*59*).

The effects that changes in vegetation have on soil carbon pools and nutrient availability are also difficult to evaluate. However, several models have been successful in predicting vegetation-soil nutrient relationships because they assume that such changes occur as a result of different rates of decomposition and nutrient release from leaf litter of different taxa (*50, 60*). Such predictions could be tested and the models refined or parameterized for new taxa by measuring soil nutrient availability and respiration in stands of different species on the same soil type. For example, fifty years ago the U.S. Civilian Conservation Corps (CCC) established such stands as species trial plots; measurements in some indicate large differences in soil nutrient availability (*48*). Further measurements in these stands would now occur at the same time-scale at which we expect the feedback between species replacement and soil processes to occur.

Information on the response of taxa to climate and the feedback between vegetation and soil nutrient availability should be synthesized and used to construct computer models operating at the same scale as GCM output (*61*). Such models should be able to do the following:

- operate at same scales as global atmospheric circulation models;

- select species or species types appropriate to new climate;

- grow species types according to changes in climate and soils;

- allow for disturbance and for invasion by early successional types with succession to climax species types;

- predict changes in soil nutrient availability caused by new types; and

- sum GPP and ecosystem respiration to yield net CO_2 release to the atmosphere.

Climate Sensitivity of Pools and Fluxes of Subfossil Carbon. A major unresolved issue of global cycling of carbon is determining whether peat and other "subfossil" outputs of ecosystems from bogs, tundra, and even some forests of the boreal zone approximate a steady state (*62, 63*). Net storage of carbon in these ecosystems has been shown (*64, 65*). Drainage and climatic change may be altering this former sink of organic humus into an extra source of CO_2.

Research is needed to quantify and assess data sets on pools and fluxes of subfossil carbon for North America, Scandinavia, and the Soviet Union where large amounts of such material exists and is vulnerable to accelerated decomposition with expected CO_2-induced climate change (*66–69*). Billings et al.(*70, 71*) performed field experiments that mimicked the changes expected to occur in the tundra as a result of climatic change. The direction of CO_2 flux was reversed from a net storage of 150 g $CO_2 \cdot m^{-2} \cdot season^{-1}$ to a net release of 300–400 g $CO_2 \cdot m^{-1} \cdot season^{-1}$. Annual liberation of as little as 1% per year of either the 300 Pg C stored in the top meter of soils above the 60° latitude band or the estimated 500 Pg C in peat (*72*) would double the current rate of increase in atmospheric CO_2.

The recent analysis by Olson (*73*) of the natural carbon cycle raised the possibility that nonequilibrium transient accumulations of humus carbon may help to explain why the net storage from ecosystems in recent millennia has substantially exceeded the longer-term average input of carbon to consolidated rocks (around 0.06 Pg C, averaged over millions of years of rock cycling during geologic time). In these humus rich ecosystems, the degree of soil saturation and, further north, the development of permafrost are key processes that determine the net exchange of CO_2 between the ecosystems and atmosphere. The degree of saturation determines the accumulation of carbon in peatlands as well as the fractionation of gaseous carbon as CO_2 or methane (*74*). The greater the degree of saturation, the slower the net accumulation rate and the greater the fraction of respired carbon that is released as methane rather than as CO_2. Since a molecule of methane has a atmospheric warming potential of 10 to 15 times that of a molecule of CO_2, the fraction released as methane is important. In peatlands, a stabilizing relationship gradually develops between soil organic matter accumulation and soil saturation. Organic matter has a high water-holding capacity. As peat accumulates, the soil becomes progressively more saturated, and production of methane is enhanced. Production of methane is also enhanced by warmer temperatures, and warming of northern peat soils (or lengthening of the decomposition season) without drainage could cause an increase in atmospheric methane. On the other hand, if climate change results in dryer conditions and lower water tables, peat will be decomposed rather than accumulated, and net carbon releases may result for a period of time, despite possible increases in ecosystem productivity.

Climate change may also affect permafrost. Melting of permafrost, in addition to releasing trapped methane, can release water that keeps the soil profile saturated. Whether this results in decreasing or increasing local soil saturation depends on whether or not the water remains or flows out to adjacent areas. Over large areas, permafrost melting may cause thermokarst slumping, changing drainage patterns, and movement of carbon across the landscape. Export of carbon and nutrients to streams, lakes, and the Arctic Ocean is an additional uncertainty in estimating carbon flux to the atmosphere. Peat is a major form of organic matter supporting the productivity of arctic rivers (*75*). Melting of permafrost and changes in drainage patterns as a result of climatic warming may divert a significant amount of organic matter into aquatic systems, where its fate is even less well known (*76*).

Researchers need to improve c der (*77*, *78*) estimates for nutrient and carbon pools and annual cycling rates. Methods are also needed for combining soils and Quaternary geology data with models for deriving improved zonal estimates for the accumulation of peat and muck or the release of CO_2. Research to accomplish these tasks will be needed (a) to understand how climate and nutrient cycling influence organic matter production and accumulation in bog, tundra, and boreal ecosystems; (b) to collect and summarize measurements of carbon flux in plots of vegetation; and (c) to extend current experimental methods of remote sensing to the difficult task of using plot or stand measures over heterogeneous areas to the landscape and global scales.

Summary.

Many climatically sensitive feedback processes could be described in addition to those outlined above. We have restricted our attention to processes that have potentially large effects. A large effect is defined as one that could change the current rate of atmospheric CO_2 increase by at least 50% ($\sim$1 Pg C·yr^{-1}).

The climate sensitivity of certain carbon cycle processes has been of scientific interest for some time (*79*). Research, however, has not progressed to a stage where research findings are useful in predicting future atmospheric CO_2. The most significant work to date on how a CO_2-enhanced climate may alter carbon cycle processes must be regarded as scientific experiments whose models and data challenge our understanding of global carbon cycle processes and their interrelationships. Most of these studies project what specific carbon cycle processes may be like at equilibrium under climatic conditions induced by a doubling of atmospheric CO_2 with all other processes remaining constant (*12, 46, 47, 52, 80*).

To move the current diverse and active research from its current state to one which can be used for making quantitative projections requires two basic steps. The first is to increase our basic understanding of carbon cycle processes and how they are affected by climate change. The second is to develop methods to extrapolate to a global scale those processes that can be studied at small spatial and temporal scales. These steps cannot usually be accomplished as separate tasks because spatial aggregation and extrapolation introduce complex linkages between processes at larger spatial scales. For example, our current knowledge is adequate to determine the equilibrium gas exchange between air and seawater for given parcels of air and seawater as functions of temperature, precipitation, and biological production. However, we cannot add up all the surface parcels of sea and arrive at a reasonable estimate of global exchanges under any climate because, at this larger scale, we must consider how ocean circulation affects exchange processes and biological production.

The research detailed in previous sections outlines productive steps toward increased certainty in global quantification of the effects that climate has on carbon cycle processes. Presented here is a short summary of future research directions.

Ocean-Atmosphere Interactions.   To determine how the ocean responds to a CO_2-induced climate forcing, it will be necessary to develop a combined ocean and atmospheric general circulation model. It will take 10–20 years to develop a model with appropriate chemistry and biology to the level of confidence necessary to make valid projections. In the interim, two approaches can be pursued in parallel with this model development.

1. Research should be conducted in order to obtain a better understanding of the current operation of the oceans. Such research would involve analysis and synthesis of observations on the contemporary ocean. Determining ocean physics and biological production are of critical importance. Large oceanographic programs under way address some of the issues that will be important for global CO_2 issues. Analysis and collection of additional tracer data will play an important role in determining of ocean physics. Research will take the intensive but spatially restricted information on biological production and provide a method for incorporating of this information into ocean GCMs and eventually ocean-atmosphere GCMs. In addition to open ocean productivity, the relationship between river flux of nutrients and continental-margin productivity and its fate must be settled.

2. Research should be conducted to understand how the oceans have operated under past climates. This would involve paleoclimatic studies including analysis of sediment and ice core records coupled with tracer-style ocean models or box models.

Atmosphere-Terrestrial Vegetation Exchanges. Regardless of the next stages in ocean and atmospheric CO_2 research or modeling, analyzing the sensitivities of terrestrial vegetation to climate change requires increased ability to extrapolate local-to-regional and monthly-to-annual vegetation responses to a global level and to decadal time-scales. This global integration is required by the spatial heterogeneity of terrestrial vegetation and its response to climate change. Research is currently underway on this task. The major deficiencies that need to be addressed are reiterated here.

1. The response of tundra, bogs, and moist or wet boreal forest to new climate regimes is expected to be large. Sufficient research to characterize the response of these ecosystems over the next 50 to 100 years is a high priority.

2. Progress in quantifying the short-term terrestrial response (seasonal and interannual) is hampered by insufficient primary data to develop and calibrate suitable models that then can be aggregated to obtain global responses. Most ecosystem measurements quantify the components of net ecosystem production (unfortunately, they are rarely done simultaneously), which incorporate both gross production and decomposition/respiration. The ecosystem carbon income and loss respond to climate in fundamentally different fashions and must be accounted for separately. Furthermore, most publications report annual rather than seasonal data. Creative analyses of the scanty available data will suffice in the short term, but additional primary measurements will also be necessary. In the meantime, researchers should further develop techniques to aggregate small-scale vegetation responses at a global scale through the use of remote sensing technology. This important technique should be coordinated with any new field measurements of ecosystems as was done in the First ISLSCP Field Experiment (*81*). Such coordination should be developed further for carbon cycle purposes.

3. Vegetation zones and composition within those zones will change with altered climate over 50 to 100 years. Our understanding of how ecosystem processes are affected by climate change is increasing rapidly for North American forests, but other ecosystems are not well understood. North American forest ecosystems are representative of ecosystems that will undergo the largest changes, given current projections for CO_2-induced temperature change. Changes in precipitation are more problematic. Additional research is needed to be able to predict vegetation changes due to altered precipitation patterns. Of special significance is the transition between forest and nonforest ecosystems at all latitudes. Climate change, particularly that affecting water availability, will have large effects in these transitional zones, shifting the balance between ecosystems with high and low carbon storage.

Acknowledgments. Research sponsored by the U.S. Department of Energy, Carbon Dioxide Research Program, Atmospheric and Climate Research Division, Office of Health and Environmental Research, and the National Science Foundation's Ecosystem Studies Program under Interagency Agreement BSR–8417923, under contract DE–AC05–84OR21400 with Martin Marietta Energy Systems, Inc. Publication No. 3655, Environmental Science Division, Oak Ridge National Laboratory.

Literature Cited

1 Berner, R. A. *Science* **1990**, *249*, 1382–1386.
2 Barnola, J. M.; Raynaud, D.; Korotkevich, Y. S.; Lorius, C. *Nature.* **1987**, *329*, 408–414.
3 Neftel, A.; Oeschger, H.; Schwander, J.; Stauffer, B.; Zumbrunn, R. *Nature* **1982**, *295*, 220–223.
4 Keeling, C. D. *Atmospheric CO_2 Concentrations—Mauna Loa, Hawaii, 1958–1987*; NDP–001/R1; Carbon Dioxide Information and Analysis Center, Oak Ridge National Laboratory: Oak Ridge, TN, 1988.
5 Friedli, H.; Lötscher, H.; Oeschger, H.; Siegenthaler, U.; Stauffer, B. *Nature* **1986**, *324*, 237–238.
6 Neftel, A.; Moor, E.; Oeschger, H.; Stauffer, B. *Nature* **1985**, *315*, 45–47.
7 Siegenthaler, U.; Friedli, H.; Lötscher, H.; Moor, E.; Neftel, A.; Oeschger, H.; Stauffer, B. *Ann. of Glaciol.* **1988**, *10*, 1–6.
8 Kasting, J. F.; Ackerman, T. P. *Science* **1986**, *234*, 1383–1385.
9 Sundquist, E. T. In *The Changing Carbon Cycle: A Global Analysis*; Trabalka, J. R.; Reichle, D. E. Eds.; Springer-Verlag: New York, NY, 1986; pp. 371-402.
10 Takahashi, T.; Broecker, W. S.; Werner, S. R.; Bainbridge, A. E. In *Isotope Marine Chemistry*; Rohakuho: Tokyo, Japan, 1980; pp. 291–326.
11 Broecker, W. S.; Kennet, J. P.; Flower, B. P.; Teller, J. T.; Trumbore, S.; Banani, G.; Wolfli, W. *Nature* **1987**, *341*, 318–320.
12 Peng, T.-H.; Broecker, W. S. *J. of Geophys. Res.* **1984**, *89*, 8170–8180.
13 Fairbanks, R. G. *Nature* **1989**, *342*, 637–642.
14 Ruddiman, W. F. *North America and Adjacent Oceans During the Last Glaciation*; Ruddiman, W. F., Wright, H. E., Jr., Eds.; Geological Society of America: Boulder, CO, 1987, Vol. K-3; pp. 463–478.
15 Sarmiento, J. L.; Toggweiler, J. R. *Nature* **1984**, *308*, 621–624.
16 Siegenthaler, U.; Wenk, T. *Nature* **1984**, *308*, 624–626.
17 Sarmiento, J. L, Thiele, G.; Key, R. M.; Moore, W. S. *J. of Geophys. Res.* **1990**, *95*, 18303–18315.
18 Dugdale, R. C.; Goering, J. J. *Limnol. and Oceanog.* **1967**, *12*, 196–206.
19 Eppley, R. W.; Peterson, B. J. *Nature* **1979**, *282*, 677–680.
20 Altabet M. A. *J. of Geophys. Res.*. **1989**, *94*, 12771–12780.
21 Toggweiler, J.R. 1989. In *Productivity of the Ocean: Past and Present*; Berger, W.H.; Smatacek, V.; Wefer, D., Eds.; Dahlem Workshop Report; John Wiley: New York, NY; pp. 65–84.
22 Martin, J. H.; Knauer, G. A.; Karl, D. M.; Broenkow, W. W. *Deep-Sea Res.* **1987**, *34*, 267–285.
23 Platt, T.; Harrison, W. G. *Nature* **1986**, *318*, 55-58.
24 Chavez, F. P.; Barber, R. T. *Deep-Sea Res.* **1987**, *34*, 1229–1243.
25 Jenkins, W. J. *Nature* **1982**, *300*, 246–248.
26 Broecker, W. S. *Chemical Oceanography*; Harcourt Brace Jovanovich: New York, NY, 1974; 214 pp.
27 Chavez, F.P. *EOS.* **1987**, *68*, 1692.
28 Packard, T. T.; Denis, M.; Rodier, M.; Garfield, P. *Deep-Sea Res.* **1988**, *35*, 371–832.
29 Chavez, F. P.; Barber R. T.; Sanderson, M. P. In *ICLARM Conference Proceedings Series, 18*; Pauly, D.; Salzwedel, H.; Muck, P.; Mendo, J., Eds.; Instituto del Mar del Peru: Callao, Peru; Deutsche Gesellschaft fur Technische Zusammenarbeit, GmbH: Eschborn, Federal Republic of Germany; and International Center for Living Aquatic Resources Management: Manila, Phillippines, 1989; pp. 50–63.
30 Glover, D. M.; Brewer, P. G. *Deep-Sea Res.* **1988**, *35*, 1525–1546.

31 Philander, S. G.; Siegel, A. D. In *Coupled Ocean–Atmosphere Models*; Nihoul, J. C. J., Ed.; Elsevier Science Publishers, B. V.: Amsterdam, The Netherlands, 1985; pp. 517–541.
32 Smith, W. O.; Nelson, D. M. *Science* **1985**, *227*, 163–166.
33 Chavez, F. P; Barber, R. T. *International Conference on the TOGA Scientific Programme*; World Climate Research Publications Series No. 4; World Meteorological Organization: Geneva, Switzerland, 1985; pp. 23–32.
34 Broecker, W. S.; Peng, T.-H. *Radiocarbon* **1986**, *28*, 309–327.
35 Keeling, C. D. In *Carbon Dioxide, Science, and Consensus*; CONF–820970; U.S. Department of Energy: Washington DC, 1983; pp. II.3–II.62.
36 Tans, P. P.; Fung, I. Y.; Takahashi, T. *Science* **1990**, *247*, 1431–1438.
37 Enting, I. G. *J. of Geophys. Res.* **1987**, *92*, 5497–5504.
38 Fung, I., Prentice, K.; Matthews, E.; Lerner, J.; Russell, G. *J. of Geophys. Res.* **1987**, *88*, 1281–1294.
39 Mook, W. M.; Koopmans, M.; Carter, A. F.; Keeling, C. D. *J. of Geophys. Res.* **1983**, *88*, 915–933.
40 Keeling, C. D.; Bacastow, R. B.; Carter, A. F.; Piper, S. C.; Whorf, T. P, Heimann; M; Mook, W. G.; Roeloffzen, H. In *Aspects of Climate Variability in the Pacific and Western Americas*; Peterson, D. H., Ed.; Geophysical Monograph 55; American Geophysical Union: Washington, DC. 1989; pp. 165–236.
41 Prentice, K. C. *The Influence of the Terrestrial Biosphere on Seasonal Atmospheric Carbon Dioxide: An Empirical Model*; Ph.D. Dissertation, Columbia University, New York, NY, 1986.
42 Tucker, C. J.; Townshend, J. R. G.; Goff, T. E. *Science* **1985**, *227*, 369–375.
43 Goward, S. N.; Tucker, C. J.; Dye, D. G. *Vegetatio* **1986**, *64*, 3–14.
44 Sellers, P. J. *Int. J. of Remote Sensing* **1985**, *6*, 1355–1372.
45 Tucker, C. J.; Fung, I. Y.; Keeling, C. D.; Gammon, R. H. *Nature* **1986**, *319*, 195–199.
46 Solomon, A. M. *Oecologia* **1986**, *68*, 567–579.
47 Pastor, J.; Post, W. M. 1988. *Nature* **1988**, *334*, 55–58.
48 Alban, D. H. *Soil Sci. Soc. of Am. J.*. **1982**, *46*, 853–861.
49 Pastor, J. J.; Aber, J. D.; McClaugherty, C. A.; Melillo, J. M. *Ecology* **1984**, *65*, 256–268.
50 Pastor, J.; Post, W. M. *Biogeochemistry* **1986**, *2*, 3–27.
51 Van Cleve, K.; Oliver, L.; Schlenter, R.; Vierek, L. A.; Dyrness, C. T. *Can. J. of For. Res.* **1983**, *13*, 747–766.
52 Emanuel, W. M.; Shugart, H. H.; Stevenson, M. P. *Clim. Change* **1985**, *7*, 29–43.
53 Leemans, R. *World Map of Holdridge Life Zones*; International Institute of Applied Systems Analysis: Laxenburg, Austria, 1989.
54 Prentice, K. C.; Fung, I. Y. *Nature* **1990**, *346*, 48–51.
55 Jacobson, G. L., Jr.; Webb, T., III; Grimm, E. C. 1987. In *North America and Adjacent Oceans During the Last Deglaciation*; W. F. Ruddiman; Wright H. E., Eds.; Geological Society of America: Boulder, CO, 1987, Vol. K-3; pp. 277–288.
56 Botkin, D. B.; Janak, J. F.; Wallis, J. R. *J. of Ecol.* **1972**, *60*, 849–872.
57 Shugart, H. H.; West, D. C. *J. of Environ. Manage.* **1977**, *5*, 161–179.
58 Bartlein, P. J.; Prentice, I. C.; Webb III, T. *J. of Biogeogr.*, **1986**, *13*, 35–57.
59 Overpeck, J. T.; Bartlein, P. J. In *The Potential Effects of Global Climate Change on the United States*; Smith, J. B.; Tirpack, D. A., Eds.; EPA-230-05-89-054; U.S. Environmental Protection Agency: Washington, DC, 1989, Appendix D; pp. 1-1 to 1-32.

60 Aber, J. D.; Melillo, J. M.; Federer, C. A. *For. Sci..* **1982**, *28*, 31–45.
61 Verstraete, M.; Graumlich, L. J.; Pastor, J.; Cook, E. R.; Martin. P.; Prentice, I. C.; Swetnam, T. R.; Valentin, K.; Webb, T., III; White, J.; Woodward, I. *Records of Past Global Change*; Bradley, R. S., Ed.; Office of Interdisciplinary Earth Studies: Boulder, CO, in press.
62 Olson, J. S. In *Beyond the Energy Crisis*; Fazzolare, R. A.; Smith, C. B., Eds.; Pergamon Press: New York, NY, 1981, Vol. 4, pp. a72–a140.
63 Trabalka, J. R.; Olson, J. S.; Gammon, R. H.; Edmonds, J. A.; Garrels, R. M.; Lovelock, J. E.; Östland, H. G.; Richards, J. F. In *Atmospheric Carbon Dioxide and the Global Carbon Cycle*. Trabalka, J. R., Ed.; DOE/ER-0239; U.S. Government Printing Office: Washington, DC, 1985; pp. 289–302.
64 *Carbon Balance in Northern Ecosystems and the Potential Effect of Carbon Dioxide Induced Climate Change*; Miller, P. C., Ed.; CONF-8003118. National Technical Information Service: Springfield, VA, 1981.
65 Silvola, U. *Ann. Bot. Fenn.* **1986**, *23*, 59–67.
66 Olson, J. S.; Watts, J. A.; Allison, L. J. *Carbon in Live Vegetation of Major World Ecosystems*; ORNL–5862; Oak Ridge National Laboratory: Oak Ridge, TN, 1983.
67 Kivinen, E.; Parkarinen, P. Ann. Acad. Sci. Fenn. **1981**, *A 132*, 1–28.
68 Matthews, E.; Fung, I. Y. 1987. *Global Biogeochem. Cycles* **1987**, *1*, 61–86.
69 Zoltai, S. C.; Vitt, D. H. *Quat. Res.* **1990**, *33*, 231–240.
70 Billings, W. C.; Luken, J. O.; Mortensen, D. A.; Peterson, K. M. *Oecologia* **1983**, *58*, 286–289.
71 Billings, W. D.; Peterson, K. M.; Luken, J. O.; Mortensen, D. A. *Oecologia* **1984**, *65*, 26–29.
72 Houghton, R. A.; Schlesinger, W. H.; Brown, S.; Richards, J. F. In *Atmospheric Carbon Dioxide and the Global Carbon Cycle*; Trabalka, J. R., Ed.; DOE/ER–0239; Carbon Dioxide Research Division, U.S. Department of Energy: Washington, DC, 1985; pp. 113–140.
73 Olson, J. S. In *The Carbon Cycle and Atmospheric CO_2: Natural Variations Archean to Present*; Sundquist, E. T.; Broecker, W. S., Eds.; Geophysical Monograph 32; American Geophysical Union: Washington DC, 1985; pp. 377–396.
74 Moore, T. R.; Knowles, R. *Can. J. of Soil Sci.* **1989**, *69*, 33–38.
75 Peterson, B. J.; Hobbie, J. E.; Hershey, A. E; Lock, T. E.; Vestal, J. R.; McKinley, J. L.; Hullar, M. A. J.; Miller, M. C.; Ventullo, R. M.; Volk, G. S. *Science* **1985**, *229*, 1383–1386.
76 Kling, G. W.; Kipphut, G. W.; Miller, M. C. *Science* **1991** *251*, 298–301.
77 Bazilevich, N. I.; Rodin, L. E.; Rozov, N. N. In *Productivity of World Ecosystems*. Reichle, D. E.; Franklin, J. F.; Goodall, D. W., Eds; National Academy of Sciences Press: Washington DC, 1971.
78 Rodin, L. Y.; Bazilevich, N. I. *Production and Mineral Cycling in Terrestrial Vegetation*; Oliver and Boyd: Edinburgh, UK, 1967.
79 Kellog, W. W. *J. Geophys. Res.* **1983** *88*, 1263–1269.
80 Lashof, D. A. *Clim. Change* **1989** *14*, 213–242.
81 Sellers, P. J.; Hall, F. G.; Asrar, G.; Strebel, D. E.; Murphy, R. E. *Bull. Am. Met. Soc.* **1988** *69*, 22–27.

RECEIVED July 23, 1991

Chapter 22

Vegetation, the Global Carbon Cycle, and Global Measures

Lloyd G. Simpson and Daniel B. Botkin

Environmental Studies Program, Department of Biological Sciences, University of California, Santa Barbara, CA 93106

Qualitatively, terrestrial vegetation is known to be an important part of the global carbon cycle. It affects the carbon cycle directly through photosynthesis, respiration, and decay of organic matter; and indirectly by affecting climate. Quantitatively, however, little is known about how vegetation fits into the global carbon budget. Computer models are the primary tools used to assess the functioning of vegetation in the global carbon cycle, but models use poor data and are too simple to give reliable results. The most commonly used estimates of global vegetation reservoir size range between 420 and 830 gigatons of carbon. However, using the most current estimates of carbon density we have calculated a new estimate of 328 gigatons of carbon. This result demonstrates that a concerted effort must be made to systematically measure the biomass of vegetation on a global scale. Until this is done, basic questions such as whether vegetation is a net source or sink of carbon in the global carbon budget will be left unresolved.

Carbon is the basic atom of all organic compounds. Life on Earth requires large amounts of carbon to produce carbohydrates, lipids, proteins, and nucleic acids. Primarily in the form of carbon dioxide (CO_2), carbon is also an important component of the Earth's atmosphere. While it makes up less that 0.04% of the atmosphere, CO_2 is significant because of its heat absorbing properties. Small changes in CO_2 concentration can change the energy budget of the atmosphere and thereby affect climate which in turn can affect life on Earth. Because carbon is so important to life and can affect climate, and because human activities are leading to a continuing increase in atmospheric CO_2 concentration, it is critical that we understand the global carbon cycle.

The global carbon cycle is the continuous movement of carbon between the living and nonliving portions of the biosphere, driven in part by biological processes and resulting in a constant supply of carbon to life (Figure 1). The

0097–6156/92/0483–0413$06.00/0
© 1992 American Chemical Society

global carbon budget quantifies the carbon cycle by describing the location of carbon reservoirs, their size, and the fluxes (rates of carbon movement) among the reservoirs. In spite of its importance, we know surprisingly little about the quantitative aspects of the carbon budget. There have been many attempts in recent years to quantify the global carbon cycle (e.g. *1, 2, 3, 4*), most of which assume that the cycle is static and in steady-state except for anthropogenic influences. Unfortunately, most of these descriptions of the carbon budget use estimates of reservoir size and flux rates that are based on little if any data appropriate for extrapolation to a global scale. The lack of good quantitative data is a fundamental problem common to all studies of biogeochemical processes at the global level.

An important issue that remains unresolved, because of the lack of adequate quantitative data on reservoirs and fluxes, is the location of the so called "missing" carbon. Missing carbon is the carbon added to the atmosphere from the burning of fossil fuel that cannot be accounted for by the measured increase in atmospheric concentration or by diffusion into the ocean (*5*).

There has been a long standing controversy about whether vegetation is a net sink or net source of excess carbon (*6*). This controversy may not be resolved until there are better assessments of the sizes of the vegetation carbon pools and fluxes associated with it. A proper assessment of the actual and potential role of vegetation in the global carbon cycle requires accurate information about carbon storage and change over time (*6, 7*).

Vegetation and the Global Carbon Cycle

Land vegetation has important effects on the biogeochemistry and energy budget of the Earth (*8*); most directly through photosynthesis and respiration. Photosynthesis of terrestrial vegetation removes carbon dioxide from the atmosphere, respiration of all life returns CO_2 to the atmosphere. Part of the carbon removed by vegetation is stored in the form of nonwoody and woody plant parts. The most striking evidence of these effects is the measurements of annual fluctuations of CO_2 concentration in the atmosphere made at Mauna Loa observatory (*9*) (Figure 2). Atmospheric concentration of CO_2 is at a minimum during the summer growing season when terrestrial photosynthesis is greatest, and at a maximum during the winter when most land vegetation is dormant and photosynthesis on the land is low. Some have estimated that as much as ten percent of atmospheric CO_2 could be taken up and released annually by vegetation (*2*), illustrating the rapidity of flux rates between the atmosphere and terrestrial ecosystems.

Marine algae and photosynthetic bacteria also remove large quantities of CO_2, but release most of this almost immediately in respiration. These organisms lack the longevity, large body size, and large storage organs that lead to storage of carbon for months and years.

Carbon dioxide has been measured at more that 30 stations, and an annual fluctuation of atmospheric carbon dioxide concentration was observed at all (*10*). However, the magnitude and timing of the fluctuations varied with geographic location (*11*). At Mauna Loa observatory, the concentration of atmospheric CO_2

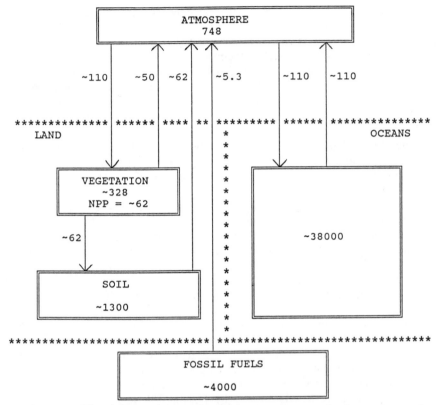

Figure 1. The global carbon cycle. Estimates of reservoir size and annual fluxes are from Post et al. (*4*). Vegetation carbon reservoir was estimated from latest carbon density estimates. All values except the atmospheric reservoir are approximate only. All values are in gigatons. Fluxes are next to the arrows and are in gigatons/year.

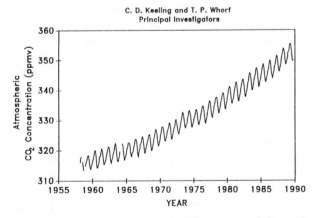

Figure 2. Concentration of atmospheric CO_2 measured from the Mauna Loa observatory, Hawaii. Data were from Boden et al. (*10*).

dropped an average of 5.8 ppmv each year between May and September from 1979 and 1989 (Figure 2). Because of the isolation of this location from large land masses, Mauna Loa represents an average of northern hemisphere fluxes. Further north, at NOAA/CMDL station in Point Barrow, Alaska, atmospheric CO_2 concentration dropped an average of 13.9 ppmv between April and August from 1979 to 1988. Point Barrow, Alaska is in a region dominated by vegetation that grows rapidly during a short growing season. In the southern hemisphere, the fluctuation is comparatively small and the decrease occurs between October and February, the southern-hemisphere summer. The small decline reflects the southern hemisphere's smaller land mass (about 30% of the Earth's land surface) and smaller amount of land vegetation. Geographical patterns of annual CO_2 fluctuations have important implications for the role of vegetation in the global carbon cycle.

Dead vegetation also affects the global carbon cycle. Dead organic matter decomposes, releasing carbon dioxide to the atmosphere. Rates of decomposition vary with material, location, and climate. Non-woody organic matter decomposes rapidly; woody organic matter slowly. Decomposition tends to occur faster at the soil surface than below. Decomposition is relatively fast in warm moist climates. In cold climates and in wetlands, decomposition is so slow that there is a net increase of stored carbon in the soil and organic soils called, "histosols," are formed.

Vegetation also affects the global carbon cycle indirectly. First, vegetation contributes raw material from which bacteria produce other trace gases such as methane and carbon monoxide (12). Methane is a byproduct of bacterial decomposition of organic matter in oxygen poor environments such as rice paddy fields, wetlands, and the intestines of ruminants and termites. Carbon monoxide is produced directly by vegetation, by burning of vegetation, and, in the atmosphere, by photochemical conversion of methane and non-methane hydrocarbons produced by vegetation such as ethylene, monoterpene, and isoprene (12, 13).

Second, vegetation protects soil from erosion and loss of nutrients and organic matter and decreases rates of decomposition. When vegetation is removed, soil decomposition and erosion often increase, because surface water runoff increases, and soil is exposed to wind and sunlight. Deforestation and clearing of grasslands at first leads to an increase in CO_2 flux to the atmosphere. Later, with the loss of soil and its nutrients, net CO_2 uptake by vegetation may proceed at a slower pace than before.

Third, vegetation affects the global carbon cycle indirectly by affecting climate -- through changes in albedo, evaporation of water, and surface roughness. Albedo, and therefore the energy budget, is influenced by the type and structure of vegetation. For example, in the northern boreal forest, stands are more open and in the spring there is significant reflectance of solar radiation from snow. This slows the warming process and delays growth (14), resulting in a shorter growing season and a reduced amount of annual carbon uptake.

The structure of vegetation also has an influence on surface roughness and on local wind patterns and rates of mixing in the boundary layer of the atmosphere. Forests have a dampening affect on wind, slowing it and causing increased turbulence. Within the canopy air movement is slower and mixing rates are reduced. The lack of vigorous mixing results in a higher concentration of CO_2 in the lower portion of a forest canopy than in the atmosphere directly above the canopy (15). Conversely, the CO_2 concentration in the air at the crown level, where all the foliage is concentrated, is lower than the atmosphere above. Some carbon released from soil respiration is reabsorbed quickly by the vegetation and does not become part of the global atmospheric carbon pool.

Changes in evapotranspiration rates of vegetation can have indirect effects. About 20% of water vapor supplied to the atmosphere annually comes from evapotranspiration of terrestrial systems (16). Some evidence suggests that in some regions, most notably the tropics, a high percentage of local precipitation comes from local evapotranspiration. A change in evapotranspiration caused by removal of vegetation could affect the amount and distribution of precipitation regionally and globally (17) and therefore affect photosynthesis and growth.

Analysis of the Global Carbon Cycle

The most common way in which the global carbon budget is calculated and analyzed is through simple diagrammatical or mathematical models. Diagrammatical models usually indicate sizes of reservoirs and fluxes (Figure 1). Most mathematical models use computers to simulate carbon flux between terrestrial ecosystems and the atmosphere, and between oceans and the atmosphere. Existing carbon cycle models are simple, in part, because few parameters can be estimated reliably.

The mathematical model of Bjorkstrom (18) is typical of those used to quantify the global carbon cycle and analyze the possible fate of missing carbon. This model is a series of first-order differential equations representing change in carbon reservoirs over time. There are only three principal reservoirs: ocean, atmosphere, and terrestrial organic carbon. The atmosphere is treated as one well mixed reservoir, while the ocean is divided into 12 interconnected reservoirs representing differences in mixing rates and movement of materials among various ocean depths and latitudes. Terrestrial carbon is divided into two biota and two soil reservoirs. One soil and one biota reservoir represent areas changing due to anthropogenic effects. Each reservoir is assumed to be homogeneous and uniform.

Fluxes are linear functions of reservoir contents. Reservoir size and the residence time of the carbon in the reservoir are the parameters used in the functions. Between the ocean and the atmosphere and within the ocean, fluxes rates are calculated theoretically using size of the reservoir, surface area of contact between reservoirs, concentration of CO_2, partial pressures of CO_2, temperature, and solubility as factors. The flux of carbon into the vegetation reservoir is a function of the size of the carbon pool and a fertilization effect of increased CO_2 concentration in the atmosphere. Flux from vegetation into the atmosphere is a function of respiration rates estimated by Whittaker and Likens (19) and the decomposition of short-lived organic matter which was assumed to be half of the gross assimilation or equal to the amount transferred to dead organic matter. Carbon in organic matter that decomposes slowly is transferred to the soil reservoir. Soil organic matter decomposition results in a flux of CO_2 from the soil to the atmosphere.

Once the model was complete, it was adjusted to a steady state condition and tested using historic carbon isotope data from the atmosphere, oceans and polar ice. Several important parameters were calculated and chosen at this stage. Sensitivity analysis indicated that results -- dispersal of the missing carbon -- were significantly influenced by the size of the vegetation carbon pool, its assimilation rate, the concentration of preindustrial atmospheric carbon used, and the CO_2 fertilization factor. The model was also sensitive to several factors related to fluxes between ocean reservoirs.

One of the most elaborate models proposed thus far was one constructed by Goudriaan and Ketner (20). This model accounted for atmospheric, ocean (subdivided into several compartments), terrestrial biosphere (subdivided into six ecosystems and six components within each ecosystem), and fossil carbon reservoirs and the fluxes among them, as well as human impact on the biosphere. This model was used to project the global carbon budget from 1870 to 2030 (20). Again, linear first-order differential equations represented fluxes of carbon among reservoirs. This model was sensitive to changes in the diffusion coefficient in the ocean, the life-span of vegetation, the rate of land clearing and reclamation, and the CO_2 fertilization effect. The CO_2 fertilization effect used in this model was relatively high and may in part account for the conclusion that vegetation is a net sink for atmospheric carbon.

Another model, first introduced by Moore, et al. (21), was used to examine the role of terrestrial vegetation and the global carbon cycle, but did not include an ocean component. This model depended on estimates of carbon pool size and rates of CO_2 uptake and release. This model has been used to project the effect of forest clearing and land-use change on the global carbon cycle (22, 23, 24).

It is interesting to note that scientists who use models with a detailed ocean component suggest that excess or missing carbon must be taken up be vegetation. They also contend that estimates of vegetation reservoirs sizes are highly suspect. Those that use models with vegetation featured prominently, on the other hand, conclude that excess carbon must be diffusing into the oceans and that ocean dynamics are poorly understood.

These models are too simple to reflect realistic dynamic properties of the carbon budget. Even so, they depend on data that are poorly measured or lacking. Many potentially important compartments are missing or assumed to be unimportant. For example, no model considers carbon transported from terrestrial systems to the oceans through rivers and streams. While the amount is very small, it is continuous and cumulative (25)

The dynamics of these models depend strictly on carbon fluxes, but the fluxes are poorly measured or are calculated from carbon reservoir size and assumptions about the residence time of the carbon in the reservoir. In addition, model fluxes are linear functions while in reality few, if any, probably are linear.

The models also assume a steady-state condition which suggests that the carbon cycle is structured, stable, and balanced and will remain so indefinitely. This mechanistic view of biogeochemistry allows for little variation even though it is known that fluctuations and variation occur seasonally. The concentration of carbon in the atmosphere is also known to have varied over thousands of years without significant anthropomorphic influence (*26*).

Furthermore, in existing global carbon cycle models, carbon flux is independent of any other factor, including climate, even though these models are used to help predict climate change. These models also fail to consider interactions of the carbon cycle with other biogeochemical cycles. In reality, living organisms require large amounts of nitrogen, phosphorus, and sulfur as well as carbon, and these affect one another. For example, phosphorus is often limiting in many ecosystems therefore an increase in phosphorus availability could result in an increase in production thus affecting the carbon cycle. Fossil fuel burning releases large amounts of sulfur to the atmosphere along with the carbon. Sulfur and carbon react together and form several compounds found in the atmosphere.

Importance of Accurate Global Measures

Land vegetation is known to play an important role in the global carbon cycle, but our knowledge about reservoir size and flux rates is very limited. In a recent review of the global carbon cycle, Post et al. (*4*) leave the question of the exact role vegetation performs in the global carbon cycle unresolved. We are not yet able to balance the global carbon budget, and different models give conflicting results. The disagreement on the role of vegetation in the global carbon cycle directly reflects uncertainties and inconsistencies in estimates of carbon pool sizes and flux rates. These estimates are based on carbon density (metric tons per hectare, or kg/m^2) and the areal extent to which the density applies. Despite their obvious importance, accurate measures of these factors are lacking for most of the Earth.

Several studies, based on models, examined the effects of land-use change on the global carbon cycle and conclude that there is a net release of carbon due to land clearing. However, the results and conclusions of these studies are based on assumed sizes of vegetation carbon pools which are inputs to the models. For example, Melillo et al. (*24*) concluded that boreal and temperate deciduous forests of the northern hemisphere are net sources of atmospheric carbon. Their analysis used values for carbon density derived by Whittaker and Likens (*19*) from work by Rodin and Bazilevich (*27*). Rodin and Bazilevich extrapolated results of small, unrelated studies in Europe and the USSR to estimate total biomass of Eurasian boreal and temperate deciduous forests. Their estimates have since been extrapolated to forests worldwide and are used often today.

Commonly used estimates of the global vegetation carbon pool range between 420 to 830 gigatons (*4*). However, the latest carbon density measurements suggest that in the past, previous estimates grossly overestimated carbon stored in land vegetation. Houghton et al. (*22*) arrived at a value of 744 gigatons for the carbon content of the global vegetation carbon pool. They computed this value by multiplying the carbon density value derived by Whittaker and Likens (*19*) for each biome by its estimated areal extent and summing the values for the biomes (Table I). We calculated a new value for the vegetation carbon pool by using the most recent carbon density values. The new value was calculated by multiplying areas of major biomes used by Houghton et al. (*22*) by the most recent estimates of carbon density for the closed tropical forest reported by Brown et al. (28) and for the boreal forest reported by Botkin and Simpson (7). In addition, it was assumed that carbon densities for tropical seasonal forest, temperate evergreen forest, and temperate deciduous forest reported by Whittaker and Likens (19) -- which were used by Houghton et al. (22) -- were overestimated. We reduced the carbon density values of these biomes by 62%, the difference between the value of the tropical forest carbon density reported by Whittaker and Likens (19) and that reported by Brown et al. (28) for tropical forests. This was the most conservative difference between the old and more recent estimates of forest biomass density. Preliminary results from our current work on the biomass of the temperate deciduous forest of eastern North America help substantiate this contention. The reduced values were then multiplied by the corresponding area. The result is a new estimate presented for the first time here, of 328 gigatons for the global vegetation carbon pool (Table I, Figure 1). This value is much lower than any previously suggested.

Table I. Estimation of the global vegetation carbon pool using the latest estimates of total carbon density for forests.

| | | Houghton et al. (22) | | This Study | |
Biome	Area[a] (10⁶ ha)	Carbon Density (ton/ha)	Total Carbon (gigatons)	Carbon Density (ton/ha)	Total Carbon (gigatons)
Tropical moist forest	1352	200	270	76[b]	103
Tropical seasonal forest	653	160	104	61[c]	40
Temperate evergreen forest	546	160	87	61[c]	33
Temperate deciduous forest	612	135	83	51[c]	31
Boreal forest	1179	90	106	23[d]	27
Trop. woodland and shrubland	945	27	26	27[e]	26
Temp. woodland and shrubland	753	27	20	27[e]	20
Tropical grassland	425	18	26	18[e]	26
Temperate grassland	2051	07	14	7[e]	14
Tundra and alpine meadow	706	03	2	3[e]	2
Desert scrub	2152	03	6	3[e]	6
Total	11374		744		328

[a] From (22).
[b] Calculated from (28).
[c] Value from (19) reduced by 62%.
[d] Value after (7); total biomass density calculated by multiplying above ground estimate by 1.23.
[e] Value after (19).

Obtaining Accurate Global Estimates

There are two types of data necessary to obtain accurate global estimates of vegetation carbon pools or biomass. First, it is important to have accurate data on the areal extent of major ecosystems. Matthews (29) found that calculations of global biomass were significantly influenced by the land cover data set used. Second, there must be accurate estimates of biomass density for terrestrial ecosystems. There is a wide range of estimates published for the same ecosystem, each derived by different methods (29), and none having statistical reliability (7).

Surprisingly, there is much confusion as to the areal extent of terrestrial vegetation on a global scale. In part, the confusion lies with different ways that vegetation is classified on maps. Various classification schemes are used, including: taxonomic, physiognomic, environmental, and functional. Taxonomic classifications are based on species. Physiognomic classifications are based on shape and form. Environmental classifications separate vegetation by the major determining environmental conditions with which they are associated. Functional classifications separate vegetation by what they do. For example, in terms of the hydrologic cycle, a functional group would be all the vegetation that evaporated water at the same rate, or at the same rate under the same environmental conditions.

Because there are different criteria, there is often disagreement on the location and extent of vegetation, especially at a global scale. For example, there is no agreement on the exact boundaries of the boreal forest in North America (30, 31). Three vegetation maps of the boreal forest (32, 33, 34), that we believe to be authoritative and to be determined by independent methods, disagree considerably as to the areal extent of the North American boreal forest. The area that all three agree is boreal forest (the intersection of the three maps) is less than one-half the area represented by the sum of the maps (the union of the maps) (Botkin, D. B.; Simpson, L. G.; Star J. L.; Estes, J. E.   In Prep. Vegetation classification and mapping: a brief summary and consideration of the potential of remote sensing) (Figure 3).

Most vegetation maps are derived from a variety of sources using different methods and made at different times. This can lead to an overlap between adjacent areas of interest, the exclusion of some areas, and the improper extrapolation of carbon densities, thus resulting in inaccurate estimates of reservoir size. We found that the biomass density of the southern North American boreal forest was over 2.5 times larger than the biomass density of the northern part of the boreal forest (35). Past estimates of boreal forest biomass density extrapolated southern biomass density values to the entire boreal forest, which in part accounts for the large overestimation (7). It is important that a consistent method be developed to map vegetation globally.

Most estimates of global vegetation biomass densities are extrapolations from studies never intended to represent large areas (e.g. 19, 36) or they were derived from questionnaires sent to botanists (37). These estimates are still used commonly in the examination and modeling of the global carbon cycle. Some of the earliest estimates were made when almost no quantitative data were available and the data or the estimates were largely speculative. Other estimates are

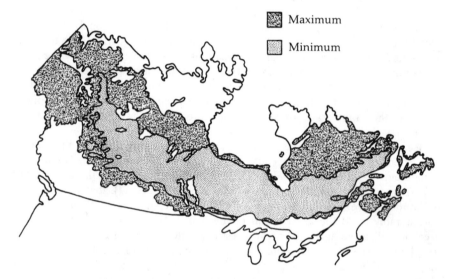

Figure 3. Maximum and minimum extent of the boreal forest of Canada from the union and intersection respectively of Anonymous (*32*), Rowe (*33*), and Anonymous (*34*).

statistically biased, extrapolating from small, restricted studies to large areas. This leads to overestimation because these studies were typically conducted in undisturbed, mature (i.e. high biomass) vegetation. Our recent work in the North American boreal forest (*7, 35*) represents the first attempt to obtain accurate large-area measures.

Conclusion

It is clear that qualitatively, vegetation plays an important role in the global carbon cycle. Quantitatively, however, the effect of vegetation is not well known. Models of the carbon budget suffer from grossly inadequate data and improper assumptions including the assumption that fluxes are only linear functions of carbon storage and that the entire budget is in steady-state except for human influences, assumptions clearly contradicted by reconstructions of the history of atmospheric CO_2 concentration and understanding of the causal of carbon flux. To determine the quantitative role of vegetation in the global carbon cycle, basic information such as carbon density and distribution must be measured accurately for the entire Earth, and realistic, non-linear models must be developed.

Acknowledgments

This research was supported by the Andrew W. Mellon Foundation. We would like to thank R. A. Nisbet and an anonymous reviewer for their helpful suggestions and comments on the manuscript; and K. E. Simpson for drafting Figure 3.

Literature Cited

1 Carbon and the Biosphere Woodwell, G. M.; Pecan, E. V. Eds; Nat. Tech. Infor. Center: Springfield, Va., 1973.
2 Bolin, B.; Degens, E. T.; Duvigneaud, P.; Kempe, S. In *The Global Carbon Cycle*; Bolin, B.; Degens, E. T.; Kempe, S.; Ketner, P., Eds.; SCOPE 13; J Wiley & Sons, New York, 1979, (pp 1-56).
3 Moore, B. III; Bolin, B. *Oceanus* **1987**, *29*, 9.
4 Post, W. M.; Peng, T.; Emanuel, W. R.; King, A. W.; Dale, V. H.; DeAngelis, D. L. *Amer. Sci.* **1990**, *78*, 310.
5 Broecker, W. S.; Takahashi, T.; Simpson, H. J.; Peng, T. H. 1979. Fate of fossil fuel carbon dioxide and the global carbon budget. *Science* **1979**, *206*, 409.
6 Detwiler, R. P.; Hall, C. A. S. 1988. Tropical forests and the global carbon cycle. *Science* **1988**, *239*, 42.
7 Botkin, D. B.; Simpson, L. G. *Biogeochemistry* **1990**, *9*, 161.
8 Botkin, D. B.; Running, S. W. *Machine Processing of Remotely Sensed Data*; Symposium; Purdue University: West Lafayette, IN, 1984, pp. 326-332.
9 Keeling, C. D.; Bacastow, R. B.; Bainbridge, A. E.; Ekdahl, Jr., C. A.; Guenther, P. R.; Waterman, L. S.; Chin, J. F. S. *Tellus* **1976**, *28*, 538.
10 Trends '90: a compendium of data on global change; Boden, T. A.; Kanciruk P.; Farrell, M. P. Eds.; ORNL/CDIAC-36; Oak Ridge Nat. Lab., Oak Ridge, TN, 1990.

11 Gammon, R. H.; Komhyr, W. D.; Peterson, J. T. In *The changing carbon cycle a global analysis*; Trabalka, J. R.; Reichle, D. E., Eds.; Springer-Verlag: New York, 1986.

12 Crutzen, P. J. In *The Major Biogeochemical Cycles and Their Interactions*; Bolin, B.; Cook, R. B., Eds.; SCOPE 21; John Wiley & Sons: New York, NY, 1983; pp 67-111.

13 Freyer, H.-D. In *The Global Carbon Cycle*; Bolin, B.; Degens, E. T.; Kempe, S.; Ketner, P., Eds.; SCOPE 13; J Wiley & Sons, New York, NY, 1979; pp 101-128.

14 Hare, F. K.; Ritchie, J. C. *The Geographical Review* **1972**, *63*, 333.

15 Oke, T. R. *Boundary Layer Climates*; Second Edition; Methuen & Co.: New York, NY, 1987.

16 Westall, J.; Strumm, W. In *The Handbook of Environmental Chemistry*; Huntzinger, O. Ed.; Springer-Verlag: New York, NY, 1980, Vol. 1 Part A; pp 17-49.

17 Waring, R. H.; Schlesinger, W. H. *Forest Ecosystems: Concepts and Management*; Academic Press: New York, NY, 1985.

18 Bjorkstrom, A. 1979. A model of CO_2 interaction between atmosphere,oceans, and land biota. In *The Global Carbon Cycle*; Bolin, B.; Degens, E. T.; Kempe, S.; Ketner, P., Eds.; SCOPE 13; J Wiley & Sons: New York, NY, 1979; pp 403-457.

19 Whittaker, R. H.; Likens, G. E. In *Carbon and the Biosphere*; Woodwell, G. M.; Pecan, E. V. Eds.; Nat. Tech. Infor. Center: Springfield, VA, 1973; pp. 281-300.

20 Goudriaan, J.; Ketner, P. *Climatic Change* **1984**, *6*, 167.

21 Moore, B.; Boone, R. D.; Hobbie, J. E.; Houghton, R. A.; Melillo, J. M.; Peterson, B. J.; Shaver, G. R.; Vorosmarty, C. J.; Woodwell, G. M. In *Carbon Cycle Modelling*; Bolin, B., Ed.; SCOPE 16; John Wiley & Sons: New York, NY, 1981; pp 365-386.

22 Houghton, R. A.; Hobbie, J. E.; Melillo, J. M.; Moore, B.; Peterson, B. J.; Shaver, G. R.; Woodwell, G. M. *Ecol. Mono.* **1983**, *53*, 235.

23 Houghton, R. A.; Boone, R. D.; Fruci, J. R.; Hobbie, J. E.; Melillo, J. M.; Palm, C. A.; Peterson, B. J.; Shaver, G. R.; Woodwell, G. M.; Moore, B.; Skole, D. L.; Myers, N. *Tellus* **1987**, *39B*, 122.

24 Melillo, J. M.; Fruci, J. R.; Houghton, R. A.; Moore III, B.; Skole, D. L. *Tellus* **1988**, *40B*, 116.

25 Lugo, A. E.; Brown, S. *Vegetatio* **1986**, *68*, 83.

26 Botkin, D. B. *Discordant Harmonies: a new ecology of the 21st century*; Oxford University Press: New York, NY, 1990.

27 Rodin, L. E.; Bazilevich, N. I. *Production and Mineral Cycling in Terrestrial Vegetation*; Oliver and Boyd: London, GB, 1967.

28 Brown, S.; Gillespie, A. J. R.; Lugo, A. E. *For. Sci.* **1989**, *35*, 881.

29 Matthews, E. *Progress in Biometeorology* **1984**, *3*, 237.

30 Larsen, J. A. *The Boreal Ecosystem*; Academic Press: New York, NY, 1980.

31 Larsen, J. A. *The Northern Forest Border in Canada and Alaska*; Springer-Verlag: New York, NY, 1989.

32 Anonymous *Physical Geographic Atlas of the World*; Acad. of Sciences U.S.S.R. and Board of Geodesy and Cartography GGK, U.S.S.R, 1964.

33 Rowe, J. S. *Forest Regions of Canada*; Can. For. Serv., Dept. Fisheries and the Environment: Ottawa, Ont. Canada, 1972.

34 Anonymous *National Atlas of Canada*; Dept. of Energy, Mines, and Resources: Ottawa, Ont., Canada, 1974.

35 Botkin, D. B.; Simpson, L. G. In *Global Natural Resource Monitoring and Assessments: preparing for the 21st century*; Cini, F. G. Ed.; . Amer. Soc. of Photo. and Remot. Sen.: Bethesda, MD, 1990, Vol. 3; pp 1036-1045.

36 Ajtay, G. L.; Ketner, P.; Duvigneaud, P. In *The Global Carbon Cycle*; Bolin, B.; Degens, E. T.; Kempe, S.; Ketner, P., Eds.; SCOPE 13; J Wiley & Sons: New York, NY, 1979; pp 129-182.

37 Olson, J. S.; Pfuderer, H. A.; Chan, Y. H. *Changes in the Global Carbon Cycle and the Biosphere*; ORNL/EIS-109, Oak Ridge National Laboratory: Oak Ridge, TN, 1978.

RECEIVED September 4, 1991

Chapter 23

Biogeochemistry of Deforestation and Biomass Burning

J. Boone Kauffman, Ken M. Till, and Ronald W. Shea

Department of Rangeland Resources, Oregon State University, Corvallis, OR 97331

Cutting and burning of the world's forests is occurring at unprecedented levels and is dramatically influencing biogeochemical cycles at local, as well as global scales. Biogeochemical cycles are altered through losses associated with wood export, volatilization, convective transport, and accelerated rates of erosion and leaching losses. These anthropogenic activities are resulting in nutrient losses that far exceed natural rates of reaccumulation. As deforestation alters microclimates and hydrological cycles, internal nutrient cycles can be influenced for decades to centuries. The ultimate results of excessive levels of deforestation and biomass burning include losses in site productivity, desertification and/or species extinctions. Biomass burning is also a significant source of CO_2, CH_4, NO_x, and other products of combustion that influence climate and atmospheric geochemistry.

Introduction: The Global Extent of Deforestation and Biomass Burning

Over the past 10,000 years it has been estimated that the area of the earth's surface covered by forests and woodlands has decreased by one-third in order to make way for crops, pastures, and cities (1). However, in the last decades of the second millenium A.D., the rates of forest loss have far exceeded that of any other time period in human history. Associated with these unprecedented rates of deforestation are unprecedented rates of species extinction (2). In addition, deforestation is often accompanied with biomass burning (or slash fires). This not only exacerbates losses in biological diversity, but is a rather dramatic biogeochemical event with local as well as global consequences. The practice of deforestation and biomass burning is common among most forest-based cultures in both developed and third world countries. Deforestation and/or intentionally set fires are used for such purposes as timber extraction and slash disposal, clearing of forests for agricultural uses, controlling weeds, insect or pathogen invasions, enhancing the productivity or value of converted pastures and grasslands, and activities associated with charcoal production and fuelwood gathering for cooking, heating or industrial use.

Accurate estimates of deforestation on a global scale are largely unavailable, if not impossible, to ascertain. Since preagricultural times, temperate

0097–6156/92/0483–0426$08.75/0

forests have lost the highest percentage of their area (32-35%), followed by subtropical forests and savannas (24-25%), and tropical forests (15-20%) (*3*). On regional scales, the rates of deforestation can be astounding. Zhang (*4*) reported that in the Xishuangbanna area of southwestern China, 10,000 km^{-2} of tropical forests were lost in the past 30 years. In India, deforestation occurred at a rate of 1.5 million ha yr^{-1} during the early 1980s (*5*). It is estimated that only 16% of Madagascar's primary forest remains. Similarly, 98% of the Atlantic rainforests of Brazil have been cleared (*6*). From 1950-1980, 23% of Africa's forests and 40% of the forests of the Himalayan watershed were lost. During this same period, approximately 40% of central America's forests disappeared (*7*). Regional levels of deforestation may affect hydrological cycles which further disrupts forest-ecosystem dynamics. For example, the majority of forest cover in Panama has been lost as a result of deforestation and a concommitant decline in total precipitation has occurred (*8*). Deforested regions of Malaysia, India, The Philippines, and The Ivory Coast have also experienced decreased amounts of precipitation during the past 30 years (*9*).

Although differences exist among estimations of the quantities of tropical forest being cleared, even the most conservative are remarkable. Currently, the majority of deforestation is occurring in the tropical forests of the world. Woodwell (*10*) reported annual rates of deforestation in tropical regions ranged from 3.3 to 20.1 million ha yr^{-1}. The average rate of tropical forest loss according to Meyers (*9*) is 9.5 million ha^{-1} yr^{-1}. In Amazonia, Meyers (*11*) estimated that 36,000 km^2 were cleared from 1966-1975. For the year 1987, Kaufman et al. (*12*) reported 350,000 fires burned >20 million ha in Amazonia alone. Based upon satellite imagery, Setzer et al. (*13*) suggested that 8 million ha of this burned area was slashed primary forest; the remaining areas were covered by second-growth forest or pasture. Because of changes in government policies and programs, coupled with above average precipitation in the dry seasons, the area of primary forests in Amazonia subjected to deforestation and fire events is estimated to have declined to 4.8 million ha in 1988 and 3 million ha in 1989 (*14*). Fearnside (*15*) estimated that by 1990, 40 million ha or 8% of the Brazilian Amazon forests have been cleared.

Land use changes in the tropics have resulted in a landscape characterized as a mosaic of logged forests, cleared fields, and successional forests. This results in the transformation from extremely fire resistant rainforest ecosystems to anthropogenic landscapes in which fire is a common event (*16, 17*). Fires occur in disturbed tropical forests because deforestation has a dramatic effect on microclimate. Deforestation results in lower relative humidities, increased wind speeds, and increased air temperatures. In addition, deforestation results in increased quantities of biomass that are susceptible to fire. This biomass may be in the form of forest slash, leaf litter, grasses, lianas or herbaceous species (*16, 18*).

Abusive forest practices are neither a recent phenomenon nor limited to developing tropical countries. Deforestation has brought about economic and social declines of civilizations for over 5,000 years (*19*). Postel and Ryan (*1*) estimated only 1.5 million ha of primary forests remain out of the 6.2 billion ha that existed prior to human dominance on earth. Virtually all of Europe's original forests have been replaced by agriculture, urban environments, and intensively managed tree plantations. In the continental United States (excluding Alaska) <5% of primary forests now remain (*1*). Deforestation can result in losses in biological diversity and increased rates of erosion and nutrient losses which threaten to permanently decrease the productivity of much of the world's forests. In many cases, areas once occupied by forests are now deserts or degraded grasslands. In addition, the combustion products from biomass burning are significant atmospheric pollutants that may influence global climate change. In this chapter we review the impacts of deforestation and biomass burning on the biogeochemistry of forests at local, regional and global scales.

Deforestation, Biomass Burning and the Biogeochemical Balance of Forests

Biogeochemical cycling in forests includes elemental inputs, exports, and a complex set of physical, chemical and biotic processes which comprise internal nutrient cycles (Fig. 1). Any disturbance, whether anthropogenic (i.e. deforestation, chemical pollution, burning, etc.) or natural (i.e. wildfire, hurricanes, flooding, etc.) will influence ecosystem nutrient dynamics. Deforestation and biomass burning influence biogeochemical cycles through alterations in: (a) hydrological cycles (i.e. declines in transpiration rates, and increases in surface or subsurface flows); (b) nutrient dynamicss (i.e. losses due to harvest, volatilization, erosion, and leaching losses); (c) disruptions in microclimate; and (d) disruptions in biotic processes (i.e. succession, species losses, internal nutrient cycles, nitrogen fixation, etc.). This section is a general review how deforestation and biomass burning can affect nutrient inputs, internal cycles, and nutrient losses.

Elemental Inputs. In order to ascertain the importance of nutrient losses associated with deforestation and fire, it is necessary to quantify rates of nutrient inputs. Nutrients are added to a forest through atmospheric inputs, mineral weathering, and biological fixation (Fig. 1). In regions in which large areas are subjected to deforestation and biomass burning, the quantity of nutrient deposition via dry fall (ash fall) can increase. In contrast to other elements, the primary source of N in most forest ecosystems is through biological fixation. Biomass burning can dramatically influence this process. Rates of symbiotic N-fixation will vary depending upon the successional status or species composition of the plant community. In Amazonian ecosystems, rates of N-fixation have been reported to vary from 2 kg ha^{-1} yr^{-1} in infertile oxisols to 200 kg ha^{-1} yr^{-1} in fertile floodplain forests (*20*). In temperate North American forests, numerous plants with symbiotic N fixing capabilities have evolved to colonize disturbed forest sites (*21*). These are principally in the Leguminosae, Betulaceae, and Rhamnaceae plant families. Rates of symbiotic fixation of N in red alder (Alnus rubra) forests may range from 32-320 kg ha^{-1} yr^{-1} (*22, 23*). Following deforestation of coniferous forests of the Pacific Northwest, USA, nitrogen accretion within early seral plant communities dominated by N-fixing plants (snowbrush [Ceanothus velutinus])

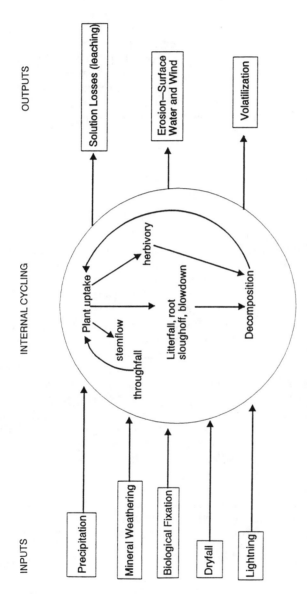

Figure 1. Generalized nutrient balance of ecosystems in the intervals between disturbance events. Natural disturbances such as wildfires, hurricanes, and floods as well as anthropogenic disturbances such as deforestation and biomass burning can dramatically influence nutrient inputs, internal cycles, and ecosystem outputs (losses).

ranged from 71-108 kg N ha yr^{-1} (*24*). In mature, well-established forests of this same ecosystem, N-fixation is relatively low (2.8 kg ha yr^{-1}) (*25*). Therefore, anthropogenic disruptions in the early seral stages of these forests that result in the removal of these species (i.e. by use of herbicides or establishing highly competitive exotic grasses) can impair the level and rate of N reaccumulation. Additionally, N-fixing activities in both temperate and tropical forests can be limited by a low availability of other nutrients (particularly P and Ca) (*26*).

With the exception of N, most nutrient inputs originate from either mineral weathering or atmospheric inputs (dryfall and precipitation) (Table I). In the coniferous forests of the Pacific Northwest, USA, the majority of P and significant quantities of ̈Mg and N are derived from atmospheric inputs (*25*). Mineral weathering of parent materials contributes the majority of inputs of Ca, Mg and Na and a significant proportion of the inputs of K and P. For example, mineral weathering accounted for inputs of 119 kg Ca ha^{-1} yr^{-1} , whereas precipitation inputs totaled 3.6 kg Ca ha^{-1} yr^{-1} (Table I) (*25*). In contrast, Jordan (*27*) reported that in highly weathered soils of Amazonian rainforests, release from parent materials was negligible; the forest nutrient balance was essentially maintained solely through atmospheric inputs.

Biomass Redistribution Associated with Deforestation and Fire. The influence of deforestation on biogeochemical cycles is dependent upon a number of factors associated with the unique characteristics of the ecosystem (climate, soils, topography, etc), the quantity of the total nutrient pool stored in aboveground biomass (Table II), and the level of disturbance (i.e. the degree of canopy removal, soil disturbance, and the quantity of wood or other forest products exported from the site). The quantity of biomass consumed by one or more slash fires following deforestation can also dramatically increase nutrient losses, influence post fire plant succession, and hence, postfire biogeochemical cycles.

Quantities of nutrients removed in wood vary depending upon the reasons for deforestation (timber, fuelwood, or shifting cultivation), methods of logging, distance to markets, and laws and regulations. The composition and structure of the forest are also important. For example, the primary (old growth or ancient) forests of the Pacific Northwest, USA, have the greatest aboveground biomass of any forest in the world. Aboveground biomass has been reported to be 3200 Mg ha^{-1} in coastal redwood (Sequoia sempervirens) forests (*28*) and 1762 Mg ha^{-1} in Douglas-fir-western hemlock (Pseudotsuga menziesii-Tsuga heterophylla) forests (Table II) (*29*). In these forests, remarkable quantities of forest biomass may be removed as a result of deforestation. Little and Ohmann (*30*) reported the total aboveground biomass following logging in Douglas-fir-western hemlock forests ranged from 71-356 kg ha^{-1}. Subsequent slash fires remove additional quantities such that the total reduction of aboveground biomass associated with deforestation and biomass burning can exceed 90%.

Negligible quantities of wood may be removed when tropical forests are cut for shifting cultivation or pasture conversion. In contrast to the temperate coniferous forests of the Northwest USA, only small quantities of wood are usually exported as a result of timber operations in tropical evergreen forests. In

Table I. Elemental inputs and losses of elements in the absence of disturbance in selected forest ecosystems*

Site	Nutrients Kg ha^{-1} yr^{-1}					Reference
	N	P	K	Ca	Mg	
Precipitation Inputs						
Venezuela-Tropical rainforest	6.1	0.25	10.59	8.83	2.44	80
Brazil-Tropical savanna	--	2.8	2.5	5.6	0.9	81
USA-Temperate coniferous forest	2.0	0.2	2.5	1.4	1.0	25
Costa Rica-Tropical moist forest	5.0	0.2	2.5	1.4	1.0	82
Canada-Temperate coniferous forest	2.3-3.8	--	0.7-1.2	3.4-8.9	--	65
Hydrologic Losses						
Venezuela-Tropical rainforest	11.6	0.0	3.7	3.5	1.0	80
Brazil-Tropical moist forest	0.2	0.01	0.4	--	--	83
USA-Temperate coniferous forest	1.5	0.8	9.5	1.2	8.6	25
Costa Rica-Tropical moist forest	19.4	0.0	3.6	5.7	8.5	84
Canada-Temperate coniferous forest	0.2-1.9	<0.1	0.9-2.1	16.6-54.3	2.6-5.9	53

* Methods for data collection vary from lysimeters to streamwater samples. Additional examples of inputs and losses may be found in Jordan (80), Melillo and Gosz (85) and Vitousek and Sanford (26).

Table II. Total aboveground biomass (Mg ha^{-1}) in selected forests of the world.

Forest	Location	Disturbance Status	Biomass	Reference
Temperate Coniferous Forest				
Coastal redwood	USA	Primary	1150-3200	28
Douglas fir-western hemlock	USA	Primary	783-1765	29, 86
	USA	Deforested	71-356	30
Lodgepole pine	North America	Primary	70-245	87
Subalpine forest	North America	Primary	144-213	87
Western juniper	USA	Primary	24-39	88
Temperate Deciduous Forest	Global Average	Primary	174	89
Boreal Coniferous Forest	Global Average	Primary	165	89
Tropical Broad-leaved Forests				
Moist evergreen forest	Neotropics	Primary	181-406	17, Kauffman and Cummings (Unpubl)
	Global Average	Primary	6-510	26
	Global Average	Primary	192	7
	Global Average	Primary	258-1051	90
	Brazil	Second growth	121	Kauffman and Cummings (Unpubl)
	Brazil	Degraded pasture	52	16
Dry deciduous forest	Global Average	Primary	68-275	90
	Brazil	Second growth	86	35

a logging operation in Amazonia, Uhl and Vieira (*31*) reported that only 2% of all trees $\geq$10 cm in diameter were harvested. Similarly, in Dipterocarp forests of southeast Asia only 3-10% of the basal area was removed by timber harvest (*32, 33*). However, in all these cases, over 50% of the canopy was destroyed by logging activities. In these ecosystems, losses in aboveground biomass are largely associated with slash fires utilized for the formation of cattle pastures and/or shifting cultivation. For example, in the eastern Amazon, aboveground biomass of tropical forests is approximately 264-292 Mg ha^{-1} (*34*, Kauffman, J. B. and Cummings, D. L. Oregon State University, unpublished data). When these disturbed forests are cut and intentionally burned, the initial slash fires are variable in the degree of biomass consumption, however, 50% loss in total aboveground biomass is not uncommon. Second-growth forests (15 years old) regrowing in abandoned cattle pastures in Amazonia have an aboveground biomass of 121 Mg ha^{-1} (Table II); much of which is residual wood debris from the primary forest. In the Amazon, Uhl and Kauffman (*16*) reported that the aboveground biomass of areas converted to cattle pastures was 52 Mg ha^{-1} (Table II). Within these degraded cattle pastures $\geq$40 Mg ha^{-1} was residual wood debris from the primary forest. Intensive manipulations of pastures in Amazonia utilizing bulldozers, herbicides, and fire result in the total removal of wood debris and an aboveground biomass consisting solely of exotic pasture grasses (8-10 Mg ha^{-1}). The aboveground mass of these pastures is <3% of the aboveground mass of the rainforests they replaced.

In the tropical dry forests of northeastern Brazil, Kauffman et al. (*35*) reported that total aboveground biomass was approximately 86 Mg ha^{-1} (Table II). Following complete cutting of all standing vegetation, 12 Mg ha^{-1} (approximately 14% of the aboveground biomass) was exported for use as fuel wood. The majority of the aboveground biomass in this ecosystem was lost through slash burning; a single slash fire resulted in the combustion of as much as 94% of the residual aboveground biomass.

Although anthropogenic disturbances vary among the world's cultures and forests, a conceptual model outlining the biomass and carbon export associated with deforestation and slash fires is possible (Fig. 2). In Fig. 2 arrow sizes represent relative magnitudes of inputs and losses. The vast majority of carbon inputs arise through photosynthesis. Deforestation, which results in the destruction of leaf area, greatly decreases C uptake from photosynthesis. In Fig. 2, timber harvest is the first significant anthropogenic export of carbon. Erosion, leaching, and microbial respiration rates are likely to increase following overstory removal. Consequently, C exports associated with these pathways will also increase. Biomass burning can result in volatilization of the majority of residual aboveground C and post fire rates of erosion, leaching, and microbial respiration can be greatly accelerated resulting in further losses of both aboveground and soil C. If land use patterns are such that deforested areas are repeatedly burned (as is the case when neotropical evergreen forests are converted to cattle pastures), the continued depletion of carbon and other nutrients will continue until land use is no longer feasible and the site is abandoned.

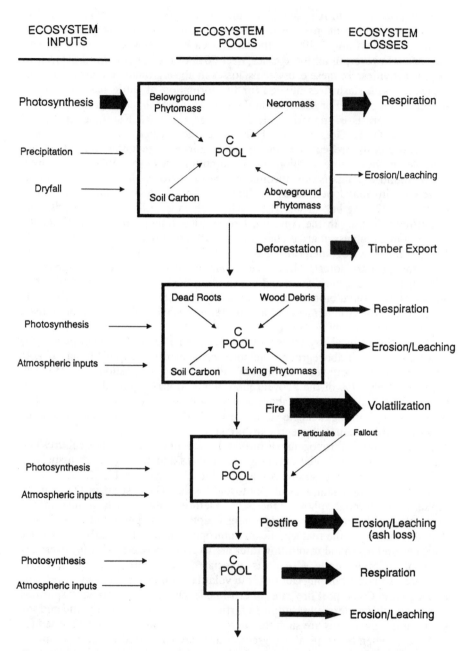

Figure 2. The carbon dynamics of a primary forest prior to and following deforestation and slash burning. Arrows represent the relative magnitude of C flux. In the primary forest (represented by the large box at the top of the figure), the C pool is in a dynamic equilibrium with inputs approximately equalling exports. With deforestation and fire, the balance is altered with exports far exceeding imports.

Effects of Deforestation and Biomass Burning on Internal Biogeochemical Cycles.
In addition to causing significant losses of aboveground biomass, deforestation
results in significant disruptions in internal biogeochemical cycles (Fig. 1). A shift
from primary forest to croplands, pasture or early seral plant communities results
in lower rates of nutrient uptake and storage within living plants. The
composition and mass of litterfall will be altered in early seral communities.
Rates of soil organic matter decomposition are increased. This can result in
declines in soil organic matter and hence, soil fertility (*36-38*). Finally,
deforestation creates a large pulse of available nutrients through the rapid
decomposition of fine roots. Vitousek and Sanford (*26*) reported belowground
biomass of roots ranged from 11-132 kg ha^{-1} in tropical moist forests (3-55 Mg ha^{-1}
were fine roots <6 mm diameter). In temperate coniferous forests of the
Pacific Northwest, USA, Grier and Logan (*29*) reported that root biomass ranged
from 105-204 Mg ha^{-1}. In this ecosystem there were 8-13 Mg ha^{-1} of readily
decomposable fine roots (<5 mm diameter). The pulse of nutrients originating
from the rapid decomposition of fine roots will either be lost through erosion or
leaching, become immobilized, or taken up by successional or planted vegetation.

Biomass burning will affect biogeochemical cycling through direct
elemental transformations during combustion processes and through
environmental changes which may affect nutrient cycling and availability for many
years following disturbance. The direct ashing of organic matter releases
significant quantities of available nutrients and can be an important source for
regrowing vegetation. Mineral ash will also influence soil pH and hence
microbial activities in soils related to decomposition and nutrient turnover.

The maximum temperature and duration of heating during fires are
important variables that influence the soil nutrient status, as well as the survival
of residual vegetation following fire (Table III). Deforestation results in the
presence of large quantities of wood debris in close proximity to the soil surface.
Fires in this scenario result in soil temperatures and magnitudes of heat flux far
in excess of those which occur in fires in uncut forests (Shea, R. W. Oregon State
University, unpublished data).

The temperature gradients generated in surface soils during fires are very
steep because the thermal conductivity of soils is low (*39*). As a consequence, the
soil surface may be heated to extremely high temperatures while soils below 10
cm in depth are little affected. Exceptions to this may be in areas in which
logging slash has been piled. During the burning of slash piles, soil surface
temperatures are as high as 1800°C (Shea, R. W. Oregon State University,
unpublished data) (Table III). Temperatures exceeding 60°C have occurred at
a soil depth of 12 cm for >20 hours under these burning slash piles. These
temperatures and durations of heat far exceed the capacity for plant and soil
microorganism survival (*40-42*).

Soil physical properties most likely to be altered by biomass burning are
soil structure, soil wettability, and clay mineralogy (Table III) (*43*). The
destruction of organic matter results in losses of soil structure, increases in bulk
density, diminished aggregate stability and decreases in macropore space (*44*).

Table III. Elemental volatilization and transformation of chemical and physical properties in the fire environment.

Phases of Combustion	Elemental or Process Transformation	Temperature Threshold (°C)	Sources
Dehydration Phase	Maximum stimulation of soil microorganisms	37	90
	Mild sterilization owing to water loss	50	90
	Breakdown of amino acids	60	91
	Lethal temperature thresholds of protoplasm in plant cells		92
	High rates of nitrate mineralization	70	91
	Maximum scarification of Ceanothus seeds in soils	90	93, 94
Endothermic Pyrolytic reactions	Soil ammonium increases through thermal decomposition of organic N	100	95
	Lethal temperatures of:		
	-Nitrosomonas and nitrobacter bacteria	100-140	41, 42
	-Hetereotrophic bacteria	110-210	41, 42
	-Actinomycetes	105-125	41, 42
	-Fungi	105-155	41, 42
	Free water is driven off between adjacent miceles of montmorillonite and illite clays	100-200	41, 96
	Volatilization of N	200	97
	Organic matter declines through pyrolysis; pyrolysis of cellulose	250-400	98, 99
	Volatilization of K	204-210	97
Exothermic pyrolytic reactions	Hydrophobic conditions begin to form in soils	200-315	100, 101, 102
	Pilot ignition temperature to flaming combustion	320	99
	Volatilization of some organic forms of P	360	57
	Average surface temperature of chaparral/brushland fires	350-370	103
	Volatilization of S	444	105
Glowing combustion	Dehydroxlization of montmorillanite (2:1 expanding) clays	500-550	96, 104

Table III (Cont'd.)

Phases of Combustion	Elemental or Process Transformation	Temperature Threshold (°C)	Sources
	Dehydroxlization of kaolinite (1:1 non-expanding soil)	500-550	104
	Volatilization of K		106
	Soil surface temperature in typical intense chaparral fire		107
	Spontaneous ignition to flaming combustion	600	99
Flaming combusion		600-1400	
	Volatilization of P (inorganic)	774	105
	Soil surface temperature of slash fires in tropical and temperate forests	800-900	35, 108, 109
	Volatilization of Na	880	40
	Irreversible conversions of clay minerals to amorphous materials	950-980	44, 110, 111
	Volatilization of Mg	1107	40
	Volatilization of Ca	1200	112
	Maximum soil surface temperature in coniferous slash-burn	1260	113
	Maximum soil surface temperatures in machine piles/windrows	1800	Shea and Kauffman (unpubl.)
	Maximum temperatures measured in wildland fires	1927-2200	41

Biomass burning will also influence soil biogeochemical cycles through increases in the solubility of surface organic matter as well as increases in the levels of available or readily mineralizable nutrients. Increases in NH_4 -N and available forms of P are very common following fire. Increased rates of mineralization (or nitrification) have also been found to occur on burned sites because of favorable soil temperatures, increased soil moisture, and increased soil pH (45, 46). Increases in available nutrients as a result of biomass burning facilitate the growth of crops in shifting cultivation systems on nutrient poor soils. These changes can also increase the quantities of nutrients lost from a site through leaching. However, both the increased solubility and levels of readily available nutrients are usually short-lived in slash-and-burned sites; a principal reason for abandonment in these agricultural systems.

Following biomass burning, an increase in soil pH is a very common occurrence (47, 48). Increases in soil pH can positively influence microbial activity (49) and are most evident in ecosystems which tend to have acidic soils, (high H^+ and Al^{+++} concentrations and low base saturation) and/or large proportions of cations released from standing biomass. Increases in soil pH may persist for many years in areas in which large quantities of biomass have been consumed by fire (50, 51). In areas with high levels of precipitation, pH increases tend to be short-lived, particularly if the cation exchange capacity of the soils has been negatively affected by fire and increased leaching losses result.

Nutrient Losses Associated with Deforestation. The impact of deforestation on biogeochemical cycles is dependent upon numerous factors including: (a) the quantity of the total nutrient pool in aboveground vegetation; (b) the quantity of this pool removed from the site; and (c) the frequency of removal from the site. In most forest ecosystems, the greatest proportion of the total nutrient pool is belowground. For example, in tropical dry forests, 22-28% of the total N pool and 11-17% of the total P pool was found in aboveground vegetation (35). In this ecosystem the nutrient loss associated with fuel wood harvest was minor (Table IV). In contrast, significant quantities of nutrients are exported when large quantities of wood debris are removed. Nitrogen exports exceeding 180-400 kg ha^{-1} are not uncommon during logging and debris removal in productive coniferous forests of the Pacific Northwest, North America (Table IV) (52, 53). Wood export may also result in the loss of 50 kg ha^{-1} of P in this same ecosystem (53). In forests over oligotrophic (nutrient poor) soils, the proportional loss of nutrient pools as a result of tree removal would be expected to be higher. Fuel wood harvest in second-growth Costa Rican rainforest resulted in the removal of 31% of ecosystem S and approximately 11-19% of P, Ca, Mg and C (37). In contrast, in a temperate deciduous forest, Hornbeck and Kropelein (54) reported that harvest removed the equivalent of approximately 2-3% of the soil capital for Ca and N and 1% of the total soil capital for K and P. Similar levels of nutrient export were reported by Johnson et al. (Table IV) (55).

Quantities of nutrients lost will also be dependent upon the type of vegetative materials harvested. Tissue nutrient concentrations are highest in fine wood debris (stems and twigs), leaves and reproductive plant parts. For example, in tropical dry forests, tissue N concentration of leaves is 2.5% and of wood debris is 0.3%. Therefore, practices which remove these finer fractions of forest vegetation (e.g. fuel wood, fodder, and whole tree removal) may remove a proportionately greater quantity of nutrients. For example, whole tree harvest in comparison to removal of only saw logs resulted in a 2-3 fold greater loss of nutrients from deforested sites (Table IV) (55-56).

Nutrient Losses Associated With Biomass Burning. Nutrient losses associated with slash fires occur through volatilization and convective losses of ash. Elements with low temperatures of volatilization (e.g. N, K, S, and some organic forms of P) will be lost in the highest quantities (Table III) (57). Conversely, Ca and Mg have volatilization temperatures higher than that recorded during most vegetation fires. Almost all fire-induced losses of these elements are due to particulate transfer by convective processes.

The burning of slash following deforestation, whether intentional or unintentional, results in far greater direct and indirect losses of nutrients than deforestation alone. This is particularly true in many tropical forests where only a small fraction (if any) of the aboveground biomass is removed prior to burning. Carbon losses from slash fires in the tropical dry forest were 4-5 fold greater than C losses from wood export (Table IV) (35). Slash fires in tropical dry forests resulted in N losses of 428-500 kg ha^{-1}, whereas fuel wood export of the relatively N-poor coarse woody debris amounted to approximately 41 kg N ha^{-1}. Losses of P increase with increasing fire severity. P losses of 10-77 kg ha^{-1} as a result of severe fires is not uncommon (Table IV) (53, 58, 60).

Because N has a low temperature of volatilization, the quantities of N lost by biomass burning are usually linearly related to the quantities of biomass consumed (57). Nitrogen losses in fire-adapted, shrub-dominated ecosystems in which low quantitites of biomass are consumed will be much smaller than N losses associated with high-consumption slash fires in coniferous forests (Table IV) (52, 53, 59). Nitrogen losses of 500-1,500 kg ha^{-1} are not uncommon in slash fires of Pacific coastal forests of North America (52, 53, 60). Similar high quantities of N loss (>600 kg ha^{-1}) are associated in slash fires in tropical rainforests (Kauffman, J. B. and Cummings, D. L. Oregon State University, unpublished data).

Erosion and Leaching Losses Following Deforestation and Biomass Burning. Accelerated rates of erosion are another significant pathway of nutrient loss following forest disturbance. Erosion losses may be the most significant pathway of loss for elements with high temperatures of volatilization and particularly following severe, high consumption fires where large quantities of nutrients are present in ash. Following fires in Eucalyptus-dominated forests, Harwood and Jackson (58) reported approximately 50% of aboveground nutrients were in the ash fraction. Similar results were found in dry forests of Brazil where 27-41% of the post fire aboveground N pools and 84% of the post fire aboveground P pools were in ash (35). Wind erosion resulted in a loss of 54% of that ash in a little

Table IV. Biomass and nutrient losses associated with wood harvest (fuel wood or timber export) and fire in selected forest ecosystems.

Plant Community/ Disturbance	Biomass (Mg ha⁻¹)	C (Mg ha⁻¹)	N (Kg ha⁻¹)	P (Kg ha⁻¹)	K (Kg ha⁻¹)	Ca (Kg ha⁻¹)	Reference
Second-growth tropical rainforest							
Costa Rica							
Harvest	29	10	111	4	90	96	37
Fire	39	16	490	0	0	0	
Tropical dry forest							
Brazil							
Harvest	12	6	41	3	–	–	35
Fire	57-70	25-32	428-530	1-21	–	–	
Western hemlock							
Canada							
Harvest	–	–	234-308	34-50	168-237	260-467	53
Fire	–	–	982	16	37	154	
Western hemlock							
Canada							
Fire	7-173	–	10-982	2-77	0-76	4-211	60
Chaparral-shrubs							
USA							
Fire	30	–	146	12	49	35	59
Eucalyptus forest							
Tazmania							
Fire	295	–	–	10	51	–	58
Subalpine forest							
Australia							
Fire	–	–	74-109	2-3	13-21	19-36	57

							Ref.
Maple-Birch **USA**							
Harvest	111	—	242	19	128	344	54
Spruce-Fir **Canada**							
Bole removal	105	—	98	16	92	181	56
Whole tree harvest	153	—	239	35	133	336	
Mixed Oak woodland **USA**							
Bole removal	64	—	110	7	36	410	55
Whole tree removal	166	—	315	22	120	1090	
Douglas-fir **USA**							
Harvest	—	—	180–400	—	—	—	52
Fire	—	—	200–550	—	—	—	
Tropical savanna (Cerrado) **Brazil**							
Fire	6.7–8.4	—	—	1.6	7.1	12.1	114, Kauffman, J. B. (Unpubl.)

Figure 3. An undisturbed primary tropical rainforest in the eastern Amazon Basin, Brazil. Although these forests only comprise 7% of the earth's surface, they contain as much as 40% of all species and are significant global C sinks.

(Photograph is by courtesy of J. Boone Kauffman).

over two weeks. This accounted for a loss of 16.7 kg P ha^{-1} (or 46% of the prefire aboveground P pools).

Much of the surface soil erosion and hence nutrient loss occurs when deforestation and biomass burning removes and/or consumes the organic materials that protect the soil surface. Significant losses may occur by dry ravel or overland water erosion associated with precipitation events. Under a shifting cultivation system in a tropical deciduous forest ecosystem in Mexico, Maass et al. (*61*) reported first year losses of N, P, K, and Ca were 187, 27, 31, and 378 kg ha^{-1}, respectively. In contrast, losses in adjacent undisturbed forests were less than 0.1 kg ha^{-1} for all nutrients except Ca (losses were 0.1-0.5 kg ha^{-1} for Ca).

Following deforestation, increased concentrations of dissolved nutrients in stream water commonly occur (*53, 62-64*). Nitrate-nitrogen (NO_3 -N) concentrations have increased greater than 200-fold following deforestation and biomass burning (*62, 64*). However, in most cases N losses through leaching and stream water transport are relatively short-lived and low in magnitude compared to losses associated with biomass removal, fire, or erosion losses. Kimmins and Feller (*65*) and Feller and Kimmins (*53*) measured hydrologic losses of nutrients in disturbed and undisturbed coniferous forests of western Canada (Tables I and IV). Following disturbance they reported significant increases in leaching losses of N, P, K, and Mg. However, losses were less than 10 kg ha^{-1} yr^{-1}. Comparatively, this was a small percentage of the nutrient losses associated with deforestation. For example, the total N lost as a result of deforestation and biomass burning was 1,293 kg ha^{-1}.

Similar results were reported in deforested Amazonian rainforests (*66*). Within three years following forest clearing and burning, nutrient concentrations of soil leachates had returned to levels typical of primary forests of the area. A combination of high rates of immobilization and storage by successional vegetation, coupled with a decline in easily decomposable substrates, was attributed to the reduction in leaching losses.

Implications of Deforestation and Fire on Long-Term Site Productivity

A major concern associated with the effects of deforestation and biomass burning centers on the effects of these activities on long term site productivity (LTSP). Declines in LTSP are manifested in: (a) excessive losses in nutrients, organic matter, and soil structure; (b) increased soil erosion and/or salinization; (c) decreased crop yields or forest growth; and (d) irreversible losses in biological diversity. Losses in LTSP can also result in a reduced capacity of forests to sequester C, and thereby decrease their potential to function as global C sinks. Land use practices that result in significant increases in nutrient loss can seriously impair the capacity of an ecosystem to recover. Prior to human settlement, natural disturbances (e.g. wildfire, flooding, windthrow, etc.) were a natural phenomena in many forests and if the rate of nutrient loss did not exceed the rate of reaccumulation between disturbances, a dynamic equilibrium of ecosystem productivity was maintained. This was the case with naturally occurring wildfires in many forest ecosystems; although significant losses associated with fires

Figure 4. Once tropical rainforests are cut, they are often burned for conversion to cattle pasture or croplands. Emissions from these fires are significant sources of CO_2, CH_4, NO_x, and other "greenhouse" gasses.

(Photograph is by courtesy of J. Boone Kauffman).

Figure 5. Amazonian tropical rainforest following slash-and-burn activities. Land use activities result in dramatic losses in biological diversity as well as soils and nutrient pools. These losses result in declines in the productive capacity of these forests.

(Photograph is by courtesy of J. Boone Kauffman).

Figure 6. An undisturbed primary temperate coniferous forest in the
Pacific Northwest, USA (Olympic National Park). The nutrient balance of
this forest is in a relative equilibrium with elemental inputs closely
approximating elemental losses.
(Photograph is by courtesy of J. Boone Kauffman).

Figure 7. Another temperate coniferous forest site of the Pacific Northwest, USA following clearcutting and slash burning. Severe levels of deforestation result in large quantities of nutrient losses through wood export, biomass burning and accelerated erosion and leaching losses. (Photograph is by courtesy of Dian L. Cummings).

occurred, nutrient accumulations during the long interval between fires was sufficient to compensate for the losses (52).

Forest regrowth can rapidly occur following deforestation if no further disturbances occur (66, 67). Buschbacher et al. (67) found the Amazon forest to be quite resilient in its capacity to recover from deforestation and pasture establishment as long as bulldozing, herbicide application or repeated fires did not follow. However, when forests are subjected to the repeated exports of large quantities of nutrients through a combination of wood or foliage removal, fire, or erosion, the potential for forest recovery can be decreased. Minimizing the quantities of biomass removed from a site during deforestation or utilizing agroforestry practices that closely mimic natural disturbance cycles have been suggested as methods to decrease the potential for losses in LTSP (68). This can be accomplished through the implementation of green tree retention (i.e. partial cuttings as opposed to clearcutting), maintenance of dead coarse woody debris on sites, and minimization of the use of biomass burning in deforested areas (31, 69, 70).

Another significant factor in the maintenance of site productivity centers upon managing the frequency of human disturbance. Increasing pressures for fuel wood, croplands, and wood products are increasing the extent and frequency of deforestation in both developed and third world countries. Within cultures that practice shifting cultivation, increasing population pressures result in shorter fallow periods. These shortened fallow periods may not be sufficient for nutrient reaccumulation to occur. In tropical dry forests the amount of P lost from a single slash fire may take well over a century to reaccumulate (Tables I and IV). However, the cropping cycles may be as frequent as 15 years. Accelerated cycles of forest exploitation resulting in a net decline in nutrient pools is an increasingly common occurrence in many tropical and temperate forests (52, 53, 71). For example, Feller and Kimmins (53) reported total P losses associated with deforestation and burning in coniferous forests of western Canada were 66 kg ha^{-1}. Based upon data from similar coniferous forests of this region (25), reaccumulation from precipitation inputs would take 220 years. At least 133 years would be required for inputs from both precipitation and mineral weathering (i.e. a rate of 0.5 kg ha^{-1} yr^{-1}) to compensate for losses from a single deforestation and fire event. The normal timber harvest cycle for these forests is 60-100 years. In addition to P, the large quantities of organic matter, C, and N lost as a result of deforestation and burning are not likely to be replaced in this period of time (52, 53). These estimates of the time required for nutrient reaccumulation are very conservative because ecosystem losses are not considered here (i.e. the assumption that all nutrient inputs are sequestered on site is highly unlikely, Table I).

Atmospheric Inputs Associated with Deforestation and Biomass Burning

Global atmospheric CO_2 has increased by approximately 25% since the industrial revolution (circa 1850). The primary source is the combustion of fossil fuels (72). However, recent estimates indicate that biomass burning may comprise 40% of the human-based sources of CO_2 (*73, 74*). Ward and Hao (*75*), estimate that 2,000-10,000 Tg (1 terragram = 10^{12} g) of biomass from all sources are burned annually (this includes combustion from fuelwood, deforestation, savanna fires, and crop residues). This relates to an estimate of 1,800-4,700 Tg of C released annually to the atmosphere via biomass burning (*73, 75*). From these data, annual emissions of CO_2 from burning are estimated to range from 1,600-4,100 Tg. Methane emissions arising from biomass burning range from 11-53 Tg yr^{-1}. This is approximately 10% of the total CH_4 production that originates from anthropogenic sources (*73, 75*). Finally, Crutzen and Andreae (*73*) recently estimated that 10-20 Tg of N are volatilized by biomass burning annually. This may represent a significant disruption in global N cycles as this is 6-20% of the terrestrial N-fixation rate of 100-170 Tg N yr^{-1} (*73, 76*).

Tropical forests and savannas are the primary source of C emissions that originate from biomass burning (*73, 75*). However, temperate forests are also sources of atmospheric carbon. Harmon et al. (*77*) reported that conversion of primary temperate forests to younger, second-growth forests lead to increases in atmospheric CO_2 levels, due to losses in long-term carbon storage within these forests. They ascertained that timber exploitation of 5 million hectares of primary forests in the Pacific Northwest of North America during the past century has resulted in the addition of 1,500 Tg of C to the atmosphere.

In summary, biomass burning is a major source of many trace gasses, especially the emissions of CO_2, CH_4, NMHC, NO_x, HCN, CH_3 CN, and CH_3 Cl (*73*). In the tropics, these emissions lead to local increases in the production of O_3. Biomass burning may also be responsible for as much as one-third of the total ozone produced in the troposphere (*74*). However, CH_3 Cl from biomass burning is a significant source for active Cl in the stratosphere and plays a significant role in stratospheric ozone depletion (*73*).

Conclusion

Through time, human civilizations have repeatedly made the same critical error: the excessive exploitation of forest resources or the failure to practice forestry on a sustainable basis. The earliest recorded cases of excessive deforestation occurred approximately 5,000 B.P. in the very cradle of western civilization, Mesopotamia (*19*). Since that period, abusive levels of forest exploitation have severely degraded or caused the complete disappearance of forests in regions of Europe, Africa, Asia, Australia and the Americas. Truly, the negative consequences of excessive levels of deforestation is a lesson that has been learned by few civilizations.

When forest vegetation is removed and converted to other uses, there are a number of changes that influence forest biogeochemical cycles. We have briefly examined how these cycles can be disrupted at local, regional, and global scales. At the local level, excessive rates of deforestation can lead to declines in biological diversity and site productivity. This is largely achieved through species extirpation and losses in soil productivity. Deforestation can alter microclimates such that air and soil temperatures may be higher, thereby increasing microbial decay while decreasing the quantity and capacity of the site to hold nutrients. Altered microclimates and edaphic conditions can prevent the reestablishment of natural forest vegetation (*34, 78*). Important linkages between the soil biota and aboveground biota can be broken, thereby further reducing the probability for reforestation (*78*). If fallow periods or harvest cycles are such that quantities of nutrients exported exceed quantities that reaccumulate, site productivity will not recover.

Regional or global changes in biogeochemical cycles occur as a result of deforestation through disruptions in hydrological cycles and radiation and chemical balances of the atmosphere. The present dynamic equilibrium of water and energy cycles in many forests is related to the vegetation cover. For example, in the Amazon Basin, approximately 49% of the precipitation is returned to the atmosphere through transpiration, 26% is returned to the atmosphere from evaporation due to canopy interception and 24% is lost as streamflow (*79*). Regional levels of deforestation would result in increased quantities of water lost through runoff and decreased quantities returned to the atmosphere. Aerosols from biomass burning can influence climate by directly changing the earth's radiation balance. Although poorly understood, smoke particles from biomass burning may have dramatic effects on the microphysical and optical properties of clouds resulting in increased cloud cover. This could influence the earth's heat balance as well as lower levels of precipitation (*73*). It is the effects of altered hydrological cycles and atmospheric chemistry that may be responsible for the often observed declines in precipitation associated with deforestation in the tropics (*8, 9*).

If the critical global geochemical and geophysical processes that are mediated by forests are to remain intact, then immediate shifts towards enlightened and sustainable forestry must be undertaken. Intact, functioning forest ecosystems are not luxury items that are solely enjoyed by a privileged elite. They provide or sustain much of the world's biological diversity, act as global carbon sinks, regulate climates, and are critical sources of a multitude of consumable and noncomsumable products. Therefore, human occupation on earth is just as dependent upon forests as those plants, insects, vertebrates, fungi, and bacteria that comprise the forest.

Acknowledgments

This paper is dedicated to the hundreds of millions of impoverished and exploited people of the forests in the developing world. Most will have little hope or opportunity to escape the misery of poverty unless the sociopolitical constraints that result in both overexploitation of natural resources and continued human suffering are overcome. This includes an increased awareness, compassion and action from the citizens, governments, and businesses of developed countries. We wish to thank Bev Clark, Dodi Reesman and Sheila Till for assistance with manuscript preparation and Drs. L. F. DeBano, D. A. Perry and one anonymous reviewer for helpful reviews of this manuscript.

Literature Cited

1. Postel, S; Ryan, J. C. *Reforming Forestry*; State of the World 1991; W.W. Norton & Company: New York, NY, 1991; pp 74-92.
2. Wilson, E.O. In *Biodiversity*; Wilson, E.O.; Peter, F.M., Eds.; National Academy Press: Washington, D.C., 1988; pp 3-18.
3. World Resources Institute. *World Resources 1990-91*; Oxford University Press: New York, NY, 1990.
4. Zhang, K. *Climatological Notes*. 1986, *35*, 223-236.
5. Repetto, R. *Sci. Am.* 1990, *262*, 36-42.
6. Meuller-Dombios; Goldammer, J.G. In *Fire in the Tropical Biota*; Goldammer, J.G., Ed.; Ecological Studies 84; Springer-Verlag: Berlin, Germany, 1990; pp 1-10.
7. Brown, S.; Gillespie, A.J.R.; Lugo, A.E. *Forest Science*. 1989, *35(4)*, 881-902.
8. Windsor, G.M.; Rand, A.S.; Rand, W.M. *Variation in Rainfall on Barro Colorado Island*; Smithsonian Tropical Research Institute: Balboa, Panama, 1986.
9. Meyers, N. *Envir. Conservation*. 1988, *15*, 293-298.
10. Woodwell, G.M., Ed.; *Scope 23*; Wiley: New York, NY; 1984; 247 p.
11. Meyers, N. *The Sinking Ark*; Pergamon Press: Oxford, 1979; 308 p.
12. Kaufman, Y.J.; Setzer, A.; Justice, C.; Tucker, C.J.; Pereira, M.G.; Fung, I. In *Fire in the Tropical Biota*; Goldammer, J.G., Ed.; Ecological Studies 84; Springer-Verlag: Berlin, Germany, 1990; pp 371-399.
13. Setzer, A.W.; Pereira, M.C.; Pereira Jr., A.C.; Almeida, S.A.O. *Relatorio de Atividades do Projeto IBDF-INPE "SEQE"*; Inst Pesquisas Espaciais (INPE), Pub No INPE-4534-RPE/565; INPE, Sao Jose dos Campos, Sao Paulo, 1988; 54 p.
14. Neto, R.B. *Nature*. 1990, 345:754.
15. Fearnside, P.M. In *Fire in the Tropical Biota*; Goldammer, J.G., Ed.; Ecological Studies 84; Springer-Verlag: Berlin, Germany, 1990; pp 106-116.
16. Uhl, C.; Kauffman, J.B. *Ecology*. 1990, *71(2)*, 437-449.
17. Kauffman, J.B.; Uhl, C. In *Fire in the Tropical Biota*; Goldammer, J.G., Ed.; Ecological Studies 84; Springer-Verlag: Berlin, Germany, 1990; pp 117-134.
18. Kauffman, J.B.; Uhl, C.; Cummings, D.L. *OIKOS*. 1988, *53(2)*, 167-175.
19. Perlin, J. In *a Forest Journey, the role of wood in the development of civilization*; NY, W.W. Norton. 1989, 445.
20. Sylvester-Bradley, R.; de Oliveira, L.A.; de Podesta Filbo, J.A.; St. John, T.V. *Agro Ecosystems*. 1980, *6*, 249-266.
21. Kauffman, J.B. In *Natural and Prescribed Fire in Pacific Northwest Forest*; Walstad, J.D.; Radosevich, S.R.; Sandberg, D.V., Eds.; Oregon State University Press: Corvallis, Oregon, 1990; pp 39-54.

22.   Cromack, Jr., K.; Delwiche, C.C.; McNabb, D.H. In *Symbiotic Nitrogen Fixation in the Management of Temperate Forests*; Gordon, J.C.; Wheeler, C.T.; Perry, D.A., Eds.; Forest Research Laboratory, Oregon State University, Corvallis, OR, 1979; pp 210-223.

23.   Franklin J.F. In *Biology of alder*; Trappe, J.M.; Franklin J.F.; Tarrant R.F.; Hansen, G.M., Eds.; Pac. Northwest For. and Rng. Exp. Stn., Portland, Oregon, 1968; 292 p.

24.   Youngberg, C.T.; Wollum II, A.G. *Soil Sci. Soc. Am. J.* 1976, *40*, 109-112.

25.   Sollins, P.; Grier, C.C.; McCorison, F.M.; Cromack, Jr., K.; Fogel, R. *Ecol. Mono.* 1980, *50(3)*, 261-285.

26.   Vitousek, P.M.; Sanford, Jr., R.L. *Ann. Rev. Ecol. Syst.* 1986, *17*, 137-167.

27.   Jordan, C.F. *Ecology.* 1982, *63(3)*, 647-654.

28.   Westman, W.E.; Whittaker, R.H. *J. Ecol.* 1975, *63*, 493-520.

29.   Grier, C.C.; Logan, R.S. *Ecol. Mono.* 1977, *47*, 373-400.

30.   Little, S.N.; Ohmann, J.L.; *For. Sci.* 1988, *34(1)*, 152-164.

31.   Uhl, C.; Vieira, I.C.G. *Biotropica.* 1989, *21(2)*, 98-106.

32.   Burgess, P.F. *Malay Nat. J.* 1971, *24*, 231-237.

33.   Johns, A.D. *Biotropica.* 1988, *20*, 31-37.

34.   Nepstad, D.C. *Forest Regrowth in Abandoned Pastures of Eastern Amazonia: Limitations to Tree Seedling Survival and Growth*; Dissertation; Yale University: New Haven, CT, 1989.

35.   Kauffman, J.B.; Sanford, R.L.; Cummings, D.L.; Salcedo, I.H.; Sampaio, E.Y.S.B. *Ecology.* 1991 (In Press).

36.   Nye, P.H.; Greenland, D.J. *The Soil Under Shifting Cultivation. Tech. Commun. 51*; Farnham Royal, England: Commonwealth Bur. Soils, Commonwealth Agric. Bur., 1960.

37.   Ewel, J.; Berish, C.; Brown, B.; Price, N.; Raich, J. *Ecology.* 1981, *62(3)*, 816-829.

38.   Sanchez, P.A.; Bandy, D.E.; Villachica, J.H.; Nicholaides, J.J. *Science.* 1982, *216*, 821-827.

39.   Frandsen, W.H.; Ryan, K.C. *Can. J. For. Res.* 1986, *16*, 244-248.

40.   Wright, H.A.; Bailey, A.W. *Fire Ecology, United States and Southern Canada*; Wiley: New York, NY, 1982; 501 p.

41.   Boyer, D.E.; Dell, J.D. *Fire effects on Pacific Northwest forest soils*; USDA For. Serv. PNW Region: Portland, OR., 1980; 57 p.

42.   DeBano, L.F.; Eberlein, E.; Dunn, P.H. *Soil Sci. Soc. Am. J.* 1979, *43*, 504-509.

43.   DeBano, L.F. *Assessing the effects of management actions on soils and mineral cycling in mediterranean ecosystems.* In Conrad, C.E.; Oechel, W.C., Tech. Coordinators. Proc. of the Symposium on Dynamics and Management of Mediterranean-Type Ecosystems, June 22-26, 1981, San Diego CA. Gen. Tech. Rep. PSW-58, USDA For. Serv. Pac. SW For. and Range Exp. Sta.: Berkeley, CA, 1982. pp 345-350.

44. Ralston, C.W.; Hatchell, G.E. *Effects of prescribed burning on physical properties of soil*; Prescribed Burning Symp. Proc.; USDA For. Serv. Southeast For. Exp. Sta.: Asheville, NC, 1971; pp 68-85.
45. White, C.S. *Biol. Fertil. Soils.* 1986, *2*, 87-95.
46. Woodmansee, R.G.; Wallach, L.S. *Effects of fire regimes on biogeochemical cycles*; In Fire Regimes and Ecosystem Properties, Proceedings. USDA, U.S. Forest Service, GTR-WO-26, 1981, pp 379-400.
47. Grier, C.C. *Can. J. For. Res.* 1975, *5*, 599-607.
48. DeByle, N.V.; Packer, P.E. *National Symposium on Watersheds in Transition.* American Water Resources Association: Bethesda, MD, 1976, pp 296-307.
49. Alexander, M. *Introduction to Soil Microbiology*, John Wiley and Sons, New York, 1977, 467 p.
50. Tarrant, R.F. *Effect of heat on soil color and pH of two forest soils*; Res. Note PNW-90; USDA For. Serv. Pac. NW For.and Rng. Exp. Sta.: Portland, OR, 1953; 5 p.
51. Tarrant, R.F. *Effect of slash burning on soil pH*; Res. Note PNW-102; USDA For. Serv. Pac. NW For. and Rng. Exp. Sta.: Portland, OR, 1954; 5 p.
52. Barnett, D. *Fire effects on Coast Range soils of Oregon and Washington and management implications; A state-of-knowledge review*; USDA Forest Service, R-6 Soils Technical Report: Portland, OR., 1989, 66 p.
53. Feller, M.C.; Kimmins, J.P. *Water Resources Research.* 1984, *20(1)*, 29-40.
54. Hornbeck, J.W.; Kropelin, W. *J. Environ. Qual.* 1982, *11(2)*, 309-316.
55. Johnson, D.W.; West, D.C.; Todd, D.E.; Mann, L.K. *Soil Sci. Soc. Am. J.* 1982, *46*, 1304-1309.

56. Freedman, B.; Morash, R.; Hanson, A.J. *Can. J. For. Res.* 1981, 11, 249-257.
57. Raison, R.J.; Khanna, P.K.; Woods, P.V. *Can. J. For. Res.* 1985, *15*, 132-140.
58. Harwood, C.E.; Jackson, W.D. *Aust. For.* 1975, *38(2)*, 92-99.
59. DeBano, L.F.; Conrad, C.E. *Ecology.* 1978, *59*, 489-497.
60. Feller, M.C. In *Proceedings of the 10th Conf. on Fire and Forest Meteorology.* Forestry Canada. Chalk River, Ontario, 1989. pp 126-135.
61. Maass, J.M.; Jordan, C.F.; Sarukhan, J. *J. Applied Ecol.* 1988, *25*, 595-607.
62. Beschta, R.L. In *Natural and Prescribed Fire in Pacific Northwest Forests*; Walstad, J.D.; Radosevich, S.R.; Sandberg D.V., Eds.; Oregon State University Press: Corvallis, OR, 1990; pp 219-232.
63. Vitousek, P.M.; Gosz, J.R.; Grier, C.C.; Melillo, J.M.; Reiners, W.A.; Todd, R.L. *Science.* 1979, *204*, 469-474.

64. Tiedemann, A.R.; Conrad, C.E.; Dieterich, J.H.; Hornbeck, J.W.; Megahan, W.F.; Viereck, L.A.; Wade, D.D. *Effects of Fire on Water; A State of Knowledge Review*; Gen. Tech. Report WO-10; National Fire Effects Workshop, Denver, Colo. USDA Forest Service, 1979. 24 p.

65. Kimmins, J.P.; Feller, M.C. *Effect of clearcutting and broadcast slashburning on nutrient budgets, streamwater chemistry and productivity in Western Canada*. XVI IUFRO World Congress Proc. Div. 1; 1976, pp 186-197.

66. Uhl, C.; Jordan, C.F. *Ecology*. 1984, *65(5)*, 1476-1490.

67. Buschbacher, R.; Uhl, C.; Serrao, E.A.S. *J. Ecol.* 1988, *76*, 682-699.

68. Anderson, A.B., Ed.; *Alternatives to Deforestation: Steps Toward Sustainable Use of the Amazon Rain Forest*; Columbia University Press: New York, NY, 1990.

69. Franklin, J.F. *American Forests*. 1989, December, 37-44.

70. Harmon, M.E.; Franklin,J.F.; Swanson, F.J.; Sollins, P.; Gregory, S.V., Lattin, G.D.; Anderson, N.H.; Cline, S.P.; Aumen, N.G.; Sedell, J.R.; Lienkaemper, G.W.; Cromack, Jr., K.; Cummins, K.W. In *Advances in Ecological Research*; MacFadyen, A.; Ford, E.D., Eds.; Academic Press: New York, NY, 1986, Vol. 15; pp 133-302.

71. Brown, S.; Lugo, A.E. *Plant and Soil*. 1990, *124*, 53-64.

72. Houghton, R.H.; Woodwell, G.M. *Sci. Am.*, 1989, *260*, 36-44.

73. Crutzen, P.J.; Andreae, M.O. *Sci.* 1990, *250*, 1669-1678.

74. Levine, J.S. *EOS*. 1990 *71(37)*, 1075-1077.

75. Ward, D.; Hao, W.M. In *Proceeding of the 1991 Annual Meeting of the Air and Waste Management Association*, Vancover, B.C., Canada. 1991. (In Press).

76. Soderlund, R.; Svensson, B.H. *Nitrogen, Phosphorus, and Sulphur*; Svensson, B.H.; Soderlund, R., Eds.; Ecol. Bull.: Stockholm; 1976, 22; 23 p.

77. Harmon, M.E.; Ferrell, W.K.; Franklin, J.F. *Science*. 1990, *247*, 699-702.

78. Perry, D.A.; Amaranthus, M.P.; Borchers, J.G.; Borchers, S.L.; Brainerd, R.E. *BioScience*. 1989, *39(4)*, 230-237.

79. Salati, E. In *The Geophysiology of Amazonia: Vegetation and Climatic Interactions*; Dickinson, R.E., Ed.; Wiley: New York, NY, 1987; pp 273-296.

80. Jordan, C.F., Ed.; *An Amazonian Rain Forest*; Man and the Biosphere Series; The Parthenon Publishing Group: Park Ridge, NJ, 1989; Vol. 2.

81. Coutinho, L.M. In *Fire in the Tropical Biota*; Goldammer, J.G., Ed.; Ecological Studies 84; Springer-Verlag: Berlin, Germany, 1990; pp 82-105.

82. Hendry, C.D.; Berish, C.W.; Edgerton, E.S. *Water Resour. Res.* 1984, *20*, 1677-84.

83. Franken, W.; Leopoldo, P.R. In *The Amazon: Limnology and Landscape Ecology of a Mighty Tropical River and its Basin*; Sioli, H., Ed.; Dordrecht: Junk, 1984; pp 501-19.

84. Parker, G.G.; *The Effect of Disturbance on Water and Solute Budgets of Hillslope Tropical Rainforest in Northeastern Costa Rica*; PhD Thesis; Univ. Georgia: Athens, Greece, 1985; 161 p.

85. Melillo, J.M.; Gosz, J.R. In *The Major Biogeochemical Cycles and Their Interactions*; Bolin, B.; Cook, R.B., Eds.; SCOPE 21; John Wiley & Sons: New York, NY, 1983; pp 177-222.

86. Agee, J.K.; Huff, M.H. *Can. J. For. Res.* 1987, *17*, 697-704.

87. Prescott, C.E.; Corbin, J.P.; Parkinson, D. *Can. J. For. Res.* 1989, *19*, 309-317.

88. Kauffman, J.B.; Cummings, D.L. *Fuelbeds and Biomass Consumption During Spring and Fall Prescribed Fires in Central Oregon Rangeland Ecosystems*. Spec. Rep. to USDA Forest Service PNW Res. Sta., Seattle, Wa. 1989, 16 p.

89. Waring, R.H.; Schlesinger, W.H. *Forest Ecosystems Concepts and Management*; Academic Press, Inc.: New York, NY, 1985; 340 p.

90. Murphy, P.G.; Lugo, A.E. *Ann. Rev. Ecol. Syst.* 1986, *17*, 67-88.

91. Funke, B.R.; Harris, J.O. *Plant Soil.* 1968, *28*, 38-48.

92. Dawson, J.R.; Johnson, R.A.H. *Ann. Appl. Biol.* 1965, *56*, 243-251.

93. Fowler, W.B.; Helvey, J.D. *Changes in the thermal regime after prescribed burning and select tree removal*; Res. Pap. PNW-234; USDA For. Serv. Pac. NW For. and Rng. Exp. Sta.: Portland, OR, 1978; 17 p.

94. Kauffman, J.B.; Martin, R.E. *N.W. Science.* (In Press).

95. Hanes, T.L. *Ecol Monogr.* 1971, *41*, 27-52.

96. Russell, J.D.; Fraser, A.R.; Watson, J.R.; Parsons, A.W. *Geoderma.* 1974, *11*, 63-66.

97. Agee, J.K. *Prescribed fire effects on physical and hydrologic properties of mixed conifer forest floor and soil*; Report 143; Univ. of CA, Water Resources Center: Davis, CA, 1973.

98. White, E.M.; Thompson, W.W.; Gartner, F.R. *J. Rng. Mgm't.* 1973, *26(1)*, 22-28.

99. Hosking, J.S. *J. Agri. Sci.* 1938, *28*, 393-400.

100. Chandler, V.; Cheney, P.; Thomas, P.; Trabaud, L.; Williams, D. *Forest Fire Management and Organization*; Fire in Forestry; John Wiley & Sons: New York, NY, 1983; Vol. II.

101. Scholl, D.G. *Soil Sci. Soc. Am. Proc.* 1975, *39*, 356-361.

102. Savage, S.M.; Lettey, J.; Osborne, J; Heaton, C. *Soil Sci. Soc. Amer. Proc.* 1972, *26(4)*, 674-678.

103. DeBano, L.F. *Water-repellent soils: a state-of-the-art*; Gen. Tech. Report PSW-46; PSW For. and Rng. Exp. Sta.: Berkeley, CA., 1981.

104. Bentley, J.R.; Fenner, R.L. *J. For.* 1958, *56*, 737-774.

105. Wells, C.G.; Campbell, R.E.; DeBano, L.F.; Lewis, C.E.; Fredrickson, R.L.; Franklin, E.C.; Froehlich, R.C.; Dunn, P.H. *Effects of fire on soil*; Gen. Tech. Report WO-7; USDA For. Serv.: Washington, DC., 1979.

106. Weast, R.C. *Handbook of Chemistry and Physics*; CRC Press Inc.: Boca Raton, FL, 1982; 60th Ed.

107.   DeBano, L.F.; Dunn, P.H.; Conrad, C.E. In *Proceedings of the Symposium on the Environmental Consequences of Fire and Fuel Management in Mediterranean Ecosystems*; Aug. 1-5, 1977, Palo Alto, CA. USDA For. Serv. Gen. Tech. Report WO-3; pp 65-74.

108.   Martin, R.E.; Davis, L.S. In *Mich. Acad. Science Arts and Letters*, Papers Vol. XLVI. 1961.

109.   Isaac, L.A.; Hopkins, H.G. *The forest soil of the Douglas-fir region and the changes wrought by logging and slash burning*; 1937.Ecology 18, 264-279.

110.   Jackson, M.L. *Soil Chemical Analysis--Advanced Course*; 5th printing; Published by author, Dept. Soil Sci., Univ. of Wisconsin; Madison, WI, 1956.

111.   DeBano, L.F.; Rice, R.M.; Conrad, C.E. *Soil heating in chaparral fires: Effects on soil properties, plant nutrients, erosion, and runoff.* Berkeley, Calif.: Pac. Southwest For. and Range Exp. Stn., Forest Service, USDA: 1979, Res. Pap. PSW-145. 21 p.

112.   Hodgman, C.D. *Handbook of Chemistry and Physics*; 44th Ed.; Chemical Rubber Publ.: Cleveland, OH, 1962.

113.   Countryman, C. *Heat conduction and wildland fire*; USDA For. Serv. PSW For. and Rng. Exp. Sta.: Berkeley, CA, 1977; 15 p.

114.   Pivello-Pompeia, V.R. *Exportacao de macronutrients para atmosfera durante queimadas realizadas no campo cerrado de Emas*. MS Thesis. Univ. Sao Paulo, 1984

RECEIVED September 4, 1991

An Earth System Science Approach to Global Environmental Chemistry Education

An Overview

Joseph M. Moran

Natural and Applied Sciences, University of Wisconsin—Green Bay, Green Bay, WI 54311

This overview of educational initiatives in global environmental chemistry argues for introduction of Earth system science at both the secondary school and college levels. Such an approach provides the holistic perspective needed to better understand contemporary environmental issues. Furthermore, problem-focused Earth system science is likely to spur student interest in science and provide a practical scientific experience for non-science majors.

Threats to stratospheric ozone, prospects for global warming, toxic and hazardous waste management, and acid deposition are several of the major environmental issues that appear with some regularity in print and electronic media. Most people are convinced that these problems are real and that something ought to be done about them. But too few individuals possess even a rudimentary understanding of the scientific basis for analyzing and ultimately solving those problems. Lack of understanding, in fact, seriously impairs their ability to participate in informed decision-making at home, at work, and at the ballot box.

The same media informs us in no uncertain terms (typically around the start of the new school year) that our school systems are woefully deficient in providing our students with sufficient background and experience in science and mathematics. We are often reminded of the decline in SAT scores and how poorly our students perform on standardized examinations in mathematics and science when compared to their cohorts in other nations. Students too often see science as an arduous field of study that focuses on an abstract collection of facts that has little if any bearing on their personal lives.

Scientific illiteracy is not only making it difficult for society to deal effectively with environmental issues, it also means that we are slipping behind other developed nations in meeting the growing demand for a scientifically and

0097–6156/92/0483–0457$06.00/0

technically skilled work force. In fact, the National Science Foundation projects a shortfall of 400,000 scientists and 275,000 engineers by the year 2006 (*1*).

What if anything can be done to spur greater student interest in science and thereby to upgrade the scientific literacy of the general population? One possible answer is Earth system science. At the secondary school level, this may inspire some students to take a second look at a possible career in science or engineering. (Choices that students make early on in their precollege curriculum ultimately determine their preparation for college level work in science and mathematics.) At the college level, Earth system science appears to have its greatest potential of reaching the most students as a component of the common (core) curriculum for non-science majors.

Simply put, Earth system science views the planet (like any other system) as consisting of numerous parts that interact in some rational way according to some basic principles. Thus Earth is made up of a biosphere, atmosphere, hydrosphere, and lithosphere. Each of these components are interrelated through a series of biogeochemical cycles whereby materials and energy continually flow from one component (reservoir) to another. As our understanding of the functioning of Earth as a system becomes more and more complete, we can better anticipate the consequences when the natural functioning of the system is disrupted either by natural events or human intervention.

Earth system science inspires a holistic perspective and thus is ideally suited for an examination of environmental issues. Consider for illustration the much publicized prospects for global warming. Predictions of global warming are based on the assumption that various human activities, especially combustion of fossil fuels, are enhancing the natural greenhouse effect. Based on an understanding of global radiative balance, an enhanced greenhouse effect may translate into warmer conditions and widespread disruption of agricultural systems. In order to fully appreciate both the causes and effects of such an event, we need to adopt a holistic perspective that follows the transport of infrared-absorbing trace gases from one component of the Earth system to another.

When applied to contemporary environmental issues, Earth system science offers practical applications of science that are more likely to appeal to students than the traditional scientific disciplines. The appeal stems from the fact that most environmental problems can be personalized even though they may be global in scope. Global warming, ozone depletion, and acid deposition, for example, can be demonstrated to impact each and every one of us. Furthermore, we can show how each and every one of us can help contribute to the solution of these problems.

While the argument is convincing that Earth system science may win over some students to science and help improve the scientific literacy of many more, actual implementation faces many formidable obstacles. Perhaps foremost among these obstacles is the interdisciplinary nature of Earth system science. Our educational systems divide and distribute the continuum of knowledge into discrete academic specialties and little incentive exists for interdisciplinary ventures. Earth system science utilizes the integrated insight provided by interdisciplinary efforts and calls for dialogue and team-teaching among faculty typically schooled in narrow disciplines.

The environmental movement of the late 1960s inspired development of interdisciplinary courses on the environment, institutes that encouraged cross-disciplinary research and teaching, and in a very few cases entire academic programs that were interdisciplinary in structure (2). By the late 1970s and early 1980s, interest in the environment waned and many of these early efforts were either downsized or abandoned entirely. By the late 1980s, however, a new environmental awareness emerged and interest in environmental problems began again to surge. Meanwhile, over the past two decades, scientists have developed a better understanding of the scientific basis of environmental problems and an appreciation of the need for an interdisciplinary/systems approach. Among the consequences was the development and gradual maturation of Earth system science.

This section of the book focuses on various efforts to incorporate interdisciplinarity and Earth system science at both the college and secondary levels. Stearns shows how a problem-focused approach can be incorporated in a traditional high school chemistry course. Winchester describes his experiences with developing modules on global change and atmospheric chemistry for college non-science majors. And Kupchella explains the advantages and difficulties encountered in revamping the college core curriculum to require an interdisciplinary, problem-focused course on the environment.

Literature Cited

1. Holden, C. *Science*, **1989**, *244*, pp. 1536-1537.
2. Weidner, E. *J. Env. Ed.*, **1970**, *2*, pp. 41-42.

Chapter 24

Helping Students Understand Global Change

John W. Winchester

Department of Oceanography, Florida State University, Tallahassee, FL 32306

Global change instruction for undergraduate college students should emphasize relationships among the natural sciences, social sciences, and humanities over specialized study of each. Potentially any of these areas of knowledge could be the starting point for multidisciplinary understanding of a changing global environment. A groundwork has been laid at Florida State University, based on experience in teaching honors students from a natural science and especially chemistry perspective, for a broader teaching program for general freshman and sophomore students who intend to major in any area.

What is meant by "global change" in the environment and its relevance for us? The term embodies an awareness by many that the world is not what it used to be, so that, as never before, we are asking governments to establish programs to assess, adapt to, or if possible control global change. Agencies responsible for science have defined new missions in the area of global change, and professional societies hold special sessions at their meetings to document the scope of global change that falls within their specialties. Increasingly attentive to news of these activities, the public and especially students are trying to understand and to plan for the future. Yet individually we all view global change from our own personal perspectives.

Among scientists, a chemist may see global scale effects on stratospheric ozone or on greenhouse gases that may change climate or the ecosystem on which we depend. A biologist may see global scale stresses on species and communities that could affect the resilience of the biosphere of which man is a part. (Following Jacques Barzun, the words man, him, etc. are used here to refer generally to humanity without specific gender, as rooted in the history of English.) A geologist may see either of these in the perspective of time and may seek to

0097–6156/92/0483–0460$06.00/0

determine how life has adjusted to similar changes in the distant past. A physicist may seek to express change in the earth system in quantitative terms so as to forecast its future magnitude and timing. All are convinced of the great human importance of their efforts to understand the natural science basis of global change so that we can adapt to or control the global environment to the advantage of all its occupants.

Among social scientists, a sociologist may see rising world population as stressing the global environment, which may attract an economist to investigate aspects of resource utilization and a political scientist to design strategies for setting public policy. Then a historian may want to reconstruct the experience of past societies in relation to their environments, and a specialist in religion may ponder the ethics of exploitation of these by man. As global change may call for action, a creative writer may see an opportunity to communicate and inspire, and a person gifted in the fine arts may re-express the call in visual or musical language. Thus, the meaning of global change can be as broad as the human imagination.

Still, common to such diversity of viewpoints must be the wish to relate observable change in the natural world on a global scale to the currently unfolding events in human affairs so as to plan for a future in harmony with our surroundings. Thus, one of the aims of education should be to help students of diverse experiences and interests to learn to deal effectively with accelerating change, not only of the environment but of man himself. By so learning, each should be better able to create his own special role for meeting his challenge. And helping him to succeed, in fact, may be the central challenge of global change instruction.

Rationale

Beginning college students, perhaps now more than ever, sense a changing world and realize that, to deal with it effectively, many different facets of change and their interrelationships have to be understood. Many already recognize that technical aspects of any particular kind of change have to be viewed in relation to the overall state of change in the world, since the whole assembly has implications that go beyond any one change alone. It is not easy for any of us to understand the complex fabric of global changes now taking place, but students look especially to their mentors for guidance in examining it.

The competence of the mentors, as college teachers, is invariably strongest in one or another of the traditional disciplines, and instruction of students has generally been through courses in one discipline without explicit reference to another. Yet the need for global change instruction is for help in understanding a multidisciplinary set of problems. Some appear to lie mainly in the natural sciences while others deal more with humanity, but all should be studied in a broad framework that embraces both science and humanities. How to achieve depth while maintaining breadth of instruction is a pedagogical challenge. How can we meet it?

One answer is by case studies of specific global change issues. These could achieve depth of understanding while considering the range of disciplines that underlie them. An instructor may, according to his knowledge and experience, address each issue from his own discipline but work toward exploring other disciplines and how they are related to the issue. From the bias of a natural scientist, an issue such as climate change could be viewed first as effects of chemical pollutants on the atmosphere from a technical standpoint, then its economic, population, and other social driving forces could be explored. An economist or a humanist could equally well approach climate change from his specialty and then work toward an understanding of technical aspects of the natural science of the earth system that seem to be important. In either case the student should benefit from sharing in the multidisciplinary exploration of such an issue with his mentor.

Let us examine more closely the first approach, viewing global environmental chemical changes in the atmosphere as a driving force for a broader range of changes in the earth system and its links with the human system. Such an approach is a case study in itself of one way to meet the pedagogical challenge of global change instruction.

Approach

In 1988 a faculty group drawn from several U.S. campuses initiated a Global Change Instruction project with coordination by the National Center for Atmospheric Research, Boulder, Colorado. The GCI group aims to develop new teaching materials on specific topics related to global change for use in the classroom. The materials, designed as modules, may be selected by instructors according to the specific needs of their classes. Modules are more flexible than books, since they can be updated and new topics can be added as our understanding advances and as instructional programs develop on the different campuses. Moreover, their formats are not restricted to chapter-like textual material but may include visual aids, suggested demonstrations for classroom, laboratory, or field work, computer software for instructional use, and other appropriate formats.

Global change instruction for undergraduates at Florida State University has been initiated as part of the GCI project coordinated by NCAR. Faculty members in the Departments of Geology, Meteorology, and Oceanography have developed modular materials for the GCI project and have used some of these and other materials in the classroom on a trial basis. With this background, formal undergraduate classes in global change are planned for the 1991-92 academic year, treating the subject as changes in the earth system viewed as natural science in relation to human affairs.

The intended student audience is the general undergraduate, mainly freshman or sophomore level, who may choose to major in any field, not necessarily science. Instruction designed for lower division students has the advantage of laying a foundation for them to build on during subsequent college years. In addition, it has the advantage of helping the instructor learn how better to interact with unspecialized students during their formative college years and, in future phases of the GCI project, more wisely adapt materials for pre-college instruction during students' even more formative younger years of learning.

At Florida State University, in addition to the regular curriculum, special classes are offered for honors students, those who have exceptional academic qualifications. One is the Natural Sciences Seminar, limited to 15 gifted freshmen or sophomores, in which initiative by the students is emphasized over mastery of assigned tasks and graded only as pass or fail. This I chose as a way to try new classroom approaches before developing a larger undergraduate formal class in global change. Two offerings of the Seminar in Global Change have been completed, and the results are being used in planning a future larger class for general undergraduates. Let us review the experience gained by this activity and plans that are currently being built upon it.

Methods

The Seminars have provided an opportunity to try methods and materials and lay a groundwork for more general instruction. Selected topics treated as case studies include:

o Energy demand and supply, our dependence on fossil fuels.
o Climate change, its causes and effects, and prediction by computer models.
o Pollution transport, acid deposition.
o Stratospheric ozone, a UV shield, destruction by chemicals, biological effects.
o Population growth, socioeconomic and environmental aspects.
o Deforestation, overfishing, and ecological resource management.
o International agreements on CFC's, acid rain, CO_2 emissions, and nuclear weapons.

Class meetings are three times weekly, two hours of lecture and one hour for group discussion. Text material includes a basic reference, World Resources 1990-91 (World Resources Institute, Oxford University Press, 1990), and supplemental references provided from time to time, including available GCI modular materials, articles from recent periodicals, and news items from the daily press.

Examples of scientific articles are "Stratospheric Ozone and the Case Against Chlorofluorocarbons" (W.H. Brune, Penn State University, 1989), "The Challenge of Acid Rain" (V.A. Mohnen, Scientific American, August 1988), "The Global Carbon Cycle" (W.M. Post et al., American Scientist, July-August 1990), "Balancing Atmospheric Carbon Dioxide" (T.J. Goreau, Ambio, August 1990),

"Deforestation in the Tropics" (Robert Repetto, Scientific American, April 1990), and "Deforestation and Agricultural Development in Brazilian Amazonia" (P.M. Fearnside, Interciencia, November-December 1990).   Examples of more humanistic articles are "The Tragedy of the Commons" (Garrett Hardin, Science, 18 December 1968) and "Winds of Change" (Wm. H. McNeill, Foreign Affairs, Fall 1990). Current news reports of global change issues are drawn especially from the New York Times, Washington Post, Christian Science Monitor, Science magazine, and the McNeal Lehrer News Hour.

The objectives simply stated are:

o To examine technical and policy aspects of global environmental changes, how they may be caused by human activities, and how they may affect human health and welfare.

o To understand the scientific basis for chemical changes in the atmosphere, linkages to the oceans and terrestrial ecosystems, and biological consequences of these changes.

o To review human population growth in developed and developing countries, its linkages to economic well-being of peoples, and its relation to global environmental change.

o To consider policy options for peoples of the world to control environmental quality, based on past experience and on present and future needs.

o To advise the instructor how he can effectively present global change issues to a large enrollment general undergraduate course.

Successful learning can be judged, after students have read about the topics in basic and supplemental references and heard information presented in lecture format, by their individual discussion during class, regular round-table discussions with short presentations by class members about global change issues, and written work by the class, including answers to short questions or quantitative problem assignments and two short papers on chosen topics for a specified audience.

Results

Honors students are highly motivated and have used their freedom to explore global change issues creatively. Although few were science majors, all were basically skilled in mathematics and quantitative reasoning. Thus, emphasis could be placed on concepts and interpretation of evidence of global change in relation to human activity. Though the majority of college students may not have all these advantages, the results of honors student instruction may still be of general interest

For the freshmen and sophomores, the Seminar appears to be the first classroom opportunity to study scientific aspects of a changing global environment in relation to social and humanistic issues and to link these to current public policy discussions reported in the press. Class members have recommended that multidisciplinary global change instruction be made a requirement for all college students, since it is no less important than classes to strengthen basic science or writing skills.

The students strongly approve of using current press accounts of global change issues, both scientific and policy related, in parallel with basic reference material. Some advised that future classes should require subscription to a high quality newspaper or journal, in addition to purchase of basic texts, for example one of those that were used in class.

The students believe that effective teaching about global change issues cannot be carried out in a large lecture hall alone but must provide for small classes that allow discussion. Class discussions have been vigorous, and some asked to present lectures themselves to the group. When urged to write papers for a larger audience than members of the class or its instructor, for example for publication, many students did.

When given freedom to redefine writing assignments, students attempted to link the natural science of global change to social or humanistic concerns. The majority wrote prose essays that summarized their information and thinking. But a sizable number chose other means, among them being an analysis of press reports about Earth Day, a questionnaire administered to a large FSU class to test environmental awareness, presentations to elementary pupils about changes in the atmosphere, letters to the President, a United Nations resolution, a television script, a lyric poem, and ideas expressed as dialogues in the style of Plato.

Future directions

Instruction in the scientific basis of global change may have several purposes. By focussing on specific types of change in the natural world, it can help a student understand some of their technical complexities and present scientific uncertainties. Equally important, the instruction should explore the relevance of these changes to human affairs. Since people may both be causes of change and be affected by them, this relevance is as important as understanding the science of change itself.

During the study of global change an instructor can also help his students become stronger scientifically, such as in mathematical expression of ideas, quantitative reasoning based on observational, experimental, or theoretical evidence, and essential information from chemistry, physics, biology, and the earth sciences. If exercises for strengthening skills are carried out while examining phenomena of change, their importance can be appreciated and effectiveness be enhanced. And if the human dimension of global change is clear, motivation will be high to learn not only the nature of change but the scientific skills needed in a society to manage or adjust to it.

An argument can be made that chemistry is a critically important science for understanding the causes and effects of much of the environmental change observed today. Consider the logical progression of ideas already discussed, i.e.

energy supply and use, atmospheric chemical basis for climate change, effects of ultraviolet radiation and pollutant deposition, perturbations on the biosphere, increases in population and exploitation of resources, and the need for international agreements to manage our commons. Chemistry is central to most of these, either as a driving force or in the nature of the effects. Thus, global environmental chemistry could be the figured bass that brings harmony and structure to the subject.

Modeling concepts are also keys for understanding global changes and rational policy responses to them. Microcomputers and software are now powerful enough to demonstrate the logic of constructing models that describe and predict energy use, climate change, and population rise for lecture demonstration and student exercises. By including modeling as a thread in the fabric under study, students will better appreciate its importance in scientific research and setting national policies. Modeling is an important linking element between natural science and the human dimension of global change.

Policy issues are now reported daily as new evidence for global change becomes public knowledge. A full discussion of them is a study in itself, but their importance during the study of the science of global change should be made clear. Regular reading of the current press can provide a way to view scientific case studies in the context of human affairs.

Perhaps the most important rationale for global change instruction in forthcoming years is to relate disparate disciplines to each other so as to better understand and deal with man's impact on the global environment. Though these disciplines, to be understood in depth, may best be taught separately from each other, understanding the relationships between them is especially important. A global change instruction program may emphasize the relationships and also serve as an introduction to each. As students are inspired to continue, they will have a stronger basis for judging in which specialty to concentrate their further efforts.

Acknowledgments. This paper was written as a result of the Global Change Instruction project coordinated by the National Center for Atmospheric Research, Boulder, Colorado, and supported by the National Science Foundation. The opportunity to test classroom ideas about global change at Florida State University was provided by the FSU Honors and Scholars Program. Encouragement and guidance by John Firor and Barbara McDonald at NCAR and Paula Barbour at FSU are greatly appreciated.

RECEIVED September 4, 1991

Chapter 25

Integrating Global Environmental Chemistry into Secondary School Curricula

Carole Stearns

Sewickley Academy, Sewickley, PA 15143

High school students should have a greater understanding of global environmental issues. This can be accomplished by using environmentally-relevant examples to teach high school chemistry. Appropriate demonstrations and laboratory experiments that illustrate these topics are suggested. To incorporate additional environmental chemistry in the secondary curriculum, help from environmental scientists will be needed.

Global environmental issues are becoming increasingly significant in our lives. Children are exposed at a young age to the ideas of pollution and recycling. Students in the 90's arrive in high school with a complex environmental vocabulary including words such as ozone and acid rain, but without the scientific background to understand them. High school courses must give students this background and help them become more environmentally-aware citizens. This paper proposes accomplishing this goal by incorporating environmentally-relevant examples in the secondary chemistry curriculum. Through this approach students will learn to apply classroom science to understanding real world issues.

Environmental Topics in the Chemistry Curriculum

There is current research in education supporting a contextual approach to high school teaching (1). When topics are presented in a context relevant to students' backgrounds and concerns, they learn more effectively. Global environmental issues provide a relevant context for high school chemistry. The biogeochemical sulfur cycle and the chemistry of natural waters offer many examples illustrating the basic chemical principles included in most high school courses. These provide students with the background to understand current issues such as acid rain and water pollution. These examples can be the subject of classroom discussions, demonstrations, and homework assignments. They should be directed towards having students apply what they learn in the classroom to significant, real-world issues. Ideally, students' interest in understanding environmental problems will make them more curious about chemistry.

0097–6156/92/0483–0467$06.00/0

Teaching Goals. Teaching general chemical principles and presenting applications to global environmental issues are realistic goals for secondary chemistry. The issues for high school teachers are: first, developing more effective classroom strategies for teaching these applications, second, modifying the traditional curriculum to accomplish this and third, learning more about environmental issues so they can teach it to their students.

High school students like the interactive quality of their history and English classes. Through discussing issues in which there are points of view rather than a right answer, they are encouraged to make judgments. Discussions of global environmental issues offer students similar opportunities in their chemistry classes. Environmental issues show them connections between science, economics, politics, and quality of life. A curriculum incorporating these issues presents chemistry, not in isolation, but as a subject integrated with the rest of their education. They begin to realize the chemical principles they have learned gives them the background to make reasoned judgements.

As class discussions relate textbook topics to the environmental issues, students become aware of the difficulty of applying what they have learned in class to more complex situation. Although frustrated by the absence of simple right answers, students can be taught to appreciate the process by which scientists evaluate data and adjust hypotheses.

Using Environmental Examples to Teach About Acids. Acid-base reactions are usually presented to secondary students as examples of aqueous equilibrium (2). In their study of acids and bases, students are expected to master the characteristic properties and reactions. They are taught to test the acidity of solutions, identify familiar acids and label them as strong or weak. The ionic dissociation of water, the pH scale and some common reactions of acids are also included in high school chemistry. All of these topics may be illustrated with examples related to acid deposition (3). A lesson plan is presented in Table I.

It is important that students begin their study of acids seeking answers to questions that interest them. This may be accomplished by assigning relevant readings or having students research the topic in the school library. Students should be made aware of the environmental issues related to acid deposition at the beginning of the acid/base unit.

Demonstrations (see below) of the acidic properties of the oxides of nitrogen and sulfur show students some of the inorganic reactions that will be background for class discussions and homework assignments. The students are also expected to know the natural and industrial sources of each gas. They must also be reminded of chemistry topics they have already studied, such as gas behavior and equilibrium, that will provide relevant background for understanding acid deposition.

My students have shown great interest in these environmental topics. They are the subject of homework problems and, as much as possible, laboratory experiments. At the end of the year students remember more descriptive chemistry because of its environmental significance. Class discussion on the effect of acid deposition on the pH of a lake often leads to a number of questions on related issues. Students become curious about factors that effect solubility of gases in water or how scientists gather reliable data about gases emitted from smokestacks. The ultimate goal is for students to develop critical thinking skills by applying chemical principles environmental issues.

Demonstrations of Environmentally-Important Reactions. Classroom demonstrations make an important contribution to students' understanding. "NOx and SOx" is a series of demonstrations illustrating the preparation and properties of

Table I. An Environmental Chemistry Lesson Plan: The Sulfur Cycle and Acid Rain

I. Descriptive Chemistry of the environmentally important oxidation states of sulfur.
    A. -2 oxidation state: H_2S
    B. +4 oxidation state: SO_2, H_2SO_3 and sulfites
    C. +6 oxidation state: SO_3, H_2SO_4 and sulfates
II. The biogeochemical sulfur cycle
    A. Background topics
        1. Oxidation reduction reactions
        2. Chemical properties of the nonmetals
        3. Reaction kinetics
    B. Enrichment topics
        1. Chemical composition of seawater
        2. Bacteria as chemical catalysts
        3. Volcanoes
        4. Chemical reactions in the atmosphere
        5. Solar energy and photoinduced reactions
III. Recent sources of environmental SO_2
    A. Fossil fuels
    B. Processing ores
IV. Acid Rain
    A. Background Topics
        1. Acids and Bases
        2. pH scale
        3. Reaction kinetics
    B. Oxidation of SO_2 in the atmosphere
    C. Measuring acidity and evaluating the data
    D. Environmental impact of acid precipitation
    E. Controlling SO_2 emission
    F. Enrichment topics
        1. Buffers
        2. Acids and the carbonate-bicarbonate equilibrium
        3. Aquatic ecosystems
        4. Weather patterns

SOURCE: Reprinted with permission from ref. 3. Copyright 1988.

the nitrogen and sulfur oxides. NO, NO_2, SO_2, and SO_3 are prepared in class and students observe the gases' colors and water solubility. The aqueous solutions formed are tested for acidity, and their characteristic reactions with reducing agents, metals and carbonates are demonstrated (4,5,6).

Observing a brown gas dissolve in water to form an acidic solution has greater relevance to a high school audience when the observation is related to the global problems of atmospheric pollution and acid precipitation. The environmental issues mean more to the students for having seen the demonstrations.

Studying Environmental Issues in the Laboratory

Although high school laboratory programs are limited by cost, time and an ever-increasing sensitivity to safety, they are important components in most high school curricula. "Hands on" has been generally accepted as the preferred approach to teaching secondary science. In the laboratory students come closest to real science. Expecting their experiments to yield right answers, they are surprised to encounter discrepant results. Laboratory work, particularly that involving sampling, helps students appreciate the process by which scientists gather and evaluate data and make decisions. Students are also surprised to discover how difficult it is to apply the results of their own simple experiments to more complex problems.

Environmental Chemistry Experiments for High School Students. High school chemistry experiments emphasize techniques of measurement, recording data, making observations and analyzing materials. These skills may be applied to the study of environmentally-relevant systems. Many of the familiar experiments can be placed in an environmental context. For example, reactions of carbonates with acid and qualitative analysis of dilute aqueous solutions, both commonly included in high school chemistry, can be related to the effect of acid deposition on building materials and water sampling, respectively.

The American Chemical Society's ChemCom (7) program has led the way in developing environmentally significant experiments for secondary school students. Other secondary laboratory programs are also starting to include environmentally-relevant experiments (8) as are college-level laboratory manuals (9). The Woodrow Wilson Foundation Chemistry Teacher Institutes have made many excellent environmentally relevant activities available to teachers through their workshops. Finally, some experiments have been developed by environmental chemists (10) working with high school teachers; two of these that have been very popular with my students are described below.

Foul Water. "Foul water" (11) is typical of Chemcom's experimental program. It provides students with familiar materials, straightforward procedures and an opportunity to relate their laboratory findings to the real world. Laboratory foul water consists of water, vegetable oil, coffee grinds and garlic salt. When mixed, these produce a dark, odorous, slimy liquid that generally produces groans from students. They perform several separations finally producing a clear, colorless liquid. Separation and purification have long been the content of high school chemistry laboratory work. The environmental context of this experiment makes these operations more relevant and encourages a discussion of how the local water supply is purified.

Sea Water. The analysis of seawater (Parravano, C., State University of New York at Purchase; Stearns, C., unpublished) is a three-part experiment employing ion exchange techniques titrations to study the salt content of this familiar substance. It combines standard laboratory techniques and environmental sampling. Students determine total cation concentration by titrating the hydrogen ions in the ion exchange elutant with standard sodium hydroxide. Two EDTA titrations come next. The first, at pH = 10, enables students to determine the combined calcium and magnesium concentrations. The second, at pH = 12, provides data for calcium ion assay.

While the calculations in this experiment are difficult, all students can readily perform the laboratory operations. Student teams work together on the challenging aspects of the calculations motivated by the fact that they are able to apply what they have learned in school to a real world substance.

Dissolved Oxygen . Few experiments have excited my students more than collecting samples and analyzing them for dissolved oxygen. They use a modified Winkler procedure (Parravano, C., State University of New York at Purchase; Stearns, C., unpublished), collecting samples in BOD bottles on a field trip to a local stream. Back in the laboratory they fix the atmospheric oxygen with a basic solution of manganese sulfate. They next add iodide and concentrated acid to liberate iodine which is titrated with standard sodium thiosulfate. Although the chemistry is very complex, the students are able to understand the purpose of each step in the procedure. The concentrations of the reagents are adjusted so that the volume of thiosulfate is numerically equal to the ppm of dissolved oxygen, making it very easy for students to compare results with one another after multiple samples have been analyzed. As part of the related discussion they consider aquatic ecosystems and problems related to water pollution.

Developing an Environmental Chemistry Curriculum

Developing a curriculum involves identifying appropriate discussion topics, experiments and demonstrations that illustrate basic principles and have relevance to students. Secondary school teachers have expertise in "packaging" science lessons for a teenage audience but little access to current environmental research. Little trickles-down! Research journals do not reach high school teachers, nor do most teachers have the time or background to read and digest these articles and convert them into class lessons. Environmental researchers do not write for the publications most familiar to high school teachers, *The Journal of Chemical Education* and *The Science Teacher.*

Good current sources of information on the environment are newspapers, *The New York Times* and *The Wall Street Journal*, and *Environment* magazine. Professional science writers have been particularly helpful to high school teachers. Several college-level texts *(12,13)* are resources for high school teachers.and, with appropriate modification, could be used as reference texts by secondary students.

Support from Environmental Scientists. High school teachers need advice in selecting the most meaningful environmental examples, a list that may have to change every few years. Support from university and industrial chemists is also needed to encourage more school boards to approve modifying the present curriculum to incorporate global environmental issues.

Some examples of successful collaborations between chemists and high school teachers were described at the 9th International Conference on Chemical Education *(14)*. Australia *(15)*, Great Britain and Canada all have national efforts underway to improve their secondary school curricula. The long term goal of each is to promote scientific literacy, and each new program draws heavily upon global environmental science for examples that are relevant to students. In each of these countries a group of professional scientists worked with secondary teachers to create the curricular materials.

At the present time a group of scientists and educators from Portland State University and Pacific University are seeking funding to establish a global environmental science program for secondary science and social science teachers, hoping to develop some curriculum initiatives. One important feature of this proposed program is the support it will offer high school teachers as they try new curricular materials by keeping them in contact through a computer network with environmental scientists. This support is very important to teachers who are trying something new.

In summary, environmental topics should be central to a high school chemistry course. Meshed with traditional topics, they provide relevance to the curriculum giving it greater meaning to students of varied backgrounds. High school teachers need help from environmental scientist in developing this perfect course that will combine the environmental issues central to our society with enough general chemistry to make the issues comprehensible to our students.

At the 1989 ACS Global Environmental Chemistry Symposium Prof. Elzerman of Clemson University described his successful practice of sending students from his lectures with a take-home message. My take-home message is:

 I.   Global environmental issues must become part of the high school curriculum.
 II. The chemistry course is a good place to begin.
 III. High school teachers will need help from professional environmental scientists to make it happen.

Literature Cited
1. Zoller, U. *The Science Teacher* 1985, 32
2. Herron, J. D.; Kukla, D. A.; Schrader, C. L.; DiSpezio, M. A.; Erickson, J. L.*Chemistry*; D. C. Heath: Lexington, MA, 1987; pp 539-580.
3. Stearns, C. *J. Chem. Educ.* 1988, 65, 232
4. Shakhashiri, B. Z. *Chemical Demonstrations,* Vol I-III; University of Wisconsin Press, Madison, WI, 1985
5. Alyea, H. N., Dutton, F. B. *Tested Demonstrations in Chemistry*; Journal of Chemical Education: Easton, PA, 1965
6. Sumerlin, L. R.; Ealy, J. L.Jr. *Chemical Demonstrations, A Sourcebook for Teachers;* American Chemical Society: Washington, DC, 1985
7. American Chemical Society; *Chemcom, Chemistry in the Community;* Kendall/Hunt: Dubuque, IA, 1988;
8. DiSpezio, M. A.; Hall, T.; Schrader, C.L.; Young, J.A.; *Heath Chemistry Laboratory Experiments*; D.C. Heath: Lexington, MA; 1987; pp 251-254.
9. Thompson, S. *Chemtrek:* Allyn and Bacon: Boston, MA 1990
10. Parravano, C. *J. Chem. Educ.* 1988, 65, 235
11. Ref. 7 pp 8-11
12. Brown, T. L., LeMay, H.E. *Chemistry: The Central Science;* Prentice-Hall: Englewood Cliffs, NJ,
13. Chiras, D.D. *Environmental Science A Framework for Decision Making 2nd Ed.;* Benjamin/Cummings: Menlo Park, CA;1988
14. *Proceedings of the Ninth International Conference on Chemical Education,* Sao Paulo, Brazil, 1987
15. Bucat, R.B.; Cole, A.R.H. *J. Chem. Educ.* 1988, 65, 777

RECEIVED September 4, 1991

Chapter 26

Education of Environmental Specialists and Generalists in American Universities

Charles E. Kupchella

Ogden College of Science Technology and Health, Western Kentucky University, Bowling Green, KY 42101

Universities must take responsibility for the general environmental education of all graduates and the preparation of greater numbers of appropriately educated environmental specialists. All university students must be environmentally educated because the health of the environment depends upon knowledge and attitudes about the environment among leaders in all walks of life. The issue here is how to fit the environment into the long list of things all students need to know. The eclectic nature of environmental problems requires that environmental specialists also need to be broadly educated. Here the issue seems to be how broad is broad enough, since breadth comes at the expense of depth. Perhaps we need a number of different ways of preparing environmental workers.

Many of the things going on today are pulling biogeochemical cycles out of balance and threaten the stability of planet, Earth. Tens of thousands of square miles of tropical forest are being burned off each year, and this is changing the chemistry of the atmosphere as well as wiping out unknown numbers of species. The world's wetlands are disappearing at an alarming rate, and this, too, distorts chemical and biological cycles and diminishes the biological richness of our planet. While urbanization continues to overrun some of the world's best farmland, many people of the world live on land that is physically and chemically abused. Thousands of lakes and millions of acres of forests are dying worldwide, most likely from the effects of acid rain. Every day it seems we have new toxic spills and old toxic disposal sites are discovered. Our atmosphere has a worrisome ozone hole in it; and there is evidence that, because of changes in atmospheric chemistry, the earth is warming up.

Our prospects for solving these and other related problems are not

0097–6156/92/0483–0473$06.00/0

good. Some are global problems whose solutions will require unprecedented international cooperation. All of them are complex problems whose solutions will require people able to grasp the big picture, people able to appreciate and deal with complex problems, and people able to support strategies having long-term impacts. We don't have many of these kinds of people: our universities aren't turning them out anymore, if indeed they ever did.

The need for environmental education at the college level has two major dimensions. One of these is the need to educate all college graduates about the environment. Environmental problems simply will not be solved by experts if government officials, leaders in business, law, medicine, and citizens, in general, have no understanding of such problems. The task here will be to determine how to add the environment to the long existing list of things all students need to know. The other major dimension has to do with the expanding need for appropriately trained and educated environmental specialists. Environmental specialists also need to have a broad appreciation of the environment built into their education. Here the issue is how much breadth is enough--since it comes at the expense of depth. The purpose of this chapter is to explore further the issues related to the education of environmental generalists and specialists at the college level.

The Environment in General Education

Much has been written lamenting the fact that college and university curricula no longer generate "educated" people. As Ernest Boyer put it in his book on The Undergraduate Experience in America (1), "The nation's colleges.....have been much less attentive to the larger, more transcendent issues that give meaning to existence and help students put their own lives in perspective." He went on to say, "This nation and the world need well-informed, inquisitive, open-minded young people who are both productive and reflective, seeking answers to life's most important questions.....educated men and women who not only pursue their own personal interests but are also prepared to fulfill their social and civic obligations," - implying that our colleges fail to generate such young people. This has especially serious implications for the environment.

A sequence of events on our campus recently provided a striking illustration of the nature and perhaps even the roots of the problem. We returned several years ago to that point in the rhythm of academic cycles at which we decided to revise our general education program. A program that had served us well for a time seemed to have gotten out of hand. The number of course alternatives had grown, and the distinctions between courses designed to educate generally and those designed to serve as foundation courses for particular majors had blurred. A task group was appointed; and when its proposed new program came out in first draft, it had a course called Planet Earth. Planet Earth was to be a course required of all students and was to be designed to achieve the important general education objective of showing the relationship of humankind to the environment. Campus-wide reaction to the proposal was distilled and a second draft was generated. Somewhere along the way, Planet Earth was deleted.

Inquiries into the reasons for this yielded several unofficial possibilities. It was suggested that some faculty feared that such a course would be too "watered down" and not have enough substance. There was some concern about who would teach it. The idea that such a course could be team taught was thought by some to be unworkable. Apparently the environment was perceived as being too big to be dealt with by any one academic specialty, too broad to be deep enough, and too complicated to be dealt with by groups of different kinds of specialists - specialists who have difficulty working together anyway. Perhaps our world is in trouble for some of the same reasons. Environmental problems are too global to be dealt with by any one country, too complex to be tackled by any single kind of specialists, too important to be left to generalists, and too complex to be appreciated by citizens, legislators, or by narrowly trained specialists.

What now? The environment simply must be made an inevitable part of the undergraduate experience, but because of very real concerns such as those just cited, this will not be easy. I would like to propose a strategy.

First of all it must be acknowledged that arguments based on the need for college graduates to know about the environment, compelling though such arguments may be, are not likely to carry the day alone. There are simply too many things students "need to know." We must begin nevertheless by developing the conviction that, as subject matter goes, the environment is at least as important as anything else in the general education curriculum. Next, we have to develop arguments for environmental education based on the conventional rationale for general education, arguments wrapped in objectives having to do with writing and related skills, quantitative and logical skills (including data analysis) social science, natural science, and the humanities.

Social sciences are found in all general education programs; perhaps a good case could be made for the idea that the proper study of man is not so much man as it is the study of humans in the system of nature. We should suggest that ecology underpins culture. It is often said that to understand the Japanese we must first understand Japanese culture. But Japanese history and culture reflect the ecology of Japan, an island nation with scarce natural resources. History is an inevitable component of college and university general education programs. One of the justifications offered for this is that those who fail to consider history are doomed to repeat it. We must make it clear that those who fail to consider ecology are doomed.

We might also link environmental science to the need for students to think and to reason. The beginning of this argument could be that environmental issues are, and will continue to be, among the most important things students will be called upon to think and reason about. Although integrative/reasoning courses are found in many general education programs, the argument may well have to begin in some cases with the need for courses specifically designed to give students integrative reasoning experiences. Perhaps every university should have an upper-level course experience wherein students are required to engage other educated people in reasoning involving complex ideas and issues. Such courses should be designed to illuminate the ways in which contending arguments are weighed and should provide practice in - so that graduates become comfortable with - substantive debate and group reasoning. Although there is some evidence that reasoning can be taught, the idea is still hotly debated (*see 2*). One view is that there are no inferential rules of reasoning, only empirical rules covering specific events and situations; a related argument is that rules of reason are specific to each individual - and thus cannot be taught. Even giving these arguments some credence, the best way to hedge all bets would be to help students learn logical reasoning skills by providing opportunities whereby they can practice and hone whatever they do when they reason.

The environment as subject matter can also help students learn how to get to the heart of issues. We often get into trouble in our society because we ask and answer questions at the wrong level with too narrow a focus. Should a certain pesticide be used? The typical approach to answering this question might focus on the toxicity and safety of the pesticide. If it is found safe, we use it. Considered at another level, however, perhaps the pesticide will result in the selection of resistant strains of pests and ultimately require more expensive, more chemically intensive strategies; perhaps the use of the pesticide will upset natural balances and end up causing more problems than it solves. Students ought to be keenly aware of the importance of asking the right questions at the right level. Issues courses can help accomplish this objective and can also help undergraduates come to appreciate the fact that they have power. Perhaps one of the things we now fail to do in educating citizens is to help them discover that they are the loci of control in our society, that people able to explore issues and to develop solidly based conviction can indeed get things done even in a big, complex world steeped in inertia. If people are to be responsible citizens, they must first believe that they can change things for better by exercising their responsibility and by bringing their intellect to bear on the search for solutions.

Could there be any better focus for an issues course than the environment? Ecology is the integrative discipline of the sciences and environmental science can be the integrative discipline of "all" the disciplines. More than 10 years ago Eugene Odum described a kind of new ecology (*3*), not as an interdiscipline but as a new "integrative discipline that deals with the supraindividual levels of organization, an arena that is little touched by other disciplines as currently bounded - that is, by disciplines with boundaries established and strongly reinforced by professional societies and departments or curricula in universities."

An environmental issues course would have the additional advantage of illuminating science in its relationship to other disciplines in the real world. We must find some way to persuade our colleagues in the sciences that environmental science is not so much a threat as it is an opportunity to help students appreciate the importance and relevance of science. Perhaps this could be done by helping them see that science teaching tends not to be very engaging and thus not very effective. In a 1979 study, one of many documenting the scientific illiteracy of the American people, it was shown that only 7% of American adults met basic criteria for scientific literacy; a 1985 follow-up study suggested that this may have deteriorated to 5% (4). Among holders of BA degrees, the figure was 12%. Science is grossly underrepresented in college curricula. According to the National Research Council, colleges "have lowered their science requirements over recent years to the alarming point where the average non-specialists student devotes only about 7% of a college course load to work in the sciences (5). Even when students take science they don't seem to get caught up in it. Science is still all too often presented as very large collections of stale, static facts, definitions, and esoteric formulas to be memorized outside of any meaningful context. A course illuminating science in the context of current environmental issues would, at the very least, show the relevance of science to daily living and help illuminate science as an important, effective way of giving shape to truth.

There is no more important product of higher education than graduates able to think and able to seek and find the truth. There is nothing more important to think about and discuss the truth about than our impacts on the chemistry of our Planet and the consequence of these impacts. Responsible environmental behavior ought to be one of the primary goals of general education.

The Education and Training of Environmental Specialists

The job outlook for environmental professionals in the United States is very good (*see* 6). Throughout our society there is a great need for people who can solve environmental problems. Federal, state, and local governments (seeking to regulate environmental quality) compete with consulting firms and with private industries (seeking to comply with regulations) for too few people with appropriate training and experience. Driving the need for environmental specialists are the significant pieces of environmental protection legislation enacted over the past 25 years. Chief among these are the Clean Air Act, the Water Pollution Control Act, the Toxic Substances Control Act, and the National Environmental Policy Act. These have created the need for trained workers in such areas as solid waste management, water quality, air quality, hazardous waste management, planning, land and water conservation, fisheries and wildlife, forestry, parks and recreation, and environmental education.

The issue of what is the best kind of university preparation for environmental work remains controversial. Some claim that environmental problem-solving requires broadly trained individuals. They argue that universities need to establish environmental specialist degrees at the bachelors, masters and doctoral levels because narrowly trained specialists are unable to deal with the social, economic, and political as well as scientific aspects of environmental problems. Others (7) have argued that environmental problems cannot be attacked effectively using the blunted lances of the well rounded. We need, they say, people who are solidly grounded in the life-sciences, chemistry, the physical sciences, and other specialties, with perhaps some additional general education in environmental matters.

In a recent survey of environmental science and environmental studies programs throughout the U.S., Judith Weis (8) of Rutgers University elucidated the characteristics of these programs. She received responses from nearly 80 programs, including 40 environmental science programs, 28 environmental studies programs, 6 environmental health programs and 2 programs in environmental engineering. (Her study did not include programs in traditional natural resources management fields such as wildlife/fisheries, or forestry). She found that about half the respondents had interdepartmental programs; the rest were housed in traditional academic departments of biology, geology, forestry, etc. Most of the programs required courses in biology, chemistry, and earth science or physics. Most also required courses in social science or law. Less than half the programs required a research experience. About half had provision for internships. Field work was required in less than half the programs but laboratory sciences were essential components in nearly all the programs. Programs using the word, "studies" in their titles tended to emphasize social, political, and economic aspects of environmental management more than the others. Environmental "science" programs tended to emphasize the importance of various laboratory courses such as microbiology, chemistry, geology, field biology, ecology, tropical biology, and physiology.

Dr. Weis' survey revealed some disagreement among the program directors themselves, as to whether or not environmental science/studies graduates did better or worse than graduates with traditional majors in the job market. Among the problems with environmental degree programs cited by Dr. Weis were the following.

1. Identity. There is considerable variation in the use of terms like, "environmentalist," "environmental science program," "environmental studies program," etc., such that no particular background is guaranteed by the use of these terms.

2. Image. In the academic world, environmental programs are perceived as weak or soft. Many apparently believe that such programs generally sacrifice narrow depth for shallow breadth.

3. Insufficient training in field/lab work. The breadth of these programs does not allow for sufficient field training or laboratory skills training.

4. Students. Many of those initially attracted to environmental careers are often not prepared for even moderately rigorous science and mathematics-based programs.

5. Staffing/organization. Interdisciplinary programs often suffer within universities because they are perceived as drains on the financial and personnel resources of the traditional departments and it is difficult to get cooperation.

These are real problems that have to be weighed against the problem of specialists who may be well-trained but who are too narrowly trained. One solution to the dilemma of how best to balance breath and depth is to offer graduate training in environmental science to complement strong, traditional undergraduate majors. This would have the effect of combining the best of both sides of the argument - graduates of these programs would retain clear academic identities, and they would also have a multidisciplinary perspective, in this case developed at the graduate level of maturity.

Another approach is to use an environmental "minor" to complement various traditional specialties. We have such an environmental studies minor at Western Kentucky University. This minor is designed to complement science majors or majors in other fields such as Journalism. Currently, we have about thirty students enrolled in this minor; it has been growing rapidly, but the jury is still out on just how effective the program will be. The minor consists of 10-12 semester hours of required courses and 12-14 hours of electives selected from a list of approved courses. The required courses consist of an introduction to environmental science (3 hrs.), either a course in environmental ethics or economics (3 hrs.), and a one credit senior environmental seminar course designed to give students practice in interacting with specialists from other disciplines. Science majors taking this minor are also required to take a 2-hr. course in "environmental sampling and measurement" and a 3-hr. course in "environmental impact assessment." Students from other disciplines are required to have a course in either chemistry or physics (3 hrs.). A course in statistics is also strongly recommended for those with science majors. Electives are chosen from lists of approved courses from the departments of biology, chemistry, geography/geology, health and safety and engineering technology. This program is supervised by a committee consisting of a biologist, a chemist, an engineer, a public health specialist, and an earth scientist. We expect that this minor will serve as an effective entryway into the work of protecting the environment.

Given the complexities of environmental issues, perhaps a number of different ways of preparing environmental workers should be available to students. Armies need the equivalents of lancers with sharp lances but they also need tacticians and the equivalents of platoon leaders, lieutenants, and generals, as well as various support personnel, each with different training needs. The point here is that there will likely be plenty of environmental work in the future for chemists, wildlife biologists, geologists, journalists, and the like. These could benefit from some broad educational exposure to environmental principles and issues as they go about the business of their specialties. There will also continue to be a need for environmental big-picture people - some of whom may even have specialized in such general subjects as environmental studies. These would benefit from substantive exposure to the scientific and technical dimensions of environmental problem solving.

Literature Cited

1. Boyer, E. *The Undergraduate Experience in America*; Harper and Row: NY, **1987**; pp 7.
2. Nisbett, R.E.; Fong, G.T.; Lehman, D.R.; and Cheng, P.W. *Science.* **1987**, *238*, 625-631.
3. Odum, E.P. *Science.* **1977**, *195*, 1289-1293.
4. Miller, J.D. *American Scientist.* **1988**, *76*(2):(editorial).
5. McDonald, K. *The Chronicle of Higher Education.* **1982**, p.6. February 24.
6. Kelley, J. *Environment Today.* **1990**, *Jan/Feb*, 27-29.
7. Nash, R.F. *J. Env. Ed.* **1977**, *8*(4), 2-3.
8. Weis, J.S. *Env. Sci. Technol.* **1990**, *24*(8), 1116-1121.

RECEIVED July 23, 1991

Indexes

Author Index

Affiliation Index

Subject Index

A

Acid, use of environmental examples for
  instruction, 468,469*t*
Acid deposition
  acidifying potential of precipitation,
    definition, 41
  acidity in relation to possible
    ecosystem response, definition, 38,41
  aquatic organic responses, 55–56
  biological responses, 51–52
  buildings, monuments, and
    materials, effects, 57–58
  characteristics, 38
  description, 38
  ecological effects, 46,48–56
  environmental benefits of emission
    controls, 58
  forms, 38
  human health effects, 56–57
  lake and stream responses, 52–53,54*f*,55
  sensitivity of ecosystem, 46,48*f*,49,50*f*
  sources of acidic pollutants, 41
  terrestrial responses, 49
Acidic pollutants, sources, 41–47
Acidification, ecological effects, 46,48–56
Acidifying potential of precipitation,
  definition, 41
Acidity, definition in relation to
  possible ecosystem responses, 38,41
Acid precipitation, role of HO·, 75
Acid rain
  identification as problem in Canada, 37
  occurrence, 21–22
  recognizing the problem, 37
  sources of acidic pollutants, 41–47
  See also Acid deposition
Aerosol
  definition, 117
  size distribution, 117,118*f*
  size modes, 117,118*t*
  See also Atmospheric dust

Agricultural crops, effect of acidification, 52
Agricultural productivity, biocides–net
  productivity relationship, 307–308
Agricultural technologies, changes, 311,313
Airborne contaminants, description, 135
Airborne pollutant, definition, 135
Air pollutants, classifications, 66
Air pollution
  effects, 166,167*t*
  scope, 21–22
  sources, 165–166
  state, 4
  U.S. Clean Air Act Amendments of
    1970, 22
Air quality, concern about deposition of
  toxic chemicals, 135
Air quality in Mexico City
  atmospheric pollution, sources, 150*t*
  carbon monoxide standards, 156*t*,157*f*
  fuel consumption in metropolitan area
    and Mexico, 153*t*,154
  fuel quality, 155
  geographical considerations, 150
  integral programs to control atmospheric
    pollution, 161
  lead standards, 156*t*,158
  meteorological considerations, 150
  monitoring network, 155,156*t*
  monitoring systems, location, 150,151*f*
  nitrogen dioxide standards, 156*t*,158
  ozone standards, 156*t*,158*t*,160*f*
  particulate matter standards, 156*t*,158,159*f*
  pollution inventory, 150*t*,153*t*,154
  standards, 155,156*t*
  sulfur dioxide standards, 156*t*
  thermal inversions, 150,152*f*
  vehicular emission standards, 154–155*t*
Air–sea exchange of CO_2, effect of
  climate, 393,396
Air toxics, description, 135
Aitken nuclei, definition, 139
Ambient air quality, 162